1. SLOVENIA
2. CROATIA
3. BOSNIA AND HERZEGOVINA
4. ALBANIA
5. MACEDONIA
6. SERBIA AND MONTENEGRO

INTRODUCTION TO
Physical Anthropology

ABOUT THE COVER IMAGE

The image on the cover is an artist's reconstruction of a fossilized partial skeleton from Ethiopia, dated to 4.4 million years ago. It represents an early member of the human ("hominin") lineage, not too long after our line diverged from that of great apes. The skeleton is that of an adult female which the press has nicknamed "Ardi."

This individual is so important because it preserves so many portions of the skeleton from which we can get better answers to some key questions such as: How big was she and how big was her brain? In both cases, she was small (only about 4 ft. tall, with a brain about the same size as a chimpanzee's).

Artist reconstruction by Jay Matternes.

2011–2012 Edition

INTRODUCTION TO
Physical Anthropology

Robert Jurmain

Professor Emeritus, San Jose State University

Lynn Kilgore

University of Colorado, Boulder

Wenda Trevathan

Professor Emerita, New Mexico State University

Russell L. Ciochon

University of Iowa

WADSWORTH
CENGAGE Learning™

Australia · Brazil · Japan · Korea · Mexico · Singapore · Spain · United Kingdom · United States

WADSWORTH
CENGAGE Learning™

Introduction to Physical Anthropology,
2011–2012 Edition
**Robert Jurmain, Lynn Kilgore, Wenda Trevathan,
Russell L. Ciochon**

Acquiring Editor: Erin Mitchell

Developmental Editor: Lin Gaylord

Assistant Editor: John Chell

Editorial Assistant: Mallory Ortberg

Media Editor: Melanie Cregger

Marketing Manager: Andrew Keay

Marketing Assistant: Dimitri Hagnere

Marketing Communications Manager: Tami Strang

Content Project Manager: Cheri Palmer

Design Director: Rob Hugel

Art Director: Caryl Gorska

Print Buyer: Judy Inouye

Rights Acquisitions Specialist: Dean Dauphinais

Production Service: Patti Zeman, Hespenheide Design

Text Designer: Gary Hespenheide,
Hespenheide Design

Photo Researcher: Patti Zeman, Hespenheide Design

Text Researcher: Isabel Alves

Copy Editor: Janet Greenblatt

Illustrator: Randy Miyake, Hespenheide Design;
Robert Greisen

Cover Designer: Gary Hespenheide,
Hespenheide Design

Cover Image: © Jay Matternes

Compositor: Hespenheide Design

For product information and technology
assistance, contact us at
**Cengage Learning Customer & Sales Support,
1-800-354-9706.**

For permission to use material from this text or product,
submit all requests online at **www.cengage.com/permissions**.
Further permissions questions can be e-mailed to
permissionrequest@cengage.com.

Library of Congress Control Number: 2010942499
Student Edition:
ISBN-13: 978-1-111-29793-0
ISBN-10: 1-111-29793-2

Loose-leaf Edition:
ISBN-13: 978-1-111-34968-4
ISBN-10: 1-111-34968-1

Wadsworth
20 Davis Drive
Belmont, CA 94002-3098
USA

Cengage Learning is a leading provider of customized learn-
ing solutions with office locations around the globe, including
Singapore, the United Kingdom, Australia, Mexico, Brazil, and
Japan. Locate your local office at **www.cengage.com/global**.

Cengage Learning products are represented in Canada by
Nelson Education, Ltd.

To learn more about Wadsworth, visit
www.cengage.com/wadsworth

Purchase any of our products at your local college store or at our
preferred online store **www.cengagebrain.com**.

Printed in the United States of America
2 3 4 5 15 14 13 12

Brief Contents

Contents

Heredity and Evolution

© The Print Collector / Alamy

Primates

© iStockphoto.com / Doug Berry

Hominin Evolution

Contemporary Human Evolution

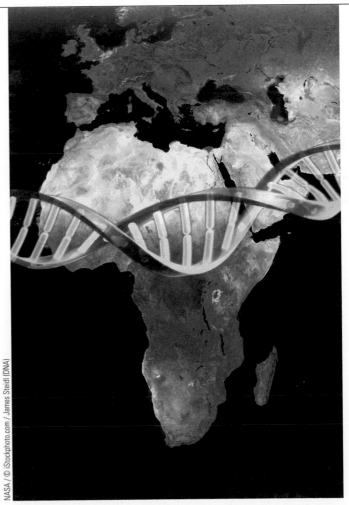

NASA / © iStockphoto.com / James Steidl (DNA)

List of Features

A Closer Look

Robert Greisen

At a Glance

What's Important

New Frontiers in Research

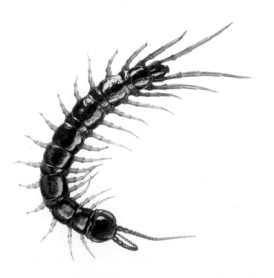

© iStockphoto.com / Tomasz Zachariasz

© iStockphoto.com / Tomasz Zachariasz

Preface

In May 2010, biologists announced they had created a synthetic bacterial cell, the first-ever human-made organism. Of course, this was a major technical achievement, but also one that raises several fundamental ethical questions, including, most obviously, What is life? And should humans try to recreate it?

The synthetic bacterial cell, just like a typical bacterial cell, contains many thousands of bits of information (stored in its DNA) that direct all the cell's functions. Scientists built a new DNA molecule that allows the cell to work normally and even to reproduce. By any biological standard, it is alive, but the researchers also had some help from nature. Even a relatively "simple" organism like a bacterium has more than half a million bits of genetic information within its DNA, all arranged in a precise sequence. This complex arrangement was molded and fine-tuned through tens of millions of years of evolution. Because the genetic information must be exact, researchers decoded DNA from a living bacterial cell and then used this "recipe" to manufacture a synthetic DNA molecule. It's not quite making life from scratch, but it's a major step in that direction.

In this book, we explore the building blocks of life, how life has evolved, and how new advances in genetic research are yielding discoveries every day that will dramatically affect our lives. This knowledge really does make a difference, and it's important to at least become familiar with the basic aspects of biology—especially evolution. This is the main goal of this text, although we will be focusing primarily on *human* evolution.

The academic discipline that studies human evolution specifically is called physical (or biological) anthropology. In this field, too, there have been major breakthroughs within the last few years. It is an exciting time in the biological sciences, of which physical anthropology is a part. However, all this very new knowledge has revealed how complicated are the genetic mechanisms that build and regulate all organisms on earth, including humans. What's more, as new fossils relating to the evolution of the human lineage are found, understanding our evolutionary history becomes all the more demanding.

These exciting developments pose a challenge for students, instructors, and textbook authors alike, but they also provide the opportunity for a deeper understanding of our subject. Each of the authors of this textbook has taught the introductory physical anthropology course for many years. From this long experience, we realize that many of the students taking this course have had little in the way of biological or anthropological instruction at the high school level and will find much of the material in this book entirely new. To help students make the transition into this new subject area, we provide clear explanations and examples enhanced by many visual aids.

Within these pages, there are many places where students can seek help in learning about topics, ideas, and developments encountered for the first time. To provide even more assistance than in previous editions, much of the artwork has been completely redrawn, and we have also added many new photos. All these changes reflect our long-term commitment to make our textbook an effective teaching and learning instrument.

Because genetic mechanisms lie at the heart of understanding evolution, we address the basic aspects of life, cells, DNA, and the ways species change in the early chapters of this text (Chapter 2 through 5). We next turn (in Chapters 6 through 8) to an exploration of our evolutionary cousins, the nonhuman primates, and how they relate to us both physically and behaviorally. In Chapter 9, we discuss the evolutionary history of early primates to help students better understand the many ways in which primates have adapted to their environments. Details of our specific human evolutionary history over the past 7 million years are covered over the next five chapters. We begin with our small-brained ancestors in Africa and follow the development of their descendants through time and over their expanding ranges into Asia and Europe and much later into Australia and the Americas.

In the last section of this book (Chapters 15 through 17), we cover the most recent part of our journey through human evolution with a discussion of modern human biology and trace the ongoing evolution of our species. Major topics include the nature of human variation (including the meaning of "race"), patterns of adaptation in recent human populations, and the developmental changes experienced by humans through the life course. In our Conclusion, "Why it Matters," we discuss how humans now adapt to and alter the planet and compare these recent developments with our species' long evolutionary past, when humans were not so numerous or so dependent on nonrenewable resources. These dramatic alterations to our world will pose enormous challenges to people throughout the twenty-first century and beyond. We hope that this book will better prepare all of you for what lies ahead.

What's New in the 2011–2012 Edition

First of all, we have updated much of the book, reflecting recent advances in virtually every field of physical anthropology. There is no area of biological research today that advances more rapidly than the study of genetics (for example, the creation of a synthetic cell in 2010). Because genetics underlies evolution and thus every topic in this book, we strive to keep our coverage as up to date as possible. At the same time, it's important to make this complicated topic understandable and (we hope) enjoyable to college students, whose lives are impacted by genetic research every day.

As genetic technology continues to grow at an unprecedented pace, it is our task to present the most relevant new discoveries in as simple a manner as possible. In addition to discussing the newly developed syn-

thetic bacterial cell in Chapter 3, we've added to Chapter 4 a new discussion of how DNA deletions and duplications impact the evolutionary process. As an example, we used changes in the skull of bull terriers over a 35-year period to show how duplications of DNA segments in developmental genes can cause dramatic and rapid anatomical changes in species if there is strong selection pressure acting on them (in this case, breeding by humans). We have added more nonhuman examples of genetic phenomena because we want to underscore the theme of biological continuity—that humans are part of a biological spectrum and that we are related to all life on earth. We have also added some new artwork and revised a number of figures in Chapters 3 and 4 to make difficult concepts clearer.

Primatologists are regularly reporting on new discoveries about our closest relatives, the nonhuman primates, revealing our continuity with them. Since many of our primate cousins are unfamiliar to our readers, we've added several new photos in all three primate chapters and replaced many others. Today, many nonhuman primates are endangered, and we hope to raise awareness of them among students who read this book. In Chapter 8, we've updated the discussion of intergroup aggression, including new findings concerning male aggression in chimpanzees. We've also broadened our discussion of nonaggressive behaviors, providing new evidence for empathy in nonhuman primates. Chapter 9 has been extensively updated to include new discoveries as well and ongoing reinterpretations of fossil primates. Among these new fossil genera are *Darwinius* (to which the provocative "Ida," touted as "the Missing Link" in early 2009, belongs) and *Saadanius*,

a recent discovery from Saudi Arabia that has helped shed light on a primate lineage closer to our own. These and other fossils have required significant changes to the way we interpret the material covered in this chapter.

In Chapter 10, we provide a new and potentially significant update—evidence of possible hominin tool use up to 1 million years earlier than previously found. Remarkable new discoveries of fossil hominins are discussed in Chapters 11 through 14. Chapter 11 covers the earliest hominins and presents controversial new interpretations of *Ardipithecus*, especially relating to the partial skeleton known as "Ardi." Exciting discoveries from South Africa of a brand-new species called *Australopithecus sediba* provide a tantalizing view of how earlier hominins may have evolved into our genus (*Homo*).

Chapter 12 has updates relating to how childhood development occurred in *Homo erectus* as well as key new dating for fossil sites in Africa and Europe. Chapters 13 and 14 have been extensively reorganized and refocused to reflect the startling new evidence obtained from the analysis of Neandertal DNA. These molecular discoveries show that Neandertals interbred with modern human populations, and their genes can still be found in many contemporary human populations! What's more, evaluation of very incomplete hominin remains from Siberia show one to be a Neandertal and the other to perhaps be a new species altogether. Lastly, newly found archaeological finds from Europe indicate that Neandertals quite possibly made use of novel materials for personal adornment, suggesting more advanced symbolic thought than previously assumed.

Chapter 14 builds on this emerging new story about the origins of modern people, and the main focus of the chapter has been modified to reflect the new evidence. What's more, physical anthropologists are learning more all the time about the little hominins from Indonesia (popularly called "hobbits"), and the most recent findings (including some new archaeological discoveries) suggest that these highly unusual hominins perhaps diverged from other hominins far earlier than previously thought.

In Chapters 15 through 17, our focus turns to modern human biology. Understanding human variation (discussed in Chapter 15) has been completely transformed by more complete DNA data, published in just the last year. We have updated and modified our main perspective in this chapter to reflect the remarkable new findings contributed by molecular biology.

In Chapter 16, there's a new discussion of recent research demonstrating a population-wide genetic mutation in Tibetan highlanders that increases their ability to adapt to living at high altitude. This chapter also considers new genetic research that suggests that cattle may have initially acquired tuberculosis from humans and also includes new evidence that the malarial parasite that infects humans evolved from one that infects gorillas, and not chimpanzees, as was previously thought.

One theme that we emphasize throughout the book is that we are the result of not only biological but also cultural evolutionary factors. In other words, we are a *biocultural* species. In Chapter 17, we focus on ways in which biology and culture act on the human life course from conception, through reproduction, to the end of life. For example, we explore the roles of genetic, nutritional, and environmental factors on growth and development. We also discuss how the rapidly growing field of *epigenetics* helps to resolve the age-old nature-nurture debate by showing how environmental factors can influence gene expression.

Finally, in our Conclusion, we focus on another theme that runs through the book—*why it matters* that we know and understand human evolutionary history and its impact on the world today. In fact, we humans and the consequences of our activities are probably the most important influences on evolution today, causing the extinction or near-extinction of thousands of other life-forms and threatening the very planet on which we live. Only by understanding how we got to this point can we begin to respond to the challenges that are in our future and the futures of our children and grandchildren.

Features

New Frontiers in Research features highlight some of the newest and most innovative research in physical anthropology.

Four areas of research are covered:

Evo-Devo: The Evolution Revolution (following Chapter 5); (updated with new illustrations

Molecular Anthropology in the Age of Genomics (following Chapter 9); new to this edition

Ancient DNA (following Chapter 13); completely rewritten and updated

Molecular Applications in Modern Human Biology (following Chapter 15); completely rewritten and updated

In-Chapter Learning Aids

A Closer Look boxes are high-interest features found throughout the book. They expand on the topic under discussion by providing a more in-depth perspective.

Key Questions appear at the beginning of each chapter and highlight the central topic of that chapter.

A running glossary in the margins provides definitions of terms immediately adjacent to the text where the term is first introduced. A full glossary is provided at the back of the book.

At a Glance boxes found throughout the book briefly summarize complex or controversial material in a visually simple fashion.

Figures, including numerous photographs, line drawings, and maps, most in full color, are carefully selected to clarify text materials and directly support the discussion in the text. Much of the art, especially anatomical drawings, have been redrawn for this edition.

Critical Thinking Questions at the end of each chapter reinforce key concepts and encourage students to think critically about what they have read.

Full bibliographical citations throughout the book provide sources from which the materials are drawn. This type of documentation guides students to published, peer-reviewed source materials and illustrates for students the proper use of references. All cited sources are listed in the comprehensive bibliography at the back of the book.

Acknowledgments

Over the years, many friends and colleagues have assisted us with our books. For this edition we are especially grateful to the reviewers who so carefully commented on the manuscript and made such helpful suggestions: Stephen Bailey, Tufts University; Eric Delson, American Museum of Natural History, New York; Arthur C. Durband, Texas Tech University; Joseph S. Eisenlauer, Pierce College; Gregg Gunnell, University of Michigan Museum of Paleontology, Ann Arbor; David Randall McCaig, Phoenix College (Maricopa Community Colleges); Jennifer Molina-Stidger, Sierra College; Kathleen A. Rizzo, University of Illinois at Chicago; and Erin B. Waxenbaum, Northwestern University.

WE WISH TO THANK THE TEAM at Cengage Learning: Erin Mitchell, Lin Marshall Gaylord, Andrew Keay, Mallory Ortberg, John Chell, Melanie Cregger, Tami Strang, Caryl Gorska, and Cheri Palmer. Moreover, for their unflagging expertise and patience, we are grateful to our copy editor, Janet Greenblatt, our production coordinator, Gary Hespenheide, and his skilled staff at Hespenheide Design: Patti Zeman, Bridget Neumayr, and Randy Miyake.

TO THE MANY FRIENDS AND colleagues who have generously provided photographs, we are greatly appreciative: Zeresenay Alemsegel, Chris Beard, David Begun, Brenda Benefit, Jonathan Bloch, C. K. Brain, Günter Bräuer, Michel Brunet, Peter Brown, Chip Clark, Desmond Clark, Ron Clarke, Bill Clemens, Raymond Dart, Henri de Lumley, Louis de Bonis, Jean DeRousseau, John Fleagle, Diane France, Robert Franciscus, David Frayer, Kathleen Galvin, Philip Gingerich, Gregg Gunnell, David Haring, Terry Harrison, John Hodgkiss, Almut Hoffman, Pat Holroyd, Ellen Ingmanson, Fred Jacobs, Don Johanson, Peter Jones, Mushtaq Kahn, John Kappelman, Richard Kay, William Kimbel, Arlene Kruse, Yutaku Kunimatsu, Richard Leakey, Carol Lofton, David Lordkipanidze, Giorgio Manzi, Margaret Maples, Monte McCrossin, Lorna Moore, Salvador Moyà-Solà, Stephen Nash, Gerald Newlands, Xijum Ni, John Oates, Bonnie Pedersen, Lorna Pierce, David Pilbeam, Judith Regensteiner, Gul Reyman, Sastrohamijoyo Sartono, Jeffrey Schwartz, Eugenie Scott, Rose Sevick, Elwyn Simons, Meredith Small, Fred Smith, Thierry Smith, Kirstin Sterner, Judy Suchey, Masanaru Takai, Heather Thew, Nelson Ting, Phillip Tobias, Erik Trinkaus, Alan Walker, Carol Ward, Dietrich Wegner, James Westgate, Randy White, Milford Wolpoff, Xinzhi Wu, and João Zilhão.

TO THE MANY STUDENTS WHO have pledged their time and expertise on Chapter 9, we would like to thank K. Lindsay Eaves for her invaluable help editing and researching this edition of the manuscript; James Rogers and Nathan Totten for their help with computer graphics; and K. Lindsay Eaves, Ian Lamb, and Hanna Roseman for their meticulous work on the related index and bibliography. Special mention goes to K. Lindsay Eaves for her valued assistance in facilitating coordination of the text and art within the context of the Ciochon Lab. These students have worked to ensure that the text is as accessible as possible for their peers. Also at the University of Iowa, Linda Maxson, Dean of the College of Liberal Arts and Sciences, provided vital support. Others who have assisted in forming the concepts that we have put into written form include John Fleagle, Eric Delson, Terry Harrison, Gregg Gunnell, Philip Rightmire, Nelson Ting, Kirstin Sterner, Iyad Zalmout, and Tim White.

ROBERT JURMAIN
LYNN KILGORE
WENDA TREVATHAN
RUSSELL CIOCHON
December 2010

Supplements

Supplements

Introduction to Physical Anthropology 2011–2012 comes with an outstanding supplements program to help instructors create an effective learning environment so that students can more easily master the latest discoveries and interpretations in the field of physical anthropology.

Supplements for the Instructor

Online Instructor's Manual with Test Bank for *Introduction to Physical Anthropology 2011–2012 Edition*

This online resource includes a sample syllabus showing how to integrate the Anthropology Resource Center with the text, as well as chapter outlines, learning objectives, key terms and concepts, lecture suggestions, enrichment topics, and 40–60 test questions per chapter.

PowerLecture™ with Exam View® (Windows/Macintosh) and JoinIn™ for *Introduction to Physical Anthropology 2011–2012 Edition*

This easy-to-use, one-stop digital library and presentation tool includes the following book-specific resources as well as direct links to many of Wadsworth's highly valued electronic resources for anthropology:

- Ready-to-use Microsoft® PowerPoint® lecture slides with photos and graphics from the text, making it easy for the instructor to assemble, edit, publish, and present customized lectures.

- ExamView® testing software, which provides all the test items from the text's test bank in electronic format, enabling the instructor to create customized tests of up to 250 items that can be delivered in print or online.
- The text's *Instructor's Resource Manual and Test Bank* in electronic format.

Anthropology CourseMate

This website for *Introduction to Physical Anthropology 2011–2012 Edition* brings chapter topics to life with interactive learning, study, and exam preparation tools, including quizzes and flash cards for each chapter's key terms and concepts. The website also provides an eBook version of the text with highlighting and note-taking capabilities. For instructors, this text's CourseMate also includes Engagement Tracker, a first-of-its-kind tool that monitors student engagement in the course. Go to login.cengage.com to access these resources.

WebTutor™ for Blackboard® and WebCT®

Instructors can jump-start their course with customizable, rich, text-specific content within your Course Management System.

- **Jump-start**—Simply load a WebTutor cartridge into your Course Management System.
- **Customize**—Easily blend, add, edit, reorganize, or delete content. The rich, text-specific content includes media assets, quizzes,

weblinks, discussion topics, interactive games and exercises, and more.

The Wadsworth Anthropology Video Library Vol. 1

The Wadsworth Anthropology Video Library drives home the relevance of course topics through short, provocative clips of current and historical events. Perfect for enriching lectures and engaging students in discussion, many of the segments on this volume have been gathered from BBC Motion Gallery. Ask your Cengage Learning representative for a list of contents.

Supplements for the Student

Anthropology CourseMate

This website for *Introduction to Physical Anthropology 2011–2012 Edition* brings chapter topics to life with interactive learning, study, and exam preparation tools, including quizzes, flash cards, videos, animations, and more! The site also provides an eBook version of the text with highlighting and note-taking capabilities. Students can access this new learning tool and all other online resources through www.cengagebrain.com.

Study Guide for *Introduction to Physical Anthropology 2011–2012 Edition*

This comprehensive student study guide includes learning objectives, chapter outlines, key terms, media suggestions, concept applications, and practice tests (answers provided) with a variety of question types—ideal for test prep!

Telecourse Course Study Guide for *Introduction to Physical Anthropology 2011–2012 Edition*

Entitled "Physical Anthropology: The Evolving Human," this distance learning course provides online and print companion study guide options that include quizzes, study aids, interactive exercises, videos, and more.

Classic and Contemporary Readings in Physical Anthropology

Edited by Mary K. Sandford and Eileen Jackson, this accessible reader presents primary articles with introductions and questions for discussion, helping students to better understand the nature of scientific inquiry. Students will read highly accessible classic and contemporary articles on key topics, including the science of physical anthropology, evolution and heredity, primates, human evolution, and modern human variation.

Lab Manual and Workbook for Physical Anthropology, Seventh Edition

Written by Diane L. France, this edition of the workbook and lab manual includes a new "Introduction to Science and Critical Thinking" that precedes the fist. Using hands-on exercises, this richly illustrated full-color lab manual balances the study of genetics, human osteology, anthropometry, and forensic anthropology with the study of primates and human evolution. In addition to providing hands-on lab assignments that apply the field's perspectives and techniques to real situations, this edition provides more explanatory information and sample exercises throughout the text to help make the concepts of physical anthropology easier to understand. Contact your Cengage sales representative to package with the text.

Virtual Laboratories for Physical Anthropology, CD-ROM, Fourth Edition, by John Kappelman

Through the use of video segments, interactive exercises, quizzes, 3-D animations, and sound and digital images, students can actively participate in 12 labs on their own terms—at home, in the library—at any time! Recent fossil discoveries are included, as well as exercises in behavior and archaeology and critical thinking and problem-solving activities. *Virtual Laboratories* includes weblinks, outstanding fossil images, exercises, and a post-lab self-quiz.

Basic Genetics in Anthropology CD-ROM: Principles and Applications, Version 2.0, by Jurmain/Kilgore/Trevathan

This student CD-ROM expands on basic biological concepts covered in the book, focusing on biological inheritance (such as genes and DNA sequencing) and its applications to modern human populations. Interactive animations and simulations bring these important concepts to life so that students can fully understand the essential biological principles underlying human evolution. Also available are quizzes and interactive flash cards for further study.

Hominid Fossils CD-ROM: An Interactive Atlas, by James Ahern

This CD-based interactive atlas includes over 75 key fossils that are important for a clear understanding of human evolution. The QuickTime® Virtual Reality (QTVR) "object" movie format for each fossil will enable students to have a near-authentic experience working with these important finds by allowing them to rotate the fossil 360°. Unlike some VR media, QTVR objects are made using actual photographs of the real objects and thus better preserve details of color and texture. The fossils used are high-quality research casts and real fossils.

The organization of the atlas is nonlinear, with three levels and multiple paths, enabling students to start with a particular fossil and work their way "up" to see how the fossil fits into the map of human evolution in terms of geography, time, and evolution. The CD-ROM offers students an inviting, authentic learning environment, one that also contains a dynamic quizzing feature that will allow students to test their knowledge of fossil and species identification as well as provide more detailed information about the fossil record.

Wadsworth Anthropology's Module Series

This series includes:

Evolution of the Brain Module: Neuroanatomy, Development, and Paleontology

The human species is the only species that has ever created a symphony, written a poem, developed a mathematical equation, or studied its own origins. The biological structure that has enabled humans to perform these feats of intelligence is the human brain. This module, created by Daniel D. White, of the University of Albany, SUNY, explores the basics of neuroanatomy, brain development, lateralization, and sexual dimorphism and provides the fossil evidence for hominin brain evolution. This module in chapter-like format can be packaged for free with the text.

Human Environment Interactions: New Directions in Human Ecology

This module by Kathy Galvin, of Colorado State University, begins with a brief discussion of the history and core concepts of the field of human ecology, the study of how humans interact with the natural environment, before looking in depth at how the environment influences cultural practices (environmental determinism) as well as how aspects of culture, in turn, affect the environment. Human behavioral ecology is presented within the context of natural selection and how ecological factors influence the development of cultural and behavioral traits and how people subsist in different environments. The module concludes with a discussion of resilience and global change as a result of human-environment interactions. This module in chapter-like format can be packaged for free with the text.

Forensic Anthropology Module

The forensic application of physical anthropology is exploding in popularity. Written by Diane L. France, this module explores the myths and realities of the search for human remains in crime scenes, what can be expected from a forensic anthropology expert in the courtroom, some of the special challenges in responding to mass fatalities, and the issues a student should consider if pursuing a career in forensic anthropology. This module in chapter-like format can be packaged for free with the text.

Molecular Anthropology Module

This module explores how molecular genetic methods are used to understand the organization and expression of genetic information in humans and nonhuman primates. Students will learn about the common laboratory methods used to study variation and evolution in molecular anthropology. Examples are drawn from up-to-date research on human evolutionary origins and comparative primate genomics to demonstrate that scientific research is an ongoing process, with theories frequently being questioned and reevaluated.

These resources are available to qualified adopters, and ordering options for student supplements are flexible. Please consult your local Cengage sales consultant for more information or to evaluate examination copies of any of these resources or to receive product demonstrations. You may also visit us at **www.cengage.com /anthropology/jurmain**.

Forensic anthropologists, including both physical anthropologists and archaeologists, recovered 114 Kurdish victims of genocide from this site in southern Iraq.

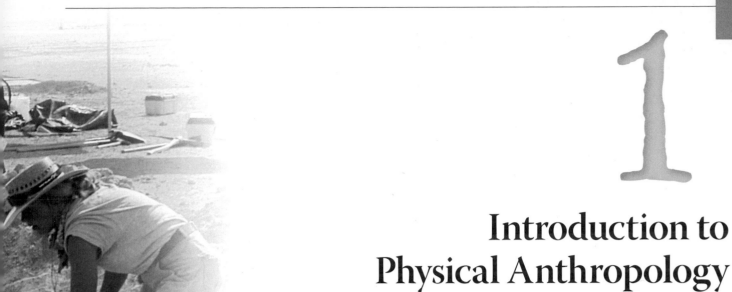

Introduction to Physical Anthropology

Key Questions

▶ How does physical anthropology help explain how humans evolved and how we are related to organisms that lived in the past as well as those living today?

▶ What is critical thinking? How does understanding and using the scientific method contribute to the development of critical thinking?

One day, perhaps during the rainy season some 3.7 million years ago, two or three animals walked across a grassland **savanna** in what is now northern Tanzania, in East Africa. These individuals were early **hominins**, members of the evolutionary lineage that also includes our own species, *Homo sapiens*. Fortunately for us, a record of their passage on that long-forgotten day remains in the form of fossilized footprints, preserved in hardened volcanic deposits.

As chance would have it, shortly after heels and toes were pressed into the damp soil, a nearby volcano erupted. The ensuing ash fall blanketed everything on the ground. In time, the ash layer hardened into a deposit that remarkably preserved the tracks of numerous animals, including those early hominins, for nearly 4 million years (**Fig. 1-1**).

These now famous prints indicate that two individuals, one smaller than the other and perhaps walking side by side, left parallel sets of tracks. But because the larger individual's prints are obscured, possibly by those of a third, it's unclear how many actually made that journey so long ago. But what is clear is that the prints were made by an animal that habitually walked **bipedally** (on two feet), and that fact tells us that those ancient travelers were hominins.

In addition to the footprints, scientists working at this site (called Laetoli) and at other locations have discovered many fossilized parts of skeletons of an animal we call *Australopithecus afarensis*. Because the remains have been extensively studied, we know that these hominins were anatomically similar to ourselves, although their brains were only about one-third the size of ours. And even though they may have used stones and sticks as simple tools, there is no evidence that they actually made stone tools. In fact, they were very much at the mercy of nature's whims. They certainly could not outrun most predators, and since their canine teeth were fairly small, they were pretty much defenseless.

We've asked hundreds of questions about the Laetoli hominins, but we will never be able to answer them all. They walked down a path into what became their future, and their immediate journey has long since ended. So it remains for

savanna (also spelled savannah) A large flat grassland with scattered trees and shrubs. Savannas are found in many regions of the world with dry and warm-to-hot climates.

hominins Colloquial term for members of the evolutionary group that includes modern humans and now extinct bipedal relatives.

bipedally On two feet; walking habitually on two legs.

species A group of organisms that can interbreed to produce fertile offspring. Members of one species are reproductively isolated from members of all other species (i.e., they cannot mate with them to produce fertile offspring).

anthropology The field of inquiry that studies human culture and evolutionary aspects of human biology; includes cultural anthropology, archaeology, linguistics, and physical, or biological, anthropology.

▼ **Figure 1-1**
Early hominin footprints at Laetoli, Tanzania. The tracks to the left were made by one individual, while those to the right appear to have been made by two individuals, the second stepping in the tracks of the first.

Peter Jones

us to learn as much as we can about them and their **species**; and as we continue to do this, their greater journey continues.

On July 20, 1969, a television audience numbering in the hundreds of millions watched as two human beings stepped out of a spacecraft onto the surface of the moon. To anyone born after that date, this event may be taken more or less for granted. But the significance of that first moonwalk can't be overstated, because it represents humankind's presumed mastery over the natural forces that govern our presence on earth. For the first time ever, people actually walked upon the surface of a celestial body that, as far as we know, has never given birth to biological life.

As the astronauts gathered geological specimens and frolicked in near weightlessness, they left traces of their fleeting presence in the form of footprints in the lunar dust (**Fig. 1-2**). On the surface of the moon, where no rain falls and no wind blows, the footprints remain undisturbed to this day. They survive as silent testimony to a brief visit by a medium-sized, big-brained creature that presumed to challenge the very forces that created it.

You may be wondering why anyone would care about early hominin footprints and how they can possibly be relevant to your life. You may also wonder why a physical **anthropology** textbook would begin by discussing two such seemingly unrelated events as hominins walking across an African savanna and a moonwalk. But the fact is, these two events are very closely related.

Physical, or biological, anthropology is a scientific discipline concerned with the biological and behavioral characteristics of human beings; our closest relatives, the nonhuman **primates** (apes, monkeys, lemurs, lorises, and tarsiers); and their ancestors. This kind of research helps us explain what it means to be human. This is an ambitious goal, and it probably isn't completely attainable, but it's certainly worth pursuing. We're the only species to ponder our own existence and question how we fit into the spectrum of life on earth. Most people view humanity as separate from the rest of the animal kingdom. But at the same time, many are curious about the similarities we share with other species. Maybe, as a child, you looked at your dog and tried to figure out how her front legs might correspond to your arms. Or perhaps during a visit to the zoo, you recognized the similarities between a chimpanzee's hands or facial expressions and your own. Maybe you wondered if he also shared your thoughts and feelings. If you've ever had thoughts and questions like these, then you've indeed been curious about humankind's place in nature.

We humans, who can barely comprehend a century, can't begin to grasp the enormity of nearly 4 million years. But we still want to know more about those creatures who walked across the savanna that day. We want to know how an insignificant but clever bipedal primate such as *Australopithecus afarensis*, or perhaps a close relative, gave rise to a species that would eventually walk on the surface of a moon, some 230,000 miles from earth.

How did *Homo sapiens*, a result of the same evolutionary forces that produced all other forms of life on this planet, gain the power to control the flow of rivers and even alter the climate on a global scale? As tropical animals, how were we able to leave the tropics and eventually occupy most of the earth's land surfaces? How did we adjust to different environmental conditions as we dispersed? How could our species, which numbered fewer than 1 billion until the mid-nineteenth century, come to number almost 7 billion worldwide today and, as we now do, add another billion people every 11 years?

These are some of the many questions that physical anthropologists try to answer through the study of human **evolution**, variation, and **adaptation**. These issues, and many others, are the topics covered directly or indirectly in this textbook, because physical anthropology is, in large part, human biology seen from an evolutionary perspective.

As biological organisms, humans are subjected to the same evolutionary forces as all other species. On hearing the term *evolution*, most people think of the appearance of new species. Certainly, new species are one important consequence of evolution; but it isn't the only one, because evolution is an ongoing biological process with more than one outcome. Simply stated, evolution is a change in the **genetic** makeup of a population from one generation to the next, and it can be defined and studied at two levels. Over time, some genetic changes in populations do result in the appearance of a new species (or *speciation*), especially when those populations are isolated from one another. Change at this level is called *macroevolution*. At the other level, there are genetic alterations *within*

▲ **Figure 1-2**
Human footprints left on the lunar surface during the *Apollo* mission.

in populations; and while this type of change may not lead to speciation, it does cause populations of a species to differ from one another in the frequency of certain traits. Evolution at this level is referred to as *microevolution*. Evolution as it occurs at both these levels will be discussed in this book.

But biological anthropologists don't just study physiological and biological systems. When these topics are considered within the broader context of human evolution, another factor must be considered, and that factor is **culture**. Culture is an extremely important concept, not only as it relates to modern humans but also because of its critical role in human evolution. Quite simply, and in a very broad sense, culture can be defined as the strategy by which humans adapt to the natural environment. In fact, culture has so altered and so dominated our world that it's become the environment in which we live. Culture includes technologies ranging from stone tools to computers; subsistence patterns, from hunting and gathering to global agribusiness; housing types, from thatched huts to skyscrapers; and clothing, from animal skins to high-tech synthetic fibers (**Fig. 1-3**). Technology, religion, values, social organization, language,

primates Members of the mammalian order Primates (pronounced "pry-may´-tees"), which includes lemurs, lorises, tarsiers, monkeys, apes, and humans.

evolution A change in the genetic structure of a population. The term is also frequently used to refer to the appearance of a new species.

adaptation An anatomical, physiological, or behavioral response of organisms or populations to the environment. Adaptations result from evolutionary change (specifically, as a result of natural selection).

genetic Having to do with the study of gene structure and action and the patterns of inheritance of traits from parent to offspring. Genetic mechanisms are the foundation for evolutionary change.

culture Behavioral aspects of human adaptation, including technology, traditions, language, religion, marriage patterns, and social roles. Culture is a set of learned behaviors transmitted from one generation to the next by nonbiological (i.e., nongenetic) means.

▶ **Figure 1-3**

Traditional and recent technologies. (**a**) An early stone tool from East Africa. This artifact represents one of the oldest types of stone tools found anywhere. (**b**) The Hubble Space telescope, a late twentieth-century tool, orbits the earth every 96 minutes at an altitude of 360 miles. Because it is above the earth's atmosphere, it provides distortion-free images of objects in deep space. (**c**) A cuneiform tablet. Cuneiform, the earliest form of writing, involved pressing symbols into clay tablets. It originated in southern Iraq some 5,000 years ago. (**d**) Text messaging, a fairly recent innovation in satellite communication, has generated a new language of sorts. Today, more than 500 million text messages are sent every day worldwide. (**e**) A Samburu woman in East Africa building a traditional but complicated dwelling of stems, small branches, and mud. (**f**) These Hong Kong skyscrapers are typical of cities in industrialized countries today.

kinship, marriage rules, gender roles, dietary practices, inheritance of property, and so on, are all aspects of culture. And each culture shapes people's perceptions of the external environment, or **worldview**, in particular ways that distinguish that society from all others.

One important point to remember is that culture isn't genetically passed from one generation to the next. We aren't born with innate knowledge that leads us to behave in ways appropriate to our own culture. Culture is *learned*, and the process of learning one's culture begins, quite literally, at birth. All humans are products of the culture they're raised in, and since most human **behavior** is learned, it follows that most human behaviors, perceptions, values, and reactions are shaped by culture.

At the same time, however, it's important to emphasize that even though culture isn't genetically determined, the human predisposition to assimilate culture and function within it is very much influenced by biological factors. Most nonhuman animals, including birds and especially primates, rely to varying degrees on learned behavior. This is especially true of the great apes (gorillas, chimpanzees, bonobos, and orangutans), which exhibit several aspects of culture.

The predisposition for culture is perhaps the most critical component of human evolutionary history, and it was inherited from our early hominin or even prehominin ancestors. In fact, the common ancestor we share with chimpanzees may have had this predisposition. But during the course of human evolution, the role of culture became exceptionally important. Over time, culture influenced many aspects of our biological makeup; and in turn, aspects of biology influenced cultural practices. For this reason, humans are the result of long-term interactions between biology and culture, and we call these interactions **biocultural**

evolution; in this respect, humans are unique (**Fig 1-4**).

Biocultural interactions have resulted in many anatomical, biological, and behavioral changes during the course of human evolution: the shape of the pelvis, increased brain size, reorganization of neurological structures, smaller teeth, and the development of language, to name a few. Today, biocultural interactions are as important as ever, especially with regard to health and disease. Air pollution and exposure to dangerous chemicals have increased the prevalence of respiratory disease and cancer. While air travel makes it possible for people to travel thousands of miles in just a few hours, we aren't the only species that can do this. Disease-causing organisms travel on airplanes with their human hosts, making it possible for infectious diseases to spread, literally within hours, across the globe.

Many human activities have changed the patterns of such infectious diseases as tuberculosis, influenza, and malaria. After the domestication of nonhuman animals, close contact with chickens, pigs, and cattle greatly increased human exposure to some of the diseases these animals carry. Through this contact we've also changed the genetic makeup of disease-causing microorganisms. For example, the H1N1 "swine flu" virus that caused the 2009 pandemic actually contains genetic material derived from bacteria that infect three different species: humans, birds, and pigs. Because we've overused antibiotics, we've made some strains of tuberculosis resistant to treatment and even deadly. Likewise, although we're making progress in treating malaria, the microorganism that causes it has developed resistance to some treatments and preventive medications. We've also increased the geographical distribution of malaria-carrying mosquitoes through agricultural practices and global climate change. But while it's clear that we humans

worldview General cultural orientation or perspective shared by members of a society.

behavior Anything organisms do that involves action in response to internal or external stimuli; the response of an individual, group, or species to its environment. Such responses may or may not be deliberate, and they aren't necessarily the result of conscious decision making (which is absent in single-celled organisms, insects, and many other species).

biocultural evolution The mutual, interactive evolution of human biology and culture; the concept that biology makes culture possible and that developing culture further influences the direction of biological evolution; a basic concept in understanding the unique components of human evolution.

8

Biocultural Evolution

▶ Figure 1-4

The Big Picture (Macroveolution): Primate/Hominin Biocultural Evolution over the last 20+ million years

For millions of years, the interaction of culture and biology has influenced human evolution. Understanding this process is a major theme of this text, and this illustration shows aspects of biocultural evolution that you will encounter in every chapter. The larger process (called "macroevolution") is shown on the outside (a-f), while more recent, microevolutionary processes are shown in the center (g-i), using the example of malaria and human cultural and biological responses to it. Macroevolution takes millions of years, and the foundations for human biocultural evolution were already developing long ago in our more distant primate ancestors. It is clear that our origins, physical and behavioral, are part of an evolutionary continuum. Building on this foundation, in the last few million years among our more immediate ancestors (d-f), culture has become far more complex and integral, to the point that humans couldn't survive without it.

Primate Social Behavior (beginning at least 20 million years ago)

Slash-and-burn agriculture creates breeding areas for mosquitoes

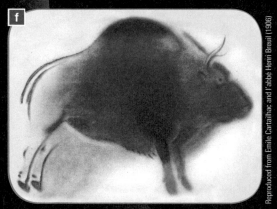

Complex Human Behavior: Symbolic Thought, Language, Larger Social Groups

Recent Biocultural Evolution (Microevolution) in Human Populations over the last two thousand years.

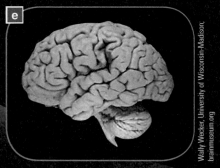

Larger, More Complex Brain

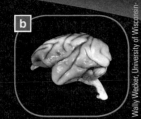

Increase in Brain Size

Wally Welker, University of Wisconsin-Madison: brainmuseum.org

Primate Tool Use

Noemi Spagnoletti / EthoCebus Project

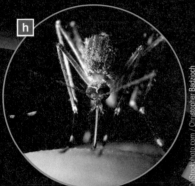

Mosquitoes Closer to Human Habitation and Infect More People with Malaria

© iStockphoto.com / Christopher Badzioch

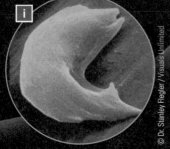

Adaptation: Sickle-cell Becomes More Common

© Dr. Stanley Flegler / Visuals Unlimited

© 2010 Photo S. Entressangle E. Daynes – Reconstruction Atelier Daynes Paris

have influenced the development and spread of infectious disease, we still don't know the many ways that changes in infectious disease patterns are affecting human biology and behavior. Anthropological research in this one topic alone is extremely relevant, and there are many other critical topics that biological anthropologists explore.

What Is Anthropology?

Many anthropology students contemplate this question when their parents or friends ask, "What are you studying?" The answer is often followed by a blank stare or a comment about Indiana Jones or dinosaurs. So, what *is* anthropology, and how is it different from several related disciplines?

Biologists also investigate human adaptation and evolution; and historians and sociologists also study aspects of human societies, past and present. But when biological or social research also considers the interactions between evolutionary and cultural factors, it's included in the discipline of anthropology.

In the United States, anthropology is divided into four main subfields: cultural, or social, anthropology; linguistic anthropology; archaeology; and physical, or biological, anthropology. Each of these, in turn, is divided into several specialized areas of interest. This four-field approach concerns all aspects of humanity across space and time. Each subdiscipline emphasizes different facets of humanity, but together, they offer a means of explaining variation in human adaptations. In addition, each of these subfields has practical applications, and many anthropologists pursue careers outside the university environment. This kind of anthropology is called **applied anthropology**, and it's extremely important today.

Cultural Anthropology

Cultural, or social, anthropology is the study of patterns of belief and behavior found in modern and historical human cultures. The origins of cultural anthropology can be traced to the nineteenth century, when travel and exploration brought Europeans in contact (and sometimes conflict) with various cultures in Africa, Asia, and the New World.

With this contact grew an interest in so-called "traditional" societies, leading many early anthropologists to study and record lifeways that are now mostly extinct. These studies produced many descriptive **ethnographies** that emphasized various phenomena, such as religion, ritual, myth, use of symbols, diet, technology, gender roles, and child-rearing practices. Ethnographic accounts, in turn, formed the basis for comparative studies of numerous cultures. By examining the similarities and differences among cultures, cultural anthropologists have been able to formulate many hypotheses regarding fundamental aspects of human behavior.

The focus of cultural anthropology shifted over the course of the twentieth century. Cultural anthropologists still worked in remote areas, but increasingly turned their gaze inward, toward their own cultures and the people around them. Increasingly, ethnographic techniques have been applied to the study of diverse subcultures and their interactions with one another in contemporary metropolitan areas (urban anthropology). The population of any city is composed of many subgroups defined by economic status, religion, ethnic background, profession, age, level of education, and so on. Even the student body of your own college or university is made up of many subcultures, and as you walk across campus, you'll see students of many nationalities and diverse religious and ethnic

applied anthropology The practical application of anthropological and archaeological theories and techniques. For example, many biological anthropologists work in the public health sector.

ethnographies Detailed descriptive studies of human societies. In cultural anthropology, an ethnography is traditionally the study of a non-Western society.

backgrounds. You may also be aware of more recent cultural identities, such as LGBT, goths, and emos, to name a few.

Linguistic Anthropology

Linguistic anthropology is the study of human speech and language, including the origins of language in general as well as specific languages. By examining similarities between contemporary languages, linguists have been able to trace historical ties between particular languages and groups of languages, thus facilitating the identification of language families and perhaps past relationships between human populations.

Because the spontaneous acquisition and use of language is a uniquely human characteristic, it's an important topic for linguistic anthropologists, who, along with specialists in other fields, study the process of language acquisition in infants. Since insights into the process may well have implications for the development of language in human evolution, as well as in growing children, it's also an important subject to physical anthropologists.

Archaeology

Archaeology is the study of earlier cultures by anthropologists who specialize in the scientific recovery, analysis, and interpretation of the material remains of past societies. Archaeologists obtain information from **artifacts** and structures left behind by earlier cultures. The remains of earlier societies, in the form of tools, structures, art, eating implements, fragments of writing, and so on, provide a great deal of information about many important aspects of a society, such as religion and social structure.

Unlike in the past (or in movies like *Tomb Raider* or *Indiana Jones*),

sites aren't excavated just because they exist or for the artifacts or "treasures" they may contain. Rather, they're excavated to gain information about human behavior. For example, patterns of behavior are reflected in the dispersal of human settlements across a landscape and in the distribution of cultural remains within them. Archaeological research questions may focus on specific localities or peoples and attempt to identify, for example, various aspects of social organization, subsistence techniques, or factors that led to the collapse of a civilization. Alternatively, inquiry may reflect an interest in broader issues relating to human culture in general, such as the development of agriculture or the rise of cities.

Archaeological techniques are used to identify and excavate not only remains of human cities and settlements but also sites that contain the remains of extinct species, including everything from dinosaurs to early hominins. Together, prehistoric archaeology and physical anthropology form the core of a joint science called *paleoanthropology*, described later in this book.

Physical Anthropology

As we've already said, *physical anthropology* is the study of human biology within the framework of evolution and with an emphasis on the interaction between biology and culture. This subdiscipline is also referred to as *biological anthropology*, and you'll find the terms used interchangeably. *Physical anthropology* is the original term, and it reflects the initial interests anthropologists had in describing human physical variation. The American Association of Physical Anthropologists, its journal, many college courses, and numerous publications retain this term. The designation *biological anthropology*

---

artifacts Objects or materials made or modified for use by hominins. The earliest artifacts are usually tools made of stone or, occasionally, bone.

reflects the shift in emphasis to more biologically oriented topics, such as genetics, evolutionary biology, nutrition, physiological adaptation, and growth and development. This shift occurred largely because of advances in the field of genetics and molecular biology since the late 1950s. Although we've continued to use the traditional term in the title of this textbook, you'll find that all of the major topics we discuss pertain to biological issues.

The origins of physical anthropology can be traced to two principal areas of interest among eighteenth- and nineteenth-century European and American scientists (at that time called *naturalists* or *natural historians*): the origins of modern species and human variation. Although most of these naturalists held religious convictions, they were beginning to doubt the literal interpretation of the biblical account of creation and to support explanations that emphasized natural processes rather than supernatural phenomena. Eventually, the sparks of interest in biological change over time were fueled into flames by the publication of Charles Darwin's *On the Origin of Species* in 1859.

Today, **paleoanthropology**, the study of anatomical and behavioral human evolution as revealed in the fossil record, is a major subfield of physical anthropology (**Fig. 1-5**). Thousands of fossilized remains of early primates, including human ancestors, are now kept in research collections. Taken together, these fossils span at least 46 million years (and maybe more!) of primate evolution. Although most of these fossils are fragmentary, they provide us with a significant wealth of knowledge that increases each year. It's the ultimate goal of paleoanthropological research to identify the various early human and humanlike species, establish a chronological sequence of

▲ **Figure 1-5**

(a) Paleoanthropologists excavating at the Drimolen site, South Africa. (b) Primate paleontologist Russ Ciochon and Le Trang Kha, a vertebrate paleontologist, examine the fossil remains of *Gigantopithecus* from a 450,000-year-old site in Vietnam. *Gigantopithecus* is the name given to the largest apes that ever lived. In the background is a reconstruction of this enormous animal.

© Kenneth Garrett / NGS Image Collection

© Russell L. Ciochon

paleoanthropology The interdisciplinary approach to the study of earlier hominins—their chronology, physical structure, archaeological remains, habitats, and so on.

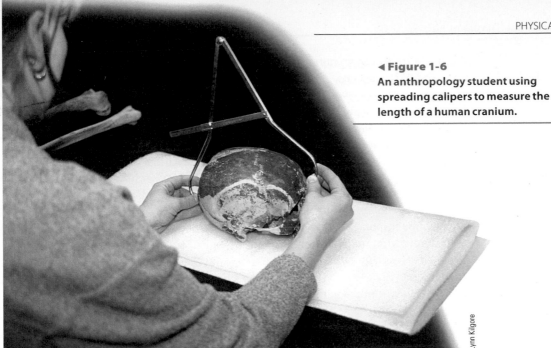

◄ **Figure 1-6**
An anthropology student using spreading calipers to measure the length of a human cranium.

relationships among them, and gain insights into their adaptation and behavior. Only then will we have a clear picture of how and when modern humans came into being.

To some extent, **primate paleontology** can be viewed as a subset of paleoanthropology. Primate paleontology is the study of the primate fossil record, which extends back to the beginning of primate evolution some 65 million years ago (mya). Virtually every year, fossil-bearing beds in North America, Africa, Asia, and Europe yield important new discoveries. By studying fossil primates and comparing them with anatomically similar living species, primate paleontologists are learning a great deal about factors such as diet or locomotion in earlier forms. They can also try to identify aspects of behavior in some extinct primates and attempt to clarify what we know about evolutionary relationships between extinct and modern species, including ourselves.

Visible physical variation was the other major area of interest for early physical anthropologists. Enormous effort was spent in measuring, describing, and explaining the obvious differences among various human populations, with particular attention being focused on skin color, body propor-

tions, and shape of the head and face. Although some approaches were misguided, they gave rise to hundreds of body measurements. The techniques of **anthropometry** are still used today, although with very different goals. In fact, they've been applied to the design of everything from wheelchairs to body armor for soldiers. (Undoubtedly, they've also been used to determine the absolute minimum amount of leg room a person needs in order to complete a 3-hour flight on a commercial airliner and remain sane.) They're also very important to the study of skeletal remains from archaeological sites (**Fig. 1-6**).

Today, anthropologists are concerned with human variation because of its possible *adaptive significance.* In other words, many traits that typify certain populations can be seen as having evolved as biological adaptations, or adjustments, to local environmental conditions, including infectious disease. Other characteristics may be the results of geographical isolation or the descent of populations from small founding groups.

Since the early 1990s, the focus of human variation studies has shifted completely away from the visible differences we see in people to the underlying genetic factors that influence

primate paleontology The study of fossil primates, especially those that lived before the appearance of hominins.

anthropometry Measurement of human body parts. When osteologists measure skeletal elements, the term *osteometry* is often used.

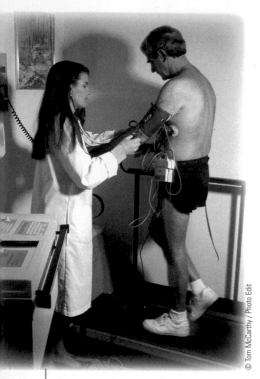

these and many other traits. This shift occurred partly because examining genetic variation between populations and individuals of any species helps explain biological change over time; and that is precisely what the evolutionary process is all about.

Modern population studies also examine other important aspects of human variation, including how various groups respond physiologically to different kinds of environmentally induced stress (**Fig. 1-7**). Such stresses may include high altitude, cold, or heat. *Nutritional anthropologists* study the relationships between various dietary components, cultural practices, physiology, and certain aspects of health and disease (**Fig. 1-8**). Investigations of human fertility, growth, and development also are closely related to the topic of nutrition. These fields of inquiry, which are fundamental to studies of adaptation in modern human populations, can provide insights into hominin evolution, too.

As you've just seen, genetics is a crucial field for physical anthropologists. As Charles Darwin discovered, it's extremely difficult (actually impossible) to effectively study evolutionary processes without knowing how traits are inherited. Therefore, modern physical anthropology wouldn't exist as an evolutionary science if it weren't for advances in the understanding of genetic mechanisms. In fact, many biological anthropologists (called molecular anthropologists) specialize in genetics.

Molecular anthropologists use cutting-edge technologies to investigate evolutionary relationships between human populations as well as between humans and nonhuman primates. To do this, they examine similarities and differences in **DNA** sequences between individuals, populations, and species. What's more, by extracting DNA from certain fossils, these researchers have contributed to our understanding of relationships

▲ **Figure 1-7**
This researcher is using a treadmill test to assess a subject's heart rate, blood pressure, and oxygen consumption.

▶ **Figure 1-8**
Dr. Kathleen Galvin measures upper arm circumference in a young Maasai boy in Tanzania. Data derived from various body measurements, including height and weight, were used in a health and nutrition study of groups of Maasai cattle herders.

DNA (deoxyribonucleic acid) The double-stranded molecule that contains the genetic code. DNA is a main component of chromosomes.

Robert Jurmain

Nelson Ting

▲ **Figure 1-9**

(a) Cloning and sequencing methods are frequently used to identify genes in humans and nonhuman primates. This graduate student is working with genetically modified bacterial clones.

(b) Molecular anthropologist Nelson Ting collecting red colobus fecal samples for a study of genetic variation in small groups of monkeys isolated from one another by agricultural clearing.

between extinct and living species. As genetic technologies continue to be developed, molecular anthropologists will play a key role in explaining human evolution, adaptation, and our biological relationships with other species (**Fig. 1-9**).

However, before genetic and molecular techniques became widespread, **osteology**, the study of the skeleton, was the only way that anthropologists could study our immediate ancestors. In fact, a thorough knowledge of skeletal structure and function is still critical to the interpretation of fossil material today. For this reason, osteology has long been viewed as central to physical anthropology. In fact, it's so important that when many people think of biological anthropology, the first thing that comes to mind is bones!

Bone biology and physiology are of major importance to many other aspects of physical anthropology besides human evolution. Many osteologists specialize in the measurement of skeletal elements, essential for identifying stature and growth patterns in archaeological populations. In the last 30 years or so, the study of human skel-

etal remains from archaeological sites has been called **bioarchaeology**.

Paleopathology, the study of disease and trauma in ancient skeletal populations, is a major component of bioarchaeology. Paleopathologists investigate the prevalence of trauma, certain infectious diseases (such as syphilis and tuberculosis), nutritional deficiencies, and numerous other conditions that may leave evidence in bone (**Fig. 1-10**). This research tells us a great deal about the lives of individuals and populations in the past. Paleopathology also yields information regarding the history of certain disease processes, and for this reason it's of interest to scientists in biomedical fields.

Forensic anthropology, an area directly related to osteology and paleopathology, has become of increasing interest to the public because of forensic TV shows like *Bones* (based on a character created by a practicing forensic anthropologist) and *Crime Scene Investigation: CSI*. Technically, this approach is the application of anthropological (usually osteological and sometimes archaeological) techniques to legal issues. Forensic anthropologists

osteology The study of skeletal material. Human osteology focuses on the interpretation of the skeletal remains from archaeological sites, skeletal anatomy, bone physiology, and growth and development. Some of the same techniques are used in paleoanthropology to study early hominins.

bioarchaeology The study of skeletal remains from archaeological sites.

paleopathology The branch of osteology that studies the evidence of disease and injury in human skeletal (or, occasionally, mummified) remains from archaeological sites.

forensic anthropology An applied anthropological approach dealing with legal matters. Forensic anthropologists work with coroners and others in identifying and analyzing human remains.

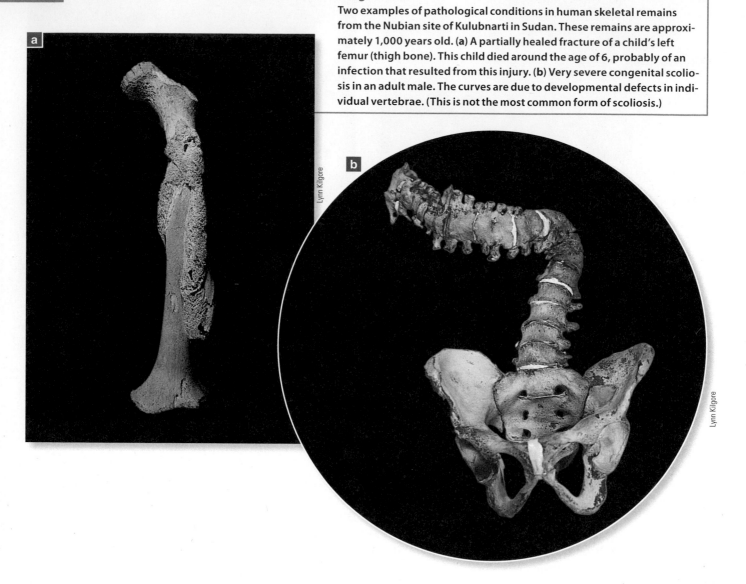

◄ **Figure 1-10**

Two examples of pathological conditions in human skeletal remains from the Nubian site of Kulubnarti in Sudan. These remains are approximately 1,000 years old. (a) A partially healed fracture of a child's left femur (thigh bone). This child died around the age of 6, probably of an infection that resulted from this injury. (b) Very severe congenital scoliosis in an adult male. The curves are due to developmental defects in individual vertebrae. (This is not the most common form of scoliosis.)

help identify skeletal remains in mass disasters or other situations where a human body has been found. They've been involved in numerous cases having important legal, historical, and human consequences (**Fig. 1-11**). They were instrumental in identifying the skeletons of most of the Russian imperial family, executed in 1918; and many participated in the overwhelming task of trying to identify the remains of victims of the September 11, 2001, terrorist attacks in the United States.

Anatomy is yet another important area of interest for physical anthropologists. In living organisms, bones and teeth are intimately linked to the soft tissues that surround and act on them. Consequently, a thorough knowledge of soft tissue anatomy is essential to understanding the biomechanical relationships involved in movement. Such relationships are important in assessing the structure and function of limbs and other components of fossilized remains. For these reasons and others, many physical anthropologists specialize in anatomical studies. In fact, several physical anthropologists are professors in anatomy departments at universities and medical schools (**Fig. 1-12**).

But humans aren't the only species studied by biological anthropolo-

© Reuters / Corbis

U.S. Army Corps of Engineers, and the Regime Crime Liaison Office

◀**Figure 1-11**
(a) Forensic anthropologists Vuzumusi Madasco (from Zimbabwe) and Patricia Bernardi (from Argentina) excavating the skeletal remains and clothing of one of many victims of a civil war massacre in El Salvador. The goal is to identify as many of the victims as possible. **(b)** These forensic anthropologists, working in a lab near Baghdad, are examining the skeletal remains of Khurdish victims of genocide. They cataloged the injuries of 114 individuals buried in a mass grave, and some of their evidence was used against Saddam Hussein during his trial in 2006.

gists. Given our evolutionary focus and the fact that we ourselves are primates, it's natural that **primatology**, the study of the living nonhuman primates, has become increasingly important since the 1960s (**Fig. 1-13**). A few scientists had begun systematically studying nonhuman primates in the 1950s, but in 1960 a young English woman named Jane Goodall went to Africa to study chimpanzees. As news of her work became popularized in *National Geographic* films and magazines, she and her research became world famous, and for the first time, people began to understand how similar we are to our closest relatives. Today, dozens of nonhuman primate species have been, and are being, studied, and because this research focuses primarily on behavior, it has implications for many scientific disciplines. Moreover, because nonhuman primates are our closest living relatives, identifying the underlying factors related to their social behavior, communication, infant

primatology The study of the biology and behavior of nonhuman primates (lemurs, lorises, tarsiers, monkeys, and apes).

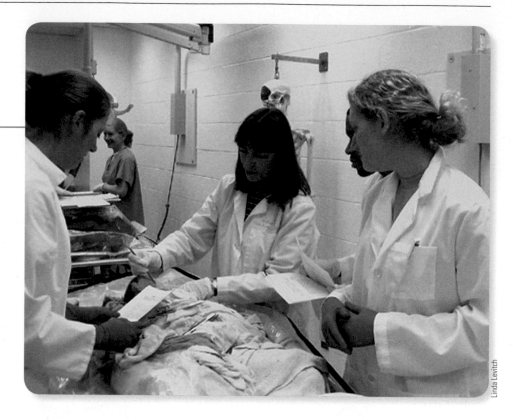

▶ **Figure 1-12**
Dr. Linda Levitch teaching a human anatomy class at the University of North Carolina School of Medicine.

Linda Levitch

care, reproductive behavior, and so on, helps us to develop a better understanding of the natural forces that have shaped so many aspects of modern human behavior.

Nonhuman primates are also important to study in their own right. This is particularly true today because the majority of primate species are threatened or seriously endangered. Only through study will scientists be able to recommend policies that can better ensure the survival of many nonhuman primates and thousands of other species as well.

Applied Anthropology

Applied approaches in anthropology are numerous. While *applied anthropology* is the practical use of anthropological theories and methods outside the academic setting, applied and academic anthropology aren't mutually exclusive approaches. In fact, applied anthropology relies on the research and theories of academic anthropologists and at the same time has much to contribute to theory and techniques.

One area of applied anthropology of interest to cultural anthropologists is the welfare of refugees and their resettlement and cultural integration (or lack thereof) in countries such as the United States or Canada. In a different approach, *medical anthropology* explores the relationship between various cultural attributes and health and disease (**Fig. 1-14**). For instance, one area of interest is how different groups view disease processes and how these views affect treatment or the willingness to accept treatment. Today, most innovative hospitals that are interested in transforming health care have cultural anthropologists on staff (Chin, pers. comm.).In fact, international corporations are increasingly hiring cultural anthropologists in particular in order to apply ethnographic techniques to a variety of issues.

While for cultural medical anthropologists the focus is primarily the social dimensions of disease, many physical anthropologists describe what they do as *biomedical anthropology.* Research topics in biomedical anthropology include population variation in susceptibility to disease; the relationship between genes, environment, diet, and health; and the evolutionary history of disease.

In the United States, there was a major expansion in archaeological research beginning in the 1970s. This applied subfield called *cultural resource management (CRM).* CRM arose from environmental legislation requiring archaeological evaluation and sometimes excavation of sites that may be threatened by development. (Canada and many European countries have similar legislation.) Many contract archaeologists (so called because their services are contracted out to builders and developers) are affiliated with private consulting firms, state or federal agencies, or educational institutions.

Within physical anthropology, forensic anthropology is probably the best example of the applied approach, and forensic anthropologists work frequently with archaeologists to search for human remains or various kinds of evidence at crime scenes.

But the practical application of the techniques of physical anthropology came about before the development of forensic anthropology. During World War II, for example, physical anthropologists, using anthropometric techniques, were extensively involved in designing gun turrets and airplane cockpits. Today, physical anthropologists pursue careers in genetic and

▲ **Figure 1-13**

(a) Primatologist Emmanuelle Grundmann using ropes and a harness to observe an orangutan in Borneo. (b) Primatologist Jill Pruetz follows a chimpanzee in Senegal, in west Africa.

Dr. Soo Young Chin

Nanette Barkey

▶ **Figure 1-14**

(a) Dr. Soo Young Chin, Lead Partner of Practical Ethnographics at Ascension Health, pointing to pilot locations for a study of a new health care plan. (b) Nanette Barkey, a medical anthropologist involved in a repatriation project in Angola, photographed this little girl being vaccinated at a refugee transit camp. Vaccinations were being administered to Angolan refugees returning home in 2004 from the Democratic Republic of Congo, where they had fled to escape warfare in their own country.

Physical Anthropology and the Scientific Method

Science is a process of explaining natural phenomena. It involves observation; developing **hypotheses** to explain what has been observed; and developing a research design or series of experiments to test the hypotheses. This is an **empirical** approach to gaining information. Because biological anthropologists are engaged in scientific pursuits, they adhere to the principles of the **scientific method** by identifying a research problem and then gathering information to solve it.

Once a question has been asked, the first step usually is to explore the existing literature (books and journals) to determine what other people have done to resolve the issue. Based on this preliminary research and other observations, one or even several tentative explanations (hypotheses) are then proposed. The next step is to develop a research design or methodology aimed at testing the hypothesis. These methods involve collecting information, or

science A body of knowledge gained through observation and experimentation; from the Latin *scientia*, meaning "knowledge."

hypotheses (*sing.*, hypothesis) A provisional explanation of a phenomenon. Hypotheses require verification or falsification through testing.

empirical Relying on experiment or observation; from the Latin *empiricus*, meaning "experienced."

scientific method An approach to research whereby a problem is identified, a hypothesis (provisional explanation) is stated, and that hypothesis is tested by collecting and analyzing data.

biomedical research, public health, evolutionary medicine, medical anthropology, and conservation of nonhuman primates. Moreover, many physical anthropologists hold positions in museums and zoos. In fact, a background in physical anthropology is excellent preparation for almost any career in the medical and biological fields.

data, that can then be studied and analyzed. Data can be analyzed in many ways, most of them involving various statistical tests. During the data collection and analysis phase, it's important for scientists to use a rigorously controlled approach so they can precisely describe their techniques and results. This precision is critical because it enables others to repeat the experiments and allows scientists to make comparisons between their study and the work of others.

For example, when scientists collect data on tooth size in hominin fossils, they must specify which teeth are being measured, how they're measured, and the results of the measurements (expressed numerically, or **quantitatively**). Then, by analyzing the data, the investigators try to draw conclusions about the meaning and significance of their measurements. This body of information then becomes the basis of future studies, perhaps by other researchers, who can compare their own results with those already obtained.

Hypothesis testing is the very core of the scientific method, and although it may seem contradictory at first, it's based on the potential to *falsify* the hypothesis. Falsification doesn't mean that the entire hypothesis is untrue, but it does indicate that the hypothesis may need to be refined and subjected to further testing.

Eventually, if a hypothesis stands up to repeated testing, it may become part of a **theory** or perhaps a theory itself. There's a popular misconception that a theory is nothing more than conjecture, or a "hunch." But in science, theories are proposed explanations of relationships between natural phenomena. Theories usually concern broader, more universal views than hypotheses, which have a narrower focus and deal with more specific relationships between phenomena. But like hypotheses, theories aren't facts. *They are tested explanations of facts.* For example, it is a fact that when you drop an object,

it falls to the ground. The explanation for this fact is the theory of gravity. But, like hypotheses, theories can be altered over time with further experimentation and by using newly developed technologies in testing. The theory of gravity has been tested many times and qualified by experiments showing how the mass of objects affects how they're attracted to one another. So far, the theory has held up.

There is one more extremely important fact about hypotheses and theories: *Any proposition that is stated as absolute or does not allow the possibility of falsification is not a scientific hypothesis and should never be considered as such.* For a statement to be considered a scientific hypothesis, there must be a way to evaluate its validity. Statements such as "Heaven exists" may well be true (that is, they may describe some actual state), but there is no rational, empirical means (based on experience or experiment) of testing them. Therefore, acceptance of such a view is based on faith rather than on scientific verification. The purpose of scientific research is not to establish absolute truths; rather, it's to generate ever more accurate and consistent explanations of phenomena in our universe based on observation and testing. At its very heart, scientific methodology is an exercise in rational thought and critical thinking (see "A Closer Look: Evaluation in Science: Lessons in Critical Thinking").

Scientific testing of hypotheses may take several years (or longer) and may involve researchers who weren't involved with the original work. What's more, new methods may permit different kinds of testing that weren't previously possible, and this is a strength, not a weakness, of scientific research. For example, since the 1970s, primatologists have reported that male nonhuman primates (as well as males of many other species) sometimes kill infants. One hypothesis has been that infanticidal males were killing the offspring of other males. But many

data (*sing.*, datum) Facts from which conclusions can be drawn; scientific information.

quantitatively Pertaining to measurements of quantity and including such properties as size, number, and capacity. When data are quantified, they're expressed numerically and can be tested statistically.

theory A broad statement of scientific relationships or underlying principles that has been substantially verified through the testing of hypotheses.

scientific testing The precise repetition of an experiment or expansion of observed data to provide verification; the procedure by which hypotheses and theories are verified, modified, or discarded.

A Closer Look

Evaluation in Science: Lessons in Critical Thinking

Every day, we're bombarded through the media with a multitude of claims relating to health, financial success, self-improvement, and just about anything else that someone wants us to believe. But we must always be careful how we evaluate such information while not being overly swayed by our personal opinions. We should also be reluctant to accept any view based solely on its personal appeal. Accepting or rejecting an idea based on personal feelings is as good a definition of bias as one could devise. Science is an approach—indeed, a tool— used to eliminate (or at least minimize) bias.

Scientific evaluation is, in fact, part of a broader framework of intellectual rigor called critical thinking. The development of critical thinking skills should be an important and lasting benefit of a college education. These skills are valuable in everyday life because they enable people to evaluate, compare, analyze, critique, and synthesize information so they won't accept everything they hear and read at face value.

The advertising industry provides an excellent illustration of the need for critical thinking. Cosmetics companies tell us, among other things, that collagen creams will reduce wrinkles because collagen is a principal protein component of connective tissue, including skin. It's true that collagen is a major protein constituent of skin tissue. Moreover, collagen fibers do break down over time, and this damage is one factor that contributes to the development of wrinkles. But the most beneficial properties of the creams are probably the UV filters and moisturizers they contain, although they won't eliminate wrinkles. What's more, the collagen isn't absorbed into skin cells, and even if it were, it still wouldn't be incorporated in a way that would replenish what's been destroyed. But most people don't know what collagen is. Thus, when they hear that it's an important component of skin tissue and therefore can help reduce wrinkles, the argument sounds reasonable; so they buy the cream, which won't reduce wrinkles and is fairly expensive.

Critical thinking skills may be most important in the area of politics. Politicians routinely make claims, frequently in 15-second sound bites that use catchphrases and misleading statistics. (Remember, their speechwriters are well informed and skillful at manipulating language, and they know they're targeting a generally uninformed public.)

An informed public can—and should— call its political leaders to task when necessary. For example, global climate change has become a political issue, especially in the United States. The vast majority of scientists worldwide now agree that global warming is happening and that it's caused by human activity. Fortunately, many governments, especially in Europe, are beginning to develop policies aimed at slowing the warming trend. However, many politicians in the United States and a few other countries continue to say that we still don't have enough scientific data to justify spending billions of dollars on preventive measures that may not even work. Given the stakes involved, if the concerns expressed by so many scientists today are real, an informed populace should take it upon itself to investigate these issues and ask why some governments are concerned while others aren't.

When politicians say, "Scientists aren't in complete agreement on the issue of global warming," what they imply—and what most people hear—is that there is widespread disagreement among scientists about climate change. Certainly, some climate scientists still aren't convinced, but most are. If you understand the nature of science and the scientific method, then you realize that much of the disagreement among scientists isn't whether warming is happening or if human activities are a factor, but rather how fast it's happening, how warm it will get, and how disastrous the consequences will be (Gregory et al., 2004).

Most people tend to be ambivalent toward science and maybe even intimidated by it. In general, people accept scientific results when they support their personal views and reject them when they don't. They're also sometimes confused because science changes so rapidly. A study in 2004,

scientists have objected to this hypothesis and have proposed several alternatives. For one thing, there was no way to know for certain that the males weren't killing their own offspring; and if they were, this would argue against the hypothesis. However, in a fairly recent study, scientists collected DNA samples from dead infants and the males who killed them and showed that most of the time, the males were not related to their victims. This result doesn't prove that the original hypothesis is accurate, but it does strengthen it. This study is described in more detail in Chapter 7, but we mention it here to emphasize that science is an ongoing process that builds on previous work and benefits from newly developed techniques (in this case,

before the presidential election, revealed that one-third of Americans had never heard of stem cells, even though stem cell research was a major political issue and had been prominent in the news. Since most respondents in the survey were older, they hadn't learned about stem cells in school, and once out of school, most people avoid scientific issues. Moreover, science and math education in the United States has suffered a deplorable decline in recent years and now ranks behind that of all European countries (Gross, 2006). And over half of high school graduates don't complete a college degree. Fortunately, most colleges and universities require at least one year of science for a degree—in fact, that may be why you're taking this course.

Education is crucial for developing the critical thinking skills that will help us make important decisions and understand the many profound issues that confront us. Moreover, critical thinkers are able to assess the evidence supporting their own beliefs (in a sense, to step outside themselves) and to identify the weaknesses in their own positions. They recognize that knowledge is not merely a collection of facts, but an ongoing process of examining information to expand our understanding of the world. Critical thinkers look beyond the often superficial or ill-informed statements made by political leaders and advertisements and ask questions aimed at assessing the claims: "Who said that?" "What is the evidence for it?" "Is there research to support that claim?" "Was the research published in a peer-reviewed journal or quoted out of context or in a biased publication?" They also may take the time to research issues before making up their minds about them.

Throughout this book, you'll be presented with the results of numerous studies using numerical data. For example, we have just said that most climate scientists agree that the climate is changing and that the change is due to human activity. It is true that most climate scientists hold this view, but until you've explored this or any issue, you should be cautious of generalizations. A person with good critical thinking skills would ask, "What's the specific nature of the argument that the climate is changing?" "What data support it? Can these data be quantified? If so, how is this information presented?" (*Note*: Always carefully read the tables that appear in textbooks or articles.)

Regardless of the discipline you ultimately study, at some point in your college career you should take a course in statistics. Many universities now make statistics a general education requirement (sometimes under the category "quantitative reasoning"). Statistics often seems like a difficult and boring subject, and many students are intimidated by the math it requires. Nevertheless, perhaps more than any other skill you'll acquire in your college years, quantitative critical reasoning is a tool you'll be able to use every day of your life.

One responsibility of an educated society is to be both informed and vigilant.

The knowledge we possess and attempt to build on is neither good nor bad; however, the ways that knowledge may be used can have highly charged moral and ethical implications. Here are some useful questions to ask in making critical evaluations about any controversial scientific topic:

1. What data are presented?
2. What conclusions are presented, and how are they organized (as tentative hypotheses or as more dogmatic assertions)?
3. Are these views simply the authors' opinions, or are they supported by a larger body of research?
4. What are the research findings? Are they adequately documented?
5. Is the information consistent with information that you already possess? If not, can the inconsistencies be explained?
6. Are the conclusions (hypotheses) testable? How might one go about testing the various hypotheses that are presented?
7. If new research findings are at odds with previous hypotheses (or theories), must these hypotheses now be modified (or completely rejected)?
8. How do your own personal views bias you in interpreting the results?
9. Once you've identified your own biases, are you able to set them aside in order to evaluate the information objectively?
10. Can you discuss both the pros and cons of a scientific topic in an evenhanded manner?

DNA testing) in ways that constantly expand our knowledge.

The scientific method not only allows for the development and testing of hypotheses, but also helps eliminate various types of *bias*. It's important to realize that bias occurs in all studies. Sources of bias include how the investigator was trained and by whom; what particular questions the researcher is asking; what specific skills and talents he or she possesses; what earlier results (if any) have been obtained, and by whom (for example, the researcher, close colleagues, or those with rival approaches or even rival personalities); and what sources of data are available (for example, accessible countries or museums) and thus what samples can be collected.

The Anthropological Perspective

Perhaps the most important benefit you'll receive from this textbook, and this course, is a wider appreciation of the human experience. To understand human beings and how our species came to be, we must broaden our viewpoint through both time and space. All branches of anthropology fundamentally seek to do this in what we call the *anthropological perspective.*

Physical anthropologists, for example, are interested in how humans both differ from and are similar to other animals, especially nonhuman primates. For example, we've defined *hominins* as bipedal primates, but what are the major anatomical components of bipedal locomotion, and how do they differ from, say, those in a **quadrupedal** ape? To answer these questions, we would need to study the anatomical structures involved in human locomotion (muscles, hips, legs, and feet) and compare them with the same structures in various nonhuman primates.

In addition to broadening perspectives over space (that is, encompassing many cultures and ecological circumstances as well as nonhuman species), an anthropological perspective also extends our horizons *through time.* For example, in Chapter 17, we'll discuss human nutrition. The vast majority of the foods people eat today (coming from domesticated plants and animals) were unavailable prior to the development of agriculture, approximately 10,000 years ago. Human physiological mechanisms for chewing and digesting foods nevertheless were already well established long before that date; these adaptive complexes go back millions of years. Moreover, earlier hominins might well have differed from humans today in average body size, metabolism, and activity patterns. How, then, does the basic evolutionary "equipment" (that is, physiology) inherited from our hominin forebears accommodate our modern diets? Clearly, the way to understand such processes is not just by looking at contemporary human responses, but by placing them in the perspective of evolutionary development through time.

Through a perspective that is broad in space and time, we can begin to grasp the diversity of the human experience within the context of biological and behavioral continuity with other species. In this way, we may better understand the limits and potentials of humankind. And by extending our knowledge to include cultures other than our own, we may hope to avoid the **ethnocentric** pitfalls inherent in a more limited view of humanity.

We hope that after reading this text, you'll have an increased understanding not only of the similarities we share with other biological organisms, but also of the processes that have shaped the traits that make us unique. We live in what may well be our planet's most crucial period in the past 65 million years. We are members of the one species that, through the very agency of culture, has wrought such devastating changes in ecological systems that we must now alter our technologies or face potentially unspeakable consequences. In such a time, it's vital that we attempt to gain the best possible understanding of what it means to be human. We believe that the study of physical anthropology is one endeavor that aids in this attempt, and that is indeed the goal of this text.

quadrupedal Using all four limbs to support the body during locomotion; the basic mammalian (and primate) form of locomotion.

ethnocentric Viewing other cultures from the inherently biased perspective of one's own culture. Ethnocentrism often results in other cultures being seen as inferior to one's own.

Summary
of Main Topics

- The major subfields of anthropology are cultural anthropology, linguistic anthropology, archaeology, and physical anthropology.
- Physical anthropology is a discipline that seeks to explain how and when human beings evolved. This requires a detailed examination of the primate, and particularly hominin, fossil record (primate paleontology). Another major topic of physical anthropology is human biological variation, its genetic basis, and its adaptive significance. In addition, physical anthropologists study the behavior and biology of nonhuman primates, partly as a method of understanding humans, but also because nonhuman primates are important in their own right.
- Because physical anthropology is a scientific approach to the investigation of all aspects of human evolution, variation, and adaptation, research in this field is based on the scientific method. The scientific method is a system of inquiry that involves the development of hypotheses to explain some phenomenon. To determine the validity of hypotheses, scientists develop research designs aimed at collecting information (data) and testing the data to see if they support the hypothesis. If the hypothesis is not supported by the data, then it may be rejected or modified and retested. If it is supported, it may also be modified or refined over time and further tested. Further tests frequently use new technologies that have been developed since the original hypothesis was proposed. If a hypothesis stands up to continued testing, then it may eventually be accepted as a theory or part of a theory.

Critical Thinking
Questions

1. Given that you've only just been introduced to the field of physical anthropology, why do you think subjects such as anatomy, genetics, nonhuman primate behavior, and human evolution are integrated into a discussion of what it means to be human?

2. Is it important to you, personally, to know about human evolution? Why or why not?

3. Do you see a connection between hominin footprints that are almost 4 million years old and human footprints left on the moon in 1969? If so, do you think this relationship is important? What does the fact that there are human footprints on the moon say about human adaptation? (Consider both biological and cultural adaptation.)

Portrait of Charles Darwin, aged 68, from a photograph taken in 1877.

2

The Development of Evolutionary Theory

Key Questions

▶ What are the basic premises of natural selection?

▶ What were three major concepts that helped Charles Darwin develop his theory of natural selection?

▶ What is meant by reproductive success? Discuss this term as it relates to natural selection.

▶ What were the technological and philosophical changes that led people to accept notions of evolutionary change?

Has anyone ever asked you, "If humans evolved from monkeys, then why do we still have monkeys?" Or maybe, "If evolution happens, then why don't we ever see new species?" These are the kinds of questions people sometimes ask if they don't understand evolutionary processes or if they don't believe evolution actually occurs. Evolution is one of the most fundamental of all biological processes, and yet it's one of the most misunderstood. The explanation for the misunderstanding is simple: Evolution isn't taught in most primary and secondary schools; in fact, it's frequently avoided. Even in colleges and universities, evolution is barely touched on, even in many biology classes. Thus, in general, it receives the most detailed treatment in biological anthropology. If you're not an anthropology or biology major and you're taking a class in biological anthropology mainly to fill a science requirement, you'll probably never study evolution again.

By the end of this course, you'll know the answers to the questions in the preceding paragraph. Briefly, no one who studies evolution would ever say that humans evolved from monkeys, because we didn't. We didn't evolve from chimpanzees either. The earliest human ancestors evolved from a species that lived some 6 to 8 million years ago (mya). That ancestral species was the *last common ancestor* we share with chimpanzees. In turn, the lineage that eventually gave rise to the apes and humans separated from a monkey-like ancestor some 20 mya, and monkeys are still around because as lineages diverged from one another, each went its separate way. Over millions of years, some of these groups became extinct while others evolved into the species we see today. So all living species are the current results of processes that go back millions of years. Because evolution takes time, and lots of it, we rarely witness the appearance of new species except in microorganisms. But we do see *microevolutionary* changes (briefly referred to in Chapter 1) in many species, including our own.

The subject of evolution is controversial, especially in the United States, because some religious views hold that evolutionary statements run counter to biblical teachings. In fact, as you're probably aware, there is strong opposition to the teaching of evolution in public schools. Opponents of evolution often say, "It's just a theory," meaning that evolution is just an idea, a hunch. As we pointed out in Chapter 1, scientific theories aren't just ideas or suppositions, although that's how the word *theory* is commonly used in everyday conversation. Actually, when dealing with scientific issues, referring to a concept as "theory" supports it. Theories have been tested and subjected to verification through accumulated evidence, and they haven't been disproved, sometimes after decades of experimentation. It's true that evolution is a theory, one that's supported by a mounting body of genetic evidence that, quite literally, grows daily. It's a theory that explains how biological change occurs in species over time, and it's stood the test of time. Today, evolutionary theory stands as the most fundamental unifying force in biological science, and evolutionary biologists are now able to explain many evolutionary processes.

Because physical anthropology is concerned with all aspects of how humans came to be and how we adapt physiologically to the external environment, the details of the evolutionary process are crucial to the field. And given the central importance of evolution to biological anthropology, it's helpful to know how the mechanics of the process came to be discovered. Also, if we want to understand and make critical assessments of the controversy that surrounds the issue today, we need to explore the social and political events that influenced the discovery of evolutionary principles.

A Brief History of Evolutionary Thought

The discovery of evolutionary principles first took place in western Europe and was made possible by advances in scientific thinking that date back to the sixteenth century. Having said this, we must recognize that Western science

borrowed many of its ideas from other cultures, especially the Arabs, Indians, and Chinese. In fact, intellectuals in these cultures and in ancient Greece had developed notions of biological evolution centuries before Charles Darwin (Teresi, 2002), but they never formulated them into a cohesive theory.

Charles Darwin was the first person to explain the basic mechanics of the evolutionary process. But while he was developing his theory of **natural selection**, a Scottish naturalist named Alfred Russel Wallace independently reached the same conclusion. That natural selection, the single most important force of evolutionary change, was proposed at more or less the same time by two British men in the mid-nineteenth century may seem like a strange coincidence. But actually, if Darwin and Wallace hadn't made their simultaneous discoveries, someone else soon would have, and that someone would probably have been British or French. That's because the groundwork had already been laid in Britain and France, and many scientists there were prepared to accept explanations of biological change that would have been unacceptable even 25 years before.

Like other human endeavors, scientific knowledge is usually gained through a series of small steps rather than giant leaps. And just as technological change is based on past achievements, scientific knowledge builds on previously developed theories. For this reason, it's informative to examine the development of ideas that led Darwin and Wallace to independently develop the theory of evolution by natural selection.

Throughout the Middle Ages, one predominant feature of the European worldview was that all aspects of nature, including all forms of life and their relationships to one another, never changed. This view was partly shaped by a feudal society that was itself a rigid class system that hadn't changed much for centuries. But the most important influence was an extremely powerful religious system

natural selection The most critical mechanism of evolutionary change, first described by Charles Darwin; refers to genetic change or changes in the frequencies of certain traits in populations due to differential reproductive success between individuals.

◀ **Figure 2-1**

Portion of a Renaissance painting depicting the execution of Father Girolamo Savonarola in 1498 in Florence, Italy. (Artist unknown.) Savonarola wasn't promoting scientific arguments—just the opposite, in fact. As virtual ruler of Florence, he was openly critical of the Renaissance and opposed the church for being worldly and materialistic. But he met the same fate as many scientists and philosophers of the day.

in which the teachings of Christianity were held to be the only "truth." Consequently, it was generally accepted that all life on earth had been created by God exactly as it existed in the present, and the belief that life-forms couldn't and didn't change came to be known as **fixity of species**. Anyone who questioned the assumptions of fixity, especially in the fifteenth and sixteenth centuries, could be accused of challenging God's perfection, and that was heresy. Generally, it was a good idea to avoid accusations of heresy because it was a crime that could be punished by a nasty and often fiery death (**Fig. 2-1**).

The plan of the entire universe was viewed as God's design. In what's called the "argument from design," anatomical structures were engineered to meet the purpose for which they were required. Limbs, internal organs, and eyes all fit the functions they performed; and they, along with the rest of nature, were a deliberate plan of the Grand Designer. Also, pretty much everybody believed that the Grand Designer had completed his works fairly recently. An Irish archbishop named James Ussher (1581–1656) analyzed the "begat" chapter of Genesis and determined that the earth was created the morning of October 23 in 4004 B.C. While Ussher wasn't the first person to suggest a recent origin of the earth, he was the first to propose a precise date for it.

The prevailing notion of the earth's brief existence, together with fixity of species, was a huge obstacle to the development of evolutionary theory. Evolution takes time; and the idea of immense geological time, which today we take for granted, simply didn't exist. In fact, until the concepts of fixity and time were fundamentally altered, it was impossible to conceive of evolution by means of natural selection.

The Scientific Revolution

So, what transformed centuries-old beliefs in a rigid, static universe to a view of worlds in continuous motion? How did the earth's brief history become an immense expanse of incomprehensible time? How did the scientific method as we know it today develop? These are important questions, but we

fixity of species The notion that species, once created, can never change; an idea diametrically opposed to theories of biological evolution.

could also ask why it took so long for Europe to break away from traditional beliefs. After all, scholars in India and the Arab world had developed concepts of planetary motion, for example, centuries earlier.

For Europeans, the discovery of the New World and circumnavigation of the globe in the fifteenth century overturned some very basic ideas about the planet. For one thing, the earth could no longer be thought of as flat. Also, as Europeans began to explore the New World, their awareness of biological diversity was greatly expanded as they became aware of plants and animals they'd never seen before.

There were other attacks on traditional beliefs. In 1514, a Polish mathematician named Copernicus challenged a notion proposed more than 1,500 years earlier by the fourth-century B.C. Greek philosopher Aristotle. Aristotle had taught that the sun and planets existed in a series of concentric spheres that revolved around the earth (**Fig. 2-2**). This system of planetary spheres was, in turn, surrounded by the stars; and this meant that the earth was the center of the universe. In fact, in India, scholars had figured out that the earth orbited the sun long before Copernicus did; but Copernicus is generally credited with removing the earth as the center of all things, including our solar system.

Copernicus' theory was discussed in intellectual circles, but it didn't attract much attention from the Catholic Church. (Catholicism was the only form of Christianity until the 1520s.) Nevertheless, the theory did contradict a major premise of church doctrine, which at that time wholeheartedly embraced the teachings of Aristotle. By the 1300s, the church had accepted this view as dogma because it reinforced the notion that the earth, and the humans on it, were the central focus of God's creation and must therefore have a central position in the universe.

However, in the early 1600s, an Italian mathematician named Galileo Galilei restated Copernicus' views in print, using logic and mathematics to support his claim. (In fact, Galileo is

▶ **Figure 2-2**
This beautifully illustrated seventeenth-century map shows the earth at the center of the solar system. Around it are seven concentric circles depicting the orbits of the moon, sun, and the five planets that were known at the time. (Note also the signs of the zodiac.)

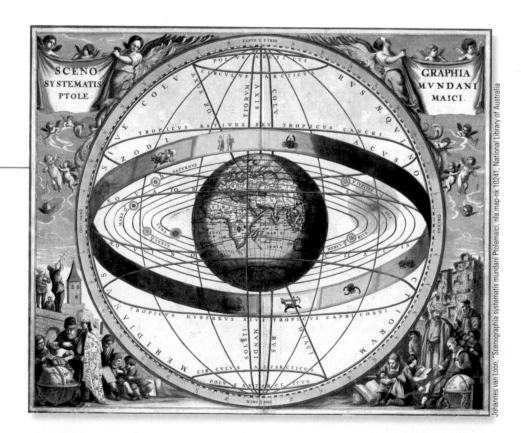

credited with having introduced the empirical approach to Western science.) To his misfortune, Galileo was eventually confronted by the highest-ranking officials of the Catholic Church (including his former friend, the pope), and he spent the last nine years of his life under house arrest. Nevertheless, in intellectual circles, the solar system had changed; the sun was now at its center, and the earth and other planets revolved around it as the entire system journeyed through space.

Throughout the sixteenth and seventeenth centuries, European scientists developed methods and theories that revolutionized scientific thought. The seventeenth century, in particular, saw the discovery of the principles of physics (such as motion and gravity), and numerous scientific instruments, including the microscope, were invented. These advances permitted the investigation of many previously misunderstood natural phenomena and opened up entire new worlds for unimagined discoveries. But even with these advances, the idea that living forms could change over time simply didn't occur to people.

Precursors to the Theory of Evolution

Before early naturalists could begin to understand the many forms of organic life, they needed to list and describe them. And as research progressed, scholars were increasingly impressed with the amount of biological diversity they saw.

The concept of species, as we think of it today, wasn't proposed until the seventeenth century, when John Ray, a minister educated at University of Cambridge, developed the concept. He recognized that groups of plants and animals could be differentiated from other groups by their ability to mate with one another and produce fertile offspring. He placed such groups of **reproductively isolated** organisms into categories, which he called species

(*sing.*, species). Thus, by the late 1600s, the biological criterion of reproduction was used to define species, much as it is today (Young, 1992).

Ray also recognized that species frequently share similarities with other species, and he grouped these together in a second level of classification he called the genus (*pl.*, genera). He was the first to use the labels *genus* and *species* in this way, and they're the terms we still use today.

Carolus Linnaeus (1707–1778) was a Swedish naturalist who developed a method of classifying plants and animals. In his famous work, *Systema Naturae* (Systems of Nature), first published in 1735, he standardized Ray's use of genus and species terminology and established the system of **binomial nomenclature**. He also added two more categories: class and order. Linnaeus' four-level system became the basis for **taxonomy**, the system of classification we continue to use.

Linnaeus also included humans in his classification of animals, placing them in the genus *Homo* and species *sapiens*. (Genus and species names are always italicized.) Placing humans in this scheme was controversial because it defied contemporary thought that humans, made in God's image, should be considered unique and separate from the rest of the animal kingdom.

For all his progressive tendencies, Linnaeus still believed in fixity of species, although in later years, faced with mounting evidence to the contrary, he came to question it. Indeed, fixity was being challenged on many fronts, especially in France, where voices were being raised in favor of a universe based on change and, more to the point, in favor of a biological relationship between similar species based on descent from a common ancestor.

A French naturalist, Georges-Louis Leclerc de Buffon (1707–1788), recognized the dynamic relationship between the external environment and living forms. In his *Natural History*, first published in 1749, he recognized that different regions have unique

reproductively isolated Pertaining to groups of organisms that, mainly because of genetic differences, are prevented from mating and producing offspring with members of other such groups. For example, dogs cannot mate and produce offspring with cats.

binomial nomenclature (*binomial*, meaning "two names") In taxonomy, the convention established by Carolus Linnaeus whereby genus and species names are used to refer to species. For example, *Homo sapiens* refers to human beings.

taxonomy The branch of science concerned with the rules of classifying organisms on the basis of evolutionary relationships.

plants and animals, a major concept in *biogeography* today. He also stressed that animals had come from a "center of origin," but he never discussed the diversification of life-forms over time. Even so, Buffon recognized that alterations of the external environment, including the climate, were agents of change in species. For this reason, the late evolutionary biologist Ernst Mayr said of him: "He was not an evolutionist, yet he was the father of evolutionism" (Mayr, 1981, p. 330).

Today, Erasmus Darwin (1731–1802) is best known as Charles Darwin's grandfather. But he was also a physician, a poet, and a leading member of an important intellectual community in England. In fact, Darwin counted among his friends some of the leading figures of the industrial revolution, a time of rapid technological and social change. In his most famous poem, Darwin expressed the view that life had originated in the seas and that all species had descended from a common ancestor. Thus, he introduced many of the ideas that his grandson would propose 56 years later. These concepts include vast expanses of time for life to evolve, competition for resources, and the importance of the environment in evolutionary processes. From letters and other sources, we know that Charles Darwin read his grandfather's writings; but the degree to which his theories were influenced by Erasmus isn't known.

Neither Buffon nor Erasmus Darwin attempted to *explain* the evolutionary process, but a French naturalist named Jean-Baptiste Lamarck (1744–1829) did. Lamarck (**Fig. 2-3**) suggested a dynamic relationship between species and the environment such that if the external environment changed, an animal's activity patterns would also change to accommodate the new circumstances. This would result in the increased or decreased use of certain body parts; consequently, those body parts would be modified. According to Lamarck, the parts that weren't used would disappear over time. However, the parts that continued to be used, perhaps in different ways, would change over time. Such physical changes would occur in response to bodily "needs," so that if a particular part of the body felt a certain need, "fluids and forces" would be directed to that point, and the structure would be modified. Since the alteration would make the animal better suited to its habitat, the new trait would be passed on to offspring. This theory is known as the *inheritance of acquired characteristics*, or the *use-disuse* theory.

One of the most frequently given hypothetical examples of Lamarck's theory is the giraffe, which, having stripped all the leaves from the lower branches of a tree (environmental change), tries to reach leaves on upper branches. As "vital forces" move to tissues of the neck, it becomes slightly longer, and the giraffe can reach higher. The longer neck is then transmitted to offspring, with the eventual result that all giraffes have longer necks than their predecessors had (**Fig. 2-4**). So, according to this theory, *a trait acquired by an animal during its lifetime can be passed on to offspring.* Today we know that this explanation is wrong because only those traits that are influenced by genetic information contained within sex cells (eggs and sperm) can be inherited (see Chapter 3).

Because Lamarck's explanation of species change isn't genetically correct, he is frequently scorned even today. But in fact, Lamarck deserves a great deal of credit because he emphasized the importance of interactions between organisms and the external environment in the evolutionary process. He also coined the term *biology* to refer to the study of living organisms, and a central feature of this

Image # 124768 American Museum of Natural History

▲ **Figure 2-3**
Lamarck believed that species change was influenced by environmental change. He is best known for his theory of the inheritance of acquired characteristics.

catastrophism The view that the earth's geological landscape is the result of violent cataclysmic events. Cuvier promoted this view, especially in opposition to Lamarck.

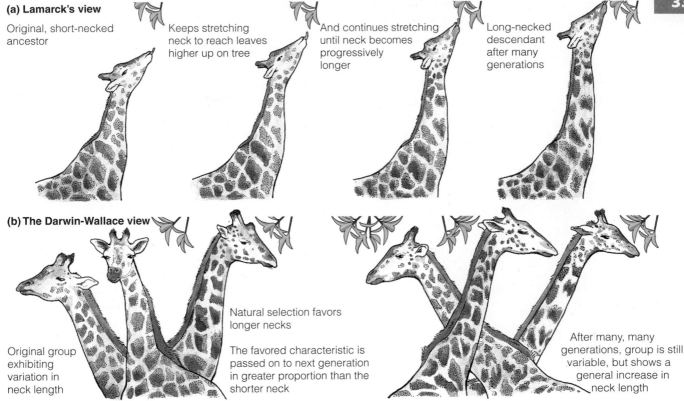

(a) Lamarck's view

Original, short-necked ancestor

Keeps stretching neck to reach leaves higher up on tree

And continues stretching until neck becomes progressively longer

Long-necked descendant after many generations

(b) The Darwin-Wallace view

Original group exhibiting variation in neck length

Natural selection favors longer necks

The favored characteristic is passed on to next generation in greater proportion than the shorter neck

After many, many generations, group is still variable, but shows a general increase in neck length

▲ **Figure 2-4**
Contrasting ideas about the mechanism of evolution. (**a**) Lamarck's theory held that acquired characteristics can be passed to offspring. Short-necked giraffes stretched to reach higher into trees for food, and their necks grew longer. According to Lamarck, this acquired trait was passed on to offspring, who were born with longer necks. (**b**) The Darwin-Wallace theory of natural selection states that among giraffes there is variation in neck length. If having a longer neck provides an advantage for feeding, the trait will be passed on to a greater number of offspring, leading to an overall increase in the length of giraffe necks over many generations.

new discipline was the idea of species change.

Lamarck's most vehement opponent was a French vertebrate paleontologist named Georges Cuvier (1769–1832). Cuvier (**Fig. 2-5**) introduced the concept of extinction to explain the disappearance of animals represented by fossils. Although he was a brilliant anatomist, Cuvier never grasped the dynamic concept of nature and continued to insist on the fixity of species. So, rather than assuming that similarities between fossil forms and living species indicate evolutionary relationships, Cuvier proposed a variation of a doctrine known as **catastrophism**.

Catastrophism was the belief that the earth's geological features are the results of sudden, worldwide cataclysmic events. Cuvier's version of catastrophism suggested that a series of regional disasters had destroyed most or all of the local plant and animal life in many places. These areas were then restocked with new, similar forms that migrated in from unaffected regions. Because he needed to be consistent with emerging fossil evidence, which indicated that organisms had become more complex over time, Cuvier proposed that after each disaster, the incoming

Mathieu-Ignace van Brée (1733–1839)

▲ **Figure 2-5**
Cuvier explained the fossil record as the result of a succession of catastrophes followed by new creation events.

migrants had a more modern appearance because they were the results of more recent creation events. (The last of these creations was the Noah flood, described in Genesis.) In this way, Cuvier's explanation of increased complexity over time avoided any notion of evolution while still accounting for the evidence of change so well preserved in the fossil record.

In 1798, an English economist named Thomas Malthus (1766–1834) wrote *An Essay on the Principle of Population* (**Fig. 2-6**). This important essay inspired both Charles Darwin and Alfred Russel Wallace in their separate discoveries of natural selection. Considering the enormous influence that Malthus had on these two men, it's noteworthy that he wasn't interested in species change at all. Instead, he was arguing for limits to human population growth. He pointed out that in nature, animal populations increase in numbers when resources are plentiful and/or there aren't many predators. Thus, the tendency for populations to increase in size is constantly being held in check by the availability of resources, with population size increasing exponentially so long as food supplies remain relatively stable. Even though humans can reduce constraints on population size by producing more food, Malthus argued that the lack of resources would always be a constant source of "misery" and famine for humankind if our numbers continued to increase. (Unfortunately, we're already testing Malthus' hypothesis as the number of humans on earth approaches 7 billion.)

Both Darwin and Wallace extended Malthus' principles to all organisms, not just humans. Moreover, they recognized the important fact that when population size is limited by resource availability, there must be constant competition for food and water. And competition between individuals is the ultimate key to understanding natural selection.

Charles Lyell (1797–1875) is considered the founder of modern geology (**Fig. 2-7**). He was a lawyer, a geologist, and, for many years, Charles Darwin's friend and mentor. Before meeting Darwin in 1836, Lyell had earned acceptance in Europe's most prestigious scientific circles, thanks to his highly praised *Principles of Geology*, first published during the years 1830–1833.

In this extremely important work, Lyell argued that the geological processes we see today are the same as those in the past. This theory, called geological **uniformitarianism**, didn't originate entirely with Lyell, having been proposed by James Hutton in the late 1700s. Even so, it was Lyell who demonstrated that forces such as wind, water erosion, local flooding, frost, decomposition of vegetable matter, volcanoes, earthquakes, and glacial movements had all contributed in the past to produce the geological landscape that we see today. What's more, these processes were ongoing, indicating that geological change was still happening and that the forces driving such change were consistent, or *uniform*, over time. In other words, various aspects of the earth's surface (for example, climate, plants, animals, and land surfaces) vary through time, but the *underlying processes* that influence them are constant.

Lyell also emphasized the obvious: namely, that for such slow-acting forces to produce momentous change, the earth must be far older than anyone had previously suspected. By providing an immense time scale and thereby changing perceptions of the earth's history from a few thousand to many millions of years, Lyell changed the framework within which scientists viewed the geological past. So the concept of "deep time" (Gould, 1987) remains one of Lyell's most significant contributions to the discovery of evolutionary principles. The immensity of geological time permitted the necessary time depth for the inherently slow process of evolutionary change (**Fig. 2-8**).

▲ **Figure 2-6**
Thomas Malthus' *Essay on the Principle of Population* led both Darwin and Wallace to the principle of natural selection.

uniformitarianism The theory that the earth's features are the result of long-term processes that continue to operate in the present just as they did in the past. Elaborated on by Lyell, this theory opposed catastrophism and contributed strongly to the concept of immense geological time.

As you can see, the roots of evolutionary theory are deeply imbedded in the late eighteenth and early nineteenth centuries. During that time, many lesser-known people also contributed to this intellectual movement. One such person was Mary Anning (1799–1847), who lived in the town of Lyme Regis, on the south coast of England (**Fig. 2-9**).

Anning's father died when she was 11 years old, leaving his wife and two children destitute. Fortunately, he had taught Mary to recognize marine fossils embedded in the cliffs near the town. Thus, she began to earn a living by collecting and selling fossils to collectors who were becoming increasingly interested in the remains of creatures that many people believed had been killed in the Noah flood.

After Anning's discovery of the first *complete* fossil of *Ichthyosaurus*, a large fishlike marine reptile, and the first *Pleiosaurus* fossil (another ocean-dwelling reptile), some of the most famous scientists in England repeatedly visited her home. Eventually, she became known as one of the world's leading "fossilists," and by sharing her

© National Portrait Gallery, London

◄ **Figure 2-7**
Portrait of Charles Lyell.

extensive knowledge of fossil species with many of the leading scientists of the day, she contributed to the understanding of the evolution of marine life that spanned over 200 million years. But because she was a woman and of lowly social position, Anning wasn't acknowledged in the numerous scientific publications she facilitated. In recent years, however, she has achieved the recognition she deserves;

Lynn Kilgore

◄ **Figure 2-8**
(a) These limestone cliffs in southern France were formed around 300 million years ago from shells and the skeletal remains of countless sea creatures. (b) Part of a block of stone cut from the same limestone containing fossilized shells.

▶ **Figure 2-9**
Portrait of
Mary Anning.

her portrait hangs prominently in the British Museum (Natural History) in London, near one of her famous *Pleiosaurus* fossils.

The Discovery of Natural Selection

Having already been introduced to Erasmus Darwin, you shouldn't be surprised that his grandson Charles grew up in an educated family with ties to intellectual circles. Charles Darwin (1809–1882) was one of six children of Dr. Robert and Susanna Darwin (**Fig. 2-10**). Being the grandson not only of Erasmus Darwin but also of the wealthy Josiah Wedgwood (of Wedgwood china fame), Charles grew up enjoying the comfortable lifestyle of the landed gentry in rural England.

As a boy, Darwin had a keen interest in nature and spent his days fishing and collecting shells, birds' eggs, and rocks. However, this interest in natural history didn't dispel the generally held view among family and friends that he was in no way remarkable. In fact, his performance at school was no more than ordinary.

After his mother's death when he was 8 years old, Darwin was raised by his father and older sisters. Because he showed little interest in anything except hunting, shooting, and perhaps science, his father sent him to Edinburgh University to study medicine. It was there that Darwin first became acquainted with the evolutionary theories of Lamarck and others.

During the 1820s, notions of evolution were becoming feared in England and elsewhere. Anything identified with postrevolutionary France was viewed with suspicion by the established order in England, and Lamarck, partly because he was French, was especially vilified by British scientists.

It was also a time of growing political unrest in Britain. The Reform Movement, which sought to undo the many inequalities of the traditional class system, was under way, and like most social movements, it had a radical faction. Because many of the radicals were atheists and socialists who also supported Lamarck's ideas, many people came to associate evolution with atheism and political subversion. The growing fear of evolutionary ideas led many to believe that if these ideas were generally accepted, "the Church would crash, the moral fabric of society would be torn apart, and civilized man would return to savagery" (Desmond and Moore, 1991, p. 34). It's unfortunate that some of the most outspoken early proponents of species change were so vehemently anti-Christian, because their rhetoric helped establish the entrenched suspicion and misunderstanding of evolutionary theory that persists today.

While at Edinburgh, Darwin studied with professors who were outspoken supporters of Lamarck. So, even though he hated medicine and left Edinburgh after two years, his experience there was a formative period in his intellectual development.

Although Darwin was fairly indifferent to religion, he next went to Cambridge to study theology. It was during his Cambridge years that he cultivated his interests in natural science, immersing himself in botany and geology. It's no wonder that following his graduation in 1831 he was invited to join a scientific expedition that would circle the globe. And so it was that Darwin set sail aboard HMS *Beagle* on December 17, 1831 (**Fig. 2-11**). The famous voyage of the *Beagle* would take almost five years and would forever change not only the course of Darwin's life but also the history of biological science (**Fig. 2-12**).

Darwin went aboard the *Beagle* believing in fixity of species. But during the voyage, he privately began to have doubts. For example, he came across fossils of ancient giant animals that, except for size, looked very much like species that still lived in the same vicinity, and he wondered if the fossils represented ancestors of those living forms.

© Bettmann / Corbis

◄ **Figure 2-10**
Charles Darwin, photographed five years before the publication of *Origin of Species*.

During the famous stopover at the Galápagos Islands, off the coast of Ecuador, Darwin noticed that the vegetation and animals (especially birds) shared many similarities with those on the mainland of South America. But they weren't identical to them. What's

▼ **Figure 2-11**
The route of HMS *Beagle*.

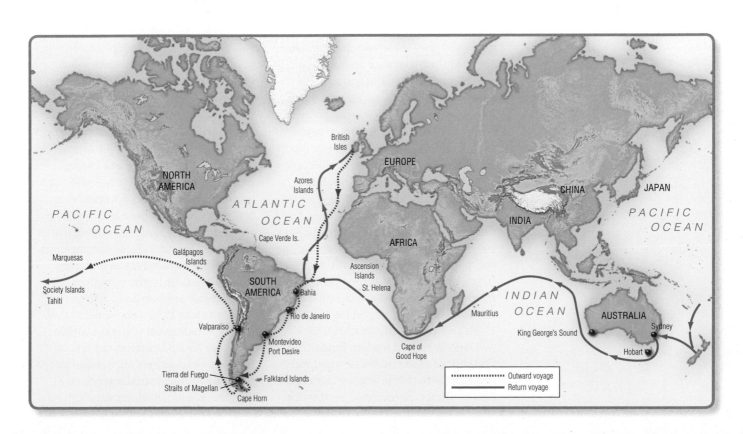

▶ **Figure 2-12**
A painting by John Chancellor of the HMS *Beagle* sailing through the Galápagos Islands in 1835.

© Gordon Chancellor

more, the birds varied from island to island. Darwin collected 13 varieties of Galápagos finches, and it was clear that they represented a closely affiliated group; but some of their physical traits were different, particularly the shape and size of their beaks (**Fig. 2-13**). Darwin also collected finches from the mainland, and these appeared to represent only one group, or species.

The insight that Darwin gained from the finches is legendary. He realized that the various Galápagos finches had all descended from a common mainland ancestor and had been modified over time in response to different island habitats and dietary preferences. But actually, it wasn't until *after* he returned to England that he recognized the significance of the variation in beak structure. In fact, during the voyage, he had paid little attention to the finches. It was only later that he considered the factors that could lead to the modification of one species into many (Gould, 1985; Desmond and Moore, 1991).

Darwin arrived back in England in October of 1836 and was immediately accepted into the most prestigious scientific circles. He married his cousin,

Emma Wedgwood, and moved to the village of Down, near London, where he spent the rest of his life writing on topics ranging from fossils to orchids (**Fig. 2-14**). But the question of species change was his overriding passion.

At Down, Darwin began to develop his views on what he called *natural selection*. This concept was borrowed from animal breeders, who choose, or "select," as breeding stock those animals that possess certain traits they want to emphasize in offspring. Animals with undesirable traits are "selected against," or prevented from breeding. A dramatic example of the effects of selective breeding can be seen in the various domestic dog breeds shown in **Figure 2-15**. Darwin applied his knowledge of domesticated species to naturally occurring ones, and he recognized that in undomesticated organisms, the selective agent was nature, not humans.

By the late 1830s, Darwin had realized that biological variation within a species (that is, differences among individuals) was crucial. Furthermore, he realized that sexual reproduction increased variation, although he

Ground finch	Tree finch	Tree finch (called woodpecker finch)	Ground finch (known as warbler finch)
Main Food: seeds	Main food: leaves, buds, blossoms, fruits	Main food: insects	Main food: insects
Beak: heavy	Beak: thick, short	Beak: stout, straight	Beak: slender

didn't know why. Then, in 1838, he read Malthus' essay; and there he found the answer to the question of how new species came to be. He accepted Malthus' idea that populations increase at a faster rate than resources do, and he recognized that in nonhuman animals, population size is always limited by the amount of food and water available. He also recognized that these two facts lead to a constant "struggle for existence." The idea that in each generation more offspring are born than survive to adulthood, coupled with the notions of competition for resources and biological diversity, was all Darwin needed to develop his theory of natural selection.

He wrote: "It at once struck me that under these circumstances favourable variations would tend to be preserved, and unfavourable ones to be destroyed. The result of this would be the formation of a new species" (F. Darwin, 1950, pp. 53–54). Basically, this quotation summarizes the entire theory of natural selection.

By 1844, Darwin had written a short summary of his hypothesis of natural selection, but he didn't think he had enough data to support it, so he continued his research without publishing. He also had other reasons for not publishing what he knew would be, to say the least, a highly controversial work.

▲ **Figure 2-13**
Beak variation in Darwin's Galápagos finches.

◄ **Figure 2-14**
Down House, as seen from the rear. *On the Origin of Species* **and numerous other publications were written here.**

▲ Figure 2-15
All domestic dog breeds share a common ancestor, the wolf. The extreme variation exhibited by dog breeds today has been achieved in a relatively short time through artificial selection. In this situation, humans allow only certain dogs to breed to emphasize specific characteristics. (We should note that not all traits desired by human breeders are advantageous to the dogs themselves.)

He was deeply troubled that his wife, Emma, saw his ideas as running counter to her strong religious convictions (Keynes, 2002). Also, as a member of the established order, he knew that many of his friends and associates were concerned with threats to the status quo, and evolutionary theory was viewed as a very serious threat.

In Darwin's Shadow

Unlike Darwin, Alfred Russel Wallace (1823–1913) was born into a family of modest means (**Fig. 2-16**). He went to work at the age of 14, and with little formal education, he moved from one job to the next. Eventually, he became interested in collecting plants and animals and joined expeditions to the Amazon and Southeast Asia, where he acquired firsthand knowledge of many natural phenomena.

In 1855, Wallace published an article suggesting that current species were descended from other species and that the appearance of new ones was influenced by environmental factors (Trinkaus and Shipman, 1992). This article caused Lyell and others to urge Darwin to publish, but he continued to hesitate.

Then, in 1858, Wallace sent Darwin another paper, "On the Tendency of Varieties to Depart Indefinitely from the Original Type." In this paper, Wallace described evolution as a process driven by competition and natural

Natural Selection

Early in his research, Darwin had realized that natural selection was the key to evolution. With the help of Malthus' ideas, he saw *how* selection in nature could be explained. In the struggle for existence, those *individuals* with favorable variations would survive and reproduce, but those with unfavorable variations wouldn't. For Darwin, the explanation of evolution was simple. The basic processes, as he understood them, are as follows:

1. All species are capable of producing offspring at a faster rate than food supplies increase.
2. There is biological variation within all species.
3. Since in each generation more offspring are produced than can survive, and because of limited resources, there is competition among individuals. (*Note*: This statement doesn't mean that there is constant fierce fighting.)
4. Individuals who possess favorable variations or traits (for example, speed, resistance to disease, protective coloration) have an advantage over those who don't have them. In other words, they have greater **fitness** because favorable traits increase the likelihood of survival and reproduction.
5. The environmental context determines whether or not a trait is beneficial. What is favorable in one setting may be a liability in another. Consequently, the traits that become most advantageous are the results of a natural process.
6. Traits are inherited and passed on to the next generation. Because individuals who possess favorable traits contribute more offspring to the next generation than others do, over time those favorable traits become more common in the population. Less

▲ **Figure 2-16**
Alfred Russel Wallace independently discovered the key to the evolutionary process.

selection. When he received Wallace's paper, Darwin realized he could wait no longer or Wallace might get credit for a theory (natural selection) that he himself had developed. He quickly wrote a paper presenting his ideas, and both men's papers were read before the Linnean Society of London. Neither author was present. Wallace was out of the country, and Darwin was mourning the recent death of his young son.

The papers received little notice at the time. But in December 1859, when Darwin completed and published his greatest work, *On the Origin of Species*,** the storm broke; and it still hasn't abated (**Fig. 2-17**). Although public opinion was negative, there was much scholarly praise for the book, and scientific opinion gradually came to Darwin's support. The riddle of species was now explained: Species could change, they weren't fixed, and they evolved from other species through the mechanism of natural selection.

---

* The full title is *On the Origin of Species by Means of Natural Selection, or the Preservation of Favoured Races in the Struggle for Life.*

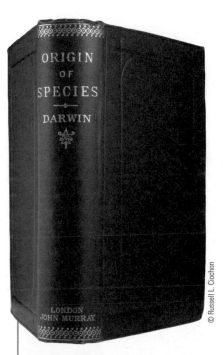

▲ **Figure 2-17**
Charles Darwin's *Origin of Species*, the book that revolutionized biological science.

fitness Pertaining to natural selection, a measure of the relative reproductive success of individuals. Fitness can be measured by an individual's genetic contribution to the next generation compared with that of other individuals. The terms genetic fitness, reproductive fitness, and *differential reproductive success* are also used.

favorable characteristics aren't passed as frequently, so they become less common over time and are "weeded out." Individuals who produce more offspring in comparison to others are said to have greater **reproductive success** or fitness.

7. Over long periods of time, successful variations accumulate in a population, so that later generations may be distinct from ancestral ones. Thus, in time, a new species may appear.

8. Geographical isolation also contributes to the formation of new species. As populations of a species become geographically isolated from one another, for whatever reasons (for example, distance or natural barriers such as oceans), they begin to adapt to different environments. Over time, as populations continue to respond to different **selective pressures** (that is, different ecological circumstances), they may become distinct species. The 13 species of Galápagos finches are presumably all descended from a common ancestor on the South American mainland, and they provide an example of the role of geographical isolation.

Before Darwin, individual members of species weren't considered important, so they weren't studied. But as we've seen, Darwin recognized the uniqueness of individuals and realized that variation among them could explain how selection occurs. Favorable variations are selected, or chosen, for survival by nature; unfavorable ones are eliminated. *Natural selection operates on individuals*, either favorably or unfavorably, but *it's the population that evolves*. It's important to emphasize that the unit of natural selection is the individual; the unit of evolution is the population. This is because individuals don't change genetically, but over time, populations do.

Natural Selection in Action

The most frequently cited example of natural selection relates to changes in the coloration of a species of moth. In recent years, the moth story has come under some criticism; but the premise remains valid, so we use it to illustrate how natural selection works.

Before the nineteenth century, the most common variety of the peppered moth in England was a mottled gray color. During the day, as the moths rested on lichen-covered tree trunks, their coloration provided camouflage (**Fig. 2-18**). There was also a dark gray variety of the same species, but since the dark moths were not as well camouflaged, they were more frequently eaten by birds and so they were less common. (In this example, the birds are the *selective agent*, and they apply *selective pressures* on the moths.) Yet, by the end of the nineteenth century, the darker form had almost completely replaced the common gray one.

The cause of this change was the changing environment of industrialized nineteenth-century England. Coal dust from factories and fireplaces settled on the trees, turning them dark gray and killing the lichen. The moths continued to rest on the trees, but the light gray ones became more conspicuous as the trees became darker, and they were increasingly targeted by birds. Since fewer of the light gray moths were living long enough to reproduce, they contributed fewer genes to the next generation than the darker moths did, and the proportion of lighter moths decreased while the dark moths became more common. A similar color shift also occurred in North America. But with the advent of clean air acts in both Britain and the United States reducing the amount of air pollution (at least from coal), the predominant color of the peppered moth once again became the light mottled gray. This kind of evolution-

reproductive success The number of offspring an individual produces and rears to reproductive age; an individual's genetic contribution to the next generation.

selective pressures Forces in the environment that influence reproductive success in individuals.

ary shift in response to environmental change is called *adaptation.*

Deer mice living in the Sand Hills of Nebraska provide another example of natural selection producing a change in coloration as a response to environmental change (Linnen et al., 2009).

Most populations of this species have a dark coat color that provides protection from predators, primarily birds, in areas with darker soil. However, coat color in populations living in the light soil of Sand Hills is much lighter, again offering camouflage.

The Sand Hills formed between 8,000 and 10,000 years ago, and biologists have now explained in detail how the lighter coat color evolved after that time. In response to this important environmental change, natural selection acted very strongly on coat color, dramatically increasing the reproductive fitness of lighter-colored mice. In fact, the advantage provided by the camouflage was so great that today, most if not all members of this mouse population have light-colored fur.

The medium ground finch of the Galápagos Islands gives us another example of natural selection. In 1977, drought killed many of the plants that produced the smaller, softer seeds favored by these birds. This forced a population of finches on one of the islands to feed on larger, harder seeds. Even before 1977, some birds had smaller, less robust beaks than others (that is, there was variation); and during the drought, because they were less able to process the larger seeds, more smaller-beaked birds died than larger-beaked birds. So, although overall population size declined, average beak thickness in the survivors and their offspring increased, simply because thicker-beaked individuals were surviving in greater numbers and producing more offspring. In other words, they had greater reproductive success. But during heavy rains in 1982–1983, smaller seeds became more plentiful again and the pattern in beak size reversed itself, demonstrating again how reproductive success is related to environmental conditions (Grant, 1986; Ridley, 1993).

The best illustration of natural selection, however—and certainly one with potentially grave consequences for humans—is the recent increase in resistant strains of disease-causing microorganisms. When antibiotics were first introduced in the 1940s, they were seen as the cure for bacterial disease. But that optimistic view didn't take into account that bacteria, like other organisms, possess genetic variability. Consequently, while an antibiotic will kill most bacteria in an infected person, any bacterium with an

▼ **Figure 2-18**
**Variation in the peppered moth.
(a) The dark form is more visible on the light, lichen-covered tree.
(b) On trees darkened by pollution, the lighter form is more visible.**

inherited resistance to that particular therapy will survive. In turn, the survivors reproduce and pass their drug resistance to future generations, so that eventually, the population is mostly made up of bacteria that don't respond to treatment. What's more, because bacteria produce new generations every few hours, antibiotic-resistant strains are continuously appearing. As a result, many types of infection no longer respond to treatment. For example, tuberculosis was once thought to be well controlled, but there's been a resurgence of TB in recent years because some strains of the bacterium that causes it are resistant to most of the antibiotics used to treat TB.

These examples (moths, mice, finches, and bacteria) provide the following insights into the fundamentals of evolutionary change produced by natural selection:

1. *A trait must be inherited if natural selection is to act on it.* A characteristic that isn't hereditary (such as a temporary change in hair color produced by the hairdresser) won't be passed on to offspring. In finches, for example, beak size is a hereditary trait.
2. *Natural selection can't occur without population variation in inherited characteristics.* If, for example, all the peppered moths had initially been gray and the trees had become darker, the survival and reproduction of the moths could have been so low that the population might have become extinct. *Selection can work only with variation that already exists.*
3. *Fitness is a relative measure that changes as the environment changes.* Fitness is simply differential reproductive success. In the initial stage, the lighter moths were more fit because they produced more offspring. But as the environment changed, the dark gray moths became more fit. Later, a further change reversed the pattern again. Likewise, the majority of Galápagos

finches will have larger or smaller beaks, depending on external conditions. So it should be obvious that statements regarding the "most fit" don't mean anything without reference to specific environments.
4. *Natural selection can act only on traits that affect reproduction.* If a characteristic isn't expressed until later in life, after organisms have reproduced, then natural selection can't influence it. This is because the trait's inherited components have already been passed on to offspring. Many forms of cancer and cardiovascular disease are influenced by hereditary factors, but because these diseases usually affect people after they've had children, natural selection can't act against them. By the same token, if a condition usually kills or compromises the individual before he or she reproduces, natural selection can act against it because the trait won't be passed on.

So far, our examples have shown how different death rates influence natural selection (for example, moths or finches that die early leave fewer offspring). But mortality is only part of the picture. Another important aspect of natural selection is **fertility**, because an animal that gives birth to more young passes its genes on at a faster rate than one that bears fewer offspring. But fertility isn't the entire story either, because the crucial element is the number of young raised successfully to the point where they themselves reproduce. We call this *differential net reproductive success.* The way this mechanism works can be demonstrated through another example.

In swifts (small birds that resemble swallows), data show that producing more offspring doesn't necessarily guarantee that more young will be successfully raised. The number of eggs hatched in a breeding season is a measure of fertility. The number of birds that mature and are eventually able to leave the nest is a measure of net repro-

fertility The ability to conceive and produce healthy offspring.

ductive success, or successfully raised offspring. The following table shows the correlation between the number of eggs hatched (fertility) and the number of young that leave the nest (reproductive success), averaged over four breeding seasons (Lack, 1966):

Number of eggs hatched (fertility)	2 eggs	3 eggs	4 eggs
Average number of young raised (reproductive success)	1.92	2.54	1.76
Sample size (number of nests)	72	20	16

As you can see, the most efficient number of eggs is three, because that number yields the highest reproductive success. Raising two offspring is less beneficial to the parents, since the end result isn't as successful as with three eggs. Trying to raise more than three is actually detrimental, since the parents may not be able to provide enough nourishment for any of the offspring. Offspring that die before reaching reproductive age are, in evolutionary terms, equivalent to never being born. Actually, death of an offspring can be a minus to the parents, because before it dies, it drains parental resources. It may even inhibit their ability to raise other offspring, thus reducing their reproductive success even further. Selection favors those genetic traits that yield the maximum net reproductive success. If the number of eggs laid is a genetic trait in birds (and it seems to be), natural selection in swifts should act to favor the laying of three eggs as opposed to two or four.

Constraints on Nineteenth-Century Evolutionary Theory

Darwin argued for the concept of evolution in general and the role of natural selection in particular. But he didn't comprehend the exact mechanisms of evolutionary change.

As we've already seen, natural selection acts on *variation* within species, but what Darwin didn't understand was where the variation came from. In the nineteenth century, this remained an unanswered question; furthermore, no one understood how parents pass traits to offspring. Almost without exception, nineteenth-century scientists believed inheritance to be a *blending* process in which parental characteristics are mixed together to produce intermediate expressions in offspring. Given this notion, we can see why the true nature of genes was unimaginable; and with no alternative explanation, Darwin accepted the blending theory of inheritance. As it turns out, however, a contemporary of Darwin's had actually worked out the rules of heredity. However, the work of this Augustinian monk named Gregor Mendel (whom you'll meet in Chapter 4) wasn't recognized until the beginning of the twentieth century.

The first three decades of the twentieth century saw the merger of natural selection theory and Mendel's discoveries. This was a crucial development because until then, scientists thought these concepts were unrelated. Then, in 1953, the structure of DNA was discovered. This landmark achievement has been followed by even more amazing advances in the field of genetics. The human **genome** was sequenced in 2003, followed by the chimpanzee genome in 2005. The genomes of many other species (including dogs, mice, and rhesus macaques, to name a few) have also now been sequenced. By comparing different species' genomes (a field called comparative genomics), scientists can examine how genetically similar (or different) the species are, and this will explain many aspects of how these species evolved. Also, since the early 1990s, several scientists have merged the fields of evolutionary and developmental biology into a new field called "evo-devo" (see p. 139). This approach, which compares the actions of different

genome The entire genetic makeup of an individual or species.

developmental genes and the factors that regulate them, are making it possible to explain evolution in ways that were impossible even 15 years ago. Scientists are truly on the threshold of revealing many secrets of the evolutionary process. The year 2009 marked the 200th anniversary of Charles Darwin's birth. How wonderful it would have been if, for Darwin's 200th birthday, we could have shown him how far the field of evolutionary biology has come!

Opposition to Evolution Today

One hundred and fifty years after the publication of *Origin of Species*, the debate over evolution is far from over, especially in the United States and, increasingly, in several Muslim countries. For most biologists, evolution is indisputable. The genetic evidence for it is solid and accumulating daily. Anyone who appreciates and understands genetic mechanisms can't avoid the conclusion that populations and species evolve. What's more, the majority of Christians don't believe that biblical depictions should be taken literally. But at the same time, some surveys show that about half of all Americans don't believe that evolution occurs. There are a number of reasons for this.

The mechanisms of evolution are complex and don't lend themselves to simple explanations. Understanding them requires some familiarity with genetics and biology, a familiarity that most people don't have unless they took related courses in school. What is more, many people want definitive, clear-cut answers to complex questions. But as you learned in Chapter 1, science doesn't always provide definitive answers to questions; it doesn't establish absolute truths; and it doesn't *prove* facts. Another thing to consider is that regardless of their culture, most people are raised in belief systems that don't emphasize **biological continuity**

between species or offer scientific explanations for natural phenomena.

The relationship between science and religion has never been easy (remember Galileo), even though both serve, in their own ways, to explain natural phenomena. As you read in Chapter 1, scientific explanations are based in data analysis, hypothesis testing, and interpretation. Religion, meanwhile, is a system of faith-based beliefs. A major difference between science and religion is that religious beliefs and explanations aren't amenable to scientific testing. Religion and science concern different aspects of the human experience, but they aren't inherently mutually exclusive approaches. That is, belief in God doesn't exclude the possibility of biological evolution; and acknowledgment of evolutionary processes doesn't preclude the existence of God. What's more, evolutionary theories aren't rejected by all religions or by most forms of Christianity.

Some years ago, the Vatican hosted an international conference on human evolution; and in 1996, Pope John Paul II issued a statement that "fresh knowledge leads to recognition of the theory of evolution as more than just a hypothesis." Today, the official position of the Catholic Church is that evolutionary processes do occur, but that the human soul is of divine creation and not subject to evolutionary processes. Likewise, mainstream Protestants don't generally see a conflict. Unfortunately, those who believe in an absolutely literal interpretation of the Bible (called *fundamentalists*) accept no compromise.

A Brief History of Opposition to Evolution in the United States

Although there are movements that argue against evolution in other parts of the world, opposition to evolution is far more prevalent in the United States, and there are historical reasons for this. Reacting to rapid cultural

biological continuity A biological continuum. When expressions of a phenomenon continuously grade into one another so that there are no discrete categories, they exist on a continuum. Color is one such phenomenon, and life-forms are another.

change after World War I, conservative Christians in the United States sought a revival of what they considered "traditional values." In their view, one way to do this was to prevent any mention of Darwinism in public schools. One result of this effort was a state law passed in Tennessee in 1925 that banned the teaching of any theory (particularly evolution) that does not support the biblical version of the creation of humankind. To test the validity of this law, the American Civil Liberties Union persuaded a high school teacher named John Scopes to submit to being arrested and tried for teaching evolution (**Fig. 2-19**). The subsequent trial, called the Scopes Monkey Trial, was a 1920s equivalent of current celebrity trials. In the end, Scopes was convicted and fined $100, though the conviction was later overturned. Although most states didn't actually forbid the teaching of evolution, Arkansas, Tennessee, and a few others continued to prohibit any mention of it until 1968, when the U.S. Supreme Court struck down the ban against teaching evolution in public schools. (One coauthor of this textbook remembers when her junior high school science teacher was fired for mentioning evolution in Little Rock, Arkansas.)

As coverage of evolution in textbooks increased by the mid-1960s, **Christian fundamentalists** renewed their campaign to eliminate evolution from public school curricula or to introduce antievolutionary material into public school classes. Out of this effort, the *creation science* movement was born.

Proponents of creation science are called "creationists" because they explain the existence of the universe as the result of a sudden creation event that occurred over the course of six 24-hour days as described in the book of Genesis. The premise of creation science is that the biblical account of the earth's origins and the Noah flood can be supported by scientific evidence.

Creationists have insisted that what they used to call "creation science" and now call "intelligent design" (ID) is a valid scientific explanation of the earth's origins. They've argued that in the interest of fairness, a balanced view should be offered in public schools: If evolution is taught as science, then creationism should also be taught as science. Sounds fair, doesn't it? But ID isn't science at all, for the simple reason that creationists insist that their view is absolute and infallible. Therefore, creationism isn't a hypothesis that can be tested, nor is it amenable to falsification. And because hypothesis testing is the basis of all science, creationism, by its very nature, cannot be considered science.

Since the 1970s, creationists have become increasingly active in local

© Bettmann / Corbis

◄ **Figure 2-19**
Photo taken at the "Scopes Monkey Trial." The well-known defense attorney Clarence Darrow is sitting on the edge of the table. John Scopes, the defendant, is sitting with his arms folded behind Darrow.

Christian fundamentalists
Adherents to a movement in American Protestantism that began in the early twentieth century. This group holds that the teachings of the Bible are infallible and that the scriptures are to be taken literally.

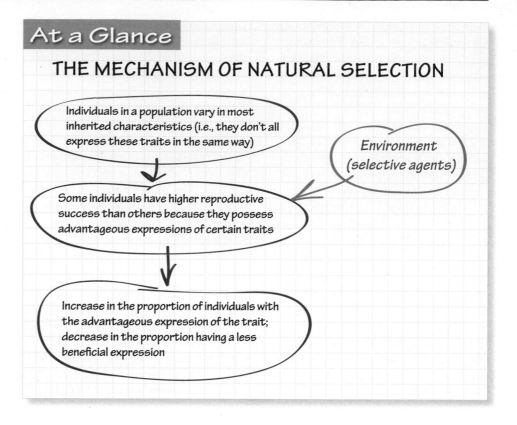

At a Glance

THE MECHANISM OF NATURAL SELECTION

Individuals in a population vary in most inherited characteristics (i.e., they don't all express these traits in the same way)

Environment (selective agents)

Some individuals have higher reproductive success than others because they possess advantageous expressions of certain traits

Increase in the proportion of individuals with the advantageous expression of the trait; decrease in the proportion having a less beneficial expression

school boards and state legislatures, promoting laws that mandate the teaching of creationism in public schools. In Dover, Pennsylvania, ID proponents suffered a setback in 2004 when voters ousted all eight of the nine-member Dover Area School Board who were up for reelection. This school board, composed entirely of ID supporters, had established a policy requiring high school teachers to discuss ID as an alternative to evolution. Then, in late 2005, a U.S. district judge struck down the policy because it violated the First Amendment to the Constitution.

In fact, state and federal courts have consistently overruled these and similar laws because they violate the "establishment clause" of the First Amendment of the U.S. Constitution, which states that "Congress shall make no law respecting an establishment of religion, or prohibiting the free exercise thereof." This statement guarantees the separation of church and state, and it means that the government can neither promote nor inhibit the practice of any religion. Therefore, the use of

public institutions (including schools) paid for by taxes to promote any particular religion is unconstitutional. Of course, this doesn't mean that individuals can't have private religious discussions or pray in publicly funded institutions; but it does mean that such places can't be used for organized religious events. The establishment clause was initially proposed to ensure that the government could neither promote nor restrict any particular religious view, as the government in England did at the time the U.S. Constitution was written. But this hasn't stopped creationists, who encourage teachers to claim "academic freedom" to teach creationism. To avoid objections based on the guarantee of separation of church and state, proponents of ID claim that they don't emphasize any particular religion. But this argument doesn't address the essential point that teaching *any* religious views in a way that promotes them in publicly funded schools is a violation of the U.S. Constitution.

It is curious that the biological process that has led to the appearance of millions of plants and animals on our planet should generate such controversy. Our current understanding of evolution is directly traceable to developments in intellectual thought in western Europe and the East over the past 400 years. Many people contributed to this shift in perspective, and we've named only a few to provide a short historical view. It is quite likely that in the next 20 years, scientists will have identified many of the secrets of our evolutionary past through advances in genetic technologies and the continued discovery of fossil material. For evolutionary science, the early twenty-first century is indeed an exciting time.

Summary of Main Topics

- Our current understanding of evolutionary processes is directly traceable to developments in intellectual thought in western Europe and the East over the past 400 years. Darwin and Wallace were able to discover the process of natural selection and evolution because of the discoveries of numerous scientists who had laid the groundwork for them. Among others, Galileo, Lyell, Lamarck, Linnaeus, and Malthus all contributed to a dramatic shift in how people viewed the planet and themselves as part of a system governed by natural processes.
- Charles Darwin and Alfred Russel Wallace recognized that there was variation among individuals in any population (human or non-human). By understanding how animal breeders selected for certain traits in cattle, pigeons, and other species, Darwin formulated the theory of natural selection. Stated in the simplest terms, natural selection is a process whereby individuals who possess favorable traits (characteristics that permit them to survive and reproduce in a specific environment) will produce more offspring than individuals who have less favorable traits. Over time, the beneficial characteristics will become more frequent in the population, and the makeup of the population (or even a species) will have changed.
- As populations of a species become reproductively isolated from one another (perhaps due to distance or geographical barriers), they become increasingly different as each population adapts, by means of natural selection, to its own environment. Eventually, the populations may become distinct enough that they can no longer interbreed; at this point, they are considered separate species.
- In the United States, and increasingly in some Muslim countries, evolutionary processes are denounced because they are seen as contradictory to religious teaching. In recent years, Christian fundamentalists in the United States have argued in favor of teaching "creation science" in public schools. So far, courts have ruled against various attempts to promote "creation science" because of separation of church and state as provided for in the U.S. Constitution.

Critical Thinking Questions

1. After having read this chapter, how would you respond to the question, "If humans evolved from monkeys, why do we still have monkeys?"
2. Given what you've read about the scientific method in Chapter 1, how would you explain the differences between science and religion as methods of explaining natural phenomena? Do you personally see a conflict between evolutionary and religious explanations of how species came to be?
3. Can you think of some examples of artificial and natural selection that weren't discussed in this chapter? For your examples, what traits have been selected for? In the case of natural selection, what was the selective agent?

Computer graphic show-
ing human chromosomes.

3

The Biological Basis of Life

Equinox Graphics / Photo Researchers, Inc.

Key Questions

▶ What is the biological basis for life? Does it vary from one species to another?

▶ What does DNA do?

▶ What is DNA replication, and why is it important?

▶ Why are regulatory genes important to the evolutionary process?

▶ What genetic evidence suggests that humans are part of a biological continuum?

You've just gotten home after a rotten day, and you're watching the news on TV. The first story, after about 20 minutes of commercials, is about genetically modified foods, a newly cloned species, synthetic DNA, or the controversy over stem cell research. What do you do? Change the channel? Press the mute button? Go to sleep? Or do you follow the story? If you watch it, do you understand it, and do you think it's important or relevant to you personally? In fact, it *is* important to you because you live in an age when genetic discoveries and genetically based technologies are advancing daily, and one way or another, they're going to profoundly affect your life.

At some point in your life, you or someone you love will probably need lifesaving medical treatment, perhaps for cancer, and this treatment will almost certainly be based on genetic research. Like it or not, you already eat genetically modified foods, and you may eventually take advantage of developing reproductive technologies. Sadly, you may also see the development of biological weapons based on genetically altered bacteria and viruses. But fortunately, you'll also live to see many of the secrets of evolution revealed through genetic research. So even if you haven't been particularly interested in genetic issues (or maybe you've been intimidated by them), you should be aware that they affect your life every day.

As you already know, this book is about human evolution, variation, and adaptation, all of which are intimately linked to life processes that involve cells, the duplication and decoding of genetic information, and the transmission of this information between generations. So before we go any further, we need to examine the basic principles of genetics. Genetics is the study of how genes work and how traits are passed from one generation to the next. Although most physical anthropologists don't specialize in this field, they're very familiar with it because genetics unifies the various subdisciplines of biological anthropology.

Cells

To discuss genetic and evolutionary principles, it's necessary to understand the basic functions of cells. Cells are the fundamental units of life in all organisms. In some life-forms, such as bacteria, the entire organism consists of only a single cell (**Fig. 3-1**). However, more complex *multicellular* forms, such as plants, insects, birds, and mammals, are composed of billions of cells. In fact, an adult human body may be composed of as many as 1 trillion (1,000,000,000,000) cells, all functioning in complex ways that ultimately promote the survival of the individual.

Life on earth began at least 3.7 billion years ago in the form of single-celled organisms, represented today by bacteria and blue-green algae. Structurally more complex cells, called *eukaryotic* cells, appeared approximately 1.2 billion years ago, and since they're the kind of cell found in multicellular organisms, they will be the focus of this chapter. Despite the numerous differences among various life-forms, it's important to understand that the cells of all living organisms

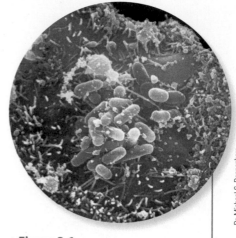

Dr. Michael S. Donnenberg

▲ **Figure 3-1**
Each one of these pink sausage-shaped structures is a single-celled bacterium.

share many similarities as a result of their common evolutionary past.

In general, a eukaryotic cell is a three-dimensional structure composed of carbohydrates, lipids (fats), nucleic acids, and **proteins**. It also contains several kinds of substructures called *organelles*, one of which is the **nucleus** (*pl.*, nuclei), a discrete unit surrounded by a thin membrane called the *nuclear membrane* (**Fig. 3-2**). Inside the nucleus

▶ **Figure 3-2**
Structure of a generalized eukaryotic cell, illustrating its three-dimensional nature. Various organelles are shown, but for simplicity, only those we discuss are labeled.

proteins Three-dimensional molecules that serve a wide variety of functions through their ability to bind to other molecules.

nucleus A structure (organelle) found in all eukaryotic cells. The nucleus contains chromosomes (nuclear DNA).

molecules Structures made up of two or more atoms. Molecules can combine with other molecules to form more complex structures.

DNA (deoxyribonucleic acid) The double-stranded molecule that contains the genetic code. DNA is a main component of chromosomes.

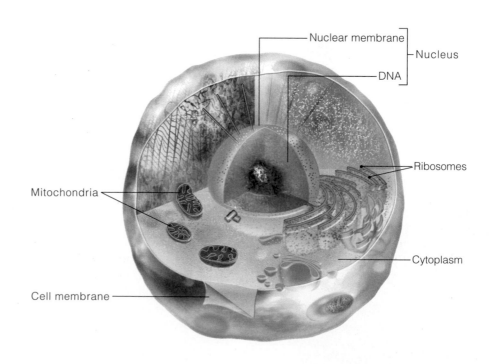

Nuclear membrane

Nucleus

DNA

Ribosomes

Mitochondria

Cytoplasm

Cell membrane

are two kinds of **molecules** that contain the genetic information that controls the cell's functions. Actually, these two molecules, **DNA (deoxyribonucleic acid)** and **RNA (ribonucleic acid)**, are not only fundamental to cellular activities; they are fundamental to life itself.

The nucleus is surrounded by a gel-like substance called **cytoplasm**, which contains many other types of organelles involved in activities related to the function of the cell and organism. These activities include breaking down nutrients and converting them to other substances, storing and releasing energy, eliminating waste, and manufacturing proteins through a process called **protein synthesis**.

Two of these organelles, **mitochondria** (*sing.*, mitochondrion) and **ribosomes**, require further mention. Mitochondria (**Fig. 3-3**) are responsible for producing energy within the cell and can be thought of as the cell's engines. Mitochondria are oval structures enclosed within a folded membrane, and they contain their own distinct DNA, called **mitochondrial DNA (mtDNA)**, which directs mitochondrial activities. Mitochondrial DNA has the same molecular structure and function as nuclear DNA (that is, DNA found in the nucleus), but it's organized somewhat differently. In recent years, mtDNA has attracted a lot of attention because of the traits it influences and because it can be used to study certain evolutionary processes. For these reasons, we'll discuss mitochondrial inheritance in more detail later. Ribosomes, which will also be discussed later, are roughly spherical and partly composed of RNA. They're important because they're essential to protein synthesis.

There are basically two types of cells: **somatic cells** and **gametes**. Somatic cells make up the body tissues, such as muscle, bone, skin, nerve, heart, and brain. Gametes, or sex cells, are specifically involved in reproduc-

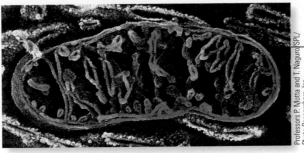

◄ **Figure 3-3**
Scanning electron micrograph of a mitochondrion.

tion and are not important as structural components of the body. There are two types of gametes: egg cells, produced in female ovaries, and sperm cells, which develop in male testes. The sole function of a sex cell is to unite with a gamete from another individual to form a **zygote**, which has the potential of developing into a new individual. In this way, gametes transmit genetic information from parent to offspring.

The Structure of DNA

DNA is the very basis of life because it directs all cellular activities. So if we want to understand these activities and how traits are inherited, we must know something about the structure and function of DNA. The exact physical and chemical properties of DNA were unknown until 1953, when, at the University of Cambridge in England, an American researcher named James Watson and three British scientists, Francis Crick, Maurice Wilkins, and Rosalind Franklin, developed a structural and functional model of DNA (**Fig. 3-4**; Watson and Crick, 1953a, 1953b). It's impossible to overstate the importance of this achievement because it completely revolutionized the fields of biology and medicine and forever altered our understanding of biological and evolutionary mechanisms (see "A Closer Look: Rosalind Franklin: The Fourth (but Invisible) Member of the Double Helix Team").

The DNA molecule is composed of two chains of even smaller units called **nucleotides**. A nucleotide, in turn, is made up of three components: a sugar molecule (deoxyribose), a phosphate

RNA (ribonucleic acid) A single-stranded molecule similar in structure to DNA. Three forms of RNA are essential to protein synthesis: messenger RNA (mRNA), transfer RNA (tRNA), and ribosomal RNA (rRNA).

cytoplasm The semifluid, gel-like substance contained within the cell membrane. The nucleus and numerous structures involved with cell function are found within the cytoplasm.

protein synthesis The manufacture of proteins; the assembly of chains of amino acids into functional protein molecules. Protein synthesis is directed by DNA.

mitochondria (*sing.*, mitochondrion) Structures contained within the cytoplasm of eukaryotic cells that convert energy, derived from nutrients, to a form that can be used by the cell.

ribosomes Structures composed of a form of RNA called ribosomal RNA (rRNA) and protein. Ribosomes are found in a cell's cytoplasm and are essential to the manufacture of proteins.

mitochondrial DNA (mtDNA) DNA found in the mitochondria. Mitochondrial DNA is inherited only from the mother.

somatic cells Basically, all the cells in the body except those involved with reproduction.

gametes Reproductive cells (eggs and sperm in animals) developed from precursor cells in ovaries and testes.

zygote A cell formed by the union of an egg cell and a sperm cell. It contains the full complement of chromosomes (in humans, 46) and has the potential of developing into an entire organism.

nucleotides Basic units of the DNA molecule, composed of a sugar, a phosphate, and one of four DNA bases.

A. Barrington Brown / Photo Researchers, Inc.

▲ Figure 3-4
James Watson (left) and Francis Crick in 1953 with their model of the structure of the DNA molecule.

stranded and is described as forming a *double helix* that resembles a twisted ladder. If we follow the twisted ladder analogy, the sugars and phosphates represent the two sides, while the bases and the bonds that join them form the rungs.

The four bases are the key to how DNA works. These bases are *adenine, guanine, thymine,* and *cytosine,* usually referred to by their initial letters: A, G, T, and C. When the double helix is formed, one type of base can pair, or bond, with only one other type: A can pair with T, and G can pair with C (Fig. 3-5). This specificity is absolutely essential to the DNA molecule's ability to **replicate**, or make an exact copy of itself.

group (a molecule composed of phosphorus and oxygen), and one of four nitrogenous *bases* (**Fig. 3-5**). In DNA, nucleotides are stacked on top of one another to form a chain that is bonded by its bases to another nucleotide chain. Together the two chains twist to form a spiral, or helical, shape. The DNA molecule, then, is double-

DNA Replication

Cells multiply by dividing, making exact copies of themselves. This, in turn, enables organisms to grow and injured tissues to heal. There are two kinds of cell division. In the simpler form, a cell divides one time to produce

▶ Figure 3-5
Part of a DNA molecule. The illustration shows the two DNA strands with the sugar (gray) and phosphate (purple) backbone and the bases (labeled T, A, G, and C) extending toward the center.

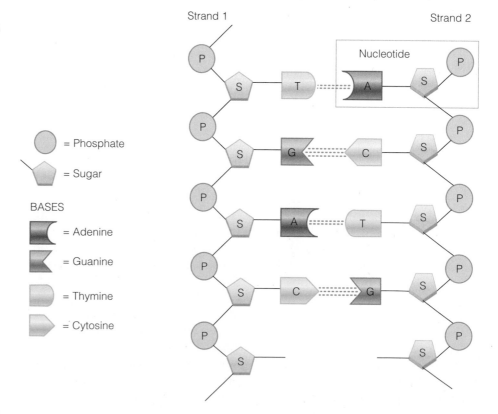

replicate To duplicate. The DNA molecule is able to make copies of itself.

Rosalind Franklin: The Fourth (but Invisible) Member of the Double Helix Team

In 1962, three men, James Watson, Francis Crick, and Maurice Wilkins, won the Nobel Prize for medicine and physiology. They earned this most prestigious of all scientific honors for their discovery of the structure of the DNA molecule, which they had published in 1953. But due credit was not given to a fourth, equally deserving but unacknowledged person named Rosalind Franklin, who had died of ovarian cancer in 1958. But even if she had been acknowledged in 1962, Franklin still wouldn't have been a Nobel recipient because the Nobel Prize isn't awarded posthumously.

Franklin was a chemist who went to the University of Cambridge in 1951, after being invited there to study the structure of DNA. Before that, she'd been in Paris using a technique called X-ray diffraction, a process that reveals the positions of atoms in crystalline structures. What Franklin didn't know was that a colleague in her Cambridge lab, Maurice Wilkins, was working on the same DNA project. To make matters worse, Wilkins hadn't been told what her position was, so he thought she'd been hired as his assistant. Needless to say, this was hardly a good way to begin a working relationship, and as you might expect, there were a few tense moments between them.

Franklin soon produced some excellent X-ray diffraction images of some DNA fibers that Wilkins had provided, and the images clearly showed that the structure was helical. Furthermore, she worked out that there were two strands, not one. Wilkins innocently (but without Franklin's knowledge) showed the

The Novartis Foundation

◀ Figure 1
Rosalind Franklin

images to Watson and Crick, who were working in another laboratory, also at Cambridge. Within two weeks, Watson and Crick had developed their now-famous model of a double-stranded helix without Franklin's knowledge.

Desperately unhappy at Cambridge, Franklin took a position at King's College, London, in 1953. In April of that year, she and a student published an article in the journal *Nature* that dealt indirectly with the helical structure of DNA. The article by Watson and Crick was published in the same issue.

During her lifetime, Franklin gained recognition for her work in carbons, coal, and viruses, topics on which she published many articles; and she was happy with the reputation she achieved. After her death, Watson made many derogative comments about Rosalind Franklin, including several in print. Even so, it appears they remained on friendly terms until she died at the age of 37. She also remained friendly with Crick, but she never knew that their revolutionary discovery was partly made possible by her photographic images.

two "daughter" cells, each of which receives a full set of genetic material. This is important, because a cell can't function properly without the right amount of DNA. But before a cell can divide, its DNA must replicate.

Replication begins when **enzymes** break the bonds between bases throughout the DNA molecule, separating the two previously joined strands of nucleotides and leaving their bases exposed (**Fig. 3-6**). These exposed bases then attract unattached DNA nucleotides that are free-floating in the cell nucleus. (These free-floating nucleotides have been made by DNA else-where in the cell nucleus.) Since each base can pair with only one other, the attraction between bases occurs in a **complementary** way. This means that the two previously joined parental nucleotide chains serve as models, or templates, for forming new strands of nucleotides. As each new strand is formed, its bases are joined to the bases of an original strand. When the process is complete, there are two double-stranded DNA molecules exactly like the original one, and each newly formed molecule consists of one original nucleotide chain joined to a newly formed chain.

enzymes Specialized proteins that initiate and direct chemical reactions in the body.

complementary In genetics, referring to the fact that DNA bases form pairs (called base pairs) in a precise manner. For example, adenine can bond only to thymine. These two bases are said to be complementary because one requires the other to form a complete DNA base pair.

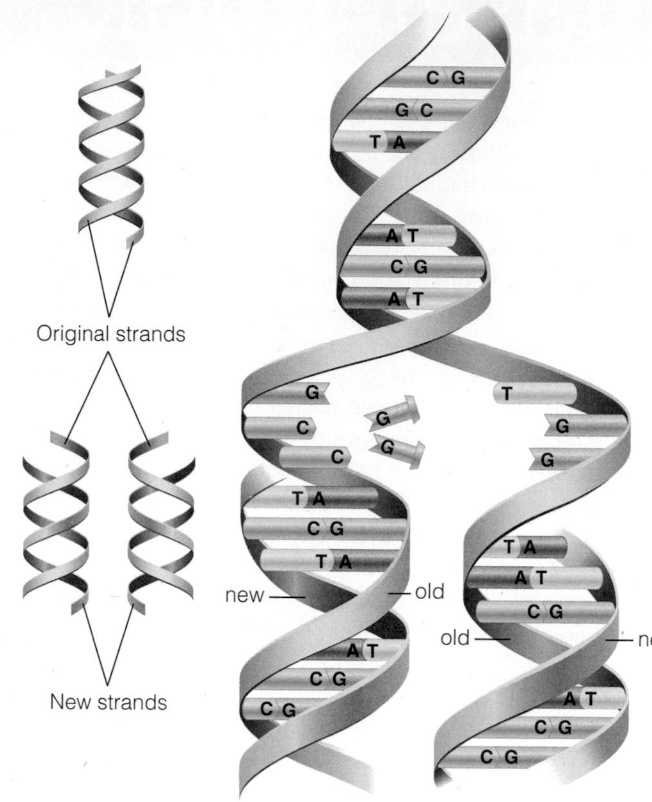

Original double-stranded DNA molecule

DNA double helix

C G
G C
T A

Original strands

Two identical double-stranded DNA molecules

A T
C G
A T

G
C
G
C
G G
G G

G
T
G
G

Replication under way

Unattached nucleotides are attracted to their complementary nucleotides and thereby form a new strand

T A
C G
T A

new — old

T A
A T
C G

old — new

New strands

A T
C G
C G

A T
C G
C G

Replication complete

▲ **Figure 3-6**
DNA replication. During DNA replication, the two strands of the DNA molecule (purple) are separated, and each strand serves as a template for the formation of a new strand (brown). When replication is complete, there are two DNA molecules, each consisting of one new strand and one original strand.

Protein Synthesis

One of the most important activities of DNA is to direct the assembly of proteins (protein synthesis) within cells. Proteins are complex, three-dimensional molecules that function through their ability to bind to other molecules. For example, the protein **hemoglobin** (Fig. 3-7), found in red blood cells, is able to bind to oxygen, which it carries to cells throughout the body.

▶ **Figure 3-7**
Diagrammatic representation of a hemoglobin molecule. Hemoglobin molecules are composed of four chains of amino acids (two alpha chains and two beta chains).

Beta chain   Beta chain

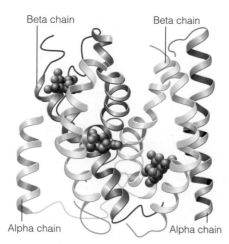

Alpha chain   Alpha chain

hemoglobin A protein molecule that occurs in red blood cells and binds to oxygen molecules.

hormones Substances (usually proteins) that are produced by specialized cells and that travel to other parts of the body, where they influence chemical reactions and regulate various cellular functions.

Proteins function in countless ways. Some, like collagen, are structural components of tissues. Collagen is the most common protein in the body and is a major component of all connective tissues. Enzymes are also proteins, and they regulate chemical reactions. For instance, a digestive enzyme called *lactase* breaks down *lactose*, or milk sugar, into two simpler sugars. Another class of proteins includes many types of **hormones**. Hormones are produced by specialized cells and then released into the bloodstream to circulate to other parts of the body, where they produce specific effects in tissues and organs. Insulin, for example, is a hormone produced by cells in the pancreas, and it causes cells in the liver to absorb energy-producing glucose (sugar) from the blood. (People whose pancreatic cells fail to produce sufficient amounts of insulin have one of the two types of diabetes.) Lastly, many kinds of proteins can enter a cell's nucleus and attach directly to its DNA. This is very important because when these proteins bind to the DNA, they can regulate its

Characteristics of the DNA Code

1. **The code is triplet.** Each amino acid is specified by a sequence of three bases in the mRNA (the codon), which in turn is coded for by three bases in the DNA (the triplet).

2. **The code is continuous, without pauses.** There are no pauses separating one triplet or codon from another. Thus, if a base is deleted, the entire frame is moved, drastically altering the message downstream for successive triplets or codons. Such a gross alteration is called a frameshift mutation. Note that although the code lacks "commas," it does contain "periods" in the form of three specific codons that act to stop translation.

3. **The code is redundant.** While there are 20 amino acids, there are 4 DNA bases and 64 possible DNA triplets or mRNA codons. Even considering the three "stop" messages, that still leaves 61 codons specifying the 20 amino acids. Thus, many amino acids are specified by more than one codon (see Table 3-1). For example, leucine and serine are each coded for by six different codons. In fact, only two amino acids (methionine and tryptophan) are coded for by a single codon. Redundancy is useful. For one thing, it serves as a safety net by helping to reduce the likelihood of severe consequences if there is a change, or mutation, in a DNA base. For example, four different DNA triplets—CGA, CGG, CGT, and CGC—code for the amino acid alanine. If, in the codon CGA, A mutates to G, the resulting triplet, CGG, will still specify alanine; thus, there will be no functional change.

4. **The code is universal.** The same DNA code applies to all life on earth, from bacteria to oak trees to humans. That is, the same DNA triplets specify the same amino acids in all forms of life. This commonality is the basis for the methods used in recombinant DNA technology, and it implies biological continuity between species.

activity. From this brief description, you can see that proteins make us what we are. So protein synthesis must occur accurately, because if it doesn't, physiological development and cellular activities can be disrupted or even prevented.

Proteins are made up of chains of smaller molecules called **amino acids**. In all, there are 20 amino acids, 8 of which must be obtained from foods (see Chapter 17). The remaining 12 are produced in cells. These 20 amino acids are combined in different amounts and sequences to produce at least 90,000 different proteins. What makes proteins different from one another is the number and sequence of their amino acids.

In part, DNA is a recipe for making a protein, since it's the sequence of DNA bases that ultimately determines the order of amino acids in a protein. In the DNA instructions, a *triplet*, or group of three bases, specifies a particular amino acid. For example, if a triplet consists of the base sequence cytosine, guanine, and adenine (CGA), it specifies the amino acid arganine (**Table 3-1**). Therefore, a small portion of a DNA recipe might look like this (except there would be no spaces between the triplets): AGA CGA ACA ACC TAC TTT TTC CTT AAG GTC.

Protein synthesis actually takes place outside the cell nucleus, in the cytoplasm at one of the previously mentioned organelles, the ribosomes. But the DNA molecule can't leave the cell's nucleus. Therefore, the first step in protein synthesis is to copy the DNA message into a form of RNA called **messenger RNA (mRNA)**, which can pass through the nuclear membrane into the cytoplasm. RNA is similar to DNA, but it's different in some important ways:

1. It's single-stranded. (This is true for the forms we discuss here, but it's not true for all forms of RNA.)

2. It contains a different type of sugar.

3. It contains the base uracil as a substitute for the DNA base thymine. (Uracil binds to adenine in the same way thymine does.)

The mRNA molecule forms on the DNA template in pretty much the same

amino acids Small molecules that are the components of proteins.

messenger RNA (mRNA) A form of RNA that's assembled on a sequence of DNA bases. It carries the DNA code to the ribosome during protein synthesis.

TABLE
3.1 The Genetic Code

Amino Acid Symbol	Amino Acid	mRNA Codon	DNA Triplet
Ala	Alanine	GCU, GCC, GCA, GCG	CGA, CGG, CGT, CGC
Arg	Arginine	CGU, CGC, CGA, CGG, AGA, AGG	GCA, GCG, GCT, GCC, TCT, TCC
Asn	Asparagine	AAU, AAC	TTA, TTG
Asp	Aspartic acid	GAU, GAC	CTA, CTG
Cys	Cysteine	UGU, UGC	ACA, ACG
Gln	Glutamine	CAA, CAG	GTT, GTC
Glu	Glutamic acid	GAA, GAG	CTT, CTC
Gly	Glycine	GGU, GGC, GGA, GGG	CCA, CCG, CCT, CCC
His	Histidine	CAU, CAC	GTA, GTG
Ile	Isoleucine	AUU, AUC, AUA	TAA, TAG, TAT
Leu	Leucine	UUA, UUG, CUU, CUC, CUA, CUG	AAT, AAC, GAA, GAG, GAT, GAC
Lys	Lysine	AAA, AAG	TTT, TTC
Met	Methionine	AUG	TAC
Phe	Phenylalanine	UUU, UUC	AAA, AAG
Pro	Proline	CCU, CCC, CCA, CCG	GGA, GGG, GGT, GGC
Ser	Serine	UCU, UCC, UCA, UCG, AGU, AGC	AGA, AGG, AGT, AGC, TCA, TCG
Thr	Threonine	ACU, ACC, ACA, ACG	TGA, TGG, TGT, TGC
Trp	Tryptophan	UGG	ACC
Tyr	Tyrosine	UAU, UAC	ATA, ATG
Val	Valine	GUU, GUC, GUA, GUG	CAA, CAG, CAT, CAC
Terminating triplets		UAA, UAG, UGA	ATT, ATC, ACT

codons Triplets of messenger RNA bases that code for specific amino acids during protein synthesis.

transfer RNA (tRNA) A type of RNA that binds to specific amino acids and transports them to the ribosome during protein synthesis.

mutation A change in DNA. The term can refer to changes in DNA bases (specifically called point mutations) as well as to changes in chromosome number and/or structure.

way that new DNA molecules are assembled. As in DNA replication, the two DNA strands separate, but only partially, and one of these strands attracts free-floating RNA nucleotides (also produced in the cell), which are joined together on the DNA template. The formation of mRNA is called *transcription* because, in fact, the DNA code is being copied, or transcribed (**Fig. 3-8**). Transcription continues until a section of DNA called a terminator region (composed of one of three specific DNA triplets) is reached and the process stops (see Table 3-1). At this point, the mRNA strand, comprising

anywhere from 5,000 to perhaps as many as 200,000 nucleotides, peels away from the DNA model, and a portion of it travels through the nuclear membrane to the ribosome. Meanwhile, the bonds between the DNA bases are reestablished, and the DNA molecule is once more intact.

As the mRNA strand arrives at the ribosome, its message is translated, or decoded (**Fig. 3-9**). Just as each DNA triplet specifies one amino acid, so do mRNA triplets, which are called **codons**. Therefore, the mRNA strand is "read" in codons, or groups of three mRNA bases at a time (see Table 3-1).

Subsequently, another form of RNA, called **transfer RNA (tRNA)**, brings each amino acid to the ribosome. The ribosome then joins that amino acid to another amino acid in the order dictated by the sequence of mRNA codons (or, ultimately, DNA triplets). In this way, amino acids are linked together to form a molecule that will eventually be a protein or part of a protein. But it's important to mention that if a DNA base or sequence of bases is changed through **mutation**, some proteins may not be made or they may be defective. In this case, cells won't function properly, if at all.

What Is a Gene?

The answer to this question is complicated, and the definition of the term **gene** is currently the subject of some debate. In the past, textbooks compared genes to a string of beads, with each bead representing one gene on a chromosome. For 50 years or so, biologists considered a gene to be an uninterrupted sequence of DNA bases responsible for the manufacture of a protein or part of a protein. Or, put another way, a gene

▶ **Figure 3-9**
Assembly of an amino acid chain in protein synthesis.

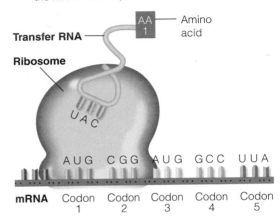

a As the ribosome binds to the mRNA, tRNA brings a particular amino acid, specified by the mRNA codon, to the ribosome.

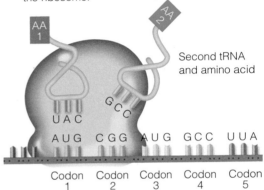

b The tRNA binds to the first codon while a second tRNA–amino acid complex arrives at the ribosome.

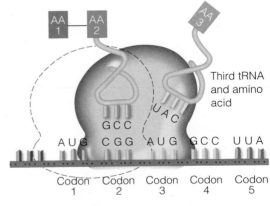

c The ribosome moves down the mRNA, allowing a third amino acid to be brought into position by another tRNA molecule. Note that the first two amino acids are now joined together.

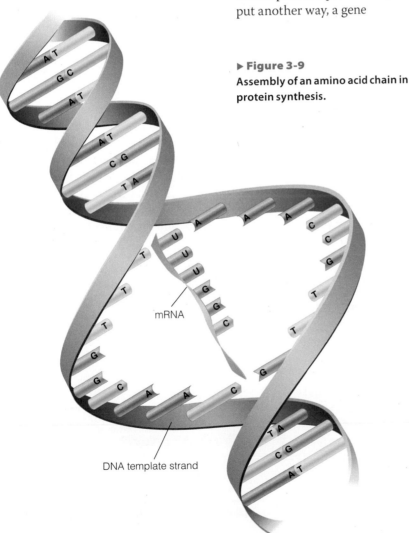

▲ **Figure 3-8**
Transcription. In this illustration, the two DNA strands have partly separated. Messenger RNA (mRNA) nucleotides have been drawn to the template strand, and a strand of mRNA is being made. Note that the mRNA strand will exactly complement the DNA template strand, except that uracil (U) replaces thymine (T).

gene A sequence of DNA bases that specifies the order of amino acids in an entire protein, a portion of a protein, or any functional product (e.g., RNA). A gene may be made up of hundreds or thousands of DNA bases organized into coding and noncoding segments.

could be defined as *a segment of DNA that specifies the sequence of amino acids in a particular protein*. This definition, based on the concept of a one gene–one protein relationship, was a core principle in biology for decades, but it's been substantially modified, partly in recognition of the fact that DNA codes not only for proteins, but also for RNA and other DNA nucleotides.

Moreover, when the human **genome** was sequenced in 2001 (International Human Genome Sequencing Consortium, 2001; Venter et al., 2001), scientists learned that humans have only about 25,000 genes, pretty much the same number as most other mammals. Yet, we produce as many as 90,000 proteins! Furthermore, protein-coding genes (also called *coding sequences*), the DNA segments that are transcribed into proteins, make up only about 2 percent of the entire human genome! Another 2 percent (approximately) regulates gene activity. The remaining 96 percent is composed of so-called "**noncoding DNA**" (Pritchard, 2010). Thus, gene action is much more complicated than previously believed and it's impossible for every protein to be coded for by a specific gene. (This shift in perspective is a good example of what we discussed in Chapter 1, that hypotheses and theories can, and do, change over time as we continue to acquire new knowledge.)

In recent years, geneticists have learned that only some parts of genes, called **exons**, are actually transcribed into mRNA and thus code for specific amino acids. In fact, most of the nucleotide sequences in genes aren't expressed during protein synthesis. (By expressed we mean that the DNA sequence is actually making a product.) Some noncoding DNA sequences, called **introns**, are initially transcribed into mRNA and then clipped out (**Fig. 3-10**). Therefore, introns aren't

translated into amino acid sequences. Moreover, the intron segments that are snipped out of a gene aren't always the same ones. This means that the exons can be combined in different ways to make segments that code for more than one protein. Genes can also overlap one another, and there can be genes within genes (**Fig. 3-11**). But they're still a part of the DNA molecule, and it's the combination of introns and exons, interspersed along a strand of DNA, that makes up the unit we call a gene. So much for beads on a string.

Clearly, the answer to the question "What is a gene?" is complicated, and a completely accurate definition may be a long time coming. However, a proposed and more inclusive definition simply states that a gene is "a complete chromosomal segment responsible for making a functional product" (Snyder and Gerstein, 2003).

In spite of all the recently obtained information that has changed some of our views and expanded our knowledge of DNA, there is one fact that doesn't change. The genetic code is *universal*, and at least on earth, DNA is the molecule that governs the expression, inheritance, and evolution of biological traits

▼ **Figure 3-10**

Diagram of a DNA sequence being transcribed. The introns are deleted from pre-mRNA before it leaves the cell's nucleus. The remaining mature RNA contains only exons, which will code for a protein or part of a protein.

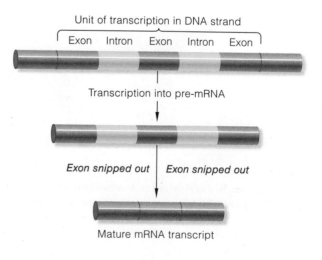

Unit of transcription in DNA strand

Exon   Intron   Exon   Intron   Exon

Transcription into pre-mRNA

Exon snipped out   Exon snipped out

Mature mRNA transcript

genome The entire genetic makeup of an individual or species. In humans, it's estimated that each individual possesses approximately 3 billion DNA bases.

noncoding DNA DNA that does not direct the production of proteins. However, such DNA segments may produce other important molecules, so the term *noncoding DNA* is not really accurate.

exons Segments of genes that are transcribed and are involved in protein synthesis. (The prefix *ex* denotes that these segments are expressed.)

introns Segments of genes that are initially transcribed and then deleted. Because they aren't expressed, they aren't involved in protein synthesis.

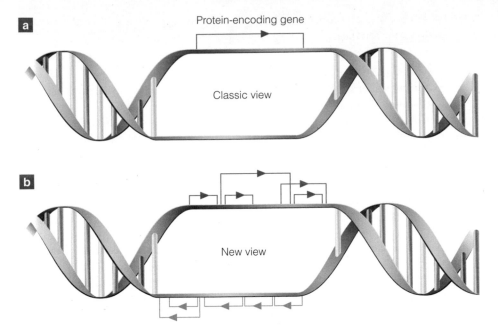

Protein-encoding gene

a

Classic view

b

New view

◄ **Figure 3-11**
Diagrammatic representation of how
our views of gene function have
changed. **(a)** According to the traditional view, genes are discrete segments of DNA, each coding for a
specific protein, and only one of the
two DNA strands are involved in protein synthesis. **(b)** We now know that as
different introns are deleted during
translation, the remaining exons can
form several overlapping coding
sequences, each of which can be considered a gene. That is, a portion of one
gene can also be part of another gene.
Also, both DNA strands are functional.

in all forms of life. The DNA of all
organisms, from bacteria to oak trees
to fruit flies to human beings, is composed of the same molecules using the
same kinds of instructions. The DNA
triplet CGA, for example, specifies the
amino acid alanine, regardless of species. These similarities imply biological
relationships between all forms of
life—and a common ancestry as well.
What makes fruit flies distinct from
humans isn't differences in the DNA
material itself, but differences in how
that material is arranged and regulated.

Regulatory Genes

Some genes act solely to control the
expression of other genes. Basically,
these **regulatory genes** make molecules
that switch other DNA segments
(genes) on or off. Thus, their functions
are critical for individual organisms,
and they also play a fundamental and
critical role in evolution. The study of
regulatory genes and their role in evolution is still in its infancy but as information about them continues to accumulate, we will be able to answer many
of the questions we still have about the
evolution of species.

DNA deactivation during embryonic development is a good example of

how regulatory genes work. As you
know, all somatic cells contain the
same genetic information; but in any
given cell, only a fraction of the DNA is
actually involved in protein synthesis.
For example, like the cells of the stomach lining, bone cells have DNA that
codes for the production of digestive
enzymes. But fortunately for us all,
bone cells don't produce digestive
enzymes. Instead, they manufacture
collagen, the main organic component
of bone. This is because cells become
specialized during embryonic development to perform only certain functions, and most of their DNA is permanently switched off by regulatory genes.
In other words, they become specific
types of cells, such as bone cells.

Homeobox genes are critically
important regulatory genes, and there
are several different kinds. Perhaps the
best know are the *Hox* genes that
direct early segmentation of embryonic
tissues, including those that give rise
to the spine and thoracic muscles.
Homeobox genes also interact with
other genes to determine the characteristics of developing body segments
and structures, but not their actual
development. For example, homeobox
genes determine where, in a developing
embryo, limb buds will appear. They
also establish the number and overall

regulatory genes Genes that influence the activity of other genes. Regulatory
genes direct embryonic development and
are involved in physiological processes
throughout life. They are extremely important to the evolutionary process.

homeobox genes An evolutionarily
ancient family of regulatory genes that
directs the development of the overall
body plan and the segmentation of body
tissues.

What's All This Junk? Or Is It Junk?

In all fields of inquiry, important discoveries always raise new questions that eventually lead to further revelations. There's probably no statement that could be more appropriately applied to the field of genetics. For example, in 1977, geneticists recognized that during protein synthesis, the initially formed mRNA molecule contains many more nucleotides than are represented in the subsequently produced protein. This finding led to the discovery of *introns*, portions of genes that don't code for, or specify, proteins. What happens is, once the mRNA molecule peels away from the DNA template, but before it leaves the cell's nucleus, enzymes snip out the introns. The original mRNA molecule is sometimes called pre-mRNA, but once the introns have been deleted, the remainder is mature mRNA. It's the mature mRNA that leaves the nucleus carrying its code for protein production.

In the 1980s, geneticists learned that only about 2 percent of human DNA is contained within *exons*, the segments that actually provide the code for protein synthesis. This means that while an estimated 28 percent of human DNA is composed of genes (including introns and exons), only 5 percent of the DNA within these genes is actually composed of coding sequences (Baltimore, 2001). We also know that a human gene can specify the production of

as many as three different proteins by using different combinations of the exons interspersed within it (Pennisi, 2005).

With only 2 percent of the human genome directing protein synthesis, and another 2 percent involved in gene regulation, humans have more noncoding DNA than any other species so far studied. Invertebrates and some vertebrates have only small amounts of noncoding sequences, and yet they're fully functional organisms. So just what does all this noncoding DNA (originally called "junk DNA") do in humans?

Almost half of all human DNA consists of noncoding segments that are repeated over and over and over. Depending on their length, these segments have been referred to as *tandem repeats*, *satellites*, or *microsatellites*, but now they're frequently lumped together and called *copy number variants (CNVs)*. Microsatellites have an extremely high mutation rate and can gain or lose repeated segments and then return to their former length. But this tendency to mutate means that the number of repeats in a given microsatellite varies between individuals. And this tremendous variation has been the basis for DNA fingerprinting, a technique commonly used to provide evidence in criminal cases. Actually, anthropologists are now using microsatellite variation for all kinds of research, from tracing migrations of populations to paternity testing in nonhuman primates.

Some of the variations in microsatellite composition are associated with various disorders, so we can't help wondering why these variations exist. One answer is that

some microsatellites influence the activities of protein coding DNA sequences. Also, by losing or adding material, they can alter the sequences of bases in genes, thus becoming a source of mutation in functional genes. And these mutations are a source of genetic variation.

Lastly, there are transposable elements (TEs), the so-called *jumping genes*. These are DNA sequences that can make thousands of copies of themselves, and these copies are then scattered throughout the genome. One family of TEs, called *Alu*, is found only in primates. About 5 percent of the human genome is made up of *Alu* sequences, and although most of these are shared with other primates, about 7,000 are unique to humans (Chimpanzee Sequencing and Analysis Consortium, 2005).

TEs mainly code for proteins that enable them to move about, and because they can land right in the middle of coding sequences (exons), TEs cause mutations. Some of these mutations are harmful, and TEs have been associated with numerous disease conditions, including some forms of cancer (Deragon and Capy, 2000). But at the same time, TEs essentially create new exons, thereby generating variations for natural selection to act on. Moreover, they also regulate the activities of many genes, including those involved in development. So, rather than being junk, TEs are increasingly being recognized as serving extremely important functions in the evolutionary process, including the introduction of genetic change that has led to the origins of new lineages.

pattern of the different types of vertebrae, the bones that make up the spine (**Fig. 3-12**).

All homeobox genes are highly conserved, meaning they've been maintained throughout much of evolutionary history. They're present in all invertebrates (such as worms and insects) and vertebrates, and they don't vary greatly from species to species.

This type of conservation means not only that these genes are vitally important, but also that they evolved from genes that were present in some of the earliest forms of life. Moreover, changes in the behavior of homeobox genes are responsible for various physical differences between closely related species or different breeds of domesticated animals. For these reasons,

At a Glance

CODING AND NONCODING DNA

CODING DNA	NONCODING DNA ("JUNK" DNA)
Codes for sequences of amino acids (i.e., functional proteins) or RNA molecules	Function not well known. A majority probably does not code for proteins. However, regulatory genes, which have been classed as noncoding, do produce proteins. This terminlogy may change.
Comprises approximately 2% of human nuclear DNA	Comprises about 98% of human nuclear DNA
Includes exons within functional genes	Includes introns within functional genes and multiple repeated segments elsewhere on chromosomes (for example, microsatellites)

homeobox genes are now a critical area of research in evolutionary and developmental biology.

There are many other types of highly conserved genes as well. For example, recent sequencing of the sea sponge genome has shown that humans share many genes with sea sponges (Srivastava et al., 2010). This doesn't mean that sponges were ancestral to humans, but it does mean that we have genes that were already in existence some 600 mya. These genes ultimately laid the foundation for the evolution of complex animals, and they're crucial to many of the basic cellular processes that are fundamental to life today. These processes include cell growth; the ability to recognize foreign cells (immunity); the development of specific cell types; signaling between cells during growth and development; and programmed cell death (related to tumor suppression).

▼ **Figure 3-12**

The differences in these three vertebrae, from different regions of the spine, are caused by the action of *Hox* genes during embryonic development. (a) The cervical (neck) vertebrae have characteristics that differentiate them from (b) thoracic vertebrae, which are attached to the ribs, and also from (c) lumbar vertebrae of the lower back. *Hox* genes determine the overall pattern not only of each type of vertebra but also of each individual vertebra.

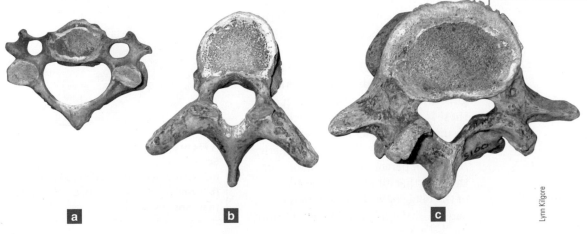

a b c

Lynn Kilgore

In Chapter 2, we saw how Charles Darwin came to recognize that variation in the finches of the Galápagos Islands was an example of natural selection. Scientists have now explained the genetic basis for some of the finch variation by identifying two of the regulatory genes involved in shape and size of bird beaks (Abzhanov et al., 2004, 2006). One of these genes (also involved in bone formation) is expressed to a greater degree during the embryonic development of wide-beaked ground finches than of finches with narrower beaks. Likewise, another gene is more active during beak development in cactus finches that have longer, narrower beaks (refer back to Fig. 2-13). Therefore, length and width of bird beaks are controlled by the activity of at least two different regulatory genes, allowing each aspect of beak size to evolve separately.

We can't overestimate the importance of regulatory genes in evolution. And the fact that these genes, with little modification, are present in all complex (and some not so complex) organisms, including humans, is the basis of biological continuity between species.

Mutation: When Genes Change

The best way to understand how genetic material functions is to see what happens when it changes, or mutates. Normal adult hemoglobin is made up of four amino acid chains (two *alpha* chains and two *beta* chains) that are the direct products of gene action. Each beta chain is in turn composed of 146 amino acids. There are several hemoglobin disorders with genetic origins, and perhaps the best known of these is **sickle-cell anemia**, which results from a defect in the beta chain. People with sickle-cell anemia inherit, from *both* parents, a mutated form of the gene that directs the formation of the beta chain. This mutation is caused by the substitution of one amino

acid (*valine*) for the amino acid that's normally present (*glutamic acid*). This single amino acid substitution on the beta chain results in the production of a less efficient form of hemoglobin called hemoglobin S (Hb^S) instead of the normal form, which is called hemoglobin A (Hb^A). In situations where the availability of oxygen is reduced, such as at high altitude, or when oxygen requirements are increased through exercise, red blood cells with Hb^S collapse and become sickle-shaped (**Fig. 3-13**). What follows is a cascade of events, all of which result in severe anemia and its consequences (**Fig. 3-14**). Briefly, these consequences include impaired circulation from blocked capillaries, red blood cell destruction, oxygen deprivation to vital organs (including the brain), and, without treatment, death.

People who inherit the altered form of the gene from only one parent don't have sickle-cell anemia, but they do have what's called *sickle-cell trait*. Fortunately for them, they're much less

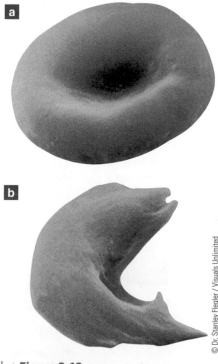

a

b

© Dr. Stanley Flegler / Visuals Unlimited

▲ **Figure 3-13**
Scanning electron micrographs of (a) a normal, fully oxygenated red blood cell and (b) a collapsed, sickle-shaped red blood cell that contains Hb^S

sickle-cell anemia A severe inherited hemoglobin disorder in which red blood cells collapse when deprived of oxygen. It results from inheriting two copies of a mutant allele. The type of mutation that produces the sickle-cell allele is a point mutation.

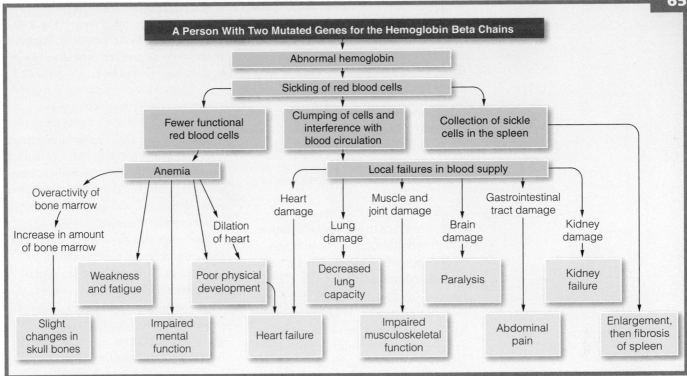

A Person With Two Mutated Genes for the Hemoglobin Beta Chains

Abnormal hemoglobin

Sickling of red blood cells

Fewer functional red blood cells | Clumping of cells and interference with blood circulation | Collection of sickle cells in the spleen

Anemia | Local failures in blood supply

Overactivity of bone marrow

Increase in amount of bone marrow

Dilation of heart

Heart damage

Muscle and joint damage

Gastrointestinal tract damage

Lung damage

Brain damage

Kidney damage

Weakness and fatigue

Poor physical development

Decreased lung capacity

Paralysis

Kidney failure

Slight changes in skull bones

Impaired mental function

Heart failure

Impaired musculoskeletal function

Abdominal pain

Enlargement, then fibrosis of spleen

▲ **Figure 3-14**
Diagram showing the cascade of symptoms that can occur in people with sickle-cell anemia.

severely affected because only about 40 percent of their hemoglobin is abnormal.

The cause of all the serious problems associated with sickle-cell anemia is a change in the *Hb* gene. Remember that the beta chains of normal hemoglobin and the sickle-cell variety each have 146 amino acids, and 145 of the amino acids in both forms are identical. What's more, to emphasize the importance of a seemingly minor alteration, consider that triplets of DNA bases are required to specify amino acids. Therefore, it takes 438 bases (146 × 3) to produce the chain of 146 amino acids that forms the adult hemoglobin beta chain. But a change in only one of these 438 bases produces the life-threatening complications seen in sickle-cell anemia. **Figure 3-15** shows

▶ **Figure 3-15**
Substitution of one base at position 6 produces sickling hemoglobin.

Point Mutation			
Normal Hemoglobin		Sickling Hemoglobin	
DNA sequence	Amino acid	Amino acid	DNA sequence
• • • • •	#1	#1	• • • • •
T G A	#4 Threonine	#4 Threonine	T G A
G G A	#5 Proline	#5 Proline	G G A
C T C	#6 Glutamic acid	#6 Valine	C A C
C T C	#7 Glutamic acid	#7 Glutamic acid	C T C
T T T	#8 Lysine	#8 Lysine	T T T
• • • • •	• • • • •	• • • • •	• • • • •
#1652 (including intron sequences)	#146	#146	#1652

the DNA base sequence and the resulting amino acid products for both normal and sickling hemoglobin. As you can see, a single base substitution (from CTC to CAC) can result in an altered amino acid sequence, from

. . . proline—*glutamic acid*—glutamic acid . . .

to

. . . proline—*valine*—glutamic acid . . .

This kind of change in the genetic code is referred to as a **point mutation**, and in evolution, it's a common and important source of new genetic variation in populations. Point mutations, like the one that causes sickle-cell anemia, probably occur fairly frequently. But for a new mutation to be evolutionarily significant, it must be passed on to offspring and eventually become more common in a population. Once point mutations occur, their fate in populations depends on the other evolutionary forces, especially natural selection. Depending on how beneficial a mutation is, it may become more common over time; if it's disadvantageous, it probably won't. Sickle-cell anemia is one of the best examples of natural selection acting on humans; it shows us how a disadvantageous mutation can become more frequent in certain environments. This is a point that we'll consider in more detail in Chapter 4.

Chromosomes

Throughout much of a cell's life, its DNA (all 6 feet of it!) directs cellular functions and exists as an uncoiled, granular substance called **chromatin**. However, at various times in the life of most types of cells, normal activities cease and the cell divides. Cell division produces new cells, and at the beginning of this process, the DNA becomes tightly coiled and is visible under a microscope as a set of discrete structures called **chromosomes** (**Fig. 3-16**).

Chromosomes are composed of a DNA molecule and proteins (**Fig. 3-17**). During normal cell function, if chromatin were organized into chromosomes, they would be single-stranded structures. However, during the early stages of cell division when they become visible, they're made up of two strands, or two DNA molecules, joined together at a constricted area called the *centromere*. The reason there are two strands is simple: The DNA molecules have *replicated*, and one strand is an exact copy of the other.

Every species has a specific number of chromosomes in somatic cells (**Table 3-2**). Humans have 46, while chimpanzees and gorillas have 48. This doesn't mean that humans have less DNA than chimpanzees and gorillas. It just means that the DNA is packaged differently.

There are two basic types of chromosomes: **autosomes** and **sex chromosomes**. Autosomes carry genetic information that governs all physical characteristics except primary sex determination. The two sex chromosomes are the X and Y chromosomes; in mammals, the Y chromosome is directly involved in determining maleness. Although the X chromosome is called a sex chromosome, it actually functions more like an autosome because it's not involved in primary sex determination, and it influences several other traits. Among mammals, all genetically normal females have two X chromosomes (XX), and they're female only because they don't have a Y chromosome. (In other words, female is the default setting.) All genetically normal males have one X and one Y chromosome (XY). In other classes of animals, such as birds or insects, primary sex determination is governed by various other chromosomal mechanisms.

Chromosomes occur in pairs, so all normal human somatic cells have 22 pairs of autosomes and one pair of sex chromosomes (23 pairs in all). Abnormal numbers of autosomes, with few exceptions, are fatal—usually soon after conception. Although abnormal

point mutation A change in one of the four DNA bases.

chromatin The form of DNA that is present when a cell is not dividing. Microscopically, chromatin appears as a granular substance; when it condenses prior to cell division, it forms chromosomes.

chromosomes Discrete structures composed of DNA and proteins found only in the nuclei of cells. Chromosomes are visible under magnification only during certain phases of cell division.

autosomes All chromosomes except the sex chromosomes.

sex chromosomes In mammals, the X and Y chromosomes.

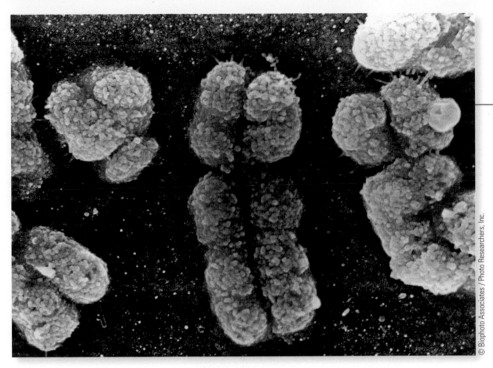

◀ **Figure 3-16**
Colorized scanning electronmicrograph of human chromosomes.

a Each of the more than 1 trillion somatic cells in the body consists of a cell membrane, cytoplasm, and a nucleus.

◀ **Figure 3-17**
A model of a human chromosome, illustrating the relationship of DNA to chromosomes.

b Each somatic cell nucleus contains 46 chromosomes—23 contributed by the mother and 23 by the father. The chromosomes consist of protein and DNA.

c A chromosome consists of two DNA molecules joined at a centromere. A chromosome is seen in this form only during cell division.

d To form the chromosome, the DNA is coiled into higher and higher levels of organization.

e The DNA is coiled around specialized proteins that provide structure to the chromosome. These proteins also interact with the DNA.

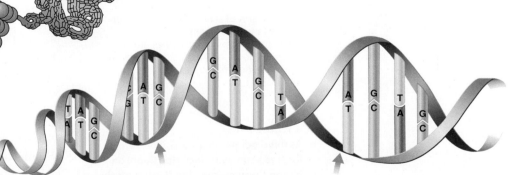

f A specific sequence of nucleotide base pairs constitutes a gene.

TABLE 3.2 Standard Chromosomal Complement in Various Organisms

Organism	Chromosome Number in Somatic Cells	Chromosome Number in Gametes
Human (*Homo sapiens*)	46	23
Chimpanzee (*Pan troglodytes*)	48	24
Gorilla (*Gorilla gorilla*)	48	24
Dog (*Canis familiaris*)	78	39
Chicken (*Gallus domesticus*)	78	39
Frog (*Rana pipiens*)	26	13
Housefly (*Musca domestica*)	12	6
Onion (*Allium cepa*)	16	8
Corn (*Zea mays*)	20	10
Tobacco (*Nicotiana tabacum*)	48	24

Source: Cummings, 2000, p. 16.

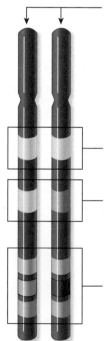

Members of a pair of chromosomes. One chromosome is from a male parent, and its partner is from a female parent.

Gene locus. The location for a specific gene on a chromosome.

Pair of alleles. Although they influence the same characteristic, their DNA varies slightly, so they produce somewhat different expressions of the same trait.

Three pairs of alleles (at three loci on this pair of chomosomes). Note that at two loci the alleles are identical (homozygous), and at one locus they are different (heterozygous).

▲ **Figure 3-18**
As this diagram illustrates, alleles are located at the same locus (position) on paired chromosomes, but they aren't always identical.

locus (*pl.*, loci) (lo'-kus, lo-sigh') The position or location on a chromosome where a given gene occurs. The term is sometimes used interchangeably with *gene*.

numbers of sex chromosomes aren't usually fatal, they may result in sterility and frequently have other consequences as well. So, to function normally, it's essential for a human cell to possess both members of each chromosomal pair, or a total of 46 chromosomes. Offspring inherit one member of each chromosomal pair from the father (the paternal chromosome) and one member from the mother (the maternal chromosome). Members of chromosomal pairs are alike in size and position of the centromere, and they carry genetic information governing the same traits. This doesn't mean that partner chromosomes are genetically identical; it just means they influence the same traits. For example, on both copies of a person's ninth chromosomes, there's a **locus**, or gene position, that determines which of the four ABO blood types (A, B, AB, or O) he or she will have. However, these two ninth chromosomes might not have identical DNA segments at the ABO locus. In other words, at numerous genetic loci,

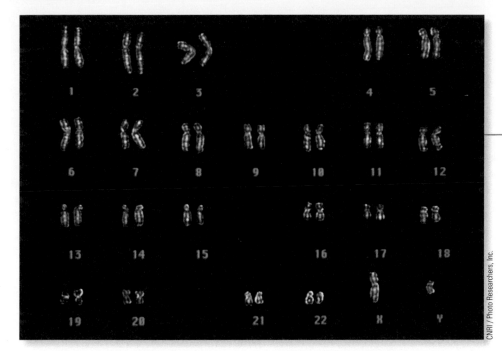

CNRI / Photo Researchers, Inc.

◀ **Figure 3-19**
A karyotype of a human male with the chromosomes arranged by size, position of the centromere, and banding patterns.

there may be more than one possible form of a gene, and these different forms are called **alleles** (**Fig 3-18**).

Alleles are alternate forms of a gene that can direct the cell to produce slightly different forms of the same product and, ultimately, different expressions of a trait—as in the hemoglobin S (Hb^S) example. At the ABO locus, there are three possible alleles: *A*, *B*, and *O*. However, since individuals have only two ninth chromosomes, only two alleles are present in any one person. And the variation in alleles at the ABO locus is what accounts for the variation among humans in ABO blood type.

Karyotyping Chromosomes

One method frequently used to examine chromosomes in an individual is to produce a **karyotype**. (An example of a human karyotype is shown in **Fig. 3-19**.) The chromosomes used in karyotypes are obtained from dividing cells. (You'll remember that chromosomes are visible only during cell division.) For example, white blood cells, because they're easily obtained, can be cultured, chemically treated, and microscopically

examined to identify the ones that are dividing. These cells are then photographed through a microscope to produce *photomicrographs* of intact, double-stranded chromosomes. Partner chromosomes are then matched up, and the entire set is arranged in descending order by size so that the largest chromosome appears first.

Karyotyping has numerous practical applications. Physicians and genetic counselors routinely use karyotypes to help diagnose chromosomal disorders in patients, and they're used in prenatal testing to identify chromosomal abnormalities in developing fetuses. Karyotype analysis has also revealed many chromosomal similarities shared by different species, including humans and nonhuman primates. However, now that scientists can compare the genomes of species directly, karyotyping probably won't continue being used for this purpose.

Cell Division

As we mentioned earlier, normal cellular function is periodically interrupted so the cell can divide. Cell division in somatic cells is called **mitosis**, and it's

alleles Alternate forms of a gene. Alleles occur at the same locus on paired chromosomes and thus govern the same trait. But because they're different, their action may result in different expressions of that trait.

karyotype The chromosomes of an individual, or what is typical of a species, viewed microscopically and displayed in a photograph. The chromosomes are arranged in pairs and according to size and position of the centromere.

mitosis Simple cell division; the process by which somatic cells divide to produce two identical daughter cells.

the way somatic cells reproduce. It occurs during growth and development; repairs injured tissues; and replaces older cells with newer ones. But while mitosis produces new somatic cells, another type of cell division, called **meiosis**, may lead to the development of new individuals, since it produces reproductive cells, or gametes.

Mitosis

In the early stages of mitosis, a human somatic cell has 46 double-stranded chromosomes, and as the cell begins to divide, these chromosomes line up along its center and split apart so that the two strands separate (**Fig. 3-20**). Once the two strands are apart, they pull away from each other and move to opposite ends of the dividing cell. At this point, each strand is a distinct chromosome, *composed of one DNA molecule*. Following the separation of chromosome strands, the cell membrane pinches in and seals, so that there are two new cells, each with a full complement of DNA, or 46 chromosomes.

Mitosis is referred to as "simple cell division" because a somatic cell divides one time to produce two daughter cells that are genetically identical to each other and to the original cell. In mitosis, the original cell possesses 46 chromosomes, and each new daughter cell inherits an exact copy of all 46. This precision is made possible by the DNA molecule's ability to replicate. Therefore, DNA replication is what ensures that the amount of genetic material remains constant from one generation of cells to the next.

We should mention here that certain types of somatic cells don't divide. Red blood cells are produced continuously by specialized cells in bone marrow, but they can't divide because they have no nucleus and no nuclear DNA. Once the brain and nervous system are fully developed, brain and nerve cells (neurons) stop dividing, although there is some debate about this. Liver cells also don't divide after growth has

stopped unless this vital organ is damaged through injury or disease. With these three exceptions (red blood cells, mature neurons, and liver cells), somatic cells are regularly duplicated through the process of mitosis.

Meiosis

While mitosis produces new cells, meiosis can lead to the development of an entire new organism because it produces reproductive cells (gametes). Although meiosis is similar to mitosis, it's more complicated. In meiosis, there are two divisions instead of one. Also, meiosis produces four daughter cells, not two, and each of these four cells contains only half the original number of chromosomes.

During meiosis, specialized cells in male testes and female ovaries divide and eventually develop into sperm and egg cells. Initially, these cells contain the full complement of chromosomes (46 in humans), but after the first division (called *reduction division*), the number of chromosomes in the two daughter cells is 23, or half the original number (**Fig. 3-21**). This reduction of chromosome number is crucial because the resulting gamete, with its 23 chromosomes, may eventually unite with another gamete that also has 23 chromosomes. The product of this union is a *zygote*, or fertilized egg, in which the original number of chromosomes (46) has been restored. In other words, a zygote inherits the exact amount of DNA it needs (half from each parent) to develop and function normally. But if it weren't for reduction division in meiosis, it wouldn't be possible to maintain the correct number of chromosomes from one generation to the next.

During the first division, partner chromosomes come together to form pairs of double-stranded chromosomes that line up along the cell's center. Pairing of partner chromosomes is essential, because while they're together, members of pairs exchange genetic information in a

meiosis Cell division in specialized cells in ovaries and testes. Meiosis involves two divisions and results in four daughter cells, each containing only half the original number of chromosomes. These cells can develop into gametes.

a The cell is involved in metabolic activities. DNA replication occurs, but chromosomes are not visible.

◄ Figure 3-20
Diagrammatic representation of mitosis. The blue images next to some of these illustrations are photomicrographs of actual chromosomes in a dividing cell.

b The nuclear membrane disappears, and double-stranded chromosomes are visible.

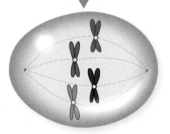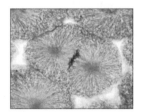

c The chromosomes align themselves at the center of the cell.

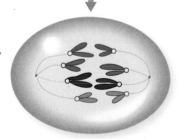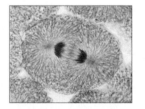

d The chromosomes split at the centromere, and the strands separate and move to opposite ends of the dividing cell.

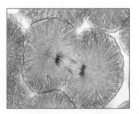

e The cell membrane pinches in as the cell continues to divide. The chromosomes begin to uncoil (not shown here).

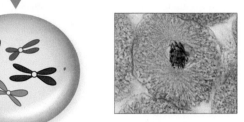

f After mitosis is complete, there are two identical daughter cells. The nuclear membrane is present, and chromosomes are no longer visible.

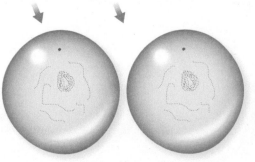

◀ **Figure 3-21**
Diagrammatic representation of meiosis. The blue squares are photomicrographs of actual chromosomes in a dividing cell.

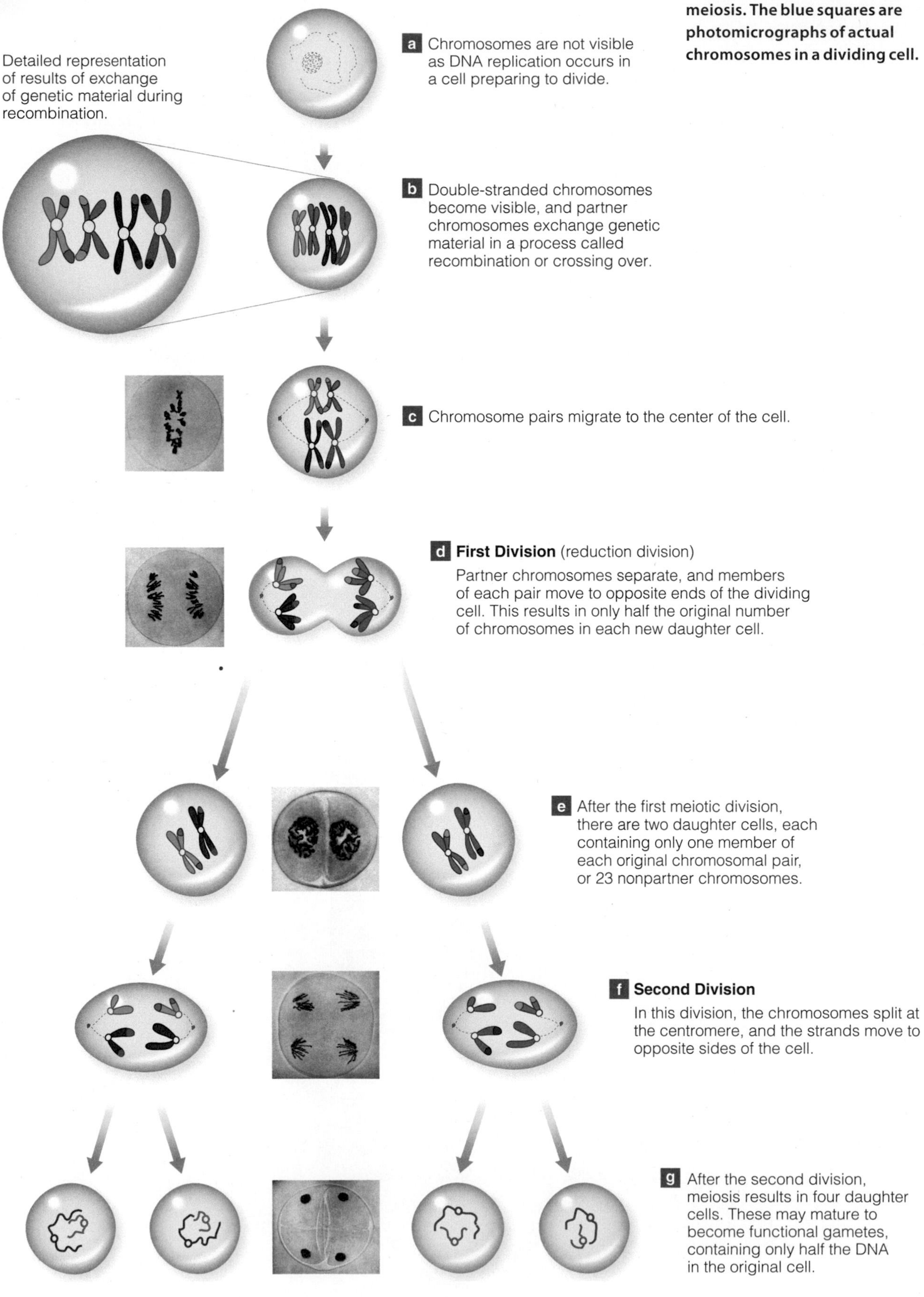

Detailed representation of results of exchange of genetic material during recombination.

a Chromosomes are not visible as DNA replication occurs in a cell preparing to divide.

b Double-stranded chromosomes become visible, and partner chromosomes exchange genetic material in a process called recombination or crossing over.

c Chromosome pairs migrate to the center of the cell.

d **First Division** (reduction division)
Partner chromosomes separate, and members of each pair move to opposite ends of the dividing cell. This results in only half the original number of chromosomes in each new daughter cell.

e After the first meiotic division, there are two daughter cells, each containing only one member of each original chromosomal pair, or 23 nonpartner chromosomes.

f **Second Division**
In this division, the chromosomes split at the centromere, and the strands move to opposite sides of the cell.

g After the second division, meiosis results in four daughter cells. These may mature to become functional gametes, containing only half the DNA in the original cell.

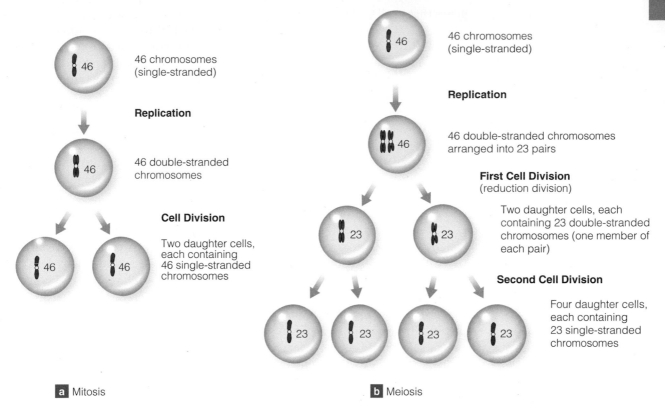

a Mitosis

b Meiosis

process called **recombination**. Pairing is also important because it ensures that each new daughter cell receives only one member of each pair.

As the cell begins to divide, the chromosomes themselves remain intact (that is, double-stranded), but *members of pairs* pull apart and move to opposite ends of the cell. After the first division, there are two new daughter cells, but they aren't identical to each other or to the parental cell. They're different because each cell contains only one member of each chromosome pair (that is, only 23 chromosomes), each of which still has two strands. Also, because of recombination, each chromosome now contains some combinations of genes it didn't have before.

The second meiotic division is similar to division in mitosis. (For a comparison of mitosis and meiosis, see **Fig. 3-22**.) In the two newly formed cells, the 23 double-stranded chromosomes line up at the cell's center, and as in mitosis, the strands of each chromosome separate and move apart. Once

this second division is completed, there are four daughter cells, each with 23 single-stranded chromosomes, or 23 DNA molecules.

The Evolutionary Significance of Meiosis Meiosis occurs in all sexually reproducing organisms, and it's an extremely important evolutionary innovation because it increases genetic variation in populations. Members of sexually reproducing species aren't genetically identical **clones** of other individuals because they receive genetic contributions from two parents. In human matings, a staggering number of genetic combinations can result in the offspring of two parents. Just from the **random assortment** of chromosome pairs during the first division of meiosis, each parent can produce around 8 million genetically different gametes. Given the combined probability accounting for both parents, the total number of possible genetic combinations for any human mating is about 70 trillion! Each individual thus represents a unique combination of

▲ **Figure 3-22**
Mitosis and meiosis compared. In mitosis, one division produces two daughter cells, each of which contains 46 chromosomes. In meiosis there are two divisions. After the first, there are two cells, each containing only 23 chromosomes (one member of each original chromosome pair). Each daughter cell divides again, so that the final result is four cells, each with only half the original number of chromosomes.

recombination The exchange of genetic material between paired chromosomes during meiosis; also called *crossing over*.

clones Organisms that are genetically identical to another organism. The term may also be used to refer to genetically identical DNA segments, molecules, or cells.

random assortment The chance distribution of chromosomes to daughter cells during meiosis. Along with recombination, random assortment is an important source of genetic variation (but not new alleles).

genes that in all likelihood has never occurred before and will never occur again.

As you can see, genetic diversity is considerably enhanced by meiosis, and this diversity is essential if species are to adapt to changing selective pressures. As we mentioned in Chapter 2, natural selection acts on genetic variation in populations; so if all individuals were genetically identical, natural selection would have nothing to act on and evolution couldn't occur. In all species, *mutation* is the only source of new genetic variation because it produces new alleles. But sexually reproducing species have an additional advantage because recombination produces new *arrangements* of genetic information, potentially providing additional material for selection to act on. In fact, the influence of meiosis on genetic variation is the main advantage of sexual reproduction. Thus, sexual reproduction and meiosis are of major evolutionary importance because they contribute to the role of natural selection in populations.

Problems with Meiosis For fetal development to occur normally, the process of meiosis needs to be exact. If chromosomes or chromosome strands don't separate during either of the two divisions, serious problems can develop. This failure to separate is called *nondisjunction*. The result of nondisjunction is that one of the daughter cells receives two copies of the affected chromosome, while the other daughter cell receives none. If such an affected gamete unites with a normal gamete containing 23 chromosomes, the resulting zygote will have either 45 or 47 chromosomes. If there are 47, then there will be three copies of one chromosome instead of two, a situation called *trisomy*.

You can appreciate the potential effects of an abnormal number of chromosomes if you remember that the zygote, by means of mitosis, ultimately gives rise to all the cells in the developing body. Consequently, every

one of these cells will inherit the abnormal chromosome number. And since most abnormal numbers of autosomes are lethal, the embryo is usually spontaneously aborted, frequently before the pregnancy is even recognized.

Trisomy 21 (formerly called Down syndrome) is the only example of an abnormal number of autosomes that's compatible with life beyond the first few years after birth. Trisomy 21 is caused by the presence of three copies of chromosome 21. It occurs in approximately 1 out of every 1,000 live births and is associated with various developmental and health problems. These problems include congenital heart defects (seen in about 40 percent of affected newborns), increased susceptibility to respiratory infections, and leukemia. However, the most widely recognized effect is mental impairment, which is variably expressed and ranges from mild to severe.

Trisomy 21 is partly associated with advanced maternal age. For example, the risk of a 20-year-old woman giving birth to an affected infant is just 0.05 percent (5 in 10,000). However, 3 percent of babies born to mothers 45 and older are affected (a 60-fold increase). Actually, most affected infants are born to women under the age of 35, but that's because the majority of women who have babies are less than 35 years old. The increased prevalence of trisomy 21 with maternal age is thought to be related to the fact that meiosis actually begins in females during their own fetal development and then stops, only to be resumed and completed at ovulation. This means that a woman's gametes are as old as she is, and age-related changes in the chromosomes themselves appear to increase the risk of nondisjunction, at least for some chromosomes.

Nondisjunction also occurs in sex chromosomes (see Table 3.3). For example, a man may have two X chromosomes and one Y chromosome (XXY) or one X chromosome and two Y chromosomes (XYY). Likewise, a

TABLE 3.3	Examples of Nondisjunction in Sex Chromosomes

Chromosomal Complement	Condition	Estimated Incidence	Manifestations
XXX	Trisomy X	1 per 1,000 female births	Affected women are usually clinically normal, but there is a slight increase in sterility and mental impairment compared to the general population. In cases with more than three X chromosomes, mental impairment can be severe
XYY	XYY syndrome	1 per 1,000 male births	Affected males are fertile and tend to be taller than average
XO	Turner syndrome	1 per 10,000 female births	Affected females are short-statured, have broad chests and webbed necks, and are sterile. There is usually no mental impairment, but concepts relating to spatial relationships, including mathematics, can pose difficulties. Between 95 and 99 percent of affected fetuses die before birth.
XXY	Klinefelter syndrome	1 per 1,000 male births	Symptoms are noticeable by puberty: reduced testicular development, reduced facial and body hair, some breast development in about half of all cases, and reduced fertility or sterility. Some individuals exhibit lowered intelligence. Additional X chromosomes (XXXY) are associated with mental impairment.

woman may have only one X chromosome (X0), or she may have more than two (XXX). Although abnormal numbers of sex chromosomes don't always result in spontaneous abortion or death, they can cause sterility, some mental impairment, and other problems. And while it's possible to live without a Y chromosome (roughly half of all people do), it's impossible for an embryo to survive without an X chromosome. (Remember, X chromosomes carry genes that influence many traits.) Clearly, normal development depends on having the correct number of chromosomes.

New Frontiers

Since the discovery of DNA structure and function in the 1950s, the field of genetics has revolutionized biological science and reshaped our understanding of inheritance, genetic disease, and evolutionary processes. For example, a technique developed in 1986, called **polymerase chain reaction (PCR)**, enables scientists to make thousands of copies of small samples of DNA that can then be analyzed. In the past, DNA samples from crime scenes or fossils were usually too small to be studied. But PCR has made it possible to examine DNA sequences in, for example, Neandertal fossils and Egyptian mummies; and it has limitless potential for many disciplines, including forensic science, medicine, and paleoanthropology.

Another application of PCR allows scientists to identify *DNA fingerprints*, so called because they appear as patterns of repeated DNA sequences that are unique to each individual (**Fig. 3-23**). For example, one person might have a segment of six bases such as ATTCTA repeated 3 times, while another person might have 20 copies of the same sequence. DNA

polymerase chain reaction (PCR)   A method of producing thousands of copies of a DNA sample.

▶ **Figure 3-23**
Eight DNA finger-
prints, one of which is
from a blood sample
left at an actual crime
scene. The other seven
are from suspects. By
comparing the band-
ing patterns, it's easy
to identify the guilty
person.

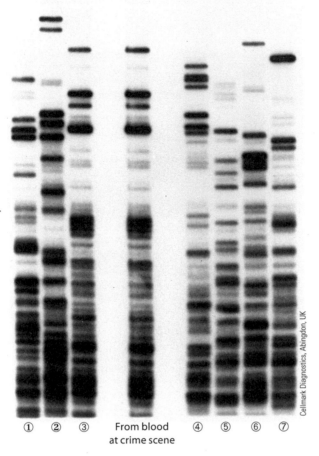

① ② ③ From blood ④ ⑤ ⑥ ⑦
at crime scene

Cellmark Diagnostics, Abingdon, UK

fingerprinting is perhaps the most
powerful tool available for human
identification. Scientists have used
it to identify scores of unidentified
remains, including members of the
Russian royal family murdered in
1918 and victims of the September
11, 2001, terrorist attacks. Moreover,
the technique has been used to exon-
erate many innocent people wrongly
convicted of crimes, in some cases
decades after they were imprisoned.

Over the last two decades, scientists
have used the techniques of *recombinant DNA technology* to transfer genes
from the cells of one species into those
of another. One common method has
been to insert human genes that direct
the production of various proteins into
bacterial cells in laboratories. The
altered bacteria can then produce
human gene products such as insulin.
Until the early 1980s, people with diabetes relied on insulin derived from
nonhuman animals. However, this

insulin wasn't plentiful, and some
patients developed allergies to it. But
since 1982, abundant supplies of
human insulin, produced by bacteria,
have been available; and bacteria-
derived insulin doesn't cause allergic
reactions.

In recent years, genetic manipula-
tion has become increasingly controversial owing to questions related to
product safety, environmental concerns, animal welfare, and concern
over the experimental use of human
embryos. For example, the insertion of
bacterial DNA into certain crops has
made them toxic to leaf-eating insects,
thus reducing the need for pesticides.
Cattle and pigs are commonly treated
with antibiotics and genetically engineered growth hormone to increase
growth rates. (There's no concrete evidence that humans are susceptible to
the insect-repelling bacterial DNA or
harmed by consuming meat and dairy
products from animals treated with
growth hormone. But there are concerns over the unknown effects of
long-term exposure.)

Cloning has been one of the most
controversial of all the new genetic
technologies. The controversy escalat-
ed in 1997 with the birth of Dolly, a
clone of a female sheep (Wilmut et al.,
1997). But cloning isn't as new as you
might think. Anyone who has ever
taken a cutting from a plant and
rooted it to grow a new one has produced a clone. Many species have now
been cloned. Cloned mammals include
mice, rats, rabbits, cats, sheep, cattle,
horses, a mule, and dogs. Moreover,
researchers recently produced clones
of dead mice that were frozen for as
long as 16 years. This gives rise to
hopes that eventually it may be possible to clone extinct animals, such as
mammoths, from the frozen bodies of
animals that died several thousand
years ago (Wakayama et al., 2008). But
don't count on visiting a *Jurassic Park*
type zoo anytime soon.

Cloning involves a technique called
nuclear transfer, a process that has several stages (**Fig. 3-24**). First, an egg cell

is taken from a donor animal, and the nucleus is removed. Then a DNA-containing nucleus is taken from a tissue cell of another animal (the animal actually being cloned). This nucleus is then inserted into the donor egg cell. The fused egg is placed in the uterus of a host mother. If all goes well, that mother eventually gives birth to an infant that's genetically identical to the animal that provided the tissue cells containing the DNA.

No one knows how successful cloning will become. Dolly, who had developed health problems, was euthanized in February 2003 at the relatively young age of 6 years (Giles and Knight, 2003). Long-term studies have yet to show whether cloned animals live out their normal life span, but some evidence from mice suggests that they don't.

As exciting as these innovations are, probably the single most important advance in genetics has been the progress made by the **Human Genome Project** (International Human Genome Sequencing Consortium, 2001; Venter et al., 2001). The goal of this international effort, begun in 1990, was to sequence the entire human genome, which consists of some 3 billion bases making up approximately 25,000 protein-coding genes. This extremely important project was completed in 2003.

The potential for anthropological applications is enormous. While scientists were sequencing human genes, the genomes of other organisms were also being studied. As of now, the genomes of hundreds of species have been sequenced, including mice (Waterston et al., 2002), chimpanzees (Chimpanzee Sequencing and Analysis Consortium, 2005), and rhesus macaques (Rhesus Macaque Genome Sequencing and Analysis Consortium, 2007).

In May 2010, researchers finished sequencing the entire Neandertal genome (Green et al., 2010). To date, the most exciting announcement stemming from this research is that modern Europeans and Asians (but

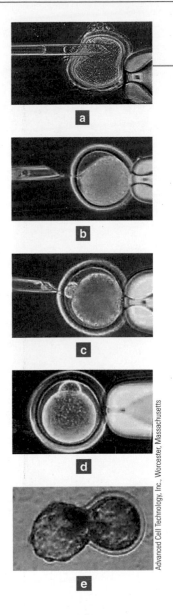

Advanced Cell Technology, Inc., Worcester, Massachusetts

◄ Figure 3-24
A series of photomicrographs showing the process of nuclear transfer. **(a)** The nucleus of an egg cell (from a donor) is drawn into a hollow needle. **(b)** Only the cytoplasm remains in the donor egg. **(c)** The nucleus of a skin cell from the individual being cloned is injected into the donor egg. **(d)** Electric shock causes the nucleus from the skin cell to fuse with the egg's cytoplasm. **(e)** The egg begins to divide, and a few days later the cloned embryo will be transferred into the uterus of a host animal.

not Africans) inherited 1 to 4 percent of their genes from ancient Neandertal ancestors. This finding sheds light on debates concerning whether or not early modern humans interbred with Neandertals. These debates have been ongoing in physical anthropology for more than 50 years, and while this new genetic evidence does not conclusively end the discussion, it strongly supports the argument that interbreeding did indeed take place and that many of us carry a few Neandertal genes (see Chapter 13).

Eventually, comparative genome analysis should provide a thorough assessment of genetic similarities and differences, and thus the evolutionary

Human Genome Project An international effort aimed at sequencing and mapping the entire human genome, completed in 2003.

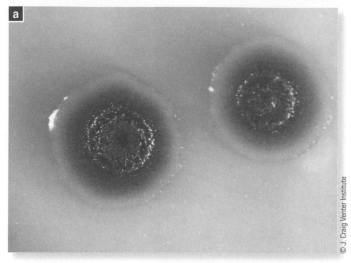

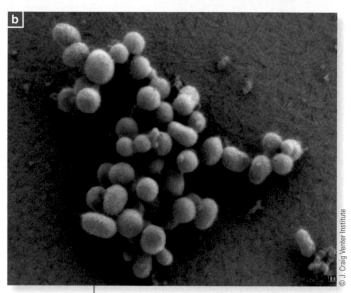

© J. Craig Venter Institute

© J. Craig Venter Institute

▲ **Figure 3-25**
Self-replicating synthetic bacteria.
(a) Researchers inserted a gene into the synthetic bacteria that makes this colony appear blue. This was so they could distinguish these cells from the original bacteria (which aren't blue) and therefore determine if the new cells were indeed replicating. **(b)** A scanning electron micrograph of a colony of the new "synthetic" bacterial cells.

scientists created a functional, synthetic bacterial genome (Gibson et al., 2010). The culmination of 10 years of effort, this synthetic genome is the first life-form ever made by humans, and it has major implications for biotechnology. (Understandably, it has also raised many ethical concerns.) Very basically, some of the geneticists involved in the Human Genome Project sequenced the 1 million bases in a bacterial chromosome. (Bacterial DNA is organized into a single ring-shaped chromosome.) They then produced an artificial chromosome by assembling DNA segments and splicing them together, interspersed with "noncoding" sequences they had invented. These noncoding sequences allowed them to distinguish the genome they had created from the natural one. And, just to show that genetic research sometimes has a lighter side, some of these sequences actually contain, in coded form, the names of some of the people involved in the project, some well-known quotations, and an e-mail address.) The new synthetic DNA was then inserted into a bacterial cell of a different species. The original DNA of the recipient cell had been removed, and the cell began to follow the instructions of the new DNA. That is, it produced proteins characteristic of a different bacterial species! Moreover, the recipient cell replicated, and there are now laboratory colonies of the "new" bacterium (**Fig. 3-25**).

It's important to emphasize that this project did not create a completely new synthetic life form because the genome had been transferred into an already existing cell. Nevertheless, the door has been opened for the development of artificial organisms. While it may never be possible to create new species as complex as birds and mammals, we can almost certainly expect to see the production of artificial, single-celled organisms, many of which will have medical applications. Others will perhaps be used to produce food or to absorb carbon dioxide. But the potential for abuse, espe-

relationships, between humans and other primates. What's more, we can already look at human variation in an entirely different light than we could even 10 years ago (see Chapter 15). Among other things, genetic comparisons between human groups can inform us about population movements in the past and what selective pressures may have been exerted on different populations to produce some of the variability we see. We may even be able to speculate on patterns of infectious disease in the past.

Completion of the Neandertal genome sequence wasn't the only groundbreaking achievement in 2010. Using some of the techniques developed in the human genome research,

cially in the development of biological weapons, will obviously be of grave concern. Still, the human development of a self-replicating bacterium with altered DNA from another species is an extraordinary milestone in biology. It is not an exaggeration to say that this is the most exciting time in the history of evolutionary biology since Darwin published *On the Origin of Species*.

Summary of Main Topics

- Cells are the fundamental units of life, and in multicellular organisms, there are basically two types. Somatic cells make up body tissues, while gametes (eggs and sperm) are reproductive cells that transmit genetic information from parents to offspring.
- Genetic information is contained in the DNA molecule, found in the nucleus of cells and in mitochondria. The DNA molecule is capable of replication, or making copies of itself. Replication makes it possible for daughter cells to receive a full complement of DNA (contained in chromosomes). DNA also controls protein synthesis by directing the cell to arrange amino acids in the proper sequence for each protein. Also involved in the process of protein synthesis is another, similar molecule called RNA.

- There are many genes that regulate the function of other genes. One class of regulatory genes, the homeobox genes, direct the development of the body plan. Other regulatory genes turn genes on and off.
- Most of our DNA doesn't actually code for protein production, and much of its function is unknown. Some of these noncoding sequences, called introns, are contained within genes. Introns are initially transcribed into mRNA but are then deleted before the mRNA leaves the cell nucleus. The function of most noncoding DNA is unknown, but some is involved in gene regulation.
- Cells multiply by dividing, and during cell division, DNA is visible under a microscope in the form of chromosomes. In humans, there are 46 chromosomes (23 pairs). If the full complement isn't precisely distributed to succeeding generations of cells, there may be serious consequences.
- Somatic cells divide during growth or tissue repair or to replace old, worn-out cells. Somatic cell division is called mitosis. A cell divides one time to produce two daughter cells, each possessing a full and identical set of chromosomes. Sex cells are produced when specialized cells in the ovaries and testes divide during meiosis. Unlike mitosis, meiosis is characterized by two divisions that produce four nonidentical daughter cells, each containing only half the amount of DNA (23 chromosomes).

Critical Thinking Questions

1. Before reading this chapter, were you aware that the DNA in your body is structurally the same as in all other organisms? Do you see this fact as having potential to clarify some of the many questions we still have regarding biological evolution? Why?

2. Do you think proteins are exactly the same in all species? If not, how do you think they would differ in terms of their composition, and why might these differences be important to physical anthropologists?

3. Do you approve of cloning? If so, would you restrict cloning to certain species? Would you have a pet cloned? Why or why not?

4. Do you approve of the recent development of a "synthetic" bacterial genome? Why or why not? How do you think this technology might be used in the future?

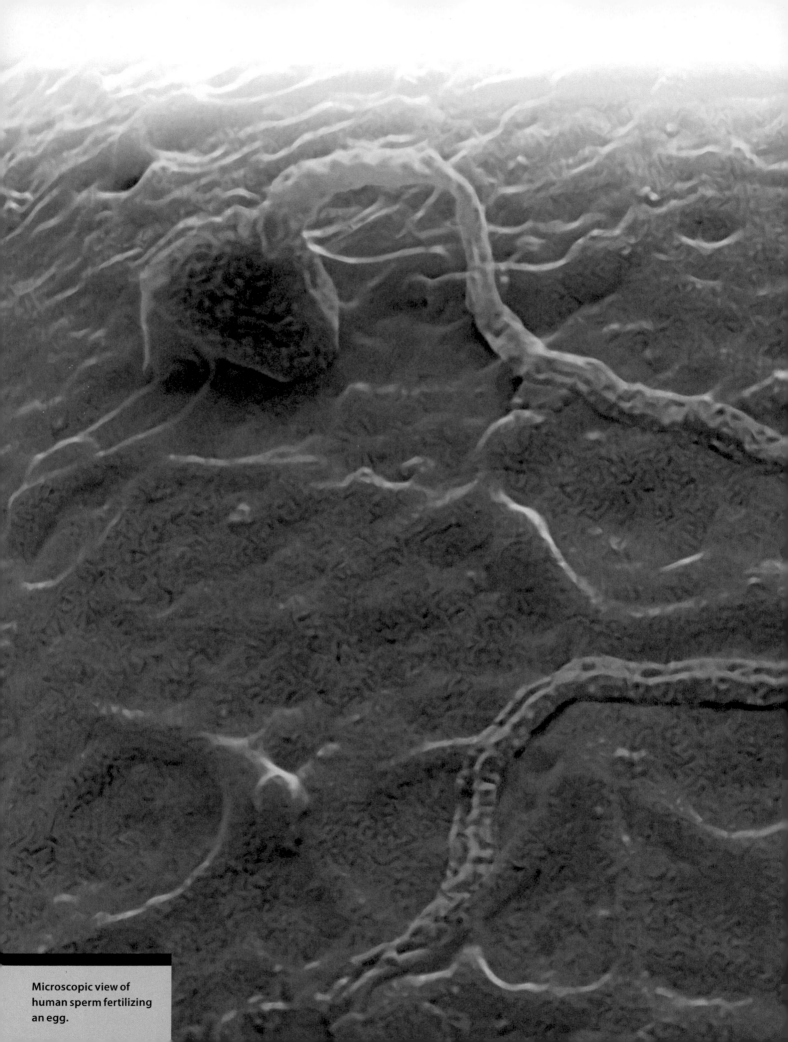

Microscopic view of
human sperm fertilizing
an egg.

Heredity and Evolution

Key Questions

▶ How do the principles of inheritance, first discovered by Gregor Mendel, help explain evolutionary processes?

▶ How do genetic drift, gene flow, mutation, and natural selection interact over time to produce evolutionary change in populations and species?

Have you ever had a cat with five, six, or even seven toes? Even if you haven't, you may have seen one, because extra toes are fairly common in cats. Maybe you've known someone with an extra finger or toe, because some people have them. Anne Boleyn, mother of England's Queen Elizabeth I and the first of Henry VIII's wives to lose her head, apparently had at least part of an extra little finger. (Of course, this had nothing to do with her early demise; that's another story.)

Having extra digits (fingers and toes) is called *polydactyly*, and it's pretty certain that one of Anne Boleyn's parents was also polydactylous (**Fig. 4-1**). It's also likely that any polydactylous cat has a parent with extra toes. But how do we know this? Actually, it's fairly simple. We know this because polydactyly is a Mendelian trait inherited in a particular way, and its pattern of inheritance is one of those discovered almost 150 years ago by a monk named Gregor Mendel (**Fig. 4-2**).

For at least 10,000 years, people have raised domesticated plants and animals. However, it wasn't until the twentieth century that scientists understood *how* **selective breeding** (see next page for definition) could increase the frequency of desirable characteristics. From the time ancient Greek philosophers considered the question of how traits were inherited until well into the nineteenth century, the most common belief was that the traits seen in offspring resulted from the *blending* of parental traits. Blending supposedly happened because of certain particles that were found in every part of the body. These particles contained miniature versions of the body part they came from (limbs, organs, bones, and so on), and they traveled through the blood to the reproductive organs and ultimately blended with particles of another individual during reproduction. There were variations on this theme, and numerous scholars, including Charles Darwin, adhered to some aspects of the theory.

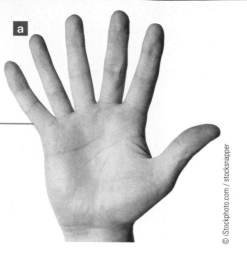

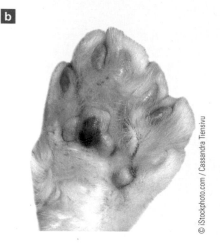

▶ **Figure 4-1**
(a) Hand of a person with polydactyly. **(b)** Front foot of a polydactylous cat.

▲ **Figure 4-2**
Portrait of Gregor Mendel.

selective breeding A practice whereby animal or plant breeders choose which individual animals or plants will be allowed to mate based on the traits (such as coat color or body size) they hope to produce in the offspring. Animals or plants that don't have the desirable traits aren't allowed to breed.

hybrids Offspring of parents who differ from each other with regard to certain traits or certain aspects of genetic makeup; heterozygotes.

The Genetic Principles Discovered by Mendel

It may seem odd that after discussing recent discoveries about DNA we now turn our attention back to the middle of the nineteenth century, but that's when the science of genetics was born. By examining how the basic principles of inheritance were discovered, we can more easily understand them. It wasn't until Gregor Mendel (1822–1884) considered the question of heredity that it began to be resolved. Mendel was living in an abbey in what is now the Czech Republic. At the time he began his research, he'd already studied botany, physics, and mathematics at the University of Vienna. He had also performed various experiments in the monastery gardens, and this background led him to investigate how physical traits, such as color or height, could be expressed in plant **hybrids**.

Mendel worked with garden peas, concentrating on seven different traits, each of which could be expressed two ways (**Fig. 4-3**). You may think it's odd that we discuss peas in an anthropology book, but they provide a simple example of the basic rules of inheritance. The principles Mendel discovered apply to all biological organisms, including humans, a fact that also illustrates biological continuity among all living things.

Segregation

First, Mendel grew groups of pea plants that were different from one another with regard to at least one trait. For example, in one group all the plants were tall, while in another they were all short. To see how the expression of height would change from one generation to the next, he crossed tall plants with short plants, calling them the *parental* generation. According to traditional views, all the hybrid offspring, which he called the F_1 *generation*, should have been intermediate in height. But they weren't; instead they were all tall (**Fig. 4-4**).

Next, Mendel let the F_1 plants self-fertilize to produce a second generation (the F_2 generation). But this time, only about ¾ of the offspring were tall, and the remaining ¼ were short. One expression (short) of the trait (height) had completely disappeared in the F_1 generation and then reappeared in the F_2 generation. Moreover, the expression that was present in all the F_1 plants was more common in the F_2 plants, occurring in a ratio of approximately 3:1 (three tall plants for every short one).

These results suggested that different expressions of a trait were con-

Raychel Ciemma and Precision Graphics

© iStockphoto.com / stocksnapper

© iStockphoto.com / Cassandra Tiensivu

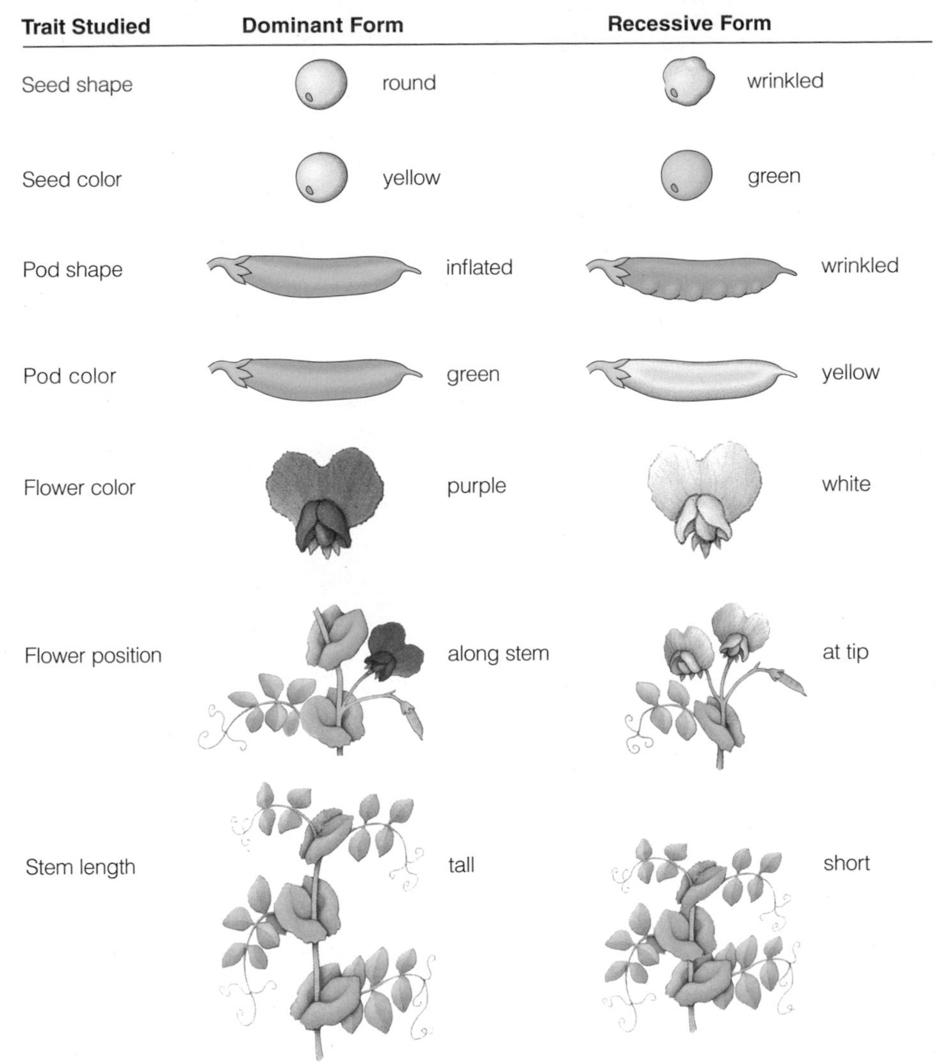

Trait Studied	Dominant Form		Recessive Form	
Seed shape		round		wrinkled
Seed color		yellow		green
Pod shape		inflated		wrinkled
Pod color		green		yellow
Flower color		purple		white
Flower position		along stem		at tip
Stem length		tall		short

◄ **Figure 4-3**
The traits Mendel studied in peas.

trolled by discrete *units* (we would call them genes) that occurred in pairs and that offspring inherited one unit from each parent. Mendel realized that the members of a pair of units that controlled a trait somehow separated into different sex cells and were again united with another member during fertilization of the egg. This is Mendel's *first principle of inheritance*, known as the **principle of segregation**.

Today we know that meiosis explains Mendel's principle of segregation. During meiosis, paired chromosomes, and the genes they carry, separate from each other and end up in different gametes. However, in the zygote, the full complement of chromosomes is restored, and both members of each chromosome pair are present in the offspring.

Dominance and Recessiveness

Mendel also realized that the "unit" for the absent characteristic (shortness) in the F_1 plants hadn't actually disappeared. It was still there, but for some reason it wasn't expressed. Mendel described the expression that seemed to be lost as "**recessive**," and he called the expressed trait "**dominant**." Thus, the important principles of *dominance* and *recessiveness* were developed, and today they're still important concepts in the field of genetics.

principle of segregation Genes (alleles) occur in pairs because chromosomes occur in pairs. During gamete formation, the members of each pair of alleles separate, so that each gamete contains one member of each pair.

recessive Describing a trait that isn't expressed in heterozygotes; also refers to the allele that governs the trait. For a recessive allele to be expressed, an individual must have two copies of it (i.e., the individual must be homozygous).

dominant In genetics, describing a trait governed by an allele that's expressed in the presence of another allele (i.e., in heterozygotes). Dominant alleles prevent the expression of recessive alleles in heterozygotes. (This is the definition of *complete* dominance.)

▶ **Figure 4-4**
Results of crosses when only one trait (height) at a time is considered.

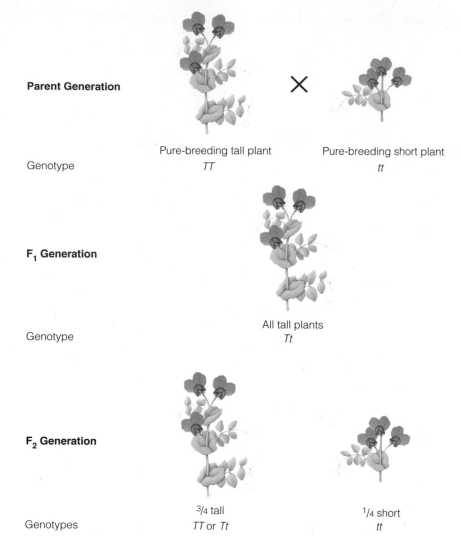

Parent Generation

Genotype

Pure-breeding tall plant
TT

×

Pure-breeding short plant
tt

F₁ Generation

Genotype

All tall plants
Tt

F₂ Generation

Genotypes

³/4 tall
TT or *Tt*

¹/4 short
tt

As it turns out, height in garden peas is controlled by two different alleles at the same genetic locus. (We'll call it the height locus.) The allele that specifies tall is dominant to the allele for short. (It's worth mentioning that height isn't controlled this way in all plants.) In Mendel's experiments, all the parent plants had two copies of the same allele, either dominant or recessive, depending on whether they were tall or short. When two copies of the same allele are present, the individual is said to be **homozygous**. Thus, all the tall parent plants were homozygous for the dominant allele, and all the short parent plants were homozygous for the recessive allele. This explains why crossing tall plants with tall plants produced only tall offspring. Likewise, all the crosses between short plants produced only

short offspring. All the plants in the parent generation had the same allele (that is, they lacked genetic variation) at the height locus. However, all the F₁ plants (hybrids) inherited one allele from each parent plant (one tall allele and one short allele). Therefore, they all inherited two different alleles at the height locus. Individuals that have two different alleles at a locus are **heterozygous**.

Figure 4-5 illustrates the crosses that Mendel initially performed. By convention, letters that represent alleles or genes are italicized, with uppercase letters referring to dominant alleles (or dominant traits) and lowercase letters referring to recessive alleles (or recessive traits). Therefore,

T = the allele for tallness
t = the allele for shortness

homozygous Having the same allele at the same locus on both members of a pair of chromosomes.

heterozygous Having different alleles at the same locus on members of a pair of chromosomes.

The same symbols are combined to describe an individual's actual genetic makeup, or **genotype**. The term *genotype* can be used to refer to an organism's entire genetic makeup or only to the alleles at a specific genetic locus. Thus, the genotypes of the plants in Mendel's experiments were

TT = homozygous tall plants
Tt = heterozygous tall plants
tt = homozygous short plants

Figure 4-5 also shows the different ways alleles can be combined when the F_1 plants are self-fertilized to produce an F_2 generation. Therefore, the figure shows all the *genotypes* that are possible in the F_2 generation, and statistically speaking, it shows that we would expect ¼ of the F_2 plants to be homozygous dominant (TT), ½ to be heterozygous (Tt), and the remaining ¼ to be homozygous recessive (tt). You can also see the proportions of F_2 **phenotypes**, the observed physical manifestations of genes, illustrating why Mendel saw approximately three tall plants for every short plant in the F_2 generation. One quarter of the F_2 plants are tall because they have the TT genotype. Furthermore, an additional ½, which are heterozygous (Tt), are also tall because T is dominant to t and so it's expressed in the phenotype. The remaining ¼ are homozygous recessive (tt), and they're short because no dominant allele is present. It's important to understand that the *only* way a recessive allele can be expressed is if it occurs with another recessive allele, that is, if the individual is homozygous recessive at the particular locus in question.

Independent Assortment

Mendel also demonstrated that different characteristics aren't necessarily inherited together by showing that plant height and seed color are independent of each other. That is, any tall pea plant had a 50-50 chance of producing either yellow or green peas. Because of this fact, he developed the **principle of independent assortment**.

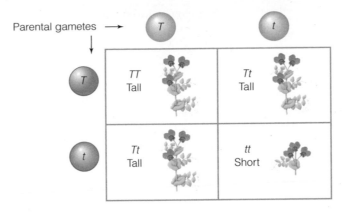

Parental gametes →

	T	t
T	TT Tall	Tt Tall
t	Tt Tall	tt Short

▲ **Figure 4-5**
Punnett square representing possible genotypes and phenotypes and their proportions in the F_2 generation. The circles across the top and at the left of the Punnett square represent the gametes of the F_1 parents. Each square receives one allele from the gamete above it and another from the gamete to the left. Thus, the square at the upper left has two dominant (T) alleles. Likewise, the upper right square receives a recessive (t) allele from the blue gamete above it and a dominant (T) allele from the orange gamete to its left. In this way, the four squares illustrate that ¼ of the F_2 plants can be expected to be homozygous tall (TT); another ½ of the plants can also be expected to be tall but will be heterozygous (Tt); and the remaining ¼ can be expected to be short because they are homozygous for the recessive "short" allele (tt). Thus, ¾ can be expected to be tall and ¼ to be short.

According to this principle, the units (genes) that code for different traits (in this example, plant height and seed color) sort out independently of each other during gamete formation (**Fig. 4-6**). Today we know that this happens because the genes that control plant height and seed color are located on different, nonpartner chromosomes, and during meiosis, the chromosomes travel to newly forming cells independently of one another in a process called **random assortment**.

But if Mendel had used just *any* two traits, his results would have been different at least some of the time. This is because genes on the same chromosome aren't independent of each other, and they usually stay together during meiosis. Even though Mendel didn't know about chromosomes, he certainly knew that all characteristics weren't independent of one another. But because he wanted to emphasize independence, he only reported on those traits that illustrated independent assortment.

In 1866, Mendel's results were published, but the methodology and

genotype The genetic makeup of an individual. Genotype can refer to an organism's entire genetic makeup or to the alleles at a particular locus.

phenotypes The observable or detectable physical characteristics of an organism; the detectable expressions of genotypes, frequently influenced by environmental factors.

principle of independent assortment The distribution of one pair of alleles into gametes does not influence the distribution of another pair. The genes controlling different traits are inherited independently of one another.

random assortment The chance distribution of chromosomes to daughter cells during meiosis. Along with recombination, random assortment is an important source of genetic variation (but not new alleles).

▼ **FIGURE 4-6**
Results of a cross when two traits (height and seed color) are considered simultaneously. These two traits are independent of each other; that is, they aren't necessarily inherited together. Also shown are the genotypes associated with each phenotype. Notice that the ratio of tall plants to short plants is ¾ to ¼, or 3:1, the same as in Figure 4-4. Likewise, the ratio of yellow seeds to green seeds is 3:1. Thus, the phenotypic ratio in the F2 generation is 9:3:3:1.

statistical nature of the research were beyond the thinking of the time, and their significance was overlooked and unappreciated. However, by the end of the nineteenth century, several investigators had made important contributions to the understanding of chromosomes and cell division. These discoveries paved the way for the acceptance of Mendel's work in 1900 when three different groups of scientists came across his paper. Regrettably, Mendel had died 16 years earlier and never saw how his work came to be appreciated.

Mendelian Inheritance in Humans

Mendelian traits, also called *discrete traits* or *traits of simple inheritance*, are controlled by alleles at only one genetic locus (or, in some cases, two or more very closely linked loci). The most comprehensive listing of Mendelian traits in humans is V. A. McKusick's (1998) *Mendelian Inheritance in Man*, first published in 1965 and now in its twelfth edition. This volume, as well as its continuously updated Internet version, *Online Mendelian Inheritance in Man* (www.ncbi.nlm.nih.gov/omim/), currently lists more than 20,000 human characteristics that are inherited according to Mendelian principles.

Although some Mendelian characteristics have readily visible phenotypic expressions (such as polydactyly), most don't. The majority of Mendelian traits are biochemical in nature, and many genetic disorders result from harmful alleles inherited in Mendelian fashion (**Table 4-1**). So if it seems like textbooks overly emphasize genetic disease in discussions of Mendelian traits, it's because many of the known Mendelian characteristics are the results of harmful alleles.

A number of genetic disorders are caused by dominant alleles (see Table 4-1). This means that if a person inherits only one copy of a harmful dominant allele, the condition it causes will be present, regardless of the presence of a different, recessive allele on the partner chromosome.

Recessive conditions are commonly associated with the lack of a substance, usually an enzyme (see Table 4-1). For a person actually to have a recessive disorder, he or she must have *two* copies of the recessive allele that causes it. People who have only one copy of a harmful recessive allele are unaffected. But even though they don't actually have the recessive condition, they can still pass the allele that causes it on to

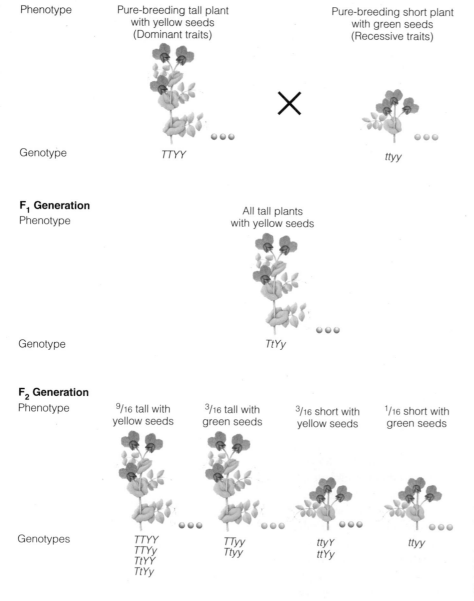

Phenotype — Pure-breeding tall plant with yellow seeds (Dominant traits)   Pure-breeding short plant with green seeds (Recessive traits)

Genotype — *TTYY*   *ttyy*

F₁ Generation
Phenotype — All tall plants with yellow seeds

Genotype — *TtYy*

F₂ Generation
Phenotype — ⁹⁄₁₆ tall with yellow seeds   ³⁄₁₆ tall with green seeds   ³⁄₁₆ short with yellow seeds   ¹⁄₁₆ short with green seeds

Genotypes — *TTYY TTYy TtYY TtYy*   *TTyy Ttyy*   *ttyY ttYy*   *ttyy*

TABLE 4.1

Some Mendelian Traits in Humans

Dominant Traits Condition	Manifestations	Recessive Traits Condition	Manifestations
Achondroplasia	Dwarfism due to growth defects involving the long bones of the arms and legs; trunk and head size usually normal.	Cystic fibrosis	Among the most common genetic (Mendelian) disorders among European Americans; abnormal secretions of the exocrine glands, with pronounced involvement of the pancreas; most patients develop obstructive lung disease. Until the recent development of new treatments, only about half of all patients survived to early adulthood.
Brachydactyly	Shortened fingers and toes.		
Familial hyper-cholesterolemia	Elevated cholesterol levels and cholesterol plaque deposition; a leading cause of heart disease, with death frequently occurring by middle age.		
Neurofibromatosis	Symptoms range from the appearance of abnormal skin pigmentation to large tumors resulting in severe deformities; can, in extreme cases, lead to paralysis, blindness, and death.	Tay-Sachs disease	Most common among Ashkenazi Jews; degeneration of the nervous system beginning at about 6 months of age; lethal by age 2 or 3 years.
Marfan syndrome	The eyes and cardiovascular and skeletal systems are affected; symptoms include greater than average height, long arms and legs, eye problems, and enlargement of the aorta; death due to rupture of the aorta is common. Abraham Lincoln may have had Marfan syndrome.	Phenylketonuria (PKU)	Inability to metabolize the amino acid phenylalanine; results in mental impairment if left untreated during childhood; treatment involves strict dietary management and some supplementation.
Huntington disease	Progressive degeneration of the nervous system accompanied by dementia and seizures; age of onset variable but commonly between 30 and 40 years.	Albinism	Inability to produce normal amounts of the pigment melanin; results in very fair, untannable skin, light blond hair, and light eyes; may also be associated with vision problems. (There is more than one form of albinism.)
Camptodactyly	Malformation of the hands whereby the fingers, usually the little finger, is permanently contracted.		
Hypodontia of upper lateral incisors	Upper lateral incisors are absent or only partially formed (peg-shaped). Pegged incisors are a partial expression of the allele.	Sickle-cell anemia	Abnormal form of hemoglobin (Hb^S) that results in collapsed red blood cells, blockage of capillaries, reduced blood flow to organs, and, without treatment, death.
Cleft chin	Dimple or depression in the middle of the chin; less prominent in females than in males.	Thalassemia	A group of disorders characterized by reduced or absent alpha or beta chains in the hemoglobin molecule; results in severe anemia and, in some forms, death.
PTC tasting	The ability to taste the bitter substance phenylthiocarbamide (PTC). Tasting thresholds vary, suggesting that alleles at another locus may also exert an influence.	Absence of permanent dentition	Failure of the permanent dentition to erupt. The primary dentition is not affected.

their children. For this reason they're frequently called *carriers*. (Remember, half their gametes will carry the recessive allele.) If their mate is also a carrier, it's possible for them to have a child who will be homozygous for the allele, and that child will be affected. In fact, in a mating between two carriers, the risk of having an affected child is 25 percent (refer back to Fig. 4-5).

Mendelian traits Characteristics that are influenced by alleles at only one genetic locus. Examples include many blood types, such as ABO. Many genetic disorders, including sickle-cell anemia and Tay-Sachs disease, are also Mendelian traits.

Blood groups, such as the ABO system, provide some of the best examples of Mendelian traits in humans. The ABO system is governed by three alleles, *A*, *B*, and *O*, found at the *ABO* locus on the ninth chromosome. These alleles determine a person's ABO blood type by coding for the production of molecules called **antigens** on the surface of red blood cells. If only antigen A is present, the blood type (phenotype) is A; if only B is present, the blood type is B; if both are present, the blood type is AB; and when neither is present, the blood type is O (**Table 4-2**).

Dominance and recessiveness are clearly illustrated by the ABO system. The *O* allele is recessive to both *A* and *B*; therefore, if a person has type O blood, he or she must have two copies of the *O* allele. However, since both *A* and *B* are dominant to *O*, an individual with blood type A can actually have one of two genotypes: *AA* or *AO*. The same is true of type B, which results from the genotypes *BB* and *BO* (see Table 4-2). However, type AB presents a slightly different situation and is an example of **codominance**.

Codominance is seen when a person has two different alleles (that is, they're heterozygous); but instead of one allele having the ability to mask the expression of the other, the products of *both* are present in the phenotype. Therefore, when both *A* and *B* alleles are present, both A and B antigens can be detected on the surface of red blood cells.

Misconceptions about Dominance and Recessiveness

Most people have the impression that dominance and recessiveness are all-or-nothing situations. This misconception especially pertains to recessive alleles, and the general view is that when these alleles occur in carriers (heterozygotes), they have no effect on the phenotype; that is, they are completely inactivated by the presence of another (dominant) allele. Certainly, this is how it appeared to Gregor Mendel.

However, various biochemical techniques available today show that many recessive alleles actually do have some effect on the phenotype, although these effects aren't usually detectable through simple observation. It turns out that in heterozygotes, the products of many recessive alleles are only reduced but not completely eliminated. Therefore, our perception of recessive alleles greatly depends on whether we examine them at the directly observable phenotypic level or the biochemical level.

Consider Tay-Sachs disease, a lethal condition resulting from the inability to produce an enzyme called hexosaminidase A (see Table 4-1). This inability, seen in people who are homozygous for a recessive allele (*ts*) on chromosome 15, invariably results in death by early childhood. Carriers

TABLE 4.2	ABO Genotypes and Associated Phenotypes	
Genotypes	**Antigens on Red Blood Cells**	**ABO Blood Type (Phenotype)**
AA, AO	A	A
BB, BO	B	B
AB	A and B	AB
OO	None	O

antigens Large molecules found on the surface of cells. Several different loci govern various antigens on red and white blood cells. (Foreign antigens provoke an immune response.)

codominance The expression of two alleles in heterozygotes. In this situation, neither allele is dominant or recessive, so they both influence the phenotype.

don't have the disease; and practically speaking, they're unaffected. But carriers, although functionally normal, actually have only about 40 to 60 percent of the amount of the enzyme seen in people with normal amounts of the enzyme. This fact has led to the development of voluntary tests to screen carriers in populations at risk for Tay-Sachs disease.

There are also a number of misconceptions about dominant alleles. Many people think of dominant alleles as somehow "stronger" or "better," and there is always the mistaken notion that dominant alleles are more common in populations because natural selection favors them. These misconceptions undoubtedly stem from the label "dominant" and its connotations of power or control. But in genetic usage, this view is misleading. Just think about it. If dominant alleles were always more common, then a majority of people would have conditions such as achondroplasia and Marfan syndrome (see Table 4-1). But obviously, that's not true.

Previously held views of dominance and recessiveness were influenced by available technologies; as genetic technologies continue to change, new theories will emerge, and our perceptions will be further altered. (This is another example of how new techniques and continued hypothesis testing can lead to a revision of hypotheses and theories.) In fact, although dominance and recessiveness will remain important factors in genetics, it's clear that the ways in which these concepts will be taught will be adapted to accommodate new discoveries.

Patterns of Mendelian Inheritance

It's important to be able to establish the pattern of inheritance of genetic traits, especially those that cause serious disease. Also, in families with a history of inherited disorders, it's important to determine an individual's risk of inher-

iting harmful alleles or expressing symptoms. The principal technique traditionally used to assess risk of genetic disease has been the construction of a **pedigree chart,** a diagram of matings and offspring in a family over the span of a few generations. Pedigree analysis helps researchers determine if a trait is Mendelian. It also helps establish the mode of inheritance. By determining whether the locus that influences a particular trait is located on an autosome or sex chromosome and whether a particular allele is dominant or recessive, researchers have identified six different modes of Mendelian inheritance in humans: *autosomal dominant, autosomal recessive, X-linked recessive, X-linked dominant, Y-linked,* and *mitochondrial.* We'll discuss the first three in some detail.

Standardized symbols are used in pedigree charts. Squares and circles represent males and females, respectively. Horizontal lines connecting individuals indicate matings, and offspring are connected to horizontal mating lines by vertical lines. Siblings are joined by a horizontal line connected to a vertical line that descends from the parents (**Fig. 4-7**).

Autosomal Dominant Traits As the term implies, autosomal dominant traits are governed by dominant alleles located on autosomes (that is, any chromosome except X or Y). One example of an autosomal dominant trait is achondroplasia, a form of dwarfism characterized by a normal sized trunk and head but shortened arms and legs (see Table 4-1 and **Fig. 4-8**). Achondroplasia occurs in approximately 1 out of every 10,000 live births. It is usually caused by a spontaneous point mutation in a gene that influences the development of cartilage and thus, bone growth.

Because achondroplasia is caused by a dominant allele, anyone who inherits just one copy of it will have the trait. (In this discussion, we'll use the symbol *A* to refer to the dominant allele

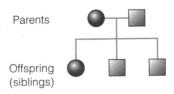

Parents

Offspring
(siblings)

▲ **FIGURE 4-7**
Typical symbols used in pedigree charts. Circles and squares represent females and males respectively. Horizontal lines connecting two individuals indicate mating. Vertical lines connect generations.

pedigree chart A diagram showing family relationships. It's used to trace the hereditary pattern of particular genetic (usually Mendelian) traits.

◄ FIGURE 4-8
This young woman inherited one copy of the dominant allele that causes achondroplasia by inhibiting bone growth, during fetal development. As a result, her legs and arms are disproportionally short. People with achondroplasia are also unable to fully extend their arms, not something that will inhibit her ability to play the violin.

► FIGURE 4-9
Inheritance of an autosomal dominant trait as illustrated by a human pedigree for achondroplasia. How can individuals 5, 11, 14, 15, and 17 be unaffected? What is the genotype of all affected individuals? (To answer the second question, let *A* = the dominant allele and *a* = the recessive allele.)

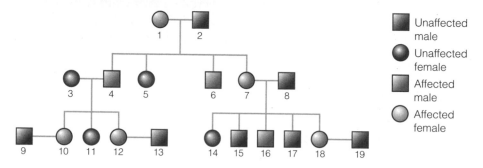

Unaffected male

Unaffected female

Affected male

Affected female

► FIGURE 4-10
The pattern of inheritance of autosomal dominant traits is the direct result of the distribution of chromosomes, and the alleles they carry, into gametes during meiosis. (a) A diagram of possible gametes produced by two parents, one with achondroplasia and another with normal development of the extremities. The achondroplastic individual can produce two types of gametes: half with the dominant allele (*A*) and half with the recessive allele (*a*). All gametes produced by the normal-height parent will carry the recessive allele. (b) A Punnett square depicting the possible genotypes in the offspring of one parent with achondroplasia (*Aa*) and one with normal extremities (*aa*). Statistically, we would expect half the offspring to have the Aa genotype and thus have achondroplasia. The other half would be homozygous recessive (*aa*) and their extremities would grow normally.

that causes the condition and *a* for the recessive, normal allele.) Since the allele is rare, virtually everyone who has achondroplasia is a heterozygote (*Aa*). Unaffected individuals (that is, almost everybody) are homozygous recessive (*aa*).

Figure 4-9 is a partial pedigree for achondroplasia. It's apparent from this pedigree that all affected members have at least one affected parent, so the condition doesn't skip generations. This pattern is true of all autosomal dominant traits. Another characteristic of autosomal dominant traits is that there is no sex bias, so males and females are more or less equally affected. Another important fact about dominant traits is that approximately half the offspring of affected parents are also affected (**Fig. 4-10**). This proportion is what we would predict for an autosomal dominant trait where only one parent is affected, because half of that parent's gametes will have the dominant but harmful allele.

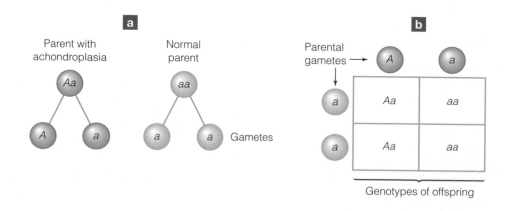

Genotypes of offspring

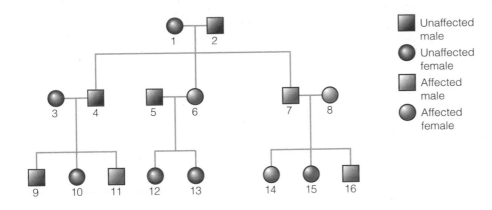

■	Unaffected male
●	Unaffected female
▨	Affected male
◗	Affected female

◀ **FIGURE 4-11**

Partial pedigree for albinism, an autosomal recessive trait. Why are some of the offspring of affected individuals unaffected? Individuals 6 and 7, children of unaffected parents, are affected. Why? Four individuals are definitely unaffected carriers. Which ones are they? Why is individual 11 affected when his parents aren't?

Autosomal Recessive Traits Autosomal recessive traits are also influenced by loci on autosomes but show a different pattern of inheritance. A good example is shown in **Figure 4-11**, a pedigree for albinism. The most common form of albinism is a metabolic disorder caused by an autosomal recessive allele that prevents the production of a pigment called melanin (see Chapter 16). Thus, albinos have unusually light hair, skin, and eyes (**Fig. 4-12**). The frequency of this type of albinism varies widely among populations, with a prevalence of about 1 in 37,000 people of European ancestry. But approximately 1 in 200 Hopi Indians are affected.

Pedigrees for autosomal recessive traits show obvious differences from those for autosomal dominant characteristics. For one thing, an affected offspring can be produced by two phenotypically normal parents. In fact, most people who express recessive conditions have unaffected parents. In addition, the proportion of affected offspring from most matings is less than half. But when both parents have the trait, all the offspring will be affected. As in the pattern for autosomal dominant traits, males and females are equally affected.

The Mendelian principle of segregation explains the pattern of inheritance

▼ **FIGURE 4-12**

(a) A Tanzanian woman with her albino young son. Tragically, since the mid-2000s, there has been a dramatic increase in the trade of albino body parts, which are used in witchcraft, especially in Tanzania. (b) This albino horse may be beautiful but with virtually no pigmentation, if kept outdoors, it is highly susceptible to sunburn and various forms of skin cancer including melanoma.

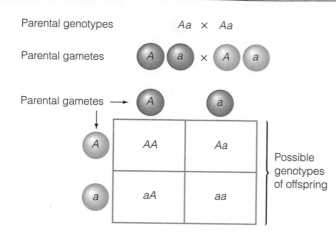

Parental genotypes $Aa \times Aa$

Parental gametes A a $\times$ A a

Parental gametes $\longrightarrow$ A a

Possible genotypes of offspring

	A	a
A	AA	Aa
a	aA	aa

▲ **FIGURE 4-13**

A cross between two phenotypically normal parents, both of them carriers of the albinism allele. From a mating such as this between two carriers, we would expect the following possible proportions of genotypes and phenotypes in the offspring: homozygous dominants (*AA*) with normal phenotype, 25 percent; heterozygotes, or carriers (*Aa*) with normal phenotype, 50 percent; and homozygous recessives (*aa*) with albinism, 25 percent. This yields the phenotypic ratio of 3 normal to 1 albino.

of autosomal recessive traits. In fact, this pattern is the very one Mendel first described in his pea experiments (look back at Fig. 4-3). Unaffected parents who produce an albino child *must both be carriers*, and their child is homozygous for the recessive allele that causes the abnormality. The Punnett square in **Figure 4-13** shows how such a mating produces both unaffected and affected offspring in predictable proportions—the typical *phenotypic ratio* of 3:1.

Sex-Linked Traits Sex-linked traits are controlled by genes located on the X and Y chromosomes. Almost all of the more than 1,000 sex-linked traits listed in *Online Mendelian Inheritance in Man* are influenced by genes on the X chromosome (**Table 4-3**). Most of the coding sequences (that is, those segments that actually specify a protein) on the Y chromosome are involved in determining maleness and testis function. Although some Y-linked genes are expressed in areas other than the testes (Skaletsky et al., 2003), their functions aren't well known. For this reason, our discussion concerns only the X chromosome.

Hemophilia, one of the best known of the X-linked traits, is caused by a recessive allele on the X chromosome. This allele prevents the formation of a clotting factor in the blood, and affected individuals suffer bleeding episodes and may actually bleed to death from injuries that most of us would consider trivial.

| TABLE 4.3 | Some Mendelian Disorders Inherited as X-linked Recessive Traits in Humans |

Condition	Manifestations
G-6-PD (glucose-6-phosphate) deficiency	Lack of an enzyme (G-6-PD) in red blood cells; produces severe, sometimes fatal anemia in the presence of certain foods (e.g., fava beans) and/or drugs (e.g., the antimalarial drug primaquin).
Muscular dystrophy	One form is X-linked; other forms can be inherited as autosomal recessives. Progressive weakness and atrophy of muscles beginning in early childhood; continues to progress throughout life; some female carriers may develop heart problems.
Red-green color blindness	Actually, there are two separate forms, one involving the perception of red and the other involving the perception of green. About 8 percent of European males have an impaired ability to distinguish green.
Lesch-Nyhan disease	Impaired motor development noticeable by 5 months; progressive motor impairment, diminished kidney function, self-mutilation, and early death.
Hemophilia	There are three forms; two (hemophilia A and B) are X-linked. In hemophilia A, a clotting factor is missing; hemophilia B is caused by a defective clotting factor. Both produce abnormal internal and external bleeding from minor injuries; severe pain is a frequent accompaniment; without treatment, death usually occurs before adulthood.
Ichthyosis	There are several forms; one is X-linked. A skin condition due to lack of an enzyme; characterized by scaly, brown lesions on the extremities and trunk. In the past, people with this condition were sometimes exhibited in circuses and sideshows as "the alligator man."

► **FIGURE 4-14**
Pedigree for Queen Victoria and some of her descendants, showing the inheritance of hemophilia, an X-linked recessive trait in humans.

The most famous pedigree illustrating this condition is that of Queen Victoria (1820–1901) of England and her descendants (**Fig. 4-14**). The most striking feature shown by this pattern of inheritance is that almost all affected people are males, because males have only one X chromosome and therefore only one copy of X-linked genes. This means that *any allele*, even a recessive one, located on their X chromosome will be expressed, because there's no possibility of a dominant allele on a partner chromosome to block it. Females, on the other hand, show the same pattern of expression of X-linked traits as for autosomal traits, because they have two X chromosomes. That is, just as with any other pair of chromosomes, the only way an X-linked recessive allele can be expressed in a female is if she has two copies of it. However, females who have one copy of the hemophilia allele are carriers, and they may have some tendency toward bleeding, even though they aren't severely affected.

Non-Mendelian Inheritance

Polygenic Inheritance

Mendelian traits are described as *discrete*, or *discontinuous*, because their phenotypic expressions don't overlap; instead, they fall into clearly defined categories (**Fig. 4-15a**). For example, in the ABO system, the four phenotypes are completely distinct from one another; that is, there is no intermediate form between type A and type B. In other words, Mendelian traits don't show *continuous* variation.

However, many traits do have a wide range of phenotypic expressions

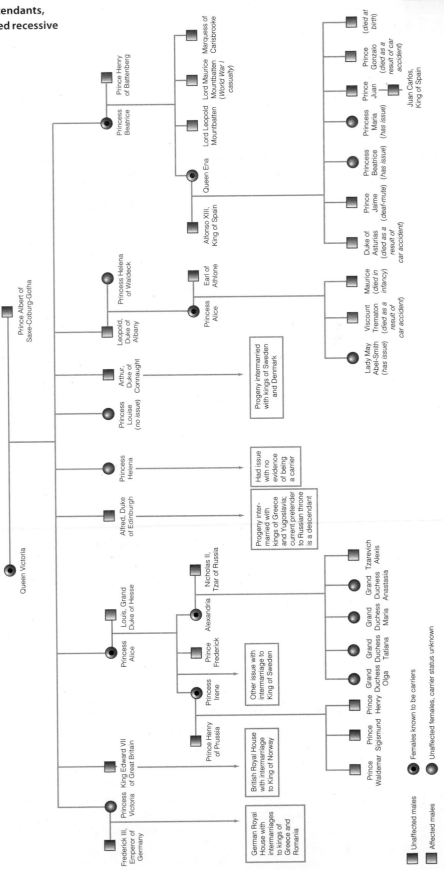

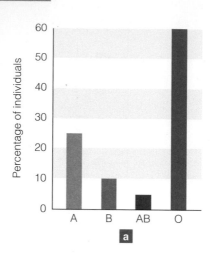

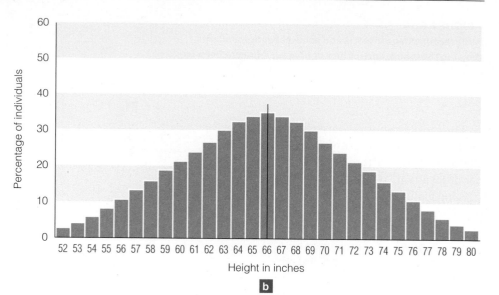

▲ Figure 4-15

(a) This bar graph shows the discontinuous distribution of a Mendelian trait (ABO blood type) in a hypothetical population. Expression of the trait is described in terms of frequencies. **(b)** This histogram represents the continuous expression of a polygenic trait (height) in a large group of people. Notice that the percentage of extremely short or tall individuals is low; most people are closer to the mean, or average, height, represented by the vertical line at the center of the distribution. **(c)** A group of male students arranged according to height. The most common height is 70 inches, which is the mean, or average, for this group.

polygenic Referring to traits that are influenced by genes at two or more loci. Examples include stature, skin color, eye color, and hair color. Many (but not all) polygenic traits are influenced by environmental factors such as nutrition and exposure to sunlight.

pigment In reference to polygenic inheritance, molecules that influence the color of skin, hair, and eyes.

that form a graded series. These are called **polygenic**, or *continuous*, traits (**Fig. 4-15b and c**). While Mendelian traits are governed by only one genetic locus, polygenic characteristics are governed by alleles at two or more loci, and each locus has some influence on the phenotype. Throughout the history of physical anthropology, the most frequently discussed examples of polygenic inheritance in humans have been skin, hair, and eye color (**Fig. 4-16**).

Coloration is determined by melanin, a **pigment** produced by specialized cells called melanocytes (see Chapter 16); and the amount of melanin that is produced determines how dark or light a person's skin will be. Melanin production is influenced by interactions between several different loci that have now been identified. A study by Lamason and colleagues (2005) showed that one single, highly *conserved* gene (called *MC1R*) with two alleles makes a greater contribution to melanin production than some other melanin-producing genes.* Moreover, geneticists know of at least four other pigmentation genes. This is very important because they can now examine the complex interactions between these genes and also how their functions are influenced by regulatory genes. So the story of melanin production is a complicated one, but it's exciting that many long-standing questions about variation in human skin color will be answered in the not too distant future. (See Chapter 6 for further discussion of variation in pigmentation.)

As we stated earlier, eye color is influenced by more than one gene, and certainly some of the genes that influence skin color are also involved. However, a gene called *OCA2*, located on chromosome 15, is apparently the most important gene in the development of blue eyes (Fig. 4-16). *OCA2* is involved in pigmentation of the iris of the eye, and mutations in this gene lead to a form of albinism. Sturm and colleagues (2008) demonstrated that this gene accounts for 74 percent of the variation in human eye color in European populations. (Northern European populations and their descendants exhibit more variability in eye color than is seen in all other human populations; and they're the only ones in which significant numbers of people have blue eyes.) Moreover, specific variations of the *OCA2* gene were found in virtually 100 percent of blue-eyed people from Denmark, Turkey, and Jordan. In addition, point mutations in one of several genes that regulate *OCA2* also are "perfectly associated" with blue eyes (Eiberg et al.,

*Highly conserved genes are those that are present in most, if not all, animal species and sometimes in plants. Genes that are found in most species are extremely important; they're evidence for shared ancestry and biological continuity. Variations in the *MC1R* gene that cause pigmentation differences occur throughout the animal kingdom in species ranging from zebra fish to dogs to humans. Similar variations have also been identified in preserved DNA of extinct species, including mammoths and Neandertals.

2007). Thus, when we examine any trait, we need to look not only at the genes traditionally associated with them, but also at the DNA sequences that regulate them. Indeed, it's looking more and more like genes don't really do much by themselves; they just follow orders, and if the orders vary, then their effects will also vary.

Polygenic traits actually account for most of the readily observable phenotypic variation in humans, and they've traditionally served as a basis for racial classification (see Chapter 6). In addition to skin, hair, and eye color, there are many other polygenic characteristics, including stature, shape of the face, and fingerprint pattern, to name a few. Because they exhibit continuous variation, most polygenic traits can be measured on a scale composed of equal increments. For example, height (stature) is measured in feet and inches (or meters and centimeters). If we were to measure height in a large number of individuals, the distribution of measurements would continue uninterrupted from the shortest extreme to the tallest (see Fig. 4-15b and c). That's what is meant by the term *continuous traits*.

Because polygenic traits can usually be measured, physical anthropologists can analyze them using certain statistical tests. The use of simple summary statistics, such as the *mean* (average) or *standard deviation* (a measure of variation within a group), permits basic descriptions of, and comparisons between, populations. For example, a physical anthropologist might be interested in average height in two different populations and whether or not differences between the two are significant, and if so, why. (Incidentally, *all* physical traits measured and statistically treated in fossils are polygenic in nature.)

These particular statistical descriptions aren't possible with Mendelian traits simply because those traits can't be measured in the same way. But this doesn't mean that Mendelian characteristics provide less information about genetic processes. Mendelian

▲ FIGURE 4-16
Eye color is a polygenic characteristic and is a good example of continuous variation.

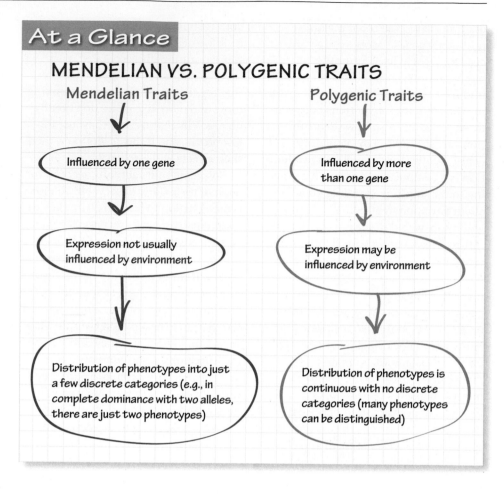

At a Glance

MENDELIAN VS. POLYGENIC TRAITS

Mendelian Traits	Polygenic Traits
Influenced by one gene	Influenced by more than one gene
Expression not usually influenced by environment	Expression may be influenced by environment
Distribution of phenotypes into just a few discrete categories (e.g., in complete dominance with two alleles, there are just two phenotypes)	Distribution of phenotypes is continuous with no discrete categories (many phenotypes can be distinguished)

characteristics can be described in terms of frequency within populations, and this makes it possible to compare groups for differences in prevalence. For example, one population may have a high frequency of blood type A, while in another group, type A may be almost completely absent. Also, Mendelian traits can be analyzed for mode of inheritance (dominant or recessive).

Lastly, for many Mendelian traits, the approximate or exact positions of genetic loci are known, and this makes it possible to examine the mechanisms and patterns of inheritance at these loci. This type of study isn't yet possible for polygenic traits because they're influenced by several genes that are only now being traced to specific loci.

Mitochondrial Inheritance

Another component of inheritance involves the organelles called *mito-* *chondria* (see Chapter 3). All cells contain several hundred of these oval-shaped structures that convert energy (derived from the breakdown of nutrients) to a form that can be used to perform cellular functions.

Each mitochondrion contains several copies of a ring-shaped DNA molecule, or chromosome. While *mitochondrial DNA (mtDNA)* is distinct from chromosomal DNA, its molecular structure and functions are the same. The entire molecule has been sequenced and is known to contain around 40 genes that direct the conversion of energy within the cell.

Like the DNA in a cell's nucleus, mtDNA is subject to mutations, and some of these mutations cause certain genetic disorders that result from impaired energy conversion. Importantly, animals of both sexes inherit all their mtDNA, and thus all mitochondrial traits, from their mothers. Because mtDNA is inherited from only one parent, meiosis and recombination don't occur. This means that all the variation in mtDNA among individuals is caused by mutation, which makes mtDNA extremely useful for studying genetic change over time. So far, geneticists have used mutation rates in mtDNA to investigate evolutionary relationships between species, to trace ancestral relationships within the human lineage, and to study genetic variability among individuals and/or populations. While these techniques are still being refined, it's clear that we have a lot to learn from mtDNA.

Pleiotropy

While polygenic traits are governed by the actions of several genes, **pleiotropy** is a situation where a single gene influences more than one characteristic. Although this might seem unusual, pleiotropic effects are probably the rule rather than the exception.

The autosomal recessive disorder phenylketonuria (PKU) provides one example of pleiotropy (see Table 4-1). Individuals who are homozygous for the *PKU* allele don't produce the enzyme involved in the initial conversion of the amino acid *phenylalanine* to another amino acid, *tyrosine*. Because of this block in the metabolic pathway, phenylalanine breaks down into substances that accumulate in the central nervous system; and without dietary management, these substances lead to mental deficiencies and several other consequences. Tyrosine is ultimately converted to several substances, including the pigment melanin; therefore, numerous other systems can also be affected. Thus, another manifestation of PKU, owing to a diminished ability to produce melanin, is that affected people usually have blue eyes, fair skin, and light hair. There are many examples of pleiotropic genes, including the allele that causes sickle-cell anemia. Clearly, the action of one gene can influence a number of seemingly unrelated traits.

Genetic and Environmental Factors

By now you may have the impression that phenotypes are entirely the expressions of genotypes; but that's not true. (Here the terms *genotype* and *phenotype* are used in a broader sense to refer to an individual's *entire* genetic makeup and *all* observable or detectable characteristics.) Genotypes set limits and potentials for development, but they also interact with the environment, and many (but not all) aspects of the phenotype are influenced by this genetic-environmental interaction. For example, adult stature is influenced by both genes and the environment. Even though the maximum height a person can achieve is genetically determined, childhood nutrition (an environmental factor) is also important. Other important environmental factors include exposure to sunlight, altitude, temperature, and, unfortunately, increasing levels of exposure to toxic waste and airborne pollutants. These and many other factors contribute in complex ways to the continuous phenotypic variation seen in traits governed by several genetic loci. However, for many characteristics, it's not possible to identify the *specific* environmental components that influence the phenotype.

Mendelian traits are less likely to be influenced by environmental factors. For example, ABO blood type is determined at fertilization and remains fixed throughout an individual's lifetime, regardless of diet, exposure to ultraviolet radiation, temperature, and so forth.

Mendelian and polygenic inheritance show different patterns of phenotypic variation. In the former, variation occurs in discrete categories, while in the latter, it's continuous. However, it's important to understand that even for polygenic characteristics, Mendelian principles still apply at

pleiotropy The capacity of a single gene to influence several phenotypic expressions.

individual loci. In other words, if a trait is influenced by six loci, each one of those loci may have two or more alleles, with some perhaps being dominant to others. It's the combined action of the alleles at all six loci, interacting with the environment, that produces the phenotype.

Modern Evolutionary Theory

By the beginning of the twentieth century, the foundations for evolutionary theory had already been developed. Darwin and Wallace had described natural selection 40 years earlier, and the rediscovery of Mendelian genetics in 1900 contributed the other major component, namely, a mechanism for inheritance. We might expect that these two basic contributions would have been combined into a consistent theory of evolution, but they weren't. For the first 30 years of the twentieth century, some scientists argued that mutation was the main factor in evolution, while others emphasized natural selection. What they really needed was a merger of the two views rather than an either-or situation; but this didn't happen until the mid-1930s (see "A Closer Look.")

The Modern Synthesis

In the late 1920s and early 1930s, biologists realized that mutation and natural selection weren't opposing processes: They *both* contributed to biological evolution. The two major foundations of the biological sciences had finally been brought together in what is called the Modern Synthesis. From such a "modern" (that is, the middle of the twentieth century onward) perspective, we define evolution as a two-stage process:

1. The production and redistribution of **variation** (inherited differences among organisms)

2. *Natural selection* acting on this variation, whereby inherited differences, or variation, among individuals differentially affect their ability to successfully reproduce

A Current Definition of Evolution

As we discussed in Chapter 2, Darwin saw evolution as the gradual unfolding of new varieties of life from preexisting ones. Certainly, this is one result of the evolutionary process. But these long-term effects can come about only through the accumulation of many small genetic changes occurring over the generations. Today, we can demonstrate how evolution works by examining some of the small genetic changes and how they increase or decrease in frequency. From this perspective, we define evolution as *a change in* **allele frequency** *from one generation to the next.*

Allele frequencies are indicators of the genetic makeup of a **population**, the members of which share a common **gene pool**. To show how allele frequencies change, we'll use a simplified example of an inherited trait, again the ABO blood types. (*Note*: There are several blood groups, not just the ABO system, and they're all controlled by different genes.)

Let's assume that the students in your anthropology class represent a population and that we've determined everyone's ABO blood type. (To be considered a population, individuals must choose mates more often from *within* the group than from outside it. Obviously, your class won't meet this requirement, but we'll overlook this point.) The proportions of the *A*, *B*, and *O* alleles are the allele frequencies for this trait. If 50 percent of all the *ABO* alleles in your class are *A*, 40 percent are *B*, and 10 percent are *O*, then the frequencies of these alleles are $A = .50$, $B = .40$, and $O = .10$.

variation In genetics, inherited differences among individuals; the basis of all evolutionary change.

allele frequency In a population, the percentage of all the alleles at a locus accounted for by one specific allele.

population Within a species, a community of individuals where mates are usually found.

gene pool All of the genes shared by the reproductive members of a population.

The Development of Modern Evolutionary Theory

Our understanding of the evolutionary process came about through contributions of biologists in the United States, Great Britain, and Russia. While "mutationists" were arguing with "selectionists" about the single primary mechanism in evolution, several population geneticists began to realize that small genetic changes and natural selection were both necessary ingredients in the evolutionary formula.

These population geneticists were largely concerned with mathematical reconstructions of evolution; in particular, they were measuring small accumulations of genetic changes in populations over just a few generations. Central figures in these early theoretical developments were Ronald Fisher and J. B. S. Haldane in Great Britain, Sewall Wright in the United States, and Sergei Chetverikov in Russia.

While these scientists produced brilliant insights, their conclusions were largely unknown to most evolutionary biologists, especially in North America. Therefore, someone had to merge the mathematical jargon of the population geneticists

American Museum of Natural History

and the general theories of evolutionary biologists. The scientist who did this was Theodosius Dobzhansky (Fig. 1). In his *Genetics and the Origin of Species* (1937), Dobzhansky integrated the mathematics of population genetics with overall evolutionary theory. His conclusions then became the basis for a period of tremendous activity in evolutionary thinking that directly led to major contributions by George Gaylord Simpson (who brought paleontology into the synthesis), Ernst Mayr, and others. In fact, the Modern Synthesis produced by these scientists stood basically unchallenged for an entire generation as the explanation of the evolutionary process. In recent years, however, some aspects of this theory have been brought under serious question (see Chapter 5).

◄ **Figure 1**
Theodosius Dobzhansky.

Since the frequencies of these alleles represent proportions of a total, it's obvious that allele frequencies can refer only to groups of individuals, or populations. Individuals don't have allele frequencies; they have either *A*, *B*, or *O* in any combination of two. Also, from conception onward, a person's genetic composition is fixed. If you start out with blood type A, you'll always have type A. Therefore, only a population can evolve over time; individuals can't.

Assume that 20 years from now, we calculate the frequencies of the *ABO* alleles for the children of our classroom population and find the following: *A* = .30, *B* = .40, and *O* = .30. We can see that the relative proportions have changed: *A* has decreased, *O* has increased, and *B* has remained the same. This wouldn't be a big deal, but in a biological sense, minor changes such as this constitute evolution. Over the short span of just a few generations, changes in the frequencies of inherited traits may be very small; but if they continue to happen, and particularly if they go in one direction as a result of natural selection, they can produce new adaptations and even new species.

Whether we're talking about the short-term effects (as in our classroom population) from one generation to the next, which is sometimes called **microevolution**, or the long-term effects through time, called speciation or **macroevolution**, the basic evolutionary mechanisms are similar. But how do allele frequencies change? Or, to put it another way, what causes evolution? As we've already said, evolution is a two-stage process. Genetic variation must first be produced by mutation, and then it can be acted on by natural selection.

microevolution Small changes occurring within species, such as changes in allele frequencies.

macroevolution Changes produced only after many generations, such as the appearance of a new species.

Factors That Produce and Redistribute Variation

Mutation

You've already learned that a mutation is a change in DNA. There are many kinds of mutations, but here we focus on *point mutations*, or substitutions of one DNA base for another. (Actually, alleles are the results of point mutations.) Point mutations have to occur in sex cells if they're going to have evolutionary consequences. This is because the mutation must be passed from one generation to the next for evolution to occur. If a mutation takes place in a person's somatic cells, but not in gametes, it won't be passed on to offspring. If, however, a genetic change occurs in the sperm or egg of one of the students in our classroom (*A* mutates to *B*, for instance), the offspring's blood type will be different from that of the parent, causing a minute shift in the allele frequencies of the next generation. In Chapter 3, we showed how a point mutation causes a change in the structure of the normal hemoglobin molecule (Hb^A) to sickling hemoglobin (Hb^S); and we also discussed how transposable elements and tandem repeats can change the structure of a gene.

Actually, except in microorganisms, it's rare for evolution to take place solely because of mutations. Mutation rates for any given trait are usually low, so we wouldn't really expect to see a mutation at the *ABO* locus in so small a population as your class. In larger populations, mutations might be observed in, say, 1 individual out of 10,000, but by themselves they would have no impact on allele frequencies. However, when mutation is combined with natural selection, evolutionary changes can occur more rapidly.

It's important to remember that mutation is the basic creative force in evolution, since it's the *only* way to pro-duce *new* genes (that is, variation). Its role in the production of variation is key to the first stage of the evolutionary process.

We discussed the importance of mutations in regulatory genes to the evolutionary process in Chapter 3. We also mentioned that many non-protein-coding DNA sequences contain variable numbers of certain segments and these segments are called *copy number variants (CNVs)* (see "A Closer Look: What's All This Junk? Or Is It Junk?" in Chapter 3). CNVs also occur in protein-coding genes; therefore, individuals and species have different numbers of certain segments within genes, and these differences influence a gene's overall effect. When CNVs occur in regulatory genes, particularly those involved in development, they can cause dramatic changes in morphology.

CNVs occur as a result of deletions or duplications of DNA segments within a gene. **Tandem repeats** are a type of duplication that has attracted a great deal of attention in recent years because they have much higher mutation rates than single alleles do and therefore could have a significant influence on rates of evolution. In one study, Fondon & Garner (2004) examined the relationship between tandem repeats in regulatory genes and phenotypic expression. Among other things, they showed how a tandem repeat in a regulatory gene involved in bone growth has dramatically influenced the shape of the cranium of bull terriers (**Fig. 4-17**).

The morphological changes in bull terrier crania are the results of artificial selection for a specific trait (the long, drooping snout), influenced by variation in a regulatory gene. While this is not speciation, it is dramatic evidence of how tandem repeats in protein-coding genes can produce significant morphological variation for natural selection to act on. Indeed, tandem repeats have played, and continue to play, a highly significant role in evolution.

tandem repeats Short, adjacent segments of DNA within a gene that are repeated several times.

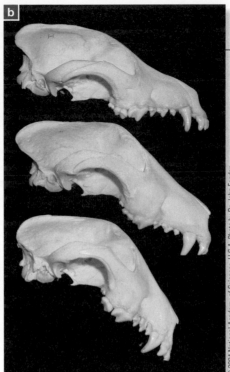

◄ **Figure 4-17**
(a) Selective breeding in bull terriers has produced dramatic changes in the shape of the head resulting in a concave profile and downward turning nose. **(b)** These three purebred bull terrier crania clearly illustrate how the shape of the head changed in this breed in just 35 years. The dates for the crania, from top to bottom, are 1931, 1950 and 1976. (The 1931 specimen, from a Swiss lab, provided DNA to use for comparison with modern bull terrier DNA.)

Gene Flow

Gene flow is the exchange of genes between populations. The term *migration* is also sometimes used; but strictly speaking, migration refers to the movement of people. In contrast, gene flow refers to the exchange of genes between groups, and this can only happen if the migrants interbreed. Also, even if individuals move temporarily and have offspring in the new population (thus leaving a genetic contribution), they don't necessarily stay there. For example, the children of U.S. soldiers and Vietnamese women represent gene flow. Even though the fathers returned to the United States after the Vietnam War, some of their genes remained behind, although not in sufficient numbers to appreciably change allele frequencies.

In humans, mating patterns are mostly determined by social factors, and cultural anthropologists can work closely with biological anthropologists to isolate and measure this aspect of evolutionary change. Human population movements (particularly in the last 500 years) have reached previously unheard of proportions, and very few breeding isolates remain. But migration on a smaller scale has been a consistent feature of human evolution since the first dispersal of our genus, and gene flow between populations (even though sometimes limited) helps explain why speciation has been rare during the past million years or so.

An interesting example of how gene flow influences microevolutionary changes in modern human populations is seen in African Americans. African Americans are largely of West African descent, but there has also been considerable genetic admixture with European Americans. By measuring allele frequencies for specific genetic loci, we can estimate the amount of migration of European alleles into the African American gene pool. Data from northern and western U.S. cities (including New York, Detroit, and Oakland) have shown that the proportion of *non*-African genes in the African American gene pool is 20 to 25 percent (Cummings, 2000). However, more restricted data from the southern United States (Charleston and rural

gene flow Exchange of genes between populations.

Georgia) have suggested a lower degree of gene flow (4 to 11 percent).

Gene flow occurs for reasons other than large-scale movements of populations. In fact, significant changes in allele frequencies can come about through long-term patterns of mate selection whereby members of a group traditionally obtain mates from certain other groups. This is especially true if mate exchange consistently occurs in one direction over a long period of time. For example, if group A chooses mates from group B, but group B doesn't reciprocate, eventually group A will have an increased proportion of group B alleles. If, however, mate exchange between groups is reciprocal, over time the two groups will become more alike genetically (**Fig. 4-18**).

Today, modern transportation plays a crucial role in determining the potential radius for finding mates. Throughout most of human history, the majority of people found mates within a few miles of their home; but today it's not uncommon to find a partner from another continent. Of course, for most people, actual patterns are somewhat more restricted. For example, data from Ann Arbor, Michigan, indicate a mean marital distance (the average distance between birthplaces of partners) of about 160 miles. This isn't a huge distance, but it's still an area large enough to include

▶ **FIGURE 4-18**
In this illustration, the colored dots represent different alleles and the circles that contain them represent two populations.

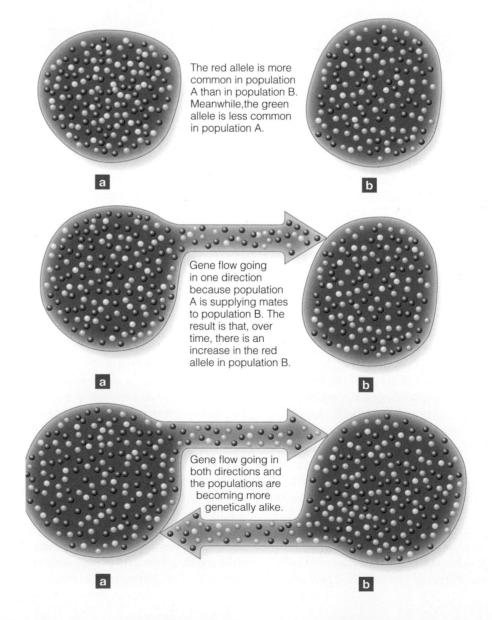

The red allele is more common in population A than in population B. Meanwhile, the green allele is less common in population A.

Gene flow going in one direction because population A is supplying mates to population B. The result is that, over time, there is an increase in the red allele in population B.

Gene flow going in both directions and the populations are becoming more genetically alike.

a tremendous number of potential marriage partners.

Genetic Drift and Founder Effect

Genetic drift is the random factor in evolution, and it's a function of population size. *Drift occurs solely because the population is small.* If an allele is rare in a population composed of only a few hundred individuals, then there's a chance it simply may not be passed on to offspring. If this happens, the allele may completely disappear from the population (**Fig. 4-19a**).

One particular kind of genetic drift, called **founder effect**, is seen in many modern human and nonhuman populations. Founder effect can occur when a small band of "founders" leaves its parent group and forms a colony somewhere else. Over time, a new population will be established, and as long as mates are chosen only from within this population, all of its members will be descended from the small original group of founders. Therefore, all the genes in the expanding group will have

Time

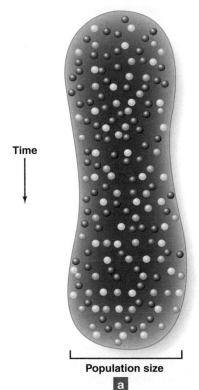

A small population with considerable genetic variability. Note that the dark green and blue alleles are less common than the other alleles.

After just a few generations, the population is approximately the same size but genetic variation has been reduced. Both the dark green and blue alleles have been lost. Also, the red allele is less common and the frequency of the light green allele has increased.

Population size

a

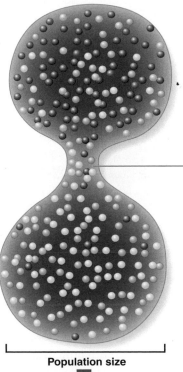

Original population with considerable genetic variation

A small group leaves to colonize a new area, or a bottleneck occurs, so that population size decreases and genetic variation is reduced.

Population size restored but the dark green and purple alleles have been lost. The frequencies of the red and yellow alleles have also changed.

Population size

b

▲ **Figure 4-19**

Small populations are subject to genetic drift, where rare alleles can be lost because, just by chance, they weren't passed to offspring. Also, although more common alleles may not be lost, their frequencies may change for the same reason. (a) This diagram represents six alleles (different-colored dots) that occur at one genetic locus in a small population. You can see that in a fairly short period of time (three or four generations), rare alleles can be lost and genetic diversity consequently reduced. (b) This diagram illustrates founder effect, a form of genetic drift where diversity is lost because a large population is drastically reduced in size and consequently passes through a genetic "bottleneck." Founder effect also happens when a small group leaves the larger group and "founds" a new population elsewhere. (In this case, the group of founders is represented by the bottleneck.) Those individuals that survive (or the founders) and the alleles they carry represent only a sample of the variation that was present in the original population. And future generations, all descended from the survivors (founders), will therefore have less variability.

genetic drift Evolutionary changes, or changes in allele frequencies, that are produced by random factors in small populations. Genetic drift is a result of small population size.

founder effect A type of genetic drift in which allele frequencies are altered in small populations that are taken from, or are remnants of, larger populations.

come from the original colonists. In such a case, an allele that was rare in the founders' parent population but was carried by even one of the founders can eventually become common among the founders' descendants (Fig. 4-18b). This is because a high proportion of people in later generations are all descended from that one founder.

Colonization isn't the only way founder effect can happen. Small founding groups may be the survivors of a larger group that was mostly wiped out by a disaster of some kind. But like the small group of colonists, the survivors possess only a sample of all the alleles that were present in the original population.

Therefore, just by chance alone, some alleles may be completely lost from a population's gene pool, while others may become the only allele at a locus that previously had two or more. Whatever the cause, the outcome is a reduction in genetic diversity, and the allele frequencies of succeeding generations may be substantially different from those of the original, larger population. The loss of genetic diversity in this type of situation is called *genetic bottleneck*, and the effects can be highly detrimental to a species.

There are many known examples (both human and nonhuman) of species or populations that have passed through genetic bottlenecks. (In fact, right now many species are currently going through genetic bottlenecks.) Genetically, cheetahs (**Fig. 4-20**) are an extremely uniform species, and biologists believe that at some point in the past, these magnificent cats suffered a catastrophic decline in numbers. For unknown reasons related to the species-wide loss of numerous alleles, male cheetahs produce a high percentage of defective sperm compared to other cat species. Decreased reproductive potential, greatly reduced genetic

Lynn Kilgore

▲ **Figure 4-20**
Cheetahs, like many other species, have passed through a genetic bottleneck. Consequently, as a species they have little genetic variation.

diversity, and other factors (including human hunting) have combined to jeopardize the continued existence of this species. Other species that have passed through genetic bottlenecks include California elephant seals, sea otters, and condors. Indeed, humans are much more genetically uniform than chimpanzees, and it appears that all modern human populations are the descendants of a few small groups.

Many examples of founder effect have been documented in small, usually isolated populations (such as island groups or small agricultural villages in New Guinea or South America). Even larger populations that are descended from fairly small groups of founders can show the effects of genetic drift many generations later. For instance, French Canadians in Quebec, who currently number close to 6 million, are all descended from about 8,500 founders who left France during the sixteenth and seventeenth centuries. Because the genes carried by the initial founders represented only a sample of the gene pool from which they were derived, a number of alleles now occur in different frequencies from those of the current population of France. These differences include an increased presence of several harmful alleles, including those that cause some of the diseases listed in Table 4-1, such as cystic fibrosis, a variety of Tay-Sachs, thalassemia, and PKU (Scriver, 2001).

Another example of genetic drift is provided by a fatal recessive condition called Amish microcephaly, in which a mutation results in abnormally small brains and heads in fetuses. The disorder is found only in the Old Order Amish community of Lancaster County, Pennsylvania, where it occurs in approximately 1 in 500 births (Kelley et al., 2002; Rosenberg et al., 2002). Genealogical research showed that affected families have all been traced back nine generations to a single couple. One member of this couple carried the deleterious recessive allele that, because of customs promoting marriage within (what was then) a small group, has greatly increased in frequency with very serious consequences.

Much insight into the evolutionary factors that have acted in the past can be gained by understanding how such mechanisms continue to operate on human populations today. In small populations, drift plays an important evolutionary role because fairly sudden fluctuations in allele frequency occur solely because of small population size. Likewise, throughout a good deal of human evolution, at least the last 4 to 5 million years, hominins probably lived in small groups, and drift probably had a significant impact.

While drift has contributed to evolutionary change in certain circumstances, the effects have been irregular and nondirectional. (Remember, drift is *random* in nature.) Certainly, the pace of evolutionary change could have been accelerated if many small populations were isolated and thus subject to drift. By modifying the genetic makeup of such populations, drift can provide significantly greater opportunities for natural selection, the only truly directional force in evolution.

Additional insight concerning the relative influences of the different evolutionary factors has emerged in recent studies of the early dispersal of modern *Homo sapiens*. Evidence suggests that in the last 100,000 to 200,000 years, our species experienced a genetic bottleneck that considerably influenced the pattern of genetic variation seen in all human populations today.

As we've seen, both gene flow and genetic drift can produce some evolutionary changes by themselves. However, these changes are usually *microevolutionary* ones; that is, they produce changes within species over the short term. To produce the kind of evolutionary changes that ultimately result in new species (for example, the diversification of the first primates or the appearance of the earliest hominins), natural selection is necessary. But natural selection can't operate independently of the other evolutionary factors: mutation, gene flow, and genetic drift.

Recombination

As we saw in Chapter 3, members of chromosome pairs exchange segments of DNA during meiosis. By itself, recombination doesn't change allele frequencies, or cause evolution. However, when paired chromosomes exchange DNA, genes sometimes find themselves in different genetic environments. (It's like they've moved to a new neighborhood.) This fact can be important because the functions of some genes can be influenced simply by the alleles they're close to. Thus, recombination not only changes the composition of parts of chromosomes but also can affect how some genes act, and slight changes of gene function can become material for natural selection to act on. (The levels of organization in the evolutionary process are summarized in **Table 4-4**.)

TABLE 4.4 Levels of Organization in the Evolutionary Process

Evolutionary Factor	Level	Evolutionary Process	Technique of Study
Mutation	DNA	Storage of genetic information; ability to replicate; influences phenotype by production of proteins	Biochemistry, recombinant DNA
Mutation	Chromosomes	A vehicle for packaging and transmitting genetic material (DNA)	Light or electron microscope
Recombination (sex cells only)	Cell	The basic unit of life that contains the chromosomes and divides for growth and for production of sex cells	Light or electron microscope
Natural selection	Organism	The unit, composed of cells, that reproduces and that we observe for phenotypic traits	Visual study, biochemistry
Drift, gene flow	Population	A group of interbreeding organisms; changes in allele frequencies between generations; it's the population that evolves	Statistical analysis

Natural Selection Is Directional and Acts on Variation

The evolutionary factors just discussed—mutation, gene flow, genetic drift, and recombination—interact to produce variation and to distribute genes within and between populations. But there is no long-term *direction* to any of these factors, and for adaptation and evolution to occur, a population's gene pool needs to change in a specific direction. This means that some alleles must consistently become more common, while others become less common, and natural selection is the one factor that can cause directional change in allele frequency *relative to specific environmental factors*. If the environment changes, then the selection pressures also change, and such a shift in allele frequencies is called *adaptation*. If there are long-term environmental changes in a consistent direction, then allele frequencies should also shift in response to those changes.

In humans, the best-documented example of natural selection involves hemoglobin S (Hb^S), an abnormal form of hemoglobin that results from a point mutation in the gene that produces part of the hemoglobin molecule. As you learned in Chapter 3, if an individual inherits the hemoglobin S (*Hb^S*) allele from both parents, he or she will have sickle-cell anemia. Worldwide, sickle-cell anemia causes an estimated 100,000 deaths each year, and in the United States, approximately 40,000 to 50,000 people, mostly of African descent, have this disease (Ashley-Koch et al., 2000).

The *Hb^S* mutation occurs occasionally in all human populations, but usually the allele is rare. However, in some populations, especially in western and central Africa, it's more common than elsewhere, with frequencies as high as 20 percent. The *Hb^S* allele is also fairly common in parts of Greece and India (**Fig. 4-21**). Given the devastating effects of hemoglobin S in homozygotes, you may wonder why it's so common in some populations. It seems like natural selection would eliminate it, but it doesn't. In fact, natural selection has actually increased its frequency, and the explanation for this situation can be summed up in one word: malaria.

Malaria is a serious infectious disease caused by a single-celled parasitic organism known as *Plasmodium* (its genus name). This parasite is transmitted to humans by mosquitoes, and it kills an estimated 1 to 3 million people worldwide every year. After an infected mosquito bite, plasmodial parasites invade red blood cells, where they obtain the oxygen they need for reproduction (**Fig. 4-22**). The consequences of this infection to the human host include fever, chills, headache, nausea, vomiting, and frequently death. In

▼ **Figure 4-21**
The distribution of the sickle-cell allele in the Old World.

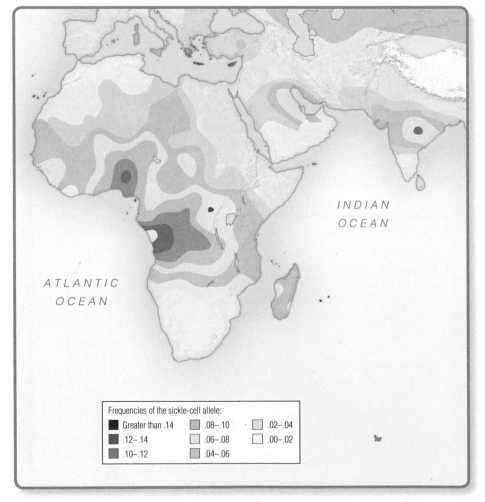

INDIAN OCEAN

ATLANTIC OCEAN

Frequencies of the sickle-cell allele:

■ Greater than .14	.08–.10	.02–.04
■ .12–.14	.06–.08	.00–.02
■ .10–.12	.04–.06	

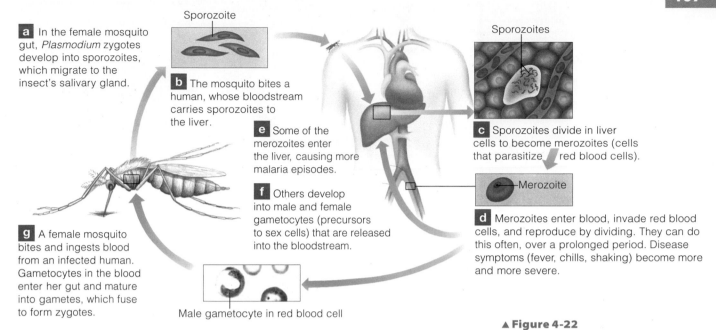

a In the female mosquito gut, *Plasmodium* zygotes develop into sporozoites, which migrate to the insect's salivary gland.

Sporozoite

b The mosquito bites a human, whose bloodstream carries sporozoites to the liver.

e Some of the merozoites enter the liver, causing more malaria episodes.

f Others develop into male and female gametocytes (precursors to sex cells) that are released into the bloodstream.

g A female mosquito bites and ingests blood from an infected human. Gametocytes in the blood enter her gut and mature into gametes, which fuse to form zygotes.

Male gametocyte in red blood cell

Sporozoites

c Sporozoites divide in liver cells to become merozoites (cells that parasitize red blood cells).

Merozoite

d Merozoites enter blood, invade red blood cells, and reproduce by dividing. They can do this often, over a prolonged period. Disease symptoms (fever, chills, shaking) become more and more severe.

▲ **Figure 4-22**
The life cycle of the parasite that causes malaria.

parts of western and central Africa, where malaria is always present, as many as 50 to 75 percent of 2- to 9-year-olds are afflicted.

In the mid-twentieth century, the geographical correlation between malaria and the distribution of the sickle-cell allele (Hb^S) was the only evidence of a biological relationship between the two (Figs. 4-21 and **4-23**). But now we know that people with **sickle-cell trait** have greater resistance to malaria than people with only normal hemoglobin. This is because people with sickle-cell trait have some red blood cells that contain hemoglobin S, and these cells don't provide a suitable environment for the malarial parasite. In other words, having some hemoglobin S is beneficial because it affords some protection from malaria. So, in areas where malaria is present, it acts as a selective agent that favors the heterozygous phenotype, since people with sickle-cell trait have higher net reproductive success than those with only normal hemoglobin, who may die of malaria. But selection for heterozygotes means that the Hb^S allele will be maintained in the population. Thus, there will always be some people with

sickle-cell anemia, and they, of course, have the lowest reproductive success, since without treatment, most die before reaching adulthood.

Review of Genetics and Evolutionary Factors

In this chapter, discussion focused on how genetic information is passed from generation to generation. We also reviewed evolutionary theory, emphasizing the crucial role of natural selection. The different levels (molecular, cellular, individual, and populational) are different components of the evolutionary process, and they're related to each other in a way that can eventually produce evolutionary change. A step-by-step example will make this clear.

Consider a population in which almost everyone has hemoglobin A. For all practical purposes, there's almost no variation regarding this trait, and without some source of new variation, evolution isn't possible. However, in every generation, a few people carry

sickle-cell trait Heterozygous condition where a person has one Hb^A allele and one Hb^S allele. Thus they have some normal hemoglobin.

▶ **Figure 4-23**
The distribution of malaria in the Old World.

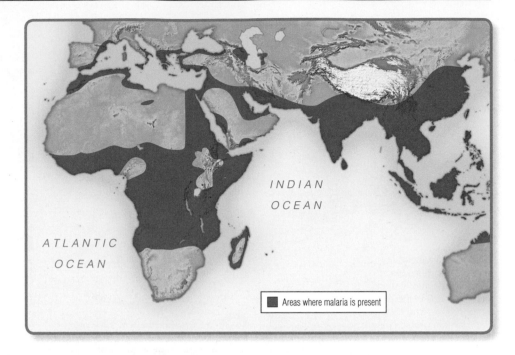

ATLANTIC OCEAN

INDIAN OCEAN

■ Areas where malaria is present

a spontaneous mutation that changes just one DNA base in the *Hb^A* gene. This single base substitution, which actually creates a new allele (*Hb^S*) in the DNA sequence, slightly alters the protein product (the hemoglobin molecule) and ultimately the phenotype of the individual. But for the mutated allele to be passed on to offspring, it must be present in the gametes. Moreover, for a mutation to have any evolutionary potential, it must be transmitted to offspring.

Once a mutation has occurred, it will exist within a chromosome, which, along with other chromosomes, may be inherited by offspring. If a person has the mutation on only one member of a pair of chromosomes, there's a 50-50 chance that the mutation will be passed on to each child he or she has.

But what does all this have to do with evolution? To repeat an earlier definition, evolution is a change in allele frequency in a population from one generation to the next. The key point here is that we are considering populations, because it's the populations that may change over time.

We know if allele frequencies have changed in a population where sickle-cell hemoglobin is found by determining the percentage of individuals with the *Hb^S* allele versus those with the normal allele (*Hb^A*). If the relative proportions of these alleles change with time, the population is evolving at the *Hb^A* locus. But in addition to knowing that evolution is happening, it's important to know why, and there are several possible explanations. First, the only way the new *Hb^S* allele could have arisen is by mutation, and we've shown how this can happen in a single individual. But this isn't an evolutionary change, since in a relatively large population, the alteration of one person's genes won't change the allele frequencies of the entire population. Somehow, this new allele must *spread* in the population; and in the case of *Hb^S*, the allele spread because it was favored by natural selection.

Summary
of Main Topics

- In the mid-nineteenth century, a monk named Gregor Mendel discovered the principles of segregation, independent assortment, and dominance and recessiveness by doing experiments with pea plants. Although the field of genetics progressed dramatically during the twentieth century, the concepts first put forth by Gregor Mendel remain the basis of our current knowledge of how traits are inherited.

- Basic Mendelian principles are applied to the study of the various modes of inheritance we're familiar with today. The most important factor in all the Mendelian modes of inheritance is the role of segregation of chromosomes, and the alleles they carry, during meiosis.

- Building on fundamental nineteenth-century contributions by Charles Darwin and the rediscovery of Mendel's work in 1900, advances in genetics throughout the twentieth century contributed to contemporary evolutionary thought. In particular, the combination of natural selection with Mendel's principles of inheritance and experimental evidence concerning the nature of mutation have all been synthesized into a modern understanding of evolutionary change, appropriately called the Modern Synthesis. In this, the contemporary theory of evolution, evolutionary change is seen as a two-stage process. The first stage is the production and redistribution of variation. The second stage is the process whereby natural selection acts on the accumulated genetic variation.

- Mutation is crucial to all evolutionary change because it's the only source of completely new genetic material (that is, new alleles), which increases variation. In addition, the factors of recombination, genetic drift, and gene flow redistribute variation within individuals (recombination), within populations (genetic drift), and between populations (gene flow).

- Natural selection is the central determining factor that influences the long-term direction of evolutionary change. How natural selection works can best be explained as differential net reproductive success, or how successful individuals are, compared to others, in leaving offspring to succeeding generations. The detailed history of the evolutionary spread of the sickle-cell allele provides the best-documented example of natural selection among recent human populations. It must be remembered that evolution is an integrated process, and this chapter concluded with a discussion of how the various evolutionary factors can be integrated into a single comprehensive view of evolutionary change.

Critical Thinking
Questions

1. If two people with blood type A, both with the *AO* genotype, have children, what *proportion* of their children would be expected to have blood type O? Why? Can these two parents have a child with AB blood? Why or why not?

2. After having read this chapter, do you understand evolutionary processes more completely? What questions do you still have?

3. Sickle-cell anemia is frequently described as affecting only Africans or people of African descent; it's considered a "racial" disease that doesn't affect other populations. How would you explain to someone that this view is wrong?

4. Give some examples of how selection, gene flow, genetic drift, and mutation have acted on populations or species in the past. Try to think of at least one human and one nonhuman example. Why do you think genetic drift might be important today to endangered species?

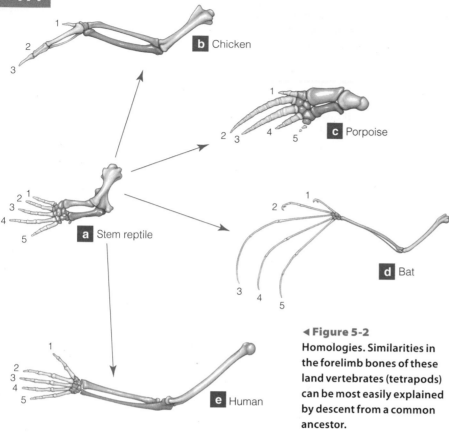

◀ **Figure 5-2**
Homologies. Similarities in the forelimb bones of these land vertebrates (tetrapods) can be most easily explained by descent from a common ancestor.

Structures that are shared by species on the basis of descent from a common ancestor are called **homologies**. Homologies alone are reliable indicators of evolutionary relationship, but we have to be careful not to draw hasty conclusions from superficial similarities. For example, both birds and butterflies have wings, but they shouldn't be grouped together on the basis of this single characteristic; butterflies (as insects) differ dramatically from birds in several other, even more fundamental ways. (For example, birds have an internal skeleton, central nervous system, and four limbs; insects don't.)

Here's what's happened in evolutionary history: From quite distant ancestors, both butterflies and birds have developed wings *independently*. So their (superficial) similarities are a product of separate evolutionary responses to roughly similar functional demands. Such similarities, based on independent functional adaptation and not on shared evolutionary descent, are called **analogies**. The process that leads to the development of analogies (also called analogous structures) such as wings in birds and butterflies is termed **homoplasy**. In the case of butterflies and birds, the homoplasy has occurred in evolutionary lines that share only very remote ancestry. Here, homoplasy has produced analogous structures separately from any homology. In some cases, however, homoplasy can occur in lineages that are more closely related (and share considerable homology as well). Homoplasy in closely related lineages is evident among the primates; for example, New and Old World monkeys show considerable homoplasy, and so do the great apes (see Chapter 6).

Constructing Classifications and Interpreting Evolutionary Relationships

Evolutionary biologists typically use two major approaches, or "schools," when interpreting evolutionary rela-

and Tabin, 1999). A few mutations in certain *Hox* genes in early vertebrates led to the basic limb plan seen in all subsequent vertebrates. With further additional, small mutations in these genes or in the genes they regulate, the varied structures that make up the wing of a chicken, the flipper of a porpoise, or the upper limb of a human developed. You should recognize that *basic* genetic regulatory mechanisms are highly conserved in animals; that is, they've been maintained relatively unchanged for hundreds of millions of years. Like a musical score with a basic theme, small variations on the pattern can produce the different "tunes" that differentiate one organism from another. This is the essential genetic foundation for most macroevolutionary change. Large anatomical modifications, therefore, don't always require major genetic rearrangements (see "New Frontiers in Research" at the end of this chapter).

homologies Similarities between organisms based on descent from a common ancestor.

analogies Similarities between organisms based strictly on common function, with no assumed common evolutionary descent.

homoplasy (*homo*, meaning "same," and *plasy*, meaning "growth") The separate evolutionary development of similar characteristics in different groups of organisms.

tionships with the goal of producing classifications. The first approach, called **evolutionary systematics**, is the more traditional. The second approach, called **cladistics**, has emerged primarily in the last three decades. While aspects of both approaches are still used by most evolutionary biologists, in recent years cladistic methodologies have predominated among anthropologists. Indeed, one noted primate evolutionist commented that "virtually all current studies of primate phylogeny involve the methods and terminology" of cladistics (Fleagle, 1999, p. 1).

Before we begin drawing distinctions between these two approaches, it's first helpful to note features shared by both evolutionary systematics and cladistics. First, both schools are interested in tracing evolutionary relationships and in constructing classifications that reflect these relationships. Second, both schools recognize that organisms must be compared using specific features (called *characters*) and that some of these characters are more informative than others. And third (deriving directly from the previous two points), both approaches focus exclusively on homologies.

But these approaches also have some significant differences—in how characters are chosen, which groups are compared, and how the results are interpreted and eventually incorporated into evolutionary schemes and classifications. The primary difference is that cladistics more explicitly and more rigorously defines the kinds of homologies that yield the most useful information. For example, at a very basic level, all life (except for some viruses) shares DNA as the molecule underlying all organic processes. However, beyond inferring that all life most likely derives from a single origin, the mere presence of DNA tells us nothing further regarding more specific relationships among different kinds of life-forms. To draw further conclusions, we need to look at particular characters that certain groups share as the result of more recent ancestry.

This perspective emphasizes an important point: Some homologous characters are much more informative than others. We saw earlier that all terrestrial vertebrates share homologies in the number and basic arrangement of bones in the forelimb. Even though these similarities are broadly useful in showing that these large evolutionary groups (amphibians, reptiles, and mammals) are all related through a distant ancestor, they don't provide information we can use to distinguish one group from another (a reptile from a mammal, for example). These kinds of characters (also called traits) that are shared through such remote ancestry are said to be **ancestral**, or primitive. We prefer the term *ancestral* because it doesn't reflect negatively on the evolutionary value of the character in question. In biological anthropology, the term *primitive* or *ancestral* simply means that a character seen in two organisms is inherited in both of them from a distant ancestor.

In most cases, analyzing ancestral characters doesn't supply enough information to make accurate evolutionary interpretations of relationships between different groups. In fact, misinterpretation of ancestral characters can easily lead to quite inaccurate evolutionary conclusions. Cladistics focuses on traits that distinguish particular evolutionary lineages; such traits are far more informative than ancestral traits. Lineages that share a common ancestor are called a **clade,** giving the name *cladistics* to the field that seeks to identify and interpret these groups. It is perhaps the most fundamental point of cladistics that evolutionary groups (that is, clades) all share one common ancestor and are thus said to be **monophyletic**. If a proposed evolutionary grouping is found to have more than one ancestor (rather than a single one shared by *all* members), it is said to be **polyphyletic**, and it represents neither a well-defined clade nor an evolutionary group actually separate from other ones. We'll encounter problems of exactly this

evolutionary systematics A traditional approach to classification (and evolutionary interpretation) in which presumed ancestors and descendants are traced in time by analysis of homologous characters.

cladistics An approach to classification that attempts to make rigorous evolutionary interpretations based solely on analysis of certain types of homologous characters (those considered to be derived characters).

ancestral Referring to characters inherited by a group of organisms from a remote ancestor and thus not diagnostic of groups (lineages) that diverged after the character first appeared; also called primitive.

clade A group of organisms sharing a common ancestor. The group includes the common ancestor and all descendants.

monophyletic Referring to an evolutionary group (clade) composed of descendants all sharing a common ancestor.

polyphyletic Referring to an evolutionary group composed of descendants with more than one common ancestor (and thus not a true clade).

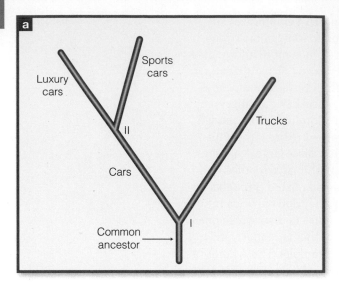
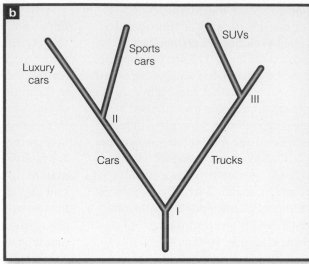

▲ **Figure 5-3**
Evolutionary "trees" showing development of passenger vehicles.

nature in Chapter 6 when we tackle the classification of a small primate called a tarsier as well as that of the great apes.

When we try to identify a clade, the characters of interest are said to be **derived**, or **modified**. Thus, while the general ancestral bony pattern of the forelimb in land vertebrates doesn't allow us to distinguish among them, the further modification of this pattern in certain groups (as hooves, flippers, or wings, for instance) does.

A simplified example might help clarify the basic principles used in cladistic analysis. **Figure 5-3a** shows a hypothetical "lineage" of passenger vehicles. All of the "descendant" vehicles share a common ancestor, the prototype passenger vehicle. The first major division (I) differentiates passenger cars from trucks. The second split (that is, diversification) is between luxury cars and sports cars (you could, of course, imagine many other subcategories). Derived characters that might distinguish trucks from cars could include type of frame, suspension, wheel size, and, in some forms, an open cargo bed. Derived characters that might distinguish sports cars from luxury cars could include engine size and type, wheel base size, and a decorative racing stripe.

Now let's assume that you're presented with an "unknown" vehicle (that

is, one as yet unclassified). How do you decide what kind of vehicle it is? You might note such features as four wheels, a steering wheel, and a seat for the driver, but these are *ancestral* characters (found in the common ancestor) of all passenger vehicles. If, however, you note that the vehicle lacks a cargo bed and raised suspension (so it's not a truck) but has a racing stripe, you might conclude that it's a car, and more than that, a sports car (since it has a derived feature presumably of *only* that group).

All this seems fairly obvious, and you've probably noticed that this simple type of decision making characterizes much of human mental organization. Still, we frequently deal with complications that aren't so obvious. What if you're presented with a sports utility vehicle (SUV) with a racing stripe (**Fig. 5-3b**)? SUVs are basically trucks; the presence of the racing stripe could be seen as a homoplasy with sports cars. The lesson here is that we need to be careful, look at several traits, decide which are ancestral and which are derived, and finally try to recognize the complexity (and confusion) introduced by homoplasy.

Our example of passenger vehicles is useful up to a point. Because it concerns human inventions, the groupings possess characters that humans can add and delete in almost any combination. Naturally occurring organ-

derived (modified) Referring to characters that are modified from the ancestral condition and thus diagnostic of particular evolutionary lineages.

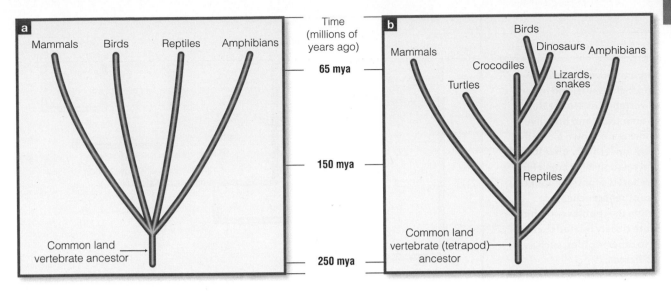

▲ Figure 5-4
Evolutionary relationships of birds and dinosaurs. (a) Traditional view, showing no close relationship. (b) Revised view, showing common ancestry of birds and dinosaurs.

ic systems are more limited in this respect. Any species can possess only those characters that have been inherited from its ancestor or that have been subsequently modified (derived) from those shared with the ancestor. So any modification in *any* species is constrained by that species' evolutionary legacy—that is, what the species starts out with.

Another example, one drawn from paleontological (fossil) evidence of actual organisms, can help clarify these points. Most people know something about dinosaur evolution, and some of you may know about the recent controversies surrounding this topic. There are several intriguing issues concerning the evolutionary history of dinosaurs, and recent fossil discoveries have shed considerable light on them. We'll mention some of these issues later in the chapter, but here we consider one of the more fascinating: the relationship of dinosaurs to birds.

Traditionally, it was thought that birds were a quite distinct group from reptiles and not especially closely related to any of them (including extinct forms, such as the dinosaurs; **Fig. 5-4a**). Still, the early origins of birds were clouded in mystery and have been much debated for more than a century. In fact, the first fossil evidence of a very primitive bird (now known to be about 150 million years

old) was discovered in 1861, just two years following Darwin's publication of *Origin of Species*. Despite some initial and quite remarkably accurate interpretations by Thomas Huxley linking these early birds to dinosaurs, most experts concluded that there was no close relationship. This view persisted through most of the twentieth century, but events of the last two decades have supported the hypothesis that birds *are* closely related to some dinosaurs. Two developments in particular have influenced this change of opinion: the remarkable discoveries in the 1990s from China, Madagascar, and elsewhere and the application of cladistic methods to the interpretation of these and other fossils. (Here is another example of how new discoveries as well as new approaches can become the basis for changing hypotheses.)

Recent finds from Madagascar of chicken-sized, primitive birds dated to 70–65 million years ago (mya) show an elongated second toe (similar, in fact, to that in the dinosaur *Velociraptor*, made infamous in the film *Jurassic Park*). Indeed, these primitive birds from Madagascar show many other similarities to *Velociraptor* and its close cousins, which together comprise a group of small- to medium-sized ground-living, carnivorous dinosaurs called **theropods**. Even more extraordinary finds have been unearthed recently

theropods Small- to medium-sized ground-living dinosaurs, dated to approximately 150 mya and thought to be related to birds.

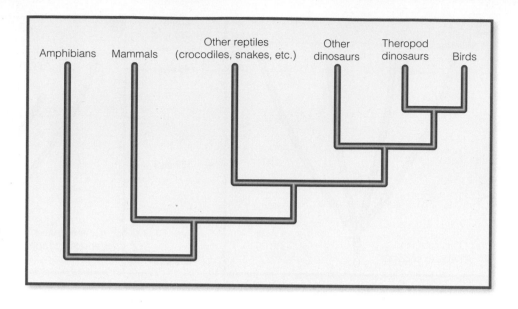

▶ **Figure 5-5**
This cladogram shows the relationships of birds, dinosaurs, and other terrestrial vertebrates. Notice that there's no time scale, and both living and fossil forms are shown along the same dimension—that is, ancestor-descendant relationships aren't indicated. The chart is slightly simplified, as there are other branches (not shown) within the reptiles (with birds slightly more closely related to crocodiles than to other reptiles, such as snakes and lizards).

in China, where the traces of what were once *feathers* have been found embossed in fossilized sediments! For many researchers, these new finds have finally solved the mystery of bird origins (**Fig. 5-4b**), leading them to conclude that "birds are not only *descended* from dinosaurs, they *are* dinosaurs (and reptiles)—just as humans are mammals, even though people are as different from other mammals as birds are from other reptiles" (Padian and Chiappe, 1998, p. 43).

There are some doubters who remain concerned that the presence of feathers in dinosaurs (145–125 mya) might simply be a homoplasy (that is, these creatures may have developed the trait independently from its appearance in birds). Certainly, the possibility of homoplasy must always be considered, as it can add considerably to the complexity of what seems like a straightforward evolutionary interpretation. Indeed, strict cladistic analysis assumes that homoplasy is not a common occurrence; if it were, perhaps no evolutionary interpretation could be very straightforward! In the case of the proposed relationship between some (theropod) dinosaurs and birds, the presence of feathers looks like an excellent example of a **shared derived** characteristic, which therefore *does* link the forms. What's

more, cladistic analysis emphasizes that several characteristics should be examined, since homoplasy might muddle an interpretation based on just one or two shared traits. In the bird/dinosaur case, several other characteristics further suggest their evolutionary relationship.

One last point needs to be mentioned. Traditional evolutionary systematics illustrates the hypothesized evolutionary relationships using a *phylogeny*, more properly called a **phylogenetic tree**. Strict cladistic analysis, however, shows relationships in a **cladogram** (**Fig. 5-5**). If you examine the charts in Figures 5-4 and 5-5, you'll see some obvious differences. A phylogenetic tree incorporates the dimension of time, as shown in Figure 5-4 (you can find many other examples in this and upcoming chapters). A cladogram doesn't indicate time; all forms (fossil and modern) are shown along one dimension. Phylogenetic trees usually attempt to make some hypotheses regarding ancestor-descendant relationships (for example, theropods are ancestral to modern birds). Cladistic analysis (through cladograms) makes no attempt whatsoever to discern ancestor-descendant relationships. In fact, strict cladists are quite skeptical that the evidence really permits such specific evolutionary hypotheses to be

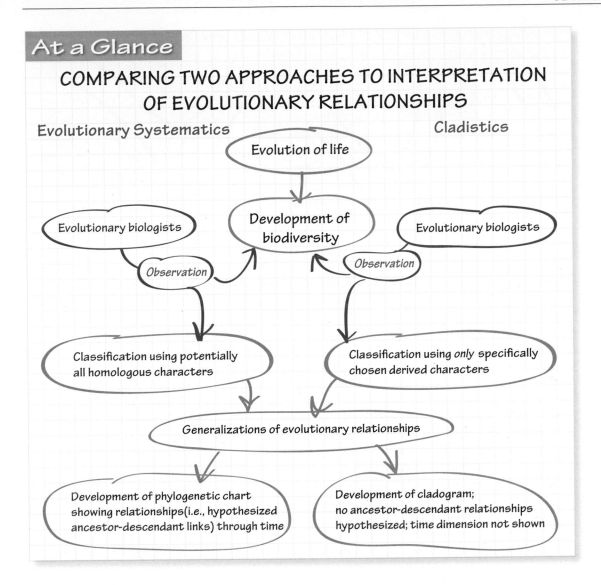

At a Glance

COMPARING TWO APPROACHES TO INTERPRETATION OF EVOLUTIONARY RELATIONSHIPS

Evolutionary Systematics

Cladistics

Evolution of life

Development of biodiversity

Evolutionary biologists

Observation

Evolutionary biologists

Observation

Classification using potentially all homologous characters

Classification using *only* specifically chosen derived characters

Generalizations of evolutionary relationships

Development of phylogenetic chart showing relationships(i.e., hypothesized ancestor-descendant links) through time

Development of cladogram; no ancestor-descendant relationships hypothesized; time dimension not shown

---

scientifically confirmed (since there are many more extinct species than living ones).

In practice, most physical anthropologists (and other evolutionary biologists) utilize cladistic analysis to identify and assess the utility of traits and to make testable hypotheses regarding the relationships between groups of organisms. They also frequently extend this basic cladistic methodology to further hypothesize likely ancestor-descendant relationships shown relative to a time scale (that is, in a phylogenetic tree). In this way, aspects of both traditional evolutionary systematics and cladistic analysis are combined to produce a more complete picture of evolutionary history.

Definition of Species

Whether biologists are doing a cladistic or more traditional phylogenetic analysis, they're comparing groups of organisms—that is, different species, genera (*sing.*, genus), families, orders, and so forth. Fundamental to all these levels of classification is the most basic, the species. It's appropriate, then, to ask how biologists define species. We addressed this issue briefly in Chapter 1, where we used the most common definition, one that emphasizes interbreeding and reproductive isolation. While it's not the only definition of species (others are discussed shortly), this view, called the **biological species concept** (Mayr, 1970), is the one preferred by most zoologists.

biological species concept A depiction of species as groups of individuals capable of fertile interbreeding but reproductively isolated from other such groups.

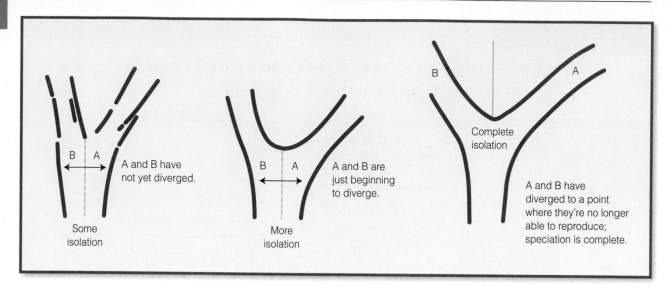

B | A   A and B have not yet diverged.

Some isolation

B | A   A and B are just beginning to diverge.

More isolation

B   A

Complete isolation

A and B have diverged to a point where they're no longer able to reproduce; speciation is complete.

▲ **Figure 5-6**
This speciation model illustrates branching evolution, or cladogenesis, which is caused by increasing reproductive isolation.

speciation The process by which a new species evolves from an earlier species. Speciation is the most basic process in macroevolution.

recognition species concept A depiction of species in which the key aspect is the ability of individuals to identify members of their own species for purposes of mating (and to avoid mating with members of other species). In theory, this type of selective mating is a component of a species concept emphasizing mating and is therefore compatible with the biological species concept.

To understand what species are, you might consider how they come about in the first place—what Darwin called the "origin of species." This most fundamental of macroevolutionary processes is called **speciation**. According to the biological species concept, the way new species are first produced involves some form of isolation. Picture a single species (baboons, for example) composed of several populations distributed over a wide geographical area. Gene exchange between populations (gene flow) will be limited if a geographical barrier, such as an ocean or a large river that changes course, effectively separates these populations. This extremely important form of isolating mechanism is called *geographical isolation.*

If one baboon population (A) is separated from another baboon population (B) by a river that has changed course, individual baboons of population A will not mate with individuals from B (**Fig. 5-6**). As time passes (perhaps hundreds or thousands of generations), genetic differences will accumulate in both populations. If population size is small, we can assume that genetic drift will also cause allele frequencies to change in both populations. And since drift is *random*, we wouldn't expect the effects to be the same. Consequently, the two populations will begin to diverge genetically.

As long as gene exchange is limited, the populations can only become more genetically different over time. What's more, further difference can be expected if the baboon groups are occupying slightly different habitats. These additional genetic differences would be incorporated through the process of natural selection. Certain individuals in population A would be more reproductively fit in their own environment, but they would show less reproductive success in the environment occupied by population B. So allele frequencies will shift further, resulting in even greater divergence between the two groups.

With the cumulative effects of genetic drift and natural selection acting over many generations, the result will be two populations that—even if they were to come back into geographical contact—could no longer interbreed. More than just geographical isolation might now apply. There may, for instance, be behavioral differences that interfere with courtship—what we call *behavioral isolation.* Using our *biological* definition of species, we would now recognize two distinct species where initially only one existed.

Another related process that can contribute to the further differentiation of populations into incipient species concerns mate recognition. This is sometimes called the **recognition**

species concept, though the crucial process, again, concerns reproduction (that is, who's mating with whom; Ridley, 1993).

Assume in our baboon example that some isolation has already occurred and that phenotypic (and genotypic) differences are beginning to be established between two populations. In this situation, coloration patterns of faces or the size, location, coloration, or even smell of the female genital swelling might vary from group to group. If so, then a female from population A might not recognize a male from population B as an appropriate mate (and vice versa, of course). Natural selection would quickly favor such discrimination if hybrids were less reproductively successful than within-population crosses. Indeed, once such "selective breeding" became established, speciation would be accelerated considerably.

Another definition of species focuses primarily on natural selection and emphasizes that speciation is the result of influences of varied habitats. In this view, called the **ecological species concept**, a species is defined as a group of organisms exploiting a single niche. Also called an **ecological niche**, this is the physical as well as biological position of an organism within the biological world (that is, within the full ecosystem).

For each population, the ecological niche will vary slightly, and different phenotypes will be slightly more advantageous in each. For example, one population might be more arboreal and another more terrestrial; but there would not be an intermediate population equally successful on the ground and in the trees.

In recent years, the ecological species concept has attracted support from several evolutionary biologists, especially among physical anthropologists. While the biological species concept emphasizes gene flow and reproductive isolation, the ecological species concept stresses the role of natural selection. Clearly, our approach in this text has been to focus on the evolutionary contribution of natural selection; thus, the ecological species concept has much to offer here. Nevertheless, our understanding of species need not entail an either-or choice between the biological species concept and the ecological species concept. Some population isolation could indeed *begin* the process of speciation, and at this stage, the influence of genetic drift could be crucial. The process might then be further influenced by mate recognition as well as by natural selection as individuals in different populations adapt to varying environments.

A final approach that biologists use to define species is primarily a practical one. How can species be defined when neither reproductive isolation nor ecological separation can be clearly tested? This type of difficulty plagues the interpretation of fossil organisms but sometimes crops up in discussions of contemporary species as well. For example, Colin Groves, of the Australian National University, has recently advocated splitting many populations of primates into separate species (Groves, 2001). He utilizes a definition of species called the **phylogenetic species concept**, based on an identifiable pattern of ancestry (that is, who is *clearly* related to whom).

For living species, characteristics that define a phylogenetic species could be phenotypic or more directly genotypic (as is becoming widely used, ascertaining differences in specific DNA sequences). For extinct groups, with a few notable exceptions (from which ancient DNA has been extracted), the *only* evidence available comes from phenotypic characters that can be identified in fossil forms.

Processes of Speciation

Now that we've seen how species can be defined in somewhat varied ways, what are some of the more explicit theories developed by evolutionary biologists to account for *how* species originate? First, you should recognize that these hypotheses are quite

ecological species concept The concept that a species is a group of organisms exploiting a single niche. This view emphasizes the role of natural selection in separating species from one another.

ecological niche The position of a species within its physical and biological environments. A species' ecological niche is defined by such components as diet, terrain, vegetation, type of predators, relationships with other species, and activity patterns, and each niche is unique to a given species. Together, ecological niches make up an ecosystem.

phylogenetic species concept Splitting many populations into separate species based on an identifiable parental pattern of ancestry.

A Closer Look

Small Changes, Big Impact

The phenomenon of island dwarfing, where body size changes can occur quite rapidly, is well recognized but not well understood. What are the precise mechanisms that cause large-bodied creatures to dwarf while many smaller creatures change in the opposite direction and become much larger in size? This occurrence has been observed and confirmed in a wide variety of animals (reptiles, including birds, and some mammals), but it's only within the past few years that anthropologists have been forced to confront the possibility that humans are not exempt.

The "island rule," as Van Valen (1973) called it, states that due to the unique adaptive pressures of islands, large-bodied vertebrates tend to become smaller over time, and smaller ones become bigger. The effects of the island rule tend to be inverse-ly proportional to the island's size (Heaney, 1978) and positively correlated with the degree of isolation from the mainland (Foster, 1964). So the smaller and more isolated the island, the bigger the size change.

Several mechanisms have been proposed to explain how evolution could produce such physical changes, though the most widely held is the "population and food availability" hypothesis. On islands or in other isolated areas, there's likely to be a decrease in resources due to reduced land area. Fewer animals can be supported by such limited resources, so mammals have fewer young and plants undergo slower growing cycles. Owing to a general absence of large predators, we find a wider array of responses to the environment both within and between species. This variety is often expressed in complex and much-accelerated patterns of body size evolution (Grant, 1982).

Because larger-bodied individuals use more resources, natural selection favors smaller sizes (Lomolino, 2005). Consider the analogy of the pioneers on the Oregon Trail. Most of the survivors who reached the West were women and children and the smaller-bodied men. The large, burly men who would have been expected to "tough it out" were actually the first to succumb to the effects of dwindling food supplies. In isolated areas with finite resources, the selection for smaller individuals over time gives way to an overall smaller-bodied population. Because of their smaller size, a bigger population of these individuals can be maintained given a constant amount of resources (Anderson and Handley, 2002).

Though just hearing the words *elephant* and *mammoth* makes people think of large size, there are many well-known examples of island dwarfing in these vertebrates. British scientist Dorothea Bate (1879–1951) spent a good deal of her paleontological career studying such curiosities. Since she worked and traveled alone in the early twentieth century, she often dressed like a man while excavating previously unheard-of species, such as pygmy hippos, dwarf elephants, and giant dormice (just like

abstract and thus difficult to test doing conventional field biology on contemporary species. Although rates of evolution vary widely among different groups of animals, the process is, by its very nature, a slow one. Some groups, such as fruit flies, members of genus *Drosophila*, seem to speciate especially slowly, taking a million years or more for a new species to be fully separate. The fastest rate of speciation in recent times may have occurred in freshwater fishes. Extreme isolation of cichlid fish populations (of which the angelfish is one of the most familiar forms) has periodically occurred in African lakes, producing "explosive speciation" in just the last few thousand years (Seehausen, 2002). We must emphasize, however, that such extreme isolation has likely never been a factor in the evolution of other vertebrates. Mammals seem to fall somewhere in between the slowly evolving fruit flies and the explosively speciating cichlids. As suggested by fossil evidence, it likely takes tens of thousands of years for speciation to occur in a free-ranging mammalian species.

Given the constraints of field testing such a slowly occurring phenomenon as macroevolution, biologists have hypothesized that speciation can occur in three different ways: by allopatric speciation, parapatric speciation, or sympatric speciation.

By far, the most widely accepted view of speciation emphasizes an **allopatric** pattern. This model requires complete reproductive isolation within a population, leading to

allopatric Living in different areas. The allopatric pattern is important in the divergence of closely related species from each other and from their shared ancestral species because it leads to reproductive isolation.

in *Alice in Wonderland*). Among her finds were mainland Mediterranean elephant populations that had become isolated on the islands of Crete and Cyprus, ultimately becoming dwarfed to only 6 feet tall at the shoulder.

Bate had such a gift for discovering island dwarfed species that one of the museum trustees who supported her wrote, "Only imagine the sensation you would make if you could walk down Piccadilly leading by a string your Pigmy [sic] Elephants, Hippopotami, Myotragus, Tortoises, etc. etc. all in one long queue, the little Elephant blowing his trumpet, and the Hippopotamus wagging its tail" (Shindler, 2006 p. 209).

Though she discovered numerous island curiosi-

ties, Bate would never see many of these animals appropriately placed in their evolutionary family tree because mainland-to-island body size comparisons make little sense without a detailed phylogeny; it's only within such a framework that any pattern can be determined. Such phylogenies are constantly being revised, with some evolutionary lineages only coming to light in recent years.

It's crucial to recognize that both natural selection and genetic drift can become more intense in isolated settings, such as islands, thus accelerating the rate of evolutionary change. Such changes begin at a microevolutionary level; but over time, they may lead to macroevolutionary changes within a lineage, leading to speciation. It's within such a phylogenetic/evolutionary framework that we will be forced to confront an interesting variant within our own genus, *Homo*. In Chapter 14, we'll discuss a provocative find from the island of Flores, in Indonesia, that brings the island rule shockingly close to home.

Drawing by Robert Greisen

◀ **Figure 1**

Scaled representation of the relative sizes of a dwarf elephant, normal hippopotamus, and Indian elephant. Redrawn from Attenborough (1987).

the formation of an incipient species separated (geographically) from its ancestral population.

In parapatric speciation, only *partial* reproductive isolation is required, so that the ranges of the populations may be partially overlapping. In this situation, a hybrid zone would form in an area between the two partially separated populations. More complete separation could then occur through reinforcement of mate recognition and selective breeding.

Interestingly, in some areas of East Africa, there's good evidence that parapatric speciation might be currently (and slowly) taking place between populations of savanna baboons and hamadryas baboons. Long-term research by Jane Phillips-Conroy and Clifford Jolly has care-

fully documented hybrid individuals produced by the mating of savanna baboons with hamadryas baboons. Traditionally, these two types of baboons have been placed in separate species (savanna as *Papio cynocephalus* and hamadryas as *Papio hamadryas*). Yet, the hybrids appear quite functional and are *fertile* (Phillips-Conroy et al., 1992; Jolly, 1993). So, what we're likely seeing here is speciation in process—and probably following a parapatric pattern. This means that we might regard these two types of baboons as incipient species. It's possible that some mate recognition differentiation may be operating as well, since male-female interactions differ considerably between savanna and hamadryas baboons.

The third type of speciation proposed, sympatric speciation, is theorized to occur completely within one population with *no* necessary reproductive isolation. In other words, two species result from one population that occupies the same geographical locality. However, this form of speciation, while possible, is not well supported by contemporary evidence and is thus considered the least significant of the three models.

A fourth type of speciation, sometimes recognized as a form of sympatric speciation, is called *instantaneous speciation*. In this pattern, chromosomal rearrangements occur (by chromosomal mutation), producing immediate reproductive barriers. This type of speciation, well documented in plants, can be rapid, and varieties can emerge with completely different numbers of chromosomes. Here, the process is one of multiplication of chromosome sets (due to mistakes in meiosis), producing a condition called *polyploidy* (the presence of more than two complete sets of chromosomes in an individual). While common in plants, such drastic reorganization of chromosome number is not a factor in the speciation of animals, where polyploidy is always lethal. However, somewhat less dramatic chromosomal alterations could accelerate speciation in animals. Certainly, chromosomal alterations may be important in speciation, and some researchers have even suggested that such processes may be a central factor in macroevolution.

Even so, demonstration in animals of the systematic influence of such large-scale mutation has been difficult. In fact, theoretical models suggest that major mutational change could not *by itself* produce speciation in animals, but would require some further mechanism to help "fix" the genetic changes within populations. Inbreeding within small population segments has been suggested by some investigators as a possible mechanism that could reinforce rapid speciation by chromosomal mutation.

Interpreting Species and Other Groups in the Fossil Record

Throughout much of this text, we'll be using various taxonomic terms for fossil primates (including fossil hominins). You'll be introduced to such terms as *Proconsul, Sivapithecus, Australopithecus*, and *Homo*. Of course, *Homo* is still a living primate. But it's especially difficult to make these types of designations from remains of animals that are long dead (and only partially preserved as skeletal remains). In these contexts, what do such names mean in evolutionary terms?

Our goal when applying species, genus, or other taxonomic labels to groups of organisms is to make meaningful biological statements about the variation that's represented. When looking at populations of living or long-extinct animals, we certainly are going to see variation; this happens in *any* sexually reproducing organism due to recombination (see Chapter 3). As a result of recombination, each individual organism is a unique combination of genetic material, and the uniqueness is often reflected to some extent in the phenotype.

Besides such *individual variation*, we see other kinds of systematic variation in all biological populations. *Age changes* alter overall body size, as well as shape, in many mammals. One pertinent example for fossil human and ape studies is the change in number, size, and shape of teeth from deciduous teeth, also known as baby or milk teeth (only 20 teeth are present), to the permanent dentition (32 are present). It would be an obvious error to differentiate two fossil forms based solely on such age-dependent criteria. If one individual were represented just by milk teeth and another (seemingly very different) individual were represented just by adult teeth, they easily could be different-aged individuals from the *same* population. Variation due to sex also plays an important role.

Differences in physical characteristics between males and females of the same species, called **sexual dimorphism**, can result in marked variation in body size and proportions in adults of the same species (we'll discuss this important topic in more detail in Chapter 6).

Recognition of Fossil Species Keeping in mind all the types of variation present within interbreeding groups of organisms, the minimum biological category we'd like to define in fossil primate samples is the *species*. As already defined (according to the biological species concept), a species is a group of interbreeding or potentially interbreeding organisms that is reproductively isolated from other such groups. In modern organisms, this concept is theoretically testable by observations of reproductive behavior. In animals long extinct, such observations are obviously impossible. Our only way, then, of getting a handle on the variation we see in fossil groups is to refer to living animals.

When studying a fossil group, we may observe obvious variation, such as some individuals being larger and with bigger teeth than others. The question then becomes: What is the biological significance of this variation? Two possibilities come to mind. Either the variation is accounted for by individual, age, and sex differences seen *within* every biological species (that is, it is **intraspecific**), or the variation represents differences *between* reproductively isolated groups (that is, it is **interspecific**). How do we decide which answer is correct? To do this, we have to look at contemporary species.

If the amount of morphological variation we observe in fossil samples is comparable to that seen today *within species of closely related forms*, then we shouldn't "split" our sample into more than one species. We must, however, be careful in choosing modern analogues, because rates of morphological evolution vary among different groups of mammals. So, for example, when studying extinct fossil primates,

we need to compare them with well-known modern primates. Even so, studies of living groups have shown that defining exactly where species boundaries begin and end is often difficult. In dealing with extinct species, the uncertainties are even greater. In addition to the overlapping patterns of variation *spatially* (over space), variation also occurs *temporally* (through time). In other words, even more variation will be seen in **paleospecies**, since individuals may be separated by thousands or even millions of years. Applying strict Linnaean taxonomy to such a situation presents an unavoidable dilemma. Standard Linnaean classification, designed to take account of variation present at any given time, describes a static situation. But when we deal with paleospecies, the time frame is expanded and the situation can be dynamic (that is, later forms might be different from earlier forms). In such a dynamic situation, taxonomic decisions (where to draw species boundaries) are ultimately going to be somewhat arbitrary.

Because the task of interpreting paleospecies is so difficult, paleoanthropologists have sought various solutions. Most researchers today define species using clusters of derived traits (identified cladistically). But owing to the ambiguity of how many derived characters are required to identify a fully distinct species (as opposed to a subspecies), the frequent mixing of characters into novel combinations, and the always difficult problem of homoplasy, there continues to be disagreement. A good deal of the dispute is driven by philosophical orientation. Exactly how much diversity should one expect among fossil primates, especially among fossil hominins?

Some researchers, called "splitters," claim that speciation occurred frequently during hominin evolution, and they often identify numerous fossil hominin species in a sample being studied. As the nickname suggests, these scientists are inclined to split groups into many species. Others,

sexual dimorphism Differences in physical characteristics between males and females of the same species. For example, humans are slightly sexually dimorphic for body size, with males being taller, on average, than females of the same population. Sexual dimorphism is very pronounced in many species, such as gorillas.

intraspecific Within species; refers to variation seen within the same species.

interspecific Between species; refers to variation beyond that seen within the same species to include additional aspects seen between two different species.

paleospecies Species defined from fossil evidence, often covering a long time span.

called "lumpers," assume that speciation was less common and see much variation as being intraspecific. These scientists lump groups together, so that fewer hominin species are identified, named, and eventually plugged into evolutionary schemes. As you'll see in the following chapters, debates of this sort pervade paleoanthropology, perhaps more than in any other branch of evolutionary biology.

Recognition of Fossil Genera The next and broader level of taxonomic classification, the **genus** (*pl.*, genera), presents another problem. To have more than one genus, we obviously must have at least two species (reproductively isolated groups), and the species of one genus must differ in a basic way from the species of another genus. A genus is therefore defined as a group of species composed of members more closely related to each other than they are to species from any other genus.

Grouping species into genera can be quite subjective and is often much debated by biologists. One possible test for contemporary animals is to check for results of hybridization between individuals of different species—rare in nature, but quite common in captivity. If members of two normally separate species interbreed and produce live (though not necessarily fertile) offspring, the two parental species probably are not too different genetically and should therefore be grouped in the same genus. A well-known example of such a cross is horses with donkeys (*Equus caballus* × *Equus asinus*), which normally produces live but sterile offspring (mules).

As previously mentioned, we can't perform breeding experiments with extinct animals, which is why another definition of genus becomes highly relevant. Species that are members of the same genus share the same broad adaptive zone. An adaptive zone represents a general ecological lifestyle more basic than the narrower ecological niches characteristic of individual species. This ecological definition of genus

can be an immense aid in interpreting fossil primates. Teeth are the most frequently preserved parts, and they often can provide excellent general ecological inferences. Cladistic analysis also helps scientists to make judgments about evolutionary relationships. That is, members of the same genus should all share derived characters not seen in members of other genera.

As a final comment, we should stress that classification by genus is not always a straightforward decision. For instance, in emphasizing the very close genetic similarities between humans (*Homo sapiens*) and chimpanzees (*Pan troglodytes*), some current researchers (Wildman et al., 2003) place both in the same genus (*Homo sapiens*, *Homo troglodytes*). This philosophy has caused some to advocate for extension of basic human rights to great apes (as proposed by members of the Great Ape Project). Such thinking might startle you. Of course, when it gets this close to home, it's often difficult to remain objective!

What Are Fossils and How Do They Form?

Much of what we know about the history of life comes from studying **fossils**. Fossils are traces of ancient organisms and can be formed in many ways. The oldest fossils found thus far date back to more than 3 billion years ago; because they are the remains of microorganisms, they are extremely small and are called *microfossils*.

These very early traces of life are fragile and very rare. Most of our evidence comes from later in time and usually in the form of pieces of shells, bones, or teeth, all of which, even in a living animal, were already partly made of mineral, giving them a head start in the fossilization process. After the organism died, these "hard" tissues were further impregnated with other minerals, being eventually transformed into a stone-like composition

genus (*pl.*, genera) A group of closely related species.

fossils Traces or remnants of organisms found in geological beds on the earth's surface.

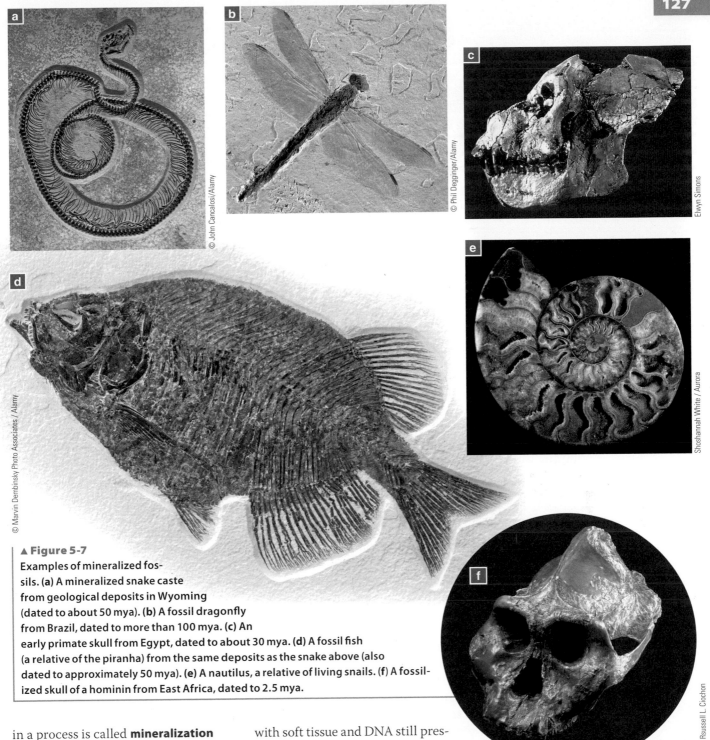

▲ **Figure 5-7**
Examples of mineralized fossils. **(a)** A mineralized snake caste from geological deposits in Wyoming (dated to about 50 mya). **(b)** A fossil dragonfly from Brazil, dated to more than 100 mya. **(c)** An early primate skull from Egypt, dated to about 30 mya. **(d)** A fossil fish (a relative of the piranha) from the same deposits as the snake above (also dated to approximately 50 mya). **(e)** A nautilus, a relative of living snails. **(f)** A fossilized skull of a hominin from East Africa, dated to 2.5 mya.

in a process is called **mineralization** (**Fig. 5-7**).

There are, however, many other ways in which life-forms have left traces of their existence. Sometimes insects were trapped in tree sap, which later became hardened and chemically altered. Because there was little or no oxygen inside the hardened amber, the insects have remained remarkably well preserved for millions of years, even

with soft tissue and DNA still present (**Fig. 5-8**). This fascinating circumstance led author Michael Crichton to conjure the events depicted in the novel (and motion picture) *Jurassic Park*.

Dinosaur footprints as well as much more recent hominin tracks, leaf imprints in hardened mud or similar impressions of small organisms, and even the traces of dinosaur feathers—all of these are fossils.

mineralization The process in which parts of animals (or some plants) become transformed into stone-like structures. Mineralization usually occurs very slowly as water carrying minerals, such as silica or iron, seeps into the tiny spaces within a bone. In some cases, the original minerals within the bone or tooth can be completely replaced, molecule by molecule, with other minerals.

▲ **Figure 5-8**
A spider fossilized in amber.

Recently, beautifully preserved theropod dinosaur feathers have been discovered in northeastern China (dated to approximately 125 mya). These remains are so superbly preserved that even microscopic cell structures have been indentified. These tiny structures directly influenced feather color in ancient dinosaurs; what's more, these same structures influence feather color in modern birds. Researchers are now able to deduce that some stripes in the feathers of one dinosaur were chestnut/reddish brown in color (Zhang et al., 2010)!

In 2009, the spectacular discovery of a 47-million-year-old early primate fossil known to the public as "Ida" burst onto the media scene. Touted first as a "missing link," the true significance of this fossil lies in its remarkable preservation. More than 95 percent of the skeleton is preserved as well as outlines of soft tissue and even the fossilized remains of Ida's last meal within the digestive tract (see Chapter 9; Franzen et al., 2009). The amazing preservation of this small primate occurred because it died on the edge of a volcanic lake in Messel, Germany, and was quickly covered with sediment. It reminds us that whether a dead animal will become fossilized and how much of it will be preserved depends to a great degree on where it dies.

Some ancient organisms have left vast amounts of fossil remains. Indeed, limestone deposits can be hundreds of feet thick and are largely made up of fossilized remains of marine shellfish (see Chapter 2). However, fossils of land animals are not nearly so common. After an animal dies—let's say it's an early hominin from 2 mya—it will probably be eaten and its bones scattered and broken, and eventually they will decompose. After just a few weeks, there will be hardly anything left to fossilize. But suppose, by chance, this recently deceased hominin became quickly covered by sediment, perhaps by sand and mud in a streambed or along a lakeshore or by volcanic ash from a nearby volcano, as Ida did. As a result, the long, slow process of mineralization may eventually turn at least some parts of the hominin into a fossil.

The study of how bones and other materials come to be buried in the earth and preserved as fossils is called **taphonomy** (from the Greek *taphos*, meaning "study of the grave"). Such studies focus on everything that happens to an organism once it has died, making it the life history of the dead, so to speak. Among the topics that taphonomists try to understand are processes of sedimentation and burial, including the action of streams, preservation properties of bone, and carnivore disturbance factors.

Vertebrate Evolutionary History: A Brief Summary

Besides the staggering array of living and extinct life-forms, biologists must also contend with the vast amount of time that life has been evolving on earth. Again, scientists have devised simplified schemes—but in this case to organize *time*, not biological diversity.

Geologists have formulated the **geological time scale** (Fig. 5-9), in which very large time spans are organized into eras that include one or

taphonomy The study of how bones and other materials come to be buried in the earth and preserved as fossils.

geological time scale The organization of earth history into eras, periods, and epochs; commonly used by geologists and paleoanthropologists.

Kazuo Unno / Minden Pictures

▼ **Figure 5-9**
Geological time scale.

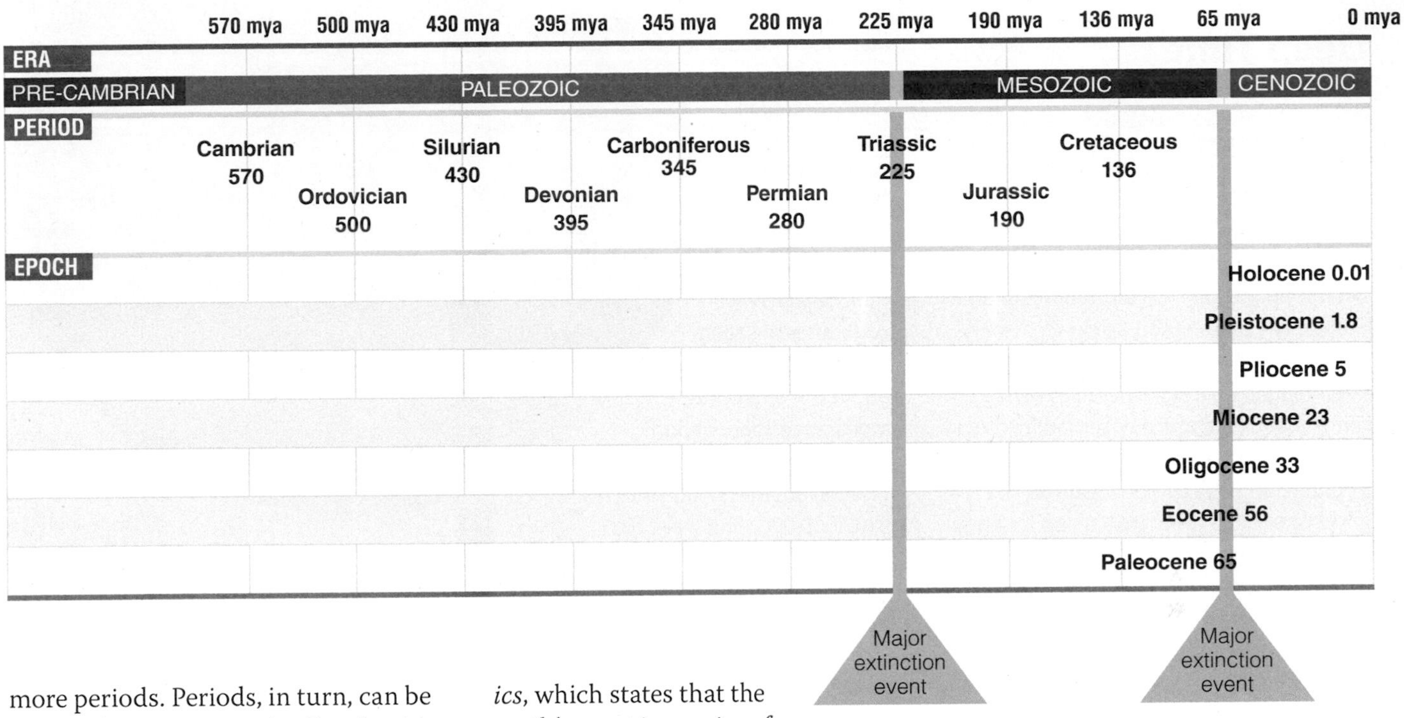

	570 mya	500 mya	430 mya	395 mya	345 mya	280 mya	225 mya	190 mya	136 mya	65 mya	0 mya
ERA											
	PRE-CAMBRIAN		PALEOZOIC					MESOZOIC		CENOZOIC	
PERIOD	Cambrian 570	Ordovician 500	Silurian 430	Devonian 395	Carboniferous 345	Permian 280	Triassic 225	Jurassic 190	Cretaceous 136		
EPOCH											Holocene 0.01
											Pleistocene 1.8
											Pliocene 5
											Miocene 23
											Oligocene 33
											Eocene 56
											Paleocene 65

Major extinction event (at Triassic/Permian boundary, ~225 mya)

Major extinction event (at ~65 mya)

more periods. Periods, in turn, can be broken down into epochs. For the time span encompassing vertebrate evolution, there are three eras: the Paleozoic, the Mesozoic, and the Cenozoic. The first vertebrates are present in the fossil record dating to early in the Paleozoic at 500 mya, and their origins are probably much older. It's the vertebrates' capacity to form bone that accounts for their more complete fossil record *after* 500 mya.

During the Paleozoic, several varieties of fishes (including the ancestors of modern sharks and bony fishes), amphibians, and reptiles appeared. At the end of the Paleozoic, close to 250 mya, several varieties of mammal-like reptiles were also diversifying. It's generally thought that some of these forms ultimately gave rise to the mammals.

The evolutionary history of vertebrates and other organisms during the Paleozoic and Mesozoic was profoundly influenced by geographical events. We know that the positions of the earth's continents have dramatically shifted during the last several hundred million years. This process, called **continental drift**, is explained by the geological theory of *plate tecton-*ics, which states that the earth's crust is a series of gigantic moving and colliding plates. Such massive geological movements can induce volcanic activity (as, for example, all around the Pacific Rim), mountain building (for example, the Himalayas), and earthquakes. Living on the juncture of the Pacific and North American plates, residents of the Pacific coast of the United States are acutely aware of some of these consequences, as illustrated by the explosive volcanic eruption of Mt. St. Helens and the frequent earthquakes in Alaska and California.

While reconstructing the earth's physical history, geologists have determined the earlier, much altered, positions of major continental landmasses. During the late Paleozoic, the continents came together to form a single colossal landmass called *Pangea*. (In reality, the continents had been drifting on plates, coming together and separating, long before the end of the Paleozoic around 225 mya.) During the early Mesozoic, the southern continents (South America, Africa, Antarctica, Australia, and India) began to split off from Pangea, forming a large southern continent

continental drift The movement of continents on sliding plates of the earth's surface. As a result, the positions of large landmasses have shifted drastically during the earth's history.

A Closer Look

Deep Time

The vast expanse of time during which evolution has occurred on earth staggers the imagination. Indeed, this fundamental notion of what John McPhee has termed "deep time" is not really understood or, in fact, widely believed. Of course, as we've emphasized beginning in Chapter 1, *belief*, as such, is not part of science. But observation, theory building, and testing are. Still, in a world populated mostly by nonscientists, the concept of deep time, crucial as it is to geology and anthropology, is resisted by many people. This situation really isn't surprising; the very notion of deep time is in many ways counterintuitive. Human beings tend to measure their existence in months, years, and the span of human lifetimes.

But what are these durations, measured against geological or galactic phenomena? In a real sense, these vast time expanses are beyond human comprehension. We can reasonably fathom the reaches of human history stretching to about 5,000 years ago. In a leap of imagination, we can perhaps even begin to grasp the stretch of time back to the cave painters of France and Spain, approximately 17,000 to 25,000 years ago. How do we relate, then, to a temporal span that's 10 times this one, back to 250,000 years ago, about the time of the earliest *Homo sapiens*—or to 10 times this span to 2,500,000 years ago (about the time of the appearance of our genus, *Homo*)? And multiply this last duration another 1,000 times (to 2,500,000,000), and we're back to a time of fairly early life-forms. And we'd have to reach still further into earth's past, another 1.5 billion years, to approach the *earliest* documented life.

The dimensions of these intervals are humbling, to say the least. The discovery in the nineteenth century of deep time (see Chapter 2), what the late Stephen Jay Gould called "geology's greatest contribution to human thought," plunged one more dagger into humanity's long-cherished view of itself as something special. Astronomers had previously established how puny our world

▲ **Figure 1**

Geological exposures at the Grand Canyon. Some of the sediments are almost 2 billion years old and have been cut through by the Colorado River over the last 6 million years.

was in the physical expanse of space, and then geologists showed that even on our own small planet, we were but residues dwarfed within a river of time "without a vestige of a beginning or prospect of an end" (from James Hutton, a founder of modern geology and one of the discoverers of deep time). It's no wonder that people resist the concept of deep time; it not only stupefies our reason, but implies a sense of collective meaninglessness and reinforces our individual mortality. Geologists, astronomers, and other scholars have struggled for over

called *Gondwanaland* (**Fig. 5-10a**). Similarly, the northern continents (North America, Greenland, Europe, and Asia) were consolidated into a northern landmass called *Laurasia*. During the Mesozoic, Gondwanaland and Laurasia continued to drift apart and to break up into smaller segments. By the end of the Mesozoic (about 65 mya), the continents were beginning to assume their current positions (**Fig. 5-10b**).

The evolutionary ramifications of this long-term continental drift were profound. Groups of animals became effectively isolated from each other by oceans, significantly influenc-ing the distribution of mammals and other land vertebrates. These continental movements continued in the Cenozoic and indeed are still happening, although without such dramatic results.

During most of the Mesozoic, reptiles were the dominant land vertebrates, and they exhibited a broad expansion into a variety of *ecological niches*, which included aerial and marine habitats. The most famous of these highly successful Mesozoic reptiles were the dinosaurs, which themselves evolved into a wide array of sizes and species and adapted to a variety of lifestyles. Dinosaur paleontology, never

a century, with modest success, to translate the tales told in rocks and hurtling stars in terms that everyone can understand. Various analogies have been attempted—metaphors, really—drawn from common experience. Among the most successful of these attempts is a "cosmic calendar" devised by eminent astronomer Carl Sagan in his book *Dragons of Eden* (1977). In this version of time's immensity, Sagan likens the passage of geological time to that of one calendar year. The year begins on January 1 with the Big Bang, the cosmic explosion marking the beginning of the universe and the beginning of time. In this version, the Big Bang is set at 15 billion years ago,* with some of the major events in the geological past as follows:

Time Unit Conversion Using the Cosmic Calendar

1 year = 15,000,000,000 years	1 hour = 1,740,000 years		
1 month = 1,250,000,000 years	1 minute = 29,000 years		*December 31 Events*
1 day = 41,000,000 years	1 second = 475 years	Appearance of early hominoids (apes and humans)	12:30 P.M.

Big Bang	January 1	
Formation of the earth	September 14	
Origin of life on earth (approx.)	September 25	
Significant oxygen atmosphere begins to develop	December 1	
Precambrian ends; Paleozoic begins; invertebrates flourish	December 17	
Paleozoic ends and Mesozoic begins	December 25	
Cretaceous period: first flowers; dinosaurs become extinct	December 28	
Mesozoic ends; Cenozoic begins; adaptive radiation of placental mammals	December 29	

First hominins	9:30 P.M.
Extensive cave painting in Europe	11:59 P.M.
Invention of agriculture	11:59:20 P.M.
Renaissance in Europe; Ming dynasty in China; emergence of scientific method	11:59:59 P.M.
Widespread development of science and technology; emergence of a global culture; first steps in space exploration; mass extinctions caused by humans	NOW: the first second of the New Year

* Recent evidence gathered by the Hubble Space Telescope has questioned the established date for the Big Bang. However, even the most recent data are somewhat contradictory, suggesting a date from as early as 16 billion years ago (indicated by the age of the oldest stars) to as recent as 8 billion years ago (indicated by the rate of expansion of the universe). Here we'll follow the conventional dating of 15 billion years; if you apply the most conservative approximation (8 billion years), the calibrations shift as follows: 1 day = 22,000,000 years; 1 hour = 913,000 years; 1 minute = 15,000 years. Using these calculations, for example, the first hominins appear on December 31 at 7:37 p.m., and modern humans (*Homo sapiens*) are on the scene at 11:42 p.m.

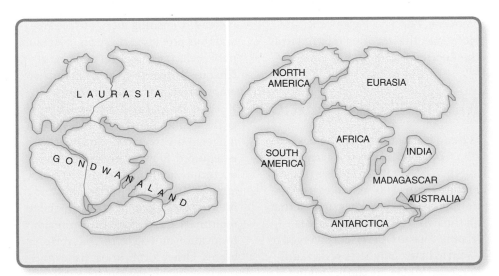

◄ **Figure 5-10**
Continental drift. (a) Positions of the continents during the Mesozoic (ca. 125 mya). Pangea is breaking up into a northern landmass (Laurasia) and a southern landmass (Gondwanaland). **(b)** Positions of the continents at the beginning of the Cenozoic (ca. 65 mya).

a

b

570 mya	500 mya	430 mya	395 mya	345 mya
ERA				
				PALEOZOIC
PERIOD				
Cambrian	**Ordovician**	**Silurian**	**Devonian**	**Carboniferous**
Trilobites abundant; also brachiopods, jellyfish, worms, and other invertebrates	First fishes; trilobites still abundant; graptolites and corals become plentiful; possible land plants	Jawed fishes appear; first air-breathing animals; definite land plants	Age of Fishes; first amphibians and first forests appear	First reptiles; radiation of amphibians; modern insects diversify

▲ **Figure 5-11**

This time line depicts major events in early vertebrate evolution.

a boring field, has advanced several startling notions in recent years: that many dinosaurs were "warm-blooded"; that some varieties were quite social and probably also engaged in considerable parental care; that many forms became extinct because of major climate changes to the earth's atmosphere from collisions with comets or asteroids; and finally, that not all dinosaurs became entirely extinct and have many descendants still living today (that is, all modern birds). (See **Fig. 5-11** for a summary of major events in early vertebrate evolutionary history.)

The Cenozoic is divided into two periods, the Tertiary (about 63 million years duration) and the Quaternary, from about 1.8 mya up to and including the present (see Fig. 5-9). Paleontologists often refer to the next, more precise level of subdivision within the Cenozoic as the **epochs**. There are seven epochs within the Cenozoic: the Paleocene, Eocene, Oligocene, Miocene, Pliocene, Pleistocene, and Holocene, the last often referred to as the Recent epoch.

Mammalian Evolution

We can learn about mammalian evolution from fossils as well as from studying the DNA of living species (Bininda-Emonds et al., 2007). Studies using both of these approaches suggest that all the living groups of mammals (that is, all the orders) had diverged by 75 mya. Later, only after several million years following the beginning of the Cenozoic, did the various current

mammalian subgroups (that is, the particular families) begin to diversify.

Today, there are over 4,000 species of mammals, and we could call the Cenozoic the Age of Mammals. It is during this era that, along with birds, mammals replaced earlier reptiles as the dominant land-living vertebrates.

How do we account for the relatively rapid success of the mammals during the late Mesozoic and early Cenozoic? Several characteristics relating to learning and general flexibility of behavior are of prime importance. Mammals were selected for larger brains than those typically found in reptiles, making them better equipped to process information. In particular, the cerebrum became generally enlarged, especially the outer covering, the **neocortex**, which controls higher brain functions (**Fig. 5-12**). In some mammals, the cerebrum expanded so much that it came to comprise most of the brain volume; the number of surface convolutions also increased, creating more surface area and thus providing space for even more nerve cells (neurons). As we'll see in Chapter 8, this is a trend even further emphasized among the primates.

For such a large and complex organ as the mammalian brain to develop, a longer, more intense period of growth is required. Slower development can occur internally (*in utero*) as well as after birth. Internal fertilization and internal development aren't unique to mammals, but the latter was a major innovation among terrestrial vertebrates. Other forms (most fishes and reptiles—including birds) lay eggs, and "prenatal" development occurs

epochs Categories of the geological time scale; subdivisions of periods. In the Cenozoic era, epochs include the Paleocene, Eocene, Oligocene, Miocene, and Pliocene (from the Tertiary Period) and the Pleistocene and Holocene (from the Quaternary Period).

neocortex The more recently evolved portions of the cortex of the brain that are involved with higher mental functions and composed of areas that integrate incoming information from different sensory organs.

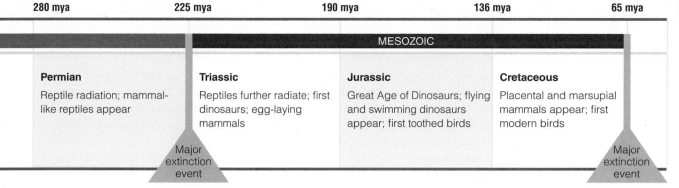

280 mya	225 mya	190 mya	136 mya	65 mya
		MESOZOIC		
Permian	**Triassic**	**Jurassic**	**Cretaceous**	
Reptile radiation; mammal-like reptiles appear	Reptiles further radiate; first dinosaurs; egg-laying mammals	Great Age of Dinosaurs; flying and swimming dinosaurs appear; first toothed birds	Placental and marsupial mammals appear; first modern birds	

Major extinction event

Major extinction event

externally, outside the mother's body. Mammals, with very few exceptions, give birth to live young. Even among mammals, however, there's considerable variation among the major groups in how mature the young are at birth; and in **placental** mammals, including ourselves, *in utero* development goes farthest.

Another distinctive feature of mammals is the dentition. While many living reptiles (such as lizards and snakes) consistently have similarly shaped teeth (called a *homodont* dentition), mammals have differently shaped teeth (**Fig. 5-13**). This varied pattern, termed a **heterodont** dentition, is reflected in the ancestral (primitive) mammalian arrangement of teeth, which includes 3 incisors, 1 canine, 4 premolars, and 3 molars in each quarter of the mouth. So, with 11 teeth in each quarter of the mouth, the ancestral mammalian dental complement includes a total of 44 teeth. Such a heterodont arrangement allows mammals to process a wide variety of foods. Incisors are used for cutting, canines for grasping and piercing, and premolars and molars for crushing and grinding.

A final point regarding teeth relates to their disproportionate representation in the fossil record. As the hardest, most durable portion of a vertebrate skeleton, teeth have the greatest likelihood of becoming fossilized (that is, mineralized), since teeth are predominantly composed of mineral to begin with. As a result, the vast majority of available fossil data for most vertebrates, including primates, consists of teeth.

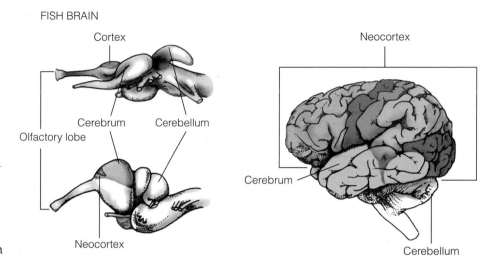

▲ **Figure 5-12**
Lateral view of the brain in fishes, reptiles, and primates. You can see the increased size of the cerebral cortex (neocortex) of the primate brain. The cerebral cortex integrates sensory information and selects responses.

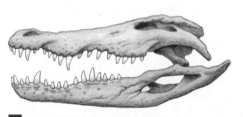

a REPTILIAN (alligator): homodont

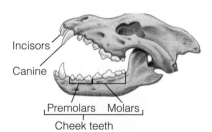

b MAMMALIAN: heterodont

▲ **Figure 5-13**
Reptilian and mammalian teeth.

Another major adaptive complex that distinguishes contemporary mammals from reptiles (except birds) is the maintenance of a constant internal body temperature. Known colloquially (and incorrectly) as warm-bloodedness, this crucial physiological adaptation is also seen in contemporary birds and may have characterized many

placental A type (subclass) of mammal. During the Cenozoic, placentals became the most widespread and numerous mammals and today are represented by upward of 20 orders, including the primates.

heterodont Having different kinds of teeth; characteristic of mammals, whose teeth consist of incisors, canines, premolars, and molars.

dinosaurs as well. Except for birds, reptiles maintain a constant internal body temperature through exposure to the sun; these reptiles are said to be *ecto-thermic*. In mammals and birds, however, energy is generated *internally* through metabolic activity (by processing food or by muscle action); for this reason, mammals and birds are said to be **endothermic**.

The Emergence of Major Mammalian Groups

There are three major subgroups of living mammals: the egg-laying mammals, or monotremes; the pouched mammals, or marsupials; and the placental mammals. The monotremes, of which the platypus is one example (**Fig. 5-14**), are extremely primitive and are considered more distinct from marsupials or placentals than these two subgroups are from each other. The recent sequencing of the full genome of the platypus

(Warren et al., 2008) has confirmed the very ancient orgins of the monotremes and their distinctiveness from other mammals.

The most notable difference between marsupials and placentals concerns fetal development. In marsupials, the young are born extremely immature and must complete development in an external pouch (**Fig. 5-15**). But placental mammals develop over a longer period of time *in utero*, made possible by the evolutionary development of a specialized tissue (the placenta) that provides for fetal nourishment.

With a longer gestation period, the central nervous system develops more completely in the placental fetus. What's more, after birth, the "bond of milk" between mother and young allows more time for complex neural structures to form. We should also emphasize that from a *biosocial* perspective, this dependency period not only allows for adequate physiological development but also provides for a wider range of learning stimuli. That is, a vast amount of information is channeled to the young mammalian brain through observation of the mother's behavior and through play with agemates. It's not enough to have evolved a brain capable of learning. Collateral evolution of mammalian social systems has ensured that young mammal brains are provided with ample learning opportunities and are thus put to good use.

Processes of Macroevolution

As we noted earlier, evolution operates at both microevolutionary and macroevolutionary levels. We discussed evolution primarily from a microevolutionary perspective in Chapter 4; in this chapter, our focus is on macroevolution. Macroevolutionary mechanisms operate more on the whole species than on individuals or populations, and they take much longer than

▲ **Figure 5-14**
A duck-billed platypus (monotreme).

© Tom McHugh / Photo Researchers, Inc.

▲ **Figure 5-15**
A wallaby with an infant in the pouch (marsupials).

© iStockphoto.com / Michael Sacco

endothermic (*endo*, meaning "within" or "internal") Able to maintain internal body temperature by producing energy through metabolic processes within cells; characteristic of mammals, birds, and perhaps some dinosaurs.

microevolutionary processes to have a noticeable impact.

Adaptive Radiation

As we mentioned in Chapter 2, the potential capacity of a group of organisms to multiply is practically unlimited, but its ability to increase its numbers is regulated largely by the availability of resources (food, water, shelter, mates, and space). As population size increases, access to resources decreases, and the environment will ultimately prove inadequate. Depleted resources induce some members of a population to seek an environment in which competition is reduced and the opportunities for survival and reproductive success are increased. This evolutionary tendency to exploit unoccupied habitats may eventually produce an abundance of diverse species.

This story has been played out countless times during the history of life, and some groups have expanded extremely rapidly. This evolutionary process, known as **adaptive radiation**, can be seen in the divergence of the stem reptiles into the profusion of different forms of the late Paleozoic and especially those of the Mesozoic. It's a process that takes place when a life-form rapidly takes advantage, so to speak, of the many newly available ecological niches.

The principle of evolution illustrated by adaptive radiation is fairly simple, but important. It may be stated this way: A species, or group of species, will diverge into as many variations as two factors allow. These factors are (1) its adaptive potential and (2) the adaptive opportunities of the available niches.

In the case of reptiles, there was little divergence in the very early stages of evolution, when the ancestral form was little more than one among a variety of amphibian water dwellers. Later, a more efficient egg (one that could incubate out of water) developed in reptiles; this new egg, with a hard, watertight shell, had great adaptive potential, but initially there were few zones to invade.

When reptiles became fully terrestrial, however, a wide array of ecological niches became accessible to them. Once freed from their attachment to water, reptiles were able to exploit landmasses with no serious competition from any other animal. They moved into the many different ecological niches on land (and to some extent in the air and sea), and as they adapted to these areas, they diversified into a large number of species. This spectacular radiation burst forth with such evolutionary speed that it may well be termed an adaptive explosion.

Of course, the rapid expansion of placental mammals during the late Mesozoic and throughout the Cenozoic is another excellent example of adaptive radiation. The worldwide major extinction event at the end of the Cenozoic left thousands of econiches vacant as the dinosaurs became extinct. Small-bodied, mostly nocturnal mammals had been around for at least 70 million years, and once they were no longer in competition with the dinosaurs, they were free to move into previously occupied habitats. Thus, over the course of several million years, there was a major adaptive radiation of mammals as they diversified to exploit previously unavailable habitats.

Generalized and Specialized Characteristics

Another aspect of evolution closely related to adaptive radiation involves the transition from *generalized* characteristics to *specialized* characteristics. These two terms refer to the adaptive potential of a particular trait. A trait that's adapted for many functions is said to be generalized, while one that's limited to a narrow set of functions is said to be specialized.

For example, a generalized mammalian limb has five fairly flexible digits adapted for many possible functions (grasping, weight support, and digging). In this respect, human hands are still quite generalized. On the other

adaptive radiation The relatively rapid expansion and diversification of life-forms into new ecological niches.

hand (or foot), there have been many structural modifications in our feet to make them suited for the specialized function of stable weight support in an upright posture.

The terms *generalized* and *specialized* are also sometimes used when speaking of the adaptive potential of whole organisms. Consider, for example, the aye-aye of Madagascar, an unusual primate species. The aye-aye is a highly specialized animal, structurally adapted to a narrow, rodent/woodpecker-like econiche—digging holes with prominent incisors and removing insect larvae with an elongated bony finger (**Fig. 5-16**).

It's important to note that only a generalized ancestor can provide the flexible evolutionary basis for rapid diversification. Only a generalized species with potential for adaptation to varied ecological niches can lead to all the later diversification and specialization of forms into particular ecological niches.

An issue that we've already raised also bears on this discussion: the relationship of ancestral and derived characters. It's not always the case, but ancestral characters *usually* tend to be more generalized. And specialized characteristics are nearly always derived ones as well.

▲ **Figure 5-16**
An aye-aye, a specialized primate native to Madagascar. Note the elongated middle finger, which is used to probe under bark for insects.

© Nigel J. Dennis; Gallo Images / Corbis

Tempos and Modes of Evolutionary Change

For many years, evolutionary biologists generally agreed that microevolutionary mechanisms could be translated directly into the larger-scale macroevolutionary changes, especially the most central of all macroevolutionary processes, speciation. However, three decades ago, this view was seriously challenged. This challenge led to the new view that macroevolution can't be explained solely in terms of slowly accumulated microevolutionary changes. Most evolutionary biologists now recognize that macroevolution is only partly understandable through microevolutionary models and that the process is much more complicated than traditionally assumed.

Gradualism versus Punctuated Equilibrium The conventional view of evolution has emphasized that change accumulates gradually in evolving lineages, an idea called *phyletic gradualism*. According to this view, the complete fossil record of an evolving group (if it could be recovered) would display a series of forms with finely graded transitional differences between each ancestor and its descendant; that is, many "missing links" would be present. The fact that such transitional forms are only rarely found is attributed to the incompleteness of the fossil record, or, as Darwin called it, "a history of the world, imperfectly kept, and written in changing dialect."

For more than a century, this perspective dominated evolutionary biology. But in the last 35 years, some biologists have called the idea into question. The evolutionary mechanisms operating on species over the long run aren't always gradual. In some cases, species persist, basically unchanged, for thousands of generations (stasis). Then, rather suddenly (at least in geological terms), a "spurt" of speciation occurs. This uneven, nongradual process of long stasis and quick spurts has been termed **punctuated equilibrium** (Gould and Eldredge, 1977). In this model, there are no "missing links" between species; the gaps are real, not artifacts of an imperfect fossil record.

What the advocates of punctuated equilibrium dispute are the tempo (rate) and mode (manner) of evolutionary change as commonly understood since Darwin's time. Rather than a slow, steady tempo, this alternate view postulates long periods of no change (that is, equilibrium, or stasis) punctuated (interrupted) only occasionally by sudden bursts. From this observa-

punctuated equilibrium The concept that evolutionary change proceeds through long periods of stasis punctuated by rapid periods of change.

tion, many researchers concluded that the mode of evolution, too, must be different from that suggested by traditional evolutionary biologists (often called "Darwinists"). Rather than gradual accumulation of small changes in a single lineage, advocates of punctuated equilibrium believe that an additional evolutionary mechanism is required to push the process along. In fact, they postulate *speciation* as the major influence in bringing about rapid evolutionary change (**Fig. 5-17**).

How well does the paleontological record agree with the predictions of punctuated equilibrium? Some fossil data do, in fact, show long periods of stasis punctuated by occasional quite rapid changes (taking from about 10,000 to 50,000 years). The best supporting evidence for punctuated equilibrium has come from marine invertebrate fossils, although not even these data are always clear (Van Bocxlaer et al., 2008). From the perspective of punctuated equilibrium, intermediate forms are rare, not so much because the fossil record is poor, but because the speciation events and longevity of these transitional species were so short that we shouldn't expect to find them very often.

To test these alternative hypotheses, long geological sequences containing well-preserved and well-dated fossils are required. It's important to recognize that in any active scientific discipline (and evolutionary biology is no exception), hypotheses continue to be tested and refined. Some nonscientists, arguing from a creationist perspective, have pointed to this dispute in an attempt to discredit the basis of evolutionary theory. These claims, however, fail to take into account not only the nature of this particular debate, but also the vast accumulation of evidence recognized by evolutionary biologists worldwide. Moreover, as we have already pointed out (see Chapter 2), the creationist perspective fundamentally fails to understand the nature of science itself. Renowned biologist Stephen Jay Gould, a cofounder of punctuated equilibrium, commented on the debate

among evolutionary biologists and the popular misunderstanding surrounding it:

> Yet amidst all this turmoil no biologist has been led to doubt the fact that evolution occurred; we are debating *how* it happened. We are all trying to explain the same thing: the tree of evolutionary descent linking all organisms by ties of genealogy (Gould, 1994, p. 256).

In summary, the critical difference between phyletic gradualism and punctuated equilibrium relates to how the timing of speciation events likely occurred in the past. Phyletic gradualism predicts slow accumulation of adaptive differences that finally

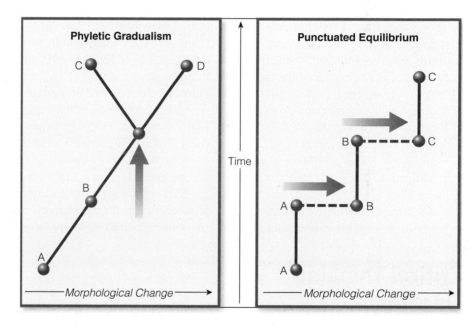

culminate in a new species, whereas punctuated equilibrium predicts that no changes occur for long periods of time until there is a sudden adaptive change, which results in a new species.

Recent molecular evidence suggests that both gradual change and rapid punctuated change occurred in the evolution of both plants and animals (Pagel et al. 2006). In all lineages, the pace assuredly speeds up and slows down due to factors that influence the size and relative isolation of populations. Environmental changes that influence the pace and direction of natural selection must also be considered.

▲ **Figure 5-17**
Phyletic gradualism compared with punctuated equilibrium. Note that in phyletic gradualism morphological change accumulates gradually with time but occurs in short bursts in punctuated equilibrium. In addition, speciation events (shown by arrows) in phyletic gradualism happen after long and slow accumulated change, but occur rapidly in punctuated equilibrium.

So, in general accordance with the Modern Synthesis and as indicated by molecular evidence, microevolution and macroevolution don't need to be considered separately, as some evolutionary biologists have suggested; both modes and tempos occur. Some groups of primates, for instance, simply have slower or faster durations of speciation, which is why Old World monkeys typically speciate more slowly than the great apes.

Summary of Main Topics

- Phylogenetic systematics and cladistics are the two major types of classification. Phylogenetic systematics uses homologous characteristics to make hypotheses regarding evolutionary relationships as well as ancestor-descendant relationships and shows the latter through time as a phylogenetic tree. Cladistics more rigorously uses only specific sorts of homologous characteristics (derived ones) and doesn't attempt to make ancestor-descendant conclusions or show evolutionary relationships through time; conclusions are shown in a cladogram.
- According to the biological species concept, species are groups of individuals capable of fertile interbreeding but reproductively isolated from other such groups. There are also other definitions of species suggested by biologists, but this one is the most widely used.
- Vertebrates are animals with a segmented backbone (vertebral column), a developed brain, and paired sensory structures. Vertebrates include fishes, amphibians, reptiles (including birds), and mammals.
- Humans are placental mammals that (along with some other mammals) are characterized by *in utero* (live) birth, differently shaped (heterodont) teeth, more complex brains, and maintenance of a constant internal body temperature (endothermic). Placental mammals, in particular, have even more complex brains (with a large neocortex), longer periods of development, and more complex social behavior.
- Macroevolution takes many hundreds or thousands of generations and can result in the appearance of new species (a process called *speciation*). Microevolution can occur within just a few generations and results in small genetic differences between populations of a species. Evolutionary biologists debate whether the two levels of evolutionary change differ in basic mechanisms. Most researchers now hypothesize that the two levels share many similarities and that both levels are crucial in producing the diversity of life that has evolved on earth.

Critical Thinking Questions

1. What are the two goals of classification? What happens when meeting both goals simultaneously becomes difficult or even impossible?

2. Remains of a fossil mammal have been found on your campus. If you adopt a cladistic approach, how would you determine (a) that it's a mammal rather than some other kind of vertebrate, (b) what kind of mammal it is, and (c) how it *might* be related to one or more living mammals?

3. For the same fossil find (and your interpretation) in question 2, draw an interpretive figure using cladistic analysis (that is, draw a cladogram). Next, using more traditional evolutionary systematics, construct a phylogenetic tree. Lastly, explain the differences between the cladogram and the phylogenetic tree (be sure to emphasize the fundamental ways the two schemes differ).

4. a. Humans are fairly generalized mammals. What do we mean by this, and what specific features (characters) would you select to illustrate this statement?

   b. More precisely, humans are *placental* mammals. How do humans and all other placental mammals differ from the other two major groups of mammals?

New Frontiers in RESEARCH

I n Chapter 4, you learned how, in the 1930s, scientists came to a better understanding of evolution once they realized that Mendel's principles and natural selection were both essential components of the process. This merger of ideas, known as the Modern Synthesis, was a major step in evolutionary science, and with the discovery of the structure of DNA in 1953, the foundations of evolutionary biology were firmly established.

(living and extinct), such as earthworms, grasshoppers, snakes, dinosaurs, sharks, frogs, birds, bats, dogs, horses, whales, and even humans. What's so remarkable is that all these animals are ultimately the descendants of a common ancestor that lived more than 600 million years ago.

In spite of how diverse these species are, they share many anatomical similarities. They're all bilaterally symmetrical, meaning that one side is like the other, except for certain aspects of internal organs. Also, and this is important, they all have a

each type of vertebra vary among species, the spine is made of repeated segments (**Fig. 2**).

Individual body parts are also modular. In all tetrapods (including all vertebrates except fishes), limbs follow a modular pattern. In humans, upper arms and thighs have one bone; forearms and lower legs have two; wrists and ankles have eight and seven, respectively; and hands and feet have five digits (see Fig. 5-2 and Appendix A). While snakes, whales, and dolphins don't have legs and feet, they're descended from animals that did, and that's why they're considered tetrapods. Moreover, some of these species, such as pythons and whales, have skeletal pelvic remnants. Although in more derived animals some of the bones in the lower limbs and feet may be reduced and/or modified, this basic pattern in limb morphology is shared by thousands of species, from sparrows to gorillas. It's the same pattern seen in dinosaur fossils, and its history goes back more than 500 million years.

Anatomical structures that have the same form, even with modifications, are called homologies, meaning that they're shared by species that ultimately inherited them from a common ancestor. Even though the last common ancestor humans share with dinosaurs lived an incomprehensibly long time ago, our limbs are homologous with dinosaur limbs. In fact, all the

Evo-Devo: The Evolution Revolution

Almost half a century after the structure of the DNA molecule was revealed, another merger of disciplines occurred (Goodman and Coughlin, 2000). In 1999, the field of evolutionary developmental biology, or evo-devo, was created by consolidating evolutionary biology with developmental biology. This combination resulted directly from research demonstrating that major evolutionary transformations involve changes in the very same regulatory genes that direct embryological development. The main goals of evo-devo are to discover how animals are put together and how the genes that control their development can, over time, produce new species.

Right now, there are millions of animal species (including insects and marine life), but they probably represent less than 1 percent of all the species that have ever existed on earth (Carroll et al., 2001). Among these many millions of species the degree of diversity is staggering, even if you only consider the ones you're familiar with

modular body plan made up of repeated segments. Arthropods (invertebrates with jointed feet, including all insects, spiders, and crustaceans) have segmented bodies and legs; and many have segmented wings, which are ultimately derived from leg-like appendages (**Fig. 1**).

Vertebrates have segmented body plans too, initially formed by the developing head and vertebral column. Although the number of vertebrae and the number of

© Tomasz Zachariasz/iStockphoto

▼ **Figure 1**
The modular body plan of insects is clearly shown in this centipede and sow bug (also known as pill bug, wood louse, and roly-poly). Their bodies, legs, and even antennae, are all composed of series of repeated segments.

© Tomasz Zachariasz/iStockphoto

Evo-Devo: The Evolution Revolution (continued)

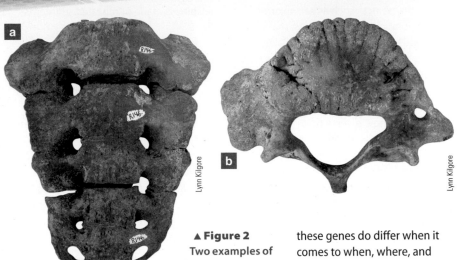

Lynn Kilgore

Lynn Kilgore

▲ **Figure 2**
Two examples of *Hox* transformations. **(a)** This sacrum, seen from the front, is composed of 6 vertebrae when there should only be 5. This was caused by the malfunction of one of the *Hox* genes involved in the initial patterning of the sacral vertebrae. **(b)** Top view of a 6th lumbar vertebra, in itself the result of a *Hox* malfunction. In addition, the left side has the morphology of a first sacral vertebra, and the opening on the right side is typical only of cervical (neck) vertebrae.

homologies shared by millions of diverse species (living and extinct) were ultimately inherited from an extremely distant common ancestor.

We know that during embryonic development, bodies are formed according to a pattern that characterizes each species; and that pattern is dictated by that species' genome. Because of advances in comparative genomics, we also now know that the coding sequences of even distantly related species are very similar. For example, around 99 percent of mouse genes have a human counterpart (Mouse Genome Sequencing Consortium, 2002). So, what is it that makes us so different from mice?

Until about 25 years ago, biologists thought that changes in protein-coding genes were the key to evolutionary change, but now it's clear that changes in regulatory genes are the real answer to the question of how macroevolution occurs. DNA sequences of regulatory genes don't differ greatly among species; however (and this is key),

these genes do differ when it comes to when, where, and how long they function. And these differences lead to major physical differences, because anatomical development depends on genes turning on and off at different times and in different places. There are many different kinds of regulatory genes, and they all instruct cells to make proteins (and different kinds of RNA) that in turn modulate the activity of yet other genes. Regulatory genes can be thought of as switches that turn other genes on or off at specific times in specific parts of the body (Carroll et al., 2008).

Many evolutionary biologists refer to the group of body-building regulatory genes as the *genetic tool kit*. This genetic tool kit is highly conserved and is shared by all vertebrates and invertebrates. Through the roughly 600 million years of animal evolution, many of the genes that make up the tool kit have been somewhat changed by mutation, and many have duplicated to produce families of genes. But given the amount of time and the huge array of descendant species, changes in the DNA sequences of tool kit genes have been extraordinarily minimal, so the roughly 10 percent of your genome that

consists of regulatory genes has the same DNA sequences as the regulatory genes of mice. It goes without saying that the tool kit genes serve as the best example of biological continuity among all animals, living and extinct.

The genetic tool kit is composed of genes that make two basic kinds of proteins: *transcription factors* and *signaling molecules*. Here we're focusing on transcription factors, protein molecules that bind to specific DNA segments called *enhancers* or *promoters*. By binding to enhancers, transcription factors switch genes on and off, and they also determine how long those genes produce proteins.

Transcription factors are produced by homeobox genes. These genes contain a highly conserved region of 180 nucleotides called the homeobox, and this sequence

> ... there are millions of animal species, but they probably represent less than 1 percent of all the species that have ever existed on earth.

codes for the proteins that bind to enhancers. There are several families of genes that contain homeoboxes, but the most familiar one is called *Hox* for short.

As we discussed in Chapter 3, *Hox* genes direct the early stages of embryonic development. Initially, they establish the identity of regions of the body and the pattern of structures along the main body axis that runs lengthwise through the embryo. These structures are actually early precursors to the head and vertebral column. Later in development, these same genes establish where limb buds will form and also determine limb polarity (that is, front, back, and sides). Mutations in these genes cause the transformation of one body part to another; we've learned about the most famous of these transformations from experiments with fruit flies, where induced mutations cause all sorts of bizarre phenotypes (such as legs where antennae should be).

Most invertebrates have 10 *Hox* genes, fruit flies have 8, but vertebrates have more. Mammals, for example, have 39, located on four different chromosomes. The reason vertebrates have more *Hox* genes than insects is that, over time, the invertebrate versions have duplicated in vertebrates. From these observations, we can see that vertebrate *Hox* genes are descended from invertebrate *Hox* genes. Just to illustrate how conserved these genes are, many experiments have shown them to be interchangeable between species. For example, one study showed that fruit flies can function normally with *Hox* proteins derived from chick embryos (Lutz et al., 1996). This indicates that these genes haven't changed much since fruit flies and chickens last shared a common ancestor some 600 millions years ago (Ayala and Rzhetskydagger, 1998).

As already stated, mutations in *Hox* genes can lead to transformations where one body segment takes on characteristics of another (like legs instead of antennae, but not so dramatic). Such anatomical changes are fairly common in humans, especially in the spine, where the fifth lumbar vertebra (the last one in the lower back) may have certain morphological similarities with the first sacral vertebra. Likewise, the first sacral vertebra may have characteristics of the fifth lumbar (Fig. 2).

The fact that *Hox* transformations in humans tend to occur more frequently between the fifth lumbar and first sacral vertebrae could lead to speculation regarding differences between human and African great ape spines. Humans typically have 12 thoracic and 5 lumbar vertebrae, while chimpanzees, gorillas, and bonobos have 13 thoracic and 4 lumbar vertebrae. The shorter

lumbar spine in apes has been explained by natural selection favoring a more stable lower back in brachiating animals. Unfortunately, we don't know for certain how many lumbar vertebrae the earliest hominins had. But we do know that the ancestral mammalian pattern is 6 or 7. It's not unreasonable to speculate, although with no supporting

> The key to this great puzzle is to understand that it all derives from simple beginnings with a set of genes that have been shared by all animals for hundreds of millions of years.

evidence at this time, that at some point in chimpanzee and gorilla evolution a *Hox* transformation, or series of transformations, effectively changed the first lumbar vertebra to a 13th thoracic vertebra. Even if this scenario isn't true, it illustrates how anatomical changes can result from *Hox* mutations. Following the evolutionary process, if mutations that produce transformations are advantageous, natural selection can act to increase their frequency in a population or species.

The science of evo-devo allows us, for the first time, to understand how morphological change and macroevolution can occur through the action of the genes that make up the genetic tool kit. This understanding has been made possible through the recently developed techniques of gene cloning and comparative genomics. By adding the evidence provided by evo-devo to comparative anatomy and fossil studies,

scientists are on the threshold of demonstrating how evolution has worked to produce the spectacular biological diversity we see today. The key to this great puzzle is to understand that it all derives from simple beginnings with a set of genes that have been shared by all animals for hundreds of millions of years. As Charles Darwin said in the last paragraph of *Origin of Species*, "There is grandeur in this view of life . . . from so simple a beginning endless forms most beautiful and most wonderful have been, and are being evolved." This quotation has been a favorite of biologists and anthropologists, not only for its eloquence, but also because we've long known that over time, life-forms have become more complex. For 150 years, we've explained this increased complexity in terms of natural selection, and we still do. But now we have the tools we need to reveal the very mechanism that allowed complexity to develop in the first place.

SOURCES

Ayala, F. J., and A. Rzhetskydagger
1998   Origin of the Metazoan phyla: molecular clocks confirm paleontological estimates. *Proceedings of the National Academy of Sciences* 95(2):606–611.

Carroll, S. B., B. Prud'homme, and N. Gompel
2008   Regulating evolution. *Scientific American* 298(5):61–67.

Carroll, S. B., J. K. Grenier, and S. D. Weatherbee
2001   *From DNA to Diversity. Molecular Genetics and the Evolution of Animal Design.* Malden, MA: Blackwell Science.

Goodman, C. S., and B. C. Coughlin
2000   The evolution of evo-devo biology. *Proceedings of the National Academy of Sciences* 97(9): 4424–4425.

Lutz, B., H. C. Lu, G. Eichele, D. Miller, and T. C. Kaufmann
1996   Rescue of **Drosophila** labial null mutant by the chicken ortholog *Hoxb-1* demonstrates that the function of *Hox* genes is phylogenetically conserved. *Genes and Development* 10:176–184.

Mouse Genome Sequencing Consortium
2002   Initial sequencing and comparative analysis of the mouse genome. *Nature* 420:520–562.

Gibbon hanging from branch while feeding.

© Ingo Arndt / Minden Pictures

6

Survey of the Living Primates

Key Questions

▶ What major groupings of animals are classified as primates?

▶ What are the major characteristics of primates?

▶ Why are humans considered primates?

▶ Why is it important to study nonhuman primates?

▶ Why are so many nonhuman primates endangered today?

Chimpanzees aren't monkeys, and neither are gorillas or orangutans. They're apes. And even though most people think that monkeys and apes are basically the same, they aren't. Yet, how many times have you seen a greeting card or magazine ad with a picture of a chimpanzee and a phrase that says something like, "Don't monkey around" or "No more monkey business"? Or maybe you've seen people at zoos making fun of primates. While these things may seem trivial, they really aren't, because they demonstrate just how little most people know about our closest relatives. This is extremely unfortunate, because by better understanding these relatives, we can better understand ourselves. And just as important, we can also try to preserve the many nonhuman primate species that are critically endangered today. Indeed, many will go extinct in the next 50 years or so if steps aren't taken now to save them.

One way to understand any organism is to compare its anatomy and behavior with that of other, closely related species. This comparative approach helps explain how and why physiological and behavioral systems evolved as adaptive responses to various selective pressures throughout the course of evolution. This statement applies to humans just as it does to any other species. So if we want to identify the components that have shaped the evolution of our species, a good starting point is to compare ourselves with our closest living relatives, the approximately 230 species of nonhuman primates (lemurs, lorises, tarsiers, monkeys, and apes).

This chapter describes the physical characteristics that define the order **Primates**, gives a brief overview of the major groups of living primates, and introduces some methods currently used to compare living primates genetically. (For a comparison of human and nonhuman skeletons, see Appendix A.) But before going any further, we again want to call attention to a few common misunderstandings about evolutionary processes.

Evolution is not a goal-directed process. Therefore, the fact that lemurs evolved before **anthropoids** doesn't mean that lemurs "progressed" or "advanced" to become anthropoids. Living primates aren't in any way "superior" to their evolutionary predecessors or to one another. Consequently, in discussions of major groupings of contemporary nonhuman primates, there's no implied superiority or inferiority of any of these groups. Each lineage or species has come to possess unique qualities that make it better suited to a particular habitat and lifestyle than others. Given that all contemporary organisms are "successful" results of the evolutionary process, it's best to completely avoid using such loaded terms as *superior* and *inferior*. Finally, you shouldn't make the mistake of thinking that contemporary primates (including humans) necessarily represent the final stage or apex of a lineage, because we all continue to evolve as lineages. Actually, the only species that represent final evolutionary stages of particular lineages are those that become extinct.

Primate Characteristics

All primates share many characteristics with other placental mammals (see Chapter 5). Some of these basic mammalian traits are body hair, a relatively long gestation period followed by live birth, mammary glands (thus the term *mammal*), different types of teeth (incisors, canines, premolars, and molars), the ability to maintain a constant internal body temperature through physiological means, or *endothermy* (see Chapter 5), increased brain size, and a considerable capacity for learning and behavioral flexibility. So, to differentiate primates as a distinct group from other mammals, we need to describe those characteristics that, taken together, set primates apart.

It isn't easy to identify single traits that define the primate order because, compared with most mammals, primates have remained quite *generalized*. This means that primates have retained several ancestral mammalian traits that many other mammals have lost over time. In response to particular selective pressures, some mammalian

groups have become increasingly specialized, or derived. For example, through the course of evolution, horses and cattle have undergone a reduction in the number of digits (fingers and toes) from the ancestral pattern of five to one and two, respectively. These species have also developed hard, protective coverings over their feet in the form of hooves (**Fig. 6-1a**). This limb structure is beneficial in prey species, because their survival depends on speed and stability, but it restricts them to only one type of locomotion. Moreover, limb function is restricted to support and movement, and the ability to manipulate objects is lost completely.

Primates can't be defined by one or even a few traits they share in common because they *aren't* so specialized. Therefore, primatologists have drawn attention to a group of characteristics that, when taken together, more or less characterize the entire primate order. Still, these are a set of *general* tendencies that aren't all equally expressed in all primates. In addition, while some of these traits are unique to primates, many others are retained ancestral mammalian characteristics shared with other mammals. The following list is meant to give you an overall structural and behavioral picture of the primates in general, focusing on those characteristics that tend to set primates apart from other mammals. Concentrating on certain ancestral mammalian traits along with more specific, derived ones has been the traditional approach of primatologists, and it's still used today. In their limbs and locomotion, teeth, diet, senses, brain, and behavior, primates reflect a common evolutionary history with adaptations to similar environmental challenges, primarily as highly social, arboreal animals.

A. *Limbs and Locomotion*
   1. *A tendency toward an erect posture (especially in the upper body).* (Derived trait) All primates show this tendency to some degree, and

primates Members of the mammalian order Primates (pronounced "pry-may´-tees"), which includes lemurs, lorises, tarsiers, monkeys, apes, and humans.

anthropoids Members of the primate infraorder Anthropoidea (pronounced "an-throw-poid´-ee-uh"), which includes monkeys, apes, and humans.

it's variously associated with sitting, leaping, standing, and, occasionally, bipedal walking.

2. *A flexible, generalized limb structure, which allows most primates to practice various locomotor behaviors.* (Ancestral trait) Primates have retained some bones (such as the clavicle, or collarbone) and certain abilities (like rotation of the forearm) that have been lost in more specialized mammals such as horses. Various aspects of hip and shoulder **morphology** also provide primates with a wide range of limb movement and function. Thus, by maintaining a generalized locomotor anatomy, primates aren't restricted to one form of movement, as are many other mammals. Primates also use their limbs for many activities besides locomotion.

3. *Prehensile hands (and sometimes feet).* (Derived trait) Lots of animals can manipulate objects, but not as skillfully as primates. All primates use their hands, and frequently their feet, to grasp and manipulate objects (**Fig. 6-1b**). This ability is variably expressed and is enhanced by several characteristics, including these:

a. *Retention of five digits on the hands and feet.* (Ancestral trait) This trait varies somewhat throughout the order, with some species having reduced thumbs or second digits.

b. *An opposable thumb and, in most species, a divergent and partially opposable big toe.* (Derived trait) Most primates are capable of moving the thumb so that it opposes or comes in contact with the second digit or with the palm of the hand (**Fig. 6-1c–e**).

c. *Nails instead of claws.* (Derived trait) This characteristic is seen in all primates except some New World monkeys (marmosets and tamarins). All lemurs and lorises also have a claw on one digit.

▲ **Figure 6-1**

(a) A horse's front foot, homologous with a human hand, has undergone reduction from five digits to one. **(b)** While raccoons are capable of considerable manual dexterity and can easily pick up small objects with one hand, they have no opposable thumb. **(c)** Many monkeys are able to grasp objects with an opposable thumb, while others have very reduced thumbs. **(d)** Humans are capable of a "precision grip." **(e)** Chimpanzees with their reduced thumbs are capable of a precision grip but frequently use a modified form.

morphology The form (shape, size) of anatomical structures; can also refer to the entire organism.

► **Figure 6-2**
This simplified diagram shows overlapping visual fields that permit binocular vision in primates with eyes positioned at the front of the face. (The green shaded area in front of the eyes represents the area of overlap.) Stereoscopic vision (three-dimensional vision) is provided in part by binocular vision and in part by the transmission of visual stimuli from each eye to both hemispheres of the brain. This is illustrated by the blue and gold lines representing nerve fibers that transmit information from each eye to visual receiving areas at the rear of *both* sides of the brain. (In non-primate mammals, most, if not all, visual information crosses over to the hemisphere opposite the eye in which it was initially received.)

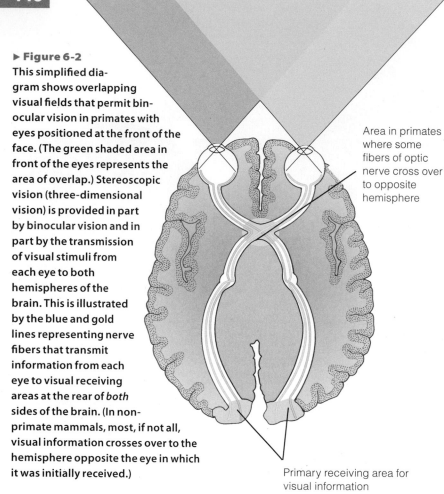

Area in primates where some fibers of optic nerve cross over to opposite hemisphere

Primary receiving area for visual information

omnivorous Having a diet consisting of many food types, such as plant materials, meat, and insects.

diurnal Active during the day.

olfaction The sense of smell.

nocturnal Active during the night.

stereoscopic vision The condition whereby visual images are, to varying degrees, superimposed. This provides for depth perception, or viewing the external environment in three dimensions. Stereoscopic vision is partly a function of structures in the brain.

binocular vision Vision characterized by overlapping visual fields provided by forward-facing eyes. Binocular vision is essential to depth perception.

hemispheres The two halves of the cerebrum that are connected by a dense mass of fibers. (The cerebrum is the large rounded outer portion of the brain.)

d. *Tactile pads enriched with sensory nerve fibers at the ends of digits.* (Derived trait) This characteristic enhances the sense of touch.

B. *Diet and Teeth*

   1. Lack of dietary specialization. (Ancestral trait) This characteristic is typical of most primates, who tend to eat a wide assortment of food items. In general, primates are **omnivorous**.

   2. *A generalized dentition.* (Ancestral trait) Primate teeth aren't specialized for processing only one type of food, a characteristic related to a general lack of dietary specialization.

C. *The senses and the brain.* Primates (**diurnal** ones in particular) rely heavily on vision and less on olfaction, especially when compared with other mammals. This emphasis is reflected in evolutionary changes in the skull, eyes, and brain. (Derived trait)

   1. *Color vision.* (Derived trait) This is a characteristic of all Old World diurnal primates. Some New World species don't have the full range of color vision, and **nocturnal** primates lack color vision.

   2. *Depth perception.* (Derived trait) Primates have **stereoscopic vision**, or the ability to perceive objects in three dimensions. This is made possible through a variety of mechanisms, including:

   a. *Eyes placed toward the front of the face (not to the sides).* This position provides for overlapping visual fields, or **binocular vision** (**Fig. 6-2**).

   b. *Visual information from each eye transmitted to visual centers in both **hemispheres** of the brain.* In nonprimate mammals, most optic nerve fibers cross to the opposite hemisphere through a structure at the base of the brain. In primates, about 40 percent of the fibers remain on the same side, so that information is shared.

   c. *Visual information organized into three-dimensional images by specialized structures in the brain itself.* The capacity for stereoscopic vision depends on each hemisphere of the brain receiving visual information from both eyes and from overlapping visual fields.

   3. *Decreased reliance on olfaction.* This trend is expressed as an overall reduction in the size of olfactory structures in the brain. Corresponding reduction of the entire olfactory apparatus has also resulted in decreased size of the snout in most species. This is related to an increased reliance on vision. Some species, such as baboons, have a large muzzle; however, this isn't related to olfaction but rather to the need to accommodate large canine teeth (see "A Closer Look: Primate Cranial Anatomy").

4. *Expansion and increased complexity of the brain.* (Derived trait) This is a general trend among placental mammals, but it's especially true of primates. In primates, this expansion is most evident in the visual and association areas of the **neocortex** (portions of the brain where information from different **sensory modalities** is combined). Expansion in regions involved with sensory and motor functions of the hand is seen in many primate species, particularly humans.

D. *Maturation, learning, and behavior*
1. *A more efficient means of fetal nourishment, longer periods of gestation, reduced numbers of offspring (with single births the norm), delayed maturation, and extension of the entire life span* (Derived trait)
2. *A greater dependence on flexible, learned behavior.* (Derived trait) This trend is correlated with delayed maturation and subsequently longer periods of infant and child dependency on at least one parent. Because of these trends, parental investment in each offspring is increased; although fewer offspring are born, they receive more intense rearing.
3. *The tendency to live in social groups and the permanent association of adult males with the group.* (Derived trait) Except for some nocturnal species, primates tend to associate with other individuals. Also, the permanent association of adult males with the group is uncommon in most mammals but widespread in primates.
4. *The tendency toward diurnal activity patterns.* (Derived trait) This is seen in most primates: Lorises, tarsiers, one monkey species, and some lemurs are nocturnal; all the rest (the other monkeys, apes, and humans) are diurnal.

Primate Adaptations

In this section, we consider how primate anatomical traits evolved as adaptations to environmental circumstances. It's important to remember that when you see the phrase "environmental circumstances," it refers to several interrelated variables, including climate, diet, habitat (woodland, grassland, forest, and so on), and predation.

Evolutionary Factors

Traditionally, the group of characteristics shared by primates has been explained as the result of an adaptation to **arboreal** living. While other mammals were adapting to various ground-dwelling lifestyles and even marine environments, the primates found their **adaptive niche** in the trees. A number of other mammals were also adapting to arboreal living; but while many of them nested in the trees, they continued to forage for food on the ground (**Fig. 6-3**). But throughout the course of evolution, primates increasingly found food (leaves, seeds, fruits, nuts, insects, and small mammals) in the trees themselves. Over time, this dietary shift enhanced a general trend toward *omnivory;* and this trend in turn led to the retention of the generalized dentition that's characteristic of primates.

Increased reliance on vision, coupled with grasping hands and feet, are also adaptations to an arboreal lifestyle. In a complex, three-dimensional environment with uncertain footholds, acute color vision with depth perception is, for obvious reasons, extremely beneficial.

An alternative to this traditional *arboreal hypothesis* is based on the fact that animals such as squirrels are also arboreal, yet they haven't evolved primate-like adaptations such as

▼ **Figure 6-3**
Gray squirrels are extremely well adapted to life in the trees, where they nest, sleep, play, and frequently eat. However, unlike primates, they don't have color vision or prehensile thumbs and big toes. They also have claws instead of nails.

© iStockphoto.com / Steve Geer

neocortex The more recently evolved portions of the cortex of the brain that are involved with higher mental functions and composed of areas that integrate incoming information from different sensory organs.

sensory modalities Different forms of sensation (e.g., touch, pain, pressure, heat, cold, vision, taste, hearing, and smell).

arboreal Tree living; adapted to life in the trees.

adaptive niche An organism's entire way of life: where it lives, what it eats, how it gets food, how it avoids predators, and so on.

A Closer Look

Primate Cranial Anatomy

Several anatomical features of the cranium distinguish primates from other mammals. The mammalian trend toward increased brain development has been further emphasized in primates, as shown by a relatively enlarged braincase. The primate emphasis on vision is further reflected in generally large eye sockets; the decreased dependence on olfaction is indicated by reduction of the snout and corresponding flattening of the face (**Fig. 1**).

Here are some of the specific anatomical details seen in modern and most fossil primate crania:

1. The primate face is shortened, and the size of the braincase, relative to that of the face, is enlarged compared with other mammals (see **Fig. 1**).
2. Unlike the eye sockets seen in other mammals, primate eye sockets are enclosed at the sides by a ring of bone called the *postorbital bar* (see Fig. 1). Also, in tarsiers, monkeys, apes, and humans, there is a plate of bone at the back of the eye orbit called the *postorbital plate*, a feature

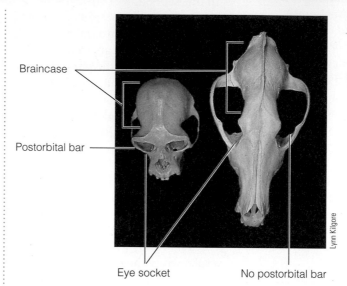

Braincase

Postorbital bar

Eye socket

No postorbital bar

Lynn Kilgore

◀ **Figure 1**
The skull of a gibbon (left) compared with that of a red wolf (right). Note that the absolute size of the braincase in the gibbon is slightly larger than that of the wolf, even though the wolf (at about 80 to 100 pounds) is six times the size of the gibbon (about 15 pounds).

that isn't present in lemurs, lorises, and other mammals. The functional significance of these structures hasn't been thoroughly explained, but it may be related to stresses on the eye orbits imposed by chewing (Fleagle, 1999).
3. The region of the skull that contains the structures of the middle ear is completely encircled by a bony structure called the *auditory bulla*. In primates, the floor of the auditory bulla is derived from a segment of the temporal bone (**Fig. 2**). Of all the skeletal

structures, most primate paleontologists consider the postorbital bar and the derivation of the auditory bulla to be the two best diagnostic traits of the primate order.
4. The base of the skull in primates is somewhat flexed, so that the muzzle (mouth and nose) is positioned lower relative to the braincase (**Fig. 3**). This arrangement provides for the exertion of greater force during chewing, particularly needed for crushing and grinding tough vegetable fibers, seeds, and hard-shelled fruits.

prehensile hands or forward-facing eyes. But visual predators, such as cats and owls, do have forward-facing eyes, and this fact may provide insight into an additional factor that could have shaped primate evolution.

Actually, forward-facing eyes (which facilitate binocular vision), grasping hands and feet, and the presence of nails instead of claws may not have come about solely as adaptive advantages in a purely arboreal setting. They may also have been the hallmarks of an arboreal visual predator. So it's possible that early primates may first have adapted to shrubby forest undergrowth and the lowest tiers of the forest

canopy, where they hunted insects and other small prey (Cartmill, 1972, 1992). In fact, many smaller primates occupy just such an econiche today.

Sussman (1991) suggested that the basic primate traits were developed in conjunction with another major evolutionary occurrence, the appearance of flowering plants that began around 140 mya. Flowering plants provide numerous resources for primates, including nectar, seeds, and fruits. Sussman argued that since visual predation isn't common among modern primates, forward-facing eyes, grasping hands and feet, omnivory, and *color vision* may have arisen in

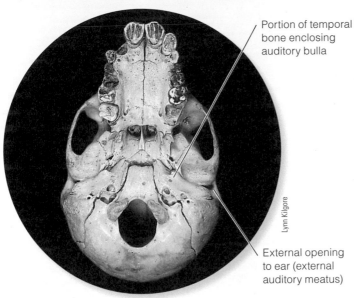

Portion of temporal bone enclosing auditory bulla

External opening to ear (external auditory meatus)

Lynn Kilgore

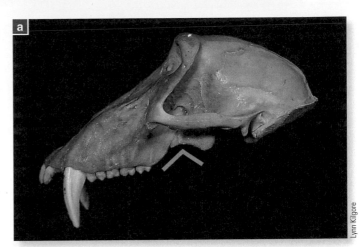

a

Lynn Kilgore

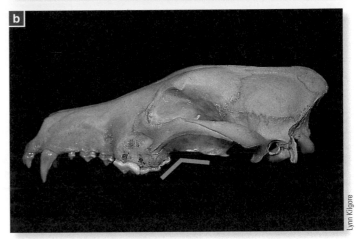

b

Lynn Kilgore

▲ **Figure 2**
The base of an adolescent chimpanzee skull. (In an adult animal, the bones of the skull would be fused together and would not appear as separate elements as shown here.)

▶ **Figure 3**
The skull of a male baboon (**a**) compared with that of a red wolf (**b**). The angle at the base of the baboon skull is due to flexion. The corresponding area of the wolf skull is relatively flat. Note the forward-facing position of the eye orbits above the snout in the baboon. Also, note that in the baboon, the enlarged muzzle does *not* reflect a heavy reliance on the sense of smell. Rather, it serves to support very large canine teeth, the roots of which curve back through the bone for as much as 1½ inches. Photos not to scale.

response to the demand for fine visual and tactile discrimination. Certainly, this type of discrimination is necessary when feeding on small food items such as fruits, berries, and seeds among branches and stems (Dominy and Lucas, 2001).

These hypotheses aren't mutually exclusive. The complex of primate characteristics might well have originated in nonarboreal settings and certainly could have been stimulated by the new econiches provided by evolving flowering plants. But at some point, primates did take to the trees, and that's where most of them still live today.

Geographical Distribution and Habitats

With just a couple of exceptions, nonhuman primates are found in tropical or semitropical areas of the New and Old Worlds. In the New World, these areas include southern Mexico, Central America, and parts of South America. Old World primates are found in Africa, India, Southeast Asia (including numerous islands), and Japan (**Fig. 6-4**).

Even though most nonhuman primates are arboreal and live in forest or woodland habitats, some Old World monkeys (for example, baboons) spend much of the day on the ground in

Howler species
(Central and South
America)

Spider monkeys
and muriquis
(Central and South
America)

Prince Bernhard's titi
(Brazil, Amazon
rain forest)

Uakari
(Brazil, near Jurua River)

Squirrel monkeys
(South America)

White-faced
capuchins
(South America)

Muriqui
(southeastern Brazil)

Marmosets and
tamarins
(South America)

▲ **Figure 6-4**
Geographical distribution of living nonhuman primates.
Much original habitat is now very fragmented.

Macaque species
(North Africa, India,
Southeast Asia,
China, and Japan)

Jean De Rousseau

Baboon species
(throughout sub-Saharan
Africa)

Bonnie Pedersen / Arlene Kruse

Gibbons and siamangs
(Southeast Asia,
islands, and China)

Lynn Kilgore

Cercopithecus
species (throughout
sub-Saharan Africa)

Robert Jurmain

Tarsier species
(southeast
Asian islands)

© Steve Bloom Images / Alamy

Loris species
(Africa, India, and
Southeast Asia)

© Ian Butler / Alamy

Mountain and lowland
gorillas (western and
central Africa)

Lynn Kilgore

Langur species
(colobines) (India,
southern Asia, and
south China)

© Cyril Ruoso / PhotoLibrary

Orangutans
(Borneo and Sumatra)

© Rolf Nussbaumer Photography / Alamy

Chimpanzees and
bonobos
(across central Africa)

Arlene Kruse / Bonnie Pedersen

Lemurs
(Madagascar)

Fred Jacobs

Galago species
(throughout sub-Saharan
Africa)

© DLILLC / Corbis

Colobus species
(throughout sub-Saharan
Africa)

Robert Jurmain

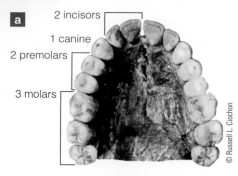

a

2 incisors
1 canine
2 premolars
3 molars

Human:
2.1.2.3.
2.1.2.3.

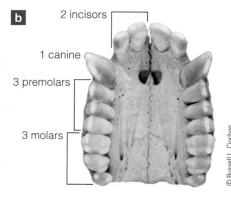

b

2 incisors
1 canine
3 premolars
3 molars

New World monkey:
2.1.3.3.
2.1.3.3.

▲ **Figure 6-5**
(a) The human maxilla illustrates a dental formula characteristic of all Old World monkeys, apes, and humans. (b) The New World monkey (*Cebus*) maxilla shows the dental formula that is typical of most New World monkeys. (Not to scale, the monkey maxilla is actually much smaller than the human maxilla.)

© Russell L. Ciochon

© Russell L. Ciochon

dental formula Numerical device that indicates the number of each type of tooth in each side of the upper and lower jaws.

cusps The bumps on the chewing surface of premolars and molars.

quadrupedal Using all four limbs to support the body during locomotion; the basic mammalian (and primate) form of locomotion.

brachiation Arm swinging, a form of locomotion used by some primates. Brachiation involves hanging from a branch and moving by alternately swinging from one arm to the other.

places where trees are sparsely distributed. And the same is true for the African apes (gorillas, chimpanzees, and bonobos). Nevertheless, no nonhuman primate is adapted to a fully terrestrial lifestyle; they all spend some time in the trees.

Diet and Teeth

Omnivory is one example of the overall lack of specialization in primates. Although the majority of primates tend to emphasize some food items over others, most eat a combination of fruits, nuts, seeds, leaves, other plant materials, and insects. Many also get animal protein from birds and amphibians. Some (capuchins, baboons, bonobos, and especially chimpanzees) occasionally kill and eat small mammals, including other primates. Others, such as African colobus monkeys and the leaf-eating monkeys (langurs) of India and Southeast Asia, have become more specialized and mostly eat leaves.

This wide and varied menu is a good example of the advantages of having a generalized diet, especially in less predictable environments; if one food source fails (for example, during drought or because of human activities), other options may still be available. The downside of being generalized is that there may be competition for resources with other species that eat the same things. Specialization, where a species has a narrow ecological niche and eats only one or two things, can be advantageous in this regard because these species don't have much competition from others; but it can be catastrophic if the food supply disappears.

Like nearly all other mammals, primates have four kinds of teeth: incisors and canines for biting and cutting, and premolars and molars for chewing and grinding. Biologists use what's called a **dental formula** to describe the number of each type of tooth that typifies a species. A dental formula indi-

cates the number of each tooth type in each quadrant of the mouth (**Fig. 6-5**). For example, all Old World anthropoids have two incisors, one canine, two premolars, and three molars on each side of the midline in both the upper and lower jaws, for a total of 32 teeth. This is represented by the following dental formula:

2.1.2.3 (upper)
2.1.2.3 (lower)

The dental formula for a generalized placental mammal is 3.1.4.3 (three incisors, one canine, four premolars, and three molars). Primates have fewer teeth than this ancestral pattern because of a general evolutionary trend toward fewer teeth in many mammal groups. Consequently, the number of each type of tooth varies between lineages. For example, in most New World monkeys, the dental formula is 2.1.3.3 (two incisors, one canine, three premolars, and three molars). In contrast, humans, apes, and all Old World monkeys share a somewhat different dental formula: 2.1.2.3. This formula differs from that of the New World monkeys in that there's one less premolar.

The overall lack of dietary specialization in primates is reflected in the lack of specialization in the size and shape of the teeth, because tooth shape and size are directly related to diet. For example, carnivores typically have premolars and molars with high, pointed **cusps** adapted for tearing meat; but herbivores, such as cattle and horses, have premolars with broad, flat surfaces suited to chewing tough grasses and other plant materials. Most primates have premolars and molars with low, rounded cusps, a molar morphology that enables them to process most types of foods. So, throughout their evolutionary history, the primates have developed a dentition adapted to a varied diet, and the capacity to exploit many foods has contributed to their overall success during the last 50 million years.

Locomotion

Almost all primates are, at least to some degree, **quadrupedal**, meaning they use all four limbs to support the body during locomotion. However, most primates use more than one form of locomotion, and they're able to do this because of their generalized anatomy.

Most of the quadrupedal primates are primarily arboreal, but terrestrial quadrupedalism is also common. The limbs of terrestrial quadrupeds are approximately the same length, with forelimbs being 90 percent (or more) as long as hind limbs (**Fig. 6-6a**). In arboreal quadrupeds, forelimbs are somewhat shorter (**Fig. 6-6b**).

Vertical clinging and leaping, another form of locomotion, is characteristic of some lemurs and tarsiers. As the term implies, vertical clingers and leapers support themselves vertically by grasping onto trunks of trees or other large plants while their knees and ankles are tightly flexed (**Fig. 6-6c**). By forcefully extending their long hind limbs, they can spring powerfully away either forward or backward.

Brachiation, or arm swinging, is a suspensory form of locomotion in which the body moves by being alternatively supported by one forelimb, then the other. (You may have brachiated as a child on "monkey bars" in playgrounds.) Because of anatomical modifications at the shoulder joint, apes and humans are capable of true brachiation. However, only the small gibbons and siamangs of Southeast Asia use this form of locomotion almost exclusively (**Fig. 6-6d**).

▶ **Figure 6-6**
Differences in skeletal anatomy and limb proportions reflect differences in locomotor patterns. (Redrawn by Stephen Nash from original art in John G. Fleagle, *Primate Adaptation and Evolution,* **2nd ed., 1999. Reprinted by permission of publisher and Stephen Nash.)**

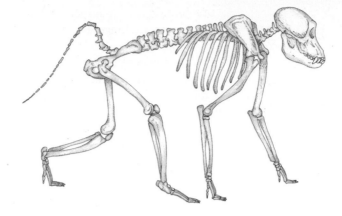

a Skeleton of a terrestrial quadruped (savanna baboon).

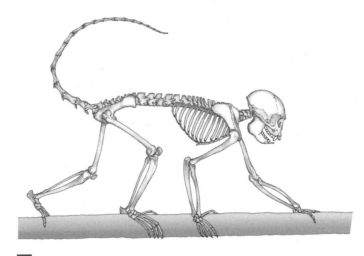

b Skeleton of an arboreal New World monkey (bearded saki).

c Skeleton of a vertical clinger and leaper (indri, a type of lemur).

d Skeleton of a brachiator (gibbon).

Brachiation is seen in species characterized by arms longer than legs, a short, stable **lumbar** spine (lower back), long curved fingers, and reduced thumbs. As these are traits seen in all the apes, it's believed that although none of the great apes (orangutans, gorillas, bonobos, and chimpanzees) habitually brachiate today, they may have inherited these characteristics from brachiating or climbing ancestors.

Some New World monkeys, such as spider monkeys and muriquis (see Fig. 6-22), are called *semibrachiators* because they practice a combination of leaping with some arm swinging. Also, some New World monkeys enhance arm swinging and other suspensory behaviors by using a *prehensile tail*, which in effect serves as an effective grasping fifth hand. It's important to mention here that prehensile tails are exclusively a New World phenomenon; they aren't seen in any Old World primates.

Lastly, all the apes, to varying degrees, have arms that are longer than legs, and some (gorillas, bonobos, and chimpanzees) practice a special form of quadrupedalism called knuckle walking. Because their arms are so long relative to their legs, instead of walking with the palms of their hands flat on the ground like some monkeys do, they support the weight of their upper body on the back surfaces of their bent fingers (**Fig. 6-7**).

▶ **Figure 6-7**
Chimpanzee knuckle walking. Note how the weight of the upper body is supported on the knuckles and not the palm of the hand.

Primate Classification

The living primates are commonly categorized into their respective subgroups, as shown in **Figure 6-8**. This taxonomy is based on the system originally established by Linnaeus (see Chapter 2). The primate order, which includes a diverse array of approximately 230 species, belongs to a larger group, the class Mammalia.

As you learned in Chapter 5, in any taxonomic system, animals are organized into increasingly specific categories. For example, the order Primates includes *all* primates. But at the next level down, the *suborder*, primates are divided into two smaller categories: **Strepsirhini** (lemurs and lorises) and **Haplorhini** (tarsiers, monkeys, apes, and humans). Therefore, the suborder distinction is narrower, or more specific. At the suborder level, the lemurs and lorises are distinct as a group from all the other primates. This classification makes the biological and evolutionary statement that all the lemurs and lorises are more closely related to one another than they are to any of the other primates. Likewise, humans, apes, monkeys, and tarsiers are more closely related to one another than they are to the lorises and lemurs.

Lynn Kilgore

lumbar Pertaining to the lower back. The lumbar area is longer in monkeys than it is in humans and apes.

Strepsirhini (strep'-sir-in-ee) The primate suborder that includes lemurs and lorises. (Colloquial form: strepsirhine.)

Haplorhini (hap'-lo-rin-ee) The primate suborder that includes tarsiers, monkeys, apes, and humans. (Colloquial form: haplorhine.)

▼ **Figure 6-8**

Primate taxonomic classification. This abbreviated taxonomy illustrates how primates are grouped from broader categories (e.g., the order Primates) into increasingly specific ones (species). Only the more general categories are shown, except for the great apes and humans.

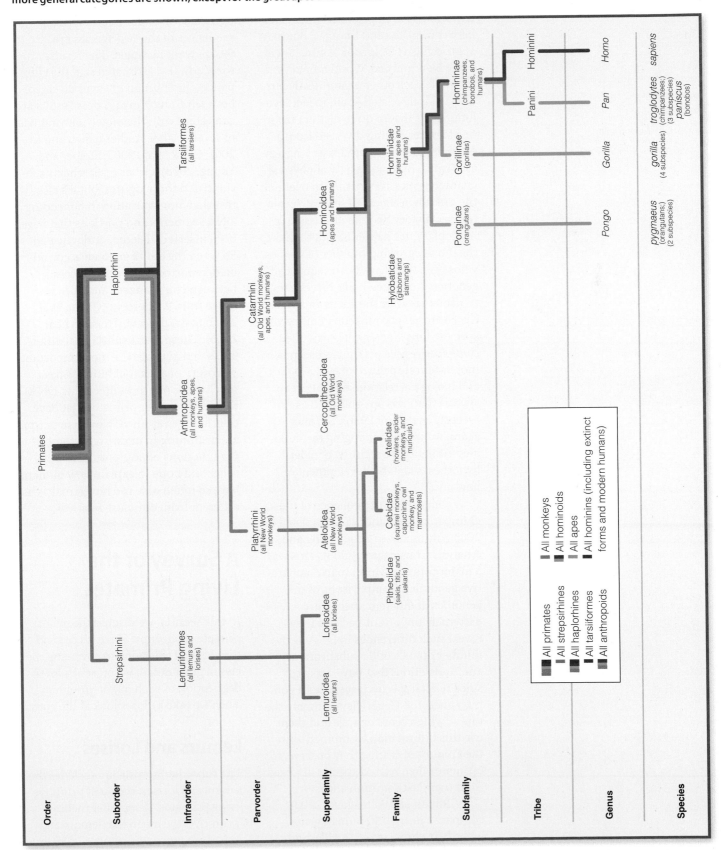

The taxonomy shown in Figure 6-8 is a modified version of a similar system that biologists and primatologists have used for decades. The traditional system was based on physical similarities between species and lineages. But that approach isn't foolproof. For instance, some New and Old World monkeys resemble each other anatomically but aren't closely related at all. In fact, evolutionarily, they're quite distinct from one another, having diverged from a common ancestor perhaps as long ago as 40 mya. By looking only at physical characteristics, it's possible to overlook the unknown effects of separate evolutionary history (see the discussion of homoplasy in Chapter 5). But thanks to the rapidly growing number of species whose genomes have been sequenced, geneticists can now make direct comparisons between the genes and indeed the entire genetic makeup of different species. This kind of analysis, called *comparative genomics*, gives us a much more accurate picture of evolutionary and biological relationships between species than was possible even as recently as the late 1990s. So, once again, we see how changing technologies influence the refining of older hypotheses and the development of new ones.

A complete draft sequence of the chimpanzee genome was completed in 2005 (Chimpanzee Sequencing and Analysis Consortium, 2005). This was a major milestone in human comparative genomics. Comparisons of the genomes of different species are extremely important because they reveal such differences in DNA as the number of nucleotide substitutions and/or deletions that have occurred since related species last shared a common ancestor. Geneticists estimate the rate at which genes change and then use this information, combined with the amount of change they observe, to estimate when related species diverged from their last common ancestor.

Wildman and colleagues (2003) compared nearly 100 human genes with their chimpanzee, gorilla, and orangutan counterparts and supported some earlier studies that concluded that humans are most closely related to chimpanzees and that the "functional elements" or protein-coding DNA sequences of the two species are 98.4 to 99.4 percent identical. The results of the study also estimated that the chimpanzee and human lineages diverged between 6 and 7 mya. These results are consistent with the molecular findings of several other studies (Chen and Li, 2001; Clark et al., 2003; Steiper and Young, 2006). Other research has substantiated these figures, but it's also revealed more variation in noncoding DNA segments and portions that have been inserted, deleted, or duplicated. So when the *entire* genome is considered, reported DNA differences between chimpanzees and humans range from 2.7 percent (Cheng et al., 2005) to 6.4 percent (Demuth et al., 2006). These aren't substantial differences, but perhaps the most important discovery of all is that humans have much more non-protein coding DNA than do the other primates that have thus far been studied. Now geneticists are beginning to understand some of the functions of non-protein coding genes and hope to explain why humans have so much of it and how it makes us different from our close relatives.

A Survey of the Living Primates

In this section, we discuss the major primate subgroups. Since it's beyond the scope of this book to cover any species in great detail, we present a brief description of each major grouping. Then we take a closer look at the apes.

Lemurs and Lorises

The suborder Strepsirhini includes the lemurs and lorises, the most primitive living primates. Remember that by "primitive" we mean that lemurs and lorises are more similar anatomically to

Lynn Kilgore

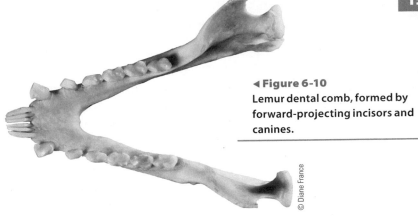

© Diane France

◀ **Figure 6-10**
Lemur dental comb, formed by forward-projecting incisors and canines.

Lynn Kilgore

▲ **Figure 6-9**
As you can see, rhinaria come in different shapes and sizes, but they all enhance an animal's sense of smell.

apart is the retention of a claw (called a "grooming claw") on the second toe.

Lemurs Lemurs are found only on the island of Madagascar and adjacent islands off the east coast of Africa (**Fig. 6-11**). As the only nonhuman primates on Madagascar, lemurs diversified into numerous and varied ecological niches without competition from monkeys and apes (see Chapter 9). Thus, the approximately 60 surviving species of lemurs on Madagascar today represent a kind of *lost world*, an evolutionary pattern that vanished elsewhere.

their earlier mammalian ancestors than are the other primates (tarsiers, monkeys, apes, and humans). For example, they retain certain ancestral characteristics, such as a more pronounced reliance on *olfaction*. Their greater olfactory capabilities (compared with other primates) are reflected in the presence of a moist, fleshy pad, or **rhinarium**, at the end of the nose and a relatively long snout (**Fig. 6-9**).

Many other characteristics distinguish lemurs and lorises from the other primates, including eyes placed more to the side of the face, differences in reproductive physiology, and shorter gestation and maturation periods. Lemurs and lorises also have a unique, derived trait called a "dental comb" (**Fig. 6-10**) formed by forward-projecting lower incisors and canines. These modified teeth are used in both grooming and feeding. One other characteristic that sets lemurs and lorises

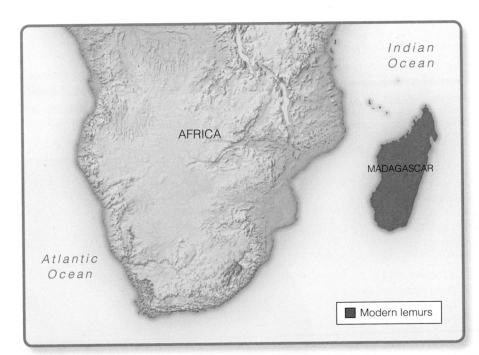

▲ **Figure 6-11**
Geographical distribution of modern lemurs.

rhinarium (rine-air´-ee-um) The moist, hairless pad at the end of the nose seen in most mammalian species. The rhinarium enhances an animal's ability to smell.

Lemurs range in size from the small mouse lemur, with a body length (head and trunk) of only 5 inches, to the indri, with a body length of 2 to 3 feet (Nowak, 1999). Typically, the larger lemurs are diurnal and eat a wide variety of foods, such as leaves, fruits, buds, bark, and shoots, but the tiny mouse and dwarf lemurs are nocturnal and insectivorous.

There is a great deal of behavioral variation among lemur species. Some are primarily arboreal, but others, such as ring-tailed lemurs (**Fig. 6-12**), are more terrestrial. Some arboreal species are quadrupeds, and others (sifakas, ring-tails, and indris) are vertical clingers and leapers (**Fig. 6-13**). Several species (for example, ring-tailed lemurs and sifakas) live in groups of 10 to 25 animals composed of males and females of all ages. However, indris live in social units made up of mated pairs and dependent offspring. Additionally, several nocturnal forms are mostly solitary.

Lorises Lorises (**Fig. 6-14**), which somewhat resemble lemurs, were able to survive in mainland areas by being nocturnal. In this way, they were (and are) able to avoid competition with more recently evolved primates (the diurnal monkeys).

There are at least eight loris species, all of which are found in tropical forest and woodland habitats of India, Sri Lanka, Southeast Asia, and Africa.

Also included in the same general category are six to nine galago species (Bearder, 1987; Nowak, 1999), also called bush babies (**Fig. 6-15**), which are widely distributed throughout most of the forested and woodland savanna areas of sub-Saharan Africa.

Locomotion in some lorises is a slow, cautious, climbing form of quadrupedalism; their flexible hip joints permit suspension by hind limbs while using the hands in feeding. All galagos, however, are highly agile vertical clingers and leapers. Some lorises and galagos are almost entirely insectivorous, while others supplement their diets with various combinations of fruits, leaves, gums, and slugs. Lorises and galagos frequently forage alone, but feeding ranges can overlap, and two or more females may feed and even nest together. Females also leave young infants behind in nests while they search for food. While "infant parking" may seem risky, many mammal mothers leave young infants alone. But lorises take an added precaution of first bathing their young with saliva that can cause an allergic reaction that discourages most predators (Krane et al., 2003).

Lemurs and lorises represent the same general adaptive level. Both groups exhibit good grasping and climbing abilities and a well-developed visual apparatus; however, vision is not completely stereoscopic, and in diurnal species, color vision may not be as well developed as in anthropoids.

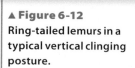

Cyril Ruoso / JH Editorial / Minden Pictures

▲ **Figure 6-12**
Ring-tailed lemurs in a typical vertical clinging posture.

▶ **Figure 6-13**
Sifakas.

Fred Jacobs

▲ **Figure 6-14**
A slow loris in Malaysia. Note the large forward-facing eyes and rhinarium.

▲ **Figure 6-15**
Galago, or "bush baby."

Tarsiers

There are five recognized tarsier species (Nowak, 1999), all of which are restricted to islands of Southeast Asia (Malaysia, Borneo, Sumatra, the Philippines), where they inhabit a wide range of habitats, from tropical forest to backyard gardens (**Figs. 6-16** and **6-17**). Tarsiers are nocturnal insectivores that use vertical clinging and leaping to surprise prey (which may also include small vertebrates) on lower branches and shrubs. They appear to form stable pair bonds, and the basic tarsier social unit is a mated pair and their young offspring (MacKinnon and MacKinnon, 1980).

Tarsiers are highly specialized (derived) animals that have several unique characteristics. In the past, primatologists believed that tarsiers were more closely related to lemurs and lorises than to other primates because they share several traits with them. Consequently, they were classified in the same suborder as lemurs and lorises. However, tarsiers actually present a complex blend of characteristics not seen in any other primate. One of the most obvious is their enormous eyes, which dominate

much of the face and are immobile within their sockets. To compensate for the inability to move their eyes, tarsiers, like owls, can rotate their heads 180°. Interestingly, each eye is about the size of a tarsier's brain (Beard, 2004).

In addition, tarsiers possess certain anthropoid characteristics, and DNA

▼ **Figure 6-16**
Bornean tarsier.

▼ **Figure 6-17**
Geographical distribution of tarsiers.

ASIA

Pacific Ocean

PHILIPPINES

SUMATRA   BORNEO

■ Tarsiers

studies have suggested that they are more closely related to monkeys, apes, and humans than to lemurs and lorises. Therefore, although there is still some debate as to the taxonomic status of tarsiers, they are now classified in the suborder Haplorhini, along with the anthropoids (see Fig. 6-8 and Appendix A).

Anthropoids: Monkeys, Apes, and Humans

Although there is much variation among anthropoids, they share certain features that, when taken together, distinguish them as a group from lemurs and lorises. Here's a partial list of these traits:

1. A larger average body size
2. Larger brain in absolute terms and relative to body weight
3. Reduced reliance on olfaction, indicated by absence of a rhinarium and a reduction in relative size of olfactory-related structures in the brain
4. Increased reliance on vision, with forward-facing eyes placed more to the front of the face
5. Greater degree of color vision
6. Back of eye socket protected by a bony plate
7. Blood supply to brain different from that of lemurs and lorises
8. Fusion of the two sides of the mandible at the midline to form one bone (in lemurs and lorises, they're two distinct bones joined by cartilage at the middle of the chin)
9. More generalized dentition, as seen in the absence of a dental comb and some other features
10. Differences in female internal reproductive anatomy
11. Longer gestation and maturation periods
12. Increased parental care
13. More mutual grooming

Approximately 85 percent of all primates are monkeys. It's thought that there are about 195 species, but it's impossible to give precise numbers because the taxonomic status of some populations remains in doubt, and primatologists are still making new discoveries. (In fact, between 1990 and 2006, 24 species and subspecies of monkeys were discovered and described.) Monkeys are divided into two groups separated by geographical area (New World and Old World) as well as at least 40 million years of separate evolutionary history (see Chapter 9).

New World Monkeys The approximately 70 New World monkey species can be found in a wide range of arboreal environments throughout most forested areas in southern Mexico and Central and South America (**Fig. 6-18**). They exhibit a wide range of variation in size, diet, and ecological adaptations (**Fig. 6-19**). In size, they vary from the tiny marmosets and tamarins (about 12 ounces) to the 20-pound howler monkeys (**Figs. 6-20** and **6-21**). New

▼ **Figure 6-18**
Geographical distribution of New World monkeys.

▼ **Figure 6-19**
Some New World monkeys.

Female muriqui with infant

Squirrel monkeys

Prince Bernhard's titi monkey (discovered in 2002)

White-faced capuchins

Male uakari

▶ **Figure 6-20**
Golden lion tamarins.

▲ **Figure 6-21**
Male, female, and infant howler monkeys illustrating why they're called "howlers." The roaring sound they make is among the loudest of mammalian vocalizations.

white-faced capuchins in Figure 6-19 with the Sykes monkey in Figure 6-24 or with your own downward-facing nostrils. This difference in nose form has given rise to the terms *platyrrhine* (flat-nosed) and *catarrhine* (downward-facing nose) to refer to New and Old World anthropoids, respectively. The more formal terminology used in primate classification is shown in Figure 6-8 and will be discussed in more detail in Chapter 9.

Marmosets and tamarins are the smallest of the New World monkeys. (In fact, they're the smallest of all monkeys.) They have claws instead of nails, and unlike other primates, they usually give birth to twins instead of a single infant. They're mostly insectivorous, although marmosets eat gums from trees, and tamarins also eat fruits. Marmosets and tamarins are quadrupedal, and they use their claws for climbing. These small monkeys live in social groups usually composed of a mated pair, or a female and two adult males, and their offspring. This type of mating pattern is rare among mammals. Indeed, marmosets and tamarins are among the few primate species in which males are extensively involved in infant care (a truly progressive society!).

World monkeys are almost exclusively arboreal, and some never come to the ground. Like the Old World monkeys, all except one species (the owl monkey) are diurnal.

One characteristic that distinguishes New and Old World monkeys is the shape of the nose. New World monkeys have broad noses with outward-facing nostrils; Old World monkeys have narrower noses with downward-facing nostrils. To verify this, compare the

Other New World species range in size from squirrel monkeys (weighing only 1.5 to 2.5 pounds and having a body length of 12 inches) to the larger howlers (as much as 22 pounds in males and around 24 inches long). Diet varies, with most relying on a combination of fruits and leaves supplemented to varying degrees with insects. Most are quadrupedal; but some, such as spider monkeys (**Fig. 6-22**), are semibrachiators. Howlers, muriquis, and spider monkeys also have prehensile tails that are used not only in locomotion but also for hanging from branches. Socially, most New World monkeys live in mixed-sex groups of all age categories. Some (such as titis) form monogamous pairs and live with their subadult offspring.

Old World Monkeys Except for humans, Old World monkeys are the most widely distributed of all living primates. They're found throughout sub-Saharan Africa and southern Asia, ranging from tropical jungle habitats to semiarid desert and even to seasonally snow-covered areas in northern Japan (**Fig. 6-23**).

Conveniently, all Old World monkeys are placed in one taxonomic

◄ **Figure 6-22**
Spider monkey. Note use of prehensile tail for suspension.

family, **Cercopithecidae**. In turn, this family is divided into two subfamilies: the **cercopithecines** and **colobines**. Most Old World monkeys are quadrupedal and primarily arboreal, but some (such as baboons) are also adapted to life on the ground. In general, they

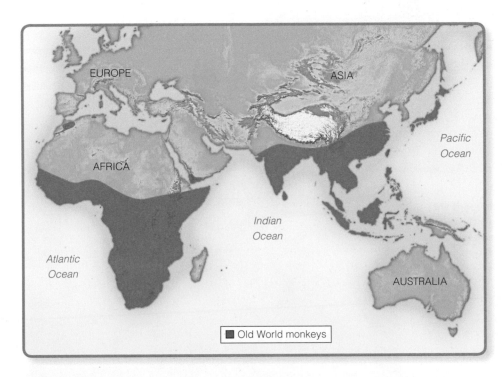

◄ **Figure 6-23**
Geographical distribution of living Old World monkeys.

Cercopithecidae (serk-oh-pith´-eh-see-dee) The taxonomic family that includes all Old World monkeys.

cercopithecines (serk-oh-pith´-eh-seens) Common name for members of the subfamily of Old World monkeys that includes baboons, macaques, and guenons.

colobines (kole´-uh-beans) Common name for members of the subfamily of Old World monkeys that includes the African colobus monkeys and Asian langurs.

spend a good deal of time feeding, sleeping, and grooming. Old World monkeys also have areas of hardened skin on the buttocks called **ischial callosities** that serve as sitting pads, which make it possible to sit and sleep on tree branches for hours at a time.

The cercopithecines are the more generalized of the two groups: They're more omnivorous and they have cheek pouches for storing food, much like hamsters. As a group, the cercopith-

ecines eat almost anything: fruits, seeds, leaves, grasses, tubers, roots, nuts, insects, birds' eggs, amphibians, small reptiles, and small mammals (the last seen in baboons).

The majority of cercopithecine species, such as the mostly arboreal guenons (Dutch for "clown"; **Fig. 6-24**) and the more terrestrial savanna and hamadryas baboons (**Fig. 6-25**), are found in Africa. The many macaque species (including the well-known rhesus

Robert Jurmain

© Corbis Super RF / Alamy

© Thomas Dobner 2006 / Alamy

▲ **Figure 6-24**
Adult male Sykes monkey, one of several guenon species.

▲ **Figure 6-25**
(a) Savanna baboons. (b) Hamadryas baboons are found in Ethiopia. Note how much larger the male (at right) is than the female. The male also has much longer hair around the head and shoulders that produces a distinctive mane.

ischial callosities Patches of tough, hard skin on the buttocks of Old World monkeys and chimpanzees.

◀ **Figure 6-26**
Black-and-white colobus monkeys.

▲ **Figure 6-27**
Male proboscis monkey. The nose (which gives the species its common name) is much larger in males than in females.

monkeys), however, are widely distributed in southern Asia and India.

Colobine species have a narrower range of food preferences and mainly eat mature leaves, which is why they're also called "leaf-eating monkeys." The colobines are found mainly in Asia, but both red colobus and black-and-white colobus are exclusively African (**Fig. 6-26**). Other colobines include several Asian langur species and the proboscis monkey of Borneo (**Fig. 6-27**)

Locomotion in Old World monkeys includes arboreal quadrupedalism in guenons, macaques, and langurs; terrestrial quadrupedalism in baboons and macaques; and semibrachiation and acrobatic leaping in colobus monkeys.

Marked differences in body size or shape between the sexes, referred to as **sexual dimorphism**, are typical of some terrestrial species and are especially pronounced in baboons and patas monkeys. In these species, male body weight (up to 80 pounds in baboons) may be twice that of females.

Females of several species (especially baboons and some macaques) have pronounced cyclical changes of the external genitalia. These changes, which include swelling and redness, are associated with estrus, a hormonally initiated period of sexual receptivity in female nonhuman mammals correlated with ovulation. They serve as visual cues to males that females are sexually receptive.

Old World monkeys live in a few different kinds of social groups. Colobines tend to live in small groups, with only one or two adult males. Savanna baboons and most macaque species are found in large social units comprising several adults of both sexes and offspring of all ages. Monogamous pairing isn't common in Old World monkeys, but it's seen in a few langur species and possibly one or two guenon species.

Old and New World Monkeys: A Case of Homoplasy

We've mentioned several differences between New and Old World monkeys, but the fact remains that they're all monkeys. That is, they're all adapted to a similar (primarily arboreal) way of life. Except for South American owl monkeys, they're all diurnal. All live in social

sexual dimorphism Differences in physical characteristics between males and females of the same species. For example, humans are slightly sexually dimorphic for body size, with males being taller, on average, than females of the same population. Sexual dimorphism is very pronounced in many species, such as gorillas.

groupings; all are omnivorous to varying degrees; and all are quadrupedal (though there are variations of this general locomotor pattern).

These similarities are even more striking when you consider that New and Old World monkeys have followed separate evolutionary paths for at least 40 million years. It was once believed that both lineages evolved independently from separate early primate ancestors; but today, the current consensus is that both New and Old World monkeys arose in Africa from a common monkey ancestor. The monkeys that gave rise to today's New World species reached South America by "rafting" over on chunks of land that had broken away from mainland areas (Hoffstetter, 1972; Ciochon and Chiarelli, 1980b). This phenomenon, which we'll explain more fully in Chapter 9, probably happened many times over the course of several million years.

Whether the last common ancestor shared by New and Old World monkeys was lemur-like, tarsier-like, or, most likely, a monkey-like animal, what's most remarkable is that the two forms haven't become more different from one another. The arboreal adaptations we see in the monkeys of both hemispheres are examples of homoplasy (see Chapter 5), resulting from adaptations in geographically distinct populations that have responded to similar selective pressures.

Hominoids: Apes and Humans

Apes and humans are classified together in the same superfamily, the **hominoids**. Apes are found in Asia and Africa. The small-bodied gibbons and siamangs live in Southeast Asia, and the two orangutan subspecies live on the islands of Borneo and Sumatra (**Fig. 6-28**). In Africa, until the mid- to late twentieth century, gorillas, chimpanzees, and bonobos occupied the forested areas of western, central, and eastern Africa, but their habitat is now extremely fragmented, and all are now threatened or highly endangered. Apes and humans differ from monkeys in numerous ways:

1. Generally larger body size (except for gibbons and siamangs)
2. No tail
3. Lower back shorter and more stable
4. Arms longer than legs (only in apes)
5. Anatomical differences in the shoulder joint that facilitate suspensory feeding and locomotion
6. Generally more complex behavior
7. More complex brain and enhanced cognitive abilities
8. Increased period of infant development and dependency

Gibbons and Siamangs The eight gibbon species and the closely related siamangs are the smallest of the apes, with a long, slender body weighing 13 pounds in gibbons (**Fig. 6-29**) and

▼ **Figure 6-28**
Geographical distribution of living Asian apes.

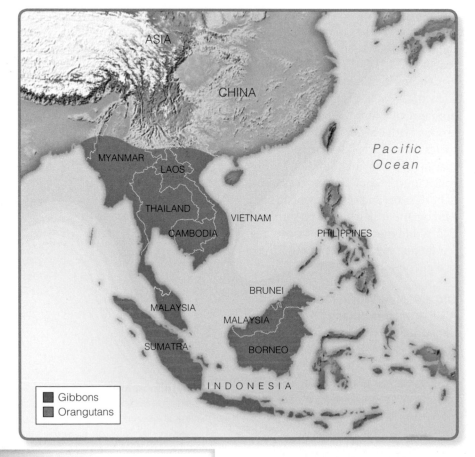

hominoids Members of the primate superfamily (Hominoidea) that includes apes and humans.

▲ **Figure 6-29**
White-handed, cream-colored gibbon. Note the extremely elongated fingers and shortened thumb, which enhances the ability to brachiate.

is an adult male and female with dependent offspring. Although they've been described as monogamous, in reality, members of a pair do sometimes mate with other individuals. As in marmosets and tamarins, male gibbons and siamangs are very much involved in rearing their young. Both males and females are highly **territorial** and protect their territories with elaborate whoops and siren-like "songs," lending them the name "the singing apes of Asia."

Orangutans Orangutans (*Pongo pygmaeus*; **Fig. 6-30**) are represented by two subspecies found today only in heavily forested areas on the Indonesian islands of Borneo and Sumatra (Fig. 6-28). The name *orangutan* (which has no final g and should never be pronounced "o-rang-oo-utang") means "wise man of the forest" in the language of

around 25 pounds in the larger siamangs. Their most distinctive anatomical features are adaptations to feeding while hanging from tree branches, or brachiation, at which gibbons and siamangs excel. In fact, gibbons and siamangs are more dedicated to brachiation than any other primate, and this fact is reflected in their extremely long arms, long, permanently curved fingers, short thumbs, and powerful shoulder muscles. (Their arms are so long that when they're on the ground, they have to walk bipedally with their arms raised to the side.) Gibbons and siamangs mostly eat fruits, although both (especially siamangs) also consume a variety of leaves, flowers, and insects.

The basic social unit of gibbons and siamangs

▲ **Figure 6-30**
Bornean orangutans. (a) Female with infant. (b) Male.

territorial Pertaining to the protection of all or a part of the area occupied by an animal or group of animals. Territorial behaviors range from scent marking to outright attacks on intruders.

the local people. But despite this somewhat affectionate-sounding label, orangutans are severely threatened with extinction in the wild due to poaching by humans and continuing habitat loss on both islands.

Orangutans are slow, cautious climbers whose form of locomotion can best be described as four-handed—referring to their tendency to use all four limbs for grasping and support. Although they're almost completely arboreal, orangutans sometimes travel quadrupedally on the ground. Orangutans exhibit pronounced sexual dimorphism; males are very large and may weigh more than 200 pounds, while females weigh less than 100 pounds. In the wild, orangutans lead largely solitary lives, although adult females are usually accompanied by one or two dependent offspring. They're primarily **frugivorous** but may also eat bark, leaves, insects, and (rarely) meat.

Gorillas The largest of all living primates, gorillas (*Gorilla gorilla*) are today confined to forested areas of western and eastern equatorial Africa (**Fig. 6-31**). There are four generally recognized subspecies, although molecular data suggest that one of these, the western lowland gorilla (**Fig. 6-32**), may be genetically distinct enough to be designated as a separate species (Ruvolo et al., 1994; Garner and Ryder, 1996).

Western lowland gorillas, the most numerous of the four subspecies, are found in several countries of west-central Africa. In 1998, Doran and McNeilage estimated their population size at perhaps 110,000, but Walsh and colleagues (2003) suggested that their numbers were far lower. Staggeringly, in August 2008, the Wildlife Conservation Society reported the discovery of an estimated 125,000 western lowland gorillas in the northern region of the Democratic Republic of the Congo (DRC—formerly Zaire)! This is extremely encouraging news, but it doesn't mean that gorillas are out of danger. To put this figure into perspective, consider that a large football stadium can hold around 70,000 spectators. So, next time you see a stadium packed with fans, think about the fact that you're perhaps looking at a crowd that numbers around half of all the western lowland gorillas on earth. Unless the DRC government, acting with wildlife conservation groups, can set aside more land as national parks and protect the gorillas from hunting and disease, it's likely that western lowland gorillas may still be facing extinction in the wild.

Cross River gorillas, a West African subspecies, were identified in the early 1900s but thought to be extinct until the 1980s, when primatologists became aware of a few small populations in areas along the border between Nigeria and Cameroon (Sarmiento and Oates, 2000). Primatologists believe that there may be only 250 to 300 of these animals; thus, Cross River gorillas are among the most endangered of all primates. Currently, the International

▼ **Figure 6-31**
Geographical distribution of living African apes.

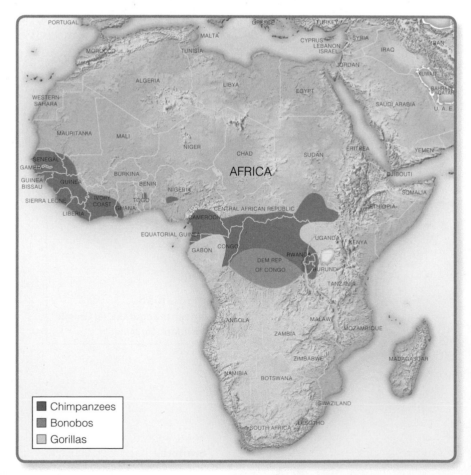

- Chimpanzees
- Bonobos
- Gorillas

frugivorous (fru-give´-or-us) Having a diet composed primarily of fruits.

© imagebroker / Alamy

© Duncan Usher / Alamy

Union for the Conservation of Nature and Natural Resources (IUCN) is developing plans to protect this vulnerable and little-known subspecies (Oates et al., 2007).

Eastern lowland gorillas, which haven't really been studied, live near the eastern border of the DRC. At present, their numbers are unknown but suspected to be around 12,000. (You wouldn't need a very large football stadium to hold this many people.) Due to warfare in the region, researchers fear that many of these gorillas have been killed, but it's impossible to know how many.

Mountain gorillas (**Fig. 6-33**), the most extensively studied of the four subspecies, are restricted to the mountainous areas of central Africa in Rwanda, the DRC, and Uganda. There have probably never been many mountain gorillas, and today they number only about 700 animals, making them one of the more endangered primate species.

Like all gorillas, Mountain gorillas exhibit marked sexual dimorphism, with males weighing up to 400 pounds and females around 150 to 200 pounds. Adult gorillas, especially males, are primarily terrestrial, and like chimpanzees, they practice a type of quadrupedalism called knuckle walking (refer back to Fig. 6-7).

Mountain gorillas live in groups consisting of one, or sometimes two, large silverback males, a variable number of adult females, and their subadult offspring. (The term *silverback* refers to the saddle of white hair across the backs of fully adult males that appears around the age of 12 or 13 years.) A silverback male may tolerate the presence of one or more young adult "blackback" males (probably his sons) in his group. Typically, but not always, both females and males leave their **natal group** as young adults. Females join other groups; and males, who appear to be less likely to emigrate, may live alone for a while or may join up with other males before eventually forming their own group.

Systematic studies of free-ranging western lowland gorillas weren't begun

▲ **Figure 6-32**
Lowland gorillas. (a) Male. **(b)** Female with infant.

natal group The group in which animals are born and raised. (*Natal* pertains to birth.)

▶ **Figure 6-33**
Mountain gorillas. (**a**) A male silver-back mountain gorilla with his group in the background. (**b**) Female.

© Thomas Marent / Minden Pictures

Lynn Kilgore

until the mid-1980s, so even though they're the only gorillas you'll see in zoos, we don't know as much about them as we do about mountain gorillas. The social structure of western lowland gorillas is similar to that of mountain gorillas, but groups are smaller and somewhat less cohesive.

All gorillas are almost exclusively vegetarian. Mountain and western lowland gorillas concentrate primarily on leaves, pith, and stalks, but western lowland gorillas eat more fruit. Western lowland gorillas, unlike mountain gorillas (which avoid water), also frequently wade through swamps while foraging on aquatic plants (Doran and McNeilage, 1998).

Perhaps because of their large body size and enormous strength, gorillas have long been considered ferocious; in reality, they're usually shy and gentle. But this doesn't mean they're never aggressive. In fact, among males, competition for females can be extremely violent. As might be expected, males will attack to defend their group from any perceived danger, whether it's another male gorilla or a human hunter. Still, the reputation of gorillas as murderous beasts is the result of uninformed myth making and little else.

◀ **Figure 6-34**
Male, female, and infant chimpanzees. Chimpanzees do not live in "nuclear families" as this photo might imply, and it's quite possible that the male at left is not the father of the infant.

Chimpanzees The three subspecies of common chimpanzee (*Pan troglodytes*) are probably the best known of all nonhuman primates, even though many people think they're monkeys, not apes (**Fig. 6-34**). Chimpanzees are often misunderstood because of zoo exhibits, circus acts, television shows, and movies; thus, their true nature didn't become known until years of fieldwork with wild chimpanzee groups provided a more accurate picture. Today, chimpanzees are found in equatorial Africa, in a broad belt from the Atlantic Ocean in the west to Lake Tanganyika in the east. But within this large geographical area, their range is very patchy, and it's becoming even more so with further habitat destruction.

In many ways, chimpanzees are anatomically similar to gorillas, with corresponding limb proportions and upper-body shape. However, the ecological adaptations and behaviors of chimpanzees and gorillas differ, with chimpanzees spending more time in the trees. Chimpanzees are also frequently excitable, active, and noisy, while gorillas tend to be placid and quiet.

Chimpanzees are smaller than orangutans and gorillas, and although they're sexually dimorphic, sex differences aren't as pronounced as in gorillas and orangutans. A male chimpanzee may weigh 150 pounds, but females can weigh at least 100 pounds. In addition to quadrupedal knuckle walking, chimpanzees (particularly youngsters) may brachiate. When on the ground, they frequently walk bipedally for short distances when carrying food or other objects.

Chimpanzees eat a huge variety of foods, including fruits, leaves, insects, nuts, birds' eggs, berries, caterpillars, and small mammals. Moreover, both males and females occasionally take part in group hunting efforts to kill small mammals such as young bushpigs and antelope. Their prey also includes monkeys, especially red colobus. When hunts are successful, the members of the hunting party share the prey.

Chimpanzees live in large, fluid communities ranging in size from 10 to as many as 100 individuals. A group of closely bonded males forms the core of chimpanzee communities in many locations, especially in East Africa (Goodall, 1986; Wrangham et al., 1992). But for some West African groups, females appear to be more central to the community (Boesch, 1996; Boesch and Boesch-Acherman, 2000; Vigilant et al., 2001). Relationships among closely bonded males aren't always peaceful or stable, yet these males cooperatively defend their territory and are highly intolerant of unfamiliar chimpanzees, especially males.

Even though chimpanzees live in communities, it's rare for all members to be together at the same time. Rather, they tend to come and go, so they don't encounter the same individuals on a daily basis. Adult females usually forage either alone or in the company of their offspring, a grouping that might include several animals, since females with infants sometimes accompany their own mothers and siblings. These associations have been reported for the chimpanzees at Gombe National Park, where about 40 percent of females remain in the group in which they were born (Williams, 1999). But in most other areas, females leave their natal group to join another community. This behavioral pattern may reduce the risk of mating with close male relatives, because males apparently never leave the group in which they were born.

Chimpanzee social behavior is extremely complex, and individuals form lifelong attachments with friends and relatives. If they continue to live in their natal group, the bond between mothers and infants can remain strong until one of them dies. This may be a considerable period of time, because many wild chimpanzees live well into their 40s and even longer.

Bonobos Bonobos (*Pan paniscus*) are found only in an area south of the Zaire River in the DRC (see **Fig. 6-35**). Not officially recognized by European scientists until the 1920s, they remain among the least studied of the great apes. Although ongoing field studies have produced much information (Susman, 1984; Kano, 1992), research has been hampered by civil war. There are currently no accurate counts of bonobos, but their numbers are believed to be between 29,000 and 50,000 (IUCN, 2008). These few are highly threatened by human hunting, warfare, and habitat loss.

Because bonobos bear a strong resemblance to common chimpanzees, but are slightly smaller, they've been called "pygmy chimpanzees." Actually, the differences in body size aren't very striking, although bonobos are less stocky. They also have longer legs relative to arms, a relatively smaller head, and a dark face from birth.

Bonobos are more arboreal than chimpanzees, and they're less excitable

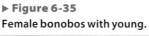

▶ **Figure 6-35**
Female bonobos with young.

Ellen Ingmanson

and aggressive. While aggression isn't unknown, it appears that physical violence both within and between groups is uncommon. Like chimpanzees, bonobos live in geographically based, fluid communities, and they eat many of the same foods, including occasional meat derived from small mammals (Badrian and Malenky, 1984). But bonobo communities aren't centered around a group of males. Instead, male-female bonding is more important than in chimpanzees and most other nonhuman primates (Badrian and Badrian, 1984). This may be related to bonobo sexuality, which differs from that of other nonhuman primates in that copulation is frequent and occurs throughout a female's estrous cycle, so sex isn't linked solely to reproduction. In fact, bonobos are famous for their sexual behavior, since they copulate frequently and use sex to defuse potentially tense situations. Sexual activity between members of the same sex is also common (Kano, 1992; de Waal and Lanting, 1997). Given this aspect of bonobo behavior, it's perhaps not surprising that they've been called the "make love, not war" primate society.

Humans Humans (*Homo sapiens*) are the only living representatives of the habitually bipedal primates (hominin tribe). Our primate heritage is evident in our overall anatomy and genetic makeup and in many behavioral aspects. Except for reduced canine size, human teeth are typical primate (especially ape) teeth. The human dependence on vision and decreased reliance on olfaction, as well as flexible limbs and grasping hands, are rooted in our primate, arboreal past (**Fig. 6-36**).

Humans in general are omnivorous, although all societies observe certain culturally based dietary restrictions. Even so, as a species with a rather generalized digestive system, we're physiologically adapted to digest an extremely wide assortment of foods. Perhaps to our detriment, we also share with our relatives a fondness for sweets that originates from the importance of

high-energy fruits eaten by many nonhuman primates.

But humans are obviously unique among primates and indeed among all animals. For example, no member of any other species has the ability to write or think about how it differs from other life-forms. This ability is rooted in the fact that during the last 800,000 years of human evolution, brain size has increased dramatically, and there have been many other neurological changes as well.

Humans are also completely dependent on culture. Without cultural innovation, it would never have been possible for us to leave the tropics. As it is, humans inhabit every corner of the planet except for Antarctica, and we've even established outposts there. And lest we forget, a fortunate few have even walked on the moon! None of the technologies (indeed, none of the other aspects of culture) that humans have developed over the last

Lynn Kilgore

▲ **Figure 6-36**
Playground equipment frequently allows children to play in ways that reflect their arboreal heritage.

several thousand years would have been possible without the highly developed cognitive abilities we alone possess. Nevertheless, the neurological basis for **intelligence** is rooted in our evolutionary past, and it's something we share with other primates. Indeed, research has demonstrated that several nonhuman primate species—most notably chimpanzees, bonobos, and gorillas—display a level of problem solving and insight that most people would have considered impossible 30 years ago (see Chapter 8).

Humans are uniquely predisposed to use spoken language, and some 5,000 years ago, we also developed writing. Our advanced capacity for language exists because during the course of human evolution, certain neurological and anatomical structures were modified in ways not seen in any other species. But while nonhuman primates aren't anatomically capable of producing speech, research has shown that to varying degrees, the great apes are able to communicate by using symbols, which is a foundation for language that humans and the great apes (to a limited degree) have in common.

Aside from cognitive abilities, the one other trait that sets humans apart from other primates (and indeed other mammals) is our unique form of striding, *habitual* bipedal locomotion. This particular trait appeared early in the evolution of our lineage, and over time, we've become more efficient at it because of related changes in the musculoskeletal anatomy of our pelvis, leg, and foot. But early hominins increasingly adopted bipedalism because they were already *preadapted* for it. That is, as primates, and especially as apelike primates, they were already behaviorally predisposed to, and anatomically capable of, at least short-term bipedal walking before they adopted it wholeheartedly. So, while it's certainly true that human beings are unique intellectually, and in some ways anatomically, we're still primates. As a matter of fact, humans are basically exaggerated African apes.

intelligence Mental capacity; ability to learn, reason, or comprehend and interpret information, facts, relationships, and meanings; the capacity to solve problems, whether through the application of previously acquired knowledge or through insight.

Endangered Primates

In September 2000, scientists announced that a subspecies of red colobus, named Miss Waldron's red colobus, had officially been declared extinct. This announcement came after a 6-year search for the 20-pound monkey that hadn't been seen for 20 years (Oates et al., 2000). Sadly, this species, indigenous to the West African countries of Ghana and the Ivory Coast, has the distinction of being the first nonhuman primate to be declared extinct in the twenty-first century, but it won't be the last. In fact, as of this writing, over half of all nonhuman primate species are now in jeopardy, and some face almost certain extinction in the wild (**Table 6-1**).

There are three basic reasons for the worldwide depletion of nonhuman primates: habitat destruction, human predation, and live capture for export or local trade. Underlying these three causes is one major factor, unprecedented human population growth, particularly in developing countries, where most nonhuman primates live. The developing nations of Africa, Asia, and Central and South America are home to over 90 percent of all nonhuman primate species; and these countries, aided in no small part by the industrialized countries of Europe and the United States, are cutting their forests at a rate of about 30 million acres per year. Unbelievably, in the year 2002, deforestation of the Amazon increased by 40 percent over that of 2001. This increase was largely due to land clearing for the cultivation of soybeans. In Brazil, the Atlantic rain forest originally covered some 385,000 square miles. Today, an estimated 7 percent is all that remains of what was once home to countless New World monkeys and thousands of other species. Fortunately, in 2008 the Brazilian government announced that in the three preceding years, deforestation decreased by 59 percent. The government also moved to enforce logging

TABLE 6.1 African Primates in Danger of Extinction

Species/Subspecies Common Name	Location	Estimated Size of Remaining Population
Barbary macaque	North Africa	23,000
Tana River mangabey	Tana River, Kenya	800–1,100
Sanje mangabey	Uzungwa Mts., Tanzania	1,800–3,000
Drill	Cameroon, Bioko	?
Preuss' guenon	Cameroon, Bioko	?
White-throated guenon	Southwest Nigeria	?
Pennant's red colobus	Bioko	?
Preuss' red colobus	Cameroon	8,000
Bouvier's red colobus	Congo Republic	?
Tana River red colobus	Tana River, Kenya	200–300
Uhehe red colobus	Uzungwa Mts. Tanzania	10,000
Zanzibar red colobus	Zanzibar	1,500
Mountain gorilla	Virunga Volcanoes (Rwanda, Uganda, and Democratic Republic of the Congo) and Impenetrable Forest (Uganda)	550–650

restrictions on public lands, but whether they will succeed or not remains to be seen (Tollefson, 2008).

The motivation behind deforestation is, of course, economic: the short-term gains from clearing forests to create immediately available (but poor) farmland or ranchland; the use of trees for lumber and paper products; and large-scale mining operations (with their necessary roads)—all causing further habitat destruction. Regionally, the loss of rain forest ranks as a national disaster for some countries. For example, the West African nation of Sierra Leone had an estimated 15,000 square miles of rain forest early in the twentieth century. Today, less than 530 square miles remain, and most of this destruction has occurred since World War II. People in many developing countries are also short of fuel and frequently use whatever firewood they can get. In addition, the demand for tropical hardwoods (such as mahogany, teak, and rosewood) in the United States, Europe, and Japan continues unabated, creating an enormously profitable market for rain forest products.

Primates are also captured live for zoos, biomedical research, and the exotic pet trade. Live capture has declined since the Convention on International Trade in Endangered Species of Wild Flora and Fauna (CITES) was implemented in 1973. By August 2005, a total of 169 countries had signed this treaty, agreeing not to allow trade in species listed by CITES as being endangered (see CITES Handbook, www.cites.org). However, even some CITES members are still occasionally involved in the illegal primate trade (Japan and Belgium, among others).

A Closer Look

Aye-Ayes: Victims of Derived Traits and Superstition

The primate order is filled with a variety of fascinating animals, although few seem as unusual as the aye-aye (*Daubentonia madagascariensis*), a type of lemur. This is because most primates aren't as derived as the aye-aye. Today, aye-ayes are the only members of their genus. A second species (a subfossil lemur) was exterminated by humans during the last few centuries, and the aye-aye was unknown (at least to Western science) until 1961. Like all lemurs, aye-ayes are found only on the island of Madagascar, where they occupy a niche similar to that of woodpeckers. Like woodpeckers, which aren't found on Madagascar, aye-ayes feed on insects and grubs that live in tree bark. On the ground they also find these same foods in logs. But instead of using a long beak to drill for hidden prey, this nocturnal primate uses an extremely specialized, elongated, bony middle finger to tap, tap, tap along a tree trunk, listening for hollow

spaces (**Fig. 1**). When an aye-aye finds a hollow space where a grub might be hiding, it tears through the bark with its continuously growing incisor teeth (a rodent trait) and scoops out the unlucky larva with the long nail at the end of its peculiar middle finger.

Aye-aye dentition is also quite derived and specialized for this particular dietary niche. The aye-aye dental formula of

$$\frac{1.0.1.3}{1.0.0.3}$$

isn't just unique among primates; it's unique among all mammals. As you can see, aye-ayes have no canine teeth and no lower premolars, although there's one upper premolar (Hershkovitz, 1977).

This perhaps strange-looking primate, which seems to have a permanent "bad hair day," is about the size of a small house cat and has little of the appeal of,

say, a galago. Unfortunately, many Malagasy (the human inhabitants of Madagascar) find the aye-aye's appearance less than endearing. In fact, many think aye-ayes are bad luck and don't realize that they're simply harmless primates making a living as best they can.

Sadly, human imagination may prove this primate's undoing. Aye-ayes are variously thought to be heralds of evil or killers who creep into thatched huts and puncture their victim's aorta with their frightening middle finger (Goodman and Schütz, 2000). And some Malagasy superstitiously believe that should an aye-aye point its long middle finger at you, you will die. So it seems that cruel fate and humans have pointed their own finger of condemnation at the aye-aye, for only about 2,500 live in the wild and only a dozen or so in captivity.

◄ **Figure 1**
This nineteenth-century drawing of an aye-aye perfectly illustrates the elongated middle finger used for digging insects and grubs from logs and tree bark.

Bushmeat and Ebola: A Deadly Combination

In many areas, habitat loss has been the single greatest cause of declining numbers of nonhuman primates. But in the past few years, human hunting has perhaps posed an even greater threat (**Fig. 6-37**). During the 1990s, primatologists and conservationists became aware of a rapidly developing trade in *bushmeat*, meat from wild animals, especially in Africa. The current slaughter, which now accounts for the loss of tens of thousands of nonhuman primates (and other animals) annually, has been compared to the near extinction of the American bison in the nineteenth century.

Wherever primates live, people have always hunted them for food. But in the past, subsistence hunting wasn't a serious threat to nonhuman primate populations, and certainly not to entire species. But now, hunters armed with automatic rifles can, and do, wipe out an entire group of monkeys or gorillas in minutes. In fact, it's now possible to buy bushmeat outside the country of origin. In major cities throughout Europe and the United States, illegal bushmeat is readily available to immigrants who want traditional foods or to nonimmigrants who think it's trendy to eat meat from exotic, and frequently endangered, animals.

It's impossible to know how many animals are killed each year, but the

John Oates

◀ **Figure 6-37**
(a) Red-eared guenons (with red tails) and Preuss' guenons for sale in a bushmeat market, Malabo, Equatorial Guinea. **(b)** Body parts, mostly from various monkey species, for sale in a West African market.

estimates are staggering. The Society for Conservation Biology estimates that about 6,000 kg (13,228 pounds) of bushmeat is taken through just seven Western cities (New York, London, Toronto, Paris, Montreal, Chicago, and Brussels) every month. No one knows how much of this meat is from primates, but this figure represents only a tiny fraction of all the animals being slaughtered, because much smuggled meat isn't detected at ports of entry. Also, the international trade is thought to account for only about 1 percent of the total (Marris, 2006).

Quite clearly, species such as primates, which number only a few hundred or a few thousand animals, cannot and will not survive this onslaught for more than a few years. In addition, hundreds of infants are orphaned and sold in markets as pets. Although a few of these traumatized orphans make it to sanctuaries, most die within days or weeks of capture (**Fig. 6-38**).

Logging has been a major factor in the development of the bushmeat trade. The construction of logging roads, mainly by French, German, and Belgian lumber companies, has opened up vast tracts of previously inaccessible forest to hunters. What has emerged is a multimillion-dollar trade in bush-meat, a trade in which logging company employees and local government officials participate with hunters, villagers, market vendors, and smugglers to cater to local and overseas markets. In other words, the hunting of wild animals for food, particularly in Africa, has quickly shifted from a subsistence activity to a commercial enterprise of international scope.

Although the slaughter may be best known in Africa, it's by no means limited to that continent. In South America, for example, hunting nonhuman primates for food is common, although it hasn't become a commercial enterprise on the scale seen in Africa and parts of Asia. Nevertheless, one report documented that in less than two years, one family of Brazilian rubber tappers killed almost 500 members of various large-bodied species, including spider monkeys, woolly monkeys, and howlers (Peres, 1990). Moreover, live capture and illegal trade in endangered primate species continue unabated in China and Southeast Asia, where nonhuman primates are not only eaten but also funneled into the exotic pet trade.

▶ **Figure 6-38**
Orphaned bonobo infants being cared for at a bonobo sanctuary in the Democratic Republic of the Congo.

But just as importantly, primate body parts also figure prominently in traditional medicines, and with increasing human population size, the enormous demand for these products (and products from other, nonprimate species, such as tigers) has placed many species in extreme jeopardy.

As a note of optimism, in November 2007, the DRC government and the Bonobo Conservation Initiative (in Washington, D.C.) created a bonobo reserve consisting of 30,500 km². This amounts to about 10 percent of the land in the DRC, and the government has stated that its goal is to set aside an additional 5 percent for wildlife protection (News in Brief, 2007). This is a huge step forward, but it remains to be seen if protection can be enforced.

But there's yet another threat to West African primates. About 80 percent of the world's remaining gorillas and most chimpanzees are found in two West African countries, Gabon and the Republic of Congo (Walsh et al., 2003; Leroy et al., 2004). Between 1983 and 2000, ape populations in Gabon declined by half, mostly because of hunting, but also due to the viral disease ebola. This devastating disease, first recognized in 1976, is believed to be maintained in wild animals, probably fruit bats (Leroy et al., 2005). Furthermore, ebola is transmitted to humans through contact with infected animals (for example, through butchering). In humans, ebola is frequently fatal, and symptoms include fever, vomiting, diarrhea, and severe hemorrhaging.

Since 1994, there have been four ebola outbreaks in Gabon, and ape carcasses were found near affected settlements in three. In one area of Gabon where large-scale hunting hasn't occurred, ape populations declined by an estimated 90 percent between 1991 and 2000. And Rouquet and colleagues (2005) reported that ebola was also the confirmed cause of death in great apes in the Republic of Congo in 2003 and 2004. But the worst news came in 2006 with a report that as many as 5,000 gorillas had died of ebola in that country (Bermejo et al., 2006). Researchers now think that the disease is spread within and between gorilla groups and not through contact with reservoir species like bats; and this fact offers some slight hope that a vaccination program might be effective. But faced with the combination of ebola and commercial hunting, it's clear that great ape populations in western Africa can't be sustained and are now being diminished to small remnant populations.

Increased Risk to Mountain Gorillas

Mountain gorillas are one of the most endangered nonhuman primate species. All of the approximately 700 mountain gorillas alive today are restricted to a heavily forested area in and around the Virunga Mountains (the Virunga Volcanoes Conservation Area) shared by three countries: Uganda, Rwanda, and the DRC. This entire area is a UNESCO (United Nations Educational, Scientific, and Cultural Organization) World Heritage Site. In addition, there is a separate, noncontiguous park in Uganda—the Bwindi Impenetrable Forest, home to about half of all the remaining mountain gorillas. Tourism has been the only real hope of salvation for these magnificent animals, and for this reason, several gorilla groups have been habituated to humans and are protected by park rangers. Nevertheless, poaching, civil war, and land clearing have continued to take a toll on these small populations.

Between January and late July 2007, 10 mountain gorillas were slaughtered in the park. Two infants orphaned in the attacks were rescued and taken to a veterinary clinic and they continue to do well. Six of the victims, including the silverback male (**Fig. 6-39**), were members of one family group of 12. The remnant of this group consists of 4 immature males and 1 immature female, and without a silverback, their future is uncertain.

The gorillas weren't shot for meat or because they were raiding crops. They were shot because the existence and protection of mountain gorillas in the park is a hindrance to people who would destroy what little remains of the forests that are home to the gorillas. One of the many reasons for cutting the forests is the manufacture of charcoal, a major source of fuel in rural Rwanda and the DRC.

In 2006, paleoanthropologist Richard Leakey and a colleague, Emmanuel de Mérode, established WildlifeDirect to help support conservationists and especially the rangers who work for little to no pay to protect the mountain gorillas. (It should be pointed out that in the past few years, more than 120 rangers have been killed while protecting wildlife in the

◄ **Figure 6-39**
Congolese villagers carrying the body of the silverback gorilla shot and killed in the July 2007 attack. His body was buried with the other members of his group who were also killed.

WildlifeDirect.org

Virungas.) You may want to go to their website (www.wildlifedirect.org), where you can read updates and see photographs and videos posted daily by the rangers. These communications offer fascinating insights into their efforts, conditions in the forest, and updates on gorillas and other species.

There are several other conservation groups that work to protect mountain gorillas. Also, in 2000, the United Nations Environmental Program established the Great Ape Survival Project (GRASP). GRASP is an alliance of many of the world's major great ape conservation and research organizations. In 2003, GRASP appealed for $25 million to be used in protecting the great apes from extinction. The money (a paltry sum) would be used to enforce laws that regulate hunting and illegal logging. It goes without saying that GRASP and other organizations must

succeed if the great apes are to survive in the wild for even 20 more years!

If you are in your 20s or 30s, you will certainly live to hear of the extinction of some of our marvelous cousins. Many more will undoubtedly slip away unnoticed. Tragically, this will occur, in most cases, before we've even gotten to know them. Each species on earth is the current result of a unique set of evolutionary events that, over millions of years, has produced a finely adapted component of a diverse ecosystem. When it becomes extinct, that adaptation and that part of biodiversity is lost forever. What a tragedy it will be if, through our own mismanagement and greed, we awaken to a world without chimpanzees, mountain gorillas, or the tiny, exquisite lion tamarin. When this day comes, we truly will have lost a part of ourselves, and we will certainly be the poorer for it.

Summary of Main Topics

- The mammalian order Primates includes humans and approximately 230 nonhuman species: apes, monkeys, tarsiers, and lemurs. Most nonhuman primates live in tropical and subtropical regions of Africa, India, Asia, Mexico, and South America.

- The order Primates is divided into two suborders: Strepsirhini (lemurs and lorises) and Haplorhini (tarsiers, monkeys, apes, and humans).

- As a group, the primates are very generalized, meaning they've retained many anatomical characteristics that were present in early ancestral mammalian species. These traits include five digits on the hands and feet, different kinds of teeth, and a skeletal anatomy and limb structure that allow for different forms of locomotion

(climbing, brachiation, quadrupedalism, and bipedalism).

- Primates have grasping hands, and most have an opposable thumb that facilitates this ability. (Some species are more specialized in that their thumbs are reduced or even absent.) Many primates, such as chimpanzees and bonobos, also have opposable big toes.

- Most primates are omnivorous, although certain species focus on only certain foods. For example, the colobines (colobus monkeys and langurs) primarily eat leaves.

- In general, primates have relatively larger, more complex brains than other mammals. Consequently, they are comparatively more intelligent and exhibit more complex behaviors. This is especially true of monkeys, apes, and humans.

- Primates rely more on vision than olfaction, and diurnal primates (with some New World exceptions) have full color vision. Correspondingly, the areas of the brain related to vision are larger and more complex than the areas related to olfaction.

- Almost all nonhuman primates are arboreal and spend at least part of the time in trees.

- Because of human hunting and habitat loss, the majority of nonhuman primates are endangered today, and some are on the verge of extinction. Without concerted efforts to preserve primate habitat and control hunting, many species, including mountain gorillas, bonobos, chimpanzees, and many monkeys, could well become extinct by 2050.

Critical Thinking Questions

1. What are some human characteristics that reflect a common ancestry between ourselves and nonhuman primates? Although we didn't really discuss this topic in the chapter, can you think of some ways in which humans are more similar to chimpanzees than to monkeys?

2. How do you think continued advances in genetic research will influence how we look at our relationship with nonhuman primates?

3. What factors threaten the existence of nonhuman primates in the wild? Is this important to you? What can you do to help save nonhuman primates from extinction?

4. How does a classification scheme reflect biological and evolutionary changes in a lineage? Can you give an example of suggested changes to how primates are classified? What do you think most people's reaction would be to hearing that scientists are placing the great apes into the same taxonomic family as humans?

important to understand that just as cats evolved as predators, horses evolved as prey animals, and their evolutionary history is littered with unfortunate animals that didn't jump at a sound in a shrub. In many cases, those ancestral horses learned, too late, that the sound wasn't caused by a breeze. This is a mistake that prey animals often don't survive, and those that don't leap first leave few if any descendants.

Obviously, this chapter isn't about cats and horses. It's about what we know and hypothesize about the individual and social behaviors of nonhuman primates. But we begin with the familiar examples of cats and horses because we want to point out that many basic behaviors have been shaped by the evolutionary history of particular species. And the same factors that have influenced many types of behavior in nonprimate animals also apply to primates. So if we want to discover the underlying principles of behavioral evolution, we first need to identify the interactions between a number of environmental and physiological variables.

Primate Field Studies

The main goal of primate field studies is to collect information on wild primates whose behavior is unaffected by human activities. Unfortunately, most, if not all, primate populations have now been exposed to human activities that influence their behavior (Janson, 2000). What's more, wild primates aren't easy to study until they've been habituated to the presence of humans, whom they generally fear, and the habituation process can take a long time. Also, habituation itself can change primate behavior. Until the last two decades, the most systematic information on free-ranging primates came from species that spend a lot of time on the ground (baboons, macaques, some lemurs, chimpanzees, and gorillas; **Fig. 7-1a**). This is because it's difficult to identify and observe arboreal primates as they flit through the forest canopy (**Fig. 7-1b**). Now, however, primatologists have accumulated a great deal of data on many arboreal species. Others have focused on nocturnal lemurs, lorises, and tarsiers. Thanks to these efforts, many of the gaps in our knowledge of nonhuman primates are being filled. But with each new discovery come new questions, so

▼ **Figure 7-1**
(a) Baboons spend a great deal of time on the ground and are much easier to observe than red colobus monkeys. **(b)** Imagine trying to recognize the red colobus monkeys as individuals. What tools and techniques would you use to identify them?

behavior Anything organisms do that involves action in response to internal or external stimuli; the response of an individual, group, or species to its environment. Such responses may or may not be deliberate, and they aren't necessarily the result of conscious decision making (which is absent in single-celled organisms, insects, and many other species).

the process will continue as long as there are wild primates to study.

The earliest studies of nonhuman primates in their natural habitats began with an American psychologist named Robert Yerkes, who, beginning in the late 1920s, sent students into the field to study gorillas, chimpanzees, and howler monkeys. Japanese scientists began their pioneering work with Japanese macaques in 1948 (Sugiyama, 1965). In 1960, Jane Goodall began her now famous field study of chimpanzees at Gombe National Park, Tanzania. This project was closely followed by Dian Fossey's work with mountain gorillas in Rwanda and by Birute Galdikas' research on orangutans in Borneo.

These initial studies were, of necessity, largely descriptive in nature. However, some early studies of savanna baboons (DeVore and Washburn, 1963), hamadryas baboons (Kummer, 1968), and geladas (Crook and Gartlan, 1966) related aspects of **social structure** and individual behavior to ecological factors. Also, most early work emphasized male behaviors, partly because of the role of males in group defense. But by the late 1970s and early 1980s, primatologists were focusing more attention on females, not only as mothers but also as individuals with an enormous influence on group dynamics.

Since then, primatologists have studied and continue to study well over 100 nonhuman primate species. Because most primates live in social groups, extensive research is devoted to primate social behavior, the costs and benefits of living in groups, and the advantages and disadvantages of specific behaviors to individuals. Behavioral research is done within an evolutionary framework, so primatologists test hypotheses relating to how behaviors have evolved. And now, the application of genetic techniques to primate behavioral research is beginning to provide answers to many questions, especially those that relate to paternity and reproductive success.

The Evolution of Behavior

Scientists study primates from an ecological and evolutionary perspective, focusing on the relationship between behaviors (both individual and social), the natural environment, and various physiological traits of the species in question. This approach is called **behavioral ecology**, and it's based on the underlying assumption that all of the biological components of ecological systems (animals, plants, and even microorganisms) evolved together. Behaviors are thus adaptations to environmental circumstances that existed in the past as well as in the present.

Briefly, the cornerstone of this perspective is that *behaviors have evolved through the operation of natural selection*. The underlying assumption is that certain behaviors are influenced by genes and are therefore subject to natural selection in the same way physical characteristics are. (Remember that within a specific environmental context, natural selection favors traits that provide a reproductive advantage to the individuals who have them. The horse that reacts quickly to a potential predator probably has greater reproductive success than one that doesn't.) Therefore, behavior constitutes a phenotype, and individuals whose behavioral phenotypes increase reproductive fitness will pass on their genes at a faster rate than others. But this doesn't mean that primatologists think that genes code for specific behaviors, such as a gene for aggression, another for cooperation, and so on. Studying complex behaviors from an evolutionary viewpoint doesn't imply a one gene—one behavior relationship, nor does it suggest that if behaviors are influenced by genes, they can't be modified through learning.

In insects and other invertebrates, behavior is mostly under genetic control. In other words, most behavioral patterns in these species aren't learned;

social structure The composition, size, and sex ratio of a group of animals. Social structure is the result of natural selection in a specific habitat, and it influences individual interactions and social relationships. In many species, social structure varies, depending on different environmental factors. Thus, in primates, social structure should be viewed as flexible, not fixed.

behavioral ecology The study of the evolution of behavior, emphasizing the role of ecological factors as agents of natural selection. Behaviors and behavioral patterns are favored by natural selection when they increase the reproductive fitness of individuals (i.e., they're adaptive) in specific environmental contexts.

they're innate. But in many vertebrates, especially birds and mammals, the proportion of behavior that's due to learning is substantially increased, while the proportion under genetic control is reduced. This is especially true of primates; and in humans, who are so much a product of culture, most behavior is learned. Still, we know that in mammals and birds, some behaviors are at least partly influenced by certain gene products, such as hormones. You may have heard about research linking increased levels of testosterone to an increase in aggression in many species. Also, some conditions, such as depression, schizophrenia, and bipolar disorder, are caused by abnormal levels of certain neurotransmitters. Neurotransmitters are chemicals produced by brain cells; when they're sent from one cell to another, they cause a response (that is, they transmit information from cell to cell). These responses range from muscle activity to the release of hormones (such as testosterone) elsewhere in the body.

Brain cells manufacture neurotransmitters as a result of the action of certain genes, and in this way, genes can influence aspects of behavior. But *behavioral genetics*, or the study of how genes affect behavior, is a relatively new field, and we don't know the extent to which genes actually influence behavior in humans or other species. What we do know is that behavior must be viewed as the product of complex interactions between genetic and environmental factors. The limits and potentials for learning and for behavioral flexibility vary considerably among species. In some species, such as primates, the potentials are extremely broad; but in others, like insects, they aren't. Ultimately, those limits and potentials are set by genetic factors that have been subjected to natural selection throughout the evolutionary history of every species. That history, in turn, has been shaped by the ecological setting not only of living species *but also of their ancestors.*

One of the main goals of primatology is to determine how behaviors influence reproductive fitness and how ecological factors have shaped the development of these behaviors. While the actual mechanics of behavioral evolution aren't yet fully understood, new technologies and methodologies are beginning to help scientists answer many questions. For example, genetic analysis has recently been used to establish paternity in a few primate groups, and this has helped support hypotheses about some behaviors. But in general, an evolutionary approach to the study of behavior doesn't provide definitive answers to many research questions. Rather, it provides a valuable framework within which primatologists analyze data to generate and test hypotheses concerning behavioral patterns. (Remember, the development and testing of hypotheses is how scientific research is done.)

Because primates are among the most social of animals, social behavior is a major topic in primate research. This is a broad subject that includes all aspects of behavior occurring in social groupings, even some you may not think of as social behaviors, like feeding or mating. To understand the function of one behavioral element, it's necessary to determine how it's influenced by numerous interrelated factors. As an example, we'll consider some of the more important variables that influence social structure. But social structure influences individual behavior, so in many cases, the distinctions between social and individual behaviors are blurred.

Some Factors That Influence Social Structure

Body Size Among the living primates, body size is extremely diverse, ranging from dwarf mouse lemurs (**Fig. 7-2**) at about 2.5 ounces to male gorillas at around 260 pounds. As a general rule, larger animals require fewer calories per unit of weight than smaller animals do. This is because larger animals have a smaller ratio of surface area to mass than do smaller animals. Since body heat is lost at the surface, larger animals can retain heat more efficiently, so they require less energy overall. It may seem strange, but two 10-pound monkeys require more food than one 22-pound monkey (Fleagle, 1999).

Russ Mittermeir

◄ **Figure 7-2**
Dwarf mouse lemur.

Basal Metabolic Rate (BMR) The BMR concerns **metabolism**, the rate at which the body uses energy to maintain all bodily functions at a resting state. Metabolism is closely correlated with body size, so in general, smaller animals have a higher BMR than larger ones. Consequently, smaller primates, such as galagos, tarsiers, marmosets, and tamarins, require an energy-rich diet high in protein (insects), fats (nuts and seeds), and carbohydrates (fruits and seeds). Some larger primates (howler monkeys, for example), which tend to have a lower BMR and reduced energy requirements relative to body size, can do well with less energy-rich foods, such as leaves.

Diet Since the nutritional requirements of animals are related to the previous two factors, all three have evolved together. Therefore, when primatologists study the relationships between diet and behavior, they consider the benefits in terms of energy (calories) derived from various food items against the costs (energy expended) of obtaining and digesting them.

As we discussed in Chapter 6, most primates eat a wide variety of foods. But each species concentrates on some kinds of foods more than others; and almost all consume some animal protein, even if it's just in the form of insects and other invertebrates. While small-bodied primates focus on high-energy foods, larger-bodied species

don't necessarily need to. For instance, mountain gorillas eat leaves, pith from bamboo stems, and other types of vegetation. Lowland gorillas do likewise, but they also consume a wider variety of items, including some water plants. These foods have less caloric value than fruits, nuts, and seeds, but they still serve these animals well because gorillas tend to spend much of the day eating. Besides, gorillas don't use a great deal of energy searching for food, since they're frequently surrounded by it (**Fig. 7-3**).

Some monkeys, especially colobines (colobus and langur species), are primarily leaf eaters. Compared with many other monkeys, they're fairly large-bodied. They've also evolved elongated intestines and pouched stomachs that enable them, with the assistance of intestinal bacteria, to digest the tough fibers and cellulose in leaves. Moreover, in at least two langur species, there's a duplicated gene that produces an enzyme that further helps with digestion. Importantly, this gene duplication isn't found in other primates that have been studied, so the duplication event probably occurred after colobines and cercopithecines last shared a common ancestor (Zhang et al., 2002). Since having a second copy

Lynn Kilgore

▲ **Figure 7-3**
This male mountain gorilla has only to reach out to find something to eat.

metabolism The chemical processes within cells that break down nutrients and release energy for the body to use. (When nutrients are broken down into their component parts, such as amino acids, energy is released and made available for the cell to use.)

of the gene was advantageous to colobine ancestors who were probably already eating some leaves, natural selection favored it to the point that it was established in the lineage. (The discovery of this gene duplication is another example of how new technologies help explain behavior, in this case, dietary differences.)

Distribution of Resources Different kinds of foods are distributed in different ways. Leaves can be plentiful and dense and support large groups of animals. Insects, on the other hand, may be widely scattered, so the animals that rely on them usually feed alone or perhaps in the company of one or two others.

Fruits, nuts, and berries in dispersed trees and shrubs occur in clumps. These can most efficiently be exploited by smaller groups of animals, so large groups frequently break up into smaller subunits while feeding. Such subunits may consist of one-male–multifemale groups (some baboons) or **matrilines** (macaques). Species that subsist on abundantly distributed resources may also live in one-male–multifemale groups (see "A Closer Look: Types of Nonhuman Primate Social Groups"), and because food is plentiful, these units are able to join with others to form large, stable communities (for example, howlers and some colobines and baboons). To the casual observer, these communities can look like multimale-multifemale groups (**Fig. 7-4**).

Some species that depend on foods distributed in small clumps tend to be protective of resources, especially if their feeding area is small enough to be defended. Some of these species live in small groups composed of a mated pair (siamangs) or a female with one or two males (marmosets and tamarins). Naturally, dependent offspring are also included. Lastly, many foods, such as fruits, nuts, seeds, and berries, are only seasonally available, and primates that rely on them must eat a variety of items. This is another factor that tends to favor smaller feeding groups.

The distribution and seasonality of water are also important. Water may be available year-round in continuously flowing rivers and streams or where there's abundant rainfall. But in areas that have a dry season, water may exist only in widely dispersed ponds that primates must share with other animals, including predators.

Predation Primates, depending on their size, are vulnerable to many types of predators, including snakes, birds of prey, leopards, wild dogs, lions, and even other primates. Their responses to predation depend on their body size and social structure and the type of predator. Typically, where predation pressure is high and body size is small, large communities are advantageous. These may be multimale-multifemale groups (see "A Closer Look") or congregations of one-male–multifemale groups.

▶ **Figure 7-4**
Gelada baboons live in one-male groups that combine to form troops that can number more than 300 animals.

matrilines Groupings of females who are all descendants of one female; a female, her daughters, granddaughters, and their offspring. Matrilines also include dependent male offspring. Among macaques, some matrilines are dominant to others, so that members of dominant matrilines have greater access to resources than do members of subordinate matrilines.

© Martin Harvey / PhotoLibrary

Types of Nonhuman Primate Social Groups

1. *One-male–multifemale*: a single adult male, several adult females, and their offspring. This is the most common primate mating structure, in which only one male actively breeds, and it's typically formed by a male joining a kin group of females. Females usually form the permanent nucleus of the group. Examples: guenons, gorillas, some pottos, some spider monkeys, patas, some langurs, and some colobus monkeys. In many species, several one-male groups may form large congregations.

2. *Multimale-multifemale*: several adult males, several adult females, and their young. Many of the males reproduce. The presence of several males in the group may lead to tension and to the formation of a dominance hierarchy. Examples: some lemurs, macaques, mangabeys, savanna baboons, vervets, squirrel monkeys, some spider monkeys, and chimpanzees. In some species (vervets, baboons, and macaques), females are members of matrilines, or groups composed of a female, her female offspring, and their offspring. These kin groups are arranged in a hierarchy, so each matriline is dominant to some other matrilines and subordinate to others.

3. *Monogamous pair*: a mated pair and its young. The term monogamous is somewhat misleading because matings with individuals other than partners aren't uncommon. Species that form pairs are usually arboreal, show minimal sexual dimorphism, and are frequently territorial. Adults don't normally tolerate other adults of the same sex. This grouping isn't found among the great apes, and it's the least common breeding structure among nonhuman primates. Examples: siamangs, gibbons, indris, titis, sakis, owl monkeys, and pottos. Males may directly participate in infant care.

4. *Polyandry*: one female and two males. This social group is seen only in some New World monkeys (marmosets and tamarins). Males participate in infant care.

5. *Solitary*: individual who forages for food alone. This is seen in nocturnal primates such as aye-ayes, lorises, and galagos. In some species, adult females may forage in pairs or may be accompanied by offspring. Also seen in orangutans.

There are also other groupings, such as foraging groups, hunting groups, all-female or all-male groups, and so on. Like humans, nonhuman primates don't always maintain one kind of group; one-male–multifemale groups may sometimes form multimale-multifemale groups, and vice versa. Hamadryas baboons, for example, are described as living in one-male groups; but they form herds of 100 or more at night as they move to the safety of sleeping cliffs.

Relationships with Other, Non-predatory Species Many primate species associate with other primate and nonprimate species for various reasons, including predator avoidance. When they do share habitats with other species, they exploit somewhat different resources.

Dispersal Dispersal is another factor that greatly influences social structure and relationships within groups. As is true of most mammals (and indeed, most vertebrates), members of one sex leave the group in which they were born (their *natal group*) about the time they become sexually mature. Male dispersal is the more common pattern in mammals, and primates are no exception (ring-tailed lemurs, vervets, and macaques, to name a few). But female dispersal is seen in some colobus species, hamadryas baboons, and chimpanzees. In species where the basic social structure is a mated pair, offspring of both sexes either leave or are driven away by their parents (gibbons and siamangs).

Dispersal may have more than one outcome. Typically, when females leave, they join another group. Males may do likewise, but in some species (such as gorillas), they may remain solitary for a time or they may temporarily join an all-male "bachelor" group until they're able to establish a group of their own. But the common result of dispersal is that individuals who disperse usually find mates outside their natal group. This commonality has led primatologists to conclude that the most valid explanations for dispersal are probably related to two major factors: reduced competition for mates (particularly between males) and, perhaps even more important, decreased likelihood of close inbreeding.

Members of the **philopatric** sex enjoy certain advantages. Individuals (of either sex) who remain in their natal group are able to establish long-term bonds with relatives and other animals, with whom they cooperate to protect resources or enhance their social position. This is well illustrated by chimpanzee males, who permanently reside in their natal groups (see further discussion in Chapter 8). Also, because female macaques are philopatric, they form stable matrilineal subgroups. Larger matrilines can have greater access to foods, and these females support each other in conflict situations.

Because some individuals remain together over a long period of time, members of a primate group get to know each other well. They learn, as they must, how to respond to a variety of actions that may be threatening, friendly, or neutral. In such social groups, individuals must be able to evaluate situations before they act. Evolutionarily speaking, this ability would have placed selective pressure on social intelligence, which in turn would have selected for brains capable of assessing social situations and storing relevant information. One result of such selection would be the evolution of proportionately larger and more complex brains, especially among the anthropoids.

Life Histories **Life history traits** are characteristics or developmental stages that typify members of a given species and influence potential reproductive rates. These traits also influence primate social structure. Examples of life history traits are length of gestation, length of time between pregnancies (interbirth interval), period of infant dependency and age at weaning, age of sexual maturity, and life expectancy.

Life history traits have important consequences for many aspects of

social life and social structure. They can also be critical to species survival. In species that live in marginal or unpredictable habitats, shorter life spans can be advantageous. Members of these species mature early and have short interbirth intervals, so reproduction can occur at a relatively fast rate in a habitat that doesn't favor longevity (Strier, 2003). Conversely, species with extended life spans are well suited to stable environmental conditions. The extended life spans of the great apes in particular, characterized by later sexual maturation and long interbirth intervals (three to five years), means that most females will raise only three or four offspring to maturity. Today, this slow rate of reproduction increases the threat of extinction to great ape populations that are now being hunted at a rate that far outpaces their replacement capacities.

Strategies **Strategies** are behaviors that increase individual reproductive success. They also influence the structure and dynamics of primate social groups. We're accustomed to using the word *strategies* to mean deliberate schemes or plans purposefully designed to achieve goals. But in the context of nonhuman behavioral ecology, strategies are seen as products of natural selection, and no conscious planning or motivation is implied (Strier, 2003). Several kinds of strategies are discussed in behavioral studies, including *life history strategies, feeding strategies, social strategies, reproductive strategies, and predator avoidance strategies.*

Distribution and Types of Sleeping Sites Gorillas are the only nonhuman primates that sleep on the ground. Primate sleeping sites can be in trees or on cliff faces, and their spacing can be related to social structure and to predator avoidance (**Fig. 7-5**).

Activity Patterns Most primates are diurnal, but galagos, lorises, aye-ayes, tarsiers, and one New World monkey

philopatric Remaining in one's natal group or home range as an adult. In most species, members of one sex disperse from their natal group as young adults, and members of the philopatric sex remain. In most nonhuman primate species, the philopatric sex is female.

life history traits Characteristics and developmental stages that influence rates of reproduction. Examples include longevity, age at sexual maturity, and length of time between births.

strategies Behaviors or behavioral complexes that have been favored by natural selection because they're advantageous to the animals that perform them. Examples include actions that enhance an animal's ability to obtain food, rear infants, or increase its social status. Ultimately, strategies influence reproductive success.

sympatric Living in the same area; pertaining to two or more species whose habitats partly or largely overlap.

(the owl monkey) are nocturnal. Nocturnal species tend to forage for food alone or in groups of two or three, and many avoid predators by hiding.

Human Activities Virtually all non-human primate populations are now affected by human hunting and forest clearing (see Chapter 6). These activities severely disrupt and isolate groups, reduce numbers, reduce resource availability, and eventually will lead to extinction.

Sympatric Species

Another issue that's basic to the behavioral ecology of primates is the differential exploitation of resources by **sympatric** species. This strategy provides a way to maximize access to food while reducing competition between different species.

Five Monkey Species in the Kibale Forest, Uganda

An early but still highly informative study of sympatric relationships between five monkey species was undertaken in the Kibale Forest (**Fig. 7-6**) of western Uganda (Struhsaker and Leland, 1979). The five species

were black-and-white colobus, red colobus, mangabey, blue monkey, and redtail monkey. In addition to these five, the Kibale Forest is home to two other monkey species as well as two galago species and chimpanzees (for a discussion of the latter, see Ghiglieri, 1984). Altogether, 11 different nonhuman primate species coexist at Kibale.

The five species in the study differ in their anatomy, behavior, and dietary preferences. Body weight varies considerably, ranging from around 8 pounds for redtail monkeys to as much as about 22 pounds for mangabey and colobus species. Diet also differs: The two colobus species mostly eat leaves, and the other three species concentrate more on fruits and insects. These differences are important because for

▲ **Figure 7-5**
Almost all primates sleep in the safety of trees or on cliffs if there are no trees around. They also often take naps during the day. The fact that many humans have a mid-afternoon "lull" may indicate a tendency for afternoon drowsiness. **(a)** Chacma baboon and **(b)** chimpanzee afternoon naps. Note that the chimpanzee is sleeping in a nest.

▼ **Figure 7-6**
Kibale Forest habitat, Uganda.

two or more species to share the same habitat and still get enough to eat, they need to exploit somewhat different resources to reduce competition for food.

Several aspects of social organization also vary. For example, red colobus and mangabeys live in multimale-multifemale groups, while only one fully adult male is typically present in the other species. There's so much variability, in fact, that researchers found little correlation between social organization and feeding ecology. The impression one gets from all this is that many primate species are quite flexible regarding group composition, a fact that makes generalizing extremely tentative. Nevertheless, the highly controlled nature of the Kibale study makes some comparisons and provisional generalizations possible:

▼ **Figure 7-7**
When a baboon strays too far from its troop, as this one has done, it's more likely to fall prey to predators. Leopards are the most serious nonhuman threat to terrestrial primates.

Time Life Pictures / Getty Images

1. The omnivores (mangabeys, redtail, and blue monkeys) move about more than the folivores (the two colobus species).
2. Among the omnivores, there's an inverse relationship between body size and group size (that is, the smaller the body size, the larger the group tends to be). Also among the omnivores, there's a direct rela-

tionship between body size and **home range** size.
3. Omnivores are more spatially dispersed than folivores.
4. Female sexual swelling is obvious only in those species (red colobus) that live in multimale-multifemale groups.
5. Feeding, spacing, dispersal, and **reproductive strategies** may be very different for males and females of the same species. These considerations have become a central focus of ecological and evolutionary research.

Why Be Social?

Group living exposes primates to competition with other group members for resources, so why don't they live alone? After all, competition can lead to injury or even death, and it's costly in terms of energy expenditure. One widely accepted answer to the question of why primates live in groups is that the costs of competition are offset by the benefits of predator defense. Multimale-multifemale groups are advantageous in areas where predation pressure is high, particularly in mixed woodlands and open savannas, where there are large predators. Leopards are the most significant predator of terrestrial primates (**Fig. 7-7**). When prey animals occur in larger groups, the chances of seeing and escaping a predator are increased simply because more pairs of eyes are looking about. (There really is safety in numbers.) This strategy also has the advantage of giving animals more time to feed because it reduces the amount of time each one spends looking around (Janson, 1990; Isbell and Young, 1993).

Savanna baboons have long been cited as an example of these principles. They live in semiarid grassland and broken woodland habitats throughout sub-Saharan Africa. To avoid nocturnal predators, savanna baboons sleep in trees, but during the day, they spend much of the time on the ground forag-

home range The total area exploited by an animal or social group; usually given for one year or for the entire lifetime of an animal.

reproductive strategies The complex of behavioral patterns that contributes to individual reproductive success. The behaviors need not be deliberate, and they often vary considerably between males and females.

At a Glance

PRIMATE SOCIAL STRATEGIES

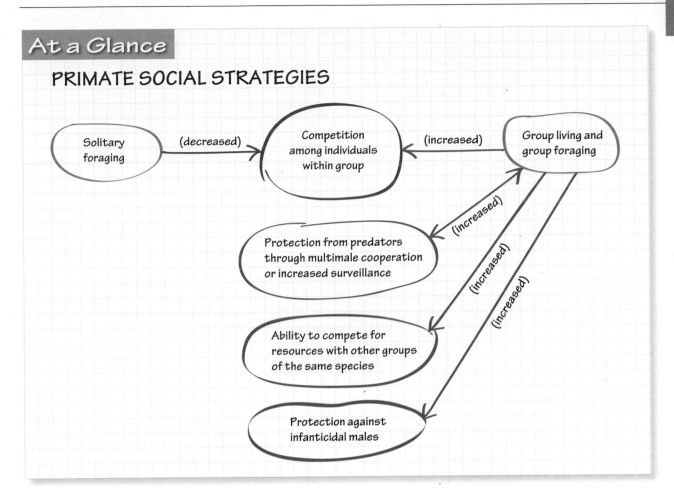

ing for food. If a nonhuman predator appears, they flee back into the trees, but if they're some distance from safety, adult males, (and sometimes females) may join forces to chase the intruder. The effectiveness of male baboons in this regard shouldn't be underestimated, because they've been known to kill domestic dogs and even to attack leopards and lions.

The benefits of larger groups are also apparent in reports of polyspecific (more than one species) associations that function to reduce predation. In the Tai National Park, Ivory Coast, red colobus monkeys, a favorite prey of chimpanzees (see Chapter 8), frequently associate with Diana monkeys (a guenon species) as a predator avoidance strategy (Bshary and Noe, 1997; Noe and Bshary, 1997). Normally, these two species don't form close associations. But when chimpanzee predation increases, new groupings

develop, and preexisting ones remain intact for longer than normal periods of time. Also, McGraw and Bshary (2002) reported that a third species, the sooty mangabey, sometimes provides additional support. The more terrestrial mangabeys live in multimale-multifemale groups of up to 100 individuals, and they detect predators earlier than the other two species. Mangabeys are in close proximity to red colobus and Diana monkeys only about 5 to 10 percent of the time, but when they're present, the other two species modify their foraging strategies. The normally arboreal red colobus, perhaps feeling more confident, even come to the ground (McGraw and Bshary, 2002). Consequently, through the strategy of associations between different species, potential prey animals are able to spend more time feeding and increase their opportunities for foraging.

As effective as increased numbers can be in preventing predation, there are other explanations for primate sociality. One is that larger social groups can outcompete smaller groups of **conspecifics** when foraging in the same area (Wrangham, 1980). Wrangham also suggests that large multimale-multifemale groups evolved because males were attracted to related females living together. And lastly, females may tolerate familiar males, since they can provide protection against other, potentially infanticidal males.

There's probably no single answer to the question of why primates live in groups. More than likely, predator avoidance is a major factor but not the only one. Group living evolved as an adaptive response to a number of ecological variables, and it has served primates well for a very long time.

Primate Social Behavior

Because primates solve their major adaptive problems in a social context, we should expect them to participate in activities that reinforce the group's integrity. The better known of these activities are described here. As you read about them, remember that all these behaviors evolved as adaptive responses during more than 50 million years of primate evolution.

Dominance

Many primate societies are organized into **dominance hierarchies**, which impose a certain degree of order by establishing parameters of individual behavior. Although aggression is frequently used to increase an individual's status, dominance hierarchies usually serve to reduce the amount of actual physical violence. Not only are lower-ranking individuals unlikely to attack or even threaten a higher-ranking one, dominant animals can frequently exert control simply by making a threatening gesture. Individual rank or status can

be measured by access to resources (food, water, and mating partners). Dominant individuals are given priority by others, and they usually don't give way in confrontations.

Many primatologists think that the primary benefit of dominance is the increased reproductive success of high-ranking animals. This may be true in some cases, but there's good evidence that lower-ranking males also successfully mate. For example, subordinate male baboons frequently establish friendships with females, and simply because of this close association, they're able to mate (sometimes surreptitiously) with their female friend when she comes into estrus.

Low-ranking male orangutans also mate frequently. These young males don't develop certain secondary sex characteristics, such as wide cheek pads and heavier musculature, as long as they live near a dominant male (**Fig. 7-8**). One theory is that this arrested development protects them from the dominant male, who doesn't view them as a threat. Nevertheless, they are a threat in terms of reproductive success because their strategy is to force females to mate with them. In fact, primatologists use the term *rape* to describe the degree of force these young males use.

Increased reproductive success is also hypothesized for high-ranking females, who have greater access to food than subordinate females do. Because they obtain more energy for the production and care of offspring (Fedigan, 1983), their reproductive success is greater. Altmann and colleagues (1988) reported that while dominant female yellow baboons in one study group didn't have higher birthrates than lower-ranking females, they did reach sexual maturity earlier (presumably because of their enhanced nutritional status), thus increasing the potential number of offspring they could produce throughout their lives.

In another example, during a drought in Kenya, dominant female vervets in two groups prevented a third

conspecifics Members of the same species.

dominance hierarchies Systems of social organization wherein individuals within a group are ranked relative to one another. Higher-ranking individuals have greater access to preferred food items and mating partners than do lower-ranking individuals. Dominance hierarchies are sometimes referred to as pecking orders.

▲ Figure 7-8
(a) Fully mature, breeding male orangutan with well-developed cheek pads. (b) "Suppressed" adult male without cheek pads.

group from gaining access to their water hole. The deprived third group resorted to licking dew from tree trunks; but even in this group, the higher-ranking members denied access to the lower-ranking members. Consequently, over half of this group died, and all of those were either adolescents or low-ranking adults (Cheney et al., 1988).

Pusey and colleagues (1997) showed that the offspring of high-ranking female chimpanzees at Gombe had significantly higher rates of infant survival. Moreover, their daughters matured faster, which meant that they had shorter interbirth intervals and thus produced more offspring.

An individual's position in the hierarchy isn't permanent and changes throughout life. It's influenced by many factors, including sex, age, level of aggression, amount of time spent in the group, intelligence, perhaps motivation, and sometimes the mother's social position (particularly true of macaques).

In species organized into groups containing a number of females associated with one or several adult males, the males are generally dominant to females. Within such groups, males and females have separate hierarchies, although very high-ranking females can dominate the lowest-ranking males (particularly young males). But there are exceptions to this pattern of male dominance. In many lemur species, females are the dominant sex. Moreover, in species that form bonded pairs (such as indris, gibbons, and siamangs), males and females are codominant.

All primates *learn* their position in the hierarchy. From birth, an infant is carried by its mother, and it observes how she responds to every member of the group. Just as importantly, it sees how others react to her. Dominance and subordination are indicated by gestures and behaviors, some of which are universal throughout the primate order (including humans), and this gestural repertoire is part of every youngster's learning experience.

Young primates also acquire social rank through play with age peers, and as they spend more time with play groups, their social interactions widen. Competition and rough-and-tumble play allow them to learn the strengths and weaknesses of other individuals, and they carry this knowledge with them throughout their lives. So, through early contact with the mother and subsequent exposure to peers, young primates learn to negotiate their way through the complex web of social interactions that make up their daily lives.

▲ Figure 7-9
A "yawn" that exposes long canine teeth is a common threat gesture in many primate species. Here an adult male baboon combines it with an "eyelid flash," closing the eyes to expose light-colored eyelids that enhance the visual effect of the threat.

© Martin B Withers / FLPA / Minden Pictures

Communication

Communication is universal among animals and includes scents and unintentional, **autonomic** responses and behaviors that convey meaning. Such things as body posture provide information about an animal's emotional state. For example, crouching indicates submission, insecurity, or fear, and this is true of many nonprimate animals (for example, dogs and cats). At the same time, a purposeful, striding gait implies confidence. Autonomic responses to threatening or novel stimuli, such as raised body hair (most species) or enhanced body odor (gorillas), indicate excitement.

Many intentional behaviors also serve as communication. In primates, these include a wide variety of gestures, facial expressions, and vocalizations, some of which we humans share. Among many primates, an intense stare is a mild threat; and indeed, people find prolonged eye contact with strangers very uncomfortable. (For this reason, people should avoid eye contact with primates in zoos.) Other threat gestures include a quick yawn to expose canine teeth (baboons, macaques; **Fig. 7-9**); bobbing back and forth in a crouched position (patas monkeys); and branch shaking (many monkey species). High-ranking baboons *mount* the hindquarters of subordinates to express dominance (**Fig. 7-10**). Mounting may also serve to defuse potentially tense situations by indicating something like, "It's okay" or "Apology accepted."

Primates also use a variety of behaviors to indicate submission, reassurance, or amicable intentions. In addition to crouching to show submission, some primates (baboons) present or turn their hindquarters to an animal they want to appease. Reassurance takes the form of touching, patting, hugging, and holding hands. **Grooming** also serves in many situations to indicate submission or reassurance.

A wide variety of facial expressions indicating emotional state are seen in chimpanzees and, especially, in bonobos (**Fig. 7-11**). These include the well-known play face (also seen in several other primate and nonprimate species),

communication Any act that conveys information, in the form of a message, to another individual. Frequently, the result of communication is a change in the recipient's behavior. Communication may not be deliberate, but may instead be the result of involuntary processes or a secondary consequence of an intentional action.

autonomic Pertaining to physiological responses that aren't under voluntary control. An example in chimpanzees would be the erection of body hair during excitement. Blushing is a human example. Both convey information regarding emotional states; but neither behavior is deliberate, and communication is not intended.

grooming Picking through fur to remove dirt, parasites, and other materials that may be present. Social grooming is common among primates and reinforces social relationships.

Lynn Kilgore

▲ Figure 7-10
One young male savanna baboon mounts another as an expression of dominance.

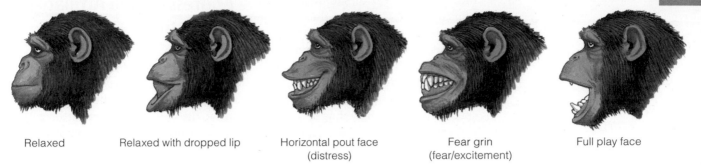

| Relaxed | Relaxed with dropped lip | Horizontal pout face (distress) | Fear grin (fear/excitement) | Full play face |

▲ **Figure 7-11**
Chimpanzee facial expressions.

associated with play behavior, and the fear grin (seen in *all* primates) to indicate fear and submission.

Not surprisingly, vocalizations play a major role in primate communication. Some, such as a baboon's bark, happen in a variety of contexts. In some cases, a bark may be little more than a startled reaction to something that isn't particularly important. When a baboon barks at the sight of a leopard, it may not actually intend to alert other troop members; but that's the effect it will have because at least some other animals will look around to see why it barked. Other vocalizations, such as the chimpanzee "food grunt," are heard only in specific contexts. But whether deliberate or not, both vocalizations convey information to other animals. The information may simply refer to the emotional state of an individual or it may alert others to the possible presence of predators or food.

Primates (and other animals) also communicate through **displays**, which are more complicated, frequently elaborate combinations of behaviors. For example, the exaggerated courtship dances of many male birds, often enhanced by colorful plumage, are displays. Common gorilla displays are chest slapping and the tearing of vegetation to indicate threat. Likewise, an angry chimpanzee, with hair on end, may charge an opponent while screaming, waving its arms, and tearing vegetation (**Fig. 7-12**).

By describing a few communicative behaviors shared by many primates (including humans), we don't mean to suggest that these gestures are dictated solely by genetic factors. Indeed, if primates aren't reared within a relatively normal social context, such behaviors may not be performed appropriately, because the contextual manifestations of communicatory actions are *learned*. But the underlying *predisposition* to learn and use them and the motor patterns involved in their execution are genetically influenced, and these factors do have adaptive significance.

© Photoshot Holdings Ltd / Alamy

Some theories about how such expressive devices evolved thus focus on motor patterns and the original context in which they occurred. Over time, certain behaviors and motor patterns that originated in specific contexts have assumed increasing importance as communicatory signals. For example, crouching initially helped avoid physical attack. But it also conveyed the information that the

▲ **Figure 7-12**
Male chimpanzee display. Note how the hair on his arms and shoulders is raised to make him look larger.

displays Sequences of repetitious behaviors that serve to communicate emotional states. Nonhuman primate displays are most frequently associated with reproductive or agonistic behavior.

individual was fearful, submissive, and nonaggressive. Crouching thus became valuable not only for its primary function but also for its role in communication, and natural selection increasingly favored it for this secondary role. In this way, over time, the expressions of specific behaviors may thus become elaborated or exaggerated because of their value in enhancing communication. Many complex displays also incorporate various combinations of **ritualized behaviors**.

Mounting, as seen in baboons, is a good example of a ritualized behavior. Higher-ranking individuals mount the hindquarters of more subordinate animals, not to mate but to express dominance. (When mounting serves a communicatory function, mounters and mountees may be members of the same sex.) In most species that live in one-male or multimale groups, males (the mounters in the mating context) are socially dominant to females. So, in the context of communication, the mounter assumes the male reproductive role. Likewise, by presenting its hindquarters to solicit mounting, the mountee indicates submission or subordination. As communication, these behavior patterns are entirely removed from their original reproductive context, and they function instead to reinforce and clarify the respective social roles of individuals in specific interactions.

All nonhuman animals use various vocalizations, body postures, and facial expressions that transmit information. But the array of communicative devices is much richer among nonhuman primates, even though they don't use language the way humans do. Communication is important because it's what makes social living possible. Through submissive gestures, aggression is reduced and physical violence is less likely. Likewise, friendly intentions and relationships are reinforced through physical contact and grooming. Indeed, we humans can see ourselves in other primate species most clearly in the familiar uses of nonverbal communication.

Aggressive and Affiliative Interactions

Within primate societies, there is an interplay between **affiliative** behaviors, which promote group cohesion, and aggressive behaviors, which can lead to group disruption. Conflict within a group frequently develops out of competition for resources, including mating partners and food. Instead of actual attacks or fighting, most **intragroup** aggression occurs in the form of various signals and displays, frequently within the context of a dominance hierarchy. Therefore, the majority of tense situations are resolved through various submissive and appeasement behaviors.

But conflicts aren't always resolved peacefully, and they sometimes have serious consequences. For example, high-ranking female macaques frequently intimidate, harass, and even attack lower-ranking females in order to restrict their access to food. In some cases, low-ranking females suffer weight loss and poor nutrition. They may also have lower reproductive success because they're less able to successfully rear offspring to maturity, partly because they're unable to obtain food (Silk et al., 2003).

Competition between males for mates frequently results in injury and even death. In species that have a distinct breeding season (such as squirrel monkeys), conflict between males is most common during that time. Male squirrel monkeys form coalitions to compete with other males, and when outright fighting occurs, injuries can be severe. In species not restricted to a mating season, competition between males can be an ongoing occurrence. In one well-known example, Dian Fossey once found the skull of an adult male mountain gorilla with a canine tooth of another male gorilla embedded in it (**Fig. 7-13**).

Even though conflict can be destructive, a certain amount of aggression is useful in maintaining order within groups and protecting either individual or group resources.

ritualized behaviors Behaviors removed from their original context and sometimes exaggerated to convey information.

affiliative Pertaining to amicable associations between individuals. Affiliative behaviors, such as grooming, reinforce social bonds and promote group cohesion.

intragroup (*intra*, meaning "within") Within the group, as opposed to between groups (intergroup).

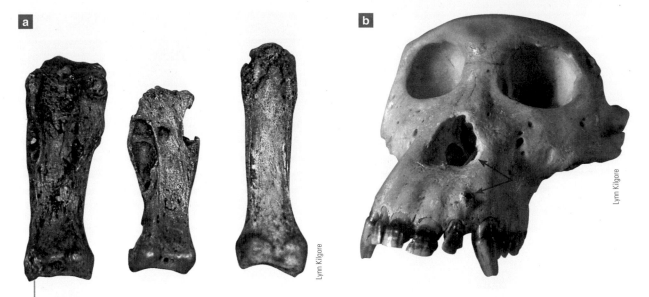

▲ Figure 7-13

(a) These finger bones are from a female chimpanzee named Gilka, a member of Jane Goodall's study group in Tanzania. On more than one occasion, observers saw another female attack Gilka, and during one attack, Gilka was badly bitten on the hand. Afterward she suffered periodically from running sores on her hand. The cavities and deformation in these bones indicate severe infection of the marrow cavity, probably resulting from the bite wound. **(b)** This male chimpanzee cranium from West Africa exhibits a healed bite wound beneath the nose (arrow) most likely inflicted by another chimpanzee. Also, the left margin of the nasal opening shows irregularities that may have been caused by an infection, perhaps related to the injury.

Fortunately, there are many affiliative behaviors that reinforce bonds between individuals, promote group cohesion, minimize actual violence, and defuse potentially dangerous situations. Thus, these behaviors are important to the maintenance of group stability.

Common affiliative behaviors include reconciliation, consolation, and simple amicable interactions between friends and relatives. Most such behaviors involve various forms of physical contact, such as touching, hand-holding, hugging, and, among chimpanzees, kissing (**Fig. 7-14**). In fact, physical contact is one of the most important factors in primate development and is crucial in promoting peaceful relationships in many primate social groups.

Grooming is one of the most important affiliative behaviors in many primate species, so much so that in 1985, primatologist Allison Jolly called it the "social cement" of primate societies. Although grooming occurs in other animal species, social grooming is mostly a primate activity, and it plays an important role in day-to-day life (**Fig. 7-15**). Because grooming involves using the fingers to pick through the fur of another individual (or one's own) to remove insects, dirt, and other materials, it serves hygienic functions. But it's also an immensely pleasurable activity that members of some species (especially chimpanzees) engage in for long periods of time.

Grooming occurs in a variety of contexts. Mothers groom infants. Males groom sexually receptive females. Subordinate animals groom dominant ones, sometimes to gain favor. And friends groom friends. In general, grooming is comforting. It restores peaceful relationships after conflict and it provides reassurance during tense situations. In short,

▲ Figure 7-14
Adolescent savanna baboons holding hands.

▲ **Figure 7-15**
Grooming primates. (a) Mandrills. (b) Longtail macaques. (c) Japanese macaques. (d) Chimpanzees.

grooming reinforces social bonds and consequently helps to maintain and strengthen a group's structure.

Conflict resolution through reconciliation is another important aspect of primate social behavior. Following a conflict, chimpanzee opponents frequently move, within minutes, to reconcile (de Waal, 1982). Reconciliation takes many forms, including hugging, kissing, and grooming. Even uninvolved animals may take part, either grooming one or both participants or forming their own grooming parties. In addition, bonobos are unique in their use of sex to promote group cohesion, restore peace after conflicts, and relieve tension within the group (de Waal, 1987, 1989).

Social relationships are crucial to nonhuman primates, and as we said earlier, bonds between individuals can last a lifetime. These relationships serve many functions. Individuals of many species form alliances in which one supports another against a third. Alliances, or coalitions, as they're also called, can be used to enhance the status of members. For example, at Gombe, the male chimpanzee Figan achieved alpha status because of his brother's support (Goodall, 1986, p. 424). In fact, chimpanzees so heavily rely on coalitions and are so skillful politically that an entire book, appropriately titled *Chimpanzee Politics: Power and Sex among Chimpanzees* (de Waal, 2007), has been devoted to the topic.

Reproduction and Reproductive Behavior

In most primate species (as in most mammals), sexual behavior is tied to the female's reproductive cycle, with females being sexually receptive to males only when they're in estrus. Estrus is characterized by behavioral changes that indicate a female is receptive. In Old World monkeys and apes that live in multimale-multifemale groups, estrus is also accompanied by swelling and changes in color of the skin around the genital area. These changes serve as visual cues of a female's readiness to mate (**Fig 7-16**).

Permanent bonding between males and females isn't common among nonhuman primates. However, male and female savanna baboons sometimes form mating *consortships*. These temporary relationships last while the female is in estrus, and the two spend most of their time together, mating frequently. Also, as we mentioned earlier, lower-ranking baboon males often form "friendships" (Smuts, 1985) with females and occasionally mate with them.

Mating consortships are sometimes seen in chimpanzees and are particularly common among bonobos. In fact, a male and female bonobo may spend several weeks mostly in each other's company. During this time, they mate often, even when the female isn't in estrus. These relationships of longer duration aren't typical of chimpanzee males and females.

Such a male-female bond may result in increased reproductive success for both sexes. For the male, there's the increased likelihood that he will be the father of any infant the female conceives. At the same time, the female potentially gains protection from predators or other members of her group and perhaps assistance in caring for offspring she may already have.

Reproductive Strategies

Reproductive strategies, especially how they differ between the sexes, have been a primary focus of primate research. The goal of such strategies is to produce and successfully rear to

◄ **Figure 7-16**
A male baboon inspects a female's estrous swelling. Note how much larger the male is than the female.

adulthood as many offspring as possible.

Primates are among the most **K-selected** of mammal species. By this we mean that individuals produce only a few young, in whom they invest a tremendous amount of parental care. Contrast this pattern with that of **r-selected** species, where large numbers of offspring are produced but parents invest little or no energy in infant care. Good examples of r-selected species include insects, most fishes, and, among mammals, mice and rabbits.

Considering the degree of care required by young, dependent primate offspring, it's clear that enormous investment by at least one parent is necessary, and in a majority of species, the mother carries most of the burden certainly before, but also after, birth. Primates are totally helpless at birth, and because they develop slowly, they're exposed to greater learning opportunities within a *social* environment. This trend has been elaborated most dramatically in great apes and humans, especially the latter. So what we see in ourselves and our close primate relatives (and presumably in our more recent ancestors as well) is a strategy in which at least one parent, usually the mother, makes an extraordinary investment to produce a few "high-quality," slowly maturing offspring.

Finding food and mates, avoiding predators, and caring for and protecting dependent young are difficult challenges for nonhuman primates. Moreover, in most species, males and females use different strategies to meet these challenges.

Female primates spend almost all their adult lives either pregnant, lactating, and/or caring for offspring, and the resulting metabolic demands are enormous. A pregnant or lactating female, although perhaps only half the size of her male counterpart, may require about the same number of calories per day. Even if these demands are met, her physical resources may be drained. For example, analysis of chim-

panzee skeletons from Gombe National Park, in Tanzania, showed significant loss of bone and bone mineral in older females (Sumner et al., 1989).

Given these physiological costs and the fact that her reproductive potential is limited by lengthy intervals between births, a female's best strategy is to maximize the amount of resources available to her and her offspring. Indeed, as we just discussed, females of many primate species (gibbons, marmosets, and macaques, to name a few) are competitive with other females and aggressively protect resources and territories. In other species (for example, chimpanzees), females distance themselves from others to avoid competition. Males, however, face a separate set of challenges. Having little investment in the rearing of offspring, it's to the male's advantage to secure as many mates and produce as many offspring as possible.

Sexual Selection

One outcome of different mating strategies is **sexual selection**, a phenomenon first described by Charles Darwin. Sexual selection is a type of natural selection that operates on only one sex, usually males. The selective agent is male competition for mates and, in some species, mate choice by females. The long-term effect of sexual selection is to increase the frequency of traits that lead to greater success in acquiring mates.

In the animal kingdom, numerous male attributes are the results of sexual selection. For example, female birds of many species are attracted to males with more vividly colored plumage. Selection has thus increased the frequency of alleles that influence brighter coloration in males, and in these species (peacocks may be the best example), males are more colorful than females (**Fig. 7-17**).

Sexual selection in primates is most important in species in which mating is polygynous and there's considerable male competition for females. In these

K-selected Pertaining to K-selection, an adaptive strategy whereby individuals produce relatively few offspring, in whom they invest increased parental care. Although only a few infants are born, chances of survival are increased for each individual because of parental investments in time and energy. Examples of nonprimate K-selected species are birds and canids (e.g., wolves, coyotes, and dogs).

r-selected Pertaining to r-selection, an adaptive strategy that emphasizes relatively large numbers of offspring and reduced parental care (compared with K-selected species). K-selection and r-selection are relative terms (e.g., mice are r-selected compared with primates but K-selected compared with most fish).

sexual selection A type of natural selection that operates on only one sex within a species. Sexual selection results from competition for mates, and it can lead to sexual dimorphism regarding one or more traits.

◄ **Figure 7-17**
The peahen is far less colorful and has shorter tail feathers than the peacock. The brilliant display of the male is a mechanism to attract mates. Thus, the brilliant coloration and long tail feathers that enhance the display are the products of sexual selection.

species, sexual selection produces dimorphism in a number of traits, most noticeably body size (**Fig. 7-18**). As you've seen, males of many primate species are considerably larger than females, and they have larger canine teeth. Conversely, in species that live in pairs (such as gibbons) or where male competition is reduced, sexual dimorphism in canine and body size is either reduced or nonexistent. For these reasons, the presence or absence of sexually dimorphic traits in a species can be a reasonably good indicator of mating structure.

Infanticide as a Reproductive Strategy?

One way males may increase their chances of reproducing is to kill infants fathered by other males. This explanation was first suggested in an early study of Hanuman langurs in India (Hrdy, 1977). Hanuman langurs (**Fig. 7-19**) typically live in groups composed of one adult male, several females, and their offspring. Males without mates form "bachelor" groups that frequently forage within sight of the one-male associations. These peripheral males occasionally attack and defeat a reproductive male and drive him from his group. Then, following such a takeover, the new male may kill some or all of the group's infants, who were fathered by the previous male.

▲ **Figure 7-18**
Female and male mandrills are one of many good examples of sexual dimorphism and sexual selection among primates. Fully adult mandrills are about twice the size of females and are much more colorful.

◄ **Figure 7-19**
Hanuman langurs.

At first glance, infanticide would seem to be counterproductive, especially for a species as a whole. However, individual animals behave in ways that maximize their *own* reproductive success, no matter what effect their actions may have on the group or even the species. Even though they aren't really aware of it, by killing infants fathered by other animals, male langurs may increase their own chances of fathering offspring. This is because while a female is producing milk and nursing an infant, she doesn't come into estrus and therefore isn't sexually available. But when an infant dies, its mother stops lactating, resumes cycling, and becomes sexually receptive again. So, by killing nursing infants, a new male avoids waiting two to three years for them to be weaned before he can mate with their mothers. This is advantageous to him, since chances are good that he won't even be in the group for two or three years. Moreover, he doesn't expend energy and put himself at risk by defending infants who don't carry his genes.

Hanuman langurs aren't the only primates that practice infanticide. It's been observed (or surmised) in many species, such as redtail monkeys, red colobus, blue monkeys, savanna baboons, howlers, orangutans, gorillas, chimpanzees, and humans. It should also be noted that infanticide occurs in many nonprimate species, including rodents, cats, and horses. In the major-ity of reported nonhuman primate examples, infanticide coincides with the transfer of a new male into a group or, as in chimpanzees, an encounter with an unfamiliar female and infant.

Numerous objections to this explanation of infanticide have been raised. Alternative hypotheses have included competition for resources (Rudran, 1973), aberrant behaviors related to human-induced overcrowding (Curtin and Dohlinow, 1978), and inadvertent killing during conflict between animals (Bartlett et al., 1993). Sussman and colleagues (1995), as well as others, have questioned the actual prevalence of infanticide, arguing that although it does occur, it's not particularly common. These authors have also suggested that if indeed male reproductive fitness is increased through the killing of infants, such increases are negligible. Yet, others (Struhsaker and Leland, 1987; Hrdy et al., 1995) maintain that both the incidence and patterning of infanticide by males are not only significant, but consistent with the assumptions established by theories of behavioral evolution.

Henzi and Barrett (2003) reported that when chacma baboon males migrate into a new group, they "deliberately single out females with young infants and hunt them down" (**Fig. 7-20**). The importance of these findings is the conclusion that, at least in chacma baboons, newly arrived males consistently try to kill infants,

▼ **Figure 7-20**
An immigrant male chacma baboon chases a terrified female and her infant (clinging to her back). Resident males interceded to stop the chase.

© Peter Henzi

and their attacks are highly aggressive and purposeful. These observations indicate that the incoming males are very motivated and are engaging in a goal-directed behavior, although they most certainly don't understand the possible reproductive advantages they may later gain. Reports like these, however, don't prove that infanticide increases a male's reproductive fitness. To do this, primatologists must demonstrate two crucial facts:

1. Infanticidal males *don't* kill their own offspring.
2. Once a male has killed an infant, he subsequently fathers another infant with the victim's mother.

These statements are hypotheses that can be tested; and to do this, Borries and colleagues (1999) collected DNA samples from the victims and the feces of infanticidal males in several groups of free-ranging langurs, specifically to determine if these males killed their own offspring. Their results showed that in all 16 cases where infant and male DNA was available, the males weren't related to the infants they either attacked or killed. Moreover, DNA analysis also showed that in 4 out of 5 cases where a victim's mother subsequently gave birth, the new infant was fathered by the infanticidal male. The application of DNA technology to a long-unanswered question has provided strong evidence suggesting that infanticide may indeed give males an increased chance of fathering offspring. However, before the question can be answered definitively, more research will be necessary.

Mothers, Fathers, and Infants

The basic social unit among all primates is a female and her infants (**Fig. 7-21**). Except in those species in which **polyandry** occurs or the social group is a bonded pair, males don't directly participate in the rearing of offspring. The mother-infant bond begins at birth. Although the exact nature of the bonding process isn't fully known, there appear to be predisposing innate factors that strongly attract a female to her infant, so long as she herself has had a sufficiently normal experience with her own mother. This doesn't mean that primate mothers have an innate knowledge of how to care for an infant. In fact, they don't. Monkeys and apes raised in captivity without contact with their mothers not only don't know how to care for a newborn infant, but may be afraid of it and attack or even kill it. For this reason, learning is essential to establishing a mother's attraction to her infant.

The role of bonding between primate mothers and infants was clearly demonstrated in a famous series of experiments at the University of Wisconsin. Psychologist Harry Harlow (1959) raised infant rhesus macaques with surrogate mothers made of wire or a combination of wire and cloth. Other infants were raised with no mother at all. Members of the first group retained an attachment to their cloth-covered surrogate mother (**Fig. 7-22**). But those raised with no mother were incapable of forming lasting attachments with other monkeys. Rather they sat passively in their cages, staring vacantly into space. None of the motherless males ever successfully copulated. Those females who were impregnated either paid little attention to their infants or reacted aggressively toward them (Harlow and Harlow, 1961). The point is that monkeys reared in isolation were denied opportunities to *learn* the rules of social and maternal behavior. Moreover, and just as essential, they were denied the all-important physical contact so necessary for normal primate psychological and emotional development.

The importance of a normal relationship with the mother is demonstrated by field studies as well. From birth, infant primates are able to cling to their mother's fur, and they're in

polyandry A mating system characterized by an association between a female and more than one male (usually two or three), with whom she mates. Among non-human primates, this pattern is seen only in marmosets and tamarins.

▶ **Figure 7-21**
Primate mothers with young.
(**a**) Mongoose lemurs.
(**b**) Chimpanzees. (**c**) Squirrel
monkeys. (**d**) Japanese
macaques. (**e**) Sykes monkeys.

more or less constant physical contact with her for several months. During this critical period, infants develop a closeness with their mothers that doesn't always end with weaning. In fact, especially among some Old World monkeys, mothers and infants may remain close until one or the other dies.

In studies that followed the Harlow research, Suomi and colleagues emphasized that social isolation initiated early in life can have devastating effects on subsequent development and behavior for many primate species. The primate deprivation syndrome that results from early isolation is characterized by displays of abnormal self-directed behavior, such as self-hugging or rocking back and forth, and by deficits in all aspects of social behavior (Suomi et al., 1983, pp. 710–786.).

Although infants are mainly cared for by their mothers, in some species, presumed fathers also participate (**Figure 7-23**). Male siamangs actively care for their offspring, and marmoset and tamarin males provide most of the direct infant care. In fact, marmoset and tamarin offspring (frequently twins) are usually carried on the male's back and are transferred to their mother only for nursing.

Even in species where adult males aren't directly involved in infant care,

◀ **Figure 7-22**
Infant macaque clinging to cloth mother.

Harlow Primate Laboratory

© Gerry Ellis / Minden Pictures

© Paul Souders / Corbis

▲ **Figure 7-23**
(**a**) This male savanna baboon is holding a very young infant as its mother looks on. (**b**) Infant mountain gorilla with silverback male. It's not certain these males are actually the fathers of the infants, but they are exhibiting parental behavior.

they may take more than a casual interest in infants, and this is especially true of hamadryas and savanna baboons. But to establish that baboons exhibit paternal care, it's necessary to establish paternity. Buchan and colleagues (2003) did just that by analyzing the DNA of subadults and males. They showed that during disputes, the fathers intervened on behalf of their offspring significantly more often than for unrelated juveniles. Because disputes can lead to severe injury, Buchan and colleagues considered the male intervention an example of true paternal care. Although this study also demonstrates that nonhuman primates can recognize relatives, the exact mechanisms of kin recognition haven't been fully identified. Clues to how nonhuman primates recognize relatives may eventually come from new molecular-based research.

What may be an extension of the mother-infant relationship has been called **alloparenting**. This behavior occurs in many animal species but is most richly expressed in primates, and some researchers believe that it's found among all social primates. Usually, alloparents crowd around an infant and attempt to groom, hold, or touch it. Some species, such as langurs, are well known for their "aunts," and several females may hold an infant during its first day of life. Occasionally, rough treatment by inexperienced or aggressive animals can result in an infant's injury or death. For this reason, mothers may attempt to shield infants from overly attentive individuals.

Several functions are suggested for alloparenting. If the mother dies, the infant stands a chance of being adopted by an alloparent or other individual. Also, it may simply be convenient for the mother to leave her infant occasionally with another female. Finally, alloparenting may help train young females in the skills of motherhood.

Because the survival of offspring is the key to individual reproductive success, parenting strategies have evolved throughout the animal kingdom. In many r-selected species, such as fishes, parenting may involve nothing more than laying large numbers of eggs. But in birds and mammals, as you've seen, there's increased care of dependent young. Alloparenting is important in some mammalian species besides primates (for example, elephants), but even so, it's most highly developed in several primate species. Likewise, males provide group defense in many mammal species, but actual paternal care is most common in primates. And with further use of genetic technologies, the role of males and other related individuals in infant care will undoubtedly become clearer.

Summary
of Main Topics

- The fundamental principle of behavioral evolution is that aspects of behavior (including social behavior) are influenced by genetic factors. Because some behavioral elements are influenced by genes, natural selection can act on them in the same way it acts on anatomical characteristics.

- In more primitive organisms, such as insects and most other invertebrates, the proportion of behavior that's directly influenced by genes is much greater than in mammals and birds.
- Behavioral ecology is the discipline that examines behavior from the perspective of complex ecological

relationships and the role of natural selection as it favors behaviors that increase reproductive fitness. This approach generates many models of behavioral evolution that can be applied to all species, including humans.

- Members of each species inherit a genome that is species-specific,

alloparenting A common behavior in many primate species whereby individuals other than the parent(s) hold, carry, and in general interact with infants.

and some part of that genome influences behaviors. But in more complex animals, the genome allows a greater degree of behavioral flexibility and learning. In humans, who rely on cultural adaptations for survival, most behavior is learned.

- Life history traits or strategies (developmental stages that characterize a species) are important to the reproductive success of individuals. These traits include length of gestation, number of offspring per birth, interbirth interval, age of sexual maturity, and longevity. Although these characteristics are strongly influenced by the genome of any species, they're also influenced by environmental and social factors, such as nutrition and

social status. In turn, nutritional requirements are affected by body size, diet, and basal metabolic rate (BMR).

- There are several types of primate social groups: one-male–multifemale groups; multimale-multifemale groups; bonded pairs consisting of one male and one female; polyandry; and more or less solitary individuals.
- Primatologists have provided various explanations for why primates live in social groups (for example, predator avoidance and competition for resources with other groups).
- Primates use various strategies that facilitate social living, including affiliative and aggressive interactions.

- Males of many primate and nonprimates species attack and kill infants. The reason for this has been debated among anthropologists for years, but one recurring explanation is that infanticide increases the male's reproductive success. While this remains to be proved, there have now been some DNA studies that have supported this hypothesis. The use of DNA sampling to test and generate hypotheses is an example of how scientific knowledge changes as new techniques become available.
- The relationship between mothers and infants is the most important interaction among primates, and there is increasing evidence that males provide more parental care than was previously thought.

Critical Thinking Questions

1. Apply some of the topics presented in this chapter to some nonprimate species that you're familiar with. Can you develop some hypotheses to explain the behavior of some domestic species? You might want to speculate on how behavior in domestic animals may differ from that of their wild ancestors.

2. In anticipation of the next chapter, can you speculate on how the behavioral ecology of nonhuman primates may be helpful in explaining human behavior?

3. We used birds as an example of sexual dimorphism resulting from sexual selection. But there are some bird species in which males, not females, sit on the nest

to warm and protect the eggs. These males are less colorful than the females. How would you explain this? (*Hint*: Sexual selection may not be the only factor involved in sexual dimorphism in bird coloration.)

A female bonobo, lying in the grass, tosses her youngster in play.

Primate Models
for the Evolution
of Human Behavior

Key Questions

▶ Which patterns of nonhuman primate behavior are the most important for understanding human evolution?

▶ How are humans unique among primates? In what ways are we not unique?

I n Chapter 1, we said that primates (chimpanzees in particular) are often used as models for early hominin behavior. But once the human and chimpanzee lineages diverged from a common ancestor, they traveled down different evolutionary paths and continued to evolve in response to different environmental pressures. Consequently, no living species, not even chimpanzees, can perfectly serve as a representative of early hominin adaptations.

Anyone who's curious about the beginnings of humankind would like to know more about our early ancestors. Drawings of early hominins, based on fossil remains, may give us a fairly accurate picture of what they looked like; but what did they *really* look like? What were their lives like? Did they have the same diseases people have today? What kinds of social groups did they live in? What did they eat? How long did they live? How did they die? Can we answer these questions? No, not completely. But we can study the complex factors that influence many behaviors in nonhuman primates. We'll also continue to make fossil discoveries, and comparative primate genomics, which has much to tell us, is still in its infancy. By combining what we learn from these approaches, we can at least have a better understanding not only of human biological evolution but also of how certain human behaviors evolved.

In the last chapter, we considered some of the factors that guided the evolutionary history of nonhuman primate behavior. In the past two decades, primatologists have agreed that certain human behavioral predispositions reflect patterns also seen in other primates (Cartmill, 1990; King, 1994, 2004; de Waal, 1996). But just because chimpanzees and humans may both show a particular behavior, we can't say for certain that it's a direct result of shared ancestry. What's important is to closely examine behavioral patterns that have evolved as adaptive responses in nonhuman primates, always keeping in mind the enormous degree of flexibility in primate behavior. Then researchers can look for similar patterns in humans and try to draw conclusions about the ecological and genetic factors that may have produced similarities (and differences) between our closest relatives and ourselves.

This approach places the study of human behavior firmly within an evolutionary context.

Certainly, human behavior is predominantly learned. But the ability to learn and behave in complex ways is ultimately rooted in biological factors. Natural selection has consistently favored the increased brain size and neurological complexity that have enhanced learning capacities and behavioral modification in the human lineage. When primatologists approach research questions from this biological perspective, they don't propose that all human abilities and behaviors are genetically determined or unalterable. Rather, they seek to explain how certain patterns may have come about and what their adaptive significance might be. Within this framework, the flexibility of human behavior is recognized and emphasized.

Human Origins and Behavior

What does it mean to be human? Clearly, certain aspects of behavior are what set humans apart from other species. Long ago, culture became our strategy for coping with life's challenges. If suddenly stripped of all cultural attributes, modern humans wouldn't be able to survive year-round in many parts of the world.

Although we share more than 98 percent of our DNA coding sequences and many anatomical and behavioral characteristics with chimpanzees, we're undeniably quite different from them, both physically and behaviorally. Humans have different limb proportions, flatter faces, smaller teeth, and, most important, relatively and absolutely bigger brains than chimpanzees. These anatomical differences are the results of changes in the behavior of regulatory genes that direct embryonic development. These genes are highly conserved throughout the animal kingdom, and they govern the same

developmental processes in all animals. But the length of time they operate to establish patterns and proportions of anatomical structures varies between species. Indeed, alterations in the activities of these developmental genes through the course of evolution may be the single most important factor in speciation. For example, chimpanzees have longer faces and larger teeth than humans because the genes that control the development of these structures cause them to develop at different rates than they do in humans (**Fig. 8-1**).

Despite these differences, humans and apes are sufficiently similar anatomically that we can identify many shared derived traits that both species inherited from our last common ancestor. For example, human and ape shoulders are anatomically quite similar, but they're different from monkey shoulders. In humans, as in many species, some systems evolved at different times and rates than others. So, human hands are less derived than ape hands because our thumbs aren't as reduced and our fingers aren't as elongated. In fact, while our shoulders are very ape-like, we have the hands of a generalized cercopithecine monkey.

So what does all this mean in terms of behavior? It means that to some extent, we shouldn't limit our behavioral comparisons to chimpanzees, any more than we should limit anatomical comparisons. Rather, we should include many species in our behavioral analogies. The selective pressures that acted on ancestral monkeys have played a role in our evolution, too, and that's something we shouldn't forget.

In the 1970s, the prevailing theory was that early hominins diverged from the apes as they moved out of a forested environment and adapted to a savanna environment. Such a move meant that they were subjected to increased predation pressure, so they adopted bipedality partly out of the need to stand upright while looking for predators (see Chapter 10). But those early hominins were already predisposed to standing upright because that is something many other primates were also able to do. The same principle applies to behavior. Although we now believe that early hominin ancestors probably exploited a more mixed woodland habitat rather than a savanna environment, they still had to have anatomical and behavioral capacities that allowed them to go there in the first place.

As a separate lineage, our own evolutionary story probably began with a behavioral shift to exploiting an econiche different from that of the great apes, and this new adaptation required spending more time on the ground and exploiting different types of resources. These factors, in turn, selected for additional behavioral and anatomical adaptations, while other hominoids were responding to different environmental pressures.

In what is now a classic study, Washburn and deVore (1961) used savanna baboons as a model of early hominin behavior because they live in open areas and spend much of the day on the ground. Savanna baboons live in large multimale-multifemale groups partly as an adaptive response to predation, and Washburn and deVore proposed that early hominins had a similar social structure (and they probably did). But because we're more closely related to chimpanzees, they, too, were used as an analogue for the development of many human behaviors, including tool use and competition for social rank. Thus, several species have been chosen for comparison based on both behavioral ecology and biological relatedness (Dunbar, 2001).

Today, primatologists still use nonhuman primate behavior to examine the evolution of human behavior, but they also study the relationships between two or more variables. For example, it's important to establish if there's a correlation between body size and basal metabolic rate. Then, having demonstrated a positive correlation, we might add another variable, such as diet. Subsequently, we could add other factors, such as increased brain size

and social structure. In other words, we look for correlations between life history traits and sociality. Once positive (or negative) correlations are ascertained, we can propose certain principles to apply to the study of human behavioral evolution.

Brain and Body Size

One predominant characteristic that clearly differentiates humans from other primates is relative brain size, by which we mean the proportion of some measure of body size, such as weight, that's accounted for by the brain. Brain size and body size are closely correlated. Clearly, an animal the size of a chimpanzee (about 100 to 150 pounds) has a larger brain than a squirrel monkey, which weighs about 2 pounds. But in cross-species comparisons, as body weight increases, brain size doesn't necessarily increase at the same rate.

The predictable relationship between body and brain size has been called the "index of **encephalization**" (Jerison, 1973). The degree of encephalization is used to estimate the expected brain size for any given body size. Most primates are close to predicted ratios for brain-body size, but there's one notable exception: ourselves. New World capuchins and squirrel monkeys also show a degree of encephalization that considerably exceeds predictions. Brain size in modern humans is well beyond what would be expected for a primate of similar body weight. It's this degree of encephalization that must be explained as a unique and central component of recent human evolution. Using the same analytical perspectives

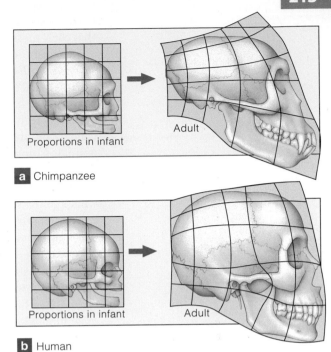

▲ Figure 8-1

Developmental changes in the skull of (a) chimpanzees and (b) humans illustrate morphological variation between two closely related species. The crania of human and chimpanzee infants are quite similar, but as chimpanzees mature, the lower face and teeth become much larger than in humans. In an adult chimpanzee, the size of the braincase is also much smaller relative to the lower face than in humans. In humans, the large upper part of the cranium reflects much more brain growth after birth than is seen in chimpanzees. These anatomical differences arise through changes in regulatory genes in one or both species since they last shared a common ancestor. In turn, regulatory genes determine the timing of development of structures.

encephalization The proportional size of the brain relative to some other measure, usually an estimate of overall body size, such as weight. More precisely, the term refers to increases in brain size beyond what would be expected given the body size of a particular species.

that are applied to the fossil materials in the next several chapters, we can see that early members of the genus *Homo*, as well as more primitive hominins (*Australopithecus*), weren't nearly as encephalized as modern humans are.

Carefully controlled comparisons are essential in making cross-species generalizations about different-sized animals (something to keep in mind when we discuss early hominins). Such controls relate to considerations of what's called scaling, or (more technically) **allometry**. These allometric comparisons have become increasingly important in understanding contemporary primate life history variables and adaptations. Moreover, similar approaches, borrowed from these primate models, are now also routinely applied to the interpretation of the primate/hominin fossil record.

Beyond simple brain size comparisons between different species, it's more appropriate to emphasize the relative size of certain structures in the brain. Primitive (ancestral) brains, such as those of reptiles, are mostly composed of structures related to basic physiological functions, and there's a small **cortex** that receives sensory (especially olfactory) information. As discussed in Chapter 5, in mammals, the relative size of the most recently evolved layer of the cortex, called the **neocortex**, has increased. This increase permits a more detailed and precise analysis and interpretation of incoming sensory information and therefore more complex behavior. In primates, expansion of the neocortex has accounted for much of the increase in brain size (**Fig. 8-2**). The primate neocortex is partly composed of many complicated association areas. It's the part of the brain that, in humans, is associated with cognitive functions related to reasoning, complex problem solving, forethought, and language. In humans, the neocortex accounts for about 80 percent of total brain volume (Dunbar, 1998).

Timing of brain growth is also important. In nonhuman primates, the most rapid period of brain growth occurs shortly before birth; but in humans, it occurs after birth. Human prenatal brain growth is restricted so that the infant can pass through the birth canal. As it is, the size of the head in human newborns makes childbirth more difficult in humans than in any other primate. Thus, in humans, the brain grows rapidly for at least the first five years after birth. Because brain tissue is the most costly of all body tissues in terms of energy consumed, the metabolic costs of such rapid and sustained neurological growth are enormous, requiring more than 50 percent of an infant's metabolic output (Aiello, 1992).

In evolutionary terms, the metabolic costs of a large brain have to be compensated for by benefits. That is, large brains wouldn't have evolved if they didn't offer some advantage (Dunbar, 1998). Various hypotheses have been proposed for the evolution of large brains in primates, and many scientists in the past focused on problems related to getting food and the kinds of foods a species eats. For example, some monkeys (with a smaller relative brain size) primarily eat leaves, which, although plentiful, aren't an energy-rich food source. Primates need a complex brain in order to be familiar with their home range; to be aware of when seasonal foods are available; and to solve the problem of extracting foods from shells, hard peels, and even underground roots. But these are problems for all foraging species (including squirrels and raccoons, for example), and yet these other animals haven't evolved such relatively large brains (**Fig. 8-3**).

Another explanation, the social brain hypothesis, proposes that primate brains increased in relative size and complexity because primates live in social groups. The demands of social living are numerous, and primates must be able to negotiate a complex web of interactions, including competition, alliance formation, forming and maintaining friendships, and avoiding certain individuals. Therefore,

allometry Also called scaling; the differential proportion among various anatomical structures (e.g., the size of the brain in proportion to overall body size during the development of an individual). Scaling effects must also be considered when comparing species.

cortex Layer. In the brain, the cortex is the layer that covers the cerebral hemispheres, which in turn cover more primitive, or older, structures related to bodily functions and the sense of smell. The cortex is composed of nerve cells called neurons, which communicate with each other and send and receive messages to and from all parts of the body.

neocortex The more recently evolved portions of the cortex of the brain that are involved with higher mental functions and composed of areas that integrate incoming information from different sensory organs.

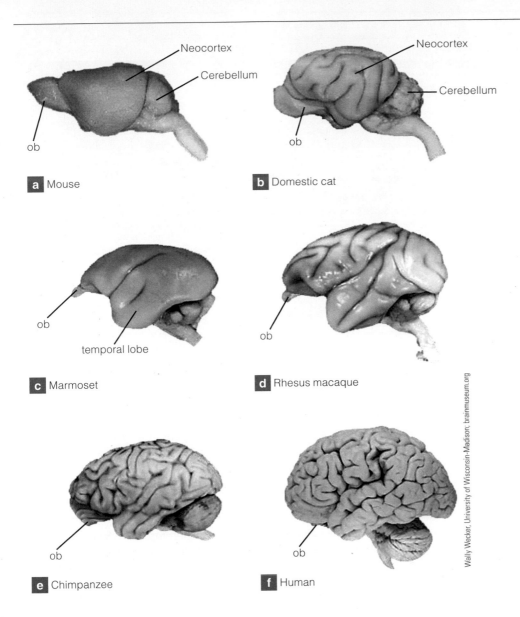

Wally Wecker, University of Wisconsin-Madison; brainmuseum.org

▲ **Figure 8-2**

Comparisons of mammalian brains as seen in these left lateral views (front is to left). Expansion of the neocortex, the outer layers of the cerebral hemispheres, has been the most significant trend during the evolution of the mammalian brain. This is especially evident in the size of the neocortex relative to that of the olfactory bulb (ob) at the front of the brain. The olfactory bulb is the termination point of sensory fibers that send olfactory information from the nose to the brain. A relatively large olfactory bulb indicates a greater dependence on the sense of smell. Compare the size of this organ, relative to the neocortex, in these brains. In the mouse and cat, it's particularly large, but it becomes smaller in primates. In humans, it's barely visible. In fact, in chimpanzees and humans, the neocortex is all that's visible from the top and sides except for the cerebellum. Also note the increasingly convoluted surface of the neocortex. This is due to cortical folding, which allows more neurons to be packed into a limited space. Increasing the number of neurons provides more interconnections between areas of the brain, allowing more information to be processed. The marmoset exhibits less cortical folding than the cat, but its temporal lobe (part of the neocortex) is better defined, and brain size relative to body size is greater. As you can see, cortical folding is most pronounced in humans. (Illustrations are shown approximately the same size and not to scale.) (Photos provided by the University of Wisconsin–Madison Comparative Mammalian Brain Collection: http://brainmuseum.org. Preparation of these images and specimens was funded by the National Science Foundation and the National Institutes of Health.)

Lynn Kilgore

► **Figure 8-3**
These young raccoons are extremely intelligent and forage for a wide assortment of foods in a complex environment. However, they don't spend their entire lives in social groups and their relative (and absolute) brain size is smaller than that of similarly sized primates.

Barton and Dunbar (1997) suggested that intelligence evolved not only to solve physical problems (such as finding food and avoiding predators), but also to analyze and use social information, such as which animals are dominant, who forms alliances with whom, and whom to avoid.

In support of the social brain hypothesis, Bergman and colleagues (2003) showed that savanna baboons in a study group in Botswana recognized that the female social hierarchy is divided into matrilines (**Fig. 8-4**) and that the matrilines are ranked rela-

tive to one another. These primates also recognized dominance relationships within each matriline. In other words, they understood the arrangement of hierarchies within hierarchies. Emphasizing the implications of such behavioral complexity for the evolution of increased intelligence in humans, the authors conclude, "The selective pressures imposed by complex societies may therefore have favored cognitive skills that constitute an evolutionary precursor to some components of human cognition" (Bergman et al., 2003, p. 1234).

But at the same time, group size is limited by brain size to the extent that a group can't be made up of more animals than individuals can recognize and interact with. Brain and group size therefore probably coevolved (Dunbar, 1998, 2001). Extrapolating from neocortical volume to the size of social groups, as seen in several nonhuman primate species, Dunbar (1998) speculates that large group size in some early members of the genus *Homo* is likely. This isn't to say that early humans always lived in large groups, but they may have formed large congregations by periodic associations of smaller groups.

Stanford (1999, 2001) has proposed that meat eating was also important in the development of increased cog-

▼ **Figure 8-4**
This bonnet macaque group is a matriline composed of a group of closely related females and their offspring.

© ephotocorp / Alamy

nitive abilities in the human lineage. Chimpanzees hunt small animals and their favorite prey is red colobus monkeys (**Fig. 8-5**). Stanford and others (Aiello and Wells, 2002) argue that if early hominins relied on a diet that increasingly contained a high proportion of meat, rich in protein and fats, such a diet would meet the nutritional demands of a lineage in which relatively large brains were becoming important. But as Stanford also points out, relatively large brain size hasn't developed in social carnivores such as wolves and lions.

So, if meat was important in the evolution of large brains in hominins, some factor other than nutrition would have had to be important. Once chimpanzees (usually males) have made a kill, they often share the meat with relatives, allies, and females. Negotiating the complexities and strategies involved in the politics of sharing meat might be viewed as one aspect of the social brain hypothesis, which holds that neurological complexity evolved as a response to complicated behavioral challenges.

Compared to most humans, chimpanzees don't really eat much meat, and there's some recent evidence that meat became an important dietary component in human ancestors sometime after chimpanzees and humans went their separate ways. In a preliminary analysis of the chimpanzee genome, Clark and colleagues (2003) discovered that several of the genes responsible for producing enzymes involved in amino acid metabolism have changed over time in both species. (Animal protein is a major source of amino acids.) This finding adds support to theories that increased meat consumption may have been important for increased brain size in early humans (Penny, 2004). At the very least, it indicates that as the two lineages diverged, both responded to different selective pressures; and selection favored enzyme mutations that enabled some hominins to digest meat more efficiently.

▲ **Figure 8-5**
Three male chimpanzees eating a red colobus monkey they've killed. The female at right is reaching out in a begging gesture. Note her facial expression (fear grin) indicating that she is very nervous about approaching the males. Note also the infant clinging to her chest.

© David Bygott

Language

One of the most significant events in human evolution was the development of language. In Chapter 7, we described several behaviors and autonomic responses that convey information in nonhuman primates. But although we emphasized the importance of communication to primate social life, we also said that nonhuman primates don't use language the way humans do.

The view traditionally held by most linguists and behavioral psychologists has been that nonhuman communication consists of mostly involuntary vocalizations and actions that convey information solely about an animal's emotional state (anger, fear, and so on). Nonhuman animals haven't been considered capable of communicating about external events, objects, or other animals, either in close proximity or removed in space or time. For example, when a startled baboon barks, other group members know only that it's startled. But they don't always know why it barked, and they can only discover this by looking around to see what provoked it. In general, then, it's been assumed that in nonhuman animals, including primates, vocalizations, facial expressions, body postures,

▶ **Figure 8-6**
Group of vervets.

Lynn Kilgore

and so on, don't refer to specific external phenomena.

But these views have been challenged for years (Steklis, 1985; King, 1994, 2004). For example, vervet monkeys (**Fig. 8-6**) use specific vocalizations to refer to particular categories of predators, such as snakes, birds of prey, and leopards (Struhsaker, 1967; Seyfarth et al., 1980a, 1980b). When researchers made tape recordings of vervet alarm calls and played them back within hearing distance of wild vervets, they saw different responses to various calls. When the vervets heard leopard-alarm calls, they climbed trees; when they heard eagle-alarm calls, they looked up; and they responded to snake-alarm calls by looking around at the ground and in nearby grass.

These results show that vervets use distinct vocalizations to refer to specific components of the external environment. Vervet calls aren't involuntary, and they don't refer solely to the individual's emotional state (alarm), although this information is certainly conveyed. While these findings dispel certain long-held misconceptions about nonhuman communication (at least for some species), they also indicate certain limitations. Vervet communication is restricted to the present; as far as we know, no vervet can refer to a predator it saw yesterday or one it might see in the future.

Other studies have demonstrated that numerous nonhuman primates produce distinct calls that have specific references. There is also compelling evidence that many birds and some nonprimate mammals use specific predator alarm calls.

Humans use *language*, a set of written and/or spoken symbols that refer to concepts, other people, objects, and so on. This set of symbols is said to be arbitrary because the symbol itself has no inherent relationship with whatever it stands for. For example, the English word *flower*, when written or spoken, neither looks, smells, nor feels like the thing it represents. Humans can also recombine their linguistic symbols in an infinite number of ways to create new meanings, and we can use language to refer to events, places, objects, and people far removed in both space and time. For these reasons, language is described as an open system of communication, based on the human ability to think symbolically.

Language, as distinct from other forms of communication, has always been considered a uniquely human achievement, setting humans apart from the rest of the animal kingdom. But work with captive apes has somewhat modified this view. Although many researchers were skeptical about the capacity of nonhuman primates to use language, reports from psychologists, especially those who work with chimpanzees, leave little doubt that apes can learn to interpret visual signs and use them in communication. Other than humans, no mammal can speak. However, the fact that apes can't speak has less to do with lack of intelligence than with differences in the anatomy of the vocal tract and language-related structures in the brain.

Beginning in the 1960s, after unsuccessful attempts by others to teach young chimpanzees to speak, psychologists Beatrice and Allen Gardner designed a study to test language capabilities in chimpanzees by teaching ASL (American Sign Language for the deaf) to an infant female named Washoe. The project began in 1966, and in three years, Washoe had acquired at least 132 signs. "She asked for goods and services, and she also asked questions about the world of objects and events around her" (Gardner et al., 1989, p. 6).

Years later, an infant chimpanzee named Loulis was placed in Washoe's care, and she adopted him. Psychologist Roger Fouts and colleagues wanted to know if Loulis would spontaneously acquire signing skills through contact with Washoe and other chimpanzees in the study group. Within just eight days, Loulis began to imitate signs the other chimps were making. Also, Washoe deliberately *taught* Loulis how to make some signs. For example, when she wanted him to sit down, "Washoe placed a small plastic chair in front of Loulis, and then signed CHAIR/SIT to him several times in succession, watching him closely throughout" (Fouts et al.,

1989, p. 290). Washoe died in 2007, but Dr. Fouts continues to study chimpanzee signing with three chimpanzees (including Loulis) at the University of Central Washington.

There have been other chimpanzee language experiments. A female named Sara was taught to recognize plastic chips as symbols for various objects. Importantly, the chips didn't resemble the objects they represented. For example, the chip that represented an apple was neither round nor red. The fact that Sara was able to use the chips to communicate is significant because her ability to associate chips with concepts and objects to which they bore no similarity implies some degree of symbolic thought. And at the Yerkes Regional Primate Research Center in Atlanta, Georgia, two male chimpanzees, Sherman and Austin, learned to communicate using a series of lexigrams, or geometric symbols, imprinted on a computer keyboard (Savage-Rumbaugh, 1986).

Other apes have also shown language capabilities. The most famous of these is Koko, a female lowland gorilla who was taught to use ASL by Dr. Francine Patterson in the 1970s. Furthermore, Michael, an adult male gorilla who was also involved in the same study until his death in 2000, had a considerable vocabulary, and the two gorillas regularly communicated with each other using sign language. Koko, who also understands spoken English, is currently the only signing gorilla in the world.

In the late 1970s, a 2-year-old male orangutan named Chantek (also at Yerkes) began to use signs after one month of training. Eventually, he acquired approximately 140 signs, which he sometimes used to refer to objects and people not present. Chantek also invented signs and recombined them in novel ways, and he appeared to understand that his signs were representations of items, actions, and people (Miles, 1990).

Several people questioned this type of experimental work. Do the apes really understand the signs they learn, or are they merely imitating their trainers? Do they learn that a symbol is a name for an object, or do they only understand that making a symbol will produce that object? Other unanswered questions concern the apes' use of grammar, especially when they combine more than just a few "words" to communicate.

Partly in an effort to address some of these questions and criticisms, psychologist Sue Savage-Rumbaugh taught the two chimpanzees Sherman and Austin to use symbols for *categories* of

▲ **Figure 8-7**
The bonobo Kanzi, as a youngster, using lexigrams to communicate with human observers.

objects, such as "food" or "tool." This was done in recognition of the fact that in previous studies, apes had been taught symbols for specific items, not categories. Using a symbol as a label isn't the same thing as understanding the *representational value* of the symbol. But if chimpanzees could classify things into groups, it would indicate that they can use symbols referentially.

Sherman and Austin were taught to recognize familiar food items, for which they routinely used symbols, as belonging to a broader category referred to by yet another sym-

bol, "food." They were then introduced to unfamiliar food items, for which they had no symbols, to see if they would place them in the food category. The fact that they both had perfect or nearly perfect scores for this task was further evidence that they could indeed categorize unfamiliar objects. More importantly, it was clear that they could assign symbols to indicate an object's membership in a broad grouping. This ability strongly indicated that the chimpanzees understood that the symbols represented not only objects but also groups of objects (Savage-Rumbaugh and Lewin, 1994).

However, subsequent work with a chimpanzee named Lana wasn't as successful. Lana had been involved in an earlier language study and clearly had the ability to use symbols to refer to objects. However, she couldn't assign generic symbols to novel items (Savage-Rumbaugh and Lewin, 1994). It became apparent that the manner in which chimpanzees are introduced to language influences their ability to understand the representational value of symbols.

One criticism of the conclusions drawn from ape language studies has been that young chimpanzees must be *taught* to use symbols, while human children spontaneously acquire language through exposure, without being deliberately taught. Therefore, it was significant when Savage-Rumbaugh and her colleagues reported that Kanzi, an infant male bonobo, was spontaneously acquiring and using symbols at the age of 2½ years (Savage-Rumbaugh et al., 1986; **Fig. 8-7**). In the same way, Kanzi's younger half sister began to use symbols spontaneously when she was only 11 months old. Both animals had been exposed to the use of lexigrams, or symbols that represent words, when they accompanied their mother to training sessions; but neither had been directly involved in these sessions, nor had they been taught the various symbols.

While Kanzi and his sister showed a remarkable degree of cognitive com-

Dr. Duane Rumbaugh, Language Research Center (photo by Elizabeth Pugh)

plexity, it's still clear that apes don't acquire and use language in the same way humans do. It also appears that not all signing apes understand the referential relationship between symbols and objects, individuals, or actions. Nonetheless, we now have abundant evidence that humans aren't the only species capable of some degree of symbolic thought and complex communication.

The Evolution of Language

From an evolutionary perspective, the ape language experiments may suggest clues to the origins of human language. It's also highly significant that free-ranging great apes use some gestures for communication (King, 2004). In fact, it's quite possible that the last common ancestor we share with the living great apes had communication capabilities similar to those we see in these species. So, we need to identify the factors that enhanced the adaptive value of these abilities in our own lineage. At the same time, it's equally important to explore why these pressures didn't operate to the same degree in our closest relatives.

While increased brain size played a crucial role in human evolution, it was changes in preexisting neurological structures that permitted the development of language. Current evidence suggests that new structures and novel connections haven't generally been the basis for most of the neurological differences we see among species. Rather, reorganization, elaboration, and/or reduction of existing structures, as well as shifts in the proportions of existing connections, have been far more important (Deacon, 1992). It's also important to understand that the neurological changes that enhanced language development in humans wouldn't have happened if early hominins hadn't already acquired the behavioral and neurological foundations that

made them possible. For reasons we don't yet fully understand, communication became increasingly important during the course of human evolution, and natural selection favored anatomical and neurological changes that enhanced our ancestors' ability to use spoken language.

Some researchers argue that language capabilities appeared late in human evolution with the wide dispersal of modern *Homo sapiens* some 100,000–30,000 years ago. Others favor a much earlier origin, possibly with the appearance of the genus *Homo* some 2 million years ago. Whichever scenario is correct, language came about as complex and efficient forms of communication gained selective value in our lineage.

As you've already learned, the metabolic costs of producing and maintaining brain tissue are high, and those costs must be offset by benefits. So we have to assume that there was intense selective pressure that favored the ability of early humans to communicate at increasingly precise levels.

In most people, language function is located in the left hemisphere, meaning it's **lateralized**. (The left hemisphere is the dominant hemisphere in most people, and since it controls motion on the right side of the body, most people are right-handed.) Two regions in particular, Broca's area in the left frontal lobe and Wernicke's area in the left temporal lobe, are directly involved in the production and perception, respectively, of spoken language (**Fig. 8-8**).

Broca's area is located in the **motor cortex** immediately adjacent to a region that controls the movement of muscles in the face, lips, larynx, and tongue. When a person is speaking, information is sent to Broca's area, where it's organized specifically for communication. Then it's sent to the adjacent motor areas, which in turn activate the muscles involved in speech. We know that Broca's area operates this way because when it's damaged, speech production is impaired, even though there's no muscle paralysis. Paralysis

lateralized Localized to one side of the brain. Lateralization is the functional specialization of the hemispheres of the brain for specific activities.

motor cortex The areas of the brain's cortex involved with movement. The motor cortex is located at the back of the frontal lobe and is composed of cells that send information to muscle cells throughout the body.

▶ **Figure 8-8**

Left lateral view of the human brain, showing major regions and areas involved in language. Information that is to be used in speech is sent from Wernicke's area, via a bundle of nerve fibers, to Broca's area.

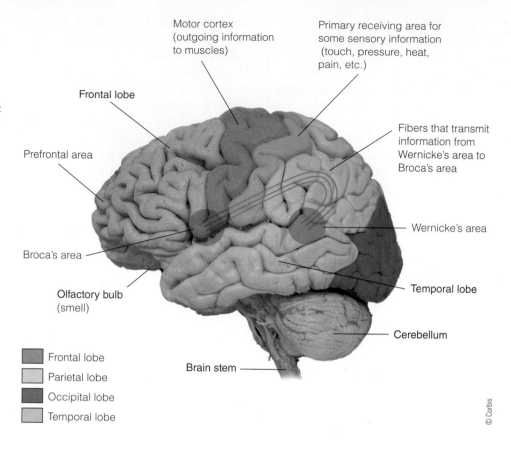

Motor cortex (outgoing information to muscles)

Primary receiving area for some sensory information (touch, pressure, heat, pain, etc.)

Frontal lobe

Prefrontal area

Fibers that transmit information from Wernicke's area to Broca's area

Wernicke's area

Broca's area

Olfactory bulb (smell)

Temporal lobe

Cerebellum

Brain stem

Frontal lobe
Parietal lobe
Occipital lobe
Temporal lobe

© Corbis

occurs only when the nearby motor areas are damaged, not when the damage is confined to Broca's area.

Wernicke's area is an association area that lies near structures involved in the reception of sound. A lesion in Wernicke's area doesn't impair hearing, but it severely affects language comprehension. This, in turn, interferes with speech production because auditory information that is related *specifically to language* is sent from Wernicke's area to Broca's area by way of a bundle of nerve fibers connecting the two regions.

But the perception and production of speech involve much more than these two areas, and the use of written language requires still other neurological structures. Eventually, information relating to all the senses (visual, olfactory, tactile, and auditory) is combined and relayed to Broca's area, where it's translated for speech production. This uniquely human ability depends on the interconnections between receiving areas for all sensory stimuli. While the

brains of other species have such areas, they don't have the ability to transform sensory information for the purpose of using language. Or maybe they do, at least to some degree.

Cantalupo and Hopkins (2001) report that magnetic resonance imaging of chimpanzee, bonobo, and gorilla brains demonstrates that in these species, a region analogous to part of Broca's area is larger on the left side than on the right. In humans, this particular area is involved in some of the motor aspects of speech production, and the report suggests that it may have also been important to the development of gestural language. These authors further report that in captive great ape studies, gestures are preferentially made by the right hand (controlled by the left hemisphere), especially when gestures are combined with vocalizations. This study suggests, therefore, that perhaps the anatomical basis for the development of left-hemisphere dominance in speech production in humans was present, at

At a Glance

EVOLUTION OF HUMAN LANGUAGE

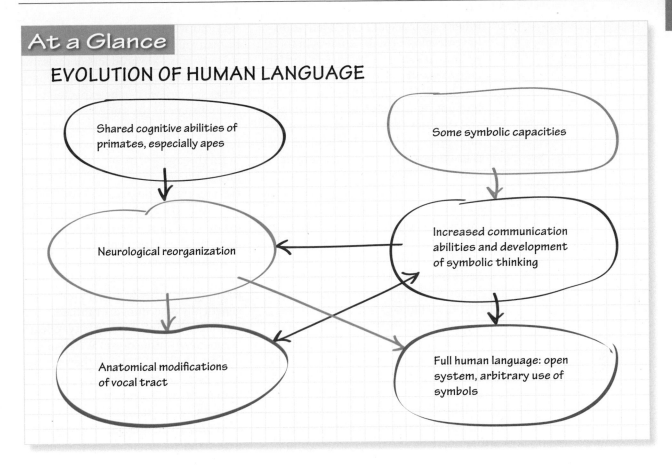

least to an incipient degree, in the last common ancestor of humans and the African great apes.

Specialization of auditory centers of the left hemisphere for language may have preceded the evolutionary divergence of humans and apes. A team of neuroscientists has shown that macaques also have this type of lateralization (Poremba et al., 2004). These researchers have demonstrated that, like humans and other species, rhesus macaques receive and process auditory information in the temporal lobes of both hemispheres. But these monkeys show greater metabolic activity in the left hemisphere specifically when they hear vocalizations of other rhesus macaques. This indicates that in macaques, the left temporal lobe is specialized for processing the vocalizations of conspecifics in particular.

This specialization may actually have an evolutionary history that extends back before the emergence of primates. Poremba and colleagues point to studies indicating that mice and birds also analyze conspecific vocalizations in the left hemisphere (Ehret, 1987; George et al., 2002). These studies don't demonstrate that this trait is as developed in mice and birds as it is in macaques; and since the studies concern only the calls of members of the same species, they don't explain the origins of language in human ancestors. However, they do indicate that in human evolution, the development of language-specific centers in the left hemisphere occurred as an elaboration of a trend that has had a very long evolutionary history.

The recent identification of a gene involved in speech may provide another piece to the puzzle of the evolution of language in humans. This gene, called *FOXP2*, produces a protein that regulates the expression of other genes. These genes, in turn, influence the embryological development of circuits in the brain that relate to language in humans. People who inherit a particular *FOXP2* mutation have developmental disorders in the brain that cause severe speech and language impairment (Lai et al., 2001).

The *FOXP2* gene isn't unique to humans. In fact, it's highly conserved; and since it's present in mice, all mammals probably have it. But while *FOXP2* is important to neurological development in nonhuman mammals, it has nothing to do with language in these species. When researchers compared the human form of the FOXP2 protein with that of chimpanzees and gorillas, they found that the human protein differed from the two ape versions by two amino acid substitutions. This means that since humans last shared a common ancestor with chimpanzees and gorillas, the gene has undergone two point mutations during the course of human evolution. But in chimpanzees and gorillas, it hasn't changed.

The *FOXP2* gene is the first gene demonstrated to influence language development. It varies between ourselves and closely related species, indicating not only that natural selection has acted on it in our lineage, but also that the FOXP2 protein may have played a role in the development of language capacities in humans.

Primate Cultural Behavior

One important trait that makes primates, and especially chimpanzees, attractive as models for early hominin behavior may be called cultural behavior. Although many cultural anthropologists and others prefer to use the term *culture* to refer specifically to human activities, most biological anthropologists consider it appropriate to use the term in discussing nonhuman primates as well (McGrew, 1992, 1998; de Waal, 1999; Whiten et al., 1999). In fact, the term *cultural primatology* is now being used more frequently.

Undeniably, most aspects of culture are uniquely human, and we should be cautious when we try to interpret nonhuman animal behavior. But again, since humans are products of the same evolutionary forces that have produced other species, we can be expected to exhibit some of the same behavioral patterns, particularly of other primates. However, because of increased brain size and learning capacities, humans express many characteristics to a greater degree. We would argue that the aptitude for culture as a means of adapting to the natural environment is one such characteristic.

Cultural behavior is passed from generation to generation through learning. (In other words, it's not genetically determined, or innate, although certainly the capacity to learn is genetically influenced.) Whereas humans deliberately teach their young, it appears that free-ranging nonhuman primates (except for a few reports) don't. But at the same time, like young nonhuman primates, human children acquire a tremendous amount of knowledge through observation rather than instruction (**Fig. 8-9a**).

Nonhuman primate infants, by observing their mothers and others, learn about appropriate food items, behaviors, and how to use and modify objects to achieve certain ends (**Fig. 8-9b**). In turn, their own offspring will observe these activities. What emerges is a cultural tradition that may eventually come to typify an entire group or even a species.

The earliest reported example of cultural behavior concerned a study group of Japanese macaques on Koshima Island, Japan. In 1952, Japanese researchers began provisioning the macaque troop with sweet potatoes. The following year, a young female named Imo began washing her potatoes in a stream before eating them. Within three years, several other monkeys were also washing their potatoes, though instead of the stream, they were using the ocean nearby. Maybe they liked the salt!

The researchers suggested that dietary habits and food preferences are learned and that potato washing was an example of nonhuman culture. Because the practice arose as an innovative solution to a problem (removing dirt) and gradually spread through the troop until it became a tradition, it was seen as containing elements of human culture.

A study of orangutans in six areas (four Bornean and two Sumatran) listed 19 behaviors that showed sufficient regional variation to be classed as "very likely cultural variants" (van Schaik et al., 2003). Four activities in the "very likely" category involved the use of nests. In five locations, nests were built exclusively for play activities and not for resting or sleeping. There was also variation in nest construction including, in some cases, the addition of sheltering roofs. Lastly, while tool use isn't as elaborate as in chimpanzees, in one Bornean locality, orangutans used sticks to scratch themselves and leaves as "napkins." And in one Sumatran area, they pushed sticks into tree holes to obtain insects.

Using tools or objects to accomplish tasks has always been considered one of the hallmarks of being human. In fact, tool use and language have traditionally been said to set humans apart from other animals. However, we now know that humans aren't the only animals that use tools. A few nonhuman primates also use tools, with chimpanzees being the most notable example. And what's more, tool use isn't even restricted to primates. New Caledonian crows modify and use leaf stems to probe for insect larvae, and in captivity, they've bent wire to make "hooks" to obtain food (Hunt, 1996; Weir et al., 2008); some bottlenose dolphins tear off chunks of sponges to wear on their noses as protection while foraging for fish on the ocean floor (Krützen et al., 2005); and sea otters use rocks to crack open abalone shells (**Fig. 8-10**). Nevertheless, tool use is most elaborate among primates, and needless to say, no other species even comes close to developing tools to the degree that humans have. But human technology had to begin somewhere, so we briefly discuss some of the many examples of tool use in nonhuman primates and how these behaviors may have come about in our own lineage.

Reports of tool use in gorillas aren't common, but Breuer and colleagues (2005) reported seeing two female lowland gorillas in the DRC using branches as tools. In one case, a gorilla used a branch to test the depth of a pool of water. Then, as she waded bipedally through the pool, she used the branch again, this time as a walking stick (**Fig. 8-11**).

▼ **Figure 8-9**
(a) This little girl is learning basic computer skills by watching her older sister. (b) A chimpanzee learns the art of termiting through intense observation.

Lynn Kilgore

Manoj Shah / The Image Bank

▶ **Figure 8-10**
This California sea otter is eating a clam it has opened with a rock. It's common for sea otters to put their shell-cracking rocks on their stomachs as they eat, just in case they need them again.

Chimpanzees exhibit more complex forms of tool use than any other nonhuman primate. They routinely insert twigs and grass blades into termite mounds in a practice primatologists call "termite fishing" (refer back to Fig. 8-9). The termites seize the twig in an attempt to protect their nest; but unfortunately for them, they become a light snack once the chimpanzee pulls the twig out of the mound. Importantly, chimpanzees frequently modify some of their stems and twigs by stripping the leaves—in effect, making a tool. For example, chimpanzees often choose a particular piece of vine, twig, or palm frond, remove leaves or other extraneous material, and then break off portions until it's the proper length. Chimpanzees have also been seen making these tools even before the termite mound is in sight.

The modification of natural objects for use as tools has several implications for nonhuman primate intelligence. First, the chimpanzees are engaged in an activity that prepares them for a future (not immediate) task at a somewhat distant location, and this action implies planning and forethought. Second, attention to the shape and size of the raw material indicates that chimpanzees have a preconceived idea of what the finished product needs to be in order to be useful. To produce a tool, even a simple tool, based on a concept is an extremely complex behavior that, as we now know, isn't the exclusive domain of humans.

Primatologists have been aware of termite fishing and similar behaviors since the 1960s, but they were surprised by the discovery that chimpanzees also use tools to catch small prey. Pruetz and Bertolani (2007) report that savanna chimpanzees in Senegal, West Africa, sharpen small branches to use as thrusting spears for capturing galagos. Prior to this study, there was no evidence that any nonhuman primate actually hunted with what is basically a manufactured (albeit simple) weapon. Yet on 22 occasions, 10 different animals repeatedly and forcefully jabbed sharpened sticks into cavities in branches and trunks to extract galagos from their sleeping nests. In much the same way they modify termiting sticks, these chimpanzees had stripped off side twigs and leaves. But they'd also chewed the ends to sharpen them, in effect producing small thrusting spears.

The spears weren't necessarily used to impale victims so much as to injure or immobilize them, because galagos are extremely agile, fast, and hard to catch. Thus, after several thrusts, the chimpanzee would reach into the opening to see if there was anything to be had. Only one galago was actually seen to be retrieved and eaten, and although it wasn't moving or vocalizing, it was unclear if it had actually been killed by the "spear" (Pruetz and Bertolani, 2007).

With the exception of two adults (one male and one female), all of the chimpanzees observed using hunting tools were subadults of both sexes. Also, the animal that was observed retrieving and eating a galago was an adolescent female. Until now, all evidence suggested that while termite fishing was largely done by females and subadults, hunting was largely done by adult males, sometimes accompanied by one or two females. The fact that females and subadults were involved in tool use, tool manufacture, and hunting may imply an increased role for females in the development of these behaviors in our own species, and this will be an important topic in future research.

There are other examples of tool use, although they don't involve modification of materials. For example, chimpanzees crumple and chew handfuls of leaves, which they dip into tree hollows where water accumulates. Then they suck the water that would otherwise be inaccessible from their newly made "leaf sponges." They also use leaves to wipe substances from fur; twigs as toothpicks; and stones as weapons. They may drag or roll various objects, such as branches and stones, to enhance displays. Lastly, in some populations, chimpanzees use sticks or leaves to help process (but not obtain) mammalian prey. In the Tai Forest (Ivory Coast), for example, chimpanzees use sticks to extract marrow from long bones (Boesch and Boesch, 1989).

Hernandez-Aguilar and colleagues (2007) report compelling evidence that savanna chimpanzees in western Tanzania use sticks and pieces of tree bark to dig for roots and tubers. These authors describe 11 digging sites, consisting of more than 200 holes. These sites were in an area inhabited by chimpanzees and in close proximity to trees containing chimpanzee sleeping nests. Although chimpanzees weren't actually seen digging the holes, there were portions of digging sticks and tree bark with adhering dirt, uneaten portions of roots, chewed wads of fibrous root remains, and chimpanzee feces and knuckle prints, all associated with the holes. Moreover, at that time, there was no evidence of other mammals in the digging areas.

Prior to this report, digging with tools had not been reported for chimpanzees. Since the digging occurred in a savanna habitat (most chimpanzees live in forests), this behavior may be an example of regional variation in food-getting behavior due to different environmental circumstances. In a somewhat marginal habitat for chimpanzees, digging makes it possible to exploit roots and tubers, which are an energy-rich food source.

▼ **Figure 8-11**
A female lowland gorilla using a "wading stick" (in her right hand) for support.

© Thomas Breuer—WCS

▼ **Figure 8-12**

Chimpanzees in Bossou, Guinea, West Africa, use a pair of stones as hammer and anvil to crack oil palm nuts. Although the youngster isn't being taught to use stone tools, it's learning about them through observation.

In several West African study groups, chimpanzees use unmodified stones as hammers and **anvils (Fig. 8-12)** to crack nuts and hard-shelled fruits (Boesch et al., 1994). Interestingly, stone hammers and platforms are used only in West African groups and not in East Africa. Likewise, termite fishing is seen in central and East Africa, but apparently it's not done in West African groups (McGrew, 1992).

The fact that chimpanzees show regional variation in their types and methods of tool use is significant because these differences, in effect, represent cultural variation from one area to another. Chimpanzees also show regional dietary preferences (Nishida et al., 1983; McGrew, 1992, 1998; Lycett et al., 2010). For example, oil palm fruits and nuts are eaten at many locations, including Gombe. But even though oil palms also grow in the Mahale Mountains (only about 90 miles from Gombe), the chimpanzees there seem to ignore them. Such regional patterns in tool use and food preferences, especially those that aren't related to environmental variation, are reminiscent of the cultural variations characteristic of humans. Moreover, it's reasonable to assume that this type of behavioral variation probably existed in early hominin groups, too.

So far, we've mainly discussed tool use and culture in great apes, but these aren't the only nonhuman primates that consistently use tools and exhibit elements of cultural behav-

ior. Primatologists have been studying tool use in capuchin (*Cebus*) monkeys for over 30 years (although indigenous human groups have been aware of the capuchin propensity for tool use long before this). Capuchins are found in South America, from Colombia and Venezuela, through Brazil, and as far south as northern Argentina. They are the most encephalized of all the monkeys, and while forest-dwelling species are arboreal, several species live in a more savanna-like habitat, and these spend a fair amount of time on the ground.

Many of the capuchin tool-using behaviors parallel those we've discussed for chimpanzees. Capuchins use leaves to extract water from cavities in trees (Phillips, 1998); they use small branches, which they modify, to probe into holes in trees and logs for invertebrates (Westergaard and Fragaszy, 1987); and they smash hard-shelled palm nuts against stones and tree trunks (Izawa and Mizuno, 1977). But what they've really become known for is using stones in a number of ways to obtain food. They use stones to smash foods into smaller pieces and crack palm nuts; to break open hollow tree branches and logs; and to dig for tubers and insects. In fact, capuchins are the only monkeys known to use stones as tools and the only nonhuman primate to dig with stones (Visalberghi, 1990; Moura and Lee, 2004; Ottoni and Izar, 2008).

When processing foods such as hard-shelled palm nuts, capuchins use stones as hammers. The anvils on which they place the nuts may be logs, flat stones, or any hard, relatively flat surface. The importance of this food source is revealed by the enormous effort expended to obtain it. Adult female capuchins weigh around 6 pounds, and the males weigh around 8 pounds, and yet they walk bipedally carrying stones that weigh as much as 2 pounds, or 25 to 40 percent of their own body weight (Fragaszy et al., 2004; Visalberghi et al., 2007)! Because the stones are so

anvils Surfaces on which an object such as a palm nut, root, or seed is placed before being struck with another object such as a stone.

heavy, it's difficult for capuchins to sit while cracking nuts with one hand, as humans and frequently chimpanzees do; and when they do sit, they use both hands. More often, they stand bipedally, raise the hammer stone with both hands (**Fig. 8-13**), and then pound the nut, basically using their entire body (Fragaszy et al., 2004).

Unlike subadult chimpanzees (especially females) who learn about termite fishing by watching their mothers, capuchin subadults tend to spend more time watching adult males, who allow youngsters to sit next to them and "scrounge" for bits of food. Even with the close attention young capuchins pay to nut cracking, it's not a skill they master until they're around 3 years old.

In addition to nut cracking, capuchins in a dry forest area of Brazil use stones to dig for roots and tubers (Moura and Lee, 2004; (**Fig. 8-14**). This is quite significant because until now, no nonhuman primate has been observed using stones for digging.

Capuchins who use stones to crack nuts and dig for roots have one extremely important thing in common with chimpanzees who dig with sticks and hunt galagos with sharpened branches: They all live in seasonally dry, open woodland environments and not in forests. In general, this is much the same habitat occupied by early hominins. Of course, capuchins and chimpanzees aren't hominins, but those populations that live in more marginal environmental settings face many of the same challenges encountered by early hominins. Moreover, chimpanzees and capuchins are among the most encephalized nonhuman primates and have manipulative abilities similar to those of early hominins. By further studying these behaviors, researchers hope to better understand how dry, open habitats, where resources are somewhat reduced and unpredictable (compared to forest environments), may have been the context that stimulated the use of tools as a means of obtaining foods that otherwise would have been inaccessible.

Noemi Spagnoletti / EthoCebus Project

Primatologist William McGrew (1992) presented eight criteria for cultural behaviors in nonhuman species (**Table 8-1**). Of these, the first six were established by the pioneering cultural anthropologist Alfred Kroeber (1928). McGrew (1992) demonstrated that Japanese macaques meet the first six criteria. However, all the macaque examples developed within the context of human interference (which isn't to say they all resulted

▲ **Figure 8-13**
This female capuchin must use most of her strength to smash a pine nut with a heavy stone, especially when carrying her infant on her back. Meanwhile, by watching her, the infant is learning the nut-smashing technique.

▼ **Figure 8-14**
A capuchin monkey using a stone as a digging tool.

Tiago Falótico / EthoCebus Project

TABLE 8.1	Criteria for Cultural Acts in Other Species
Innovation	New pattern is invented or modified.
Dissemination	Pattern is acquired (through imitation) by another from an innovator.
Standardization	Form of pattern is consistent and stylized.
Durability	Pattern is performed without presence of demonstrator.
Diffusion	Pattern spreads from one group to another.
Tradition	Pattern persists from innovator's generation to the next.
Nonsubsistence	Pattern transcends subsistence.
Naturalness	Pattern is shown in absence of direct human influence.

Source: Adapted from Kroeber (1928) and McGrew and Tutin (1978). In McGrew (1992).

directly from human intervention). To avoid this difficulty, the last two criteria were added later (McGrew and Tutin, 1978).

Capuchins and chimpanzees unambiguously meet the first six criteria, although not all groups meet the last two because most study groups have been at least minimally provisioned. However, all criteria are met by at least some chimpanzees in some instances (McGrew, 1992). While it's obvious that chimpanzees don't possess human culture, we can't overlook the possibility that human culture probably originated in exactly the same kinds of behaviors we've just described in several nonhuman primates. In fact, it's quite possible that these behaviors had already developed before the chimpanzee and human lineages diverged. While sticks and unmodified stones don't remain to tell tales, our early ancestors surely used these same objects as tools in much the same ways as chimpanzees and capuchins do today.

We've made it clear that even though chimpanzees and capuchins modify sticks to make tools, they haven't been observed modifying the stones they use. However, Kanzi, the signing bonobo, learned to strike two stones together to produce sharp-edged flakes. In a study conducted by Sue Savage-Rumbaugh and archaeologist Nicholas Toth, Kanzi was allowed to watch as Toth produced stone flakes, which were then used to open a transparent plastic food container (Savage-Rumbaugh and Lewin, 1994).

Bonobos don't commonly use objects as tools in the wild, and as far as we know, they don't use stones. But Kanzi readily appreciated the usefulness of the flakes in getting food. What's more, he was able to master the basic technique of producing flakes without having been taught the various components of the process, although at first his progress was slow. But eventually, Kanzi realized that if he threw the stone onto a hard floor, it would shatter and he would have an abundance of cutting tools. Although his solution wasn't the one that Savage-Rumbaugh and Toth expected, it more importantly provided an excellent example of bonobo insight and problem-solving ability. Kanzi did eventually learn to strike two stones together to make flakes, and he then used them to obtain food. This behavior is not only an example of tool manufacture and tool use, albeit in a captive situation; it's also a very sophisticated, goal-directed activity and provides a wonderful example of bonobo problem-solving abilities.

As we said earlier, culture has become the environment in which modern humans live. Quite clearly, catching termites with sticks and cracking nuts with stones are hardly comparable to modern human technology. Even so, modern human technology had its beginnings in these very sorts of behaviors. But this doesn't mean that nonhuman primates are "on their way" to becoming human. Remember, evolution is not goal directed, and if it were, there's nothing to dictate that modern humans necessarily constitute an evolutionary goal. Such a conclusion is a purely **anthropocentric** view, and it has no validity in discussions of evolutionary processes.

Aggression

For many primate species, especially those whose ranges are small, contact with one or more other groups of conspecifics is a daily occurrence; and the nature of these encounters can vary from one species to another. Primate groups are associated with a *home range*, where they remain permanently. (Although individuals may leave their home range and join another community, the group itself remains in a particular area.) Within the home range is a portion called the **core area**. This area contains the highest concentration of predictable resources, and it's where the group is most likely to be found. Although portions of the home range may overlap with that of one or more other groups, core areas of adjacent groups don't overlap. The core area can also be said to be a group's **territory**, and it's the portion of the home range defended against intrusion. In some species, however, other areas of the home range may also be defended.

Not all primates are territorial. In general, territoriality is associated with species whose ranges are sufficiently small to permit patrolling and protection (such as gibbons and vervets). But male chimpanzees are highly intolerant of unfamiliar chimpanzees, especially other males, and fiercely defend their territories and resources. Therefore, chimpanzee intergroup interactions almost always include aggressive displays, chasing, and sometimes fighting.

In recent years, a good deal of attention has been focused on lethal attacks by male coalitions on other chimpanzees. Such attacks occur when a number of individuals attack and sometimes kill one or two others who may or may not be members of the same group. Lethal aggression is relatively common between groups of chimpanzees, and it's also been reported for red colobus monkeys (Starin, 1994); spider monkeys, although no actual killings have been observed (Aureli et al., 2006; Campbell, 2006); and capuchin monkeys (Gros-Louis et al., 2003).

Groups of male chimpanzees, sometimes accompanied by one or two females, patrol the boundaries of their home range and sometimes enter another group's territory (Wrangham, 1999; Wilson et al., 2004). When patrolling, chimpanzees travel silently in compact groupings (**Fig. 8-15**). They stop frequently to sniff, look around, or climb tall trees, where they may sit for an hour or more surveying the region. During such times, they appear to be tense, and a sudden sound, such as a snapping twig, causes them to touch or embrace each other for reassurance (Goodall, 1986). It's apparent from their nervous behavior and uncharacteristic silence that they know they're venturing into a potentially dangerous situation.

Before they enter peripheral areas, chimpanzees usually hoot and display to determine if other animals are present. If members of another community appear, some form of aggression occurs until one group retreats. But if the intruders encounter a female with an infant or a lone male, they will almost certainly attack, and chances are good

anthropocentric Viewing nonhuman organisms in terms of human experience and capabilities; emphasizing the importance of humans over everything else.

core area The portion of a home range containing the highest concentration and most reliable supplies of food and water. The core area is frequently the area that will be most aggressively defended.

territory The portion of a home range actively defended against intrusion, particularly by members of the same species.

that an infant or a single male will be killed. (Mothers of killed infants are frequently allowed to escape.)

Beginning in 1974, Jane Goodall and her colleagues witnessed at least five unprovoked and extremely brutal attacks by groups of chimpanzees (usually, but not always, males) upon lone individuals. To explain these attacks, we must point out that by 1973, the original Gombe community had split into two distinct groups, one in the north and the other in the

▼ **Figure 8-15**
A chimpanzee border patrol. Note the bristling hair of the animal in front. This is an indication of excitement.

© Juergen Ritterbach / Alamy

south of what was once the original group's home range. In effect, the southern splinter group had denied the others access to part of their former home range.

By 1977, all seven males and one female of the splinter group were either known or suspected to have been killed. All observed incidents involved several animals, usually adult males, who brutally attacked lone individuals (**Fig. 8-16**). It's impossible to know exactly what motivated the attacks, but it was clear that the attackers intended to incapacitate their victims (Goodall, 1986). Whether chimpanzees intend to actually kill their victims is difficult to ascertain, since we don't know to what degree they have a concept of death.

The violence at Gombe has continued over the years, although the actual number of observed attacks is low. Wilson and colleagues (2004) have described four cases of aggression between groups at Gombe between 1993 and 2002. In these incidents, two infants were killed and eaten, and two young adult males were severely injured and presumed dead, as they weren't seen again. In all these attacks, the victims were either lone males or mothers with dependent young. And there were always at least four attackers; thus, the risk of injuries to attackers was minimal.

A situation similar to the one at Gombe was also reported for a group of chimpanzees in the Mahale Mountains south of Gombe. Over a 17-year period, all the males of a small community disappeared. Although no attacks were actually observed, there was circumstantial evidence that most of these males met the same fate as the Gombe attack victims (Nishida et al., 1985, 1990).

Mitani and colleagues (2010) document a third such situation in a large chimpanzee community at Ngogo, Kibale National Park, Uganda. Between 1999 and 2009, members of this group were observed killing or fatally wounding 18 individuals from other groups, and all but one of the observed attacks were made by coalitions of males on patrol. There was also convincing evidence of three additional lethal attacks. The entire Ngogo community now regularly uses the area where they frequently conducted border patrols and where 13 of the attacks occurred; meanwhile the former residents have not been seen. In effect, these chimpanzees have increased their territory by 2.5 square miles, or 22 percent. Given this fact, the researchers attribute the attacks on a neighboring group to territorial expansion, which increases their resource base and in turn may lead to greater reproductive success.

Even though chimpanzees clearly engage in lethal attacks, the actual number of observed incidents is low. In the period between 1966 and 1999 at Mahale, aggression accounted for 16 percent of known (not presumed) deaths. In all, 18 individuals are known to have been killed by adult males, and all but one were infants. Actually, the major cause of death among the Mahale chimpanzees was disease (Nishida et al., 2003), and this is probably typical of most chimpanzee populations and perhaps early hominin populations as well. Certainly, in preindustrial modern humans, infant childhood and adolescent mortality was at least 50 percent for most groups.

Efforts to identify the social and ecological factors that predispose males of some species to engage in lethal attacks have led to hypotheses that attempt to explain the function and adaptive value of these activities (Manson and Wrangham, 1991; Nishida, 1991). In this context, the benefits and costs of extreme aggression must be identified. The principal benefits to aggressors are protection and acquisition of territory (thus reduced competition for resources) and perhaps the acquisition of mating partners, especially in cases of infanticide. Costs include risk of injury or death and loss of energy expended in performing aggressive acts, but these risks are greatly reduced, since attacks occur only when the attackers considerably outnumber their victim.

Although we may never have a precise explanation for lethal raiding, it appears that protection and acquisition of resources are of major importance (Goodall, 1986; Nishida et al., 1990; Manson and Wrangham, 1991; Nishida, 1991; Aureli et al., 2006; Mitani et al., 2010). Early hominins and chimpanzees may have inherited from a common ancestor the predispositions that have resulted in shared patterns of strife between populations. It's difficult to draw direct comparisons between nonhuman primate conflict and human warfare, partly because of elaborations of human culture including symbols (such as flags), religion,

and language. But it's important to speculate on the fundamental issues that may have led to the development of similar patterns in different species, and the acquisition and protection of resources was undoubtedly crucial. In fact, even though nations go to war for many stated reasons, such as religion or retaliation, the underlying causes very often have to do with increased access to resources, be they water, land, or oil.

Prosocial Behaviors: Affiliation, Altruism, and Cooperation

In Chapter 7, we briefly discussed affiliative behaviors and the role they play in maintaining group cohesion by reinforcing bonds between individuals. There are also **prosocial behaviors** that indicate just how important social bonds are, and these include assistance, sharing, care giving, and perhaps even compassion. Humans are by far the most prosocial of species. It's not uncommon for people to risk their lives to save the lives of others, even strangers. On a simpler level, we pick things up for each other; we help strangers who've fallen down; we contribute to charities that help people we've never met; we open doors for people; and we especially come to the assistance of children and the elderly (**Fig. 8-17**). Why we have a propensity to do this isn't well understood, but studying these behaviors in other primates can help clarify this important issue.

Laboratory studies have been instrumental in testing food-sharing

Lynn Kilgore

▲ **Figure 8-16**
The right ulna (the long bone on the little finger side of the forearm) of a female Gombe chimpanzee called Madam Bee. Madam Bee was one of the 1970s attack victims. The enlarged area of the shaft is the site of a healing fracture near the wrist. Apparently, the bone was broken in one attack, then rebroken in a subsequent episode. (As her left arm had been paralyzed by polio, she only had her right arm to defend herself.) Madam Bee died within a few days of this last attack.

prosocial behaviors Actions that benefit another individual even when there is no reward to the performer. Prosocial behaviors include sharing, assisting, and comforting and in humans are motivated in part by empathy and compassion.

tendencies in nonhuman primates. These studies have shown that bonobos and some monkeys, in particular, engage in sharing behaviors similar to that seen in humans. When given the option to perform tasks to obtain food solely for themselves or for themselves and another animal, both capuchins and bonobos most frequently chose the latter option (Lakshminarayanan and Santos, 2008; Hare and Kwetuenda, 2010). Indeed, bonobos showed a clear preference for eating with another, unrelated individual, even when it meant sharing highly desirable food items. Interestingly, although chimpan-

zees share meat after killing prey, they don't share to the degree that bonobos do in testing situations (Silk, 2005).

Altruism

Altruism is behavior that benefits another individual while involving some risk or sacrifice to the performer. Cooperation, assistance, and altruism are fairly common in many primate species, and altruistic acts sometimes contain elements of compassion. It's somewhat risky to use the term *compassion* because in humans, compassion is motivated by **empathy** for another individual. We don't know whether nonhuman primates can empathize with another's situation, but many researchers believe they do. Certainly, there are many examples, mostly from chimpanzee studies, of actions that resemble compassionate behavior in humans. Examples include protecting victims during attacks, helping younger siblings, and remaining near ill or dying relatives or friends.

In a poignant example from Gombe, the young adult female Little Bee brought food to her mother, Madam Bee, at least twice while the latter lay dying of wounds inflicted by attacking males (Goodall, 1986). When chimpanzees have been observed sitting near a dying relative, they were seen occasionally shooing flies away or grooming the other, as if trying to help in some way.

Some other examples involve chimpanzees attempting to rescue others who have fallen into water. Because chimpanzees can't swim, jumping into water is a life-threatening action. Nevertheless, there are several reports of chimpanzees doing just that, especially in zoos where water-filled moats sometimes surround portions of chimpanzee exhibits. In one case, an adult male actually drowned while trying to save an infant that had fallen into the water (de Waal, 2007).

The most fundamental of altruistic behaviors, protecting dependent offspring, is ubiquitous among mammals and birds; and in most species,

▶ **Figure 8-17**
(a) Children often try to help others. (b) This man is carrying an elderly neighbor to safety during a flood in Utah.

altruism Behavior that benefits another individual at some potential risk or cost to oneself.

empathy The ability to identify with the feelings and emotions of others.

altruistic acts are confined to this context. Among primates, however, recipients of altruistic acts may include individuals who aren't offspring and who may not even be closely related to the performer.

Chimpanzees routinely come to the aid of relatives and friends; female langurs join forces to protect infants from infanticidal males; and male baboons protect infants and cooperate to chase predators. In fact, the primate literature abounds with examples of altruistic acts—individuals placing themselves at risk to protect others from attack.

One very intriguing report concerns the attempted rescue of a young adult male baboon who, at some distance from his group, was being chased by a hyena. Suddenly, observers saw an adult female racing toward the hyena in what turned out to be a vain attempt to rescue the male (Stelzner and Strier, 1981; Strier, 2003). The female wasn't the victim's mother, and a female baboon is no match for a hyena. So why would she place herself in serious danger to help an animal to whom, as far as we know, she wasn't closely related? We don't know, but this was clearly an altruistic, albeit unsuccessful, act.

Adopting orphans is a form of altruism that has been reported for capuchins, macaques, baboons, and especially chimpanzees. When chimpanzee youngsters are orphaned, they're routinely adopted, usually by older siblings, who are solicitous and highly protective. Adoption is crucial to the survival of orphans, who certainly wouldn't survive on their own. In fact, it's extremely rare for a chimpanzee orphan less than 3 years old to survive, even if it is adopted.

Evolutionary explanations of altruism are based on the premise that individuals are more likely to perform risky or self-sacrificing behaviors for the benefit of a relative, who shares genes with the performer. According to this hypothesis, known as *kin selection*, an individual may enhance his or her reproductive success by saving the life of a relative. Even if the performer's life

is lost because of the act, the relative may survive to reproduce and pass on genes that both individuals shared.

There's also the hypothesis of reciprocal altruism, where the recipient of an altruistic act (that is, the one who benefits) may later return the favor (the debt to be paid in the future). Coalitions, or alliances between two or more individuals, are an often-cited example of reciprocal altruism, and it's common in baboons and chimpanzees. As we mentioned in Chapter 7, members of alliances support and defend one another in conflicts with others and may use the alliance to increase their status within the group hierarchy. In chimpanzees, members of coalitions are sometimes, but not always, related. Even though reciprocal altruism may occur, it's a hypothesis that needs further testing.

Group selection is a third hypothesis that some primatologists have supported. According to this model, an individual may act altruistically to benefit other group members because ultimately it's to the performer's benefit that the group be maintained. If the altruist dies, genes he or she shares with other group members may still be passed on (as in kin selection). But there's a problem with group selection theory: According to natural selection theory, individual reproductive success is enhanced by acting selfishly, and the individual is the object of natural selection.

Although the group selection issue hasn't been resolved, we do know that for many reasons discussed in Chapter 7, primates, including humans, have a better chance of surviving and reproducing if they live in groups. Given this important fact, any behavioral mechanism that reinforces the integrity and cohesion of social groupings is to the advantage of individual group members. These mechanisms include altruism, perhaps a form of compassion, and a certain degree of empathy (de Waal, 2005).

Primatologist Frans de Waal, has published extensively on empathy and altruism in chimpanzees. He points out that theories of kin selection, reciprocal altruism, and group selection ultimately explain altruism and cooperation in terms of selfishness. But this is the *explanation of how the behaviors evolved*, not the motivation of the animal performing the altruistic act, and de Waal views the immediate motivation as a function of "sensitivity to the needs of others," or empathy. He states, "In humans, the most commonly assumed motivation behind altruism is empathy. We identify with another in need, pain, or distress, which induces emotional arousal that may translate into sympathy and helping. Inasmuch as there are signs of empathy in other animals, from rodents to primates, the same hypothesis may apply" (de Waal, 2007).

The issue of empathy is much discussed, and not all primatologists agree that nonhuman primates possess a true capacity for it. Nonetheless, many behaviors certainly support the hypothesis that empathy is a behavioral trait that other species have, at least to some degree. Further studies no doubt will clarify the issue and provide yet another example of behavioral continuity between other primates and ourselves.

The Primate Continuum

It's unfortunate that humans generally view themselves as separate from the rest of the animal kingdom. This perspective is, in no small measure, due to a prevailing lack of knowledge about other species' behaviors and abilities. To make matters worse, we're exposed to advertising, movies, and television programs that continuously reinforce these notions.

For decades, behavioral psychology taught that animal behavior represents nothing more than a series of conditioned responses to specific stimuli. (This perspective is convenient for those who exploit nonhuman animals,

for whatever purposes, and remain free of guilt.) Fortunately, this attitude has been changing in recent years to reflect a growing awareness that humans, although in many ways unquestionably unique, are nevertheless part of a biological continuum. Indeed, we're also part of a behavioral continuum.

Where do humans fit, then, in this biological continuum? Are we at the top? The answer depends on the criteria used. Certainly, we're the most intelligent species if we define intelligence in terms of problem-solving abilities and abstract thought. But if we look more closely, we recognize that the differences between our primate relatives and ourselves (especially chimpanzees and bonobos) are primarily quantitative, not qualitative.

Although the human brain is absolutely and relatively larger than the brains of other primates, neurological processes are functionally the same. The need for close bonding with at least one parent and for physical contact are essentially the same. Developmental stages and dependence on learning are strikingly similar. Indeed, even in the capacity for cruelty and aggression combined with compassion, tenderness, and altruism exhibited especially by chimpanzees, we see a close parallel to the dichotomy between "evil" and "good" so long recognized in ourselves. The main difference between how chimpanzees and humans express these qualities (and thus the dichotomy) is one of degree. Humans are much more adept at cruelty, enormously compassionate, and able to reflect on their behavior in ways that chimpanzees can't. Like the cat in Chapter 7 that plays with a mouse, chimpanzees don't seem to understand the suffering they inflict on others; but humans do. Likewise, while an adult chimpanzee may sit next to and protect a dying relative or friend, it doesn't seem to feel intense grief and a sense of loss to the extent a human normally does.

To arrive at any understanding of what it is to be human, it's important to recognize that many of our behaviors are elaborate extensions of those of our hominin ancestors and close primate relatives. The fact that so many of us prefer to bask in the warmth of the "sun belt" with literally thousands of other people reflects our heritage as social animals adapted to life in the tropics. Likewise, the "sweet tooth" seen in so many humans is a direct result of our earlier primate ancestors' predilection for high-energy sugar contained in desirably sweet, ripe fruit. Recognizing our primate heritage is a significant aspect in our exploration of how humans came to be and how we continue to adapt.

Summary of Main Topics

- Biological anthropologists (including primatologists) apply what they've learned about nonhuman primate evolution, life history traits, and behavior to the study of early hominin behavior and adaptations.
- Although we humans share a common ancestry with all nonhuman primates, our complex behavior and use of language are unique. This uniqueness is related to expansion of the neocortex of the brain since the divergence of the hominin lineage from that of the African great apes.
- Because of the importance of neocortical expansion in human evolution, we emphasized some of the evolutionary changes that have occurred in the brain, particularly as they relate to language. Because the brain is such a metabolically expensive organ to maintain, selective pressures favoring increased behavioral complexity would have been enormous. An important source of these pressures may have been living in social groups.
- There is considerable evidence of cultural behavior in nonhuman primates, particularly regarding tool use in various populations. For example, while West African chimpanzees use stones to crack palm nuts, East African populations don't. Some savanna chimpanzees use sharpened sticks to hunt for galagos, and others use sticks to dig for roots. But neither of these behaviors has been seen in forest-dwelling chimpanzees. Likewise, capuchins that inhabit savanna-like environments crack nuts and dig for roots with stones, but forest-dwelling capuchins don't.
- Variation in cultural behavior and the transmission of these behaviors from one individual to another through observation and learning are hallmarks of human culture. Nonhuman primates exhibit certain aspects of culture, and so do several nonprimate species, although none of these species have adopted culture as an adaptive strategy the way humans have.

Critical Thinking Questions

1. Do you think that knowing about aggression between groups of chimpanzees is useful in understanding conflicts between human societies? Why or why not?

2. What are some examples of cultural behavior in nonprimate species that weren't mentioned in this chapter? Have you personally witnessed such behaviors?

3. Knowing what you currently know, how would you explain the presence of tool-using behaviors in chimpanzees and capuchin monkeys who live in savanna-like environments, while these activities aren't seen in forest-dwelling chimpanzees and capuchins?

The extremely well preserved fossil of *Darwinius* from Germany, dated to about 47 mya.

9

Overview of the Fossil Primates

Key Questions

▶ What were the oldest primates like, and how do they compare with the most primitive of the living primates (the lemurs and lorises)?

▶ Who are the oldest members of Hominoidea (apes and humans), and how do they compare with their modern counterparts? How do they fit into the primate family tree?

When gazing into the eyes of a great ape, we see in them something unique that we feel inside ourselves. Often, however, when looking into the eyes of a galago ("bush baby"), we see nothing but a cuddly animal that we might like to take home as a pet (see Fig. 6-14). When most of us think back to the origins of our own species, we generally stop once we've evoked the idea of an upright-walking ape ancestor. But have you ever considered extending your family tree to the baboons you may see in a wildlife park or to the lemurs or bush babies you see in the zoo? You might think, "How can a creature so small and, well, *animal*-like have anything to do with us or our evolutionary background?" In this chapter, we focus on bridging the gap between these creatures and ourselves—between **strepsirhines** and **haplorhines**—to help us better understand our own evolutionary history.

As we've seen in Chapters 6 through 8, some of our primate cousins share many of the traits we generally think of as uniquely human. Many of these similarities can be traced to shared origins in highly social groups living in the trees. We see these origins in the structure of our body and in the retention of many primitive features, such as pentadactyly (five fingers and toes) and unfused lower arm bones, but also in more "derived" skeletal traits that came later. Among the most important of these derived primate traits are a more **orthograde** (upright) body position and forward-facing eyes. Distinguishing these uniquely primate features in the fossil record as being different from those traits found in more distantly related mammalian cousins is the first step in recognizing our own beginnings. As we move in time through the Cenozoic era (see Chapter 5), we see in rough form the recapitulation of our own (primate) order from "primitive" to highly derived. We'll also trace the development of mammals that resemble us more and more over time until we conclude this chapter in the Miocene, 23 to 5 million years ago (mya), with the emergence of the first hominoids (apes) and then the first possible hominins (humans). As you'll see, our ability to recognize primate families in the fossil record not only uses the same skills that allow us to discover our later human origins, but also enables us to organize these creatures into meaningful groups.

This organization means that you'll face a multitude of taxonomic designations. These names aren't meant to scare you, but they should impress upon you how successful past lineages of primates have been—in fact, much more so than they are now. As you'll see, learning about the earliest beginnings and recent past of our primate order can lend powerful perspective and meaning to our own origins, even though most of the fossil groups discussed in this chapter never led to any living forms, and even fewer are related to our own hominin ancestors.

Background to Primate Evolution: Late Mesozoic

The exact origins of the earliest primates aren't well understood; in fact, they're shrouded in some amount of mystery. We *do* know that following the extinction of the dinosaurs at the end of the Mesozoic, the reign of the giant reptiles was over and the Age of Mammals had begun. Primates were just one of the many groups of small mammals that were left to diversify and explore the many niches left vacant with the passing of the dinosaurs.

It was during the last period of the Mesozoic era (the Cretaceous) that primates began to diverge from closely related mammalian lineages. Some scientists place these closely related ("sister") lineages into a group known as **Euarchonta**. Euarchonta is the **superorder** designated for the sister orders of tree shrews, flying lemurs (also known as the colugos, which don't fly and aren't lemurs), and primates (**Fig. 9-1**). **Sister groups** are two new clades that result from the splitting of a single common lineage. It's interesting to note that the closest relatives of Euarchonta are rabbits, rodents, and their relatives.

This diversification of early mammals took place in a global, tropical climate that accompanied the emergence of modern plants—although neither the exact region where primates first evolved nor the precise pressures that molded their adaptations are known. These uncertainties continue to intrigue scientists even today.

strepsirhines (strep-sir´-rines) Members of the primate suborder Strepsirhini, which includes lemurs and lorises.

haplorhines (hap-lore´-ines) Members of the primate suborder Haplorhini, which includes tarsiers, monkeys, apes, and humans.

orthograde Referring to an upright body position. This term relates to the position of the head and torso during sitting, climbing, etc., and doesn't necessarily mean that an animal is bipedal.

Euarchonta The superorder designated for the sister (closely related) orders of tree shrews, flying lemurs, and primates.

superorder A taxonomic group ranking above an order and below a class or subclass.

sister groups Two new clades that result from the splitting of a single common lineage.

▼ **Figure 9-1**
Euarchonta, the superorder designated for the sister orders of tree shrews, flying lemurs, and primates.

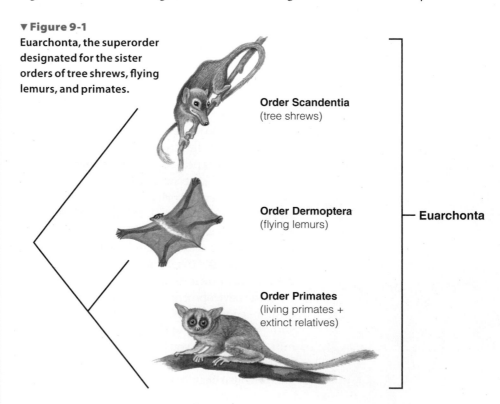

Order Scandentia
(tree shrews)

Order Dermoptera
(flying lemurs)

Order Primates
(living primates + extinct relatives)

Euarchonta

Primate Origins

The Cenozoic era is the broad time period during which most of primate evolution has unfolded (and continues to unfold) (see **Fig. 9-2**). This time period is divided into seven epochs, the oldest of which is called the Paleocene (beginning 65 mya). For each of these broad epochs, we can roughly attribute a particular phase of primate evolution and development. However, evolution knows no temporal bounds, so the time line for these phases will always be imperfectly defined (more precise dates and particular fossil primate groups will be discussed later in this chapter):

- Paleocene (65–55.8 mya): first archaic primates, plesiadapiforms
- Eocene (55.8–33 mya): first euprimates, early strepsirhines and haplorhines
- Oligocene (33–23 mya): early catarrhines, precursors to monkeys and apes
- Miocene (23–5.3 mya): monkeys and apes; first humanlike creatures
- Pliocene (5.3–1.8 mya): early hominin diversification
- Pleistocene (1.8–0.01 mya): early *Homo*
- Holocene (0.01 mya–present): modern humans

Paleontological evidence indicates that the first indisputable primates emerged just before the Eocene epoch (56 mya). Given that this is the first fossil occurrence, it has led many primate biologists to hypothesize that the initial radiation of archaic primates must have occurred long before this, perhaps during the early Paleocene epoch (65–55.8 mya; Miller et al., 2005; Bloch et al., 2007). Recent molecular evidence, however, has been used to predict the origins of primates to be as early as 90–80 mya, during the Cretaceous period (Tavaré et al., 2002; Martin et al., 2007; Soligo et al., 2007). This disparity in dates arises from the difficulty in reconciling morphological and molecular data in our search for the key time of evolutionary divergence—that is, the time when the last common ancestor of primates and their closest (euarchontan) relatives lived. The **last common ancestor (LCA)** is the hypothetical species that was the last to exist before it speciated into the myriad of sister orders related to primates. This critical species is often difficult to pinpoint morphologically, since it doesn't yet have the shared derived traits found in the **crown group**. This means that researchers can't confidently associate it with any given fossil. A crown group is easier to identify because it includes all of the taxa that come *after* a major speciation event. All extant groups and fossils sharing their specific derived traits are crown. Despite its lack of the clade's derived traits, the LCA also belongs to the crown group. On the other hand, the **stem group** includes all of the taxa in a clade *before* a major speciation event. For this reason, like the LCA, stem group taxa are often difficult to recognize in the fossil record. In spite of this, many scientists feel more comfortable classifying uncertain taxa as stem rather than committing them to the crown group (see Chapter 5 for a more complete discussion of phylogenetic concepts).

Thus, the time when we can first *confidently* identify an archaic primate is almost assuredly an underestimate of the actual time of divergence (the assumed date when the last common ancestor lived). Molecular data, on the other hand, provides us with what is often an overestimate of this time (Steiper and Young, 2008). What is important to realize, however, is that since molecular estimates are calibrated using known fossil dates, the two approaches are inextricably linked. Together, these two approaches (morphological and molecular) enable us to bracket the origins of indisputable primates at sometime between 90 and 65 mya (Steiper and Young, 2008)—a very large swath of time, indeed! However, until more fossil evidence emerges in support of the more ancient genetically predicted date of 90 mya,

last common ancestor (LCA) The final evolutionary link between two related groups.

crown group All of the taxa that come after a major speciation event. Crown groups are easier to identify than stem groups because the members possess the clade's shared derived traits.

stem group All of the taxa in a clade before a major speciation event. Stem groups are often difficult to recognize in the fossil record, since they don't often have the shared derived traits found in the crown group.

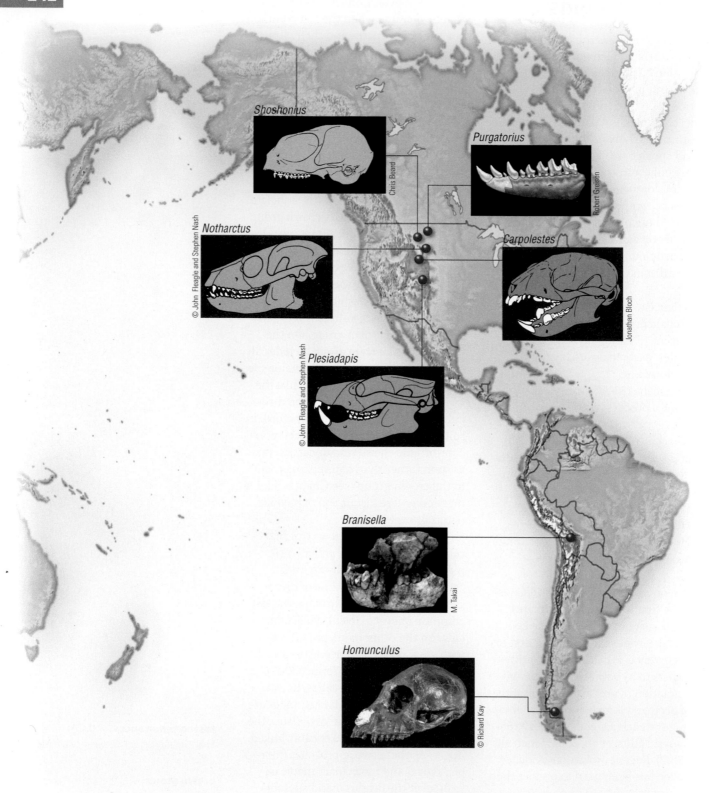

▲ **Figure 9-2**
A map showing the location of the fossil
primates discussed in this chapter.

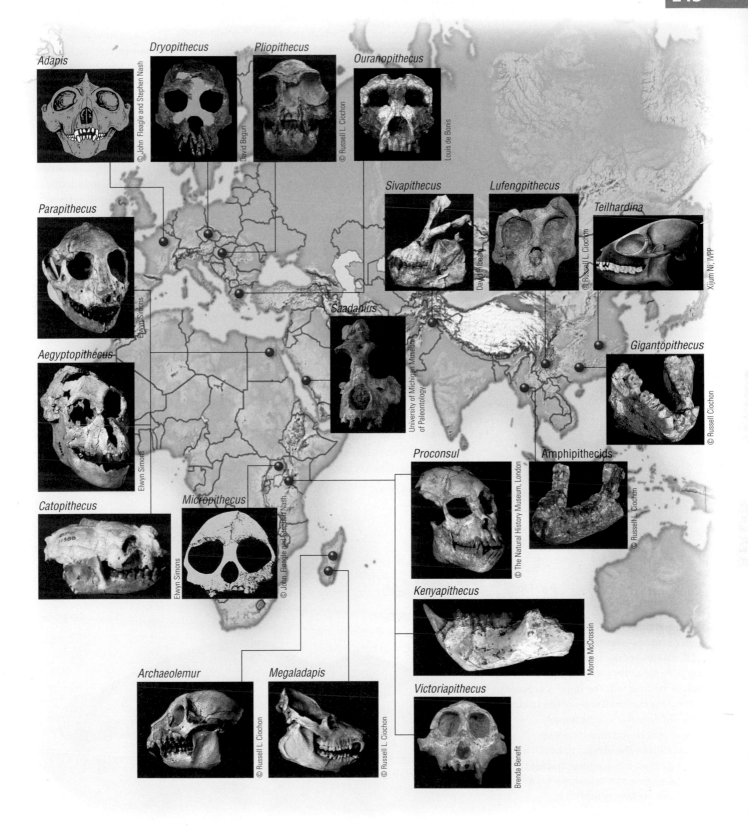

Adapis
© John Fleagle and Stephen Nash

Dryopithecus
David Begun

Pliopithecus

Ouranopithecus
© Russell L. Ciochon

Louis de Bonis

Parapithecus
Elwyn Simons

Sivapithecus
David Pilbeam

Lufengpithecus
© Russell L. Ciochon

Teilhardina
Xijum Ni, IVPP

Aegyptopithecus
Elwyn Simons

Saadanius
University of Michigan Museum of Paleontology

Gigantopithecus
© Russell Ciochon

Catopithecus

Micropithecus
© John Fleagle and Stephen Nash

Elwyn Simons

Proconsul
© The Natural History Museum, London

Amphipithecids
© Russell L. Ciochon

Kenyapithecus
Monte McCrossin

Archaeolemur
© Russell L. Ciochon

Megaladapis
© Russell L. Ciochon

Victoriapithecus
Brenda Benefit

65 mya remains the conservative estimate—although there are important implications related to which of the two dates one accepts with regard to what characteristics most properly define our order (see "Evolution of True Lemurs and Lorises" later in this chapter).

Made to Order: Archaic Primates

Fossil evidence indicates that between 65 and 52 mya, a major radiation of archaic primates, known as the plesiadapiforms, occurred. Plesiadapiforms are members of an extinct group that occupies a controversial position in primate phylogeny. When first discovered, these creatures were considered early members of the primate order, but in the 1960s, this conclusion was reversed and they were treated as their own order, Plesiadapiformes. In recent years, however, the careful analysis of an amazing array of recently discovered fossils has once again placed plesiadapiforms back within Primates (Bloch and Silcox, 2001; Silcox, 2001; Bloch and Boyer, 2002; Bloch et al., 2007). They are now gaining acceptance as a **semiorder** within Primates that is separate from the later **euprimates** (Silcox, 2007).

Plesiadapiforms are best known from a large number of fossil finds from the American West (especially Montana and Wyoming). Some of the more recent finds of these Paleocene mammals, particularly those from Clarks Fork Basin, Wyoming, have yielded a variety of nearly complete skeletons. Some members of this group exhibit a striking continuity of traits with some of the earliest strepsirhines from the later Eocene epoch. Although as many as six families are commonly recognized within this group, we'll concentrate on the three families that are most pertinent for this discussion.

The first family, Purgatoriidae, counts among their numbers the oldest recognized archaic primate, *Purgatorius* (Clemens, 1974; **Fig. 9-3**). Members of this extinct genus are believed to have been about the size of modern rats, and at least two (and

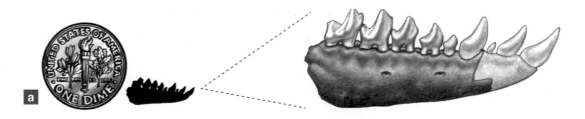

▶ **Figure 9-3**

Artist's representations of *Purgatorius*. **(a)** Rendering of the best-preserved jaw of *Purgatorius* with the front portion reconstructed. The dime is present to indicate the small scale of the specimen. **(b)** An artist's depiction of *Purgatorius* based on our current knowledge of the groups to which it belongs. Note in particular, the feet as they tread over the Paleocene sycamore and hackberry leaf litter.

Drawings by Robert Greisen/Designed by Russell L. Ciochon

semiorder The taxonomic category above suborder and below order.

euprimates "True primates." This term was coined by Elwyn Simons in 1972.

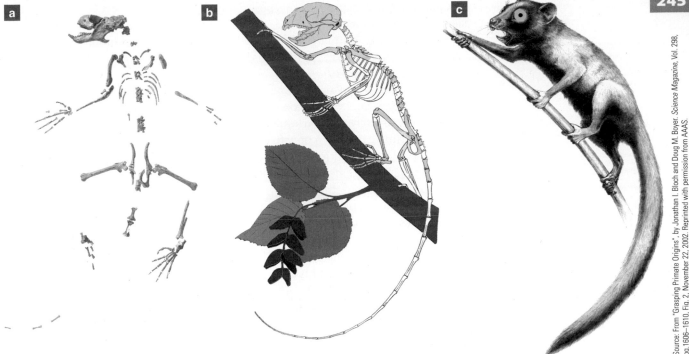

Source: From "Grasping Primate Origins", by Jonathan I. Bloch and Doug M. Boyer. *Science Magazine*, Vol. 298, pg.1606–1610, Fig. 2, November 22, 2002. Reprinted with permission from AAAS.

▲ Figure 9-4

Nearly complete skeleton of *Carpolestes* discovered in the Clarks Fork Basin of Wyoming. (a) *Carpolestes* as it was discovered. (b) Reconstructed skeleton of *Carpolestes*. (c) Artist's rendering of *Carpolestes* as it might have looked in life.

perhaps as many as four) species lived in the American Northwest during the earliest Paleocene about 65 mya (Lofgren, 1995; Clemens, 2004; Bloch et al., 2007). Evidence of a radiation of this kind, however, most likely indicates an origin in the late Cretaceous. Based on its placement at the base of Euarchonta lineages (think "stem group"), we can hypothesize that unpublished **postcranial** material from the Bug Creek Anthills site (rich in Purgatoriidae) in Montana will include evidence for nails; only time will tell.

Another family, Plesiadapidae, was among the more successful plesiadapiform groups. They were chipmunk- to marmot-sized mammals with large incisors similar to those of a rodent. However, unlike rodents, the plesiadapids had incisors that weren't continuously growing and didn't self-sharpen, suggesting that they used their incisors for a purpose other than gnawing. Some have suggested that this family subsisted on a vegetative diet of leaves supplemented with fruits. The best-known of this family is the genus *Plesiadapis*, which probably originated in North America but went on to colonize Europe via a land bridge across Greenland before eventually dying out.

The last family we'll look at, Carpolestidae (whose name means "fruit stealer"), was quite common during the Paleocene in North America and Asia, although its members were never as successful as the plesiadapids. These creatures were much smaller, generally mouse- to rat-sized, though they exhibit the typical enlarged incisors. They also have specialized dental traits that allowed them to efficiently process fibrous vegetation as well as nuts and insects. For a long time, carpolestids were known only from fossil teeth and jaws, but our knowledge of them changed recently when a nearly complete skeleton of *Carpolestes* (**Fig. 9-4**) was discovered in the Clarks Fork Basin, in Wyoming (Bloch and Boyer, 2002). This specimen is estimated at about 3.5 ounces, the size of the average hamster, and its postcranial anatomy reveals many traits adapted to a highly arboreal environment (particularly since it had opposable, grasping big toes with nails instead of claws). But unlike later euprimates that were fully adapted to living in the trees, *Carpolestes* displays no adaptations for leaping, though it was almost certainly a terminal branch feeder (Sargis et al., 2007).

postcranial Referring to all or part of the skeleton not including the skull. The term originates from the fact that in quadrupeds, the body is posterior to the head; the term literally means "behind the head."

One apparent exception to this plesiadapiform prominence is the oldest of the potential "primates of modern aspect" (Simons, 1972, p. 174); this presumed euprimate, *Altiatlasius*, is from the very latest Paleocene of Morocco (Sigé et al., 1990; Silcox, 2008). Unfortunately, this earliest possible true primate is known only from a handful of teeth. Additionally, there is no other terrestrial mammalian fossil record known from this time in Africa, making comparisons difficult. Some have suggested that its primate-like teeth may be a homoplasy rather than evidence of true euprimate affiliation (Rasmussen, 2007). This complicates our view of euprimate origins, as it would place their origin in Africa rather than in Asia, as the bulk of later material from the Eocene appears to do (see discussion of *Teilhardina*). Only more fossils will help clarify this ongoing mystery.

Eocene Euprimates

During the Eocene epoch (55.8–33 mya), we see the gradual extinction of the plesiadapiforms and their replacement by the euprimates (**Fig. 9-5**). These mammals, unlike the plesiadapiforms, have definite recognizable and modern derived primate traits, such as forward-facing eyes, greater encephalization, a postorbital bar, nails instead of claws at the ends of their fingers and toes, and an opposable big toe (see Chapter 6). These and other basic primate features suggest an adaptation to environmental conditions that were fundamentally different from those experienced by the plesiadapiforms: a warmer climate with year-round rainfall and lush, broad-leaved evergreen forests.

At the beginning of the Eocene epoch, North America and Europe were connected; they didn't split apart until the middle Eocene. Meanwhile, during the middle to late Eocene, North America was sporadically connected to Asia via the Bering land bridge. These early connections between these three continents meant that they shared many species in common. In contrast, the continents of Africa, Antarctica, Australia, and South America remained isolated by large bodies of water. These connections and isolations led to the evolution of a variety of animals of very different characters. In fact, following the end of the reign of dinosaurs, the Eocene was a time of rapid diversification for *all* mammals, not just the primates. As a result, the variety of animals known from this time period is much greater than that known from the earlier Paleocene.

Euprimates were part of this wave of diversification. They came on the scene around 56 mya—nearly simultaneously, it seems—in North America, Europe, and Asia. There are two main branches of euprimates, grouped into different superfamilies (Adapoidea and Omomyoidea). These two superfamilies include primitive primates that are described as being either more lemur-like (adapoid) or tarsier- or galago-like (omomyoid). Both groups are well known from cranial, dental, and post-cranial remains from North America, Europe, and, increasingly, Asia and Africa.

Lemur-like Adapoids

The adapoids are the best known of the Eocene stem strepsirhines and include more than 35 genera that we know of; the actual biodioversity at this time was surely far greater. These are the most primitive of the euprimates, as recognized by their dental anatomy. Their primitive dental formula (2.1.4.3; see Chapter 6) provided a generalized ancestral baseline from which many later, more derived varieties of dental specializations could evolve. The adapoids are divided into five families, based mostly on biogeographical distinctions. The most prominent are the amphipithecids of Asia, the notharctids of North America (predominantly), and the adapids of Europe.

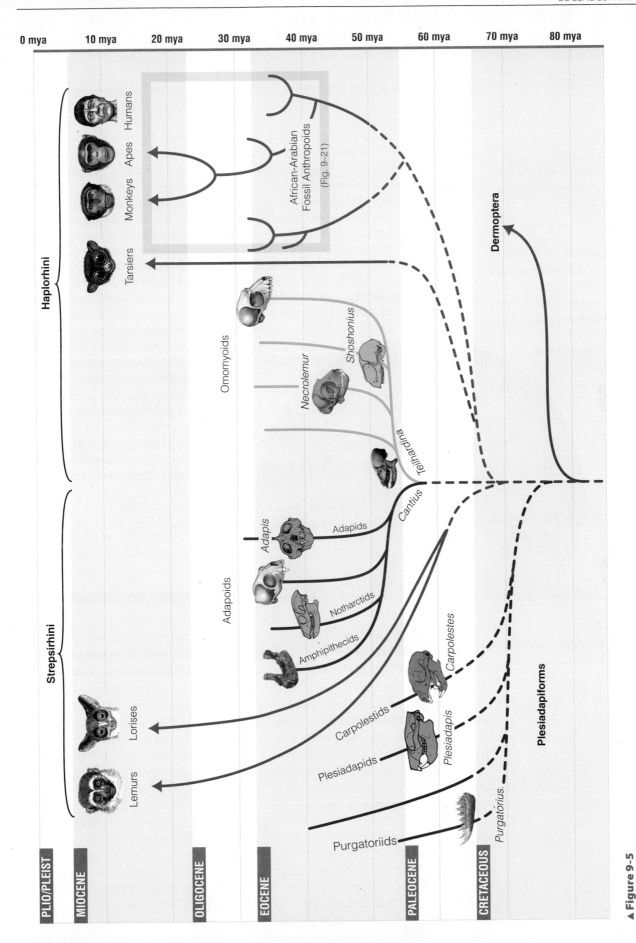

▲ **Figure 9-5**

Family tree of euprimates and their relationships to modern strepsirhine and haplorhine groups. Colors represent major groupings within the primates. Red is for the lemur-like adapoids; green is for the tarsier-like omomyoids; purple is for the plesiadapiforms; and blue represents the Fayum early anthropoid radiation. For a taxonomy of living and extinct primates, see Appendix B.

"Ida"-latry

It was the press release heard 'round the world: "WORLD RENOWNED SCIENTISTS REVEAL A REVOLUTIONARY SCIENTIFIC FIND THAT WILL CHANGE EVERYTHING" (Switek, 2009). She's been described variously as "a Rosetta Stone," "the Eighth Wonder of the World," and "an asteroid falling down to Earth." Her name is *Darwinius masillae*, nicknamed "Ida," and for a short time at the beginning of 2009, she was hailed as the "missing link" between lower and higher primates (Switek, 2010).

A few things mark Ida as a rare specimen, the first being the circumstances of the fossil's discovery. This remarkable fossil was apparently discovered and excavated illegally by amateur rock collectors in 1983 from the Messel Shale, in Germany. A completely flattened specimen, Ida was split into two mirrored slabs: B, which was sold to a Wyoming collector before being described in 1994, and A, the more complete of the two, recently acquired by the University of Oslo's Natural History Museum. Reunited, the two sides provide us with one of the best-preserved fossils of early primate history (**Fig.1**).

The name *Darwinius* was chosen to commemorate the bicentennial of Charles Darwin's birth, a source of celebration in scientific communities around the world. Also, Ida's description was not published in *Nature* or *Science* as might be expected, but rather in an online journal, *PLoS One* (Franzen et al., 2009). In fact, Henry Gee,

© Atlantic Productions Ltd.

the biology editor of *Nature*, gave faint praise, stating, "It's extremely nice to have a new find and it will be well-studied." To date, however, this fossil has not been studied by anyone outside of the original authors, interfering with the normal peer review analyses that are such an essential component of scientific research.

Another peculiarity was the media machine that drove the announcement of the new fossil. Within days of publication, Ida was off on a whirlwind media tour, including a splashy television documentary narrated by Sir David Attenborough, a book (*The Link: Uncovering Our Earliest Ancestor*), the cover of *People Magazine*, and her own website (www.revealingthelink.com). And in May of 2009, Google, the online search engine, even featured homage to the fossil on its homepage (**Fig. 2**)! In fact, the hullaballoo surrounding Ida seemed less like a scientific announcement and more like a commercial product launch! Matt Cartmill, of Duke University, commented, "The P.R. campaign on this fossil is I think more of a

◄ Figure 1

The hands of *Darwinius*, which indicate grasping adaptations, are extremely well preserved.

The amphipithecid family members from Myanmar (Burma) and Thailand, which in turn belong to the superfamily Adapoidea, don't fit neatly with any of the preconceived notions about early primates. Amphipithecids had generally been accepted as a dead-end lineage that had its heyday in the Eocene with no later Oligocene descendants. However, in the last few years, just such a primate has been found in Pakistan (Marivaux et al., 2005). Still, even with the addition of new material, this curious family of animals from Asia has many challenging features that are difficult to interpret, with hazy evolutionary affiliations. Some researchers say that these creatures are stem anthropoids

of some kind (Marivaux et al., 2005; Bajpai et al., 2008; Williams et al., 2010), while most say they're adapoids. Why the disagreement?

Remember that in Chapter 5 we introduced the terms *homology* (similar traits based on descent) and *homoplasy* (similar traits that evolve independently in different groups) and talked about the example of theropod dinosaurs and birds sharing derived traits. Unlike dinosaurs and birds, however, the amphipithecids are a textbook example of convergent evolution: Their seemingly "anthropoid" traits are actually homoplasies, not shared derived traits. Their teeth, in particular, can be somewhat deceiving. Since both early anthropoids and

story than the fossil itself." We might also mention that along with (and fueling) all the popular glitz, money was also a major driving force. Rumor has it that the museum in Oslo paid a million dollars for the fossil, creating outrage in the scientific community (Simons et al., 2009). It's no wonder the scientific process was so greatly accelerated.

After all the glitter settled, the scientific community got to work evaluating the grandiose claims surrounding Ida's announcement. Though the original researchers have not allowed other independent scientists to study the original material, careful evaluations of the description and high-quality photos reveal Ida's

affinity to the lemur-like adapoids and not to anthropoids. So, Ida's not the "missing link"—but so what? This should not downplay the importance of this exquisitely preserved fossil. As a 95 percent complete skeleton, Ida has much to tell us regarding the adaptations of her now long-extinct lineage. So excellent is her preservation that the soft tissue outline of her body can be seen, as well as the fossilized contents of her digestive tract. This has allowed a full-body reconstruction (**Fig. 3**). Future studies will focus on aspects of Ida's life history, including timing of maturation, giving us some estimate as to life expectancy of members of the *Darwinius* genus. So, while Ida may not live up to all the hype, she still sheds light on a dimly illuminated part of our primate past.

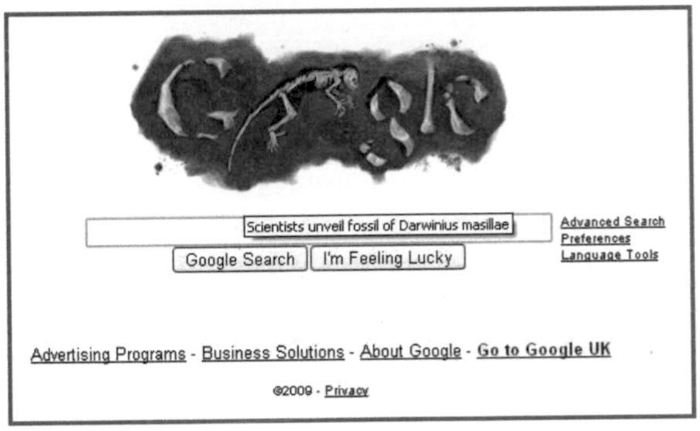

▲ **Figure 3**
An artist's reconstruction of what Ida might have looked like in real life.

▲ **Figure 2**
Google's homage to Ida, the supposed missing link, in May 2009.

Google

amphipithecids were exploiting the same dietary niche, they developed similar dental patterns. On the other hand, the postcranial skeleton and mandibles (**Fig. 9-6**) of amphipithecids betray their true affiliation as more primitive but specialized adapoids that exploited a slow-moving arboreal niche (Ciochon and Gunnell, 2002). For many years, the amphipithecid dental pattern confounded researchers; but with the discovery of more complete specimens, this mystery has now been solved. It seems that these remarkable adapoids, evolving in Asia in the absence of anthropoids, converged on the anthropoid dental pattern (this pattern of dietary and dental convergence was apparently fairly

common in early groups; see discussion of *Afradapis*).

The second major adapoid family, the notharctids, includes the genus *Cantius*. This was the earliest notharctid and one of the earliest adapoids in general. This small- to medium-sized animal is known primarily from North America, with just two species from Europe. Cranial and skeletal remains indicate that it was a diurnal creature, foraging during the day. It also probably traveled very rapidly through the trees, leaping quadrupedally. Traits of its mandible and its primitive dental formula of 2.1.4.3 indicate that it was probably a fruit eater. Another prominent notharctid was unveiled in 2009 to great fanfare.

▶ **Figure 9-6**
The teeth of the amphipithecids are misleading, but their mandibles betray their true phylogenetic affinity as lower primates.

© Russell L. Ciochon

This 47-million-year-old creature, *Darwinius* (nicknamed, "Ida"), does not appear to have had a dental comb or a grooming claw, which its scientific proponents argue is evidence that the adapoids are much more than mere lemur relatives (**Fig. 9-7**). In fact, these researchers went on to sensationally assert that Ida and other adapoids were basal haplorhines, a position not supported by the preponderance of scientific evidence (Franzen et al., 2009; see "A Closer Look: 'Ida'-latry"). Ironically, just months later, a new adapid from Egypt solidified the adapoid position as a stem strepsirhine group and helped bolster the hypothesis that apparent similarities to higher primates are indicative of convergent evolution (Seiffert et al., 2009).

This informative fossil, dating to about 37 mya, represents a previously unknown large-bodied adapiform genus,

▼ **Figure 9-7**
Skeleton of *Darwinius*, nicknamed "Ida."

© Martin Shields / Alamy

Afradapis. This fossil belongs to the third major family of adapoids, appropriately called the adapids. This group abruptly appeared in Europe near the end of the Eocene and just as quickly became extinct. For this reason, phylogenetic relations for this group are not well understood, although the adapids probably emigrated from another continent, most likely Asia. As the largest nonanthropoid primate known from Afro-Arabia, *Afradapis* is believed by some to indicate that adapoids were probably the first primates to exploit anthropoid-like feeding niches in Africa, in this case folivory (Seiffert et al., 2010). If true, this could have some important implications with regard to the role that potential ecological competition might have played in the early evolution of stem strepsirhine and haplorhine groups, explaining some of these early apparent convergences (Seiffert et al., 2009). Perhaps the best known of this group is *Adapis*. Not only was it the first nonhuman fossil primate named, but it was also first described by the well-known nineteenth-century naturalist Georges Cuvier. As you may remember from Chapter 2, Cuvier didn't believe in evolving lineages, even going so far as to state in 1812, *"l'homme fossile n'existe pas"* ("fossil man does not exist"; by this he also meant fossil primates). So it's ironic that in 1822, it was Cuvier who described and named the first fossil primate. Unfortunately for him, he confused the remains for that of an ungulate (a hoofed mammal); shortly after his death in 1837, the fossil was correctly identified as a primate. *Adapis'* dental formula remains primitive (2.1.4.3), and some have argued that an incipient dental comb (a lemur feature) could be recognized in this fossil genus. (You may recall from Chapter 6 that a dental comb is a specialization of the front teeth in the lower jaw; the teeth are elongated and project forward like a small comb.) A slow, arboreal quadruped, *Adapis* most likely spent its time foraging for leaves during the daytime hours.

Evolution of True Lemurs and Lorises

As we've mentioned, the adapoids were fairly lemur-like in their overall pattern, and they show distinctive primate tendencies. Although the ancient adapoids do resemble lemurs in overall anatomical body plan, this is mostly due to modern lemurs retaining some ancestral traits. The adapoid fossils don't show the same specializations seen in crown members of lemurs, galagos, and lorises, such as development of the dental comb. For this reason, we may say that modern-day lemurs, galagos, and lorises have retained many "primitive" aspects of anatomy, though there's no clear evolutionary relationship between the Eocene adapoids and these latter-day creatures (but see Kay et al., 2004; Ross et al., 2004).

It's important to note that the evolution of lemurs and other strepsirhines is of great interest to researchers because of their basal position as the sister group to all other primate lineages (Horvath and Willard, 2007; Horvath et al., 2008). Accordingly, information related to their initial emergence and dispersal can be used to time subsequent primate divergence dates.

Lorisoids (lorises and galagos) are the earliest examples of strepsirhine primates in the fossil record. These small, primitive creatures have been found in late Eocene deposits of the Fayum Depression in Egypt, an area that we'll discuss in more detail next. A late Eocene (circa 34 mya) fossil find from Egypt appears to have had a dental comb (Stevens and Heesy, 2006). This and other features have led to the conclusion that it's a stem galagid. When combined with molecular evidence (Seiffert et al., 2003), it can be inferred that lorises and galagos (also known as "bush babies") likely diverged by the close of the middle Eocene.

The existence of an early African bush baby in Egypt during this time indicates that stem strepsirhines initially evolved on the African mainland. These primates likely colonized Madagascar to give rise to crown lemuriforms. This would mean that lemurs have *never* existed outside of this tiny island (Seiffert et al., 2005a). The colonization itself most likely occurred by crossing the Mozambique Channel, perhaps by unintentionally rafting over on drifting debris (Yoder et al., 1996, 2003; Kappeler, 2000; Ali and Huber, 2010), though other biogeographical mechanisms, such as "island-hopping," have been suggested (McCall, 1997; Arnason et al., 2000). These related migrational phenomena are described in "A Closer Look: The Lost World." As you'll see, this is also the suggested explanation for how monkeys originally colonized South America.

There are few, if any, truly fossilized lemur remains in Madagascar; but there are numerous **subfossil** lemurs. These unfossilized skeletal remains are too recent to have become completely mineralized into fossils. Many of these extinct subfossil lemurs were colossal compared with the lemurs of today—indeed, some of them were up to five times as big! Despite their large size, they were mostly tree-dwelling and possibly even diurnal. Most

subfossil Bone not old enough to have become completely mineralized as a fossil.

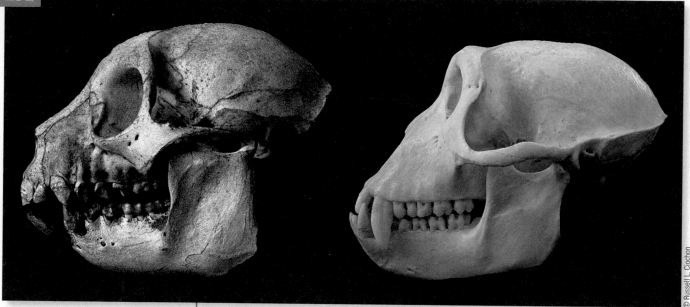

▲ Figure 9-8
Comparison of the skull of *Archaeolemur* (left) and a macaque monkey. Note how the lemur resembles the monkey in the shape of the jaw, teeth, and overall cranial form. This is an excellent example of convergent evolution.

interesting of all, many filled unusual ecological niches not shared by any living lemurs. Many of these peculiar adaptations provide examples of convergence with higher primate niches found elsewhere in the Old World. For instance, the extinct *Archaeolemur* (**Fig. 9-8**), with its fused mandible and **bilophodont** molars, in many ways more closely resembled a monkey than the 37-pound lemur that it was (Fleagle, 1999). What's more, the sulcal (grooved) pattern of *Archaeolemur*'s brain was similar to that seen in higher primates (Martin, 1990). Based on this evidence, we can see this group as converging on a monkey-like role on a monkey-less island.

The best known of the giant lemurs, however, is the 170-pound *Megaladapis*. Built more like a gorilla than a lemur (another incident of convergence), this specialized forest dweller lost its livelihood when the trees were cleared for farmland with the appearance of humans on the island. Sadly, the *Megaladapis* story isn't unusual; most of the 16 subfossil species discovered went extinct within the last 2,000 years—at the same time that humans began colonizing the island. As these large-bodied lemurs (over 22 pounds) had low reproduc-

tive rates, the predation and deforestation carried out by these early peoples rapidly caused the extinction of these massive animals (Catlett et al., 2010). Unfortunately, the remaining lemurs of Madagascar will meet the same fate unless the continued destruction of their habitat ceases.

Tarsier-like Omomyoids

The tarsier-like omomyoids, the earliest haplorhine group, are more taxonomically diverse than the adapoids. They're often called tarsier-like because the European specimens of this group more closely resemble the tarsier, though no specific phylogenetic connection has been made. They have a similar dental formula (1.1.3.3), large orbits, and small snouts. Earlier members of this group are somewhat more generalized than later ones, and some researchers hypothesize that they represent the stock for all later haplorhines—that is, tarsiers, New World monkeys, Old World monkeys, apes, and humans (Ross, 2000). **Paleoprimatologists** have traced this successful radiation from primarily the Eocene and early Oligocene of North America and Europe, with a small number also known from Asia.

bilophodont Referring to molars that have four cusps oriented in two parallel rows, resembling ridges, or "lophs." This trait is characteristic of Old World monkeys.

paleoprimatologists Anthropologists specializing in the study of the nonhuman primate fossil record.

Members of the genus *Teilhardina* (**Fig. 9-9**) are found on three continents (although a new analysis disputes whether all the attributed material belongs in the same genus; see Tornow, 2008). With the possible exception of African *Altiatlasius*, from the latest Paleocene, the fossil record appears to show that the earliest euprimates (including all adapoids and omomyoids) engaged in a rapid westward dispersal, with evidence pointing to Asia as the euprimates' starting point. In fact, analysis of related species of *Teilhardina* has shown that the oldest and most primitive members were from Asia, while the youngest were from North America. This evidence would tend to support a westward migration of euprimates from Asia, through Europe, and eventually to North America (Smith et al., 2006; **Fig. 9-10**). A brand new species of *Teilhardina* recently unearthed in Mississippi, however, has challenged this view. If the fossils of this coastal dweller are as old as they are purported to be, it would predate those in Europe, meaning that the genus actually moved from Asia to North America before finally moving into western Europe (Beard, 2008). It is important to recognize, however, that standard carbon isotope evidence has been notably omitted from the published study (Gingerich et al., 2008). Without this evidence, it's difficult to accept the early date of the Mississippi *Teilhardina* on face value.

Other Eocene fossils of the family Omomyidae from North America (*Shoshonius*) and Europe (*Necrolemur*) are also thought to be closely related to the tarsier. Like modern tarsiers, these animals apparently possessed large convergent eye orbits as well as details of the ear region that unite them to the tarsier group. In addition, there is some evidence that *Necrolemur* may have had a fused tibia and fibula as well as an elongated calcaneus, a lever-like construction (much like that seen in a jackrabbit) that gives modern tarsiers their fantastic leaping abilities. However, many researchers believe that these similarities are superficial ones, not necessarily indicating any unique (that is, shared derived) relationship. Even so, at least one feature, the position of the olfactory portion of the brain that processes scent, links these Eocene forms with later tarsiers, though not with anthropoids (Fleagle, 1999).

Evolution of True Tarsiers

For many years, "the 'living fossil' [had] no fossil record!" (Schwartz, 1984, p. 47). However, the situation has recently improved. Fragmentary

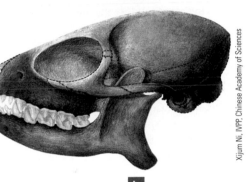

▲ **Figure 9-9**
Teilhardina. (**a**) View of the skull of *Teilhardina* from the top. (**b**) An artist's reconstruction of *Teilhardina*, with areas in gray representing missing fragments.

Xijum Ni, IVPP, Chinese Academy of Sciences

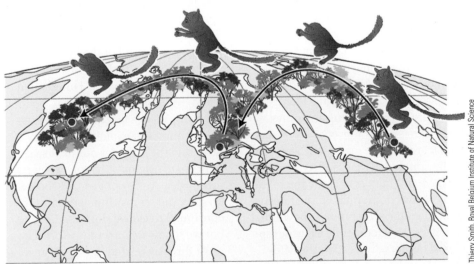

Thierry Smith, Royal Belgium Institute of Natural Science

◄ **Figure 9-10**
The rapid westward dispersal of euprimates of the genus *Teilhardina*. Analysis of related species of *Teilhardina* shows that the oldest and most primitive members were from Asia, while the youngest were from North America.

A Closer Look

The Lost World

In many ways, Madagascar is the island that time left behind. Just off the eastern coast of the African nation of Mozambique, Madagascar has proved an incubator for all manner of curious creatures. Over 70 percent of the 250,000 species native to Madagascar are found nowhere else in the world! Among its living menagerie are the *Brookesia* chameleon—at just over an inch long, one of the world's smallest reptiles; the fossa, perhaps best described as a mongoose on steroids; and the strange hedgehog- and shrew-like tenrecs. Absent are the standard African fare of apes, monkeys, elephants, giraffes, lions, and rhinoceroses, among many others. Now vanished from the island are the giant tortoises, pygmy hippopotamuses, and flightless elephant birds (the world's largest birds, over 10 feet tall!) of the past, as well as fully one-third of all identified lemur species that are known to have ever existed, including all species over 22 pounds (Goodman et al., 2003).

Unlocking the key to Madagascar's diversity has long been a holy grail of biologists. The insular nature of island environments is known to have dramatic effects on the animals within their bounds (see Chapter 5). The microclimates found within this Texas-sized island contribute to the differences seen; highland areas are hot and humid, while low-lying regions are arid. Among living lemurs, larger species tend to inhabit the higher, wetter regions, whereas smaller species tend to inhabit the lower, arid regions (Godfrey et al., 1990). This phenomenon has led to limited distribution of many species within Madagascar, a condition known as "micro-endemism" (Goodman, 2008).

The subfossil lemurs are in many ways even more fantastic than their already amazing living relatives. Coupled with the effects of island gigantism and the general supersizing of animals toward the Ice Age, subfossil lemurs are known to have grown to gargantuan proportions! But for a long time, it was questioned just how lemur-like these ancient forms were, given that their body size more closely resembled that of larger primates and other mammals. Indeed, the "sloth" lemur (for example, *Archaeoindris*; **Fig. 1**), "koala" lemur (for example, *Megaladapis*), and "monkey" lemur (for example, *Archaeolemur*) (see Fig. 9-8), as well as the giant aye-aye

▲ **Figure 1**
Life restoration of the sloth lemur *Archaeoindris*. A modern-day indri from Madagascar appears in silhouette for a size comparison.

(*Daubentonia robusta*), all were lost forms of strepsirhines sometimes two or even three times as large as their modern counterparts! These mammoth forms possessed some unique qualities. Despite their size, most of the sloth lemurs (with the possible exception of *Archaeoindris*, which may have been more like a ground sloth) were highly suspensory. In fact, the extreme curvature of their fingers had led some scientists to

remains of fossil tarsiers (a single jaw and isolated teeth) are now known from Egypt, China, Myanmar, and Thailand. In addition, the first cranial remains of an early tarsier have been described. Amazingly enough, these remains are "virtually identical to the corresponding anatomy in living tarsiers" (Rossie et al., 2006, p. 4381). From these fossils, it's been generally concluded that modern tarsiers have retained essentially the same body plan that they had in the Eocene. Biomolecular evidence has shown that the five extant (currently existing) species of tarsiers diverged in the Miocene (Wright et al., 2003); and as you learned in Chapter 6, all living tarsiers are now limited to a few islands in Southeast Asia.

Toward the end of the Eocene, there was a shift from tropical to drier and more seasonal climates. This change led to more diverse landscapes, opening many niches for the highly adaptable primates to exploit. This backdrop sets the stage for our next saga in primate origins—that of our own infraorder, Anthropoidea. Of course, tarsiers and strepsirhine primates have continued to evolve since the Eocene, but we'll now focus on those primates most directly related to our own evolution as humans.

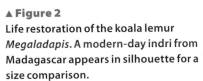

▲ Figure 2
Life restoration of the koala lemur *Megaladapis*. A modern-day indri from Madagascar appears in silhouette for a size comparison.

believe that they were one of the most suspensory clades of mammals ever to evolve (Jungers et al., 1997)! There is even some speculation that the brief contemporaneity of *Megaladapis* (**Fig. 2**) with the early human immigrants of Madagascar has been passed down to the present in Malagasy accounts of the "Tokandia," a large arboreal crypto-species said to have a cry like a human (Eberhart, 2002).

While un-lemur-like in their size, the subfossil giants actually had much in common with their latter-day forms. Like living lemurs, the subfossils are found in forested environments and may have exhibited female dominance in their social structure—an extraordinary display of "girl power," where females win the majority of aggressive confrontations with males. Their victories, however, are not related to their superior size or strength, so the pattern of sexual dimorphism in these species is not reversed, but neither is it marked. The resulting lack of big canines relative to body size makes the subfossil and living lemurs very different from most living anthropoids (Godfrey et al., 2006).

Subfossil lemurs, because of their size and reconstructed positional and locomotor behavior, also likely shared a relatively energy-conserving lifestyle with their modern counterparts. This means that they probably lived in small groups, exploiting only locally available resources that were subject to Madagascar's notoriously extreme seasonality. This seasonality of resources has been present for thousands of years, precipitating many unique adaptations in the island's animal inhabitants. Unlike many living lemurs, omnivorous forms were more prevalent in the past, often eating hard seeds and other fibrous foods along with the ubiquitous leaves. Additionally, all ancient forms were diurnal, unusual for many strepsirhines, though their eyesight was unlikely to have been as sharp as that of anthropoids of the same size. In all, the picture of subfossil lemurs emerges as a group similar in size to anthropoids, but with great affinity to their more petite strepsirhine relatives in daily life and behavior (Godfrey et al., 2006).

Unfortunately, the large size, slow locomotion, and diurnality of subfossil lemurs may have contributed to their destruction by humans. Evidence abounds of lemur bones scarred with cut marks like those associated with skinning, disarticulation, and filleting. This evidence of megafaunal butchery coincides with the earliest period of human colonization of the island around 2,300 years ago (Perez et al., 2005). The same constrained island bounds that led to the subfossil lemurs' diversity and success likely had a role in their annihilation. Hunting them was probably like "shooting monkeys in a barrel."

Eocene and Oligocene Early Anthropoids

It's important to realize that when we're trying to interpret the past, things aren't as straightforward as they first seem. In addition to the debate about the earliest emergence of strepsirhines and tarsiers (and therefore the most "primitive" members of Primates), we're equally unsure about the origins of anthropoid primates—the ones that eventually led to apes and monkeys as well as to our own lineage.

In recent years, new discoveries have led scientists to dispute an adapoid or even omomyoid origin of anthropoids, with some advocating that crown haplorhines (tarsiers and anthropoids) are a sister group to omomyoids as a whole (Bajpai et al., 2008; Williams et al., 2010). However, some recent molecular evidence indicates that anthropoid primates probably emerged *separately* from either of these two groups; and at 77 mya, they may have a time depth as ancient as either (Miller et al., 2005). Unfortunately, fossil anthropoid remains aren't known from that time, so the cradle of anthropoid origins remains hotly debated. Some paleoprimatologists have suggested an Asian origin, while most now support an African source, which was an island continent in the late Cretaceous.

The Fayum Depression in Egypt (see "A Closer Look: Primate Diversity in the Fayum"), an arid region today, provides most of our early anthropoid record for the Eocene and Oligocene. Over the last five decades, paleoprimatologist Elwyn Simons and colleagues have excavated this rich area and found a remarkable array of fossil primates. One of the most recent discoveries, a new species of *Biretia*, is precisely dated to 37 mya and repre-

▼ Figure 9-11
Three specimens of *Catopithecus*, the earliest anthropoid genus to preserve a skull. These elements give us our first view of early catarrhine cranial anatomy, including fully enclosed orbits.

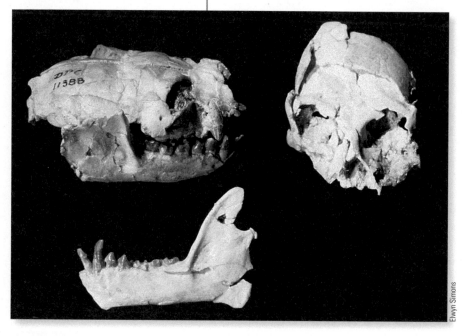

Elwyn Simons

sents the most complete remains of an early African anthropoid. This small primate, weighing just under a pound, exhibits dental morphology typical of that expected for a basal (most primitive) anthropoid. Surprisingly, though, the structure of the upper molar tooth roots points to large orbits, implying that *Biretia* was nocturnal (Seiffert et al., 2005b). This is interesting because as discussed in Chapter 6, the general trend for Anthropoidea is toward a diurnal activity pattern. Simons has placed these fossils, based on their dental characters, into the extinct superfamily Parapithecoidea. This superfamily is significant as the most primitive anthropoid group and there-

fore the possible root stock from which the entire New World anthropoid evolutionary group (that is, clade) evolved.

The later Oligocene evolution of these very early anthropoids (Seiffert et al., 2005b) is discussed in the next section. Somewhat more recent (dating to around 35 mya) are the Fayum primate genera from the family Oligopithecidae, including *Catopithecus* (**Fig. 9-11**), which clearly possessed anthropoid features (such as complete postorbital closure) and some derived **catarrhine** features (such as a 2.1.2.3 dental formula). These Fayum discoveries help fill in the gap between later (more derived) anthropoids and the middle Eocene anthropoids of Algeria. The earliest fossil anthropoids are known from Africa, and current molecular and biogeographical data agree that anthropoids had an African origin, much like the African origin of our own genus, *Homo* (Miller et al., 2005).

Oligocene Primates

The vast majority of Old World primate fossils of the Oligocene epoch (33–23 mya) come from just one region, the Fayum Depression in Egypt—the same area that has yielded abundant late Eocene remains. Altogether, well over 1,000 specimens have been retrieved from the Fayum, representing a remarkable paleontological record of what was once an extremely rich primate ecosystem.

True Anthropoids

The early primates of the Oligocene are generally placed into three families: the oligopithecids, parapithecids, and propliopithecids. Members of the oligopithecid family are among the earliest catarrhine anthropoid primates, with some also known from the late Eocene of the Fayum in Egypt. One of these early taxa, *Catopithecus* (mentioned earlier), is represented by several

catarrhine Member of Catarrhini, a parvorder of Primates, one of the three major divisions of the suborder Haplorhini. It contains the Old World monkeys, apes, and humans.

At a Glance

LEMURIFORM VS. ANTHROPOID CHARACTERISTICS

General Lemuriform Characteristics

1. Smaller body size
2. Longer snouts with greater emphasis on smell
3. Eye sockets not completely enclosed in bone
4. Dental comb
5. Small, simple premolars
6. Primitive triangle-shaped molars
7. Grooming claw
8. Artery running through the bone of the middle ear
9. Unfused mandible
10. Unfused frontal bone
11. Smaller brain size relative to body size

See Appendix A, Fig. A-9A and A-9B for illustrations of these differences.

General Anthropoid Characteristics

1. Generally larger body size
2. Shorter snouts with greater emphasis on vision
3. Back of eye socket formed by bony plate
4. Less specialized dentition, as seen in absence of dental comb and some other features
5. Larger and more complex premolars
6. Derived square-shaped molars with new cusp
7. Nails instead of claws on all digits
8. Loss of the artery running through the bone of the middle ear
9. Fusion of the two sides of the mandible to form one bone
10. Fusion of the two sides of the frontal bone
11. Larger brain (in absolute terms and relative to body weight)

crushed crania. Analyses of these fragmentary remains, with their complete postorbital closure and derived 2.1.2.3 dental formula, have led paleoprimatologists to conclude that *Catopithecus* is the earliest catarrhine.

The most abundant of the Oligocene fossils from the Fayum are from the parapithecid family, and they belong to the genus *Apidium*. About the size of a squirrel, *Apidium* had several anthropoid-like features, but it also possessed some unusual dental features. *Apidium* fossils exhibit a dental formula of 2.1.3.3, indicating that *Apidium* probably appeared before the Old and New World anthropoids diverged. As noted, this makes the early relatives of *Apidium* a possible candidate as an ancestor of New World anthropoids (that is, **platyrrhines**; Fig. 9-12). The teeth also suggest a diet composed of fruits and probably some seeds. Another interesting feature suggests something about this animal's social behavior; an unusually large degree of sexual dimorphism in canine size may indicate that *Apidium* lived

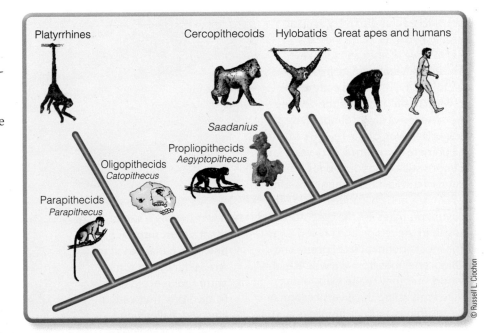

in polygynous social groups of a single male and multiple females and offspring. Limb remains show that this creature was a small arboreal quadruped, adept at leaping and springing. We now know much more about the cranial anatomy of the parapithecids, thanks to the discovery of a complete skull of

▲ **Figure 9-12**
Diagram of the phyletic relationships (cladogram) of Fayum early anthropoids and living catarrhines (monkeys, apes, and humans). (Adapted from Fig. 13-18 Fleagle, 1999, p. 418.)

platyrrhines Members of Platyrrhini, a parvorder of Primates, one of the three major divisions of the suborder Haplorhini. It contains only the New World monkeys.

© Russell L. Ciochon

A Closer Look

Primate Diversity in the Fayum

Today El-Fayuom, or the Fayum, is an Egyptian province about 40 miles southwest of Cairo. In the Eocene and Oligocene epochs, it was a swampy forest playground for primates. Now all that's left of that primate Eden is chunks of petrified wood, flotsam adrift in the vast desert of the Sahara. The name Fayum probably comes from the ancient Egyptian word *Baym*, meaning "lake or sea" and referring to the area's proximity to a large lake near the Nile. Nowadays, though, the last thing anyone would associate with this arid region is a body of water.

In 1906, the first primate ever discovered in Egypt was unearthed and later identified as *Apidium*. Many considered this discovery, hailed as a "dawn ape," to be the earliest relative of apes and monkeys. Though several primate fossils were discovered in the early 1900s, it wasn't until 1961 that the dogged persistence of Elwyn Simons led to the unearthing of the Fayum's true fossil primate abundance. Fifty years later, Simons still coaxes dry bones from the sand of the Fayum. Through the efforts of Simons and colleagues (**Fig. 1**), the Fayum primates are the best-studied fossils in the region and far and away the most abundant late Eocene and Oligocene finds from anywhere in the world, and they shape many of our views regarding the diversification of strepsirhines, tarsiers, monkeys, and apes. These fossils are often referred to as the "lower-sequence primates" and "upper-sequence primates," according to their placement in the stratigraphic section. From these Eocene (lower) and Oligocene (upper) sediments, over 17 genera are known, presenting us with a wide variety of dietary niches.

© Russell L. Ciochon

Figure 1

Elwyn Simons and colleagues toil in the harsh heat of the Fayum in Egypt while collecting fossils of the earliest anthropoids. These fossils are so small that workers must excavate with their faces pressed close to the ground.

© Russell L. Ciochon

What's most surprising, however, is that both the strepsirhines and some anthropoids exploited a frugivorous (fruit-eating) lifestyle, challenging the idea that ecological changes might account for the emergence of the latter group (Kirk and Simons, 2001). So, for the time being, anthropoid origins remain as enigmatic as the Sphinx.

© Russell L. Ciochon

At a Glance

NEW WORLD MONKEY VS. OLD WORLD MONKEY CHARACTERISTICS

General New World Monkey Characteristics

1. Sideways-facing nostrils
2. Ringlike ear hole with no tube
3. Dental formula of 2.1.3.3
4. Grasping tail
5. Distribution: Mexico and South America

See Appendix A, Fig. A-10 for illustrations of these differences.

General Old World Monkey Characteristics

1. Downward-facing nostrils
2. Tubelike ear hole
3. Dental formula of 2.1.2.3
4. Ischial callosities
5. Distribution: Africa, southern Asia, and Japan

---

the genus *Parapithecus* (**Fig. 9-13**), a close relative of *Apidium.*

Members of the third major family are called the propliopithecids. They include possibly the most significant fossil genus from the Fayum, *Aegyptopithecus* (**Fig. 9-14**). This genus has been proposed as the ancestor of both later Old World monkeys and hominoids. *Aegyptopithecus* is known from several well-preserved crania, numerous jaw fragments, and a fair number of limb bones. The largest of the Fayum anthropoids, *Aegyptopithecus* was roughly the size of a modern howler monkey at 13 to 18 pounds, with considerable sexual dimorphism. With a dental formula of 2.1.2.3, *Aegyptopithecus* shares the derived catarrhine (Old World anthropoid) dental formula. The skull is small and resembles a modern monkey skull in certain details, while the brain size appears to have been at best strepsirhine-like; some even consider it so primitive as to be non-primate-like. In fact, a reappraisal of intracranial size has determined that given the small brain size of this genus, greater encephalization must have evolved independently within the two anthropoid parvorders,

Platyrrhini and Catarrhini (Simons et al., 2007). Postcranial evidence reveals that *Aegyptopithecus* was likely a short-limbed, heavily muscled, slow-moving arboreal quadruped.

Aegyptopithecus was long viewed as the best candidate from the Fayum to have given rise to Old World monkeys, apes, and humans. This was because there was a distressing lack of substantive fossil material immediately following them that was more than fragmentary teeth (and we know from the adapoids how prone teeth can be to convergence and homoplasy). However, a recent discovery from the Afro-Arabian region, this time

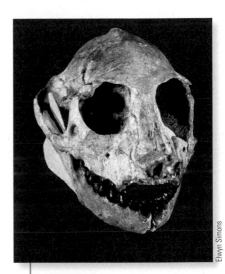

▲ **Figure 9-13**
Parapithecus belongs to the group of Fayum anthropoids most closely related to the ancestry of New World monkeys.

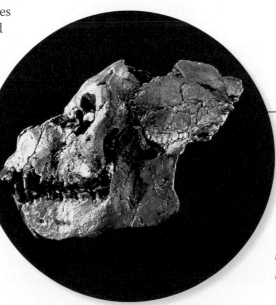

◄ **Figure 9-14**
Skull of *Aegyptopithecus.* This genus has historically been proposed as the ancestor of *both* Old World monkeys and hominoids.

University of Michigan Museum of Paleontology

▲ **Figure 9-15**
Skull of *Saadanius*. This genus has recently been proposed as the ancestor of *both* Old World monkeys and hominoids.

from Saudi Arabia, has helped shed important light on the timing of the cercopithecoid-hominoid split. This new anthropoid find, assigned to the new genus *Saadanius*, defies current attribution to any existing catarrhine family or superfamily (**Fig. 9-15**). What's more, its date of 29–28 mya is within a critical period in the evolution of our lineage. This time period is so crucial because it bridges much of the evidence of the earliest stem catarrhines that we've just summarized with the later Miocene fossils that definitively indicate that the major split between Old World monkeys and hominoids had already occurred.

Until the discovery of this new and surprising fossil, scientists faced a puzzling gap of many millions of years, with very few fossils available between 30 and 23 mya to provide insight. *Saadanius* dates to within this gap, and lacking derived features of either cercopithecoids or hominoids, suggests that the split between these lines had not yet occurred. *Saadanius*' most significant features, in this respect, include a projecting midface, a tubelike middle ear, and large, broad molars. The tubelike middle ear is especially important, as it is a characteristic that it shares with crown catarrhines (monkeys, apes, and humans) to the exclusion of the propliopithecids. This would make *Saadanius* an advanced stem catarrhine, though perhaps inter-

mediate between *Aegyptopithecus* and Miocene apes (Zalmout et al., 2010).

Early Platyrrhines: New World Anthropoids

The earliest primates yet found in the New World date to around 27 mya, about 10 million years after fossil evidence for the first anthropoids appears in the Fayum of Egypt. However, they probably evolved from ancestors similar to those seen within the parapithecids of the Fayum primate radiation. The earliest platyrrhine (New World anthropoid) fossils are found in the late Oligocene of Bolivia and have been placed in the genus *Branisella*. Members of this genus appear to have been small monkeys (about 2 pounds), with diets comprised primarily of fruits. The evolutionary relationships of these first fossil platyrrhines are still greatly debated. *Branisella* is thought to be so primitive that it's not placed in any living platyrrhine lineage; it perhaps represents a remnant of the first platyrrhine radiation. Molecular evidence supports this view, as living platyrrhines converge on a shared ancestor that is only 20 million years old (Hodgson et al., 2009a). Another member of this mysterious early radiation—*Homunculus* (meaning "miniature human")—appears in the middle Miocene. A cranium of this creature was found in Argentina in 2004 embedded in volcanic ash dated to 16.5 mya (**Fig. 9-16**). *Branisella* and *Homunculus* represent different side branches from the clade of living New World monkeys that includes the last common ancestor of extant platyrrhines (**Fig. 9-17**). But this doesn't mean that they have nothing to tell us about modern platyrrhines. As remnants of the earliest New World radiation, these fossils open a window through which we can begin to view the first primate colonizers of South America.

Based on the presence of the first platyrrhines in South America at 27 mya, it's likely that the very first

▶ **Figure 9-16**
Skull of *Homunculus*, a middle Miocene descendant of the earliest platyrrhine radiation.

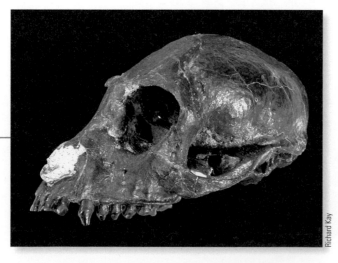

Richard Kay

anthropoids arrived in the New World somewhat earlier, probably during the late Eocene (45–35 mya). In fact, recent molecular data indicate that the platyrrhine-catarrhine (New World–Old World anthropoid) lineages diverged approximately between 50 and 35 mya, with a conservative estimate of 43 mya (Steiper and Young, 2006). This estimate is further bolstered by fossil and molecular evidence concerning the arrival and diversification of caviomorph rodents (for example, guinea pigs, chinchillas, New World porcupines, and their relatives). "Cavies" also originate from African stock and were the only other group of terrestrial mammals to colonize South America at the same time as platyrrhines (Poux et al., 2006). The early transatlantic migration of both groups would have involved the crossing of some sort of oceanic barrier, since South America was an island continent until 5–3 mya. We know that these two groups overcame this boundary, but how platyrrhines arrived in the New World in general, and in South America in particular, remains one of the most fascinating questions in primate evolution (**Fig. 9-18**). Several competing theories have been proposed in an attempt to explain the mysterious arrival of platyrrhines in South

▼ **Figure 9-17**

Cladogram of extant groups of New World monkeys based on biomolecular evidence, with dates of divergence noted in the yellow nodes (Hodgson et al., 2009a; Wildman et al., 2009). *Branisella* and *Homunculus* have been plotted relative to their positions regarding living groups and can be seen as representing separate side branches of a more basal adaptive radiation of New World monkeys, unrelated to the species living today.

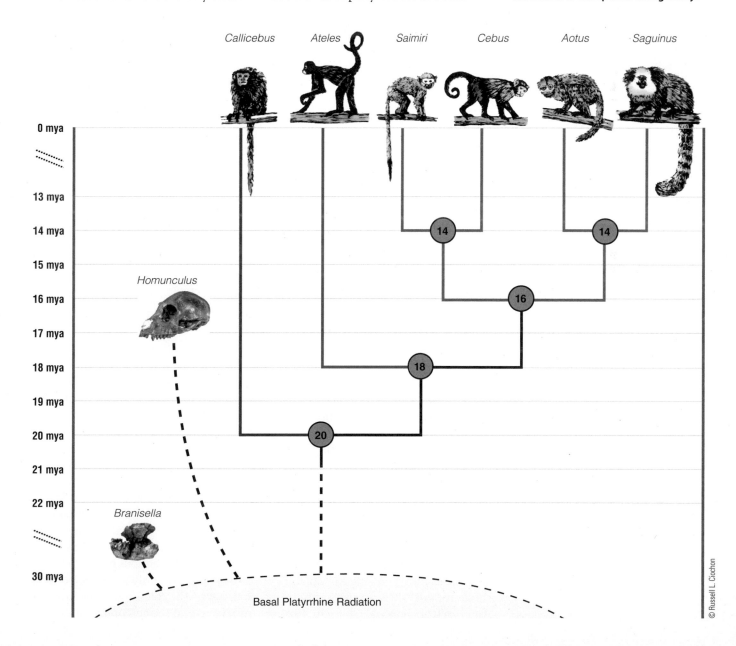

© Russell L. Ciochon

▶ **Figure 9-18**
Here are the continental relationships during the late Eocene. Several competing theories have been proposed in an attempt to explain the arrival of platyrrhines in South America: North American migration, Antarctic migration, and South Atlantic migration (by way of island-hopping). The broken white line and surrounding shades of blue in the ocean represent seafloor spreading, which caused the continents to drift apart.

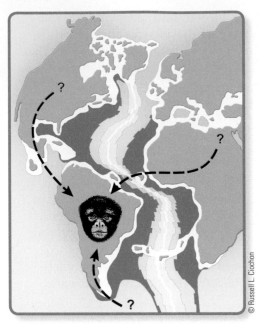

© Russell L. Ciochon

America: North American migration, Antarctic migration, and South Atlantic "**island-hopping**."

The scenario for a North American migration route argues that one of the North American tarsier-like omomyoids journeyed down to South America, giving rise to the later platyrrhines. An alternative scenario contends that migration could have been accomplished by passing through the Antarctic—first crossing by water from Africa south to Antarctica and then crossing a land bridge that linked Antarctica to South America.

The most likely scenario for the arrival of platyrrhines to South America, however, involves their floating between closely spaced islands across the Atlantic Ocean from Africa to South America on rafts made of naturally formed mats of vegetation (see "A Closer Look: Island-Hopping and Primate Evolution"). The rafting scenario is supported by the fact that during the Eocene, South America and Africa were closer to each other than they are today. An additional drop in sea level would have further decreased the distance between Africa and South America and may have exposed mid-Atlantic islands, allowing early platyrrhines to "raft" their way to South America (Ciochon and Chiarelli, 1980a;

Houle, 1999; Poux and Douzery, 2004). Further, recent paleo-oceanographic modeling has indicated that paleocurrent directions at this time may have favored this method of dispersal (Ali and Huber, 2010).

Miocene Primates

Throughout the Miocene, we see diversification of the anthropoids into the groups we're familiar with today. The cercopithecoid monkeys and the hominoids competed for the dominant position on the primate landscape in the Old World, with the former finally emerging victorious. Today, the number of ape groups is very limited compared with the diversity they enjoyed in the Miocene, while cercopithecoids remain relatively varied.

Monkeying Around

Following the emergence of Afro-Arabian stem catarrhines like *Aegyptopithecus* and *Saadanius*, we have evidence of further diversification of later catarrhines—namely, the Old World monkeys and the hominoids. The cercopithecoids, as the Old World monkeys are known, fall into two families—one extinct (called the victoriapithecids) and the other being the living cercopithecids. The late Miocene was a highly successful time for the radiation of monkeys in the Old World. Their more immediate descendants, which evolved during the Pliocene and the Pleistocene, were much more varied in size, locomotion, and diet than their counterparts today.

The extinct family Victoriapithecidae represents the earliest members of the lineage leading to present-day Old World monkeys. The victoriapithecids were found throughout northern and eastern Africa as early as 19 mya, predating the split between the two extant subfamilies of Old World monkeys—the colobines (leaf-eating monkeys) and the cercopithecines

island-hopping Traveling from one island to the next.

Island-Hopping and Primate Evolution

Despite the peculiar images this statement might conjure, island-hopping and the associated phenomenon of rafting are actually well-recognized methods of animal migration for some vertebrates. In fact, there's documented evidence of a natural raft carrying a crocodile 685 miles from Java to the Cocos Islands in 1930 (Ciochon and Chiarelli, 1980b). Admittedly, such instances of natural rafting are rare; but given the geological span of time, even unlikely events (such as you winning the lottery or monkeys floating to South America) become likely. This idea is known as the sweepstakes model, and it was popularized by evolutionist G. G. Simpson (contributor to the Modern Synthesis, discussed in Chapter 4).

As better information regarding the rare availability of land bridges has been absorbed, scientists are relying more and more on sweepstakes models such as rafting to explain events that are otherwise impossible to explain. Such is the case for the lemur population of Madagascar and the New World monkeys. In both circumstances, we have the relatively sudden appearance of primates in areas where no ancestor is present and for which migration could only have been predominantly over a large body of water. The existence of now-submerged islands as intermediates accompanied by short instances of natural rafting could have accommodated such an otherwise unlikely route of travel. Coincidentally, Africa is the apparent source of both the lemur and platyrrhine root stock.

The scenario goes like this: A female primate and her mate live on the edge of a river. During one particularly nasty storm, their home is disconnected from the mainland, becoming a natural houseboat of sorts. The storm rages, and the entire raft is carried out to sea. Days later, the bedraggled primates wash ashore at their new home (**Fig. 1**). The rest is history. Or is it?

Recently, scientists reevaluated this sweepstakes model, exposing some serious flaws. To be a lucky ticket holder, the primates would have to actually survive the voyage, or the whole model is useless. In 1976, Simons calculated that it would take only 4 to 6 days for most small primates to succumb to the combined effects of lacking food and water and experiencing salt imbalance and exposure (Simons, 1976). The shortest distance today from the African mainland to Madagascar is 249 miles. Even with a stiff continuous wind, it would take 10 days to make the journey, so the migrant lemurs would be comatose days before. The first platyrrhines would have had to cross 870 miles—that's an intolerable amount of time for a thirsty primate.

Despite these shortcomings, rafting is still viewed by many to be the best explanation that we have for these dispersals— short of some even more obscure method of transportation. Combined with the probable existence of islands intermediate to Madagascar and the New World during the times of these voyages, it's quite possible that the primates were first washed up on one of these isles and only later rafted to their current residences. This would mean that they would not have to cross the entire span in one daunting voyage, but would instead engage in island-hopping. In addition, Alain Houle (1998) has researched the idea of "floating islands" as a mode of distant dispersal of small- to medium-sized vertebrates. These vegetation rafts could have supported microhabitats that would have permitted small vertebrates, such as primates, to cross ocean barriers and reach far-distant islands. Additional random dispersals on vegetation rafts from these distant islands ultimately would have allowed primates to colonize the New World.

▲ **Figure 1**

An artist's rendering of the South Atlantic populating scenario called island-hopping, which would allow primates to take their time in moving from one island to another before finally reaching South America.

Drawing by Robert Greisen/Design by Russell L. Ciochon

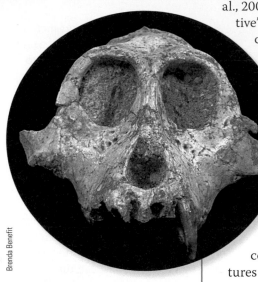

Brenda Benefit

▲ **Figure 9-19**
Skull of *Victoriapithecus*, the first Old World monkey.

(cheek-pouch monkeys)—which occurred around 15 mya (Sterner et al., 2006). Since they're more "primitive" in many features than either colobines or cercopithecines, the victoriapithecids may represent a basal cercopithecoid and therefore the last common ancestors of all living Old World monkeys; but it's also possible that they represent an extinct sister group. The best known of the victoriapithecids is *Victoriapithecus* (**Fig. 9-19**), a small monkey whose cranium exhibits a mosaic of later colobine and cercopithecine features that place it close to the root of both subfamilies. The molars of *Victoriapithecus* exhibit bilophodonty, like all living Old World monkeys, indicating a diet of hard fruits and seeds. Meanwhile, postcranial skeletal features demonstrate similarities to living terrestrial monkeys (Benefit and McCrossin, 1997; Miller et al., 2009).

By 12 mya, the victoriapithecids had been replaced by Old World forms whose direct descendants are still alive today—that is, cercopithecines and colobines (see Chapter 6). Fossils of the first true colobine are found in African deposits dating to approximately 9 mya. These monkeys were smaller than most living forms, though at 8 to 9 pounds, they weren't lightweights. Following their first appearance in Africa, the colobines quickly radiated into Europe and Asia. As you'll see, this was when Eurasian ape groups also began reentering Africa.

You may not know it, but you're probably already familiar with members of Cercopithecinae, a subfamily of the family Cercopithecidae. This subfamily includes monkeys such as today's macaques (for example, the rhesus monkeys used in labs) and baboons. Most fossil macaques appear remarkably similar to each other and to living forms, indicating that ancestral macaque morphology has been retained for more than 5 million years. This is bolstered by biomolecular evidence indicating that *Macaca* diverged from *Papio* (the modern baboon) about 10 mya (Raaum et al., 2005).

In East Africa, the baboon-like *Theropithecus* was the dominant cercopithecine genus of the Plio-Pleistocene (**Fig. 9-20**). Adaptations of

At a Glance

OLD WORLD MONKEY VS. APE CHARACTERISTICS

General Old World Monkey Characteristics	General Ape Characteristics
1. Narrow nose and palate	1. Broader nose and palate
2. Smaller brain (in absolute terms and relative to body weight)	2. Larger brain (in absolute terms and relative to body weight)
3. Bilophodont molars	3. Y-5 molars
4. Smaller average body size	4. Larger average body size
5. Longer torso	5. Shorter torso
6. Shorter arms	6. Longer arms
7. Tail	7. No tail

See Appendix A, Fig. A-11 for illustrations of these differences.

the hands and teeth indicate that all species of *Theropithecus* exploited a dietary niche consisting almost exclusively of grasses—a unique diet among primates that feed on small objects. This group contains some notable fossil specimens, among them the largest monkey that ever lived (225 pounds). *Theropithecus* was an incredibly successful genus throughout much of the Pliocene and Early Pleistocene; but sometime during the Middle Pleistocene, most of its members went extinct, leaving a single remaining species—the gelada (*Theropithecus gelada*). While we don't completely understand exactly what caused these extinctions, many researchers hypothesize that competition with the closely related *Papio* baboons of today was a major factor. Today, the living gelada is confined to the high, wet grasslands of the Amhara Plateau, in Ethiopia, an ecological zone where no *Papio* baboons are found.

Aping Monkeys

By the end of the Oligocene, the world's major continents were located about where they are today. During the Miocene (23–5.3 mya), however, the drifting of South America and Australia away from Antarctica significantly altered ocean currents. At the same time, the South Asian Plate continued to ram into Asia, producing the Himalayan Plateau. Together, these major paleogeographical modifications significantly affected the climate, causing the early Miocene to be considerably warmer and wetter than the Oligocene. As a result, rain forests and dense woodlands became the dominant environments of Africa during the early Miocene. It was in this forested environment of Africa that the first apelike primates evolved.

Molecular evidence suggests that the evolutionary lineages leading to monkeys and apes diverged

▼ **Figure 9-20**
Skull of *Theropithecus brumpti*, the most bizarre fossil monkey (inset). An artist's rendering of *Theropithecus* on the landscape in the Omo Basin of Ethiopia about 3 mya.

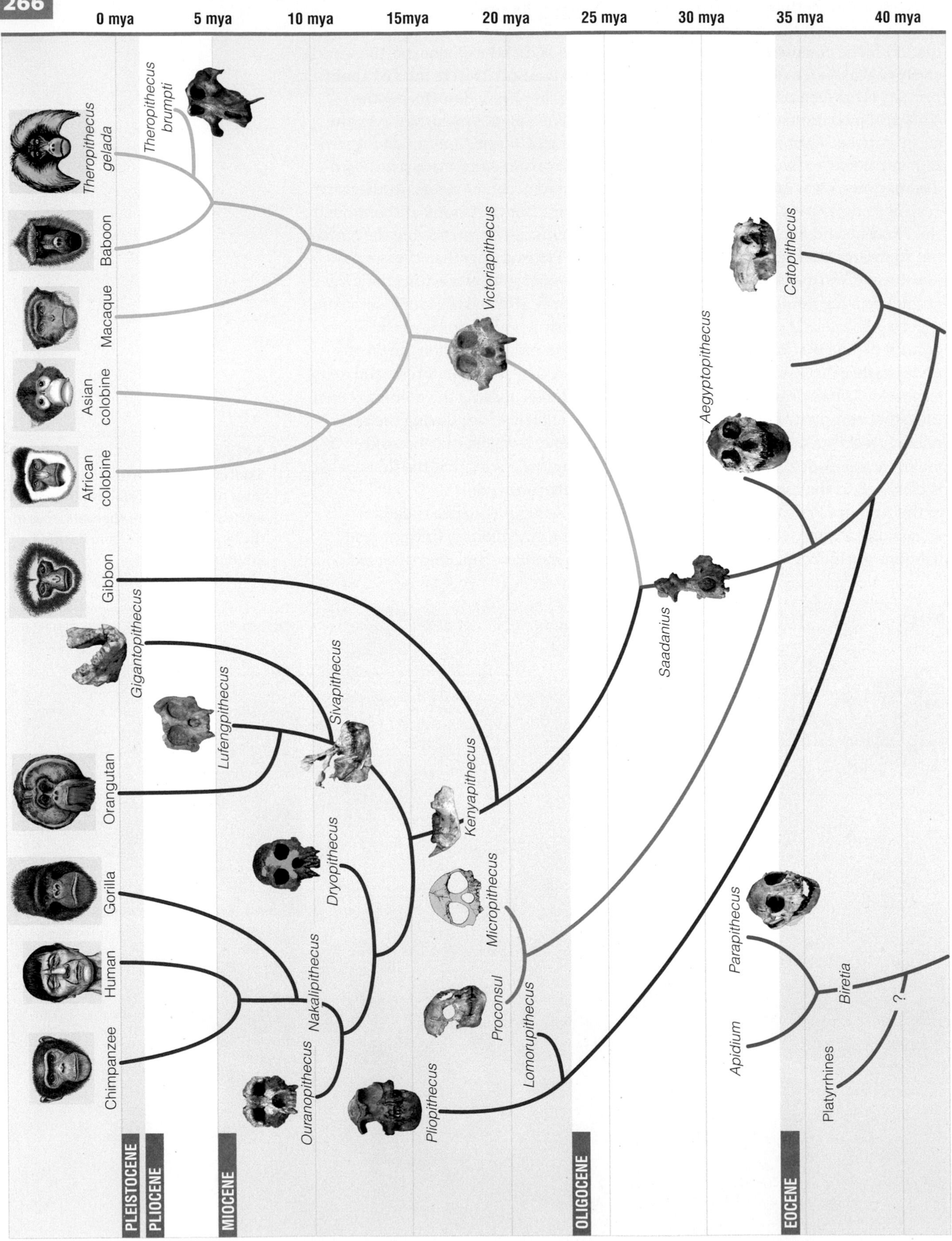
0 mya
5 mya
10 mya
15mya
20 mya
25 mya
30 mya
35 mya
40 mya
PLEISTOCENE
PLIOCENE
MIOCENE
OLIGOCENE
EOCENE
Chimpanzee
Human
Gorilla
Orangutan
Gibbon
African colobine
Asian colobine
Macaque
Baboon
Theropithecus gelada
Theropithecus brumpti
Victoriapithecus
Catopithecus
Aegyptopithecus
Saadanius
Gigantopithecus
Lufengpithecus
Sivapithecus
Kenyapithecus
Dryopithecus
Nakalipithecus
Ouranopithecus
Micropithecus
Proconsul
Lomorupithecus
Pliopithecus
Parapithecus
Biretia
Apidium
Platyrrhines
?

approximately 27 mya (Janečka et al., 2007; **Fig. 9-21**), which is consistent with the fossil evidence following the recent discovery of the Oligocene advanced stem catarrhine, *Saadanius* (Zalmout et al., 2010). Not surprisingly, the first apelike fossils share many anatomical characteristics with monkeys. In fact, in many of these early forms of the superfamily Proconsuloidea, the only apelike feature is the presence of the **Y-5 molar** pattern. As shown in **Figure 9-22**, the ape molars have five cusps separated by a "Y" groove, as opposed to the monkey's typical four bilophodont cusps. Consequently, proconsuloids were once commonly called dental apes, reflecting their apelike teeth but monkey-like postcranial skeleton. Today, proconsuloids are generally viewed as general precursors to all later hominoids (Harrison, 2010; but see Zalmout et al., 2010).

Nearly all of the proconsuloid fossils come from East Africa, although some fossils have been recovered as far south and west as Namibia, on the southern coast of Africa. The fossil record shows that these early apelike creatures were a highly diverse group, varying greatly in both size and locomotor patterns. They ranged in size from 22 to 110 pounds in *Proconsul* to the tiny *Micropithecus*, which probably weighed no more than 6 to 8 pounds, making it the smallest ape ever known to have lived (Ruff et al., 1989; Rafferty et al., 1995; **Fig. 9-23**). The fossil record suggests a considerable diversity of locomotor patterns among the proconsuloids, including suspensory locomotion (swinging by their arms) as well as quadrupedalism either in trees or on the ground (Gebo et al., 1997; Fleagle, 1999).

The best known of the proconsuloids is the genus *Proconsul*, which lived in Africa 20–17 mya. The first example of *Proconsul*, a skull, was discovered on Rusinga Island, Kenya, in 1948 by esteemed fossil hunter Mary Leakey. For a long time, it was considered the first ape, but that position has been recently challenged. This fruit-eating, apelike creature roamed a wide range of environments from rain forest to open woodlands. Though generally considered small-bodied, various *Proconsul* species actually ranged in size from 10 to 150 pounds (Harrison, 2002). *Proconsul* exhibits a generalized cranium (**Fig. 9-24**) and an apelike Y-5 dental pattern, but postcranial remains show that *Proconsul's* limbs and long torso retained adaptations for quadrupedal locomotion similar to that of monkeys. Scientists are increasingly accepting that *Proconsul* may not have had a tail, which could indicate that this particular hominoid characteristic had a relatively ancient origin (Begun, 2003; Nakatsukasa et al., 2004; Ward, 2005). However, the proconsuloids' uncertain position has caused many researchers to place them outside of Hominoidea (in Proconsuloidea), just prior to the divergence of hominoids and cercopithecoids (Harrison, 2010; but see McCollum et al., 2010 and Zalmout et al., 2010). This would mean not only that *Proconsul's* lack of tail was due to convergence, but also that the time depth of tail-lessness within Hominoidea itself is still unknown.

Members of the superfamily Pliopithecoidea, like the proconsuloids, also are generally known from the early Miocene, though they're more primitive in their features than all other

◄ **Figure 9-21 (opposite page)** Family tree of early catarrhines and their relationships to modern Old World monkeys and apes. Red is for living apes and their immediate ancestors (Hominoidea); green is for the Old World monkeys and their immediate ancestors (Cercopithecoidea); orange is for precursors to apes (Proconsuloidea); purple is for the primitive catarrhines (Pliopithecoidea); and blue represents the Fayum early anthropoid radiation.

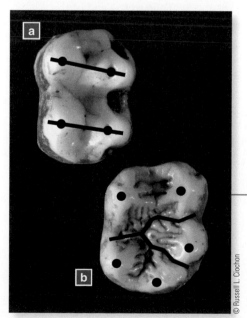

© Russell L. Ciochon

◄ **Figure 9-22** Comparison of (a) bilophodont molars, as found in cercopithecoids, and (b) Y-5 molars, as seen in hominoids. (a) Notice that the four cusps are positioned in two parallel rows or lobes. (b) See how the five cusps are arranged so that a Y-shaped valley runs between them.

Y-5 molar Molar that has five cusps with grooves running between them, forming a Y shape. This is characteristic of hominoids.

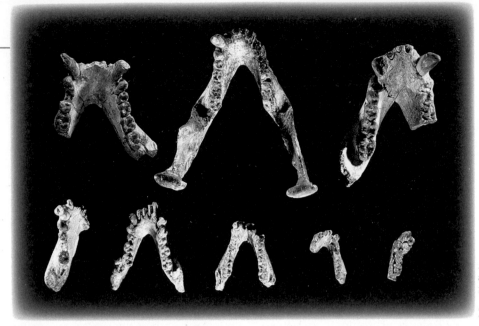

▶ **Figure 9-23**
Diversity of early Miocene ape mandibles. The shapes and sizes of these mandibles and teeth illustrate the adaptive diversity of apes during this time. The apes ranged in size from that of a male orangutan to half the size of a modern gibbon and ate foods as varied as hard roots and soft fruits.

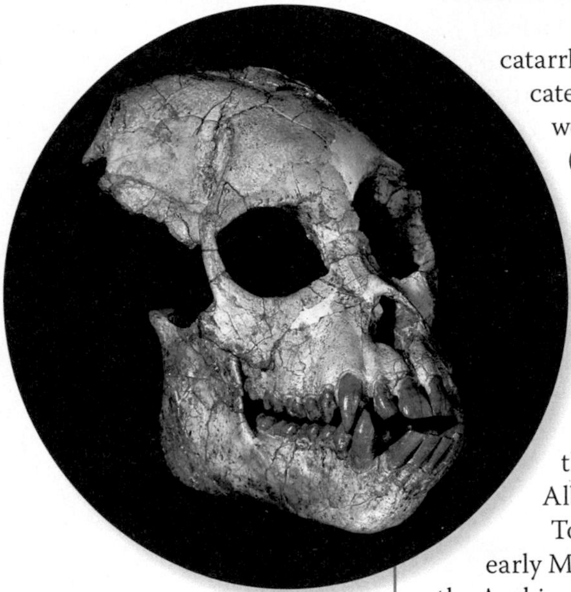

© Russell L. Ciochon

© The Natural History Museum, London

▲ **Figure 9-24**
Skull of *Proconsul*, the best known of the early Miocene precursors to apes.

catarrhines. Most evidence indicates that the pliopithecoids were an early, small-bodied (6 to 44 pounds) group of stem catarrhines that branched off prior to the cercopithecoid-hominoid split. A highly successful group once thought to be related to extant hylobatids, they underwent a rapid adaptive radiation in the Miocene (Begun, 2002; Alba et al., 2010).

Toward the end of the early Miocene, around 19 mya, the Arabian Plate moved to its current location, forming a land bridge between Africa and Eurasia. Major animal migrations could then take place between the two previously separated landmasses. It's thought that African pliopithecoids were among the first transcontinental migrants and, importantly, represent the first anthropoids to colonize both Asia and Europe. Researchers thus commonly agree that the pliopithecoids were the first catarrhines to leave Africa. Until recently, however, this migration was only assumed, since pliopithecoid fossil remains were known only from Eurasia. However, a more recently discovered possible genus of pliopithecoid, *Lomorupithecus*, could be the earliest member of this group, dating to the early Miocene (nearly 20 mya), and (as predicted) it's from Uganda, in Africa (Rossie and MacLatchy, 2006)! Though still more recent in age than *Saadanius*, the pliopithecoids' more primitive features indicate that they actually diverged earlier, possibly giving rise to the early primitive catarrhine group to which *Saadanius* belongs, among others (Begun, 2002; Alba et al., 2010). This find could provide the proof that pliopithecoids had their roots in Africa, bringing this idea from the realm of conjecture into reality.

Dating to the middle Miocene, *Pliopithecus* is the best-known pliopithecoid and is known from Europe. Robust features of the mandible indicate that *Pliopithecus* probably ate a diet consisting of relatively tough foods, most likely leaves (**Fig. 9-25**). Postcranially, it appears that *Pliopithecus* possessed some features for suspensory locomotion (arm hanging) similar to that of some large platyrrhines, although it clearly lacked the grasping prehensile tail of New World monkeys. There are some indications that *Pliopithecus* may have possessed a short tail (making it decidedly un-apelike), but this feature has been and is still greatly debated (Ankel, 1965).

Despite the intensity of their radiation early on, it appears that later, during the Pliocene, the success of the pliopithecoids ended. All forms went extinct with no living descendants.

True Apes

The first true apes, those belonging to the superfamily Hominoidea, appear in Africa during the middle Miocene, approximately 16 mya. Probably the best known of these early African hominoids was for years simply known as *Kenyapithecus*. Later finds from the Nachola Hills of Kenya have led many researchers more recently to split this genus into three separate forms (McNulty, 2010). Of these three taxa, the one retaining the name *Kenyapithecus* is still the most significant, as it best indicates affinities with more recent apes. Anatomical evidence indicates that *Kenyapithecus* was a large-bodied terrestrial quadruped, possibly the first hominoid to adapt to life on the ground, with specialized adaptations in the humerus, wrist, and hands (McCrossin and Benefit, 1994; McCrossin et al., 1998; Ward et al., 1999). Evidence from hand bones thought by many researchers to belong to *Kenyapithecus* indicates that this ape may have employed a form of locomotion similar to the knuckle-walking gait typical of living gorillas and chimpanzees. The jaw and dentition of *Kenyapithecus* also exhibit greater similarities to extant great apes than to earlier Miocene forms such as *Proconsul*.

Soon after the pliopithecoids became the first anthropoids to leave Africa, the hominoids probably also began to migrate out of Africa. Like the pliopithecoids, the hominoids rapidly colonized the Old World and quickly produced two highly successful adaptive radiations in both Europe and Asia, though, at the same time, fossil evidence from the late Middle Miocene in Africa became more scant, leaving us with less certain knowledge about their African cousins.

West Side Story: European Radiation Europe was likely the first stop on the hominoid radiation outside of Africa around 16 mya; the colonization of Asia actually occurred later, at around 15 mya (Heizmann and Begun, 2001). Although this radiation was widespread geographically, so far we've found only scant evidence of it from scattered localities in France, Spain, Italy, Greece, Austria, Germany, and Hungary. The best-known middle Miocene (circa 12–9 mya) hominoid from Europe is *Dryopithecus*, from southern France and northern Spain (**Fig. 9-26**). *Dryopithecus* resembles modern hominoids in many cranial and postcranial features, including long arms, large hands, and long fingers—all signifying an ability to brachiate, or swing through the trees. The teeth of *Dryopithecus* imply an unusual diet of both fruits and leaves (Begun, 1994). The skeletal and dental remains suggest that unlike most other apes, *Dryopithecus* was a highly arboreal species, rarely descending from its high-canopy forested habitat.

A recently discovered middle Miocene (circa 11.9 mya) hominoid, *Anoiapithecus*, has been described from a partial face with mandible of an adult male individual (**Fig. 9-27**). This early ape is known from northeastern Spain and exhibits a unique array of features. It has some classic ape traits, like the heavy browridges, low forehead, and large canine teeth, but what is striking about *Anoiapithecus* is its very short face. Its level of orthognathism or flat-facedness is unparalleled in the extant apes and even in early hominins like *Sahelanthropus*. Its describers state that this find lends support to those who favor a Eurasian origin for apes and humans (Moyà-Solà et al., 2009), though this ignores the distinct possibility of homoplasy.

▲ **Figure 9-25**
Pliopithecus, from the middle Miocene of Europe. The pliopithecoids were the first catarrhines to leave Africa.

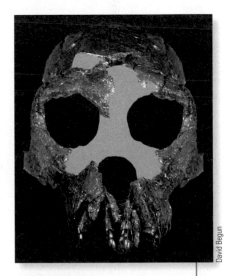

▲ **Figure 9-26**
Skull of *Dryopithecus*, the earliest European ape. The left side is reconstructed as a mirror image of the complete right side.

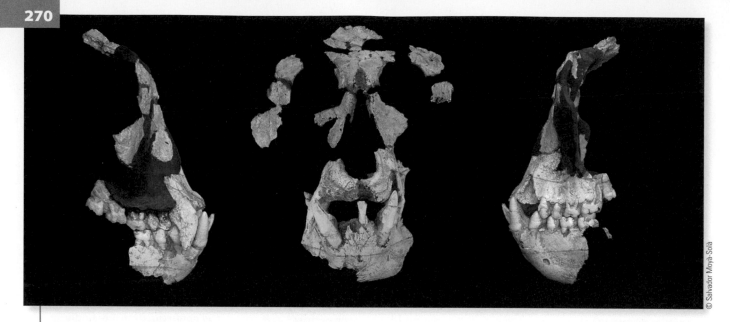

© Salvador Moyà-Solà

▲ Figure 9-27
Three views of the face of *Anoiapithecus*, an early ape closely related to *Dryopithecus*.

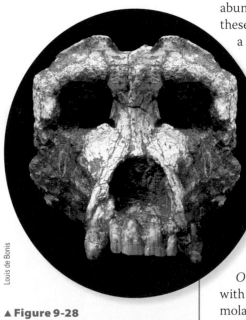

Louis de Bonis

▲ Figure 9-28
Ouranopithecus, possible extinct relative of the African apes. Notice that the face shares many features with living African great apes, including large browridges and a wide distance between the eye orbits. The upper left side is reconstructed as a mirror image of the complete right side.

One late Miocene (9.6–8.7 mya) European fossil hominoid is *Ouranopithecus*, unique in that the first fossils were discovered in Greece during World War I when Allied soldiers were digging trenches to protect themselves from enemy troops. The abundance of the fossils found within these trenches led Camille Arambourg, a French commander (and paleontologist), to order his machine-gun-toting soldiers to unearth fossils until they were redeployed elsewhere (de Bonis and Koufos, 1994).

The face of *Ouranopithecus* shares many features with living African great apes, including large browridges and a wide distance between the eye orbits (**Fig. 9-28**). Some of these traits are even shared by some early fossil hominins. *Ouranopithecus'* powerful jaws, with small canines and extremely thick molar enamel, led some researchers to postulate that these hominoids subsisted on a diet consisting of relatively hard foods, such as nuts (Ungar and Kay, 1995). The variation in both body and canine size indicates a range of sexual dimorphism comparable to that of the modern gorilla, which they resemble in size.

East Side Story: Asian Radiation

The hominoids of the middle and late Miocene of Asia represent one of the most varied Miocene fossil ape assemblages. These Asian fossil apes are geographically dispersed from Turkey in the west to China in the east.

Sivapithecus dates to the middle and late Miocene and has been recovered from southern Asia, in the Siwalik Hills of India and Pakistan. Over the last 30 years, paleoanthropologists led by David Pilbeam have recovered numerous specimens from the Potwar Plateau of Pakistan. Included in this large collection are a multitude of mandibles, many postcranial remains, and a partial cranium, including most of the face. *Sivapithecus* was a large hominoid, ranging from 70 to 150 pounds, and probably inhabited a mostly arboreal niche. The most characteristic anatomical aspects of *Sivapithecus* are seen in the face, which exhibits a concave profile (dished face), broad **zygomatics** (cheekbones), and procumbent (projecting) maxilla and incisors, remarkably resembling that of the modern orangutan (Pilbeam, 1982; **Fig. 9-29**). It's important to note that the body of *Sivapithecus* is distinctly unlike living orangutans or any other known hominoid, for that matter. For example, the forelimb exhibits a unique

zygomatics Cheekbones.

mixture of traits, probably indicating some mode of arboreal quadrupedalism with no ability for brachiation (Pilbeam et al., 1990).

One of *Sivapithecus'* descendants from the late Miocene through the Pleistocene, *Gigantopithecus* ("Giganto"), was discovered in a rather unconventional way. For thousands of years, Chinese pharmacists have used fossils as ingredients in potions intended to cure ailments ranging from backache to sexual impotence. In 1935, Dutch paleoanthropologist Ralph von Koenigswald came across a large fossil primate molar in a Hong Kong apothecary shop. He named the fossil tooth *Gigantopithecus*, meaning "gigantic ape," and the species *blacki*, in honor of his late friend and colleague Davidson Black (the discoverer of "Peking Man"). Subsequent researchers were able to source the teeth to China's southernmost Guangxi Province, a karstic (eroded limestone) region of great rock towers riddled with caves.

While four lower jaws and 1,500 isolated teeth of the extinct ape have been found, no other bones have turned up (**Fig. 9-30**). Based only on the jaws and teeth, however, researchers can attempt to reconstruct both the animal and its way of life. Estimates based on the massive mandibles indicate that the Chinese species of Giganto likely weighed more

than 800 pounds and was possibly 9 feet tall when standing erect on its hind legs (though it was most likely a terrestrial fist walker). This makes *Gigantopithecus* the largest primate that ever lived. But Giganto wasn't always the king of apes that it became in later years. Evidence shows that this great ape increased in size as the genus evolved, which follows a trend seen in other large Pleistocene mammals, such as the mammoth. The earlier Indian and Pakistani *Gigantopithecus giganteus* (8.5 mya), despite its specific name, was about half the size of the later Chinese and Southeast Asian *Gigantopithecus blacki* (around 2 mya).

The comparatively small incisors and canines, very thick enamel on the cheek teeth, and massive, robust jaws lead to the inevitable conclusion that the animal was adapted to the consumption of tough, fibrous foods by cutting, crushing, and grinding them. Some researchers have argued that Giganto's huge mandible and dentition were an adaptation for a diet consisting primarily of bamboo, much like that of the giant panda. More current research has supported this claim and also concludes that its diet may have included the durian, a tropical fruit with a tough outer skin (Ciochon et al., 1990; **Fig. 9-31**).

Sadly, sometime near the end of the Middle Pleistocene, around 200,000 years ago (ya), Giganto went extinct. The animal had flourished for more than 8.5 million years, but climatic

▼ **Figure 9-29**
Comparison of a modern chimpanzee (left), *Sivapithecus* (middle), and a modern orangutan (right). Notice that both *Sivapithecus* and the orangutan exhibit a dished face, broad cheekbones, and projecting maxilla and incisors.

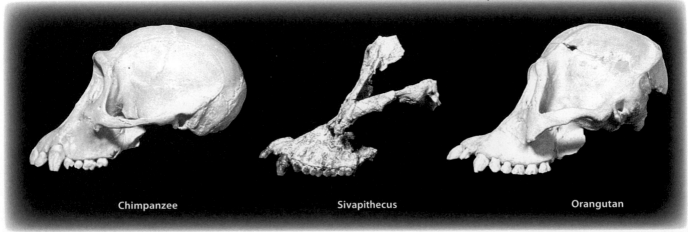

Chimpanzee   Sivapithecus   Orangutan

David Pilbeam

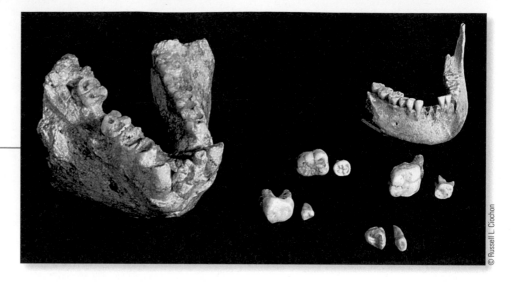

▶ **Figure 9-30**
Comparison of the mandibles and teeth of *Gigantopithecus* and *Homo sapiens*. Notice that Giganto's jaw is almost three times the size of the human's, as are the teeth.

or other environmental change may have proved too much for the vegetarian giant.

A final ape from Asia, *Lufengpithecus*, has been recovered from localities in southern China and dated to the late Miocene/early Pliocene (9–5 mya). This medium-sized ape, with an estimated adult body weight of about 110 pounds, is known from one of the most complete fossil ape assemblages: 5 crania, 41 mandibles, over 650 iso-lated teeth, and, most recently, post-crania including finger bones and a femur (Xu and Lu, 2007). With its narrow interorbital distance, ovoid orbits, and procumbent incisors (**Fig. 9-32**), some researchers have argued that *Lufengpithecus* is related to the modern orangutan, while others believe that it is related to the European *Dryopithecus*. If not for its location in southern China, *Lufengpithecus* would just be another of the many apes that faced extinction at the end of the Miocene. However, this, in conjunction with its newly described curved phalanges, has catapulted this genus to prominence. It now appears that *Lufengpithecus* is most properly considered a stem orangutan (Harrison et al., 2008; Harrison, 2010).

Lufengpithecus is also noted for its existence within a protected area created by the uplift of the Tibetan Plateau—the result of Himalayan mountain building (Harrison et al., 2002). Within this refuge, a sort of "lost world," *Lufengpithecus* survived until at least 5 mya—or at least that's what conventional wisdom leads us to believe. In recent years, however, Pleistocene cave sites in southern China that have long yielded teeth belonging to *Gigantopithecus* have now also produced more diminutive teeth initially identified as belonging to an early human. These same teeth, following more rigorous analysis, are now

▼ **Figure 9-31**
An artist's rendering of *Gigantopithecus* enjoying a meal of the tasty, but tough, tropical fruit known as durian.

thought to be those of a previously unknown, medium-sized Pleistocene ape. The teeth are too small to be those of either Giganto or the orangutan, *Pongo*. Could these mystery ape teeth be a descendant of *Lufengpithecus* (Ciochon, 2009)? In fact, the strongest evidence points to the existence of three distinct great ape lineages in Asia: the massive *Gigantopithecus*, the large-bodied *Pongo*, and the medium-sized *Lufengpithecus* descendant. But as you've seen in Chapter 6, this Asian hominoid diversity has dwindled, just as it has in Africa and elsewhere in the world.

Evolution of Extant Hominoids

Hylobatids: The Lesser Apes

Biomolecular evidence indicates that the gibbon–great ape split occurred approximately 18–15 mya. This would place their divergence around the time that migration into Eurasia from Africa would have first become geographically possible (Pilbeam, 1996; Raaum et al., 2005). The molecular evidence also shows that the radiation of the current hylobatids (lesser apes, such as gibbons) occurred only 10.5 mya (Chatterjee, 2006), with newly discovered 9-million-year-old *Yuanmoupithecus* supporting that date (Harrison et al., 2008). Before this new find, various researchers had previously considered pliopithecoids as a possible gibbon ancestor due to similarities in the shape of the face. But pliopithecoids and Oligocene catarrhines actually share numerous primitive features, including the lack of a tube-like middle ear, the presence of a small tail, and an elbow joint that's strikingly similar to those of various Fayum primates. These features, as well as their monkey-like limb proportions, clearly remove pliopithecoids from consideration as the ancestors of modern gibbons. From molecular evidence and from fossil remains of the small-bodied Chinese stem hylobatid *Yuanmoupi-*

thecus (Harrison et al., 2008), however, we can determine that the gibbon radiation began 10.5–9 mya in China before dispersing southward to Malaysia and Sumatra. Once in Sumatra, gibbons differentiated into two taxa, including the modern *Hylobates*, which eventually made its way into Borneo and Java around 5–3 mya (Chatterjee, 2006; Harrison et al., 2008).

The African Great Apes

Recent molecular studies suggest that gorillas diverged from humans and chimpanzees between 9 and 8 mya (Kumar et al., 2005), with the divergence between humans and chimpanzees occurring between 6 and 5 mya (Steiper and Young, 2006, 2008). If these estimates are right, then the late Miocene (11–5 mya) becomes a crucial period for understanding African great apes and human origins. Strangely, after beginning their migration into Asia and Europe, hominoids disappear from the African fossil record around 13 mya, not to reappear until the late Miocene, around 10.5–10 mya (in the form of *Chororapithecus*). Since there is no evidence of a mass extinction of hominoids in the middle Miocene, this "ape gap" (Hill, 2007) in the fossil record has led some researchers to hypothesize that the reappearance of hominoids in

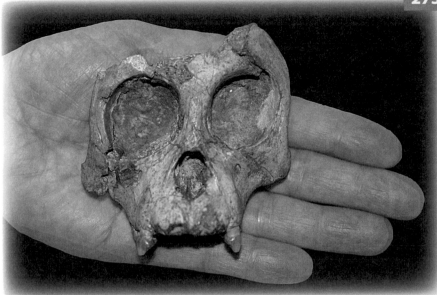

▲ **Figure 9-32**
Skull of a *Lufengpithecus* juvenile from the late Miocene of Yunnan Province, China. Note the orangutan-like oval eye orbits and narrow distance between the eyes.

Africa during the late Miocene was the result of Eurasian fossil apes migrating back into Africa at the same time the colobine monkeys were leaving. This has been the prevailing paradigm for the past decade or so.

For this reason, *Ouranopithecus* (9.6–8.7 mya), the large-bodied hominoid from Greece, was long thought to be a stem African ape/human ancestor. This argument is based primarily on the facial similarities discussed earlier. This would make an ape similar to *Ouranopithecus* a kind of prodigal son who returned to Africa from a long stay (and evolution) in Europe. This out-of-Europe ape line would then later diverge in the late Miocene of Africa, producing the human line (see Chapter 11).

However, given some provocative finds from Kenya, many researchers are shifting from an out-of-Europe scenario to a plausible African origin for the living African apes (Bernor, 2007). The oldest of these African specimens is the fairly recently described Ethiopian *Chororapithecus*, dating to 10.5–10 mya. This genus is notable as the first representative of a large-bodied Miocene ape in eastern Africa following the "ape gap." Its dental morphology and apparent adaptation to a hard, fibrous diet have caused some to suggest that it represents the basal stock for the modern gorilla (Suwa et al., 2007). In fact, its discoverers have gone so far as to say that the eight molars and one canine "are collectively indistinguishable from modern gorilla subspecies" (Dalton, 2007, p. 844; **Fig. 9-33**). If this genus represents a gorilla ancestor to the exclusion of humans, this would place the divergence of the two groups at 11–10 mya, more than 2 million years earlier than generally accepted.

Another more recently described genus, dated to 9.9–9.8 mya, is *Nakalipithecus*, from Kenya, thought by some to be close to the last common ancestor of the African great apes and humans (but see previous discussion of *Chororapithecus*). Though slightly older than *Ouranopithecus* (9.9–9.8 mya ver-

sus 9.6–8.7 mya), *Nakalipithecus* shares many features with *Ouranopithecus*, as they both lived in similar environments. *Nakalipithecus* is reconstructed as comparable in size to that of a female gorilla, with dental features that indicate a hard-object diet. Both of these features are suggestive of a **terrestrial** lifestyle (substantial ground living; Kunimatsu et al., 2007; Nakatsukasa and Kunimatsu, 2009). Despite its still-ambiguous phylogenetic affiliation, it is clear that the Samburu Hills of northern Kenya, from which *Nakalipithecus* was found, were a hotbed of hominoid diversity with at least two other genera known from this region during the Miocene (Nakatsukasa and Kunimatsu, 2009).

Nakalipithecus' and *Ouranopithecus'* morphological similarities have led some to propose a possible ancestor-descendant relationship between the two (Kunimatsu et al., 2007). Coupled with *Nakalipithecus'* and *Chororapithecus'* East African origins and earlier ages when compared with *Ouranopithecus*, this would appear to indicate an African rather than Eurasian origin for the living African apes (**Fig. 9-34**).

In 2005, researchers discovered several teeth of a fossil chimpanzee at a site near Lake Baringo, in Kenya. This discovery adds some fossil time depth to at least the *Pan* lineage. These fossil chimpanzee teeth date to approximately 500,000 ya and represent the first and only fossils belonging to the genus *Pan* (such fossils are rare because tropical forest environments aren't conducive to preserving organic remains). Also note that these fossils are quite late, several million years after the chimpanzee lineage diverged from hominins. Although currently not assigned to a particular chimpanzee species, the fossil teeth exhibit greater similarities to the common chimpanzee (*Pan troglodytes*) than to bonobos (*Pan paniscus*) (McBrearty and Jablonski, 2005).

Another reason why African ape and chimpanzee fossils in particular

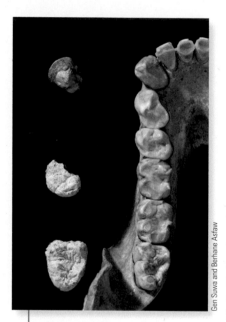

▲ **Figure 9-33**
Comparison of three mandibular teeth belonging to *Chororapithecus* (left) with a modern gorilla mandible (right).

Gen Suwa and Berhane Asfaw

are so rare is the difficulty in identifying them as such and not as early hominins. As a preview to Chapter 11, let us spend a few moments on the controversial and now iconic rebranding of the previously described *Ardipithecus*. Though known for some 15 years and purported by its discoverers, including the legendary Tim White (also famous for his role in the "Lucy" discovery), to be considered a hominin, the scientific community awaited tangible proof of this assessment. In 2009, an entire issue of *Science* devoted to the genus and its related paleoecology was published largely due to one influential partial skeleton dated to 4.4 mya (though other members of this genus are dated to much earlier in the late Miocene, to 5.8–5.2 mya). *Ardipithecus* (or "Ardi," as the mostly complete female skeleton of this genus was nicknamed) provided an entirely new way of looking at the origins of hominins, as she revealed a complex and unexpected mix of primitive and derived traits, meaning that the

last common ancestor of the African apes and humans may not have looked like either group as we know them now (Lovejoy, 2009; Shreeve, 2009). However, many in the scientific community are still skeptical given the high degree of reconstruction, and in a series of terse communications within *Science* the next year, some of this professional sniping aired itself openly (see Sarmiento, 2010; White et al., 2010). Many believe that this genus, once open to inspection, will be revealed not as a hominin, but rather as another late Miocene African ape. However, given the paucity of the African hominoid record at that time, why can't that be good enough? Still, if these aren't our distant relatives, where *do* we come from? In the next part of the text, we'll seek answers to this question.

Asia's Lone Great Ape Of all the living apes, the orangutan's ancestry is probably the best documented. Current evidence indicates that *Sivapithecus* gave rise to

▼ **Figure 9-34**
Cladogram of Homininae showing the relationships of gorillas, chimpanzees, and humans with their fossil ape relatives.

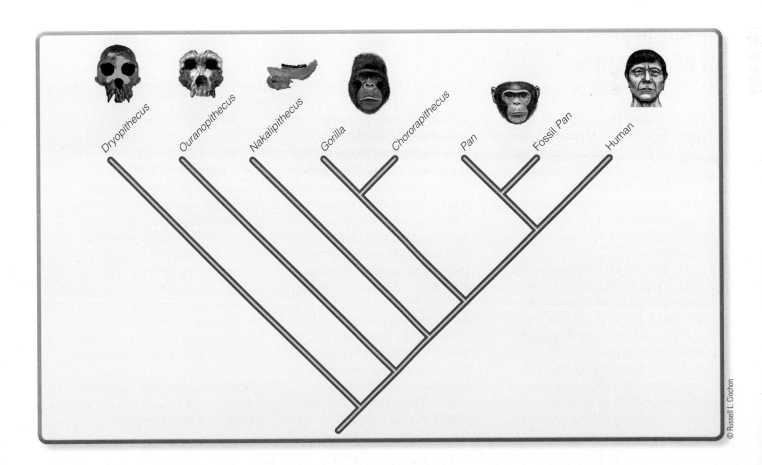

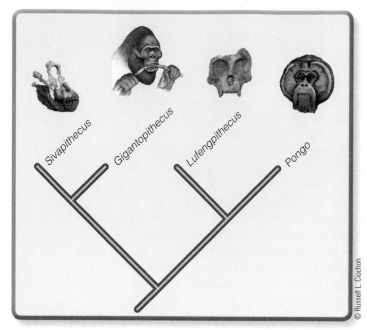

Sivapithecus Gigantopithecus Lufengpithecus Pongo

© Russell L. Ciochon

▲ **Figure 9-35**
Cladogram of Ponginae showing the relationship of the orangutan with its fossil ape relatives.

Gigantopithecus (sometime before 9 mya) as well as to *Lufengpithecus* and then finally to the orangutans (*Pongo*) possibly in the Pliocene. Since the earliest *Sivapithecus* fossils date to more than 12 mya, it's clear that the branching event separating orangutans and the lineage leading to the African great apes and humans must have occurred before then. In fact, biomolecular evidence indicates that this divergence took place approximately 14 mya (Raaum et al., 2005). The relationship between *Sivapithecus* and *Pongo* is based primarily on cranial similarities, though their vastly differing postcranial anatomies raise questions regarding their evolutionary proximity to each another. As mentioned earlier, the face of *Lufengpithecus* is also very similar to that of the modern orangutan. However, it's the postcrania of *Lufengpithecus* (particularly its curved phalanges) that indicate its closer relationship to *Pongo* than to *Sivapithecus* (Harrison et al., 2008). Several other Asian hominoids have been suggested as more recent orangutan ancestors, but there's as yet little evidence to support these assertions (**Fig. 9-35**).

Summary of Main Topics

- Beginning in the late Cretaceous, the earliest primate ancestors were probably little more than arboreally adapted insectivores, much like the modern tree shrews.
- In the Paleocene, no indisputable euprimates are yet apparent, despite these claims for *Altiatlasius*.
- In the Eocene, we see an abundant diversification of readily identifiable euprimates, with the lemurlike adapoids and the tarsier-like omomyoids beginning their evolutionary radiations.
- As demonstrated by recent evidence from the Fayum and other locations in Africa, early anthropoid origins also date to sometime in the middle Eocene.

- Old and New World anthropoids apparently shared their last common ancestry in the Eocene or early Oligocene and have gone their separate evolutionary pathways ever since that time. In the Old World, the Oligocene reveals numerous possible early anthropoid ancestors, again mostly at the Fayum, but none of the modern lineages (Old World monkeys, gibbons, large-bodied apes) can definitely be traced to this time.
- The Miocene reveals the first Old World monkeys and a highly complex array of ape forms; many large-bodied varieties are represented from remains discovered in Africa, Asia, and Europe. Some early forms from Kenya

and Uganda (the proconsuloids) are more primitive than all of the hominoids from Eurasia.
- Though there's little firm evidence tying Miocene fossil forms to living apes or humans, morphological evidence suggests that *Yuanmoupithecus* may be related to the gibbon, and *Lufengpithecus* is probably closely related to the orangutan. The more recently discovered *Chororapithecus* and *Nakalipithecus* might be the ancestors of the African apes.

The most important fossil discoveries discussed in this chapter are summarized in What's Important.

What's Important

Key Discoveries of Fossil Primates

EPOCH	GENUS OR SUPER-FAMILY NAME	SITES/REGIONS	THE BIG PICTURE
Paleocene	*Purgatorius*	American Southwest, Bug Creek Anthills (Montana)	Plesiadapiform; first known archaic primate
Mainly Eocene	Adapoidea	North America, Europe	Lemur-like stem strepsirhines; one of the two main branches of euprimates; may or may not have had a tooth comb
Mainly Eocene	Omomyoidea	North America, Europe, and (more rarely) Africa and Asia	Tarsier- or galago-like stem strepsirhines; one of the two main branches of euprimates
Oligocene	*Aegyptopithecus*	North Africa, the Fayum (Egypt)	Has 2.1.2.3 dental formula; ancestor of both later catarrhines and hominoids
Oligocene	*Saadanius*	Afro-Arabia (Saudi Arabia)	First stem catarrhine; has ear tube
Middle Miocene	*Victoriapithecus*	East Africa	Has bilophodont molar pattern; ancestor of all Old World monkeys
Late Miocene	*Lufengpithecus*	China, East Asia	Fossil great ape; closely related to the modern orangutan
Late Miocene	*Ouranopithecus*	Greece, Europe	Fossil great ape; believed by many to have returned to Africa to give rise to the living great apes
Miocene-Pleistocene	*Gigantopithecus*	China, India, Pakistan, Vietnam, Burma	The largest ape that ever lived; only great ape to go extinct in the Pleistocene

Critical Thinking Questions

1. How do biomolecular and direct estimates of dating fossil lineages differ? How can they be used to give us a more complete view of the past?

2. Why is it difficult to distinguish the earliest members of the primate order from other placental mammals? If you found a nearly complete skeleton of an early Paleocene mammal, what structural traits might lead you to determine that it was a euprimate?

3. Compare and contrast the adapoids and omomyoids with living members of the primate order. Why do we call them lemur- or tarsier-like and not lemurs and tarsiers?

4. Where is the Fayum Depression, and why is it significant in primate evolution? Are there any other sites where so many fossil primates have been found? Why or why not?

5. What are proconsuloids, and why are they no longer considered to be true hominoids?

6. Compare *Gigantopithecus* in Asia with the modern gorilla in Africa. How do their dietary niches differ?

New Frontiers in RESEARCH

Building Family Trees from Genes

Molecular anthropology is the branch of anthropology that uses genetics to investigate the biology and evolution of humans and our closest relatives—the nonhuman primates. Before we can test more specific hypotheses about primate evolution and adaptation, we need to know how different primate species are related to one another. Nearly 50 years ago, the late Morris Goodman was among the pioneering figures to use molecular data to help better explain primate relationships (**Fig. 1**). During the 1960s, he and his colleagues used immunological data to suggest that humans, chimpanzees, and gorillas were genetically very similar and closely related to one another. In fact, humans and chimpanzees appeared to be more closely related to one another than either was to gorillas. This challenged the then prevailing view that the human species was highly diverged from other nonhuman primates—in a class of their own, you might say. Since this time, molecular anthropologists have used proteins, genes, and even genomes to test hypotheses regarding the relationships within the primate order. The use of molecular methods in this manner has revolutionized our knowledge of primate systematics and has revealed evolutionary relationships

that have been difficult to resolve using other methods. This new and more scientifically substantiated family tree (**Fig. 2**) is compiled from the research of a number of molecular anthropologists (Raaum et al., 2005; Steiper and Young, 2006; Sterner et al., 2006; Janečka et al., 2007; Hodgson et al., 2008; Hodgson et al., 2009b, Wildman et al., 2009).

Phylogenetic hypotheses can be tested by comparing DNA (nucleotide) sequences from various primate species to deduce a gene tree of primate family relationships. When using DNA to test phylogenetic hypotheses, it's important to construct gene trees from various genetic loci because different parts of the genome can have unique evolutionary histories. For example, studies on macaques and colobines have shown that mitochondrial, sex-linked, and autosomal gene trees from the same individuals can show very different relationships. Determining the cause of these different evolutionary histories across the genome, as well as which gene trees most accurately reflect the relationships among primate species, requires careful interpretation.

Molecular anthropologists can also use sequences of DNA to infer how long it has been since primate species last shared a common ancestor. Because mutations in DNA occur at a relatively constant rate of change, the amount of difference between two samples is proportional to the amount of time elapsed since their last common ancestor existed. This is often referred to as the "molecular clock." When parts of the fossil record are fairly complete *and* well dated, they can be used to calibrate this "clock" by telling us how long ago two or more species on a tree diverged from one another and thus how long it takes for a certain number of mutations to occur. This information can then be used to reason when in time other

▼ Figure 1
The late Morris Goodman and Kirstin Sterner (Wayne State University's School of Medicine) use genomics to examine the evolutionary relationships of extant primates and to test for evidence of adaptive evolution in the primate clade.

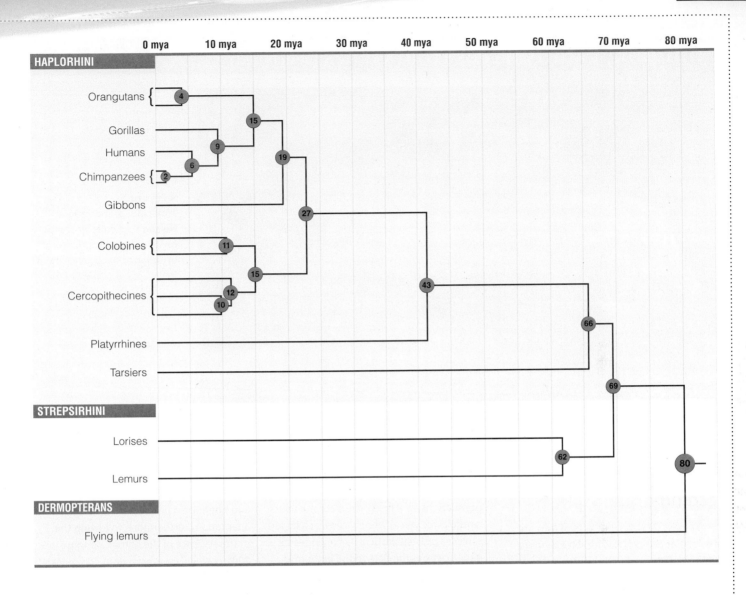

Time scale (top): 0 mya, 10 mya, 20 mya, 30 mya, 40 mya, 50 mya, 60 mya, 70 mya, 80 mya

HAPLORHINI

Orangutans — 4
Gorillas
Humans — 9 — 6 — 2
Chimpanzees
Gibbons — 15 — 19
Colobines — 11
Cercopithecines — 15 — 12 — 10
— 27
— 43
Platyrrhines — 66
Tarsiers — 69

STREPSIRHINI

Lorises — 62 — 80
Lemurs

DERMOPTERANS

Flying lemurs

▲ **Figure 2**
Molecular primate family tree based on the works of various researchers (see text). Dates of divergence are noted in the gold-colored nodes.

less documented primate species across the tree last shared a common ancestor. As with the construction of gene trees, molecular divergence dates are best inferred from various parts of the genome to ensure that divergences calculated from one region are consistent with those calculated from others. In many cases, primate divergence dates inferred from molecular data are

much farther back in time than expected, which leaves the exciting possibility that we are missing even more of the primate fossil record than previously thought.

A relatively recent molecular method for the inference of primate evolutionary relationships is the use of transposable genomic elements (see Chapter 4). These are regions of DNA that are replicated and inserted into different areas of the genome. They have therefore been called "jumping genes," and each "jump" to a different part of the genome can be used as a character for phylogenetic analysis. The presence of a transposable element in a specific part of the genome in two species

could represent a shared derived trait that reveals a close evolutionary relationship. One type of transposable element, called an *Alu* element, is particularly common in primate genomes. In fact, there are over 1 million copies of this repetitive element in humans, making up approximately 10 percent of our genome. Because their mode of evolution is unidirectional and free of homoplasy, transposable elements, and *Alu* elements in particular, are becoming prominent in phylogenetic analyses. However, because their replication and jumping do not follow a "clock," they cannot be used to infer divergence dates among primate species.

Building Family Trees from Genes (continued)

◄ Figure 3
Molecular primatologist
Nelson Ting collects samples
in Africa for genomic study
in his lab at the University of
Iowa.

Primate Molecular Ecology

In the past 10 years, the field of primate molecular ecology has grown exponentially as biological anthropologists have begun to use genetics to investigate the evolution and ecology of wild primate populations (**Fig. 3**). This includes working out evolutionary relationships among different populations, determining species boundaries, quantifying population structure and gene flow, deducing demographic history, and approximating population size. Such research is important not only to understand evolutionary processes in natural settings, but also to aid in the designation of conservation priorities for species threatened with extinction. One major limitation in this field is that researchers can typically use only noninvasively collected samples such as hair or feces. This constraint exists because sedating wild primates to draw blood can disrupt delicate social relationships, risk injury to study

animals, and facilitate the spread of disease from humans to nonhuman primate populations (or if researchers are not *very* careful, vice versa). Noninvasively collected samples present particular challenges to geneticists, as the DNA found in them is often degraded. Luckily, technological advances continue to aid researchers in obtaining genetic information from such samples.

Molecular Anthropology in the Age of Genomics

Advances in sequencing technology now allow for the collection of an unprecedented amount of molecular data (**Fig. 4**). The same time and money used to collect 500 base pairs of DNA 10 years ago can now be used to collect tens of thousands of base pairs. This large amount of data provides us with increasing confidence that the gene trees and divergence dates we infer are accurate representations of primate

evolutionary history and allows us to test more specific hypotheses about human and nonhuman primate evolution and adaptation. Furthermore, following the draft sequence of the human genome in 2001, molecular anthropology has quickly moved into the age of genomics, and many additional primate genome projects have since been initiated. At the time of this printing, large amounts of genomic data are available for the following nonhuman primates: common chimpanzee, gorilla, orangutan, rhesus macaque, baboon, small-eared galago, white-tufted-ear marmoset, Philippine tarsier, and mouse lemur. Sequencing projects for the bonobo, gibbon, vervet monkey, long-tailed macaque, and squirrel monkey have been initiated or are planned for the immediate future (see www.genome.gov/10002154 for the most up-to-date information regarding ongoing projects), and there is a current initiative to sequence the genomes of 10,000 different vertebrate species (http://www.genome10k.org/). In addition, many more

Amy M. Boddy

▲ **Figure 4**
The late Morris Goodman and Kirstin Sterner (Wayne State University's School of Medicine) view evolutionary relationships of primates on this genomic phylogenetic tree.

human genomes have been sequenced, providing essential information about human diversity and evolution. Advances in ancient DNA extraction and sequencing have even made it possible to sequence large portions of the Neandertal genome! Genomic data are now being collected so rapidly that we are having a difficult time keeping up with the development of new analytical methods. The merging of computer programming and biology has become essential to sort through all of these data, making the field of bioinformatics extremely important. With this age of genomics upon us, molecular anthropologists can now use genomic-scale data to further examine the relationships of extant primate species and the timing of their divergence from one another, as well as to examine genotypes that underlie distinctly modern human characteristics.

Sources

Hodgson, J. A., K. N. Sterner, et al.
2008   Phylogenetic relationship of the Platyrrhini inferred from complete mitochondrial genome sequences. *American Journal of Physical Anthropology* S46:118–119.

Hodgson, J. A., L. Pozzi, et al.
2009b   Molecular divergence dates suggest an origin of crown primates near the K/T boundary. *American Academy of Sciences* 138(S48):227.

Janečka, J., W. Miller, et al.
2007   Molecular and genomic data identify the closest living relative of primates. *Science* 318:792–794.

Raaum, R., K. Sterner, et al.
2005   Catarrhine primate divergence dates estimated from complete mitochondrial genomes: Concordance with fossil and nuclear DNA evidence. *Journal of Human Evolution* 48:237–257.

Steiper, M. E., and N. M. Young
2006   Primate molecular divergence dates. *Molecular Phylogenetics and Evolution* 41(2):384–394.

Sterner, K., R. Raaum, et al.
2006   Mitochondrial data support an odd-nosed colobine clade. *Molecular Phylogenetics and Evolution* 40:1–7.

Wildman, D. E., N. M. Jameson, et al.
2009   A fully resolved genus level phylogeny of neotropical primates. *Molecular Phylogenetics and Evolution* 53:694–702.

Excavations in northern Kenya of a fossil hominin skull, conducted by Meave Leakey (on right) and crew.

10

Paleoanthropology: Reconstructing Early Hominin Behavior and Ecology

Key Questions

▶ How did the development of culture alter the nature of human evolution, and how does human biocultural evolution compare with that of our close primate cousins?

A portion of a pig's tusk, a small sample of volcanic sediment, a battered rock, a primate's molar: What do these seemingly unremarkable remains have in common, and more to the point, why are they of interest to paleoanthropologists? First of all, if they're all discovered at sites in Africa or Eurasia, they *may* be quite ancient—indeed, perhaps millions of years old. Further, some of these materials actually inform scientists directly of quite precise dating of the finds. Last, and most exciting, some of these finds may have been modified, used, and discarded by bipedal creatures who looked and behaved in some ways like ourselves (but were in other respects very different). And what of that molar? Is it a fossilized remnant of an ancient hominin? These are the kinds of questions asked by paleoanthropologists, and to answer them, these researchers travel to remote locales across the Old World.

How do we distinguish possible hominins from other types of animals (most notably, from other primates), especially when all we have are fragmentary fossil remains from just a small portion of a skeleton? How do humans and our most distant ancestors compare with other animals? In the last four chapters, we've seen how humans are classified as primates, both structurally and behaviorally, and how our evolutionary history coincides with that of other mammals and, specifically, other primates. Even so, we're a unique kind of primate, and our ancestors have been adapted to a particular lifestyle for several million years. Some late Miocene fossil apes probably began this process close to 7 mya, though better-preserved fossil discoveries reveal more definitive evidence of hominins shortly after 5 mya.

We're able to determine the hominin nature of these remains by more than the structure of teeth and bones; we know that these animals are hominins also because of the way they behaved—emphasizing once again the *biocultural* nature of human evolution. In this chapter, we'll discuss the methods scientists use to explore the secrets of early hominin behavior and ecology, and we'll demonstrate these methods through the example of the best-known early hominin site in the world: Olduvai Gorge, in East Africa.

283

Definition of Hominin

The earliest evidence of hominins that has been found dates to the end of the Miocene and mainly includes dental and cranial pieces. But dental features alone don't describe the special features of hominins, and they certainly aren't distinctive of the later stages of human evolution. Modern humans, as well as our most immediate hominin ancestors, are distinguished from the great apes by more obvious features than tooth and jaw dimensions. For example, various scientists have pointed to such distinctive hominin characteristics as bipedal locomotion, large brain size, and toolmaking behavior as being significant (at some stage) in defining what makes a hominin a hominin.

It's important to recognize that not all these characteristics developed simultaneously or at the same pace. In fact, over the last several million years of hominin evolution, quite a different pattern has been evident, in which the various components (dentition, locomotion, brain size, and toolmaking) have developed at quite different rates. This pattern, in which physiological and behavioral systems evolve at different rates, is called **mosaic evolution**. As we first pointed out in Chapter 1 and will emphasize in this and the next chapter, the single most important defining characteristic for the full course of hominin evolution is bipedal locomotion. In the earliest stages of hominin emergence, skeletal evidence indicating bipedal locomotion is the only truly reliable indicator that these fossils were indeed hominins. But in later stages of hominin evolution, other features, especially those relating to brain development and behavior, become highly significant (**Fig. 10-1**).

These behavioral aspects of hominin emergence—particularly toolmaking—are what we'd like to emphasize in this chapter. Important structural attributes of the hominin brain, teeth, and especially locomotor apparatus are discussed in the next chapter, where we investigate early hominin anatomical adaptations in greater detail.

What's in a Name?

Throughout this book, we refer to members of the human family as hominins (the technical name for members of the tribe Hominini). Most professional paleoanthropologists now prefer this terminology, since it more accurately reflects evolutionary relationships. As we mentioned briefly in Chapter 6, the more traditional classification of hominoids is not as accurate and actually misrepresents key evolutionary relationships.

In the last several years, detailed molecular evidence clearly shows that the great apes (traditionally classified as pongids and including orangutans, gorillas, chimpanzees, and bonobos) do not make up a coherent evolutionary group sharing a single common ancestor and thus are not a *monophyletic* group. Indeed, the molecular data indicate that the African great apes (gorillas, chimpanzees, and bonobos) are significantly more closely related to humans than is the orangutan. What's more, at an even closer evolutionary level, we now know that chimpanzees and bonobos are yet more closely linked to humans than is the gorilla. Hominoid classification has been significantly revised to show these more complete relationships, and two further taxonomic levels (subfamily and tribe) have been added (**Fig. 10-2**).

We should mention a couple of important ramifications of this new classification. First, it further emphasizes the *very* close evolutionary relationship of humans with African apes and most especially with chimpanzees and bonobos. Second, the term *hominid*, which has been used for decades to refer to our specific evolutionary lineage, has a quite different meaning in the revised classification; now it refers to *all* great apes and humans together.

Unfortunately, during the period of transition to the newer classification

mosaic evolution A pattern of evolution in which the rate of evolution in one functional system varies from that in other systems. For example, in hominin evolution, the dental system, locomotor system, and neurological system (especially the brain) all evolved at markedly different rates.

culture Behavioral aspects of human adaptation, including technology, traditions, language, religion, marriage patterns, and social roles. Culture is a set of learned behaviors transmitted from one generation to the next by nonbiological (i.e., nongenetic) means.

scheme, confusion is bound to result. For this reason, we won't use the term *hominid* in this book except where absolutely necessary (for example, in a formal classification; see Fig. 6-6 and Appendix B). To avoid confusion, we'll simply refer to the grouping of great apes and humans as "large-bodied hominoids." And when you see the term *hominid* in earlier publications (including earlier editions of this text), simply regard it as synonymous with *hominin*, the term we use in this book.

Biocultural Evolution: The Human Capacity for Culture

One of the most distinctive behavioral features of humans is our extraordinary elaboration of and dependence on **culture**. Certainly other primates, and many other animals, for that matter, modify their environments. As we saw in Chapter 8, chimpanzees especially are known for such behaviors as using

▼ **Figure 10-1**
Mosaic evolution of hominin characteristics: a postulated time line.

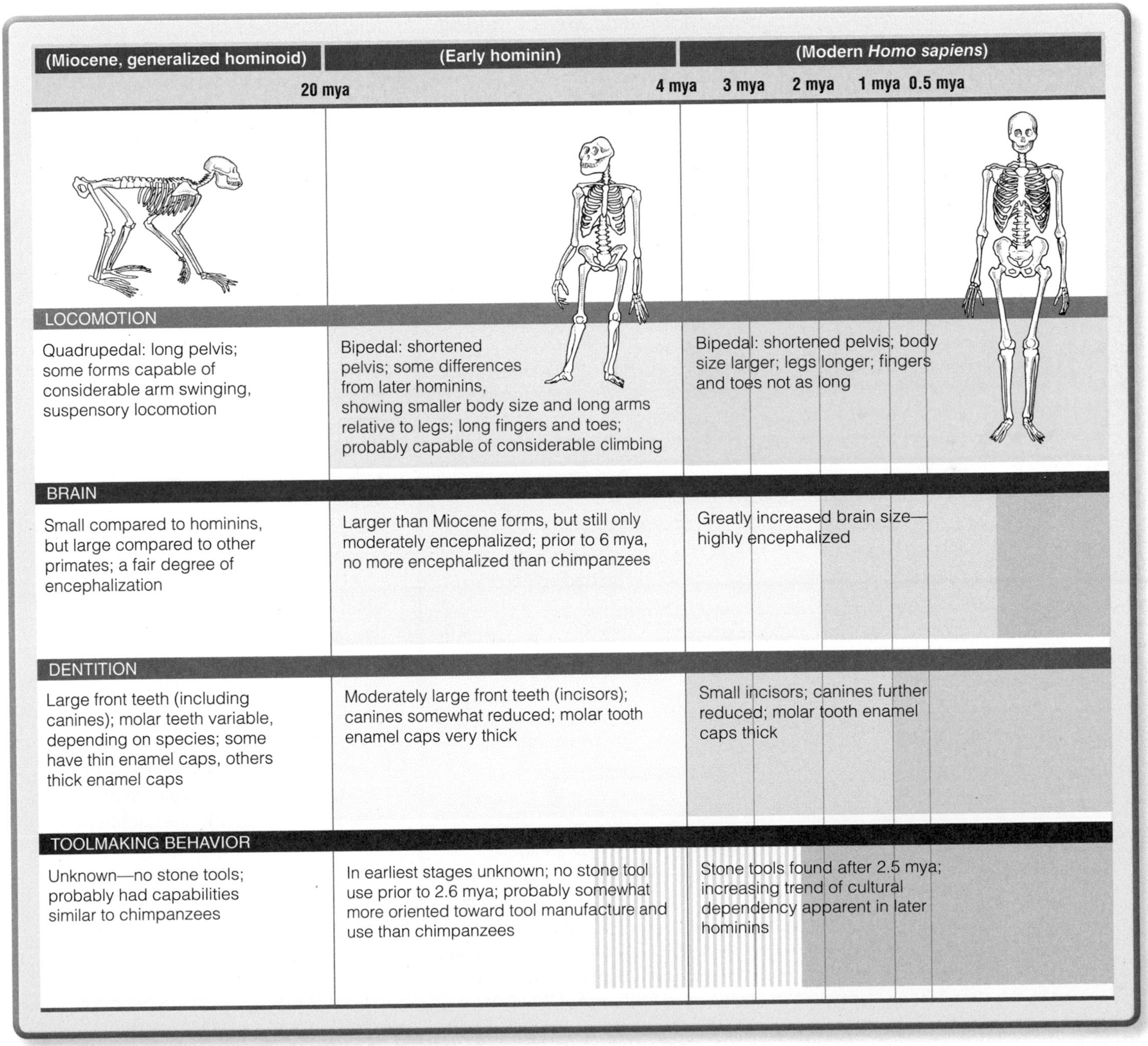

(Miocene, generalized hominoid)	(Early hominin)	(Modern *Homo sapiens*)				
20 mya		4 mya	3 mya	2 mya	1 mya	0.5 mya
LOCOMOTION						
Quadrupedal: long pelvis; some forms capable of considerable arm swinging, suspensory locomotion	Bipedal: shortened pelvis; some differences from later hominins, showing smaller body size and long arms relative to legs; long fingers and toes; probably capable of considerable climbing	Bipedal: shortened pelvis; body size larger; legs longer; fingers and toes not as long				
BRAIN						
Small compared to hominins, but large compared to other primates; a fair degree of encephalization	Larger than Miocene forms, but still only moderately encephalized; prior to 6 mya, no more encephalized than chimpanzees	Greatly increased brain size—highly encephalized				
DENTITION						
Large front teeth (including canines); molar teeth variable, depending on species; some have thin enamel caps, others thick enamel caps	Moderately large front teeth (incisors); canines somewhat reduced; molar tooth enamel caps very thick	Small incisors; canines further reduced; molar tooth enamel caps thick				
TOOLMAKING BEHAVIOR						
Unknown—no stone tools; probably had capabilities similar to chimpanzees	In earliest stages unknown; no stone tool use prior to 2.6 mya; probably somewhat more oriented toward tool manufacture and use than chimpanzees	Stone tools found after 2.5 mya; increasing trend of cultural dependency apparent in later hominins				

termite sticks, and some chimpanzees as well as capuchin monkeys even carry rocks to use for crushing nuts. Because of such observations, we're on shaky ground when it comes to drawing sharp lines between early hominin toolmaking behavior and that exhibited by other animals.

Another point to remember is that human culture, at least as it's defined in contemporary contexts, involves much more than toolmaking capacity. For humans, culture integrates an entire adaptive strategy involving cognitive, political, social, and economic components. *Material culture*—or the tools humans use—is but a small portion of this cultural complex.

Still, when we examine the archaeological record of earlier hominins, what's available for study is almost exclusively limited to material culture, especially the bits and pieces of broken stone left over from tool manufacture. This is why it's extremely difficult to learn anything about the earliest stages of hominin cultural development before the regular manufacture of stone tools. As you'll see, this most crucial cultural development has been traced to approximately 2.6 mya (Semaw et al., 2003). Yet because of our contemporary primate models, we can assume that hominins were undoubtedly using other kinds of tools (made of perishable materials) and displaying a whole array of other cultural behaviors long before then. But with no "hard" evidence preserved in the archaeological record, our understanding of the early development of these nonmaterial cultural components remains elusive.

The fundamental basis for human cultural success relates directly to our cognitive abilities. Again, we're not dealing with an absolute distinction, but a relative one. As you've already learned, other primates, as documented in the great apes, have some of the language capabilities exhibited by humans. Even so, modern humans display these abilities in a complexity several orders of magnitude beyond that of any other animal. And only humans are so completely dependent on symbolic communication and its cultural by-products that contemporary *Homo sapiens* could not survive without them.

At this point you may be wondering when the unique combination of cognitive, social, and material cultural adaptations became prominent in human evolution. In answering that question, we must be careful to recognize the manifold nature of culture; we can't expect it to always contain the same elements across species (as when comparing ourselves with nonhuman primates) or through time (when trying to reconstruct ancient hominin behavior). Richard Potts (1993) has critiqued such overly simplistic perspectives and suggests instead a more dynamic approach, one that incorporates many subcomponents (including aspects of behavior, cognition, and social interaction).

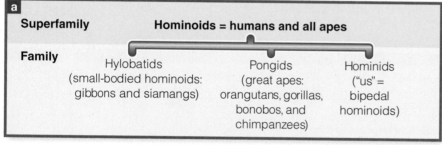

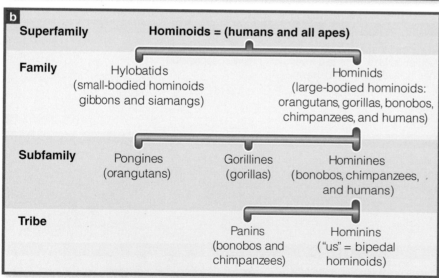

▲ **Figure 10-2**

(a) Traditional classification of hominoids. **(b)** Revised classification of hominoids. Note that two additional levels of classification are added (subfamily and tribe) to show more precisely and more accurately the evolutionary relationships among the apes and humans. In this classification, "hominin" is synonymous with the use of "hominid" in part **(a)**.

We know that the earliest hominins almost certainly didn't regularly manufacture stone tools (at least, none that have been found and identified as such). These earliest members of the hominin lineage, dating back to approximately 7–5 mya, may have carried objects such as naturally sharp stones or stone flakes, parts of carcasses, and pieces of wood around their home ranges. At the very least, we would expect them to have displayed these behaviors to at least the same degree as that exhibited in living chimpanzees.

Also, as you'll see in the next chapter, by 6 mya—and perhaps as early as 7 mya—hominins had developed one crucial advantage: They were bipedal and so could more easily carry all kinds of objects from place to place. Ultimately, the efficient exploitation of resources widely distributed in time and space would most likely have led to using "central" spots where key components—especially stone objects—were cached, or collected (Potts, 1991; see "A Closer Look").

What we know for sure is that over a period of several million years, during the formative stages of hominin emergence, many components interacted, but not all of them developed simultaneously. As cognitive abilities developed, more efficient means of communication and learning resulted. Largely because of consequent neurological reorganization, more elaborate tools and social relationships also emerged. These, in turn, selected for greater intelligence, which in turn selected for further neural elaboration. Quite clearly, these mutual dynamic interactions are at the very heart of what we call hominin *biocultural* evolution.

The Strategy of Paleoanthropology

To adequately understand human evolution, we obviously need a broad base of information. It's the paleoanthropologist's task to recover and interpret all the clues left by early hominins. *Paleoanthropology* is defined as "the study of ancient humans." As such, it's a diverse **multidisciplinary** pursuit seeking to reconstruct every possible bit of information concerning the dating, anatomy, behavior, and ecology of our hominin ancestors. In the past few decades, the study of early humans has marshaled the specialized skills of many different kinds of scientists. This growing and exciting adventure includes, but is not limited to, geologists, vertebrate paleontologists, archaeologists, physical anthropologists, and paleoecologists (**Table 10-1**).

TABLE 10.1 Subdisciplines of Paleoanthropology

Physical Sciences	Biological Sciences	Social Sciences
Geology	Physical anthropology	Archaeology
Stratigraphy	Paleoecology	Ethnoarchaeology
Petrology	Paleontology	Cultural anthropology
(rocks, minerals)	(fossil animals)	Ethnography
Pedology (soils)	Palynology (fossil pollen)	Psychology
Geomorphology	Primatology	
Geophysics		
Chemistry		
Taphonomy		

multidisciplinary Pertaining to research involving mutual contributions and cooperation of experts from various scientific fields (i.e., disciplines).

A Closer Look

Who Was Doing What at Olduvai and the Other Plio-Pleistocene Sites?

Many years ago, the popular interpretation of the bone refuse and stone tools discovered at Olduvai suggested that most, if not all, of these materials resulted from hominin activities. However, a later and more comprehensive reanalysis of the bone remains from Olduvai localities has challenged this view (Binford, 1981, 1983). Archaeologist Lewis Binford criticizes those drawn too quickly to concluding that these bone scatters are the remnants of hominin behavior patterns while simultaneously ignoring the possibility of other explanations.

From information concerning the kinds of animals present, which body parts were found, and the differences in preservation among these skeletal elements, Binford has concluded that much of what's preserved can be explained by carnivore activity. This conclusion has been reinforced by certain details observed by Binford himself in Alaska—details on animal kills, scavenging, the transportation of elements, and preservation that are the result of wolf and dog behaviors. Binford describes his approach:

I took as "known," then, the structure of bone assemblages produced in various settings by animal predators and scavengers; and as "unknown" the bone deposits excavated by the Leakeys at Olduvai Gorge. Using mathematical and statistical techniques I considered to what degree the finds from Olduvai Gorge could be accounted for in terms of the results of predator behavior and how much was "left over." (Binford, 1983, pp. 56–57)

Binford isn't arguing that all of the remains found at Olduvai resulted from non-hominin activity. In fact, he recognizes that "residual material" was consistently found on surfaces with high tool concentration "which could not be explained by what we know about African animals" (Binford, 1983).

Support for the idea that early hominins utilized at least some of the bone refuse has come from a totally different perspective. Researchers have analyzed (both macroscopically and microscopically) the cut marks left on fossilized bones. By experimenting with modern materials, they've been able to delineate more clearly the differences between marks left by stone tools and those left by animal teeth or other factors (Bunn, 1981; Potts and Shipman, 1981). Analyses of bones from several early localities at Olduvai have shown unambiguously that hominins used these specimens and left telltale cut marks from their stone

tools. The sites investigated so far reveal a somewhat haphazard cutting and chopping, apparently unrelated to deliberate disarticulation. So the conclusion (Shipman, 1983) is that hominins scavenged carcasses, probably of carnivore kills, and did not hunt large animals themselves. As we'll see in a moment, new evidence of likely cut marks as well as indications of pounding to get at the marrow has been found at a site in Ethiopia dating as far back as 3.4 mya.

Following and expanding on the experimental approaches pioneered by Binford, Bunn, and others, Robert Blumenschine, of Rutgers University, has more recently conducted a more detailed analysis of the Olduvai material. Like his predecessors, Blumenschine has also concluded that the cut marks on animal bones are the result of hominin processing (Blumenschine, 1995). Blumenschine and colleagues further surmise that most meat acquisition (virtually all from large animals) was the result of scavenging (from remains of carnivore kills or from animals that died from natural causes). In fact, these researchers suggest that scavenging was a crucial adaptive strategy for early hominins and considerably influenced their habitat usage, diet, and stone tool utilization (Blumenschine and Cavallo, 1992; Blumenschine and Peters, 1998). What's more, Blumenschine and colleagues have developed a model detailing how scavenging and other early hominin adaptive strategies integrate into

Geologists, usually working with other paleoanthropologists, do the initial surveys to locate potential early hominin sites. Many sophisticated techniques aid in this search, including aerial and satellite imagery (**Fig. 10-3**), though the most common way to find these sites is simply to trip over fossil remains. Vertebrate paleontologists are usually involved in this early survey work, helping find fossil beds containing faunal (animal) remains, because where conditions are favorable for the

preservation of bone from such species as pigs and elephants, hominin remains may also be preserved. Paleontologists also can (through comparison with known faunal sequences) give quick and dirty approximate age estimates of fossil sites in the field without having to wait for the results of more time-consuming (though more accurate) analyses that will later be performed in a lab (**Fig. 10-4**)

Once identified, fossil beds likely to contain hominin finds are subjected to

patterns of land use (that is, differential utilization of various niches in and around Olduvai). From this model, they formulated specific hypotheses concerning the predicted distribution of artifacts and animal remains in different areas at Olduvai. Ongoing excavations at Olduvai are now aimed specifically at testing these hypotheses.

If early hominins (close to 2 mya) weren't hunting consistently, what did they obtain from scavenging the kills of other animals? One obvious answer is, whatever meat was left behind. However, the position of the cut marks suggests that early hominins were often hacking at non-meat-bearing portions of the skeletons. Perhaps they were after bone marrow and brain, substances not fully exploited by other predators and scavengers (Binford, 1981; Blumenschine and Cavallo, 1992).

Exciting discoveries from the Bouri Peninsula of the Middle Awash of Ethiopia provide the best evidence yet for meat and marrow exploitation by early hominins. Dated to 2.5 mya (that is, as old as the oldest known artifacts), antelope and horse fossils from Bouri show telltale incisions

© DUILLC / Corbis

▲ **Figure 1**

Hyenas scavenging a buffalo carcass in East Africa. Early hominins also scavenged animals that had been killed by predators. In so doing, they almost certainly competed with hyenas and other scavengers.

and breaks, indicating that bones were not only smashed to extract marrow but also cut, ostensibly to retrieve meat (de Heinzelin et al., 1999). The researchers who analyzed these materials have suggested that the greater dietary reliance on animal products may have been important in stimulating brain enlargement in the lineage leading to genus *Homo*.

Another recent research twist relating to the reconstruction of early hominin diets

has come from biochemical analysis of hominin teeth from South Africa (dating to about the same time range as hominins from Olduvai—or perhaps slightly earlier). In an innovative application of stable carbon isotope analysis, Matt Sponheimer and Julia Lee-Thorp found that these early hominin teeth revealed telltale chemical signatures relating to diet (Sponheimer and Lee-Thorp, 1999). In particular, the proportions of stable carbon isotopes indicated that these early hominins either ate grass products (such as seeds) or ate meat/marrow from animals that in turn had eaten grass products (that is, the hominins might well have derived a significant portion of their diet from meat or other animal products). This evidence comes from an exciting new perspective that provides a more direct indicator of early hominin diets. While it's not clear how much meat these early hominins consumed, these new data do suggest that they were consistently exploiting more open regions of their environment. Moreover, a new laser technology makes it possible to detect, from a single tooth, what sorts of foods were eaten from year to year and even seasonally within the same year. Sponheimer, Thorp, and colleagues have used this new approach to show that some early hominins were able to flexibly move between different environments and exploit seasonally available foods (Sponheimer et al., 2006).

extensive field surveying. For some sites, generally those postdating 2.6 mya (roughly the age of the oldest identified human artifacts), archaeologists take over in the search for hominin material traces. We don't necessarily have to find remains of early hominins themselves to know that they consistently occupied a particular area. Such material clues as **artifacts** inform us directly about early hominin activities. Modifying rocks according to a consistent plan or simply carrying

them around from one place to another over fairly long distances (to be later discovered by archaeologists distributed in a manner not explicable by natural means, like streams or glaciers) is characteristic of no other animal but a hominin. So, when we see such material evidence at a site, we know without a doubt that hominins were present.

Because organic materials such as wood or fiber aren't usually preserved in the archaeological record of the oldest hominins, we have no solid

artifacts Objects or materials made or modified for use by hominins. The earliest artifacts are usually tools made of stone or, occasionally, bone.

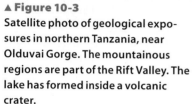

▲ Figure 10-3
Satellite photo of geological exposures in northern Tanzania, near Olduvai Gorge. The mountainous regions are part of the Rift Valley. The lake has formed inside a volcanic crater.

Goddard Space Flight Center, NASA

Institute of Human Origins, photo by Nanci Kahn

▲ Figure 10-4
A geologist is shown making entries on a detailed map as he surveys a large area of exposures in the Hadar region of northeastern Ethiopia.

evidence of the earliest stages of hominin cultural modifications. On the other hand, our ancestors at some point around 2.6 mya started showing a veritable fascination with stones, partly because they could be used as convenient objects for throwing or for holding down other objects, such as skins and windbreaks. Even more crucially, they also provided the most durable and sharpest cutting edges available at that time. Luckily for us, stone is almost indestructible, and some early hominin sites are strewn with thousands of stone artifacts. The earliest sites that have consistently made artifacts are from the Gona and Bouri areas in northeastern Ethiopia, dating to 2.6 mya (de Heinzelin et al., 1999; Semaw et al., 2003). Other contenders for the "earliest" stone assemblage come from the adjacent Hadar and Middle Awash areas, immediately to the south in Ethiopia, dated 2.5–2.0 mya.

We've suspected for awhile that hominins likely used stone and other materials for a long time prior to when they began modifying rock to a consistent (and recognizable) pattern. After all, chimpanzees carry rocks short distances and bash nuts with them (see Chapter 8). New evidence from Ethiopia now strongly indicates hominins were using stone in an even more

sophisticated way as far back as 3.4 mya (McPherron et al., 2010). No stone tools were found, but two animal bones show distinctive cut marks (see "A Closer Look," pp. 288–289), as well as other marks, suggesting the bones were pounded with unmodified rocks (ostensibly to slice away meat and to retrieve marrow). While it's true that this evidence doesn't mean hominins were yet modifying rocks consistently to make tools, it does show advanced behavior, including scavenging, meat eating, and marrow extraction that have not previously been considered possible for very early hominins. These finds are extremely important and have been very carefully investigated. However, just the two bones by themselves (and no stone tools) are not enough evidence for many paleoanthropologists to be entirely convinced that meat eating and marrow eating were yet typical behaviors of such ancient hominins.

If an area is clearly demonstrated to be a hominin site, much more concentrated research will then begin. We should point out that a more mundane but significant aspect of paleoanthropology not reflected in Table 10-1 is the financial one. Just the initial survey work in usually remote areas costs many thousands of dollars, and mounting a concentrated research project costs several hundred thousand dollars more. This is why many projects are undertaken in areas where promising surface finds have been made; massive financial support is required from government agencies and private donations, and it's unrealistic to simply dig at random. A great deal of a paleoanthropologist's effort and time is necessarily devoted to writing grant proposals or speaking on the lecture circuit to raise the required funds for this work.

Once the financial hurdle has been cleared, a coordinated research project can begin. Usually headed by an archaeologist or physical anthropologist, the field crew continues to survey and map the target area in great detail. In addition, field crew members begin searching carefully for bones and artifacts eroding out of the soil, taking pollen and soil samples for ecological analysis, and carefully collecting rock and other samples for use in various dating techniques. If, in this early stage of exploration, members of the field crew find fossil hominin remains, they will feel very lucky indeed. The international press usually considers human fossils the most exciting kind of discovery, a fortunate circumstance that produces wide publicity and often ensures future financial support. More likely, the crew will accumulate much information on geological setting, ecological data (particularly faunal remains), and, with some luck, artifacts and other archaeological traces.

Although paleoanthropological fieldwork is typically a long and arduous process, the detailed analyses of collected samples and other data back in the laboratory are even more time-consuming. Archaeologists must clean, sort, label, and identify all artifacts, and vertebrate paleontologists must do the same for all faunal remains. Knowing the kinds of animals represented—whether forest browsers, woodland species, or open-country forms—greatly helps in reconstructing the local *paleoecological* settings in which early hominins lived. Analyzing

the fossil pollen collected from hominin sites by a scientist called a palynologist further aids in developing a detailed environmental reconstruction. All these paleoecological analyses can assist in reconstructing the diet of early humans. Also, the **taphonomy** of the site must be worked out to understand its depositional history—that is, how the site formed over time and if its present state is in a *primary* or *secondary* **context**.

In the concluding stages of interpretation, the paleoanthropologist draws together these essentials:

1. *Dating*: geological, paleontological, geophysical
2. *Paleoecology*: paleontology, palynology, geomorphology, taphonomy
3. *Archaeological traces of behavior*
4. *Anatomical evidence from hominin remains*

By analyzing all this information, scientists try to "flesh out" the kind of creature that may have been our direct ancestor (or at least a very close relative). Primatologists may assist here by showing the detailed relationships between the anatomical structure and behavior of humans and that of contemporary nonhuman primates. Cultural anthropologists and ethnoarchaeologists (who study the "archaeology" of living groups by examining their material remains) may contribute ethnographic information concerning the varied nature of modern human behavior, particularly ecological adaptations of those contemporary hunter-gatherer groups exploiting roughly similar environmental settings as those reconstructed for a hominin site.

The end result of years of research by dozens of scientists will (we hope) produce a more complete and accurate understanding of human evolution—how we came to be the way we are. Both biological and cultural aspects of our ancestors contribute to this investigation, each process developing in relation to the other.

taphonomy (*taphos*, meaning "tomb") The study of how bones and other materials came to be buried in the earth and preserved as fossils. Taphonomists study the processes of sedimentation, the action of streams, preservation properties of bone, and carnivore disturbance factors.

context The environmental setting where an archaeological trace is found. Primary context is the setting in which the archaeological trace was originally deposited. A secondary context is one to which it has been moved (such as by the action of a stream).

Paleoanthropology in Action— Olduvai Gorge

Several paleoanthropological projects of the scope just discussed have recently been pursued in diverse places in the Old World, including East and South Africa, Indonesia, and the Republic of Georgia in eastern Europe. Of all these localities, the one that has yielded the finest quality and greatest abundance of paleoanthropological information concerning early hominin behavior has been Olduvai Gorge.

First "discovered" in the early twentieth century by a German butterfly collector, Olduvai was soon scientifically surveyed and its wealth of paleontological evidence recognized. In 1931, Louis Leakey made his first trip to Olduvai Gorge and almost immediately realized its significance for studying early humans. From 1935, when she first worked there, until she retired in 1984, Mary Leakey directed the archaeological excavations at Olduvai.

Located in the Serengeti Plain of northern Tanzania, Olduvai is a steep-sided valley resembling a miniature version of the Grand Canyon. A deep ravine cut into an almost mile-high grassland plateau of East Africa, Olduvai extends more than 25 miles in total length. Climatically, the semi-arid pattern of present-day Olduvai is believed to be similar to what it has been for the last 2 million years. The surrounding countryside is a grassland savanna broken occasionally by scrub bushes and acacia trees.

Geographically, Olduvai is located on the eastern branch of the Great Rift Valley of Africa. The geological processes associated with the formation of the Rift Valley make Olduvai (and other East African sites) extremely important to paleoanthropological investigation. Three of these processes of geological rifting are most significant:

1. Faulting, or earth movement, exposes geological beds near the surface that are normally hidden by hundreds of feet of accumulated sediment called overburden.
2. Active volcanic processes cause rapid sedimentation, which often yields excellent preservation of bone and artifacts that normally would be scattered by carnivore activity and erosion forces.

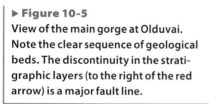

▶ **Figure 10-5**
View of the main gorge at Olduvai. Note the clear sequence of geological beds. The discontinuity in the stratigraphic layers (to the right of the red arrow) is a major fault line.

Robert Jurmain

3. Volcanic activity provides a wealth of radiometrically datable material.

As a result, Olduvai is a site of superb preservation of ancient hominins, portions of their environment, and their behavioral patterns in datable contexts, all of which are readily accessible.

The greatest contribution Olduvai has made to paleoanthropological research is the establishment of an extremely well-documented and correlated sequence of geological, paleontological, archaeological, and hominin remains over the last 2 million years. At the very foundation of all paleoanthropological research is a well-established geological context. At Olduvai, the geological and paleogeographical context is known in minute detail. Today, Olduvai is a geologist's delight, containing sediments in some places 350 feet thick, accumulated from lava flows (basalts), tuffs (windblown or waterborne fine deposits from nearby volcanoes), sandstones, claystones, and limestone conglomerates, all neatly stratified like a layer cake (**Fig. 10-5**). A hominin site can therefore be accurately dated relative to other sites in the Olduvai Gorge by cross-correlating with known marker beds that have already been dated and can be quite quickly identified by geologists in the field. At the most general geological level, the stratigraphic sequence at Olduvai is broken down into four major geological strata called beds (Beds I–IV).

Paleontological evidence of fossilized animal bones also has come from Olduvai in great abundance. More than 150 species of extinct animals have been recognized, including fishes, turtles, crocodiles, pigs, giraffes, horses, and many birds, rodents, and antelopes. Careful analysis of such remains has yielded voluminous information concerning the ecological conditions of early human habitats. What's more, the precise analysis of bones directly associated with artifacts can sometimes tell us about the early hominin diet as well

as the various ways bone was handled and modified by early hominins. (There are some reservations, however; see "A Closer Look.")

The archaeological sequence is also well documented for the last 2 million years. Beginning at the earliest hominin site in Olduvai (circa 1.85 mya), there is already a well-developed stone tool kit, consisting primarily of numerous small flake tools (Leakey, 1971). Such a tool industry is called *Oldowan* (after Olduvai), and it continues into later beds with some small modifications.

Finally, partial remains of several fossilized hominins have been found at Olduvai, ranging in time from the earliest occupation levels to fairly recent *Homo sapiens*. Of the more than 40 individuals represented, many are quite fragmentary, but a few are excellently preserved. While the center of hominin discoveries has now shifted to other areas of East Africa, it was the initial discovery by Mary Leakey of the *Zinjanthropus* (nicknamed "Zinj") skull at Olduvai in July 1959 that focused the world's attention on this remarkably rich area (**Fig. 10-6**).

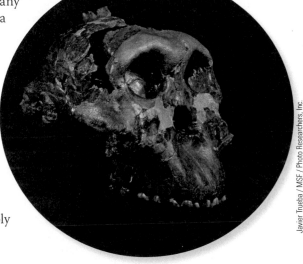

Javier Trueba / MSF / Photo Researchers, Inc.

▼ **Figure 10-6**
Zinjanthropus cranium, discovered by Mary Leakey at Olduvai Gorge in 1959. As we will see in Chapter 11, this fossil is now included as part of the genus *Paranthropus*.

Dating Methods

An essential objective of paleoanthropology is to place sites and fossils into a time frame. In other words, we want to know how old they are. How, then, do we date sites—or more precisely, the geological strata, or layers, in which sites are found? The question is both reasonable and important, so let's examine the dating techniques used by paleontologists, archaeologists, and other scientists involved in paleoanthropological research.

Scientists use two kinds of dating for this purpose: relative dating and

chronometric dating (also known as *absolute dating*). Relative dating methods tell us that something is older or younger than something else, but not by how much. If, for example, a cranium is found at a depth of 50 feet and another cranium at 70 feet at the same site, we usually assume that the specimen discovered at 70 feet is older. We may not know the date (in years) of either one, but we'd know that one is older (or younger) than the other. Although this may not satisfy our curiosity about the actual number of years involved, it would give some idea of the evolutionary changes in cranial morphology (structure), especially if we found several crania at different levels and compared them.

This method of relative dating is based on **stratigraphy** and was one of the first techniques to be used by scientists working with the vast period of geological time. Stratigraphy, in turn, is based on the **principle of superposition**, which states that a lower stratum (layer) is older than a higher stratum. Because much of the earth's crust has been laid down by layer after layer of sedimentary rock, much like the layers of a cake, stratigraphy has been a valuable aid in reconstructing the history of the earth and the life upon it.

Stratigraphic dating does, however, have some problems. Earth disturbances, such as volcanic activity, river activity, and mountain building, may shift strata and the objects within them, and the chronology of the material may be difficult or even impossible to reconstruct. What's more, it's impossible to accurately determine the time period of a particular stratum—that is, how long it took to accumulate.

Another method of relative dating is *fluorine analysis*, which applies only to bones (Oakley, 1963). Bones in the earth are exposed to the seepage of groundwater that usually contains fluorine. The longer a bone lies in the earth, the more fluorine it will incorporate during the fossilization process. Bones deposited at the same time in the same location thus should contain the same amount of fluorine. Professor Kenneth Oakley, of the British Museum, used this technique in the early 1950s to expose the Piltdown (England) hoax by demonstrating that a human skull was considerably older than the jaw (ostensibly also human) found with it (Weiner, 1955). When a discrepancy in fluorine content led Oakley and others to more closely examine the bones, they found that the jaw was not that of a hominin at all but of a young adult orangutan!

Unfortunately, fluorine analysis is useful only with bones found at the same location. Because the amount of fluorine in groundwater is based on local conditions, it varies from place to place. Also, some groundwater may not contain any fluorine. For these reasons, it's impossible to use fluorine analysis when comparing bones from different localities.

In both stratigraphy and fluorine analysis, it's impossible to calculate the actual age of the rock stratum and the objects in it. To determine the age in years, scientists have developed various chronometric techniques based on the phenomenon of radioactive decay. Actually, the theory is pretty simple: Certain radioactive isotopes of elements are unstable, causing them to decay and form an isotopic variation of another element. Since the rate of decay follows a definite mathematical pattern, the radioactive material forms an accurate geological time clock of sorts. By measuring the amount of decay in a particular sample, scientists can calculate the number of years it took for that amount of decay to accumulate. Chronometric techniques have been used for dating the immense age of the earth as well as artifacts less than 1,000 years old. Several techniques have been employed for a number of years and are now quite well known.

The most important chronometric technique used to date early hominins involves potassium-40 (^{40}K), which has

---

chronometric dating (*chrono*, meaning "time," and *metric*, meaning "measure") A dating technique that gives an estimate in actual numbers of years; also known as absolute dating.

stratigraphy Study of the sequential layering of deposits.

principle of superposition In a stratigraphic sequence, the lower layers were deposited before the upper layers. Or, simply put, the stuff on top of a heap was put there last.

a **half-life** of 1.25 billion years and produces argon-40 (^{40}Ar). Known as the K/Ar or potassium-argon method, this procedure has been extensively used by paleoanthropologists in dating materials in the 1- to 5-million-year range, especially in East Africa, where past volcanic activity makes this dating technique possible. A variant of this technique, the ^{40}Ar/^{39}Ar method, also has been used to date several hominin localities. The ^{40}Ar/^{39}Ar method allows analysis of smaller samples (even single crystals), reduces experimental error, and is more precise than standard K/Ar dating. Consequently, it can be used to date a wide chronological range—indeed, the entire hominin record, even up to modern times. Recent applications have provided excellent dates for several early hominin sites in East Africa (discussed in Chapter 11) as well as somewhat later sites in Java (discussed in Chapter 12). In fact, the technique was used to date the famous Mt. Vesuvius eruption of A.D. 79, which destroyed the city of Pompeii as documented by ancient historians. Remarkably, the midrange date obtained by the ^{40}Ar/^{39}Ar technique was A.D. 73, just six years from the known date (Renne et al., 1997)! And still another radiometric dating method, this one measuring the decay of uranium into lead (the U/Pb method, with a half-life of 4.47 million years), has been used recently in South Africa to date hominin sites (De Ruiter et al., 2009; Dirks et al., 2010). Organic material, such as bone, can't be measured by these techniques; but the rock matrix in which the bone is found can be. Scientists used K/Ar dating to obtain a minimum date for the deposit containing the *Zinjanthropus* cranium by dating a volcanic layer above the fossil.

Rocks that provide the best samples for K/Ar and ^{40}Ar/^{39}Ar are those heated to an extremely high temperature, such as that generated by volcanic activity. When the rock is in a molten state, argon, a gas, is driven off. As the rock cools and solidifies, potassium-40 con-

tinues to break down to argon; but now the gas is physically trapped in the cooled rock. To obtain the date of the rock, scientists reheat it and measure the escaping gas. Because the rock must in the past have been exposed to extreme heat, this limits these techniques to areas where sediments have been superheated, such as regions of past volcanic activity or meteorite falls.

A well-known radiometric method popular with archaeologists makes use of carbon-14 (^{14}C), with a half-life of 5,730 years. Carbon-14 has been used to date organic materials (such as wood, bone, cloth, and plant remains) from less than 1,000 years to as old as 75,000 years, although accuracy is reduced for materials more than 40,000 years old. Since this technique applies to the latter stages of hominin evolution, its applications relate to material discussed in Chapters 13 and 14.

Some inorganic artifacts can be directly dated through the use of **thermoluminescence (TL)**. This method, too, relies on the principle of radiometric decay. Stone material used in manufacturing tools invariably contains trace amounts of radioactive elements, such as uranium or thorium. As the rock gets heated (perhaps by accidentally falling into a campfire or by deliberately being heated to help in its production), the rapid heating releases displaced beta particles trapped within the rock. As the particles escape, they emit a dull glow known as thermoluminescence. After that, radioactive decay resumes within the fired stone, again building up electrons at a steady rate. To determine the age of an archaeological sample, the researcher must heat the sample to 500°C and measure its thermoluminescence; from that, the date can be calculated. Used especially by archaeologists to date ceramic pots from recent sites, TL can also be used to date burned flint tools from earlier hominin sites.

Like TL, two other techniques used to date sites from the latter phases of

half-life The time period in which one-half the amount of a radioactive isotope is converted chemically to a daughter product. For example, after 1.25 billion years, half the 40K remains; after 2.5 billion years, one-fourth remains.

thermoluminescence (TL) (ther-mo-loo-min-ess´-ence) Technique for dating certain archaeological materials (such as stone tools) that were heated in the past and that release stored energy of radioactive decay as light upon reheating.

A Closer Look

Chronometric Dating Estimates

Chronometric dates are usually determined after testing several geological samples. The dates that result from such testing are combined and expressed statistically. For example, say that five different samples are used to give the K/Ar date 1.75 ± 0.2 mya for a particular geological bed. The individual results from all five samples are totaled together to give an average date (here, 1.75 mya), and the standard deviation is calculated (here, 0.2 million years; that is, 200,000 years). The dating estimate is then reported as the mean plus or minus (±) one standard deviation. Those of you who have taken statistics will realize that (assuming a normal distribution) 67 percent of a distribution of dates is included within 1 standard deviation (±) of the mean. Thus, the chronometric result, as shown in the reported range, is simply a probability statement that 67 percent of the dates from all the samples tested fell within the range of dates from 1.55 to 1.95 mya. You should carefully read chronometric dates and study the reported ranges. It's likely that the smaller the range, the more samples were analyzed. Smaller ranges mean more precise estimates; better laboratory controls will also increase precision.

hominin evolution (where neither K/Ar nor radiocarbon dating is possible) are uranium series dating and electron spin resonance (ESR) dating. Uranium series dating relies on radioactive decay of short-lived uranium isotopes, and ESR is similar to TL because it's based on measuring trapped electrons. However, while TL is used on heated materials such as clay or stone tools, ESR is used on the dental enamel of animals. All three of these dating methods have been used to provide key dating controls for hominin sites discussed in Chapters 12 through 14.

You should realize that none of these methods is precise. Each one has problems that must be carefully considered during laboratory measurement and when collecting material to be analyzed. Because the methods aren't perfectly accurate, approximate dates are given as probability statements with an error range. For example, a date given as 1.75 ± 0.2 mya should be read as having a 67 percent chance that the actual date lies somewhere between 1.55 and 1.95 mya (see "A Closer Look," above).

To sum up, there are two ways of answering the question of age. We can say that a particular fossil is x number of years old, a date usually determined by chronometric dating. Or we can say that fossil X lived before or after fossil Y, as determined by relative dating.

Applications of Dating Methods: Examples from Olduvai

Olduvai has been a rich proving ground for numerous dating techniques. As a result, it has some of the best-documented chronology for any hominin site in the Early or Middle Pleistocene.

As we've noted, the potassium-argon (K/Ar) method is an extremely valuable tool for dating early hominin sites and has been widely used in areas containing suitable volcanic deposits (mainly in East Africa) or superheated debris from meteorites (mainly in Indonesia). At Olduvai, K/Ar has given several reliable dates of the underlying basalt and several tuffs in Bed I, including the one associated with the "Zinj" find (now dated at 1.79 ± 0.03 mya).

Due to several potential sources of error, K/Ar dating must be cross-checked using other independent methods. Once again, the sediments at Olduvai provide some excellent examples of the use of many of these other dating techniques.

An important means of cross-checking dates is called **paleomagnetism**. This technique is based on the constantly shifting nature of the earth's magnetic pole. Of course, the earth's magnetic pole is now oriented in a northerly direction, but this hasn't always been so. In fact, the orientation and intensity of the geomagnetic field have undergone numerous documented changes in the last few million years. From our current viewpoint, we call a northern orientation "normal" and a southern one "reversed." Here are the major epochs (also called "chrons") of recent geomagnetic time for the last few million years:

0.7 mya–present	Normal
2.6–0.7 mya	Reversed
3.4–2.6 mya	Normal
?–3.4 mya	Reversed

Paleomagnetic dating is accomplished by carefully taking samples of sediments that contain magnetically charged particles. Since these particles maintain the magnetic orientation they had when they were consolidated into rock (millions of years ago), we have a kind of "fossil compass" (**Fig. 10-7**). Then the paleomagnetic sequence is compared against the K/Ar dates to see if they agree. Some complications may arise, for during an epoch, a relatively long period of time can occur when the geomagnetic orientation is the opposite of what's expected. For example, during the reversed epoch from 2.6 to 0.7 mya (the Matuyama epoch), there was an event lasting about 210,000 years when orientations were normal. (Because this phenomenon was first conclusively demonstrated at Olduvai, it's appropriately called the *Olduvai* event.) But once these oscillations in the geomagnetic pole are worked out, the sequence of paleomagnetic orientations can provide a valuable cross-check for K/Ar age determinations. Paleomagnetic dating has also been used recently in South Africa to confirm the U/Pb dates

◀ **Figure 10-7**
A geologist carefully takes a sample of sediment containing magnetically charged particles for paleomagnetic dating. He must very precisely record the exact compass orientation so that it can be correlated with the sequence of magnetic orientations.

from a newly discovered hominin site (Dirks et al., 2010).

A final dating technique used at Olduvai and other African sites is based on the regular evolutionary changes in well-known groups of mammals. This technique, called *faunal correlation* or **biostratigraphy**, provides yet another means of cross-checking the other methods. This technique employs some of the same methods used in relative stratigraphic dating, but it incorporates information on sequences of faunal remains from different sites. For instance, the presence of particular fossil pigs, elephants, antelopes, rodents, and carnivores in areas where dates are known (by K/Ar, for example) can be used to extrapolate an approximate age for other, more hard-to-date sites by noting which genera and species are present at those sites.

All these methods—K/Ar dating, paleomagnetism, and biostratigraphy—have been used in dating sites at Olduvai. So many different dating techniques are necessary because no single method is perfectly reliable by itself. Sampling error, contamination, and experimental error can all introduce ambiguities into our so-called

paleomagnetism Dating method based on the earth's shifting magnetic pole.

biostratigraphy A relative dating technique based on the regular changes seen in evolving groups of animals as well as the presence or absence of particular species.

absolute dates. Because the sources of error are different for each technique, however, cross-checking among several independent methods is the most reliable way of authenticating the chronology for early hominin sites.

Excavations at Olduvai

Because the vertical cut of the Olduvai Gorge provides a cross section of 2 million years of earth history, sites can be excavated by digging "straight in" rather than first having to remove tons of overlying dirt (**Fig. 10-8**). In fact, as mentioned before, sites are usually discovered by merely walking the exposures and observing what bones, stones, and so forth, are eroding out.

Several dozen hominin sites (at a minimum, they are bone and tool scatters) have been surveyed at Olduvai, and Mary Leakey extensively excavated close to 20 of these. An incredible amount of paleoanthropological information has come from these excavated areas.

There has been much controversy regarding how to interpret the types of activities early hominins carried out at these sites (**Fig. 10-9**). Archaeologists had thought, as suggested by Mary

Leakey and others, that many of the sites functioned as "campsites." Lewis Binford has forcefully critiqued this view and has alternatively suggested that much of the refuse accumulated is the result of nonhominin (that is, predator) activities. Another possibility, suggested by Richard Potts (1984), is that these areas served as collecting points (caches) for some tools. This last interpretation has received considerable support from other archaeologists in recent years.

A final interpretation, incorporating aspects of the hypotheses proposed by Binford and Potts, has been suggested by Robert Blumenschine. He argues that early hominins were gatherers and scavengers, and the bone and stone scatters reflect these activities (Blumenschine, 1986; Blumenschine and Cavallo, 1992).

Experimental Archaeology

Simply classifying artifacts into categories and types is not enough. We can learn considerably more about our ancestors by understanding how they made and used their tools. It is, after all, the artifactual traces of prehistoric tools of stone (and, to a lesser degree,

▶ **Figure 10-8**
Excavations in progress at Olduvai. This site, more than 1 million years old, was located when a hominin ulna (arm bone) was found eroding out of the side of the gorge.

◄ **Figure 10-9**
A dense scatter of stone and some fossilized animal bone from a site at Olduvai, dated at approximately 1.6 mya. Some of these remains are the result of hominin activities.

bone) that provide much of our information concerning early human behavior. Tons of stone debris litter archaeological sites worldwide. A casual walk along the bottom of Olduvai Gorge could well be interrupted every few seconds by tripping over prehistoric tools!

So, archaeologists are presented with a wealth of information revealing at least one part of human material culture. What do these artifacts tell us about our ancestors? How were these tools made, and how were they used? To answer these questions, contemporary archaeologists have tried to reconstruct prehistoric techniques of stone toolmaking, butchering, and so forth. In this way, experimental archaeologists are, in a sense, trying to re-create the past.

Stone Tool (Lithic) Technology

Stone is by far the most common residue of prehistoric cultural behavior. For this reason, archaeologists have long been keenly interested in this material.

When struck properly, certain types of stone will fracture in a con-trolled way; these nodules are called **blanks**. The smaller piece that comes off is called a **flake**, while the larger remaining chunk is called a **core** (**Fig. 10-10**). Both core and flake have sharp edges useful for cutting, sawing, or scraping. The earliest hominin cultural inventions probably used nondurable materials that didn't survive archaeologically (such as a digging stick or an ostrich eggshell used as a watertight container). Still, a basic human invention was the recognition that stone can be fractured to produce sharp edges.

For many years, it's been assumed that in the earliest known stone tool industry (that is, the Oldowan), both core and flake tools were deliberately manufactured as final, desired products. Such core implements as "choppers" were thought to be central artifactual components of these early **lithic** assemblages (in fact, the Oldowan is often depicted as a "chopping tool industry"). However, detailed reevaluation of these artifacts has thrown these traditional assumptions into doubt. By carefully analyzing the attributes of Oldowan artifacts from Olduvai, Potts (1991, 1993) concluded that the so-called core tools really weren't tools after all. He suggests instead that early

flake   core

▲ **Figure 10-10**
Flake and core.

blanks In archaeology, stones suitably sized and shaped to be further worked into tools.

flake Thin-edged fragment removed from a core.

core Stone reduced by flake removal. A core may or may not itself be used as a tool.

lithic (*lith*, meaning "stone") Referring to stone tools.

hominins were deliberately producing flake tools, and the various stone choppers were simply "incidental stopping points in the process of removing flakes from cores" (Potts, 1993, p. 60). As Potts concludes, "The flaked stones of the Oldowan thus cannot be demonstrated to constitute discrete target designs, but can be shown to represent simple by-products of the repetitive act of producing sharp flakes" (Potts, 1993, pp. 60–61).

Breaking rocks by bashing them together is one thing. Producing consistent results, even apparently simple flakes, is quite another. You might want to give it a try, just to appreciate how difficult making a stone tool can be. It takes years of practice before modern stone **knappers** learn the intricacies—the type of rock to choose, the kind of hammer to employ, the angle and velocity with which to strike, and so on. Such experience allows us to appreciate how skilled in stoneworking our ancestors truly were.

Flakes can be removed from cores in various ways. The object in making a tool, however, is to produce a usable cutting surface. By reproducing results similar to those of earlier stoneworkers, experimental archaeologists can infer which kinds of techniques *might* have been employed.

For example, the nodules (now thought to be blanks) found in sites in Bed I at Olduvai (circa 1.85–1.2 mya) are flaked on one side only (that is, *unifacially*). It's possible, but by no means easy, to produce such implements by hitting one stone—the hammerstone—against another—the core—in a method called **direct percussion** (Fig. 10-11).

In Bed IV sites (circa 400,000 ya*), however, most of the tools are flaked on both sides (that is, *bifacially*) and have long rippled edges. Such a result can't be reproduced by direct percussion with just a hammerstone. The edges must have been straightened

_____
*ya = years ago.

("retouched") with a "soft" hammer, such as bone or antler.

Reproducing implements similar to those found in later stages of human cultural development calls for even more sophisticated techniques. Tools such as the delicate **microliths** found in the uppermost beds at Olduvai (circa 17,000 ya), the superb Solutrean blades from Europe (circa 20,000 ya), and the expertly crafted Folsom projectile points from the New World (circa 10,000 ya) all require a mastery of stone matched by few knappers today.

To reproduce implements like those just mentioned, the knapper must remove extremely thin flakes. This can be done only through **pressure flaking**—for example, using a pointed piece of bone, antler, or hard wood and pressing firmly against the stone (**Fig. 10-12**).

Once the tools were manufactured, our ancestors used them in ways that we can infer through further experimentation. For example, archaeologists from the Smithsonian Institution successfully butchered an entire elephant (which had died in a zoo) using stone tools they had made for that purpose (Park, 1978). Other archaeologists have cut down (small) trees using stone axes they had made.

Ancient tools themselves may carry telltale signs of how they were used. Lawrence Keeley performed a series of experiments in which he manufactured flint tools and then used them in diverse ways—whittling wood, cutting bone, cutting meat, and scraping skins. Viewing these implements under a microscope at fairly high magnification revealed patterns of polishes, striations, and other kinds of **microwear**. What's most intriguing is that these patterns varied, depending on how the tool was used and which material was worked. For example, Keeley was able to distinguish among tools used on bone, antler, meat, plant materials, and hides. In the latter case, he was even able to determine if the hides were fresh or dried! Orientations of microwear

▲ **Figure 10-11**
Direct percussion.

▲ **Figure 10-12**
Pressure flaking.

knappers People (frequently archaeologists) who make stone tools.

direct percussion Striking a core or flake with a hammerstone.

microliths (*micro*, meaning "small," and *lith*, meaning "stone") Small stone tools usually produced from narrow blades punched from a core; found especially in Africa during the latter part of the Pleistocene.

pressure flaking A method of removing flakes from a core by pressing a pointed implement (e.g., bone or antler) against the stone.

microwear Polishes, striations, and other diagnostic microscopic changes on the edges of stone tools.

markings also give some indication of how the tool was used (such as for cutting or scraping). Because these experiments into stone tool manufacture and use reveal valuable information about variations in microwear morphology, researchers are able to use the experimentally produced data to infer about specific stone tool usage in the past—such as for the 9,000-year-old Paleo-Indian flake from Nebraska shown in **Figure 10-13**, which shows microwear polish from cutting antler or bone. Evidence of microwear polish has been examined on even the extremely early hominin stone tools from Koobi Fora (East Lake Turkana), in Kenya (Keeley and Toth, 1981).

Recent advances in tool use studies include the application of scanning electron microscopy (SEM). Working at 10,000× magnification, researchers have found that the edges of stone implements sometimes retain plant fibers and amino acids, as well as nonorganic residues, including **phytoliths**. Because phytoliths produced by different plant species are distinctive, there is good potential for identifying the botanical materials that came in contact with the tool during its use (Rovner, 1983). Such work is most exciting; for the first time, we may be able to make definite statements concerning the uses of ancient tools.

Analysis of Bone

Experimental archaeologists are also interested in the ways bone is altered by human and natural forces. Other scientists are vitally concerned with this process as well; in fact, it has produced an entire new branch of paleoecology—taphonomy. Taphonomists have carried out comprehensive research on how natural factors influence bone deposition and preservation. In South Africa, C. K. Brain collected data on contemporary African butchering practices, carnivore (dog) disturbances, and so forth, and then correlated these factors with the kinds and

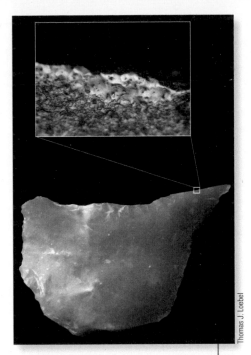

Thomas J. Loebel

▲ **Figure 10-13**
Photomicrograph (200×) showing polish resulting from bone modification on a 9,000-year-old stone tool excavated from the O. V. Clary site in Nebraska by Dr. M.G. Hill, of Iowa State University.

numbers of elements usually found in bone accumulations (Brain, 1981). In this way, he was able to account for the accumulation of most (if not all) of the bones in South African cave sites. Likewise, in East African game parks, observations have been made on decaying animals to measure the effects of weathering, predator chewing, and trampling (Behrensmeyer et al., 1979; Perkins, 2003).

Further insight into the many ways bone is altered by natural factors has come from experimental work in the laboratory (Boaz and Behrensmeyer, 1976). In an experiment conducted at the University of California, Berkeley, human bones were put into a running-water trough. Researchers observed how far the water carried different pieces and recorded how much and what kind of damage was done. Such information is extremely useful in interpreting early hominin sites. For example, the distribution of

phytoliths (*phyto*, meaning "hidden," and *lith*, meaning "stone") Microscopic silica structures formed in the cells of many plants, particularly grasses.

hominin fossils at Olduvai suggests that active water transport was less prevalent there than in the Omo River Valley in southern Ethiopia.

Detailed examination of bones may also provide evidence of butchering and bone breakage by hominins, including cut marks and percussion marks left by stone tools. Great care must be taken to distinguish marks left on bone by carnivore or rodent gnawing, weathering processes, hoof marks, or even normal growth. High magnification of a cut made by a stone tool may reveal a minutely striated and roughened groove scored into the bone's surface. Many such finds have been recognized at early hominin sites, including Olduvai Gorge (Bunn, 1981; Potts and Shipman, 1981; see "A Closer Look," earlier in this chapter).

Reconstruction of Early Hominin Environments and Behavior

Now that we've reviewed the various methods used by paleoanthropologists to collect their varied data, we can look at the intriguing ways this information is *interpreted*. Be aware that much of this interpretation is quite speculative and less amenable to scientific verification than more concrete sources of data (for example, that relating to dating, geology, or hominin anatomy). (In Chapter 1, we discussed how hypotheses are developed and tested by scientists, noting the requirement that *scientific* explanations be falsifiable.)

Paleoanthropologists are keenly interested not just in *how* early hominins evolved but also in *why* the process occurred the way it did. Accordingly, they frequently use the data available as a basis for broad, speculative scenarios that try to explain both early hominin adaptations to a changing environment and

the new behaviors that these hominins adopted. Such scenarios are fascinating, and paleoanthropologists enjoy constructing them (and certainly many in the general public enjoy reading them). Without doubt, for scientists and laypersons alike, our curiosity inevitably leads to intriguing and sweeping generalizations. Still, in the following discussion, we'll focus on what is *known* from the paleoanthropological record itself and separate that from the more speculative conclusions. You, too, should evaluate these explanations with a critical eye and try to identify the empirical basis for each type of reconstruction. It's important not to accept a scenario merely because it's appealing (often because it's simple) or just because it seems plausible. We always need to ask ourselves what kinds of evidence support a particular contention, how generally the explanation fits the evidence (that is, how consistent it is with different types of data from varied sources), and what types of new evidence might either help to verify or potentially falsify the interpretation.

Environmental Explanations for Hominin Origins

As we'll discuss in the next chapter, the earliest hominins evolved late in the Miocene or very early in the Pliocene (7–5 mya). What were the environmental conditions at that time? Can these general ecological patterns help explain the origins of the first hominins (as they diversified from other kinds of hominoids)?

Before continuing, we'll give you one more word of caution. Many students have the common misconception that a single large environmental change is related clearly to a major adaptive change in a type of organism (in other words, environmental change X produced adaptation Y in a particular lifeform). This oversimplification is a form of **environmental determinism**, and it grossly underestimates the true complexity of the evolutionary process. It's clear that the environment influences evolutionary change, as seen in the process of natural selection; but organisms are highly complex systems, composed of thousands of genes, and any adaptive shift to changing environmental circumstances is likely to be a compromise, balancing several selective factors simultaneously (such as temperature requirements, amount and distribution of food and water, predators, and safe sleeping sites). In our discussion of the socioecological dynamics of nonhuman primate adaptations in Chapter 7, we made this same point.

There's some evidence that at about the same time the earliest hominins were diverging, some major ecological changes *may* have been occurring in Africa. Could these ecological and evolutionary changes be related to each other? As we'll see, such a sweeping generalization has produced much debate. For most of the Miocene, Africa was generally tropical, with heavy rainfall persisting for most of the year; consequently, most of the continent was heavily forested. However, beginning later in the Miocene and intensifying up to the end of the epoch (about 5 mya), the climate became cooler, drier, and more seasonal.

We should also mention that in other regions of the world, paleoecological evidence reveals a distinct cooling trend at the end of the Miocene. But our focus is on Africa, particularly eastern and central Africa, for it's from these regions that we have the earliest evidence of hominin diversification. We've already noted that one method paleoanthropologists use to reconstruct environments is to analyze animal remains and fossilized pollen. Using another innovative technique, scientists study the chemical pathways utilized by different plants. In particular, **stable carbon isotopes** are produced by plants in differing proportions, depending part-

ly on temperature and aridity (plants adapted to warmer, wetter climates—such as most trees, shrubs, and tubers—versus plants requiring hotter, drier conditions, as typified by many types of grasses). Animals eat the plants, and the differing concentrations of the stable isotopes of carbon are incorporated into their bones and teeth, thus providing a "signature" of the general type of environment in which they lived.

Through a combination of these analytical techniques, paleoecologists have gained a reasonably good handle on worldwide and continent-wide environmental patterns of the past. For example, one model postulates that as climates grew cooler in East Africa 12–5 mya, forests became less continuous. As a result, forest "fringe" habitats and transitional zones between forests and grasslands became more widespread. It's hypothesized that in such transitional environments, some of the late Miocene hominoids may have more intensively exploited the drier grassland portions of the fringe (these would be the earliest hominins); conversely, other hominoids concentrated more on the wetter portions of the fringe (these presumably were the ancestors of African great apes). In the incipient hominins, further adaptive strategies would have followed, including bipedalism, increased tool use, dietary specialization (perhaps with an emphasis on hard items such as seeds and nuts), and changes in social organization.

Such assertions concerning interactions of habitat, locomotion, dietary changes, and social organization are not really testable (since we don't know which changes came first). Still, some of the more restricted contentions of this "climatic forcing" theory are amenable to testing, though some of the model's more basic predictions haven't been confirmed. Most notably, further analyses using stable carbon isotopes from several East African localities suggest that during the late Miocene,

environmental determinism An interpretation that links simple environmental changes directly to a major evolutionary shift in an organism. Such explanations tend to oversimplify the evolutionary process.

stable carbon isotopes Isotopes of carbon that are produced in plants in differing proportions, depending on environmental conditions. By analyzing the proportions of the isotopes contained in fossil remains of animals (who ate the plants), it's possible to reconstruct aspects of ancient environments (particularly temperature and aridity).

environments across the area were consistently quite densely forested (that is, grasslands never predominated, except perhaps at a local level).

You should be aware that at the local level, there can be wide fluctuations in temperature, rainfall, and vegetation as well as in the animals exploiting the vegetation. For example, local uplift, like a mountain, can produce a rain shadow, dramatically altering rainfall and temperature in a region. River and related lake drainages also have major impacts in some areas, and these topographical features are often influenced by highly localized geological factors. To generalize about climates in Africa, good data from several regions are required.

So it would seem, given current evidence and available analytical techniques, that our knowledge of the factors influencing the appearance of the *earliest* hominins is very limited. Considering the constraints, most hypotheses relating to potential factors are best kept restricted in scope and directly related to actual data. In this way, scientists can more easily evaluate the usefulness of these hypotheses, and the hypotheses themselves can be modified and built upon.

Other environmentally oriented hypotheses have been proposed for somewhat later stages of hominin evolution in Africa. Analysis of faunal remains from South African sites led Elizabeth Vrba, of Yale University, to suggest an *evolutionary pulse theory*. In this view, at various times during the Pliocene and Early Pleistocene, the environment all across Africa became notably more arid. Vrba hypothesized that these major climatic shifts may have played a central role in stimulating hominin evolutionary development at key stages.

At one group of later hominin sites in Java, Indonesia, researchers are seeking to discover something about the plants and animals that they believe may have *enticed* our ancestors away from Africa, rather than thinking that harsh environments drove them out.

The long sedimentary sequence of this region, known as the Sangiran Dome, allows for stable isotope analyses of the large and varied fossil assemblage—everything from mammals to clams and snails to fossil pollen and other plant remains. It's here, in these favorable circumstances, that nearly 100 fossils of the extinct human *Homo erectus* have been found, spanning a 700,000-year time span from 1.6 to 0.9 mya. This unique co-occurrence makes Sangiran an outstanding locality to test the effects of climate change on the evolving human lineage. The surrounding sites provide a wealth of information about climatic conditions and the environment that attracted and sustained *H. erectus* in central Java. This region offers scientists a rare opportunity to determine just how flexible the adaptations of our hominin cousins might have been.

This new view of humans—as just one of many animals lured out of Africa by the promise of open niches—is more in line with additional data derived from thousands of animal fossils from various sites in East Africa (Behrensmeyer et al., 1997). Analysis of these remains have failed to show that the environmental transitions that Vrba (1992) and others suggested were as widespread as initially proposed. Further detailed analysis by Richard Potts, of the Smithsonian Institution, has in fact shown that ecosystems changed rapidly and often unpredictably throughout various areas of Africa (Bower, 2003; Potts, 2003). Rather than large-scale environmental changes "forcing" hominins into new adaptive strategies, perhaps our ancestors flourished and evolved because they were flexible opportunists.

Why Did Hominins Become Bipedal?

As we've noted several times, the adaptation of hominins to bipedal locomotion was *the* most fundamental adaptive shift among the early members of our lineage. But what were the factors that initiated this crucial change? Ecological theories similar to some of those just discussed have long been thought to be central to the development of bipedalism. Clearly, however, environmental influences would have to occur *before* documented evidence of well-adapted bipedal behavior. In other words, the major shift would have been at the end of the Miocene. Although the evidence indicates that no *sudden* wide ecological change took place at that time, locally forests probably did become patchier as rainfall became more seasonal. Given the changing environmental conditions, did hominins come to the ground to seize the opportunities offered in these more open habitats? Did bipedalism quickly ensue, stimulated somehow by this new way of life? At a very general level, the answer to these questions is yes. Obviously, hominins did at some point become bipedal, and this adaptation took place on the ground. Likewise, hominins are more adapted to mixed and open-country habitats than are our closest modern ape cousins. Successful terrestrial bipedalism probably made possible the further adaptation to more arid, open-country terrain. Still, this rendition simply tells us *where* hominins found their niche, not *why*.

As always, it's wise to be cautious when speculating about causation in evolution. It is all too easy to draw superficial conclusions. For example, scientists often surmise that the mere fact that ground niches were available (and perhaps lacked direct competitors) inevitably led the earliest hominins to terrestrial bipedalism. But consider this: Plenty of mammalian species, including some nonhuman primates, also live mostly on the ground in open country—and they aren't bipedal. Clearly, beyond such simplistic environmental determinism, some more complex explanation for hominin bipedalism is required. There must have been something more than just an environmental opportunity to explain this adaptation to such a unique lifestyle.

Another issue sometimes overlooked in the discussion of early hominin bipedal adaptation is that these creatures did not suddenly become completely terrestrial; but they also didn't slouch about, as illustrations of a linear progression of human evolution would suggest. We know, for example, that all terrestrial species of nonhuman primates (including savanna baboons, hamadryas baboons, and patas monkeys; see Chapter 7) regularly seek out safe sleeping sites off the ground. These safe havens help protect against predation and are usually found in trees or on cliff faces. Likewise, early hominins almost certainly sought safety at night in the trees, even after they became well adapted to terrestrial bipedalism during daytime foraging. What's more, the continued opportunities for feeding in the trees would most likely have remained significant to early hominins, well after they were also utilizing ground-based resources.

Various hypotheses explaining why hominins initially became bipedal have been suggested and are summarized in **Table 10-2**. The primary influences claimed to have stimulated the shift to bipedalism include acquiring the ability to carry objects (and offspring); hunting on the ground; gathering of seeds and nuts; feeding from bushes; improved thermoregulation (that is, keeping cooler on the open savanna); having a better view of open country (to spot predators); walking long distances; and provisioning by males of females with dependent offspring.

These are all creative scenarios, but once again they're not very conducive to rigorous testing and verification. Still, two of the more ambitious scenarios proposed by Clifford Jolly (1970) and Owen Lovejoy (1981) deserve further mention. Both of these views sought to link several aspects of early hominin ecology, feeding, and social behavior, and both utilized models

TABLE 10.2 Possible Factors Influencing the Initial Evolution of Bipedal Locomotion in Hominins

Factor	Speculated Influence	Comments
Carrying (objects, tools, weapons, infants)	Upright posture freed the arms to carry various objects (including offspring).	Charles Darwin emphasized this view, particularly relating to tools and weapons; however, evidence of stone tools is found much later in the record than first evidence of bipedalism.
Hunting	Bipedalism allowed carrying of weapons, more accurate throwing of certain weapons, and improved long-distance walking.	Systematic hunting is now thought not to have been practiced until after the origin of bipedal hominins (see Issue, Chapter 12).
Seed and nut gathering	Feeding on seeds and nuts occurred while standing upright.	Model initially drawn from analogy with gelada baboons (see text).
Feeding from bushes	Upright posture provided access to seeds, berries, etc., in lower branches; analogous to adaptation seen in some specialized antelope.	Climbing adaptation already existed as prior ancestral trait in earliest hominins (i.e., bush and tree feeding already was established prior to bipedal adaptation).
Thermoregulation (cooling)	Vertical posture exposes less of the body to direct sun; increased distance from ground facilitates cooling by increased exposure to breezes.	Works best for animals active midday on savanna; moreover, adaptation to bipedalism may have initially occurred in woodlands, not on savanna.
Visual surveillance	Standing up provided better view of surrounding countryside (view of potential predators as well as other group members).	Behavior seen occasionally in terrestrial primates (e.g., baboons); probably a contributing factor, but unlikely as "prime mover."
Long-distance walking	Covering long distances was more efficient for a biped than for a quadruped (during hunting or foraging); mechanical reconstructions show that bipedal walking is less energetically costly than quadrupedalism (this is not the case for bipedal running).	Same difficulties as with hunting explanation; long-distance foraging on ground also appears unlikely adaptation in earliest hominins.
Male provisioning	Males carried back resources to dependent females and young.	Monogamous bond suggested; however, most skeletal data appear to falsify this part of the hypothesis (see text).

derived from studies of contemporary nonhuman primates.

Jolly's seed-eating hypothesis used the feeding behavior and ecology of gelada baboons as an analogy for very early hominins. Seed eating is an activity that requires keen hand-eye coordination, with presumed bipedal shuffling potentially improving efficiency of foraging. In this view, early hominins are hypothesized to have adapted to open country and bipedalism as a result of their primary adaptation to eating seeds and nuts (found on the ground). The key assumption is that early hominins were eating seeds acquired in similar ecological conditions to those of contemporary gelada baboons.

Lovejoy, meanwhile, has combined presumed aspects of early hominin ecology, feeding, pair bonding, infant care, and food sharing to devise his creative scenario. This view hinges on these assumptions: (1) that the earliest hominins had offspring at least as K-selected (see Chapter 7) as other large-bodied hominoids; (2) that hominin males ranged widely and provisioned females and their young, who remained more tied to a "home base"; and (3) that males were paired monogamously with females.

As we've noted, while not strictly testable, such scenarios do make certain predictions that can be potentially falsified or upheld. Accordingly, aspects of each scenario can be evaluated in light of more specific data (obtained from the paleoanthropological record). Regarding the seed-eating hypothesis, predictions relating to size of the back teeth in most early hominins are met, but the proportions of the front teeth in many forms aren't what we'd expect to see in a committed seed eater. Besides, the analogy with gelada baboons is not as informative as once thought; these animals actually don't eat that many seeds and certainly aren't habitual bipeds. Finally, many of the characteristics that Jolly suggested were restricted to hominins (and geladas) are also found in several late

Miocene hominoids (who weren't hominins—nor obviously bipeds). Thus, regarding the seed-eating hypothesis, the proposed dental and dietary adaptations don't appear to be linked specifically to hominin origins or bipedalism.

Further detailed analyses of data have also questioned crucial elements of Lovejoy's male-provisioning scenario. The evidence that appears to most contradict this view is that all early hominins were quite sexually dimorphic (McHenry, 1992). According to Lovejoy's model (and analogies with contemporary monogamous nonhuman primates such as gibbons), there shouldn't be such dramatic differences in body size between males and females. Recent studies (Reno et al., 2003, 2005) have questioned this conclusion regarding sexual dimoprhism, suggesting, at least for one species (*Australopithecus afarensis*), that sexual dimorphism was only very moderate. Further evaluation of another, even earlier hominin (*Ardipithecus*) has led Lovejoy to continue to forcefully argue for his male-provisioning model (Lovejoy, 2009). From a wider perspective, these conclusions appear at odds with most of the evidence regarding early hominins. What's more, the notions of food sharing (presumably including considerable meat), home bases, and long-distance provisioning are questioned by more controlled interpretations of the archaeological record.

Another imaginative view is also relevant to this discussion of early hominin evolution, since it relates the adaptation to bipedalism (which was first) to increased brain expansion (which came later). This interpretation, proposed by Dean Falk, suggests that an upright posture put severe constraints on brain size (since blood circulation and drainage would have been altered and cooling would consequently have been more limited than in quadrupeds). Falk thus hypothesizes that new brain-cooling mechanisms must have coevolved with bipedalism, articulated in what she calls the "radiator theory" (Falk, 1990). Falk further surmises that the requirements for better brain cooling would have been particularly marked as hominins adapted to open-country ground living on the hot African savanna. Another interesting pattern observed by Falk concerns two different cooling adaptations found in different early hominin species. She thus suggests that the type of "radiator" adapted in the genus *Homo* was particularly significant in reducing constraints on brain size—which presumably limited some other early hominins. The radiator theory works well, since it not only helps explain the relationship of bipedalism to later brain expansion but also explains why only some hominins became dramatically encephalized.

The radiator theory, too, has been criticized by some paleoanthropologists. Most notably, the presumed species distinction concerning varying cooling mechanisms is not as obvious as suggested by the hypothesis. Both types of venous drainage systems can be found in contemporary *Homo sapiens* as well as within various early hominin species (that is, the variation is intraspecific, not just interspecific). Indeed, in some early hominin specimens, both systems can be found in the same individual (expressed on either side of the skull). Besides, as Falk herself has noted, the radiator itself didn't lead to larger brains; it simply helped reduce constraints on increased encephalization among hominins. It thus requires some further mechanism (prime mover) to explain why, in some hominin species, brain size increased the way it did.

As with any such ambitious effort, it's all too easy to find holes. Falk aptly reminds us that "the search for such 'prime movers' is highly speculative, and these theories do not lend themselves to hypothesis testing" (Falk, 1990, p. 334). Even so, the attempt to interrelate various lines of evidence, the use of contemporary primate models, and predictions concerning further evidence obtained from paleoanthropological contexts all conform to sound scientific methodology. All the views discussed here have contributed to this venture—one not just aimed at understanding our early ancestors but also seeking to refine its methodologies and scientific foundation.

Summary of Main Topics

- The most important subfields of paleoanthropology are geology, paleontology, archaeology, and physical anthropology.
- The two types of dating techniques are relative dating and chronometric dating. Stratigraphy and paleomagnetism are the two most important examples of relative dating; potassium-argon dating and radiocarbon (^{14}C) dating are the most important examples of chronometric dating.
- The first stone tools thus far discovered date to about 2.6 mya. The tools include mostly simple flake implements and the discarded cores from which they were struck.
- Bipedal locomotion is thought to have been significantly influenced by one or more of the following: carrying objects, seed gathering or feeding from bushes, visual spotting of predators, and long-distance walking (the latter coming more recently in human evolution).

Critical Thinking Questions

1. You are leading a paleoanthropological expedition aimed at discovering an early hominin site dating to the Pliocene. In what part of the world will you pick your site, and why? After selecting a particular region, how will you identify which area(s) to survey on foot?

2. Why is it important to have accurate dates for paleoanthropological localities? Why is it necessary to use more than one kind of dating technique?

3. What do we mean when we say that early hominins displayed cultural behavior? What types of behavior do you think this would have included? (Imagine that you've been transported back in time by a time machine, and you're sitting in a tree watching a group of hominins at Olduvai Gorge 1.5 mya.)

4. Now put yourself in the same place, this time leading an archaeological excavation. What would be left for you to detect of the cultural behavior you observed in question 3? What happened to the remainder of this behavioral repertoire?

5. What do we mean when we say that human evolution is biocultural? How do paleoanthropologists investigate early hominins using such a biocultural perspective?

11

Hominin Origins in Africa

Key Questions

▶ Who are the oldest members of the human lineage, and how do these early hominins compare with modern humans? With modern apes? How do they fit within a biological continuum?

Our species today dominates our planet as we use our brains and cultural inventions to invade every corner of the earth. Yet, 5 million years ago, our ancestors were little more than bipedal apes, confined to a few regions in Africa. What were these creatures like? When and how did they begin their evolutionary journey?

In Chapter 10, we discussed the techniques paleoanthropologists use to locate and excavate sites, as well as the multidisciplinary approaches used to interpret discoveries. In this chapter, we turn to the physical evidence of the hominin fossils themselves. The earliest fossils identifiable as hominins are all from Africa. They date from as early as 6+ mya, and after 4 mya, varieties of these early hominins become more plentiful and widely distributed in Africa. It's fascinating to think about all these quite primitive early members of our family tree living side by side for millions of years, especially when we also try to figure out how they managed to coexist with their different adaptations. Most of these species became extinct. But why? What's more, were some of these apelike animals possibly our direct ancestors?

Hominins, of course, evolved from earlier primates (dating from the Eocene to late Miocene), and in Chapter 9 we discussed the fossil evidence of prehominin primates. These fossils provide us with a context within which to understand the subsequent evolution of the human lineage. In recent years, paleoanthropologists from several countries have been excavating sites in Africa, and many exciting new finds have been uncovered. However, because many finds have been made so recently, detailed evaluations are still in progress, and conclusions must remain tentative.

One thing is certain, however. The earliest members of the human lineage were confined to Africa. Only much later did their descendants disperse from the African continent to other areas of the Old World. (This "out of Africa" saga will be the topic of the next chapter.)

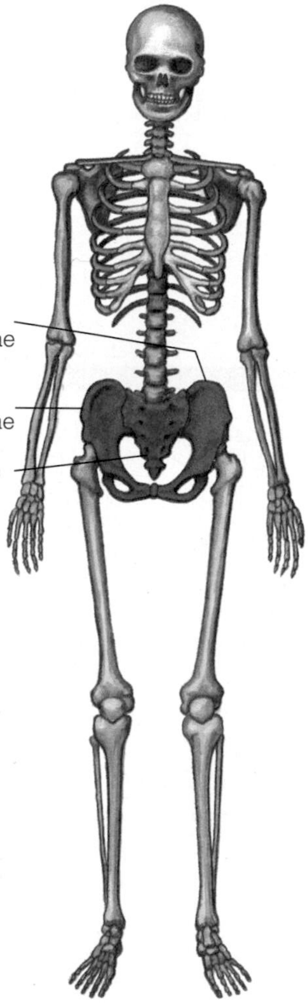

The Bipedal Adaptation

In our overview in Chapter 10 of behavioral reconstructions of early hominins, we highlighted several hypotheses that attempt to explain *why* bipedal locomotion first evolved in the hominins. Here we turn to the specific anatomical (that is, **morphological**) evidence that shows us when, where, and how hominin bipedal locomotion evolved. From a broader perspective, we've noted a tendency in all primates for erect body posture and some bipedalism. Of all living primates, however, efficient bipedalism as the primary (habitual) form of locomotion is seen *only* in hominins. Functionally, the human mode of locomotion is most clearly shown in our striding gait, where weight is alternately placed on a single fully extended hind limb. This specialized form of locomotion has developed to a point where energy levels are used to near peak efficiency. Our manner of bipedal locomotion is a far cry from what we see in nonhuman primates, who move bipedally with hips and knees bent and maintain balance clumsily and inefficiently, tottering along rather than striding.

From a survey of our close primate relatives, it's apparent that while still in the trees, our ancestors were adapted to a fair amount of upper-body erectness. Prosimians, monkeys, and apes all spend considerable time sitting erect while feeding, grooming, or sleeping. Presumably, our early ancestors displayed similar behavior. What caused these forms to come to the ground and embark on the unique way of life that would eventually lead to humans is still a mystery. Perhaps natural selection favored some Miocene hominoids coming occasionally to the ground to forage for food on the forest floor and forest fringe. In any case, once they were on the ground and away from the immediate safety offered by trees, bipedal locomotion could become a tremendous advantage. (For a discussion of some specific hypotheses that have tried to explain the early evolution of bipedal locomotion, see Chapter 10.)

Our mode of locomotion is indeed extraordinary, involving, as it does, a unique kind of activity in which "the body, step by step, teeters on the edge of catastrophe" (Napier, 1967, p. 56). In this way, the act of human walking is the act of *almost falling* repeatedly! The problem is to maintain balance on the "stance" leg while the "swing" leg is off the ground. In fact, during normal walking, both feet are simultaneously on the ground only about 25 percent of the time, and this figure becomes even less as we walk (or run) faster.

Maintaining a stable center of balance in this complex form of locomotion calls for many drastic structural/anatomical alterations in the basic primate quadrupedal pattern. The most dramatic changes are seen in the pelvis. The pelvis is composed of three elements: two hip bones, or ossa coxae (*sing.*, os coxae), joined at the back to the sacrum (**Fig. 11-1**). In a quadruped, the ossa coxae are vertically elongated bones positioned along each side of the lower portion of the spine and oriented more or less parallel to it. In hominins, the pelvis is comparatively much shorter and broader and extends around to the side (**Fig. 11-2**). This configuration helps to stabilize the line of weight transmission in a bipedal posture from the lower back to the hip joint (**Fig. 11-3**).

Several consequences resulted from the remodeling of the pelvis during early hominin evolution. Broadening the two sides and extending them around to the side and front of the body produced a basin-shaped structure that helps support the abdominal organs (*pelvis* means "basin" in Latin). These alterations also repositioned the attachments of several key muscles that act on the hip and leg, changing their mechanical function. Probably the most important of these altered relationships is that involving the gluteus maximus, the largest muscle in the body, which in humans forms the bulk

Left os coxae

Right os coxae

Sacrum

▲ **Figure 11-1**
The human pelvis: various elements shown on a modern skeleton.

morphological Pertaining to the form and structure of organisms.

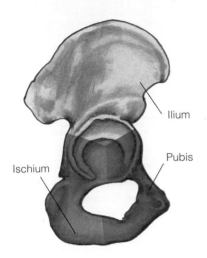

▲ Figure 11-2
The human os coxae, composed of three bones (right side shown).

Ilium

Ischium

Pubis

Ossa coxae. (a) *Homo sapiens*. (b) Early hominin (australopith) from South Africa. (c) Great ape. Note especially the length and breadth of the iliac blade (boxed) and the line of weight transmission (shown in red).

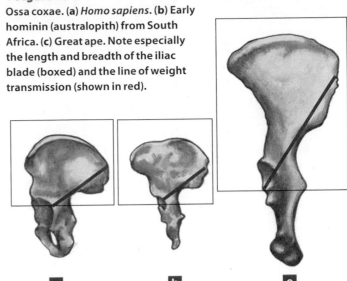

a   b   c

of the buttocks. In quadrupeds, the gluteus maximus is positioned to the side of the hip and functions to pull the thigh to the side and away from the body. In humans, this muscle is positioned behind the hip; this arrangement allows it, along with the hamstrings, to extend the thigh, pulling it to the rear during walking and running (**Fig. 11-4**). The gluteus maximus is a truly powerful extensor of the thigh and provides additional force, particularly during running and climbing.

Modifications also occurred in other parts of the skeleton because of the shift to bipedalism. The most significant of these, summarized in "A Closer Look: Major Features of Bipedal Locomotion," include (1) repositioning of the foramen magnum, the opening at the base of the skull through which the spinal cord emerges; (2) the addition of spinal curves that help to transmit the weight of the upper body to the hips in an upright posture; (3) shortening and broadening of the pelvis and the stabilization of weight transmission (discussed earlier); (4) lengthening of the hind limb, thus increasing stride length; (5) angling of the femur (thighbone) inward to bring the knees and feet closer together under the body; and (6) several structural changes in the foot, including the development of

a longitudinal arch and realignment of the big toe in parallel with the other toes (that is, it was no longer divergent).

As you can appreciate, the evolution of hominin bipedalism required complex anatomical reorganization. For natural selection to produce anatomical change of the magnitude seen in hominins, the benefits of bipedal locomotion must have been significant indeed! We mentioned in Chapter 10 several possible adaptive advantages that bipedal locomotion may have

▼ Figure 11-4

Comparisons of important muscles that act to extend the hip. Note that the attachment surface (origin, shown in black) of the gluteus maximus in humans (a) is farther in back of the hip joint than in a chimpanzee standing bipedally (b). Conversely, in chimpanzees, the hamstrings are farther in back of the knee.

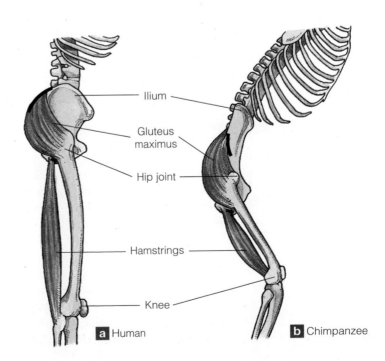

Ilium

Gluteus maximus

Hip joint

Hamstrings

Knee

a Human   b Chimpanzee

A Closer Look

Major Features of Bipedal Locomotion

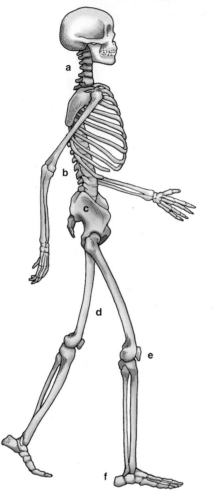

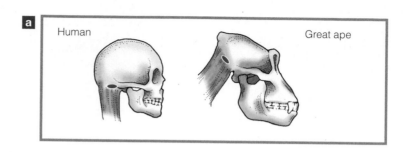

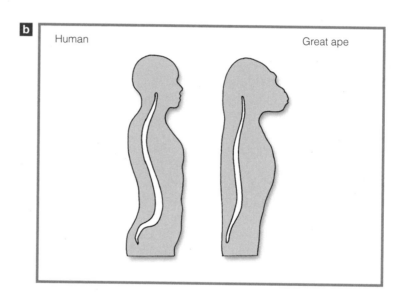

During hominin evolution, several major structural features throughout the body have been reorganized (from that seen in other primates), facilitating efficient bipedal locomotion. These are illustrated here, beginning with the head and progressing to the foot: (**a**) The foramen magnum (shown in blue) is repositioned farther underneath the skull, so that the head is more or less balanced on the spine (and thus requires less robust neck muscles to hold the head upright). (**b**) The spine has two distinctive curves—a backward (thoracic) one and a forward (lumbar) one—that keep the trunk (and weight) centered above the pelvis. (**c**) The pelvis is shaped more in the form

conferred upon early hominins. But these all remain hypotheses (even more accurately, they could be called scenarios), and we have inadequate data for testing the various proposed models.

Still, given the anatomical alterations required for efficient bipedalism, some major behavioral stimuli must have been influencing its development. When interpreting evolutionary history, biologists are fond of saying that

form follows function. In other words, during evolution, organisms don't undergo significant reorganization in structure *unless* these changes—over many generations—assist individuals in some functional capacity (and in so doing increase their reproductive success). Such changes didn't necessarily occur all at once, but probably evolved over a fairly long period of time. Even so, once behavioral influences initiated

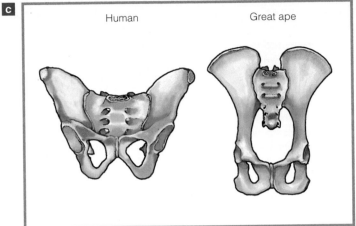

c. Human — Great ape

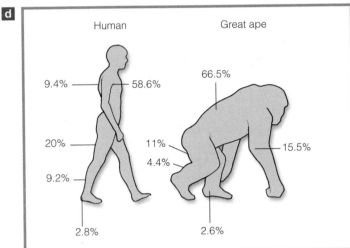

d. Human — Great ape

9.4% — 58.6%

66.5%

20% — 11% — 15.5%

4.4%

9.2%

2.8% — 2.6%

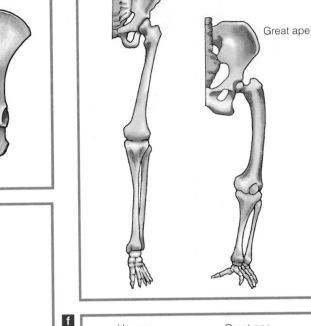

e. Human — Great ape

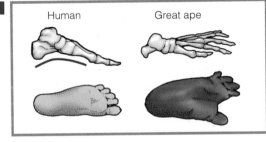

f. Human — Great ape

of a basin to support internal organs; the ossa coxae (specifically, iliac blades) are also shorter and broader, thus stabilizing weight transmission. (**d**) Lower limbs are elongated, as shown by the proportional lengths of various body segments (for example, in humans the thigh comprises 20 percent of body height, while in gorillas it comprises only 11 percent. (**e**) The femur is angled inward, keeping the legs more directly under the body; modified knee anatomy also permits full extension of this joint. (**f**) The big toe is enlarged and brought in line with the other toes; a distinctive longitudinal arch also forms, helping absorb shock and adding propulsive spring.

certain structural modifications, the process gained momentum and proceeded irreversibly.

We say that hominin bipedalism is both habitual and obligate. By **habitual bipedalism**, we mean that hominins, unlike any other primate, move bipedally as their standard and most efficient mode of locomotion. By **obligate bipedalism**, we mean that hominins are committed to bipedalism and cannot locomote efficiently in any other way. For example, the loss of grasping ability in the foot makes climbing much more difficult for humans (although by no means impossible). The central task, then, in trying to understand the earliest members of the hominin lineage is to identify anatomical features that indicate bipedalism and to interpret to what degree these organisms were committed to this form of locomotion

habitual bipedalism Bipedal locomotion as the form of locomotion shown by hominins most of the time.

obligate bipedalism Bipedalism as the *only* form of hominin terrestrial locomotion. Since major anatomical changes in the spine, pelvis, and lower limb are required for bipedal locomotion, once hominins adapted this mode of locomotion, other forms of locomotion on the ground became impossible.

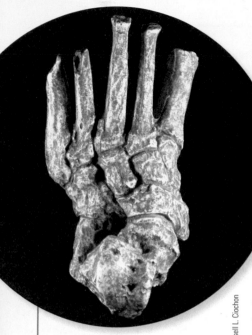

▲ **Figure 11-5**
A nearly complete hominin foot
(OH 8) from Olduvai Gorge, Tanzania.
(See Appendix C for an explanation of
how specimen numbers such as OH 8
are assigned.)

© Russell L. Ciochon

(that is, was it habitual and was it obligate?).

What structural patterns are observable in early hominins, and what do they imply regarding locomotor function? By at least 4 mya, all the major structural changes required for bipedalism are seen in early hominins from Africa (at least as far as the evidence permits conclusions to be made). In particular, the pelvis, as clearly documented by several excellently preserved specimens, was dramatically remodeled to support weight in a bipedal stance (see Fig. 11-3b).

Other structural changes shown after 4 mya in the earliest relatively complete hominin postcranial remains further confirm the pattern seen in the pelvis. For example, the vertebral column (as known from specimens in East and South Africa) shows the same curves as in modern hominins. The lower limbs are also elongated, and they seem to be proportionately about as long as in modern humans (although the arms are longer in these early hominins). Further, the carrying angle of weight support from the hip to the knee is very similar to that seen in *Homo sapiens*.

Fossil evidence of early hominin foot structure has come from two sites in South Africa; especially important are some fossils from **Sterkfontein** (Clarke and Tobias, 1995). These specimens, consisting of four articulating elements from the ankle and big toe, indicate that the heel and longitudinal arch were both well adapted for a bipedal gait. But the paleoanthropologists (Ron Clarke and Phillip Tobias) who analyzed these remains also suggest that the large toe was *divergent*, unlike the hominin pattern shown in "A Closer Look: Major Features of Bipedal Locomotion." If the large toe really did possess this anatomical position (and this is disputed), it most likely would have aided the foot in grasping. In turn, this grasping ability (as in other primates) would have enabled early hominins to more effectively exploit arbor-

eal habitats. Finally, since anatomical remodeling is always constrained by a set of complex functional compromises, a foot highly capable of grasping and climbing is less capable as a stable platform during bipedal locomotion. Some researchers therefore see early hominins as perhaps not quite as fully committed to bipedal locomotion as were later hominins.

Further evidence for evolutionary changes in the foot comes from two sites in East Africa where numerous fossilized elements have been recovered (**Fig. 11-5**). As in the remains from South Africa, the East African fossils suggest a well-adapted bipedal gait. The arches are developed, but some differences in the ankle also imply that considerable flexibility was possible (again, probably indicating some continued adaptation to climbing). From this evidence, some researchers have recently concluded that many forms of early hominins probably spent considerable time in the trees. What's more, they may not have been quite as efficient bipedally as has previously been suggested. Nevertheless, most researchers maintain that early hominins from Africa displayed both habitual and obligate bipedalism (despite the new evidence from South Africa and the earliest traces from central and East Africa, all of which will require further study).

Finding Early Hominin Fossils

As we've discussed, paleoanthropology is a multidisciplinary science, and the finding, surveying, and eventual excavation of hominin sites is a time-consuming and expensive undertaking. What's more, since hominin fossils are never common anywhere and are usually at least partially buried under sediment, finding them also requires no small portion of good luck.

In Africa, most fossil discoveries have come from either East or South

Sterkfontein (sterk´-fawn-tane)

Africa. As we'll soon see, a few extremely important discoveries have recently come from central Africa. Nevertheless, more than 99 percent of the early African hominin fossils so far discovered come from the eastern and southern portions of the continent.

In East Africa, early hominin sites are located along the Great Rift Valley. Stretching over more than 2,000 miles, the Rift Valley was formed by geological shifting (actually separation, producing the "rift") between two of the earth's tectonic plates. That is, it's the same geological process as that leading to "continental drift" (discussed in Chapter 5). The outcome of these geological upheavals leads to faulting (with earthquakes), volcanoes, and sometimes rapid sedimentation. Paleoanthropologists see all this as a major plus, since it produces a landscape that has many geological exposures revealing at surface level ancient beds that just might contain fossils of all sorts—including hominins. What's more, the chemical makeup of the volcanic sediments makes accurate chronometric dating much more possible.

Paleoanthropological discoveries along the East African branch of the Rift Valley extend from northern Ethiopia, through Kenya, and finally into northern Tanzania (**Fig. 11-6**). Key locales within the Rift Valley, where in total more than 2,000 hominin fossils have been found, include the extremely productive Middle Awash area of northeastern Ethiopia (containing Aramis, Hadar, and Dikika). In Kenya, crucial discoveries have come from the east and west sides of Lake Turkana and just a bit to the south from the Tugen Hills. Lastly, in northern Tanzania, the remarkably informative paleoanthropological site of Olduvai Gorge has been explored for several decades, and nearby, the Laetoli site has yielded other key fossils as well as extraordinarily well-preserved hominin footprints.

South Africa has also been a very productive area for early hominin discoveries. Over the last 80 years, paleoanthropologists have explored numerous sites, which together have yielded several hundred hominin specimens. The most important South African hominin sites are Taung, Sterkfontein, Swartkrans, and Malapa.

It's important to recognize that the geological context of all the South African sites is quite different from that in East Africa. The Rift Valley does not extend into southernmost Africa, where, instead, the sediments are composed of layer upon convoluted layer of accumulated limestones. As a result, the geological layers are extremely complex and do not form into such recognizable strata as seen in sites along the East African Rift Valley. In the South African landscape, caves and fissures form, into which animals fall or perhaps are dragged by predators. Consequently, the hominins accumulated in these caverns and fissures, where they eventually became encased in a rock matrix. Decades ago, the hominins were removed by dynamite. Today, they are retrieved using small hand tools, and only then with extraordinarily painstaking effort (**Fig 11-7**).

Because the geological setting is so much more complicated in South Africa than in East Africa, the fossils are generally more difficult to locate and usually not as well preserved, and chronometric dating is typically far more difficult. Still, there are some exceptions, as exemplified by an extremely well-preserved skeleton still being excavated at Sterkfontein (see Fig. 11-7) and the extraordinary (and well-dated) new finds from Malapa.

Early Hominins from Africa

As you are now well aware, a variety of early hominins lived in Africa, and we'll cover their comings and goings over a 5-million-year period, from at least 6 to 1 mya. It's also important to keep in mind that these hominins were geographically widely distributed, with

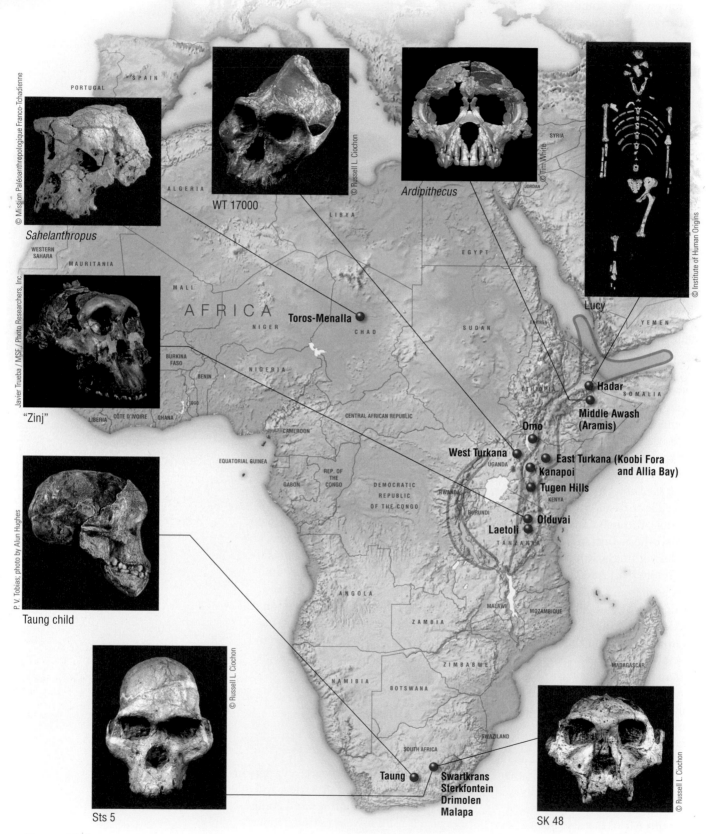

Sahelanthropus

WT 17000

Ardipithecus

Lucy

"Zinj"

Taung child

Toros-Menalla

Hadar

Middle Awash (Aramis)

Omo

West Turkana

East Turkana (Koobi Fora and Allia Bay)

Kanapoi

Tugen Hills

Olduvai

Laetoli

Sts 5

Taung

Swartkrans
Sterkfontein
Drimolen
Malapa

SK 48

▲ **Figure 11-6**
Early hominin fossil finds (pre-australopith and australopith localities).
The Rift Valley in East Africa is shown in gold.

◄ **Figure 11-7**
Paleoanthropologist Ronald Clarke carefully excavates a 2-million-year-old skeleton from the limestone matrix at Sterkfontein Cave. Clearly seen are the cranium (with articulated mandible) and the upper arm bone.

John Hodgkiss

fossil discoveries coming from central, East, and South Africa. Paleoanthropologists generally agree that among these early African fossils, there were at least 6 different genera, which in turn comprised upward of 13 different species. At no time, nor in any other place, were hominins ever as diverse as were these very ancient members of our family tree. As you'll see in a minute, some of the earliest fossils thought by many researchers to be hominins are primitive in some ways and unusually derived in others. In fact, some paleoanthropologists remain unconvinced that they are really hominins.

As you've already guessed, there are quite a few different fossils from many sites, and you'll find that their formal naming can be difficult to pronounce and not easy to remember. So we'll try to discuss these fossil groups in a way that's easy to understand. Our primary focus will be to organize them by time and by major evolutionary trends. In so doing, we recognize three major groups:

- Pre-australopiths— the earliest and most primitive (possible) hominins (6.0+–4.4 mya)
- Australopiths—diverse forms, some more primitive, others highly derived (4.2–1.2 mya)
- Early *Homo*—the first members of our genus (2.0+–1.4 mya)

Pre-Australopiths (6.0+–4.4 mya)

The oldest and most surprising of these earliest hominins is represented by a cranium discovered at a central African site called Toros-Menalla in the modern nation of Chad (Brunet et al., 2002; **Fig. 11-8**). Provisional dating using faunal correlation (biostratigraphy) suggests a date of between 7 and 6 mya (Vignaud et al., 2002). Closer examination of the evidence used in obtaining this biostratigraphic date now has led many paleoanthropologists to suggest that the later date (6 mya) is more likely.

The morphology of the fossil is unusual, with a combination of characteristics unlike that found in other early hominins. The braincase is small, estimated at no larger than a modern chimpanzee's (preliminary estimate in the range of 320 to 380 cm^3), but it is massively built, with huge browridges in front, a crest on top, and large muscle attachments in the rear. Yet, combined with these ape-like features is a smallish vertical face containing front teeth very unlike an ape's. In fact, the lower face, being more tucked in under the brain vault (and not protruding, as in most other early hominins), is more of a *derived* feature more commonly expressed in

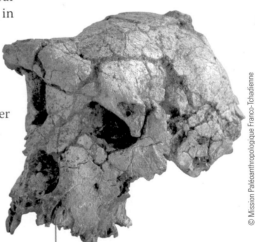

© Mission Paléoanthropologique Franco-Tchadienne

▲ **Figure 11-8**
A nearly complete cranium of *Sahelanthropus* from Chad, dating to approximately 6 mya or somewhat older.

much later hominins (especially members of genus *Homo*). What's more, unlike the dentition seen in apes (and some early hominins), the upper canine is reduced and is worn down from the tip (rather than shearing along its side against the first lower premolar).

In recognition of this unique combination of characteristics, paleoanthropologists have placed the Toros-Menalla remains into a new genus and species of hominin, *Sahelanthropus tchadensis* (Sahel being the region of the southern Sahara in North Africa). These new finds from Chad have forced an immediate and significant reassessment of early hominin evolution. Two cautionary comments, however, are in order. First, as we noted, the dating is only approximate, based, as it is, on biostratigraphic correlation with sites in Kenya (1,500 miles to the east). Second, and perhaps more serious, is the hominin status of the Chad fossil. Given the facial structure and dentition, it's difficult to see how *Sahelanthropus* could be anything but a hominin. However, the position of its foramen magnum is intermediate between that of a quadrupedal ape and that of a bipedal hominin (**Fig. 11-9**); for this and other reasons, some researchers (Wolpoff et al., 2002) suggest that at this time, "ape" may be a better classification for *Sahelanthropus*. As we have previously said, the best-defining anatomical characteristics of hominins relate to bipedal locomotion. Unfortunately, no postcranial elements have been recovered from Chad—at least not yet. Consequently, we do not yet know the locomotor behavior of *Sahelanthropus*, and this raises even more fundamental questions: What if further finds show this form not to be bipedal? Should we still consider it a hominin? What, then, are the defining characteristics of our lineage? For all these reasons, several paleoanthropologists have recently grown more skeptical regarding the hominin status of all the pre-australopith finds, and Bernard Wood (2010) prefers to call them "possible hominins."

Probably living at about the same time as *Sahelanthropus*, two other very early (possible) hominin genera have been found at sites in central Kenya in the Tugen Hills and from the Middle Awash area of northeastern Ethiopia. The earlier of these finds (dated by radiometric methods to around 6 mya) comes from the Tugen Hills and includes mostly dental remains, but also some quite complete lower limb bones. The fossils have been placed in a separate early hominin genus called *Orrorin*. The postcranial remains are especially important, since they seem to indicate bipedal locomotion (Pickford and Senut, 2001; Senut et al., 2001; Galik et al., 2004; Richmond and Jungers, 2008). As a result of these further analyses, *Orrorin* is the pre-australopith generally recognized as having the best evidence to establish it

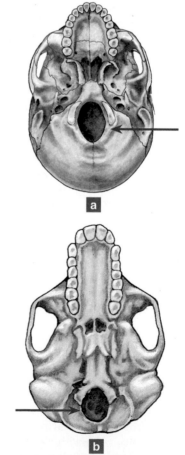

▲ **Figure 11-9**
Position of the foramen magnum in (a) a human and (b) a chimpanzee. Note the more forward position in the human cranium.

as a hominin (compared to less clear evidence for *Sahelanthropus* and *Ardipithecus*).

The last group of possible hominins dating to the late Miocene (that is, earlier than 5 mya) comes from the Middle Awash in the Afar Triangle of Ethiopia. Radiometric dating places the age of these fossils in the very late Miocene, 5.8–5.2 mya. The fossil remains themselves are very fragmentary. Some of the dental remains resemble some later fossils from the Middle Awash (discussed shortly), and Yohannes Haile-Selassie, the researcher who first found and described these earlier materials, has provisionally assigned them to the genus *Ardipithecus* (Haile-Selassie et al., 2004; see "At a Glance: Pre-Australopith Discoveries"). In addition, some postcranial elements have been preserved, most informatively a toe bone, a phalanx from the middle of the foot (see Appendix A, Fig. A-8). From clues in this bone, Haile-Selassie concludes that this primate was a well-adapted biped (once again, the best-supporting evidence of hominin status).

From another million years or so later in the geological record in the Middle Awash region, a very large and significant assemblage of fossil hominins has been discovered at a site called **Aramis**. Radiometric dating firmly places these remains at about 4.4 mya. The site, represented by a 6-foot-thick bed of bones, has yielded more than 6,000 fossils. This abundant find reveals both large and small vertebrates—birds and other reptiles and even very small mammals. Additionally, fossil wood and pollen samples have been recovered. All this information is important for understanding the environments in which these ancient hominins lived.

Hominin fossil remains from Aramis include several individuals, the most noteworthy being a partial skeleton. At least 36 other hominins are represented by isolated teeth, cranial bones, and a few limb bones. All the bones were extremely fragile and frag-mentary and required many years of incredibly painstaking effort to clean and reconstruct. Indeed, it took 15 years before the partial skeleton was in adequate condition to be intensively studied. But the wait was well worth it, and in 2009, Tim White and colleagues published their truly remarkable finds. By far, the most informative fossil is the partial skeleton. Even though it was found crushed and basically pulverized, the years of work and computer imaging have now allowed researchers to interpret this 4.4-million-year-old individual. The skeleton, nicknamed "Ardi," has more than 50 percent of the skeleton represented; however, since it was found in such poor condition, any reconstruction must be seen as provisional and open to varying interpretations. Ardi has been sexed as female and contains several key portions, including a skull, a pelvis, and almost complete hands and feet (White et al., 2009; **Fig. 11-10**).

Brain size, estimated between 300 and 350 cm^3, is quite small, being no larger than a chimpanzee's. However, it is much like that seen in *Sahelanthropus*, and overall, the skulls of the two hominins also appear to be similar. The fact that remains of the postcranial skeleton are preserved is potentially crucial, because key body elements, such as the pelvis and the foot, are only very rarely discovered. This is the *earliest* hominin for which we have so many different parts of the body represented, and it permits researchers to hypothesize more confidently about body size and proportions and, perhaps most crucially of all, the mode of locomotion.

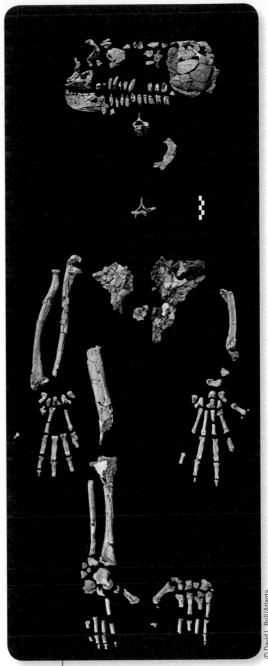

© David L. Brill/Atlanta

▲ **Figure 11-10**
A mostly complete (but fragmented) skeleton of *Ardipithecus*. Dating to about 4.4 mya, this is the earliest hominin skeleton yet found containing so many different portions of the body.

Aramis (air-ah-miss)

Height is estimated at close to 4 feet, with a body weight of around 110 pounds. Compared to other early hominins, such a body size would be similar to that of a male and well above average for a female (**Table 11-1**). The pelvis and foot are preserved well enough to allow good-quality computer reconstructions. According to Tim White and colleagues, both areas of the body show key anatomical changes indicating that *Ardipithecus* was a competent biped. For example, the ilium is short and broad (see Figs. 11-2 and 11-3), and the foot has been modified to act as a prop for propulsion during walking.

However, Ardi also contains some big surprises. While the shape of the ilium seems to show bipedal abilities, other parts of the pelvis show more ancestral ("primitive") hominoid characteristics. In fact, the paleoanthropologists who analyzed the skeleton concluded that Ardi likely walked quite adequately, but might well have had difficulty running (Lovejoy et al., 2009a, 2009b). The foot is also an odd mix of features, showing a big toe that is highly divergent and capable of considerable grasping. Some researchers are not convinced that Ardi was bipedal, and considering all her other primitive characteristics, some have questioned whether *Ardipithecus* was really a hominin at all (Sarmiento, 2010). The extreme degree of reconstruction that was required (for the skull and pelvis especially) adds further uncertainty to understanding this crucial discovery. One thing that everyone agrees on is that Ardi was an able climber who likely was well adapted to walking on all fours along the tops of branches. It seems clear that she spent a lot of time in the trees.

Accepting for the moment that *Ardipithecus* was a hominin, it was a very primitive one, displaying an array of characteristics quite distinct from all later members of our lineage. In fact, its combination of characteristics is very odd and unique among our lineage. The new evi-

dence that Ardi provides has not convinced all paleoanthropologists that *Ardipithecus* or any of the other very early pre-australopiths are hominins; indeed, Ardi's very odd anatomy has caused doubts to increase. One thing is for sure: It would take a considerable adaptive shift in the next 200,000 years to produce the more derived hominins we'll discuss in a moment. All of these considerations have not only intrigued professional anthropologists; they have also captured the imagination of the general public. When did the earliest member of our lineage first appear? The search still goes on, and professional reputations are made and lost in this quest.

Another intriguing aspect of all these late Miocene/early Pliocene locales (that is, Toros-Menalla, Tugen Hills, early Middle Awash sites, and Aramis) relates to the ancient environments associated with these earliest hominins. Rather than the more open grassland savanna habitats so characteristic of most later hominin sites, the environment at all these early locales is more heavily forested. Perhaps we are seeing at Aramis and these other ancient sites the very beginnings of hominin divergence, not long after the division from the African apes.

Australopiths (4.2–1.2 mya)

The best-known, most widely distributed, and most diverse of the early African hominins are colloquially called **australopiths**. In fact, this diverse and very successful group of hominins is made up of two closely related genera, *Australopithecus* and *Paranthropus*. These hominins have an established time range of over 3 million years, stretching back as early as 4.2 mya and not becoming extinct until apparently close to 1 mya—making them the longest-enduring hominins yet documented. In addition, these hominins have been found in all the

australopiths A colloquial name referring to a diverse group of Plio-Pleistocene African hominins. Australopiths are the most abundant and widely distributed of all early hominins and are also the most completely studied.

TABLE 11.1	Estimated Body Weights and Stature in Plio-Pleistocene Hominins

| | Body Weight | | Stature | |
	Male	Female	Male	Female
A. afarensis	45 kg (99 lb)	29 kg (64 lb)	151 cm (59 in.)	105 cm (41 in.)
A. africanus	41 kg (90 lb)	30 kg (65 lb)	138 cm (54 in.)	115 cm (45 in.)
A. robustus	40 kg (88 lb)	32 kg (70 lb)	132 cm (52 in.)	110 cm (43 in.)
A. boisei	49 kg (108 lb)	34 kg (75 lb)	137 cm (54 in.)	124 cm (49 in.)
H. habilis	52 kg (114 lb)	32 kg (70 lb)	157 cm (62 in.)	125 cm (49 in.)

Source: After McHenry, 1992. *Note:* Reno et al. (2003) conclude that sexual dimorphism in *A. afarensis* was considerably less than shown here.

major geographical areas of Africa that have, to date, produced early hominin finds, namely, South Africa, central Africa (Chad), and East Africa. From all these areas combined, there appears to have been considerable complexity in terms of evolutionary diversity, with numerous species now recognized by most paleoanthropologists.

There are two major subgroups of australopiths, an earlier one that is more anatomically primitive and a later one that is much more derived. These earlier australopiths, dated 4.2–3.0 mya, show several more primitive (ancestral) hominin characteristics than the later australopith group, whose members are more derived,

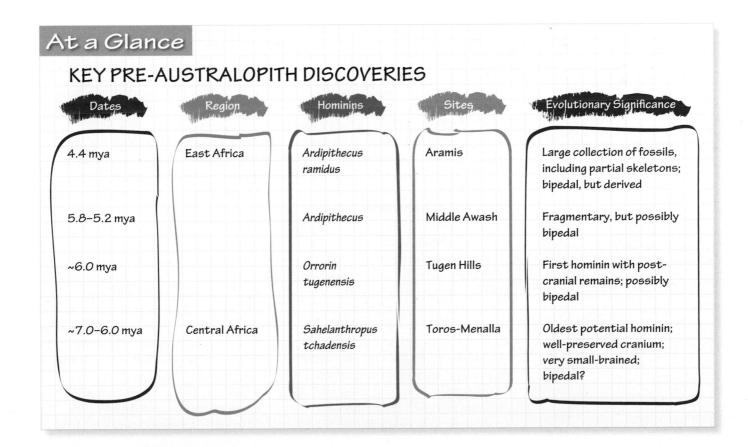

At a Glance

KEY PRE-AUSTRALOPITH DISCOVERIES

Dates	Region	Hominins	Sites	Evolutionary Significance
4.4 mya	East Africa	*Ardipithecus ramidus*	Aramis	Large collection of fossils, including partial skeletons; bipedal, but derived
5.8–5.2 mya		*Ardipithecus*	Middle Awash	Fragmentary, but possibly bipedal
~6.0 mya		*Orrorin tugenensis*	Tugen Hills	First hominin with post-cranial remains; possibly bipedal
~7.0–6.0 mya	Central Africa	*Sahelanthropus tchadensis*	Toros-Menalla	Oldest potential hominin; well-preserved cranium; very small-brained; bipedal?

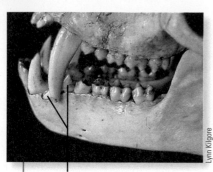

Sectorial lower first premolar

▲ **Figure 11-11**
Sectorial lower first premolar. Left lateral view of the teeth of a male patas monkey. Note how the large upper canine shears against the elongated surface of the sectorial lower first premolar.

some extremely so. These more derived hominins lived after 2.5 mya and are composed of two different genera, together represented by at least five different species (see Appendix C for a complete listing and more information about early hominin fossil finds).

Given the 3-million-year time range as well as quite varied ecological niches, there are numerous intriguing adaptive differences among these varied australopith species. We'll discuss the major adaptations of the various species in a moment. But first let's emphasize the major features that all australopiths share:

1. They are all clearly bipedal (although not necessarily identical to *Homo* in this regard).
2. They all have relatively small brains (at least compared to *Homo*).
3. They all have large teeth, particularly the back teeth, with thick to very thick enamel on the molars.

In short, then, all these australopith species are relatively small-brained, big-toothed bipeds.

The earliest australopiths, dating to 4.2–3.0 mya, come from East Africa from a couple of sites in northern Kenya. Among the fossil finds of these earliest australopiths so far discovered, a few postcranial pieces clearly indicate that locomotion was bipedal. There are, however, a few primitive features in the dentition, including a large canine and a **sectorial** lower first premolar (**Fig. 11-11**).

Since these particular fossils have initially been interpreted as more primitive than all the later members of the genus *Australopithecus*, paleoanthropologists have provisionally assigned them to a separate species. This important fossil species is now called *Australopithecus anamensis*, and some researchers suggest that it is a potential ancestor for many later australopiths as well as perhaps early members of the genus *Homo* (White et al., 2006).

Australopithecus afarensis Slightly later and much more complete remains of *Australopithecus* have come primarily from the sites of Hadar (in Ethiopia) and Laetoli (in Tanzania). Much of this material has been known for three decades, and the fossils have been very well studied; indeed, in certain instances, they are quite famous. For example, the Lucy skeleton was discovered at Hadar in 1974, and the Laetoli footprints were first found in 1978. These hominins are classified as members of the species *Australopithecus afarensis*.

Literally thousands of footprints have been found at Laetoli, representing more than 20 different kinds of animals (Pliocene elephants, horses, pigs, giraffes, antelopes, hyenas, and an abundance of hares). Several hominin footprints have also been found, including a trail more than 75 feet long made by at least two—and perhaps three—individuals (Leakey and Hay, 1979; **Fig. 11-12**). Such discoveries of well-preserved hominin footprints are extremely important in furthering our understanding of human evolution. For the first time, we can make *definite* statements regarding the locomotor pattern and stature of early hominins.

Studies of these impression patterns clearly show that the mode of locomotion of these hominins was bipedal (Day and Wickens, 1980). Some researchers, however, have concluded that *A. afarensis* was not bipedal in quite the same way that modern humans are. From detailed comparisons with modern humans, estimates of stride length, cadence, and speed of walking have been ascertained, indicating that the Laetoli hominins moved in a slow-moving ("strolling") fashion with a rather short stride.

One extraordinary discovery at Hadar is the Lucy skeleton (**Fig. 11-13**), found eroding out of a hillside by Don Johanson. This fossil is scientifically designated as Afar Locality (AL) 288-1, but is usually just called Lucy (after the Beatles song "Lucy in the Sky with Diamonds"). Representing almost 40 percent of a skeleton, this is one of the

sectorial Adapted for cutting or shearing; among primates, refers to the compressed (side-to-side) first lower premolar, which functions as a shearing surface with the upper canine.

◀ **Figure 11-12**
Hominin footprint from Laetoli, Tanzania. Note the deep impression of the heel and the large toe (arrow) in line (adducted) with the other toes.

John Reader / Photo Researchers, Inc.

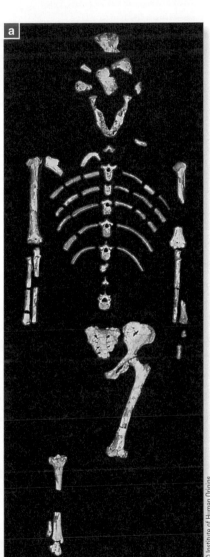

most complete individuals from any-where in the world for the entire period before about 100,000 years ago.

Because the Laetoli area was covered periodically by ashfalls from near-by volcanic eruptions, accurate dating is possible and has provided dates of 3.7–3.5 mya. Dating from the Hadar region hasn't proved as straight-forward; however, more complete dating calibration using a variety of techniques has determined a range of 3.9–3.0 mya for the hominin discoveries from this area.

Several hundred *A. afarensis* specimens, representing a minimum of 60 individuals (and perhaps as many as 100), have been removed from Laetoli and Hadar. At present, these materials represent the largest *well-studied* collection of early hominins and as such are among the most significant of the hominins discussed in this chapter.

Without question, *A. afarensis* is more primitive than any of the other later australo-pith fossils from South or East Africa (discussed shortly). By "primitive" we mean that *A. afarensis* is less evolved in any particular direction than are later-occurring hominin species. That is, *A. afarensis* shares more primitive features

with other late Miocene apes and with living great apes than do later homi-nins, who display more derived characteristics.

For example, the teeth of *A. afaren-sis* are quite primitive. The canines are often large, pointed teeth. Moreover, the lower first premolar is semisectori-al (that is, it provides a shearing surface for the upper canine), and the tooth

© 2010 Photo E. Daynes – Reconstruction Atelier Daynes Paris

© Institute of Human Origins

▲ **Figure 11-13**
(a) "Lucy," a partial hominin skele-ton, discovered at Hadar in 1974. This individual is assigned to *Australopithecus afarensis.*
(b) Artist's reconstruction of a female *A. afarensis* derived from study of the Lucy skeleton.

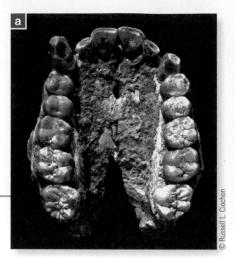

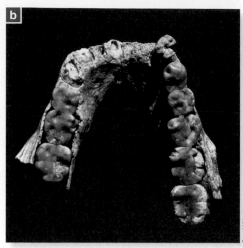

▶ **Figure 11-14**

Jaws of *Australopithecus afarensis.*
(a) Maxilla, AL 200-1a, from Hadar,
Ethiopia. (Note the parallel tooth
rows and large canines.) (b)
Mandible, LH 4, from Laetoli,
Tanzania. This fossil is the type
specimen for the species
Australopithecus afarensis.

rows are parallel, even converging somewhat toward the back of the mouth (**Fig. 11-14**).

The cranial portions that are preserved also display several primitive hominoid characteristics, including a crest in the back as well as several primitive features of the cranial base. Cranial capacity estimates for *A. afarensis* show a mixed pattern when compared with later hominins. A provisional estimate for the one partially complete cranium—apparently a large individual—gives a figure of 500 cm³, but another, even more fragmentary cranium is apparently quite a bit smaller and has been estimated at about 375 cm³ (Holloway, 1983). Thus, for some individuals (males?), *A. afarensis* is well within the range of other australopith species (see "A Closer Look: Cranial Capacity"), but others (females?) may have a significantly smaller cranial capacity. However, a detailed depiction of cranial size for *A. afarensis* is not possible at this time; this part of the skeleton is unfortunately too poorly represented. One thing is clear: *A. afarensis* had a small brain, probably averaging for the whole species not much over 420 cm³.

On the other hand, a large assortment of postcranial pieces representing almost all portions of the body of *A. afarensis* has been found. Initial impressions suggest that relative to lower limbs, the upper limbs are lon-

ger than in modern humans (also a primitive Miocene ape condition). (This statement does not mean that the arms of *A. afarensis* were longer than the legs.) In addition, the wrist, hand, and foot bones show several differences from modern humans (Susman et al., 1985). From such excellent postcranial evidence, stature can be confidently estimated: *A. afarensis* was a short hominin. From her partial skeleton, Lucy is estimated to be only 3 to 4 feet tall. However, Lucy—as demonstrated by her pelvis—was probably a female, and there is evidence of larger individuals as well. The most economical hypothesis explaining this variation is that *A. afarensis* was quite sexually dimorphic: The larger individuals are male, and the smaller ones, such as Lucy, are female. Estimates of male stature can be approximated from the larger footprints at Laetoli, inferring a height of not quite 5 feet. If we accept this interpretation, *A. afarensis* was a very sexually dimorphic form indeed. In fact, for overall body size, this species may have been as dimorphic as *any* living primate (that is, as much as gorillas, orangutans, or baboons).

Significant further discoveries of *A. afarensis* have come from Ethiopia in the last few years, including two further partial skeletons. The first of these is a mostly complete skeleton of an *A. afarensis* infant discovered at the

Cranial Capacity

Cranial capacity, usually reported in cubic centimeters, is a measure of brain size, or volume. The brain itself, of course, doesn't fossilize. However, the space once occupied by brain tissue (the inside of the cranial vault) does sometimes preserve, at least in those cases where fairly complete crania are recovered.

For purposes of comparison, it's easy to obtain cranial capacity estimates for contemporary species (including humans) from analyses of skeletonized specimens in museum collections. From studies of this nature, estimated cranial capacities for modern hominoids have been determined as follows (Tobias, 1971, 1983):

	Range (cm³)	Average (cm³)
Human	1150–1750*	1325
Chimpanzee	285–500	395
Gorilla	340–752	506
Orangutan	276–540	411
Bonobo	—	350

*The range of cranial capacity for modern humans is very large—in fact, even greater than that shown (which approximates cranial capacity for the majority of contemporary *H. sapiens* populations).

These data for living hominoids can then be compared with those obtained for early hominins:

	Average (cm³)
Sahelanthropus	~350
Orrorin	Not currently known
Ardipithecus	~420
Australopithecus anamensis	Not currently known
Australopithecus afarensis	438
Later australopiths	410–530
Early members of genus *Homo*	631

As the tabulations indicate, cranial capacity estimates for australopiths fall within the range of most modern great apes, and gorillas actually average slightly greater cranial capacity than *that seen in most early hominins*. It's important to remember, however, that gorillas are very large animals, whereas most early hominins probably weighed on the order of 100 pounds (see Table 11-1). Since brain size is partially correlated with body size, comparing such different-sized animals can't be justified. Compared to living chimpanzees (most of which are slightly larger than early hominins) and bonobos (which are somewhat smaller), australopiths had *proportionately* about 10 percent bigger brains, and so we would say that these early hominins were more *encephalized*.

Dikika locale in northeastern Ethiopia, very near the Hadar sites mentioned earlier (**Fig. 11-15**). What's more, the infant comes from the same geological horizon as Hadar, with very similar dating: 3.3–3.2 mya (Alemseged et al., 2006).

This find of a 3-year-old infant is remarkable because it's the first example of a very well-preserved immature hominin prior to about 100,000 years ago. From the infant's extremely well-preserved teeth, scientists hypothesize that she was female. A comprehensive study of her developmental biology has already begun, and many more revelations are surely in store as the Dikika infant is more completely cleaned and studied. For now, and accounting for her immature age, the skeletal pattern appears to be quite similar to what we'd expect in an *A. afarensis* adult. What's more, the limb proportions,

anatomy of the hands and feet, and shape of the scapula (shoulder blade) reveal a similar "mixed" pattern of locomotion. The foot and lower limb indicate that this infant would have been a terrestrial biped; yet, the shoulder and (curved) fingers suggest that she was also capable of climbing about quite ably in the trees.

The second recently discovered *A. afarensis* partial skeleton comes from the Woranso-Mille research area in the central Afar, only about 30 miles north of Hadar (Haile-Selassie et al., 2010). The dating places the find at close to 3.6 mya (almost 400,000 years earlier than Lucy). Moreover, the individual was considerably larger than Lucy and likely was male. Analysis of

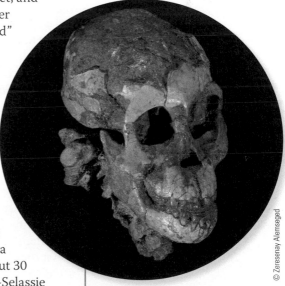

© Zeresenay Alemseged

▲ **Figure 11-15**
Complete skull with attached vertebral column of the infant skeleton from Dikika, Ethiopia (dated to about 3.3 mya).

bones preserved in this new find reinforces what was previously known about *A. afarensis* as well as adding some further insights. The large degree of sexual dimorphism and well-adapted bipedal locomotion agree with prior evidence. What's more, a portion of a shoulder joint (with a scapula; see Appendix A) confirms that suspensory locomotion was not a mode of arboreal locomotion; nevertheless, arboreal habitats could still have been effectively exploited.

What makes *A. afarensis* a hominin? The answer is revealed by its manner of locomotion. From the abundant limb bones recovered from Hadar and other locales, as well as those beautiful footprints from Laetoli, we know unequivocally that *A. afarensis* walked bipedally when on the ground. (At present, we do not have nearly such good evidence concerning locomotion for *any* of the earlier hominin finds.) Whether Lucy and her contemporaries still spent considerable time in the trees and just how efficiently they walked have become topics of some controversy. Most researchers, however, agree that *A. afarensis* was an efficient habitual biped while on the ground. These hominins were also clearly *obligate* bipeds, which would have hampered their climbing abilities but would not necessarily have precluded arboreal behavior altogether.

Australopithecus afarensis is a crucial hominin group. Since it comes after the earliest, poorly known group of pre-australopith hominins, but prior to all later australopiths as well as *Homo*, it is an evolutionary bridge, linking together much of what we assume are the major patterns of early hominin evolution. The fact that there are many well-preserved fossils and that they have been so well studied also adds to the paleoanthropological significance of *A. afarensis*. The consensus among most experts over the last several years has been that *A. afarensis* is a potentially strong candidate as the ancestor of *all* later hominins. Some ongoing analysis has recently chal-

lenged this hypothesis (Rak et al., 2007), but at least for the moment, this new interpretation has not been widely accepted. Still, it reminds us that science is an intellectual pursuit that constantly reevaluates older views and seeks to provide more systematic explanations about the world around us. When it comes to understanding human evolution, we should always be aware that things might change. So stay tuned.

Later More Derived Australopiths (3.0–1.2 mya) Following 3.0 mya, hominins became more diverse in Africa. As they adapted to varied niches, australopiths became considerably more derived. In other words, they show physical changes making them quite distinct from their immediate ancestors.

In fact, there were at least three separate lineages of hominins living (in some cases side by side) between 2.0 and 1.2 mya. One of these is a later form of *Australopithecus*; another is represented by the highly derived three species that belong to the genus *Paranthropus*; and the last consists of early members of the genus *Homo*. Here we'll discuss *Paranthropus* and *Australopithecus*. *Homo* will be discussed in the next section.

The most derived australopiths are the various members of *Paranthropus*. While all australopiths are big-toothed, *Paranthropus* has the biggest teeth of all, especially as seen in its huge premolars and molars. Along with these massive back teeth, these hominins show a variety of other specializations related to powerful chewing (**Fig. 11-16**). For example, they all have large, deep lower jaws and large attachments for muscles associated with chewing. In fact, these chewing muscles are so prominent that major anatomical alterations evolved in the architecture of their face and skull vault. In particular, the *Paranthropus* face is flatter than that of any other australopith; the broad cheekbones (to which the masseter muscle attaches)

sagittal crest A ridge of bone that runs down the middle of the cranium like a short Mohawk. This serves as the attachment for the large temporal muscles, indicating strong chewing.

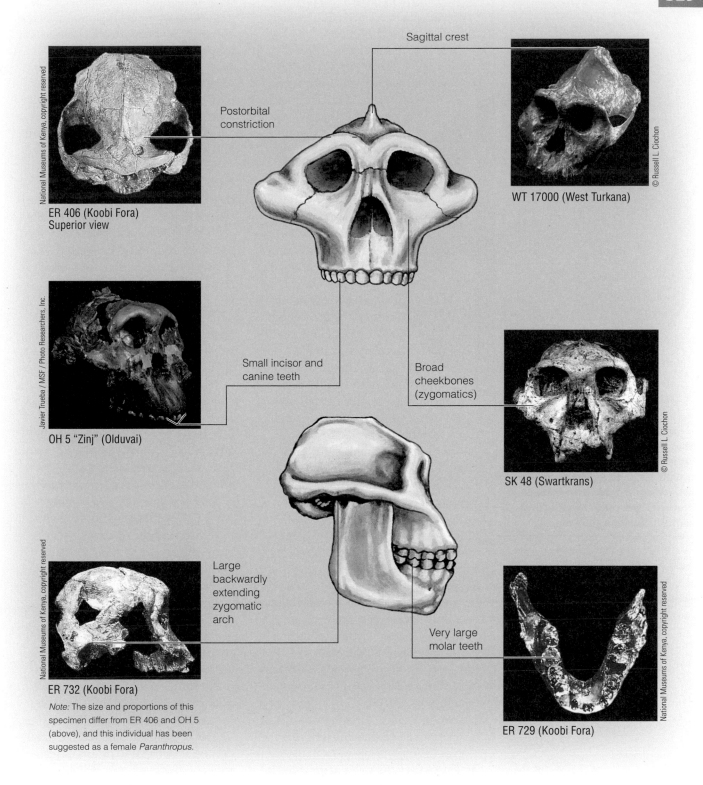

Sagittal crest

Postorbital constriction

Small incisor and canine teeth

Broad cheekbones (zygomatics)

Large backwardly extending zygomatic arch

Very large molar teeth

ER 406 (Koobi Fora) Superior view

WT 17000 (West Turkana)

OH 5 "Zinj" (Olduvai)

SK 48 (Swartkrans)

ER 732 (Koobi Fora)

Note: The size and proportions of this specimen differ from ER 406 and OH 5 (above), and this individual has been suggested as a female *Paranthropus*.

ER 729 (Koobi Fora)

▲ **Figure 11-16**

Morphology and variation in *Paranthropus.* **(Note both typical features and range of variation as shown in different specimens.)**

flare out; and a ridge develops on top of the skull (this is called a **sagittal crest**, and it's where the temporal muscle attaches).

All these morphological features suggest that *Paranthropus* was adapted for a diet emphasizing rough vegetable foods. However, this does not mean that these very big-toothed hominins did not also eat a variety of other foods, perhaps including some meat. In fact, sophisticated recent chemical analyses of *Paranthropus* teeth suggest that their diet may have been quite varied (Sponheimer et al., 2006).

The first member of the *Paranthropus* evolutionary group (clade) comes from a site in northern Kenya on the west side of Lake Turkana. This key find is that of a nearly complete skull, called the "Black Skull" (owing to chemical staining during fossilization), and it dates to approximately 2.5 mya (**Fig. 11-17**). This skull, with a cranial capacity of only 410 cm³, is among the smallest for any hominin known, and it has other primitive traits reminiscent of *A. afarensis*. For example, there's a compound crest in the back of the skull, the upper face projects considerably, and the upper dental row converges in back (Kimbel et al., 1988).

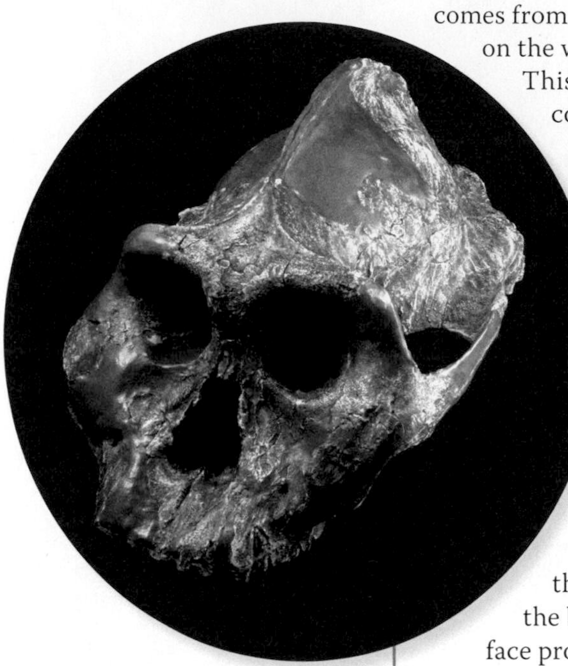

But here's what makes the Black Skull so fascinating: Mixed into this array of distinctively primitive traits are a host of derived ones that link it to other, later *Paranthropus* species (including a broad face, a very large palate, and a large area for the back teeth). This mosaic of features seems to place this individual between earlier *A. afarensis* on the one hand and the later *Paranthropus* species on the other. Because of its unique position in hominin evolution, the Black Skull (and the population it represents) has been placed in a new species, *Paranthropus aethiopicus*.

Around 2 mya, different varieties of even more derived members of the *Paranthropus* lineage were on the scene in East Africa. As well documented by finds dated after 2 mya from Olduvai and East Turkana, *Paranthropus* continues to have relatively small cranial capacities (ranging from 510 to 530 cm³) and very large, broad faces with massive back teeth and lower jaws. The larger (probably male) individuals also

show that characteristic raised ridge (sagittal crest) along the midline of the cranium. Females are not as large or as robust as the males, indicating a fair degree of sexual dimorphism. In any case, the East African *Paranthropus* individuals are all extremely robust in terms of their teeth and jaws—although in overall body size they are much like other australopiths. Since these somewhat later East African *Paranthropus** fossils are so robust, they are usually placed in their own separate species, *Paranthropus boisei*.

Paranthropus fossils have also been found at several sites in South Africa. As we discussed earlier, the geological context in South Africa usually does not allow as precise chronometric dating as is possible in East Africa. Based on less precise dating methods, *Paranthropus* in South Africa existed about 2.0–1.2 mya.

Paranthropus in South Africa is very similar to its close cousin in East Africa, but it's not quite as dentally robust. As a result, paleoanthropologists prefer to regard South African *Paranthropus* as a distinct species—one called *Paranthropus robustus*.

What became of *Paranthropus*? After 1 mya, these hominins seem to vanish without descendants. Nevertheless, we should be careful not to think of them as "failures." After all, they lasted for 1.5 million years, during which time they expanded over a considerable area of sub-Saharan Africa. Moreover, while their extreme dental/chewing adaptations may seem peculiar to us, it was a fascinating "evolutionary experiment" in hominin evolution. And it was an innovation that worked for a long time. Still, these big-toothed cousins of ours did eventually die out. It remains to us, the descendants of another hominin lineage, to find their fossils, study them, and ponder what these creatures were like.

---

* Note that these later East African *Paranthropus* finds are at least 500,000 years later than the earlier species (*P. aethiopicus*, exemplified by the Black Skull).

© Russell L. Ciochon

▲ **Figure 11-17**
The "Black Skull," discovered at West Lake Turkana. This specimen is usually assigned to *Paranthropus aethiopicus*. It's called the Black Skull due to its dark color from the fossilization (mineralization) process.

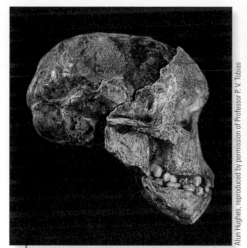

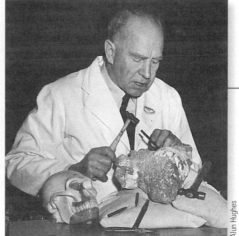

◀ **Figure 11-19**
Raymond Dart, shown working in his laboratory.

▲ **Figure 11-18**
The Taung child's skull, discovered in 1924. There is a fossilized endocast of the brain in back, with the face and lower jaw in front.

From no site dating after 3 mya in East Africa have fossil finds of the genus *Australopithecus* been found. As you know, their close *Paranthropus* kin were doing quite well during this time. Whether *Australopithecus* actually did become extinct in East Africa following 3 mya or whether we just haven't yet found their fossils is impossible to say.

South Africa, however, is another story. A very well-known*Australopithecus* species has been found at four sites in southernmost Africa, in a couple of cases in limestone caves very close to where *Paranthropus* fossils have also been found.

In fact, the very first early hominin discovery from Africa (indeed, from *anywhere*) came from the Taung site and was discovered back in 1924. The story of the discovery of the beautifully preserved child's skull from Taung is a fascinating tale (**Fig. 11-18**). When first published in 1925 by a young anatomist named Raymond Dart (**Fig. 11-19**), most experts were unimpressed. They thought Africa to be an unlikely place for the origins of hominins. These skeptics, who had been long focused on European and Asian hominin finds, were initially unprepared to acknowledge Africa's central

place in human evolution. Only years later, following many more African discoveries from other sites, did professional opinion shift. With this admittedly slow scientific awareness came the eventual consensus that Taung (which Dart classified as *Australopithecus africanus*) was indeed an ancient member of the hominin family tree.

Like other australopiths, the "Taung baby" and other *A. africanus* individuals (**Fig. 11-20**) were small-brained, with an adult cranial capacity of about 440 cm³. They were also big-toothed, although not as extremely so as in *Paranthropus*. Moreover, from very well-preserved postcranial remains from Sterkfontein, we know that they also were well-adapted bipeds. The ongoing excavation of the remarkably complete skeleton at Sterkfontein should tell us about *A. africanus'* locomotion, body size and proportions, and much more.

The precise dating of *A. africanus*, as with most other South African hominins, has

▼ **Figure 11-20**
Australopithecus africanus adult cranium from Sterkfontein.

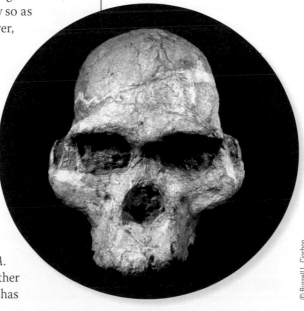

been disputed. Over the last several years, it's been assumed that this species existed as far back as 3.3 mya. However, the most recent analysis suggests that *A. africanus* lived approximately between 3 and 2 mya (Walker et al., 2006; Wood, 2010; **Fig. 11-21**).

A Transitional Australopith? As we'll see in the next section, almost all the evidence for the earliest appearance of our genus, *Homo*, has come from East Africa. So it's no surprise that most researchers have assumed that *Homo* probably first evolved in this region of Africa.

However, new and remarkably well-preserved fossil discoveries from South Africa have significantly challenged this view. In 2008, paleoanthropologists discovered two partial skeletons at the Malapa Cave, located just a few miles from Sterkfontein and Swartkrans (see Fig. 11-6). Actually, the first find was made by the lead researcher's 9-year-old son, Matthew. His father (Lee Berger, from the University of Witwatersrand) and colleagues have been further investigating inside the cave, where several skeletons may be buried, and they announced and described these finds in 2010 (Berger et al., 2010).

Using more precise radiometric techniques than have been used before in South Africa (Dirks et al., 2010; see

Chap. 10), the fossils are dated to just a little less than 2 mya and show a fascinating mix of australopith characteristics along with many features more suggestive of *Homo*. Because of this unique anatomical combination, these fossils have been assigned to a new species, *Australopithecus sediba* (*sediba* means "wellspring" or "fountain" in the local language). Australopith-like characteristics seen in *A. sediba* include a small brain (estimated at 420 cm³), the australopith shoulder joint, long arms with curved fingers, and several primitive traits in the feet. In these respects *A. sediba* most resembles its potential immediate South African predecessor, *A. africanus*.

On the other hand, many other aspects of *A. sediba* more resemble *Homo*. Among these characteristics are smaller teeth, narrower cheekbones (zygomatics), less postorbital constriction of the cranium (see Figs. 11-17 and **11-22**), several aspects of the pelvis, and proportionately less robust upper limbs (as compared to lower limbs; **Fig. 11-23**). These latter two traits might indicate that *A. sediba* was becoming adapted to a more fully terrestrial niche and was thus less arboreal than other australopiths (and more like *Homo*).

All this is very new and quite complex. Indeed, initial paleoanthropologi-

▼ **Figure 11-21**
Time line of early African hominins. Note that most dates are approximations. Question marks indicate those estimates that are most tentative.

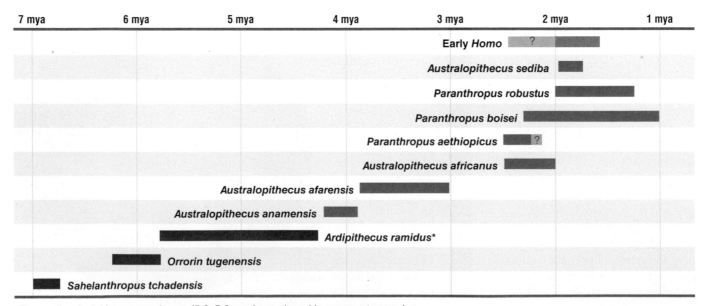

*The earlier *Ardipithecus* specimens (5.8–5.2 mya) are placed in a separate species.

cal interpretations are highly varied (Balter, 2010). It will take some time for experts to figure it out. Remember, too, that there are more fossils still in the cave. For the moment, the initial consensus among paleoanthropologists is that *A. sediba* is very different from other australopiths. In particular, it's more like genus *Homo* than any other known australopith species. So, was *A. sediba* the immediate ancestor of *Homo*, and did this transition take place in South Africa? Perhaps. But let's look at the fossils that many researchers have considered the earliest evidence of the evolution of *Homo*—and these come from East Africa.

Early *Homo* (2.0+–1.4 mya)

In addition to the australopith remains, there's another largely contemporaneous hominin that is quite distinctive and thought to be more closely related to us. In fact, as best documented by fossil discoveries from Olduvai and East Turkana, these materials have been assigned to the genus *Homo*—and thus are different from all species assigned to either *Australopithecus* or *Paranthropus*.

The earliest appearance of genus *Homo* in East Africa may date back well before 2 mya (and thus considerably before *A. sediba*). A discovery in the 1990s from the Hadar area of Ethiopia suggested to many paleoanthropologists that early *Homo* was present in East Africa by 2.3 mya; however, we must be cautious, since the find is quite incomplete (including only one upper jaw). The recent discovery of *A. sediba* provides better evidence of a transition from *Australopithecus* to *Homo* in South Africa than anything yet found in East Africa.

Better-preserved evidence of a **Plio-Pleistocene** hominin with a significantly larger brain than seen in aus-

tralopiths was first suggested by Louis Leakey in the early 1960s on the basis of fragmentary remains found at Olduvai Gorge. Leakey and his colleagues gave a new species designation to these fossil remains, naming them *Homo habilis*. There may, in fact, have been more than one species of *Homo* living in Africa during the Plio-Pleistocene. So, more generally, we'll refer to them all as "early *Homo*." The species *Homo habilis* refers particularly to those early *Homo* fossils from Olduvai and the Turkana Basin. There is no evidence of transitional fossils in East Africa, so it's entirely possible that just after 2 mya, *H. habilis* first evolved in South Africa and then quite quickly spread to East Africa (see **Fig. 11-24**).

The *Homo habilis* material at Olduvai dates to about 1.8 mya, but due to the fragmentary nature of the fossil remains, evolutionary interpretations have been difficult. The most immediately obvious feature distinguishing the *H. habilis* material from the australopiths is cranial size. For all the measurable early *Homo* skulls, the estimated average cranial capacity is 631 cm³, compared to 520 cm³ for all measurable *Paranthropus* specimens and 442 cm³ for *Australopithecus* crania (McHenry, 1988), including *A. sediba* (see "A Closer Look: Cranial Capacity"). Early *Homo*, therefore, shows an increase in cranial size of about 20 percent over the larger of the

◀ **Figure 11-22**
A. sediba skull, found at Malapa Cave, South Africa. The morphology of this and another well-preserved individual suggests this species may have been transitional between australopiths and *Homo*.

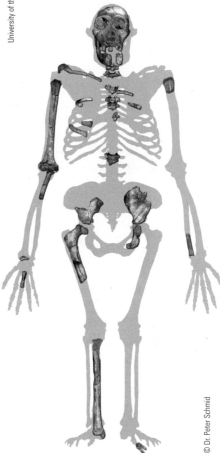

▲ **Figure 11-23**
One of the two partial *A. sediba* skeletons so far discovered at Malapa Cave, showing those elements that were preserved.

Plio-Pleistocene Pertaining to the Pliocene and first half of the Pleistocene, a time range of 5–1 mya. For this time period, numerous fossil hominins have been found in Africa.

▲ **Figure 11-24**
Artist's reconstruction of a female *Homo habilis* based on a cranium from East Lake Turkana (skull 1813; see photo of this specimen in Figure 11-26.)

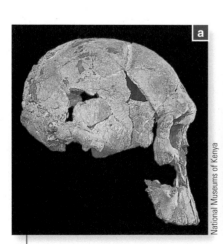

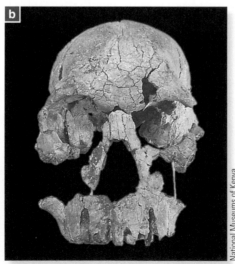

▲ **Figure 11-25**
A nearly complete early *Homo* cranium from East Lake Turkana (ER 1470), one of the most important single fossil hominin discoveries from East Africa. (a) Lateral view. (b) Frontal view.

australopiths and an even greater increase over some of the smaller-brained forms. In their initial description of *H. habilis*, Leakey and his associates also pointed to differences from australopiths in cranial shape and in tooth proportions (with early members of genus *Homo* showing larger front teeth relative to back teeth and narrower premolars).

The naming of this fossil material as *Homo habilis* ("handy man") was meaningful from two perspectives. First of all, Leakey argued that members of this group were the early Olduvai toolmakers. Second, and most significantly, by calling this group *Homo*, Leakey was arguing for at least *two separate branches* of hominin evolution in the Plio-Pleistocene. Clearly, only one could be on the main branch eventually leading to *Homo sapiens*. By labeling this new group *Homo* rather than *Australopithecus*, Leakey was guessing that he had found our ancestors.

Because the initial evidence was so fragmentary, most paleoanthropologists were reluctant to accept *H. habilis* as a valid species distinct from all australopiths. Later discoveries, especially from Lake Turkana, of better-preserved fossils have shed further light on early *Homo* in the Plio-Pleistocene.* The most important of this additional material is a nearly complete cranium (**Fig. 11-25**). With a cranial capacity of 775 cm³, this individual is well outside the known range for australopiths and actually overlaps the lower boundary for later species of *Homo* (that is, *H. erectus*, discussed in the next chapter). In addition, the shape of the skull vault is in many respects unlike that of australopiths. However, the face is still quite robust (Walker, 1976), and the fragments of tooth crowns that are pre-

---

* Some early *Homo* fossils from East Turkana are classified by a minority of paleoanthropologists as a different species (*Homo rudolfensis*; see Appendix C). These researchers often identify both *H. habilis* and *H. rudolfensis* at Turkana but only *H. habilis* at Olduvai.

served indicate that the back teeth in this individual were quite large.[†] The East Turkana early *Homo* material is generally contemporaneous with the Olduvai remains. The oldest date back to about 1.8 mya, but a newly discovered specimen dates to as recently as 1.44 mya, making it by far the latest surviving early *Homo* fossil yet found (Spoor et al., 2007). In fact, this discovery indicates that a species of early *Homo* coexisted in East Africa for several hundred thousand years with *H. erectus*, with both species living in the exact same area on the eastern side of Lake Turkana. This new evidence raises numerous fascinating questions regarding how two closely related species existed for so long in the same region.

As in East Africa, early members of the genus *Homo* have also been found in South Africa, and these fossils are considered more distinctive of *Homo* than is the *transitional* australopith, *A. sediba*. At both Sterkfontein and Swartkrans, fragmentary remains have been recognized as most likely belonging to *Homo* (**Fig. 11-26**)

On the basis of evidence from Olduvai, East Turkana, and Hadar, we can reasonably postulate that at least one species (and possibly two) of early *Homo* was present in East Africa around 2.0-1.8 mya, developing in parallel with an australopith species. These hominin lines lived contemporaneously for a minimum of 1 million years, after which time the australopiths apparently disappeared forever. One lineage of early *Homo* likely evolved into *H. erectus* about 1.8 mya. Any other species of early *Homo* became extinct sometime after 1.4 mya. In South Africa, the situation is quite different. It's possible that early *Homo* evolved there first, deriving from *A. sediba*. This, however, is not yet certain.

[†] In fact, some researchers have suggested that all these "early *Homo*" fossils are better classified as *Australopithecus* (Wood and Collard, 1999a).

Interpretations: What Does It All Mean?

By this time, you may think that anthropologists are obsessed with finding small scraps buried in the ground and then assigning them confusing numbers and taxonomic labels impossible to remember. But it's important to realize that the collection of all the basic fossil data is the foundation of human evolutionary research. Without fossils, our speculations would be largely hollow—and most certainly not scientifically testable. Several large, ongoing paleoanthropological projects are now collecting additional data in an attempt to answer some of the more perplexing questions about our evolutionary history.

The numbering of specimens, which may at times seem somewhat confusing, is an effort to keep the designations neutral and to make reference to each individual fossil as clear as possible. The formal naming of finds as *Australopithecus*, *Paranthropus*, or *Homo habilis* should come much later, since it involves a lengthy series of complex interpretations. Assigning generic and specific names to fossil finds is more than just a convenience; when we attach a particular label, such as *A. afarensis*, to a particular fossil, we should be fully aware of the biological implications of such an interpretation.

From the time that fossil sites are first located until the eventual interpretation of hominin evolutionary patterns, several steps take place. Ideally, they should follow a logical order, for if interpretations are made too hastily, they confuse important issues for many years. Here's a reasonable sequence:

1. Selecting and surveying sites
2. Excavating sites and recovering fossil hominins

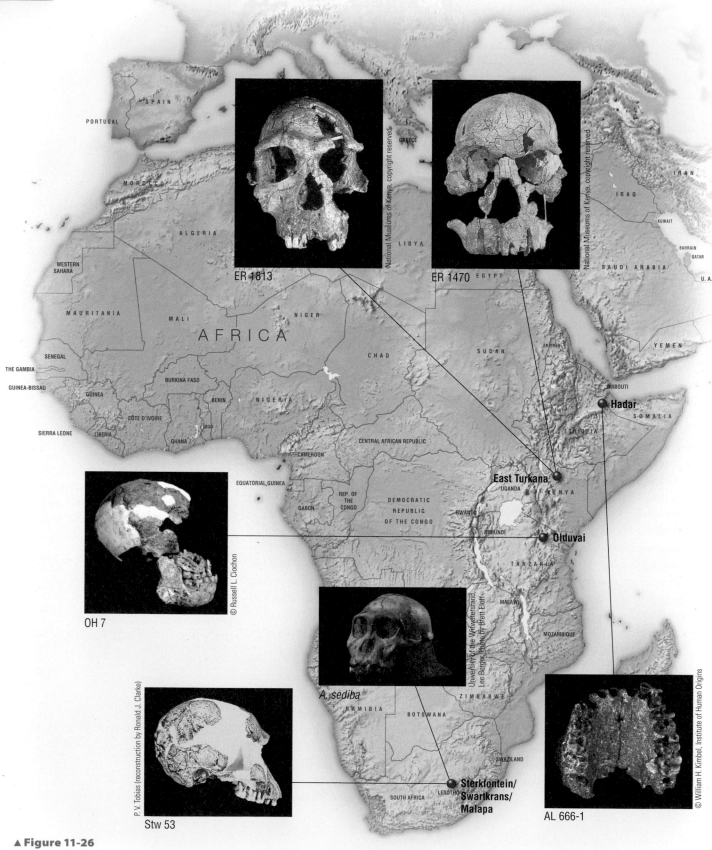

ER 1813

ER 1470

OH 7

A. sediba

Stw 53

AL 666-1

Hadar

East Turkana

Olduvai

Sterkfontein/
Swartkrans/
Malapa

▲ **Figure 11-26**
Early *Homo* and transitional *A. sediba*
fossil finds.

3. Designating individual finds with specimen numbers for clear reference

4. Cleaning, preparing, studying, and describing fossils

5. Comparing with other fossil material—in a chronological framework if possible

6. Comparing fossil variation with known ranges of variation in closely related groups of living primates and analyzing ancestral and derived characteristics

7. Assigning taxonomic names to fossil material

But the task of interpretation still isn't complete, for what we really want to know in the long run is what happened to the populations represented by the fossil remains. In looking at the fossil hominin record, we're actually looking for our ancestors. In the process of eventually determining those populations that are our most likely antecedents, we may conclude that some hominins are on evolutionary side branches. If this conclusion is accurate, those hominins necessarily must have become extinct. It's both interesting and relevant to us as hominins to try to find out what influenced some earlier members of our family tree to continue evolving while others died out.

Although a clear evolutionary picture is not yet possible for organizing all the early hominins discussed in this chapter, there are some general patterns that for now make good sense (**Fig. 11-27**). New finds may of course require serious alterations to this scheme. Science can be exciting but can also be frustrating to many in the general public looking for simple answers to complex questions. For well-informed students of human evolution, it's most important to grasp the basic principles of paleoanthropology and *how* interpretations are made and *why* they sometimes must be revised. This way you'll be prepared for whatever shows up tomorrow.

Seeing the Big Picture: Adaptive Patterns of Early African Hominins

As you are by now aware, there are several different African hominin genera and certainly lots of species. This, in itself, is interesting. Speciation was occurring quite frequently among the various lineages of early hominins—more frequently, in fact, than among later hominins. What explains this pattern?

Evidence has been accumulating at a furious pace in the last decade, but it's still far from complete. What's clear is that we'll never have anything approaching a complete record of early hominin evolution, so some significant gaps will remain. After all, we're able to discover hominins only in those special environmental contexts where fossilization was likely. All the other potential habitats they might have exploited are now invisible to us.

Still, patterns are emerging from the fascinating data we do have. First, it appears that early hominin species (pre-australopiths, *Australopithecus*,

▼ **Figure 11-27**

A tentative early hominin phylogeny. Note the numerous question marks, indicating continuing uncertainty regarding evolutionary relationships.

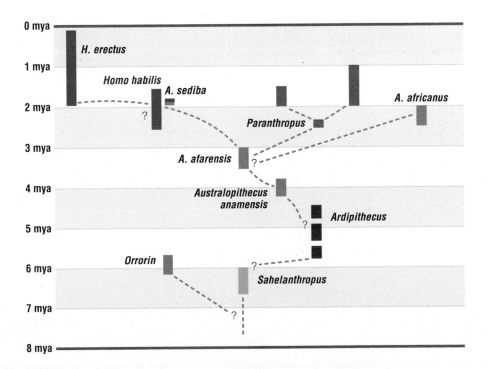

Paranthropus, and early *Homo*) all had restricted ranges. It's therefore likely that each hominin species exploited a relatively small area and could easily have become separated from other populations of its own species. So genetic drift (and to some extent natural selection) could have led to rapid genetic divergence and eventual speciation.

Second, most of these species appear to be at least partially tied to arboreal habitats, although there's disagreement on this point regarding early *Homo* (see Wood and Collard, 1999b; Foley 2002). Also, *Paranthropus* was probably somewhat less arboreal than *Ardipithecus* or *Australopithecus*. These very large-toothed hominins apparently concentrated on a diet of coarse, fibrous plant foods, such as roots. Exploiting such resources may have routinely taken these hominins farther away from the trees than their dentally more gracile—and perhaps more omnivorous—cousins.

Third, except for some early *Homo* individuals, there's very little in the way of an evolutionary trend of increased body size or of markedly greater encephalization. Beginning with *Sahelanthropus*, brain size was no more than that in chimpanzees—although when controlling for body size, this earliest of all known hominins may have had a proportionately larger brain than any living ape. Close to 5 million years later (that is, the time of the last surviving australopith species), relative brain size increased by no more than 10 to 15 percent. Perhaps tied to this relative stasis in brain capacity, there's no absolute association of any of these hominins with patterned stone tool manufacture (see Chapter 10).

Although conclusions are becoming increasingly controversial, for the moment, early *Homo* appears to be a partial exception. This group shows both increased encephalization and numerous occurrences of likely association with stone tools (though at many of the sites, australopith fossils were *also* found). Moreover, some researchers now hypothesize that the earliest *Homo* didn't evolve until around 2 mya. If so, we need to account for 600,000 years prior to this time during which stone tools were already being produced—but

What's Important

Key Early Hominin Fossil Discoveries from Africa

DATES	HOMININS	SITES/REGIONS	THE BIG PICTURE
1.8–1.4 mya	Early *Homo*	Olduvai; E. Turkana (E. Africa)	Bigger-brained; possible ancestor of later *Homo*
1.9 mya	*Australopithecus sediba*	Malapa (S. Africa)	Possibly a transitional species between *Australopithecus* and *Homo*
2.5–2.0 mya	Later *Australopithecus* (*A. africanus*)	Taung; Sterkfontein (S. Africa)	Quite derived; likely evolutionary dead end
2.0–1.0 mya	Later *Paranthropus*	Several sites (E. and S. Africa)	Highly derived; very likely evolutionary dead end
2.4 mya	*Paranthropus aethiopicus*	W. Turkana (E. Africa)	Earliest robust australopith; likely ancestor of later *Paranthropus*
3.6–3.0 mya	*Australopithecus afarensis*	Laetoli; Hadar (E. Africa)	Many fossils; very well studied; earliest well-documented biped; possible ancestor of all later hominins
4.4 mya	*Ardipithecus ramidus*	Aramis (E. Africa)	Many fossils; not yet well studied; bipedal, but likely quite derived; any likely ancestral relationship to later hominins not yet possible to say
~7.0 mya	*Sahelanthropus*	Toros-Menalla (Central Africa)	The earliest hominin; bipedal?

by whom? It would likely have been one or more of the australopith species.

Lastly, all of these early African hominins show an accelerated developmental pattern (similar to that seen in African apes), one quite different from the *delayed* developmental pattern characteristic of *Homo sapiens* (and our immediate precursors). This apelike development is also seen in some early *Homo* individuals (Wood and Collard, 1999a). Rates of development can be accurately reconstructed by examining dental growth markers (Bromage and Dean, 1985), and these data may provide a crucial window into understanding this early stage of hominin evolution.

These African hominin predecessors were rather small, able bipeds, but still closely tied to arboreal and/or climbing niches. They had fairly small brains and, compared to later *Homo*, matured rapidly. It would take a major evolutionary jump to push one of their descendants in a more human direction. For the next chapter in this more human saga, read on.

Summary of Main Topics

- The earliest possible members of our lineage date back to about 6 mya, and for the next 4 million years, they stayed geographically restricted to Africa, where they diversified into many different forms.
- During this several-million-year span, at least 6 different hominin genera and upward of 13 species have been identified from the available fossil record.
- These early African hominins fit into three major groupings:

    Pre-australopiths (6.0+–4.4 mya), including three genera of very early, and still primitive, possible hominins (*Sahelanthropus*, *Orrorin*, and *Ardipithecus*)

    Australopiths (4.2–1.2 mya): Early, more primitive australopith species (4.2–3.0 mya), including *Australopithecus anamensis* and *Australopithecus afarensis*. These are the earliest definite hominins.

    Later, more derived australopith species (2.5–1.2 mya), including two genera (*Paranthropus* and later species of *Australopithecus*). One of these species, just recently discovered (*A. sediba*), seems to be transitional between *Australopithecus* and early *Homo*.

    Early *Homo* (2.0+–1.4 mya), including the first members of our genus, who around 2 mya likely diverged into more than one species

The most important fossil discoveries discussed in this chapter are summarized in "What's Important."

Critical Thinking Questions

1. In what ways are the remains of *Sahelanthropus* and *Ardipithecus* primitive? How do we know that these forms are hominins? How sure are we?

2. Assume that you are in the laboratory analyzing the "Lucy" *A. afarensis* skeleton. You also have complete skeletons from a chimpanzee and a modern human. (a) Which parts of the Lucy skeleton are more similar to the chimpanzee? Which are more similar to the human? (b) Which parts of the Lucy skeleton are *most informative*?

3. Discuss the first thing you would do if you found an early hominin fossil and were responsible for its formal description and publication. What would you include in your publication?

4. Discuss two current disputes regarding taxonomic issues concerning early hominins. Try to give support for alternative positions.

5. What is a phylogeny? Construct one for early hominins (6.0–1.0 mya). Make sure you can describe what conclusions your scheme makes. Also, try to defend it.

Dr. David Lordkipanidze, director of the Georgian National Museum, holds a skull of *Homo erectus*, found at the Dmanisi site, Republic of Georgia.

12

The First Dispersal of the Genus *Homo*: *Homo erectus* and Contemporaries

Key Questions

▶ Who were the first members of the human lineage to disperse from Africa, and what were they like (behaviorally and anatomically)?

▶ How do these hominins compare with modern *Homo sapiens*, and what do they tell us about human evolution?

Today it's estimated that more than 1 million people cross national borders every day. Some travel for business, some for pleasure, and others may be seeking refuge from persecution in their own countries. Regardless, it seems that modern humans have wanderlust—a desire to see distant places. Our most distant hominin ancestors were essentially homebodies, staying in fairly restricted areas, exploiting the local resources, and trying to stay out of harm's way. In this respect, they were much like other primate species.

One thing is certain: All these early hominins were restricted to Africa. When did hominins first leave Africa? What were they like, and why did they leave their ancient homeland? Did they differ physically from their australopith and early *Homo* forebears, and did they have new behavioral and cultural capabilities that helped them successfully exploit new environments?

It would be a romantic misconception to think of these first hominin transcontinental emigrants as "brave pioneers, boldly going where no one had gone before." They weren't deliberately striking out to go someplace in particular. It's not as though they had a map! Still, for what they did, deliberate or not, we owe them a lot.

Sometime close to 2 mya, something decisive occurred in human evolution. As the title of this chapter suggests, for the first time, hominins expanded widely out of Africa into other areas of the Old World. Since all the early fossils have been found *only* in Africa, it seems that hominins were restricted to that continent for perhaps as long as 5 million years. The later, more widely dispersed hominins were quite different both anatomically and behaviorally from their African ancestors. They were much larger, were more committed to a completely terrestrial habitat, used more elaborate stone tools, and probably ate meat.

There is some variation among the different geographical groups of these highly successful hominins, and anthropologists still debate how to classify them. In particular, new discoveries from Europe are forcing a major reevaluation of exactly which were the first to leave Africa (**Fig. 12-1**).

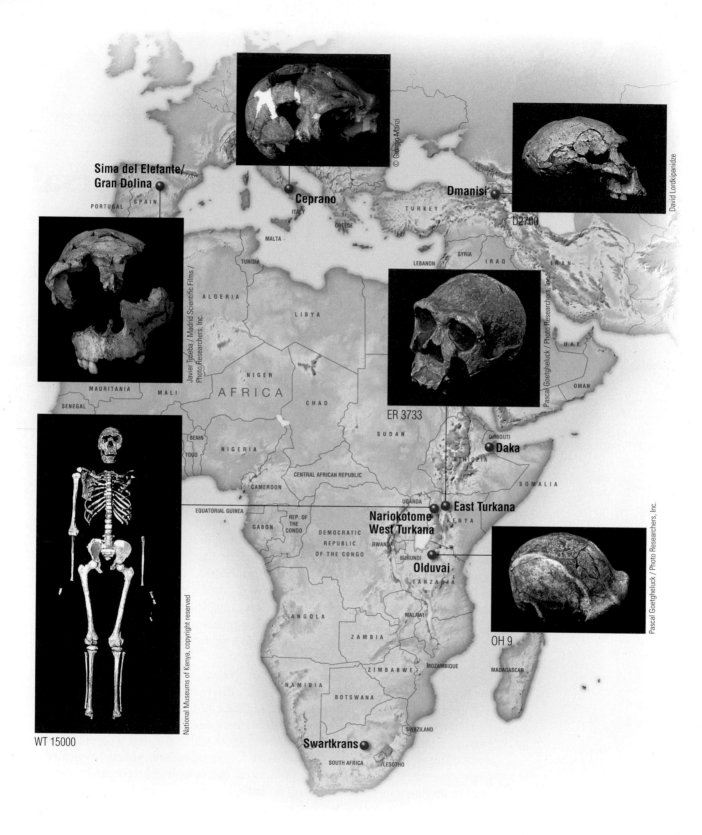

▲ Figure 12-1
Major *Homo erectus* sites and localities of
other contemporaneous hominins.

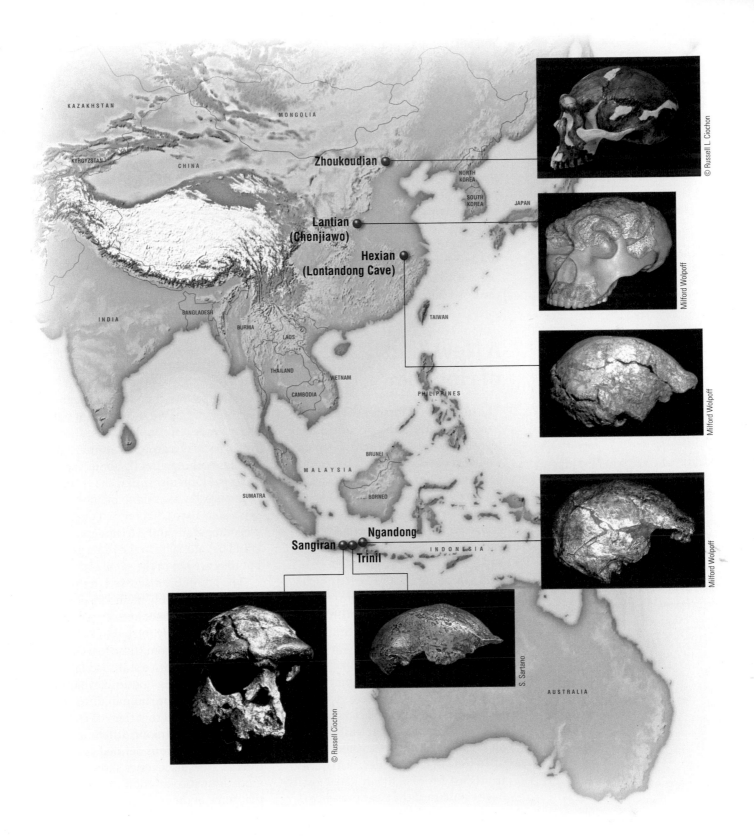

KAZAKHSTAN

KYRGYZSTAN

MONGOLIA

CHINA

Zhoukoudian

NORTH KOREA

SOUTH KOREA

JAPAN

Lantian (Chenjiawo)

Hexian (Lontandong Cave)

TAIWAN

INDIA

BANGLADESH

BURMA

LAOS

THAILAND

VIETNAM

CAMBODIA

PHILIPPINES

MALAYSIA

BRUNEI

SUMATRA

BORNEO

Ngandong

Sangiran

INDONESIA

Trinil

AUSTRALIA

© Russell L. Ciochon

Milford Wolpoff

Milford Wolpoff

Milford Wolpoff

© Russell Ciochon

S. Sartano

Nevertheless, after 2 mya, there's less diversity among these hominins than is apparent in their pre-australopith and australopith predecessors. Consequently, there is universal agreement that the hominins found outside of Africa are all members of genus *Homo*. Thus, taxonomic debates focus solely on how many species are represented. The species for which we have the most evidence is called *Homo erectus*. Furthermore, this is the one group that most paleoanthropologists have recognized for decades and still agree on. Thus, in this chapter we'll focus our discussion on *Homo erectus*. We will, however, also discuss alternative interpretations that "split" the fossil sample into more species.

A New Kind of Hominin

The discovery of fossils now referred to as *Homo erectus* began in the nineteenth century. Later in this chapter, we'll discuss the historical background of these earliest discoveries in Java and the somewhat later discoveries in China. For these fossils, as well as several from Europe and North Africa, a variety of taxonomic names were suggested.

It's important to realize that such taxonomic *splitting* was quite common in the early years of paleoanthropology. More systematic biological thinking came to the fore only after World War II and with the incorporation of the Modern Synthesis into paleontology. Most of the fossils that were given these varied names are now placed in the species *Homo erectus*—or at least they've all been lumped into one genus (*Homo*).

In the last few decades, discoveries from East Africa of firmly dated fossils have established the clear presence of *Homo erectus* by 1.7 mya. Some researchers see several anatomical differences between these African representatives of an *erectus*-like hominin

and their Asian cousins (hominins that almost everybody refers to as *Homo erectus*). Thus, they place the African fossils into a separate species, one they call *Homo ergaster* (Andrews, 1984; Wood, 1991).

While there are some anatomical differences between the African specimens and those from Asia, they are all clearly *closely* related and quite possibly represent geographical varieties of a single species. We'll thus refer to them collectively as *Homo erectus*.

All analyses have shown that *H. erectus* hominins represent a different **grade** of evolution than their more ancient African predecessors. A grade is an evolutionary grouping of organisms showing a similar adaptive pattern. Increase in body size and robustness, changes in limb proportions, and greater encephalization all indicate that these hominins were more like modern humans in their adaptive pattern than their African ancestors were. We should point out that a grade only implies general adaptive aspects of a group of animals; it implies nothing directly about shared ancestry. Organisms that share common ancestry are said to be in the same *clade* (see Chapter 5). For example, orangutans and African great apes could be said to be in the same grade, but they are not in the same clade.

The hominins discussed in this chapter are not only members of a new and distinct grade of human evolution; they're also closely related to each other. It's clear from these fossils that a major adaptive shift had taken place—one setting hominin evolution in a distinctly more human direction.

We mentioned that there is considerable variation among different regional populations defined as *Homo erectus*. New discoveries show even more dramatic variation, suggesting that some of these hominins may not fit closely with this general adaptive pattern (more on this presently). For the moment, however, let's review what most of these fossils look like.

grade A grouping of organisms sharing a similar adaptive pattern. Grade isn't necessarily based on closeness of evolutionary relationship, but it does contrast organisms in a useful way (e.g., *Homo erectus* with *Homo sapiens*).

The Morphology of *Homo erectus*

Homo erectus populations lived in very different environments over much of the Old World. They all, however, shared several common physical traits.

Body Size

Anthropologists estimate that some *H. erectus* adults weighed well over 100 pounds, with an average adult height of about 5 feet 6 inches (McHenry, 1992; Ruff and Walker, 1993; Walker and Leakey, 1993). Another point to keep in mind is that *H. erectus* was quite sexually dimorphic—at least as indicated by the East African specimens. Some adult males may have weighed considerably more than 100 pounds.

Increased height and weight in *H. erectus* are also associated with a dramatic increase in robusticity. In fact, a heavily built body was to dominate hominin evolution not just during *H. erectus* times, but through the long transitional era of premodern forms as well. Only with the appearance of anatomically modern *H. sapiens* did a more gracile skeletal structure emerge, one that still characterizes most modern populations.

Brain Size

While *Homo erectus* differs in several respects from both early *Homo* and *Homo sapiens*, the most obvious feature is cranial size—which is closely related to brain size. Early *Homo* had cranial capacities ranging from as small as 500 cm³ to as large as 800 cm³. *H. erectus*, on the other hand, shows considerable brain enlargement, with a cranial capacity of about 700*° to

---

*Even smaller cranial capacities are seen in recently discovered fossils from the Caucasus region of southeastern Europe at a site called Dmanisi. We'll discuss these fossils in a moment.

1,250 cm³ (and a mean of approximately 900 cm³).

As we've discussed, brain size is closely linked to overall body size. So it's important to note that along with an increase in brain size, *H. erectus* was also considerably larger than earlier members of the genus *Homo*. In fact, when we compare *H. erectus* with the larger-bodied early *Homo* individuals, *relative* brain size is about the same (Walker, 1991). What's more, when we compare the relative brain size of *H. erectus* with that of *H. sapiens*, we see that *H. erectus* was considerably less encephalized than later members of the genus *Homo*.

Cranial Shape

Homo erectus crania display a highly distinctive shape, partly because of increased brain size, but probably more correlated with increased body size. The ramifications of this heavily built cranium are reflected in thick cranial bone (in most specimens), large browridges (supraorbital tori) above the eyes, and a projecting **nuchal torus** at the back of the skull (**Fig. 12-2**).

The braincase is long and low, receding from the large browridges with little forehead development. Also, the cranium is wider at the base compared with earlier *and* later species of genus *Homo*. The maximum cranial breadth is below the ear opening, giving the cranium a pentagonal shape (when viewed from behind). In contrast, the skulls of early *Homo* and *H. sapiens* have more vertical sides, and the maximum width is *above* the ear openings.

Most specimens also have a sagittal keel running along the midline of the skull. Very different from a sagittal crest, the keel is a small ridge that runs front to back along the sagittal suture. The sagittal keel, browridges, and nuchal torus don't seem to have served an obvious function, but most likely reflect bone buttressing in a very robust skull.

nuchal torus (nuke´-ul) (*nucha*, meaning "neck") A projection of bone in the back of the cranium where neck muscles attach. These muscles hold up the head.

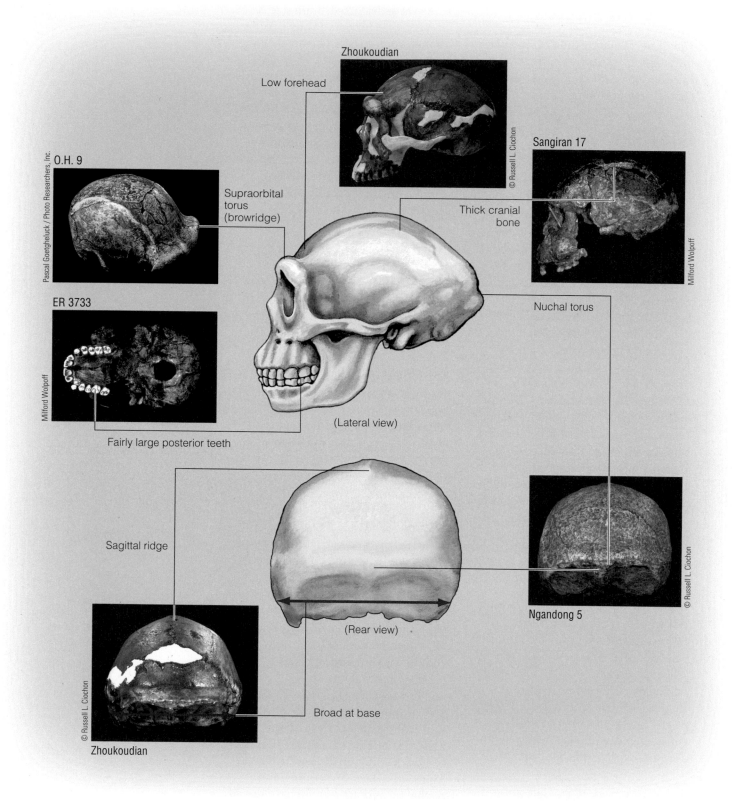

▲ **Figure 12-2**
Morphology and variation in *Homo erectus.*

The First *Homo erectus: Homo erectus* from Africa

Where did *Homo erectus* first appear? The answer seems fairly simple: Most likely, this species initially evolved in Africa. Two important pieces of evidence help confirm this hypothesis. First, *all* of the earlier hominins prior to the appearance of *H. erectus* come from Africa. What's more, by 1.7 mya, there are well-dated fossils of this species at East Turkana, in Kenya, and not long after that at other sites in East Africa.

But there's a small wrinkle in this neat view. We now know that at about 1.8 mya, similar populations were already living far away in southeastern Europe, and by 1.6 mya, in Indonesia. So, adding these pieces to our puzzle, it seems likely that *H. erectus* first arose in East Africa and then very quickly migrated to other continents; nevertheless, as we'll see shortly, the dating of sites from Africa and elsewhere does not yet clearly confirm this hypothesis. Let's first review the African *H. erectus* specimens dated at 1.7–1 mya, and then we'll discuss those populations that emigrated to Europe and Asia.

The earliest of the East African *H. erectus* fossils come from East Turkana, from the same area where earlier australopith and early *Homo* fossils have been found (see Chapter 11). Indeed, it seems likely that in East Africa around 2.0–1.8 mya, some form of early *Homo* evolved into *H. erectus*.

The most significant *H. erectus* fossil from East Turkana is a nearly complete skull (ER 3733; **Fig. 12-3**). Recently redated at 1.7 mya, this fossil has been regarded as the oldest *H. erectus* specimen ever found (but new dates from elsewhere have changed this); it certainly is the oldest known member of this species from Africa (Lepre and Kent, 2010). The cranial capacity is estimated at 848 cm³, in the lower range for *H. erectus* (700 to 1,250 cm³),

which isn't surprising considering its early date. A second very significant new find from East Turkana is notable because it has the smallest cranium of any *H. erectus* specimen from anywhere in Africa. Dated to around 1.5 mya, the skull has a cranial capacity of only 691 cm³. As we'll see shortly, there are a couple of crania from southeastern Europe that are even smaller. The small skull from East Turkana also shows more gracile features (such as smaller browridges) than do other East African *H. erectus* individuals, but it preserves the overall *H. erectus* vault shape. It's been proposed that perhaps this new find is a female and that the variation indicates a very high degree of sexual dimorphism in this species (Spoor et al., 2007).

Another remarkable discovery was made in 1984 by Kamoya Kimeu, a member of Richard Leakey's team known widely as an outstanding fossil hunter. Kimeu discovered a small piece of skull on the west side of Lake Turkana at a site known as **Nariokotome**. Excavations produced the most complete *H. erectus* skeleton ever found (**Fig. 12-4**). Known properly as WT 15000, the almost complete skeleton includes facial bones, a pelvis, and most of the limb bones, ribs, and vertebrae and is chronometrically dated to about 1.6 mya. Such well-preserved postcranial elements make for a very unusual and highly useful discovery, because these elements are scarce at other *H. erectus* sites. The skeleton is that of an adolescent about 8 years of age with an estimated height of about 5 feet 3 inches (Walker and Leakey, 1993; Dean and Smith, 2009).

Some estimates have hypothesized that the adult height of this individual could have been about 6 feet. However, this conclusion is contentious, since it assumed that the growth pattern of

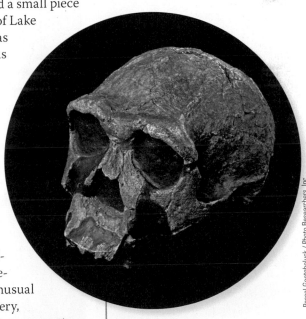

Pascal Goetgheluck / Photo Researchers, Inc.

▲ **Figure 12-3**
Nearly complete skull of *Homo erectus* from East Lake Turkana, Kenya, dated to approximately 1.7 mya.

Nariokotome (nar´-ee-oh-koh´-tow-may)

this species was similar to that of modern humans. But more recent and more detailed analyses find the developmental pattern in this and other *H. erectus* individuals to actually be more like that of an ape (Dean and Smith, 2009). What's more, it now seems unlikely that this individual would have experienced the typical adolescent growth spurt seen in modern humans (see Chapter 17). Indeed, the most recent estimates suggest that had he lived, the Nariokotome youth would have grown to a full adult stature of perhaps only about 64 inches (Graves et al., 2010). This may be a minimum estimate, and other paleoanthropologists think that the adult stature may have been closer to 69 inches.

Nevertheless, the postcranial bones look very similar, though not quite identical, to those of modern humans. The cranial capacity of WT 15000 is estimated at 880 cm³; brain growth was nearly complete, and the adult cranial capacity would have been approximately 909 cm³ (Begun and Walker, 1993).

Other important *H. erectus* finds have come from Olduvai Gorge, in Tanzania, and they include a very robust skull discovered there by Louis Leakey back in 1960. The skull is dated at 1.4 mya and has a well-preserved cranial vault with just a small part of the upper face. Estimated at 1,067 cm³, the cranial capacity is the largest of all the African *H. erectus* specimens. The browridge is huge, the largest known for any hominin, but the walls of the braincase are thin. This latter characteristic is seen in most East African *H. erectus* specimens; in this respect, they differ from Asian *H. erectus*, in which cranial bones are thick.

Three other sites from Ethiopia have yielded *H. erectus* fossils, the most noteworthy coming from the Gona area and the Daka locale, both in the Awash River region of eastern Africa (Gilbert and Asfaw, 2008). As you've seen, numerous remains of earlier hominins have come from this area (see Chapter 11 and Appendix C).

A recently discovered nearly complete female *H. erectus* pelvis comes from the Gona area in Ethiopia and is dated to approximately 1.3 mya (Simpson et al., 2008). This find is particularly interesting because *H. erectus* postcranial remains are so rare, and this is the first *H. erectus* female pelvis yet found. This fossil also reveals some tantalizing glimpses of

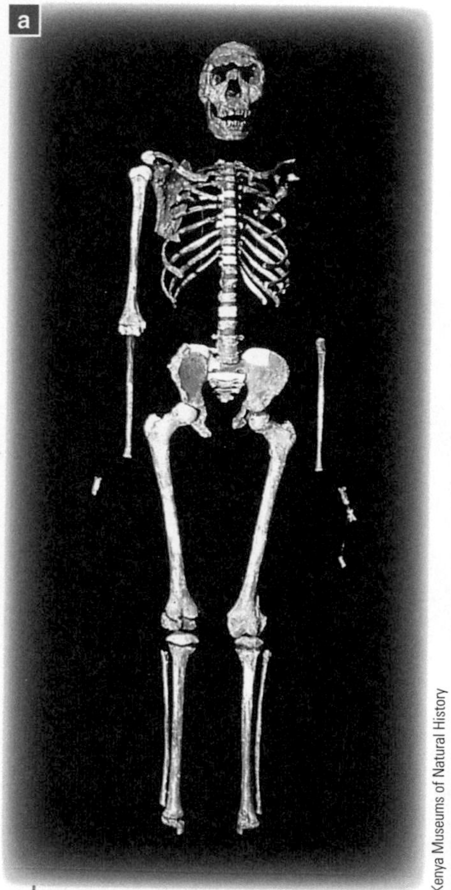

Kenya Museums of Natural History

▲ **Figure 12-4**
(a) WT 15000 from Nariokotome, Kenya: the most complete *H. erectus* specimen yet found. **(b)** Artist's reconstruction of the 8-year-old *H. erectus* boy from Nariokotome, based on a nearly complete skeleton.

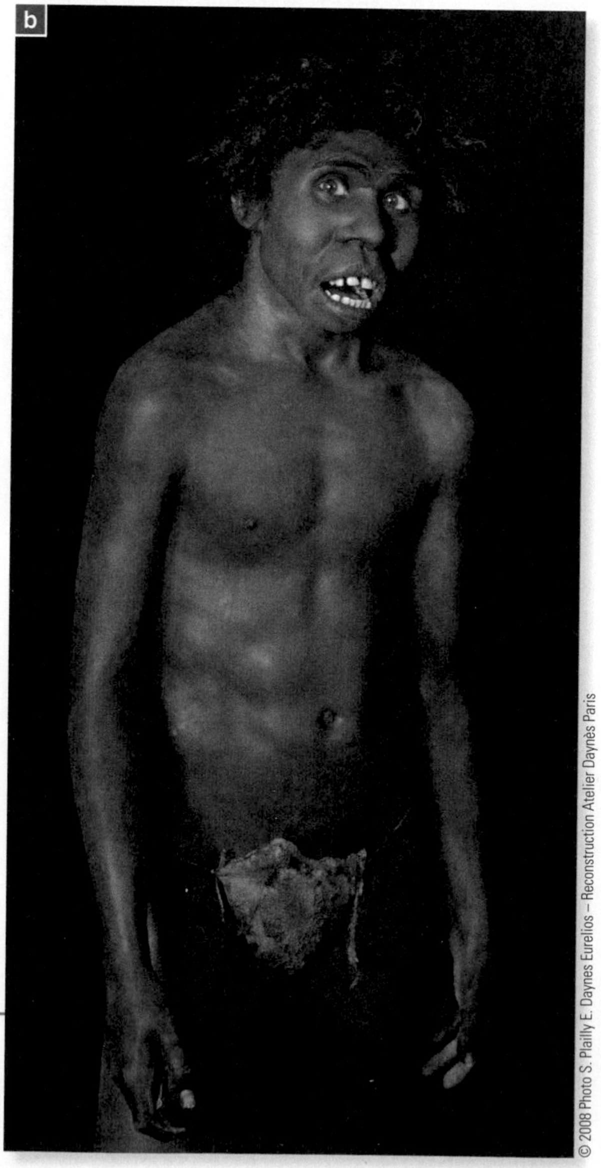

© 2008 Photo S. Plailly E. Daynes Eurelios – Reconstruction Atelier Daynès Paris

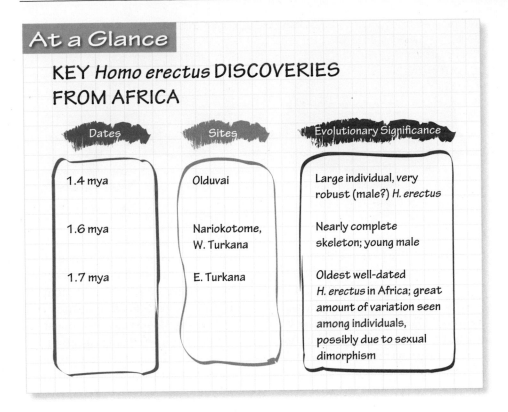

At a Glance

KEY *Homo erectus* DISCOVERIES FROM AFRICA

Dates	Sites	Evolutionary Significance
1.4 mya	Olduvai	Large individual, very robust (male?) *H. erectus*
1.6 mya	Nariokotome, W. Turkana	Nearly complete skeleton; young male
1.7 mya	E. Turkana	Oldest well-dated *H. erectus* in Africa; great amount of variation seen among individuals, possibly due to sexual dimorphism

likely *H. erectus* development. The pelvis has a very wide birth canal, indicating that quite large-brained infants could have developed *in utero* (before birth); in fact, it's possible that a newborn *H. erectus* could have had a brain that was almost as large as what's typical for modern human babies.

This evidence has led Scott Simpson and his colleagues to suggest that *H. erectus* prenatal brain growth was more like that of later humans and quite different from that found in apes *or* in australopiths such as Lucy. However, it's also evident that *H. erectus* brain growth after birth was more rapid than in modern humans. This new pelvis is very different from that of the Nariokotome pelvis and may reflect considerable sexual dimorphism in skeletal anatomy linked to reproduction as well as body size. However, the Gona female was in some ways quite primitive, especially her unusually small body size (approximately 81 pounds, as estimated by the size of her hip joint). Some anthropologists conclude from this evidence that the Gona pelvis may actually have come from an australoptith rather than from *H. erectus*

(or any other species of *Homo*) (Ruff, 2010).

Another recent discovery from the Middle Awash of Ethiopia of a mostly complete cranium from Daka is also important because this individual (dated at approximately 1 mya) is more like Asian *H. erectus* than are most of the earlier East African remains we've discussed (Asfaw et al., 2002). Consequently, the suggestion by several researchers that East African fossils are a different species from (Asian) *H. erectus* isn't supported by the morphology of the Daka cranium.

Who Were the Earliest African Emigrants?

The fossils from East Africa imply that a new grade of human evolution appeared in Africa not long after 2 mya. Until recently, *H. erectus* sites outside Africa all have shown dates later than the earliest finds of this species in Africa, leading paleoanthropologists to assume that the hominins who migrated to Asia and Europe descended from earlier African ancestors. Also, these

a

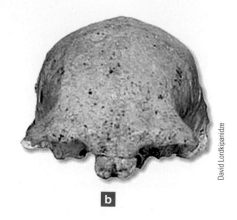

b

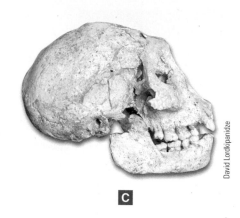

c

David Lordkipanidze

▲ **Figure 12-5**
Dmanisi crania discovered in 1999 and 2001 and dated to 1.8–1.7 mya. **(a)** Specimen 2282. **(b)** Specimen 2280. **(c)** Specimen 2700.

travelers look like *Homo*, with longer limbs and bigger brains. Since *H. erectus* originated in East Africa, they were close to land links to Eurasia (through the Middle East) and thus were probably the first to leave the continent. We can't be sure why these hominins left—were they following animal migrations, or was it simply population growth and expansion?

What we do know is that we're seeing a greater range of physical variation in the specimens outside of Africa and that the emigration out of Africa happened earlier than we had previously thought. Current evidence shows *H. erectus* in East Africa about 1.7 mya, while similar hominins were living in the Caucasus region of southeastern Europe *even a little earlier*, about 1.8 mya.* Eventually, hominins made it all the way to the island of Java, Indonesia, by 1.6 mya! It took *H. erectus* less than 200,000 years to travel from East Africa to Southeast Asia. Let's review the evidence.

The site of **Dmanisi**, in the Republic of Georgia, has produced several individuals, giving us a unique look at these first possible travelers. The age of this crucial site has recently been radiometrically redated to 1.81 mya (Garcia et al., 2010). The Dmanisi crania are similar to those of *H. erectus* (for example, the long, low braincase, wide base, and sagittal keeling; see especially **Fig. 12-5b**, and compare with Fig. 12-2). However,

─────────

* Note that these dates are based solely on what has been discovered so far.

other characteristics of the Dmanisi individuals are different from other hominins outside Africa. In particular, the most complete fossil (specimen 2700; see **Fig. 12-5c**) has a less robust and thinner browridge, a projecting lower face, and a relatively large upper canine. At least when viewed from the front, this skull is more reminiscent of the smaller early *Homo* specimens from East Africa than it is of *H. erectus*. Also, specimen 2700's cranial capacity is very small—estimated at only 600 cm³, well within the range of early *Homo*. In fact, all four Dmanisi crania so far described have relatively small cranial capacities—the other three estimated at 630 cm³, 650 cm³, and 780 cm³.

Probably the most remarkable find from Dmanisi is the most recently discovered skull, excavated by researchers in 2002 (and published in 2005). This nearly complete cranium is of an older adult male; and surprisingly for such an ancient find, he died with only one tooth remaining in his jaws (Lordkipanidze et al., 2006). Because his jawbones show advanced bone loss (which occurs after tooth loss), it seems that he lived for several years without being able to efficiently chew his food (**Fig. 12-6**). As a result, it probably would have been difficult for him to maintain an adequate diet.

Researchers have also recovered some stone tools at Dmanisi. The tools are similar to the Oldowan industry from Africa, as would be expected for a site dated earlier than the beginning of the **Acheulian** industry; this later and

Dmanisi (dim´-an-eese´-ee)

Acheulian (ash´-oo-lay-en) Pertaining to a stone tool industry from the Early and Middle Pleistocene; characterized by a large proportion of bifacial tools (flaked on both sides). Acheulian tool kits are common in Africa, Southwest Asia, and western Europe, but they're thought to be less common elsewhere. Also spelled Acheulean.

very important tool industry is first found associated with African *H. erectus* after 1.4 mya.

The newest evidence from Dmanisi includes several postcranial bones coming from at least four individuals (Lordkipanidze et al., 2007). This new evidence is especially important because it allows us to make comparisons with what is known of *H. erectus* from other areas. The Dmanisi fossils have an unusual combination of traits. They weren't especially tall, having an estimated height ranging from about 4 feet 9 inches to 5 feet 5 inches. Certainly, based on this evidence, they seem much smaller than the full *H. erectus* specimens from East Africa or Asia. Yet, although very short in stature, they still show body proportions (such as leg length) like that of *H. erectus* (and *H. sapiens*) and quite different from that seen in earlier hominins.

Based on the evidence from Dmanisi, we can assume that *Homo erectus* was the first hominin to leave Africa. While the Dmanisi specimens are small in both stature and cranial capacity, they have specific characteristics that identify them as *H. erectus* (for example, a sagittal keel and low braincase). So, for now, the Dmanisi hominins are thought to be *H. erectus*, although an early and quite different variety from that found almost anywhere else.

While new and thus tentative, the recent evidence raises important and exciting possibilities. The Dmanisi findings suggest that the first hominins to leave Africa were quite possibly a small-bodied very early form of *H. erectus*, possessing smaller brains than later *H. erectus* and carrying with them a typical African Oldowan stone tool culture.

Also, the Dmanisi hominins had none of the adaptations hypothesized to be essential to hominin migration—that is, being tall and having relatively large brains. Another explanation may be that there were *two* migrations out of Africa at this time: one consisting of the small-brained, short-statured Dmanisi hominins and an almost immediate second migration that founded the well-recognized *H. erectus* populations of Java and China. However, there is yet another possibility now being considered by some paleoanthropologists: Since the oldest as well as most primitive and smallest *H. erectus* individuals occur at Dmanisi, this area may actually be close to the center of origin for the species. All this evidence is so new, however, that it's too soon even to predict what further revisions may be required.

Homo erectus from Indonesia

After the publication of *On the Origin of Species*, debates about evolution were prevalent throughout Europe. While many theorists simply stayed home and debated the merits of natural selection and the likely course of human evolution, one young Dutch anatomist decided to go find evidence of it. Eugene Dubois (1858–1940) enlisted in the Dutch East Indian Army and was shipped to the island of Sumatra, Indonesia, to look for what he called "the missing link."

In October 1891, after moving his search to the neighboring island of Java, Dubois' field crew unearthed a skullcap along the Solo River near the town of Trinil—a fossil that was to become internationally famous as the first recognized human ancestor (**Fig. 12-7**). The following year, a human femur was recovered about 15 yards upstream in what Dubois claimed was the same level as the skullcap, and he assumed that the skullcap (with a cranial capacity of slightly over 900 cm^3)

David Lordkipanidze

▲ **Figure 12-6**
Most recently discovered cranium from Dmanisi, almost totally lacking in teeth (with both upper and lower jaws showing advanced bone resorption).

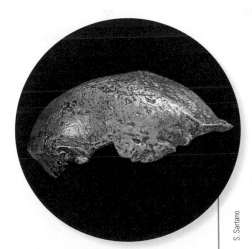

S. Sartano

▲ **Figure 12-7**
The famous Trinil skullcap discovered by Eugene Dubois near the Solo River in Java. Discovered in 1891, this was the first fossil human found outside of Europe or Africa.

A Closer Look

In Search of Ancient Human Ancestors— and a Little Shade

"Whoops!" Upon hearing this exclamation, my colleagues halt their progress along the narrow earthen walkways that outline the flooded rice paddies and make an emerald patchwork quilt on the Java landscape. They turn around and see that I've slipped. Again. Each misstep comes with some good-hearted ribbing as my comrades heave me back onto dry land. Each day we traverse the paddies by way of the thin dikes en route to our research site in central Java. Around us rise great cliffs of ancient soil, striated like an intricately layered cake. Rich green jewel tones dazzle the eye as we pass by peasants laboring in the fields under the hot sun. We, too, are in Java to work, but we toil for a different kind of produce—we seek answers about our early ancestor, Homo erectus. As we tread across the paddies to a dusty oxcart path, our eyes comb the adjacent outcrops for darkened silhouettes of fossils—carefully, we note their locations. By the time we reach our destination, our backpacks are filled with curious remains—this one a tooth of a fossil deer, that one a piece of ancient crocodile bone—but no humans. All the fossils are stained crimson or black by the very soils in which they have lain for nearly a million years. As we begin to examine the exposed sediments, we resume our search for more fossils, our sweat-soaked shirts sticking to our skin. It's 9 A.M. and we're already tired and hot, but we quickly brush these distractions away. Our search has just begun.

For the past twelve years, my colleagues and I have been conducting fieldwork in the rice paddies of central Java. You might think it unusual to conduct scientific research in a rice paddy, but you have to "follow the fossils." Ancient sediments in our field area, the Sangiran Dome, were forced to the surface by the pressure of subterranean mud volcanoes about 120,000 years ago. What attracts us to the Sangiran Dome? It's the 1- to 2-million-year-old fossils and sediments that have been unearthed by erosion and other natural processes. This special series of events means that the Sangiran Dome is prime for both discovering the fossils of early humans in their original environmental context and for radiometrically dating them using volcanic sediments—a common occurrence in Java, an island formed by volcanoes.

If the cradle of human origins is Africa, then Asia was one of the playgrounds where our species grew and matured. Around 2 mya, Homo erectus, our first widely traveled ancestor, left the African savanna homeland to expand its horizons in the larger world. The first stop on this species' journey was in what is now the Republic of Georgia in southeastern Europe, where four skulls and a partial skeleton have been found. From here, we know that Homo erectus ventured onward to East Asia and eventually Java. We know little about the features that attracted these hominins to the Javanese landscape or when the first migration to this island occurred. We do know that over time, the descendants of original Homo erectus immigrants evolved, giving us both full-sized primitive peoples with thick skulls and projecting browridges and later the diminutive "Hobbits" on the island of Flores (you'll meet them in Chapter 14).

Every good realtor will tell you that it's "location, location, location!" What was it

and the femur belonged to the same individual.

So far, all the *H. erectus* fossil remains have come from six sites in eastern Java. The dating of these fossils has been hampered by the complex nature of Javanese geology, but it's generally accepted that most of the fossils belong to the Early to Middle **Pleistocene** and are between 1.6 and 1 million years old. What's more, there was also a very late surviving *H. erectus* group in Java at the Ngandong site, where the fossils are dated to just 70,000–40,000 years ago (ya) (Yokoyama et al., 2008).

The earliest *H. erectus* fossils from Java come from the central part of the island. Beginning with Dubois' famous discovery at Trinil, over 80 different specimens have been located, with many coming from an area called the Sangiran Dome, located just west of Trinil. Several crania have been found, although only one preserves the face. Cranial capacities range between 813 and 1,059 cm³, with an average slightly larger than that of African *H. erectus*. These specimens have thick cranial vaults, sagittal keels, browridges, and nuchal tori, and often these traits are a bit more pronounced than in African *H. erectus*. The Sangiran Dome gives us a picture of a sustained population of *H. erectus* from 1.6 to 1 mya living on the banks of rivers, in the shadows of erupting volcanoes. This environment doesn't seem so different from

Pleistocene The epoch of the Cenozoic from 1.8 mya until 10,000 ya. Frequently referred to as the Ice Age, this epoch is associated with continental glaciations in northern latitudes.

about this Asian setting—particularly the island of Java—that drew these ancient immigrants to colonize, as evidenced by the nearly 100 fossils of *Homo erectus* that have been unearthed there over the past century? Was it, perhaps, the rich volcanic soils and the vegetation they fostered that attracted our distant relatives to the Sangiran Dome, or did *Homo erectus* simply follow land-loving animals to the newly emergent environment of central Java? Our research centers on this very issue, using visual and geochemical clues from soils and plant and animal fossils to reconstruct the landscape of Java when *Homo erectus* first arrived millions of years ago.

As the sun dips low on the horizon, the valley of the Sangiran Dome dims. At the end of the day, our team reassembles for the trek back to our van, joking and chatting about the day's finds. Our packs are heavy with samples of ancient soils, fossil shells and teeth, and rocks from ancient volcanic eruptions, all being hauled back for analysis. We watch our shadowy likenesses in the murky water of the paddies as we trudge out of the mists of time. In an hour we'll return to the hustle and bustle of Solo and wash away the dirt of ages. But before reentering civilization, we cast one last look into the past and wonder—"What was this place like during the time of our very ancient ancestors?" Was the landscape dominated by palms, mahogany, and cashew-bearing trees, as it is today, or was the countryside completely foreign? The full answers are just beyond our grasp. Perhaps today we carry in our backpacks the answers to these questions. Some day soon we'll be able to look at this landscape as our ancestors did, linking our common histories with modern technology.

—*Russell L. Ciochon*

© Russell L. Ciochon

◀ **Figure 1**
The Sangiran Dome Team, composed of researchers from the University of Iowa and the Bandung Institute of Technology, shown here doing a paleoecological analysis of the ancient strata of the dome.

that of Lake Turkana at that time: water, grassland, and roaming animals.

By far, the most recent group of *H. erectus* fossils from Java come from Ngandong, in an area to the east of the finds already mentioned. At Ngandong, an excavation along an ancient river terrace produced 11 mostly complete hominin skulls. Two specialized dating techniques, discussed in Chapter 10, have determined that animal bones found at the site—and presumably associated with the hominins—are only about 25,000–50,000 years old (Swisher et al., 1996). These dates are controversial, but further evidence is now establishing a *very* late survival of *H. erectus* in Java, long after the species had disappeared elsewhere. So these individuals would be contemporary with *H. sapiens*—which, by this time, had expanded widely throughout the Old World and into Australia around 60,000–40,000 ya. Recent work on the old excavation site of Ngandong (first excavated in the early 1930s) has led to a rediscovery of the fossil bed where the 14 individuals had been found (Ciochon et al., 2009). New dating techniques and fossil identification will be undertaken to better understand site formation and taphonomy. As we'll see in Chapter 14, even later—and very unusual—hominins have been found not far away, apparently evolving while isolated on another Indonesian island.

Homo erectus from China

The story of the first discoveries of Chinese *H. erectus* is another saga filled with excitement, hard work, luck, and misfortune. Europeans had known for a long time that "dragon bones," used by the Chinese as medicine and aphrodisiacs, were actually ancient mammal bones. Scientists eventually located one of the sources of these bones near Beijing at a site called **Zhoukoudian**. Serious excavations were begun there in the 1920s, and in 1929, a fossil skull was discovered. The skull turned out to be a juvenile's, and although it was thick, low, and relatively small, there was no doubt that it belonged to an early hominin.

Zhoukoudian *Homo erectus*

The fossil remains of *H. erectus* discovered in the 1920s and 1930s, as well as some more recent excavations at Zhoukoudian (**Fig. 12-8**), are by far the largest collection of *H. erectus* material found anywhere. This excellent sample includes 14 skullcaps (**Fig. 12-9**), other cranial pieces, and more than 100 isolated teeth, but only a scattering of postcranial elements (Jia and Huang, 1990). Various interpretations to account for this unusual pattern of preservation have been offered, rang-

ing from ritualistic treatment or cannibalism to the more mundane suggestion that the *H. erectus* remains are simply the leftovers of the meals of giant hyenas. The hominin remains were studied, and casts were made immediately, which proved invaluable, since the original specimens were lost during the American evacuation of China at the start of World War II.

The hominin remains belong to upward of 40 adults and children and together provide a good overall picture of Chinese *H. erectus*. Like the materials from Java, they have typical *H. erectus* features, including a large browridge and nuchal torus. Also, the skull has thick bones, a sagittal keel, and a protruding face and is broadest near the bottom. This site, along with others in China, has been difficult to date accurately. Although Zhoukoudian was previously dated to about 500,000 ya, a new radiometric dating technique that measures isotopes of aluminum and beryllium shows that Zhoukoudian is actually considerably older, with a dating estimate of approximately 780,000 ya (Ciochon and Bettis, 2009; Shen et al., 2009).

Cultural Remains More than 100,000 artifacts have been recovered from this vast site, which was occupied intermittently for many thousands of years. The earliest tools are generally crude and shapeless, but they become more refined over time. Common tools at the site are choppers and chopping tools, but retouched flakes were fashioned into scrapers, points, burins, and awls (**Fig. 12-10**).

The way of life at Zhoukoudian has traditionally been described as that of hunter-gatherers who killed deer, horses, and other animals. Fragments of charred ostrich eggshells and abundant deposits of hackberry seeds unearthed in the cave suggest that these hominins supplemented their diet of meat by gathering herbs, wild fruits, tubers, and eggs. Layers of what has long been thought to be ash in the cave (over 18 feet deep at one point) have been inter-

▼ **Figure 12-8**
Zhoukoudian cave.

© Russell L. Ciochon

▶ **Figure 12-9**
Composite cranium of Zhoukoudian *Homo erectus*, reconstructed by Ian Tattersall and Gary Sawyer, of the American Museum of Natural History in New York.

© Russell L. Ciochon

| Graver, or burin | Flint awl | Flint point | Quartzite chopper |

◄ **Figure 12-10**
Chinese tools from Middle Pleistocene sites. (Adapted from Wu and Olsen, 1985.)

preted as indicating the use of fire by *H. erectus.*

More recently, several researchers have challenged this picture of Zhoukoudian life. Lewis Binford and colleagues (Binford and Ho, 1985; Binford and Stone, 1986a, 1986b) reject the description of *H. erectus* as hunters and argue that the evidence clearly points more accurately to scavenging. Using advanced archaeological analyses, Noel Boaz and colleagues have even questioned whether the *H. erectus* remains at Zhoukoudian represent evidence of hominin habitation of the cave. By comparing the types of bones, as well as the damage to the bones, with that seen in contemporary carnivore dens, Boaz and Ciochon (2001) have suggested that much of the material in the cave likely accumulated through the activities of extinct giant hyenas. In fact, they hypothesize that most of the *H. erectus* remains, too, are the leftovers of hyena meals.

Boaz and his colleagues do recognize that the tools in the cave, and possibly the cut marks on some of the animal bones, provide evidence of hominin activities at Zhoukoudian. They also recognize that more detailed analysis is required to test their hypotheses and to "determine the nature and scope" of the *H. erectus* presence at Zhoukoudian (see "A Closer Look: Dragon Bone Hill: Cave Home or Hyena Den?").

Probably the most intriguing archaeological aspect of the presumed

hominin behavior at Zhoukoudian has been the long-held assumption that *H. erectus* deliberately used fire inside the cave. Controlling fire was one of the major cultural breakthroughs of all prehistory. By providing warmth, a means of cooking, light to further modify tools, and protection, controlled fire would have been a giant technological innovation. While some potential early African sites have yielded evidence that to some have suggested hominin control of fire, it's long been assumed that the first *definite* evidence of hominin fire use comes from Zhoukoudian. Now even this assumption has been challenged.

In the course of further excavations at Zhoukoudian during the 1990s, researchers carefully collected and analyzed soil samples for distinctive chemical signatures that would show whether fire had been present in the cave (Weiner et al., 1998). They determined that burnt bone was only rarely found in association with tools. And in most cases, the burning appeared to have taken place *after* fossilization—that is, the bones weren't cooked. In fact, it turns out that the "ash" layers mentioned earlier aren't actually ash, but naturally accumulated organic sediment. This last conclusion was derived from chemical testing that showed absolutely no sign of wood having been burnt inside the cave. Finally, the "hearths" that have figured so prominently in archaeological reconstructions of presumed fire control at

Zhoukoudian (Zhoh´-koh-dee´-en)

A Closer Look

Dragon Bone Hill: Cave Home or Hyena Den?

About 30 miles southwest of Beijing, near Zhoukoudian, is the locality known as Dragon Bone Hill. In the 1920s and 1930s, this cave site yielded the first (and still the largest) cache of fossils of *Homo erectus*, historically known as Peking Man. The remains of about 45 individuals, along with thousands of stone tools, debris from tool manufacture, and thousands of animal bones, were contained within the 100-foot-thick deposits that once completely filled the original cave. Some evidence unearthed at the site suggests to many researchers that these creatures, who lived from about 800,000 to 400,000 ya, had mastered the use of fire and practiced cannibalism. Still, despite years of excavation and analysis, little is certain about what occurred here long ago.

To most of the early excavators, the likely scenario was that these particular early humans lived in the cave where their bones and stone tools were found. The animal bones were likely the remains of meals—proof of their hunting expertise. A more sensational view, first advanced in 1929, was that the cave contained evidence of cannibalism. Skulls were conspicuous among the remains, suggesting to Chinese paleoanthropologist Jia Lanpo that these might be the trophies of headhunters.

But another Chinese paleoanthropologist—Pei Wenzhong, who codirected the early Zhoukoudian excavations—believed that the skulls and accompanying damage were due to hyena chewing, not human killers. In 1939, his views were bolstered by the emerging science of taphonomy, which

▲ **Figure 1**
These illustrations demonstrate the two interpretations of the remains from Dragon Bone Hill: **(a)** the more traditional cave home model and **(b)** the newer, and probably more accurate, hyena den model.

this site are apparently not hearths at all. They are simply round depressions formed in the past by water.

Another provisional interpretation of the cave's geology suggests that the cave wasn't open to the outside like a habitation site, but was accessed only through a vertical shaft. This theory has led archaeologist Alison Brooks to remark, "It wouldn't have been a shelter, it would have been a trap" (quoted in Wuethrich, 1998). These serious doubts about control of fire, coupled with the suggestive evidence of bone accumulation by carnivores, have led anthropologists Boaz and Ciochon to conclude that "Zhoukoudian cave was neither hearth nor home" (Boaz and Ciochon, 2001).

Other Chinese Sites

More work has been done at Zhoukoudian than at any other Chinese site. Even so, there are other paleoanthropological sites worth mentioning. Three of the more important regions outside of Zhoukoudian are Lantian County (including two sites, often simply referred to as Lantian), Yunxian County, and several discoveries in

is the study of how, after death, animal and plant remains become modified, moved, buried, and fossilized (see Chapter 10). Published observations on the way hyenas at the Vienna zoo fed on cow bones led later scientists to reject the idea of cannibalism, although they continued to look upon the cave as a shelter used by early humans equipped with stone tools and fire (as reflected in the title of *The Cave Home of Peking Man*, published in 1975).

In the mid- to late 1970s, however, Western scientists began to better appreciate and develop the field of taphonomy. One assumption of taphonomy is that the most common species at a fossil site and/or the best-preserved animal remains at the site are most likely the ones to have inhabited the area in life. Of all the mammal fossils from the cave, very few belonged to *H. erectus*—perhaps only 0.5 percent, suggesting that most of the time, this species did not live in the cave. What's more, none of the *H. erectus* skeletons are complete. There's a lack of limb bones—especially of forearms, hands, lower leg bones, and feet—indicating that these individuals died somewhere else and that their partial remains were later carried to the cave. But how?

The answer is suggested by the remains of the most common and complete animal

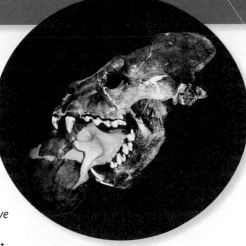

© Russell L. Ciochon

skeletons in the cave deposit—those of the giant hyena, *Pachycrocuta brevirostris*. Had *H. erectus*, instead of being the mighty hunter of anthropological lore, simply met the same unhappy fate as the deer and other prey species in the cave? To test the giant hyena hypothesis, scientists reexamined the fossil casts and a few actual fossils of *H. erectus* from Zhoukoudian for evidence of carnivore damage. Surprisingly, two-thirds of the *H. erectus* fossils displayed puncture marks from a carnivore's large, pointed front teeth, most likely the canines of a hyena. What's more, there were long, scraping bite marks, typified by U-shaped grooves along the bone, and fracture patterns comparable to those modern hyenas make when they chew bone. One of the *H. erectus* bones, part of a femur, even

reveals telltale surface etchings from stomach acid, indicating it was swallowed and then regurgitated.

Cut marks (made by stone tools) observed on several mammal bones from the cave suggest that early humans did sometimes make use of Zhoukoudian, even if they weren't responsible for accumulating most of the bones. Stone tools left near the cave entrance also attest to their presence. Given its long history, the cave may have served a variety of occupants or at times have been configured as several separate, smaller shelters. Another possibility is that, in a form of time sharing, early humans ventured partway into the cave during the day to scavenge on what the hyenas had not eaten and to find temporary shelter. They might not have realized that the animals, which roamed at twilight and at night, were sleeping in the dark recesses a couple of hundred feet away.

Hexian County (usually referred to as the Hexian finds).

Dated to 1.15 mya, Lantian is older than Zhoukoudian (Zhu et al., 2003). From the Lantian sites, the cranial remains of two adult *H. erectus* females have been found in association with fire-treated pebbles and flakes as well as ash (Woo, 1966; **Fig. 12-11a**). One of the specimens, an almost complete mandible containing several teeth, is quite similar to those from Zhoukoudian.

Two badly distorted crania were discovered in Yunxian County, Hubei Province, in 1989 and 1990 (Li and

Etler, 1992). A combination of ESR and paleomagnetism dating methods (see Chapter 10) gives us an average dating estimate of 800,000–580,000 ya. If the dates are correct, this would place Yunxian at a similar age to Zhoukoudian in the Chinese sequence. Due to extensive distortion of the crania from ground pressure, it was very difficult to compare these crania with other *H. erectus* fossils; recently, however, French paleoanthropologist Amélie Vialet has restored the crania using sophisticated imaging techniques (Vialet et al., 2005). And from a recent analysis of

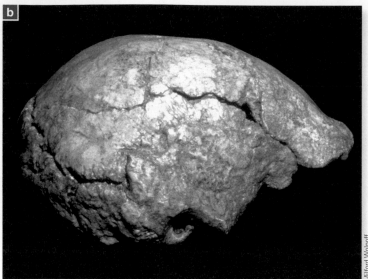

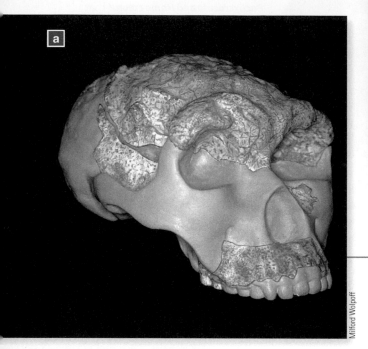

◀ **Figure 12-11**

(**a**) Reconstructed cranium of *Homo erectus* from Lantian, China, dated to approximately 1.15 mya. (**b**) Hexian cranium.

At a Glance

KEY *Homo Erectus* DISCOVERIES FROM ASIA

Dates	Sites	Evolutionary Significance
70,000-40,000 ya	Ngandong (Java)	Very late survival of *H. erectus* in Java
780,000 ya	Zhoukoudian (China)	Large sample; most famous *H. erectus* site; shows some *H. erectus* populations well adapted to temperate (cold) environments
1.6 mya	Sangiran (Java)	First discovery of *H. erectus* from anywhere; shows dispersal out of Africa into southeast Asia by 1.6 mya

the fauna and paleoenvironment at Yunxian, the *H. erectus* inhabitants are thought to have had limited hunting capabilities, since they appear to have been restricted to the most vulnerable prey, namely, the young and old animals.

In 1980 and 1981, the remains of several individuals, all bearing some resemblance to similar fossils from Zhoukoudian, were recovered from Hexian County, in southern China (Wu and Poirier, 1995; see Fig. 12-11b). A close relationship has been postulated between the *H. erectus* specimens from the Hexian finds and from Zhoukoudian (Wu and Dong, 1985). Dating of the Hexian remains is unclear, but they appear to be later than Zhoukoudian, perhaps by several hundred thousand years.

The Asian crania from Java and China share many similar features, which could be explained by *H. erectus* migration from Java to China perhaps around 1 mya. Asia has a much longer *H. erectus* habitation than Africa (1.8 mya–40,000 or 70,000 ya versus 1.7–1 mya), and it's important to understand the variation seen in this geographically dispersed species. It's also possible that *H. erectus* populations in Java and China were always distinct and perhaps resulted from separate migrations from Africa (Ciochon and Bettis, 2009).

Asian and African *Homo erectus*: A Comparison

The *Homo erectus* remains from East Africa show several differences from the Javanese and Chinese fossils. Some African cranial specimens—particularly ER 3733, presumably a female, and WT 15000, presumably a male—aren't as strongly buttressed at the browridge and nuchal torus, and their cranial bones aren't as thick. Indeed, some researchers are so impressed by these differences, as well as others in the postcranial skeleton, that they're arguing for a *separate* species status for the African material, to distinguish it from the Asian samples. Bernard Wood, the leading proponent of this view, has suggested that the name *Homo ergaster* be used for the African remains and that *H. erectus* be reserved solely for the Asian material (Wood, 1991). In addition, the very early dates now postulated for the dispersal of *H. erectus* into Asia (Java) would argue that the Asian and African populations were separate (distinct) for more than 1 million years.

With the discovery of the Daka cranium in Ethiopia and continued comparison of these specimens, this species division has not been fully accepted; the current consensus (and the one we prefer) is to continue referring to all these hominins as *Homo erectus* (Kramer, 1993; Conroy, 1997; Rightmire, 1998; Asfaw et al., 2002). So, as with some earlier hominins, we'll have to accommodate a considerable degree of variation within this species. Regarding variation within such a broadly defined *H. erectus* species, Wood has concluded that "it is a species which manifestly embraces an unusually wide degree of variation in both the cranium and postcranial skeleton" (Wood, 1992, p. 783).

Later *Homo erectus* from Europe

We've talked about *H. erectus* in Africa, the Caucasus region, and Asia, but there are European specimens as well, found in Spain and Italy. While not as old as the Dmanisi material, fossils from the Atapuerca region in northern Spain are significantly extending the antiquity of hominins in western Europe. There are several caves in the Atapuerca region, two of which (Sima del Elefante and Gran Dolina) have yielded hominin fossils contemporaneous with *H. erectus*.

The earliest find from Atapuerca (from Sima del Elefante) has been recently discovered and dates to 1.2 mya, making it clearly the oldest hominin yet found in western Europe (Carbonell et al., 2008). So far, just one specimen has been found here, a partial jaw with a few teeth. Very provisional analysis suggests that it most closely resembles the Dmanisi fossils. There are also tools and animal bones from the site. As at the Dmanisi site, the implements are simple flake tools similar to that of the Oldowan. Some of the animal bones also bear the scars of hominin activity, with cut marks indicating butchering (similar to what we discussed in Chapter 10 for Olduvai).

Gran Dolina is a later site, and based on specialized techniques discussed in Chapter 10, it is dated to approximately 850,000–780,000 ya (Parés and Pérez-González, 1995; Falguères et al., 1999). Because all the remains so far identified from both these caves at Atapuerca are fragmentary, assigning these fossils to particular species poses something of a problem. Spanish paleoanthropologists who have studied the Atapuerca fossils have decided to place these hominins

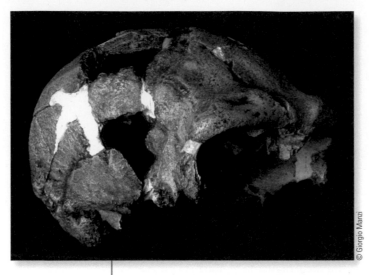

© Giorgio Manzi

▲ **Figure 12-12**

The Ceprano *Homo erectus* cranium from central Italy, recently dated to 450,000 ya. This is the best evidence for *Homo erectus* in Europe.

(**Fig. 12-12**), but more recent paleomagnetic studies have indicated a date of 450,000 ya (Muttoni et al., 2009). Philip Rightmire (1998) has concluded that cranial morphology places this specimen quite close to *H. erectus*. Italian researchers have proposed a different interpretation that classifies the Ceprano hominin as a species separate from *H. erectus*. For the moment, the exact relationship of the Ceprano find to *H. erectus* remains to be fully determined.

After about 400,000 ya, the European fossil hominin record becomes increasingly abundant. More fossils mean more variation, so it's not surprising that interpretations regarding the proper taxonomic assessment of many of these remains have been debated, in some cases for decades. In recent years, several of these somewhat later "premodern" specimens have been regarded either as early representatives of *H. sapiens* or as a separate species, one immediately preceding *H. sapiens*. These enigmatic premodern humans are discussed in Chapter 13. A time line for the *H. erectus* discoveries discussed in this chapter, as well as other finds of more uncertain status, is shown in **Figure 12-13**.

into another (separate) species, one they call *Homo antecessor* (Bermúdez de Castro et al., 1997; Arsuaga et al., 1999). However, it remains to be seen whether this newly proposed species will prove to be distinct from other species of *Homo*.

Finally, the southern European discovery of a well-preserved cranium from the Ceprano site in central Italy may be the best evidence yet of *H. erectus* in Europe (Ascenzi et al., 1996). Provisional dating of a partial cranium from this important site suggested a date between 900,000 and 800,000 ya

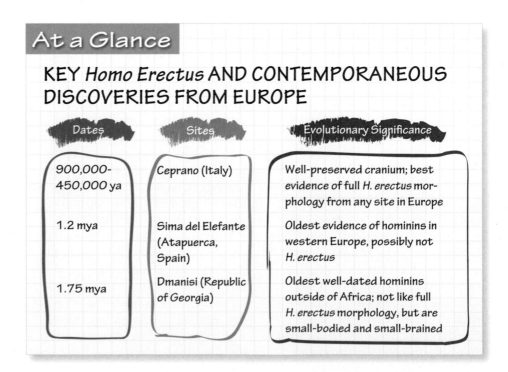

At a Glance

KEY *Homo Erectus* AND CONTEMPORANEOUS DISCOVERIES FROM EUROPE

Dates	Sites	Evolutionary Significance
900,000–450,000 ya	Ceprano (Italy)	Well-preserved cranium; best evidence of full *H. erectus* morphology from any site in Europe
1.2 mya	Sima del Elefante (Atapuerca, Spain)	Oldest evidence of hominins in western Europe, possibly not *H. erectus*
1.75 mya	Dmanisi (Republic of Georgia)	Oldest well-dated hominins outside of Africa; not like full *H. erectus* morphology, but are small-bodied and small-brained

▼ Figure 12-13
Time line for *Homo erectus* discoveries and other contemporary hominins. (*Note*: Most dates are only imprecise estimates. However, the dates from East African sites are chronometrically determined and are thus much more secure. The early dates from Java are also radiometric and are gaining wide acceptance.)

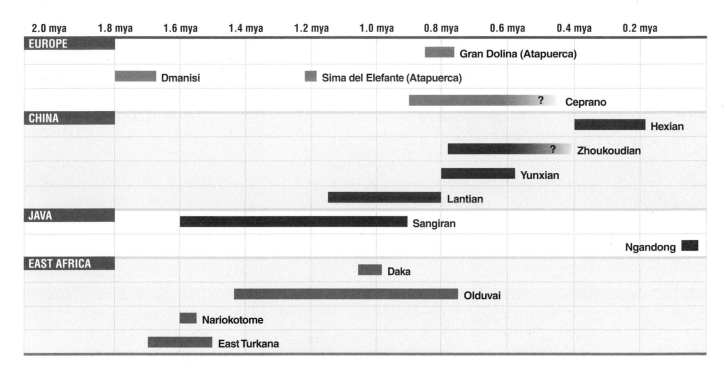

Technological Trends in *Homo erectus*

The temporal span of *H. erectus* includes two different stone tool industries, one of which was probably first developed by *H. erectus*. Earlier finds indicate that *H. erectus* started out using Oldowan tools, which the *H. erectus* emigrants took with them to Dmanisi, Java, and Spain. The newer industry was invented (about 1.4 mya) *after* these early African emigrants left their original homeland for other parts of the Old World. This new kit is called the Acheulian. The important change in this kit was a core worked on both sides, called a *biface* (known widely as a hand axe or cleaver; **Fig. 12-14**). The biface had a flatter shape than seen in the rounder earlier Oldowan cores (which were worked to make quick and easy flakes and were soon discarded).

William Turnbaugh

▲ Figure 12-14
Acheulian biface ("hand axe"), a basic tool of the Acheulian tradition.

A Closer Look

The Sky Is Falling

The blazing red soil of Guangxi, in southwest China, is all that remains of a powerful conflagration in the wake of a violent meteor impact some 800,000 ya. As it struck the ground somewhere in Indochina, the asteroid liquefied the terrain and sent it spewing skyward in a hailstorm of fire that scarred land as far south as Australia. The remnants of this event can be found scattered across China, Indonesia, and Australia and are known collectively as the Australasian Tektite Strewn Field (Paine, 2001). The tektites themselves are the fragments of ejecta fused in the furnace of the impact and flung across the landscape. These onyx spheroids resemble miniature meteorites; and, most crucially for paleoanthropology, they allow us to date the appearance of bifacial tools (that is, the Acheulian industry) in China. Because tektites are superheated, as in volcanic eruptions, they can be radiometrically dated using the potassium-argon technique (see Chapter 10). Consequently, we can also get a date for the stone tools lying alongside them in the Bose Basin of China.

The "Movius Line" (named after Harvard archaeologist Hallum Movius) was long believed to represent an imaginary, though very real, technological barrier separating the primitive residents of Asia from the western makers of bifacial hand axes. Underlying this dichotomy was the implicit conviction that a lack of Acheulian-type tools throughout eastern Eurasia was more a function of reduced intelligence than resource scarcity. Recent excavations in the Bose Basin, in Guangxi, have thrown this scheme into doubt with the revelation that at least some Asian *H. erectus* populations were fully capable of making bifacial tools and were doing so as early as 800,000 ya (Hou et al., 2000).

More important still, the tektites represent an underlying reason that these tools exist at all. As molten earth showered the region, it scoured the landscape of the dense and impenetrable forest that had long excluded habitation by *H. erectus* populations, previously restricting them to more open river valleys. A cataclysmic natural event opened a new world for human hands to exploit. Outcroppings of stone materials ideal for biface manufacture were left bare and steaming. An event

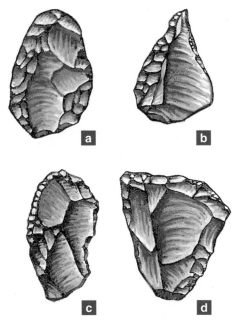

▲ **Figure 12-15**
**Small tools of the Acheulian industry.
(a)** Side scraper. **(b)** Point. **(c)** End scraper. **(d)** Burin.

Beginning with the Acheulian culture, we find the first evidence that raw materials were being transported more consistently and for longer distances. When Acheulian tool users found a suitable piece of stone, they often would take it with them as they traveled from one place to another. This behavior suggests foresight: They likely knew that they might need to use a stone tool in the future and that this chunk of rock could later prove useful. This is a major change from the Oldowan, where all stone tools are found very close to their raw-material sources. With the biface as a kind of "Acheulian Swiss army knife," these tools served to cut, scrape, pound, and dig. This most useful tool has been found in Africa, parts of Asia, and later in Europe. Note that Acheulian tool kits also include several types of small tools (**Fig. 12-15**).

For many years, scientists thought that a cultural "divide" separated the Old World, with Acheulian technology found *only* in Africa, the Middle East, and parts of Europe (elsewhere, the Acheulian was presumed to be absent). But recently reported excavations from more than 20 sites in southern China have forced reevaluation of this hypothesis (Hou et al., 2000). The new archaeological assemblages from southern China are securely dated at about 800,000 ya and contain numerous bifaces, very similar to contemporaneous Acheulian bifaces from Africa (see Fig. 12-14). It now appears likely that cultural traditions relating to stone tool technology were largely equivalent over the *full* geographical range of *H. erectus* and its contemporaries (see "A Closer Look: The Sky Is Falling").

Evidence of butchering is widespread at *H. erectus* sites, and in the past, such evidence has been cited in arguments for consistent hunting (researchers formerly interpreted any association of bones and tools as evidence of hunting). But many studies

that so nearly ended life in the region—a small-scale version of the asteroid impact that ended the reign of dinosaurs—became a reason for it to prosper. Far from dim-witted country cousins, *Homo erectus* in Asia represents a population of savvy opportunists who turned a potential doomsday into the heyday of stone tool manufacture in the region.

▶ **Figure 1**

The red laterite soils of Guangxi in southwest China, from which many important Acheulian-style hand axes have been discovered alongside tektites used to date the site to 800,000 ya.

now suggest that cut marks on bones from the *H. erectus* time period often overlay carnivore tooth marks. This means that hominins weren't necessarily hunting large animals but were scavenging meat from animals killed by carnivores. It's also crucial to mention that they obtained a large amount of their daily calories from gathering wild plants, tubers, and fruits. Like hunter-gatherers of modern times, *H. erectus* individuals were most likely consuming most of their daily calories from plant materials.

Seeing the Big Picture: Interpretations of *Homo erectus*

Several aspects of the geographical, physical, and behavioral patterns shown by *Homo erectus* seem clear.

But new discoveries and more in-depth analyses are helping us to reevaluate our prior ideas. The fascinating fossil hominins discovered at Dmanisi are perhaps the most challenging piece of this puzzle.

Past theories suggest that *H. erectus* was able to emigrate from Africa owing to more advanced tools and a more modern anatomy (longer legs, larger brains) compared to earlier African predecessors. Yet, the Dmanisi cranial remains show that these very early Europeans still had small brains; and *H. erectus* in both Dmanisi and Java was still using Oldowan-style tools.

So it seems that some key parts of earlier hypotheses are not fully accurate. At least some of the earliest emigrants from Africa didn't yet show the entire suite of *H. erectus* physical and behavioral traits. How different the Dmanisi hominins are from the full *H. erectus* pattern remains to be seen, and the discovery of more complete postcranial remains will be most illuminating.

Going a step further, the four crania from Dmanisi are extremely variable; one of them, in fact, does look more like *H. erectus*. It would be tempting to conclude that more than one type of hominin is represented here, but they're all found in the same geological context. The archaeologists who excavated the site conclude that all the fossils are closely associated with each other. The simplest hypothesis is that they're all members of the *same* species. This degree of apparent intraspecific variation is biologically noteworthy, and it's influencing how paleoanthropologists interpret all of these fossil samples.

This growing awareness of the broad intraspecific variation among some hominins brings us to our second consideration: Is *Homo ergaster* in Africa a separate species from *Homo erectus*, as strictly defined in Asia? While this interpretation was popular in the last decade, it's now losing support. The finds from Dmanisi raise fundamental issues of interpretation. Among these four crania from one locality (see Fig. 12-5), we see more variation than between the African and Asian forms, which many researchers have interpreted as different species. Also, the new discovery from Daka (Ethiopia) of a young African specimen with Asian traits further weakens the separate-species interpretation of *H. ergaster*.

The separate-species status of the early European fossils from Spain (Sima del Elefante and Gran Dolina) is also not yet clearly established. We still don't have much good fossil evidence from these two sites; but dates going back to 1.2 mya for the earlier site are well confirmed. Recall also that no other western European hominin fossils are known until at least 500,000 years later, and it remains to be seen if any of these European hominins dating prior to 500,000 ya are ancestors of any later hominin species. Nevertheless, it's quite apparent that later in the Pleistocene, well-established hominin populations were widely dispersed in both Africa and Europe. These later premodern humans are the topic of the next chapter.

When looking back at the evolution of *H. erectus*, we realize how significant this early human was. *H. erectus* had greater limb length and thus more efficient bipedalism; was the first species with a cranial capacity approaching the range of *H. sapiens*; became a more efficient scavenger and exploited a wider range of nutrients, including meat; and ranged across the Old World, from Spain to Indonesia. In short, it was *H. erectus* that transformed hominin evolution to human evolution. As Richard Foley states, "The appearance and expansion of *H. erectus* represented a major change in adaptive strategy that influenced the subsequent process and pattern of human evolution" (1991, p. 425).

Summary of Main Topics

- *Homo erectus* remains have been found in Africa, Europe, and Asia dating from about 1.8 mya to at least 100,000 ya—and probably even later—and thus this species spanned a period of more than 1.5 million years.
- *H. erectus* likely first appeared in East Africa and later migrated to other areas. This widespread and highly successful hominin defines

a new and more modern grade of human evolution.
- *H. erectus* differs from early *Homo*, with a larger brain, taller stature, robust build, and changes in facial structure and cranial buttressing.
- *H. erectus* and contemporaries introduced more sophisticated tools (as part of the Acheulian industry) and probably ate novel foods processed in new ways. By

using these new tools and—at later sites possibly fire as well—they were also able to move into different environments and successfully adapt to new conditions.

The most important fossil discoveries discussed in this chapter are summarized in "What's Important."

What's Important

Key Fossil Discoveries of *Homo erectus*

DATES	REGION	SITE	THE BIG PICTURE
1.6 mya–25,000 ya	**Asia** Indonesia	Java (Sangiran and other sites)	Shows *H. erectus* early on (by 1.6 mya) in tropical areas of Southeast Asia; *H. erectus* persisted here for more than 1 million years
780,000–(?)400,000 ya	China	Zhoukoudian	Largest, most famous sample of *H. erectus*; shows adaptation to colder environments; conclusions regarding behavior at this site have been exaggerated and are now questioned
900,000–450,000 ya	**Europe** (Italy)	Ceprano	Likely best evidence of full-blown *H. erectus* morphology in Europe
1.8–1.7 mya	Republic of Georgia)	Dmanisi	Very early dispersal to southeastern Europe (by 1.8 mya) of small-bodied, small-brained *H. erectus* population; may represent an earlier dispersal from Africa than one that led to wider occupation of Eurasia
1.6 mya	**Africa** (Kenya)	Nariokotome	Beautifully preserved nearly complete skeleton; best postcranial evidence of *H. erectus* from anywhere
1.7 mya		East Turkana	Earliest *H. erectus* from Africa; some individuals more robust, others smaller and more gracile; variation suggested to represent sexual dimorphism

Critical Thinking Questions

1. Why is the nearly complete skeleton from Nariokotome so important? What kinds of evidence does it provide?

2. Assume that you're in the laboratory and have the Nariokotome skeleton, as well as a skeleton of a modern human. First, given a choice, what age and sex would you choose for the comparative human skeleton, and why? Second, what similarities and differences do the two skeletons show?

3. What fundamental questions of interpretation do the fossil hominins from Dmanisi raise? Does this evidence completely overturn the earlier views (hypotheses) concerning *H. erectus* dispersal from Africa? Explain why or why not.

4. How has the interpretation of *H. erectus* behavior at Zhoukoudian been revised in recent years? What kinds of new evidence from this site have been used in this reevaluation, and what does that tell you about modern archaeological techniques and approaches?

An imaginative reconstruction by artist, Elisabeth Daynes, showing a Neandertal band's camp site in a cave.

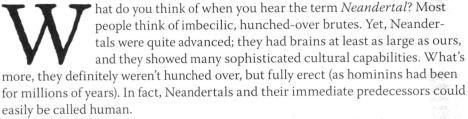

13

Premodern
Humans

Key Question

▶ Who were the immediate precursors to modern *Homo sapiens*, and how do they compare with modern humans?

What do you think of when you hear the term *Neandertal*? Most people think of imbecilic, hunched-over brutes. Yet, Neandertals were quite advanced; they had brains at least as large as ours, and they showed many sophisticated cultural capabilities. What's more, they definitely weren't hunched over, but fully erect (as hominins had been for millions of years). In fact, Neandertals and their immediate predecessors could easily be called human.

That brings us to possibly the most basic of all questions: What does it mean to be human? The meaning of this term is highly varied, encompassing religious, philosophical, and biological considerations. As you know, physical anthropologists primarily concentrate on the biological aspects of the human organism. All living people today are members of one species, sharing a common anatomical pattern and similar behavioral potentials. We call hominins like us "modern *Homo sapiens*," and in the next chapter, we'll discuss the origin of forms that were essentially identical to people living today.

When in our evolutionary past can we say that our predecessors were obviously human? Certainly, the further back we go in time, the less hominins look like modern *Homo sapiens*. This is, of course, exactly what we'd expect in an evolutionary sequence.

We saw in Chapter 12 that *Homo erectus* took crucial steps in the human direction and defined a new *grade* of human evolution. In this chapter, we'll discuss the hominins who continued this journey. Both physically and behaviorally, they're much like modern *Homo sapiens*, though they still show several significant differences. So while most paleoanthropologists are comfortable referring to these hominins as "human," we need to qualify this recognition a bit to set them apart from fully modern people. Thus, in this text, we'll refer to these fascinating immediate predecessors as "premodern humans."

When, Where, and What

Most of the hominins discussed in this chapter lived during the **Middle Pleistocene**, a period beginning 780,000 ya and ending 125,000 ya. In addition, some of the later premodern humans, especially the Neandertals, lived well into the **Late Pleistocene** (125,000–10,000 ya).

The Pleistocene

The Pleistocene has been called the Ice Age because, as had occurred before in geological history, it was marked by periodic advances and retreats of massive continental **glaciations**. During glacial periods, when temperatures dropped dramatically, ice accumulated as a result of more snow falling each year than melted, causing the advance of massive glaciers. As the climate fluctuated, at times it became much warmer. During these **interglacials**, the ice that had built up during the glacial periods melted, and the glaciers retreated back toward the earth's polar regions. The Pleistocene was characterized by numerous advances and retreats of ice, with at least 15 major and 50 minor glacial advances docu-

mented in Europe alone (Delson et al., 1988).

These glaciations, which enveloped huge swaths of Europe, Asia, and North America as well as Antarctica, were mostly confined to northern latitudes. Hominins living at this time—all still restricted to the Old World—were severely affected as the climate, flora, and animal life shifted during these Pleistocene oscillations. The most dramatic of these effects were in Europe and northern Asia—less so in southern Asia and in Africa.

Still, the climate also fluctuated in the south. In Africa, the main effects were related to changing rainfall patterns. During glacial periods, the climate in Africa became more arid, while during interglacials, rainfall increased. The changing availability of food resources certainly affected hominins in Africa; but probably even more importantly, migration routes also swung back and forth. For example, during glacial periods (**Fig. 13-1**), the Sahara Desert expanded, blocking migration in and out of sub-Saharan Africa (Lahr and Foley, 1998).

In Eurasia, glacial advances also greatly affected migration routes. As the ice sheets expanded, sea levels dropped, more northern regions became uninhabitable, and some

▶ **Figure 13-1**
Changing Pleistocene environments in Africa.

Middle Pleistocene The portion of the Pleistocene epoch beginning 780,000 ya and ending 125,000 ya.

Late Pleistocene The portion of the Pleistocene epoch beginning 125,000 ya and ending approximately 10,000 ya.

glaciations Climatic intervals when continental ice sheets cover much of the northern continents. Glaciations are associated with colder temperatures in northern latitudes and more arid conditions in southern latitudes, most notably in Africa.

interglacials Climatic intervals when continental ice sheets are retreating, eventually becoming much reduced in size. Interglacials in northern latitudes are associated with warmer temperatures, while in southern latitudes the climate becomes wetter.

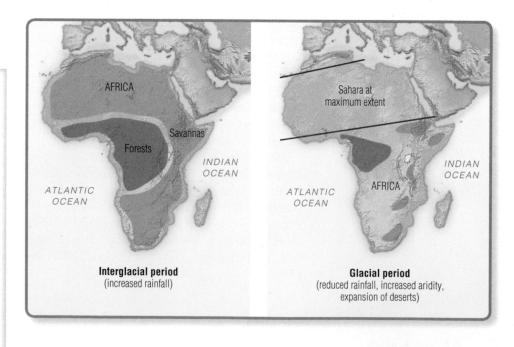

Interglacial period
(increased rainfall)

Glacial period
(reduced rainfall, increased aridity, expansion of deserts)

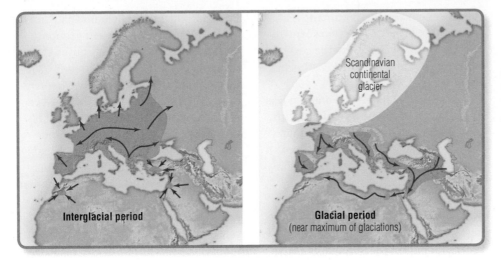

◄ **Figure 13-2**
Changing Pleistocene environments in
Eurasia. Orange areas show regions of
likely hominin occupation. White areas
are major glaciers. Arrows indicate
likely migration routes.

key passages between areas became
blocked by glaciers. For example, during glacial peaks, much of western
Europe would have been cut off from
the rest of Eurasia (**Fig. 13-2**).

During the warmer—and, in the
south, wetter—interglacials, the ice
sheets shrank, sea levels rose, and certain migration routes reopened (for
example, from central Europe into
western Europe). Clearly, to understand
Middle Pleistocene hominins, it's crucial to view them within their shifting
Pleistocene world.

Dispersal of Middle Pleistocene Hominins

Like their *Homo erectus* predecessors,
later hominins were widely distributed in the Old World, with discoveries coming from three continents—
Africa, Asia, and Europe. For the first
time, Europe became more permanently and densely occupied, as Middle
Pleistocene hominins have been discovered widely from England, France,
Spain, Germany, Italy, Hungary, and
Greece. Africa, as well, probably continued as a central area of hominin
occupation, and finds have come from
North, East, and South Africa. Finally,
Asia has yielded several important
finds, especially from China (see Fig.
13-6). We should point out, though,
that these Middle Pleistocene premodern humans didn't vastly extend the

geographical range of *Homo erectus*,
but rather largely replaced the earlier
hominins in previously exploited habitats. One exception appears to be the
more successful occupation of Europe,
a region where earlier hominins have
only sporadically been found.

Middle Pleistocene Hominins: Terminology

The premodern humans of the Middle
Pleistocene (that is, after 780,000 ya)
generally succeeded *H. erectus*. Still,
in some areas—especially in Southeast Asia—there apparently was a long
period of coexistence, lasting 300,000
years or longer; you'll recall the very
late dates for the Javanese Ngandong
H. erectus (see Chapter 12).

The earliest premodern humans
exhibit several *H. erectus* characteristics: The face is large, the brows are
projected, the forehead is low, and in
some cases the cranial vault is still
thick. Even so, some of their other
features show that they were more
derived toward the modern condition than were their *H. erectus* predecessors. Compared with *H. erectus*,
these premodern humans possessed an
increased brain size, a more rounded
braincase (that is, maximum breadth
is higher up on the sides), a more vertical nose, and a less angled back of the
skull (occipital). We should note that
the time span encompassed by Middle

Pleistocene premodern humans is at least 500,000 years, so it's no surprise that over time we can observe certain trends. Later Middle Pleistocene hominins, for example, show even more brain expansion and an even less angled occipital than do earlier forms.

We know that premodern humans were a diverse group dispersed over three continents. Deciding how to classify them has been disputed for decades, and anthropologists still have disagreements. However, a growing consensus has recently emerged. Beginning perhaps as early as 850,000 ya and extending to about 200,000 ya, the fossils from Africa and Europe are placed within *Homo heidelbergensis*, named after a fossil found in Germany in 1907. What's more, some Asian specimens possibly represent a regional variant of *H. heidelbergensis*.

Until recently, many researchers regarded these fossils as early, but more primitive, members of *Homo sapiens*. In recognition of this somewhat transitional status, the fossils were called "archaic *Homo sapiens*," with all later humans also belonging to the species *Homo sapiens*. However, most paleoanthropologists now find this terminology unsatisfactory. For example,

Phillip Rightmire concludes that "simply lumping diverse ancient groups with living populations obscures their differences" (1998, p. 226). In our own discussion, we recognize *H. heidelbergensis* as a transitional species between *H. erectus* and later hominins (that is, primarily *H. sapiens*). Keep in mind, however, that this species was probably an ancestor of both modern humans and Neandertals. It's debatable whether *H. heidelbergensis* actually represents a fully separate species in the *biological* sense, that is, following the biological species concept (see Chapter 5). Still, it's useful to give this group of premodern humans a separate name to make this important stage of human evolution more easily identifiable. (We'll return to this issue later in the chapter when we discuss the theoretical implications in more detail.)

Premodern Humans of the Middle Pleistocene

Africa

In Africa, premodern fossils have been found at several sites. One of the best known is Kabwe (Broken Hill). At this site in Zambia, fieldworkers discovered a complete cranium (**Fig. 13-3**), together with other cranial and postcranial elements belonging to several individuals. In this and other African premodern specimens, we can see a mixture of primitive and more derived traits. The skull's massive browridge (one of the largest of any hominin), low vault, and prominent occipital torus recall those of *H. erectus*. On the other hand, the occipital region is less angulated, the cranial vault bones are thinner, and the cranial base is essentially modern. Dating estimates of Kabwe and most of the other premodern fossils from Africa have ranged throughout the Middle and Late Pleistocene, but recent estimates have given dates

▶ **Figure 13-3**
The Kabwe (Broken Hill) *Homo heidelbergensis* skull from Zambia. Note the very robust browridges.

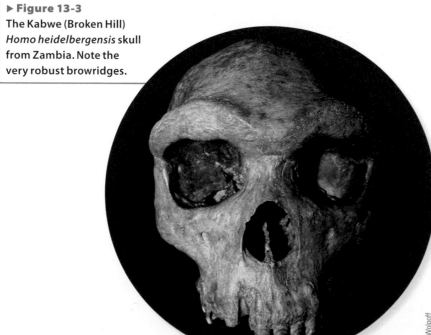

Milford Wolpoff

for most of the sites in the range of 600,000–125,000 ya.

Bodo is another significant African premodern fossil (**Fig. 13-4**). A nearly complete cranium, Bodo has been dated to relatively early in the Middle Pleistocene (estimated at 600,000 ya), making it one of the oldest specimens of *H. heidelbergensis* from the African continent. The Bodo cranium is particularly interesting because it shows a distinctive pattern of cut marks, similar to modifications seen on butchered animal bones. Researchers have thus hypothesized that the Bodo individual was defleshed by other hominins, but for what purpose is not clear. The defleshing may have been related to cannibalism, though it also may have been for some other purpose, such as ritual. In any case, this is the earliest evidence of deliberate bone processing of hominins *by* hominins (White, 1986).

A number of other crania from South and East Africa also show a combination of retained ancestral with more derived (modern) characteristics, and they're all mentioned in the literature as being similar to Kabwe. The most important of these African finds come from the sites of Florisbad and Elandsfontein (in South Africa) and Laetoli (in Tanzania).

The general similarities in all these African premodern fossils indicate a close relationship between them, almost certainly representing a single species (most commonly referred to as *H. heidelbergensis*). These African premodern humans also are quite similar to those found in Europe.

© Robert Franciscus

▲ **Figure 13-4**
Bodo cranium, the earliest evidence of *Homo heidelbergensis* in Africa.

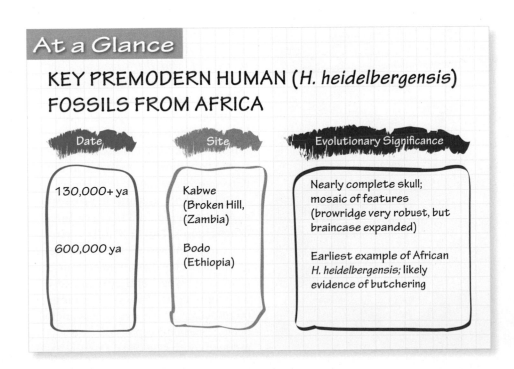

At a Glance

KEY PREMODERN HUMAN (*H. heidelbergensis*) FOSSILS FROM AFRICA

Date	Site	Evolutionary Significance
130,000+ ya	Kabwe (Broken Hill, (Zambia)	Nearly complete skull; mosaic of features (browridge very robust, but braincase expanded)
600,000 ya	Bodo (Ethiopia)	Earliest example of African *H. heidelbergensis*; likely evidence of butchering

► **Figure 13-5**
Artist's reconstruction of a *Homo heidelbergensis* adult male, based on a skull found in Arago France.

Europe

More fossil hominins of Middle Pleistocene age have been found in Europe than in any other region. Maybe it's because more archaeologists have been searching longer in Europe than anywhere else. In any case, during the Middle Pleistocene, Europe was more widely and consistently occupied than it was earlier in human evolution.

The time range of European premodern humans extends the full length of the Middle Pleistocene and beyond. At the earlier end, the Gran Dolina finds from northern Spain (discussed in Chapter 12) are definitely not *Homo erectus*. The Gran Dolina remains may, as proposed by Spanish researchers, be members of a new hominin species. However, Rightmire (1998) has suggested that the Gran Dolina hominins may simply represent the earliest well-dated occurrence of *H. heidelbergensis*, possibly dating as early as 850,000 ya.

More recent and more completely studied *H. heidelbergensis* fossils have been found throughout much of Europe. Examples of these finds come from Steinheim (Germany), Petralona (Greece), Swanscombe (England), Arago (France), and another cave site at Atapuerca (Spain) known as Sima de los Huesos (**Fig. 13-5**). Like their African counterparts, these European premoderns have retained certain *H. erectus* traits, but they're mixed with more derived ones—for example, increased cranial capacity, less angled occiput, parietal expansion, and reduced tooth size (**Figs. 13-6** and **13-7**).

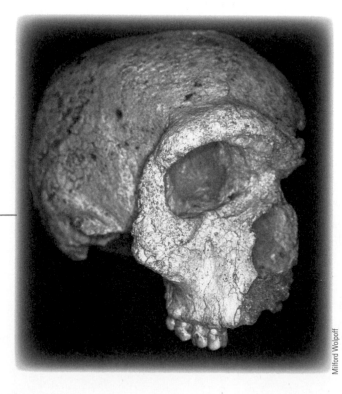

► **Figure 13-6**
Steinheim cranium, a representative of *Homo heidelbergensis* from Germany.

The hominins from the Atapuerca site of Sima de los Huesos are especially interesting. These finds come from another cave in the same area as the Gran Dolina discoveries, but are slightly younger, likely dating to between 500,000 and 400,000 ya. Using a different dating method, a date as early as 600,000 ya has been proposed (Bischoff et al., 2007), but most researchers prefer the more conservative later dating (Green et al., 2010; Wood, 2010). A total of at least 28 individuals have been recovered from Sima de los Huesos, which literally means "pit of bones." In fact, with more than 4,000 fossil fragments recovered, Sima de los Huesos contains more than 80 percent of all Middle Pleistocene hominin remains in the world (Bermúdez de Castro et al., 2004). Excavations continue at this remarkable site, where bones have somehow accumulated within a deep chamber inside a cave. From initial descriptions, paleoanthropologists interpret the hominin morphology as showing several indications of an early Neandertal-like pattern, with arching browridges, projecting midface, and other Neandertal features (Rightmire, 1998).

Asia

Like their contemporaries in Europe and Africa, Asian premodern specimens discovered in China also display both earlier and later characteristics. Chinese paleoanthropologists suggest that the more ancestral traits, such as a sagittal ridge and flattened nasal bones, are shared with *H. erectus* fossils from Zhoukoudian. They also point out that some of these features can be found in modern *H. sapiens* in China today, indicating substantial genetic continuity. That is, some Chinese researchers have argued that anatomically, modern Chinese didn't evolve from *H. sapiens* in either Europe or Africa; instead, they evolved locally in China from a separate *H. erectus* lineage. Whether such regional evolution occurred or whether anatomically modern migrants from Africa displaced local populations is the subject of a major ongoing debate in paleoanthropology. This important controversy will be a central focus of the next chapter.

Dali, the most complete skull of the later Middle or early Late Pleistocene fossils in China, displays *H. erectus* and *H. sapiens* traits, with a cranial capacity of 1,120 cm³ (**Fig. 13-8**). Like Dali, several other Chinese

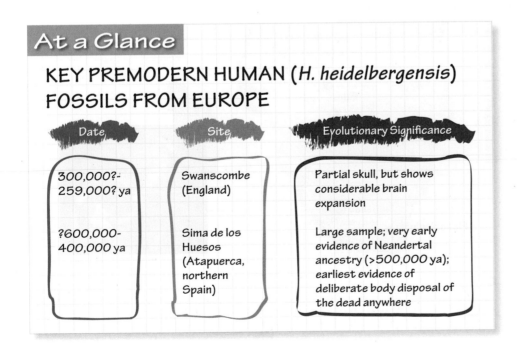

At a Glance

KEY PREMODERN HUMAN (*H. heidelbergensis*) FOSSILS FROM EUROPE

Date	Site	Evolutionary Significance
300,000?-259,000? ya	Swanscombe (England)	Partial skull, but shows considerable brain expansion
?600,000-400,000 ya	Sima de los Huesos (Atapuerca, northern Spain)	Large sample; very early evidence of Neandertal ancestry (>500,000 ya); earliest evidence of deliberate body disposal of the dead anywhere

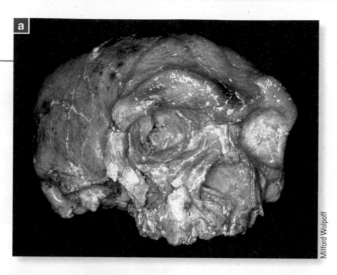

▶ **Figure 13-8**
(a) Dali skull and
(b) Jinniushan skull,
both from China.
These two crania are
considered by some to
be Asian representa-
tives of *Homo
heidelbergensis*.

Milford Wolpoff

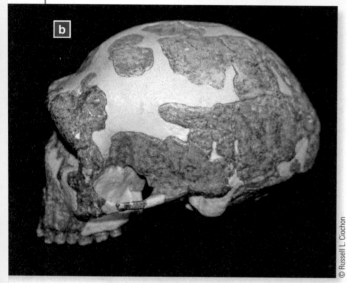

© Russell L. Ciochon

specimens combine both earlier and later traits. In addition, a partial skeleton from Jinniushan, in northeast China, has been given a provisional date of 200,000 ya (Tiemel et al., 1994). The cranial capacity is fairly large (approximately 1,260 cm³), and the walls of the braincase are thin. These are both modern features, and they're somewhat unexpected in an individual this ancient—if the dating estimate is indeed correct. Just how to classify these Chinese Middle Pleistocene hominins has been a sub-

ject of debate and controversy. More recently, though, a leading paleoanthropologist has concluded that they're regional variants of *H. heidelbergensis* (Rightmire, 2004).

A Review of Middle Pleistocene Evolution

Premodern human fossils from Africa and Europe resemble each other more than they do the hominins from Asia. The mix of some ancestral characteristics—retained from *Homo erectus* ancestors—with more derived features gives the African and European fossils a distinctive look; thus, Middle Pleistocene hominins from these two continents are usually referred to as *H. heidelbergensis*.

The situation in Asia isn't so tidy. To some researchers, the remains, especially those from Jinniushan, seem more modern than do contemporary fossils from either Europe or Africa. This observation explains why Chinese paleoanthropologists and some American colleagues conclude that the Jinniushan remains are early members of *H. sapiens*. Other researchers (for example, Rightmire, 1998, 2004) suggest that they represent a regional branch of *H. heidelbergensis*.

The Pleistocene world forced many small populations into geographical

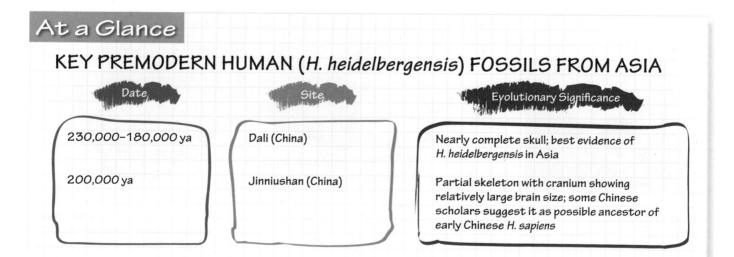

At a Glance

KEY PREMODERN HUMAN (*H. heidelbergensis*) FOSSILS FROM ASIA

Date	Site	Evolutionary Significance
230,000–180,000 ya	Dali (China)	Nearly complete skull; best evidence of *H. heidelbergensis* in Asia
200,000 ya	Jinniushan (China)	Partial skeleton with cranium showing relatively large brain size; some Chinese scholars suggest it as possible ancestor of early Chinese *H. sapiens*

▼ **Figure 13-9**
Time line of Middle Pleistocene hominins. Note that most dates are approximations.
Question marks indicate those estimates that are most tentative.

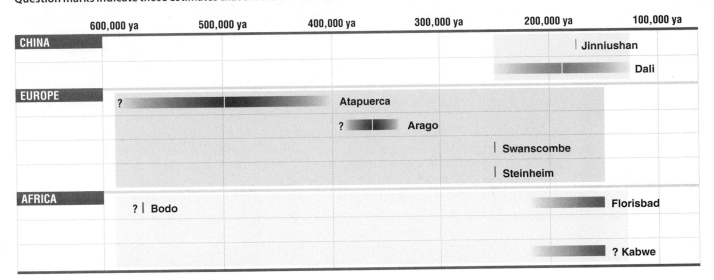

	600,000 ya	500,000 ya	400,000 ya	300,000 ya	200,000 ya	100,000 ya
CHINA						Jinniushan
						Dali
EUROPE	?			Atapuerca		
			?	Arago		
					Swanscombe	
					Steinheim	
AFRICA	? Bodo					Florisbad
						? Kabwe

isolation. Most of these regional populations no doubt died out. Some, however, did evolve, and their descendants are likely a major part of the later hominin fossil record. In Africa, *H. heidelbergensis* is hypothesized to have evolved into modern *H. sapiens*. In Europe, *H. heidelbergensis* evolved into Neandertals. Meanwhile, the Chinese premodern populations may all have met with extinction. Right now, though, there's no consensus on the status or the likely fate of these enigmatic Asian Middle Pleistocene hominins (**Fig. 13-9**).

Middle Pleistocene Culture

The Acheulian technology of *H. erectus* carried over into the Middle Pleistocene with relatively little change until near the end of the period, when it became slightly more sophisticated. Bone, a high-quality tool material, remained practically unused during this time. Stone flake tools similar to those of the earlier era persisted, possibly in greater variety. Some of the later premodern humans in Africa and Europe invented a method—the Levallois technique (**Fig. 13-10**)—for controlling flake size and shape, resulting in a "turtle-back" profile. The Levallois technique required several complex and coordinated steps, suggesting increased cognitive abilities in later premodern populations.

Interpreting the distribution of artifacts during the later Middle Pleistocene has generated considerable discussion among archaeologists. As we noted in Chapter 12, a general geographical distribution characterizes the

▼ **Figure 13-10**
The Levallois technique.

Nodule

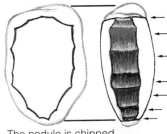

The nodule is chipped on the perimeter.

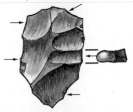

Flakes are radially removed from top surface.

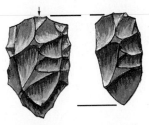

A final blow struck at one end removes a large flake. The flake on the right is the goal of the whole process and is the completed tool.

Early Pleistocene, with bifaces (mostly hand axes) found quite often at sites in Africa, at several sites in parts of Asia, but not at all among the rich assemblage at Zhoukoudian. Also, where hand axes proliferate, the stone tool industry is referred to as Acheulian. At localities without hand axes, various other terms are used—for example, *chopper/chopping tool*, which is a misnomer, since most of the tools are actually flakes and not the cores for which they were named.

Acheulian assemblages have been found at many African sites as well as numerous European ones—for example, Swanscombe (England) and Arago (France). Even though there are broad geographical patterns in the distribution of what we call Acheulian, this shouldn't blind us to the considerable intraregional diversity in stone tool industries. Clearly, a variety of European sites do show a typical Acheulian complex, rich in bifacial hand axes and cleavers. However, at other contemporaneous sites in Germany and Hungary, fieldworkers found a variety of small retouched flake tools and flaked pebbles of various sizes, but no hand axes. So it seems that different stone tool industries coexisted in some areas for long periods, and various explanations (Villa, 1983) have been offered to account for this apparent diversity. Some say that different groups of hominins may have produced the tool industries; others suggest that the same group may have produced them when performing different activities at different sites. The type of stone tool manufactured was also affected by the amount and quality of workable rock in the area. In an area without large cores, it's harder to produce hand axes, since the material to make them has to be brought in from another area.

Premodern human populations continued to live both in caves and in open-air sites, but they may have increased their use of caves. Did these hominins control fire? Klein (1999), in interpreting archaeological evidence from France, Germany, and Hungary,

suggests that they did. What's more, Chinese archaeologists insist that many Middle Pleistocene sites in China contain evidence of human-controlled fire. Still, not everyone is convinced.

We know that Middle Pleistocene hominins built temporary structures, because researchers have found concentrations of bones, stones, and artifacts at several sites. We also have evidence that they exploited many different food sources—fruits, vegetables, seeds, nuts, and bird eggs, each in its own season. Importantly, they also exploited marine life, a new innovation in human biocultural evolution.

The hunting capabilities of premodern humans, as for earlier hominins, are still greatly disputed. Most researchers have found little evidence supporting widely practiced advanced hunting. Some more recent finds, however, are beginning to change this view—especially the discovery in 1995 of remarkable wood spears from the Schöningen site, in Germany (Thieme, 1997). These large, extremely well-preserved weapons (provisionally dated to about 400,000 ya) were most likely used as throwing spears, presumably to hunt large animals. Also interesting in this context, the bones of numerous horses were recovered at Schöningen.

As documented by the fossil remains as well as artifactual evidence from archaeological sites, the long period of transitional hominins in Europe continued well into the Late Pleistocene (after 125,000 ya). But with the appearance and expansion of the Neandertals, the evolution of premodern humans took a unique turn.

Neandertals: Premodern Humans of the Late Pleistocene

Since their discovery more than a century ago, the Neandertals have haunted the minds and foiled the best-laid theories of paleoanthropologists. They fit into the general scheme of human evolution, and yet they're misfits. Classified variously either as *H. sapiens* or as belonging to a separate species, they are like us and yet different. It's not easy to put them in their place. Many anthropologists classify Neandertals within *H. sapiens*, but as a distinctive subspecies, *Homo sapiens neanderthalensis,*[*] with modern *H. sapiens* designated as *Homo sapiens sapiens*. However, not all experts agree with this interpretation. The most recent genetic evidence of interbreeding between Neandertals and early modern humans (Green et al., 2010) suggests that complete speciation was never attained. This argues against a clear designation of Neandertals as a species separate from *H. sapiens*. We'll discuss in a moment this important evidence in more detail.

Thal, meaning "valley," is the old spelling; due to rules of taxonomic naming, this spelling is retained in the formal species designation *Homo neanderthalensis* (although the *h* was *never* pronounced). The modern spelling, *tal*, is used today in Germany; we follow contemporary usage in the text with the spelling of the colloquial *Neandertal*.

Neandertal fossil remains have been found at dates approaching 130,000 ya; but in the following discussion of Neandertals, we'll focus on those populations that lived especially during the last major glaciation, which began about 75,000 ya and ended about 10,000 ya (**Fig. 13-11**). We should also note that the evolutionary roots of Neandertals apparently reach quite far back in western Europe, as evidenced by the 400,000+-year-old remains from Sima de los Huesos, Atapuerca, in northern Spain. The majority of fossils have been found in Europe, where they've been most studied. Our description of Neandertals is based primarily on those specimens, usually called *classic* Neandertals, from western Europe. Not all Neandertals—including others from eastern Europe and western Asia and those from the interglacial period just before the last glacial one—exactly fit our description of the classic morphology. They tend to be less robust, possibly because the climate in which they lived was not as cold as in western Europe during the last glaciation.

▼ **Figure 13-11**
Correlation of Pleistocene subdivisions with archaeological industries and hominins. Note that the geological divisions are separate and different from the archaeological stages (e.g., Late Pleistocene is not synonymous with Upper Paleolithic).

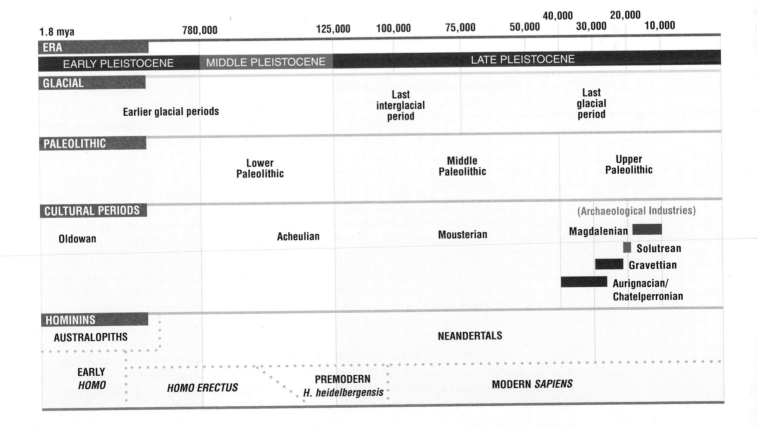

One striking feature of Neandertals is brain size, which in these hominins actually was larger than that of *H. sapiens* today. The average for contemporary *H. sapiens* is between 1,300 and 1,400 cm³, while for Neandertals it was 1,520 cm³. The larger size may be associated with the metabolic efficiency of a larger brain in cold weather. The Inuit (Eskimo), also living in very cold areas, have a larger average brain size than most other modern human populations. We should also point out that the larger brain size in both premodern and contemporary human populations adapted to cold climates is partially correlated with larger body size, which has also evolved among these groups (see Chapter 16).

The classic Neandertal cranium is large, long, low, and bulging at the sides. Viewed from the side, the occipital bone is somewhat bun-shaped, but the marked occipital angle typical of many *H. erectus* crania is absent. The forehead rises more vertically than that of *H. erectus*, and the browridges arch over the orbits instead of forming a straight bar (see **Fig. 13-12**).

Compared with anatomically modern humans, the Neandertal face stands out. It projects almost as if it were pulled forward. Postcranially, Neandertals were very robust, barrel-chested, and powerfully muscled. This robust skeletal structure, in fact, dominates hominin evolution from *H. erectus* through all premodern forms. Still, the Neandertals appear particularly robust, with shorter limbs than seen in most modern *H. sapiens* populations. Both the facial anatomy and the robust postcranial structure of Neandertals have been interpreted by Erik Trinkaus, of Washington University in St. Louis, as adaptations to rigorous living in a cold climate.

For about 100,000 years, Neandertals lived in Europe and western Asia (see **Fig. 13-13**), and their coming and going have raised more questions and controversies than for any other hominin group. As

we've noted, Neandertal forebears were transitional forms dating to the later Middle Pleistocene. However, it's not until the Late Pleistocene that Neandertals become fully recognizable.

Western Europe

One of the most important Neandertal discoveries was made in 1908 at La Chapelle-aux-Saints, in southwestern France. A nearly complete skeleton was found buried in a shallow grave in a **flexed** position (**Fig. 13-14**). Several fragments of nonhuman long bones had been placed over the head, and over them, a bison leg. Around the body were flint tools and broken animal bones.

The skeleton was turned over for study to a well-known French paleontologist, Marcellin Boule, who depicted the La Chapelle Neandertal as a brutish, bent-kneed, not fully erect biped. Because of this exaggerated interpretation, some scholars, and certainly the general public, concluded that all Neandertals were highly primitive creatures.

Why did Boule draw these conclusions from the La Chapelle skeleton? Today, we think he misjudged the Neandertal posture because this adult male skeleton had arthritis of the spine. Also, and probably more important, Boule and his contemporaries found it difficult to fully accept as a human ancestor an individual who appeared in any way to depart from the modern pattern.

The skull of this male, who was possibly at least 40 years of age when he died, is very large, with a cranial capacity of 1,620 cm³. Typical of western European classic forms, the vault is low and long; the browridges are immense, with the typical Neandertal arched shape; the forehead is low and retreating; and the face is long and projecting. The back of the skull is protuberant and bun-shaped (see Figs. 13-12 and **13-15**).

flexed The position of the body in a bent orientation, with arms and legs drawn up to the chest.

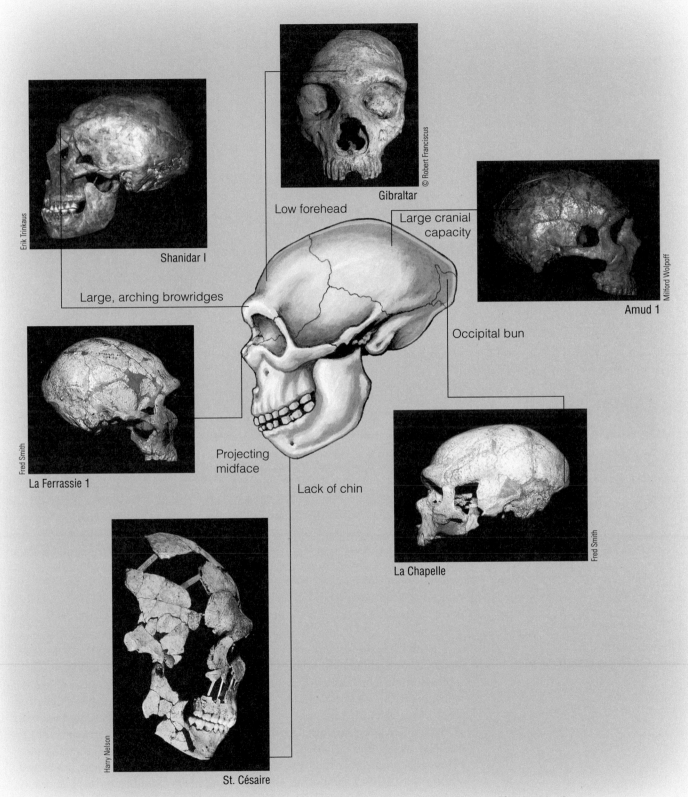

Shanidar I

Low forehead

Gibraltar

Large cranial capacity

© Robert Franciscus

Large, arching browridges

Amud 1

Milford Wolpoff

Occipital bun

La Ferrassie 1

Fred Smith

Projecting midface

Lack of chin

La Chapelle

Fred Smith

St. Césaire

Harry Nelson

Erik Trinkaus

▲ Figure 13-12
Morphology and variation in Neandertal crania.

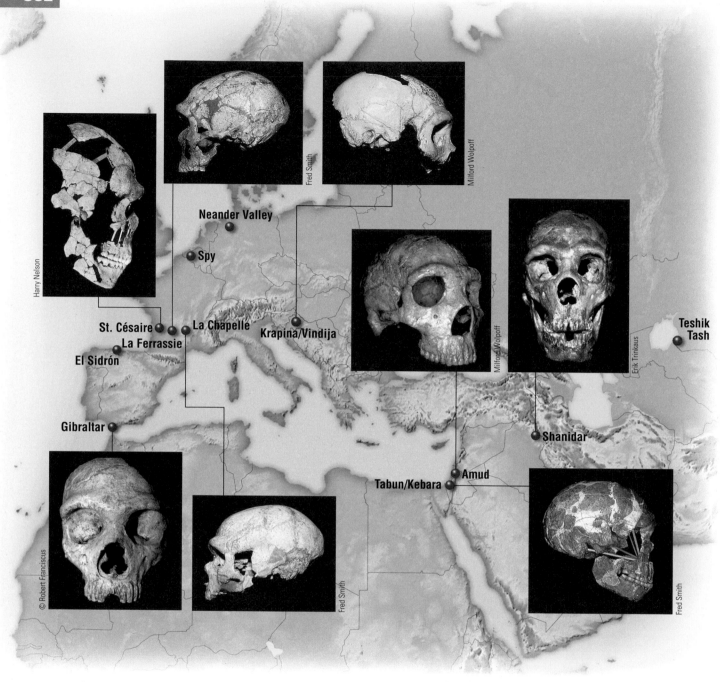

▲ **Figure 13-13**
Fossil discoveries of Neandertals.

The La Chapelle skeleton isn't a typical Neandertal, but an unusually robust male who "evidently represents an extreme in the Neandertal range of variation" (Brace et al., 1979, p. 117). Unfortunately, this skeleton, which Boule claimed didn't even walk completely erect, was widely accepted as "Mr. Neandertal." But few other Neandertal individuals possess such exaggerated expression of Neandertal traits as the "Old Man of La Chapelle-aux-Saints."

Dramatic new evidence of Neandertal behavior comes from the El Sidrón site in northern Spain. Dated to about 49,000 ya, fragmented remains of 12 individuals show bone changes indicating they were smashed, butchered, and likely cannibalized—presumably by other Neandertals (Lalueza-Fox et al., 2011).

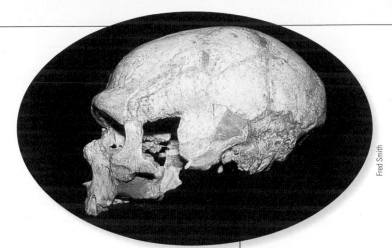

▲ **Figure 13-14**
Artist's reconstruction of an adult male Neandertal based on skeletal remains from La Chapelle France.

▲ **Figure 13-15**
La Chapelle-aux-Saints. Note the occipital bun, projecting face, and low vault.

Because the remains of all 12 individuals were found together in a cave where they had accidentally fallen, they all probably died (were killed) at about the same time. Lying there undisturbed for almost 50,000 years, these individuals reveal several secrets about Neandertals. First, they are hypothesized to all have belonged to the same social group, representing a band of hunter-gatherers. Their ages and sex support this interpretation: three adult males, three adult females, five children/adolescents, and one infant.

What's more, genetic evidence shows that the adult males were all closely related, but the females weren't. It seems that Neandertals practiced a patrilocal form of mating, where related males stay together and mate with females from other groups (see New Frontiers in Research at the end of this chapter).

Some of the most recent of the western European Neandertals come from St. Césaire, in southwestern France, and are dated at about 35,000 ya (**Fig. 13-16**). At St. Césaire, Neandertal remains were recovered from an archaeological level that also included discarded chipped blades, hand axes, and other stone tools of an **Upper Paleolithic** tool industry associated with Neandertals. Perhaps the most recent Neandertal remains yet recovered come from central Europe, at the site of Vindija, in Croatia. Radiocarbon dating suggests that the Vindija remains may date as late as 33,000–32,000 ya (Smith et al., 1999).

The St. Césaire and Vindija sites are important for several reasons. Anatomically modern humans were living in both western and central Europe by about 35,000 ya or a bit earlier. So it's possible that Neandertals and modern *H. sapiens* were living quite close to each other for several thousand years (**Fig. 13-17**). How did these two groups interact? Evidence from a number of French sites indicates that Neandertals may have borrowed technological methods and tools (such as blades) from the anatomically modern populations and thereby modified their own tools, creating a new industry, the **Chatelperronian**. It's also possible, of course, that early modern *H. sapiens* borrowed cultural innovations from the Neandertals (who, as we'll soon see, were in many ways also quite sophisticated). What's more, we know they very likely were *interbreeding* with each other!

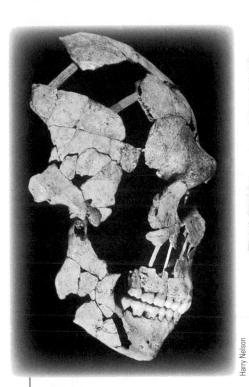

▲ **Figure 13-16**
St. Césaire, among the "last" Neandertals.

Upper Paleolithic A cultural period usually associated with modern humans, but also found with some Neandertals, and distinguished by technological innovation in various stone tool industries. Best known from western Europe, similar industries are also known from central and eastern Europe and Africa.

Chatelperronian Pertaining to an Upper Paleolithic industry found in France and Spain, containing blade tools and associated with Neandertals.

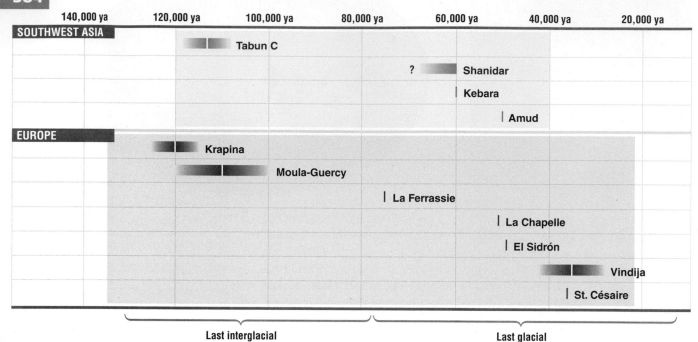

	140,000 ya	120,000 ya	100,000 ya	80,000 ya	60,000 ya	40,000 ya	20,000 ya
SOUTHWEST ASIA		Tabun C					
					? Shanidar		
					Kebara		
					Amud		
EUROPE		Krapina					
			Moula-Guercy				
				La Ferrassie			
					La Chapelle		
					El Sidrón		
						Vindija	
						St. Césaire	

Last interglacial   Last glacial

▲ **Figure 13-17**
Time line for Neandertal fossil discoveries.

Central Europe

There are quite a few other European classic Neandertals, including significant finds from central Europe (see Fig. 13-13). At Krapina, Croatia, researchers have recovered an abundance of bones—1,000 fragments representing up to 70 individuals—and 1,000 stone tools or flakes (Trinkaus and Shipman, 1992). Krapina is an old site, possibly the earliest showing the full suite of classic Neandertal morphology (**Fig. 13-18**), dating back to the beginning of the Late Pleistocene (estimated at 130,000–110,000 ya). Krapina is also important as an intentional burial site—one of the oldest on record.

About 30 miles from Krapina, Neandertal fossils have also been discovered at Vindija. The site is an excellent source of faunal, cultural, and hominin materials stratified in *sequence* throughout much of the Late Pleistocene. Neandertal fossils from Vindija consist of some 35 specimens dated to between 42,000 and 32,000 ya, making them some of the most recent

▶ **Figure 13-18**
Krapina cranium. (a) Lateral view showing characteristic Neandertal traits. (b) Three-quarters view.

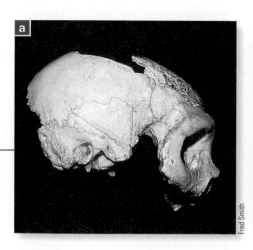

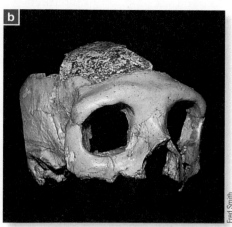

Neandertals ever discovered (Higham et al., 2006). While the overall anatomical pattern is definitely Neandertal, some features of the Vindija individuals, such as smaller browridges and slight chin development, approach the morphology seen in early modern south-central European *H. sapiens*. These similarities have led some researchers to suggest a possible evolutionary link between the late Vindija Neandertals and modern *H. sapiens*.

Western Asia

Israel In addition to European Neandertals, many important discoveries have been made in southwest Asia. Neandertal specimens from Israel are less robustly built than the classic Neandertals of Europe, though again, the overall pattern is clearly Neandertal. One of the best known of these discoveries is from Tabun—short for Mugharet-et-Tabun, meaning "cave of the oven"—at Mt. Carmel, a short drive south from Haifa (**Fig. 13-19**). Tabun, excavated in the early 1930s, yielded a female skeleton, recently dated by thermoluminescence (TL) at about 120,000–110,000 ya (TL dating is discussed in Chapter 10). If this

dating is accurate, Neandertals at Tabun were generally contemporary with early modern *H. sapiens* found in nearby caves.

A more recent Neandertal burial of a large male comes from Kebara, a neighboring cave at Mt. Carmel. A partial skeleton, dated to 60,000 ya, contains the most complete Neandertal thorax and pelvis so far recovered, providing us with valuable information regarding body shape. Also recovered at Kebara is a hyoid—a small bone located in the throat, and the first ever found from a Neandertal; this bone is especially important because of its usefulness in reconstructing language capabilities.*

Iraq A most remarkable site is Shanidar Cave, in the Zagros Mountains of northeastern Iraq, where fieldworkers found partial skeletons of nine individuals, four of them deliberately buried. One of the more interesting skeletons recovered from Shanidar is that of a male (Shanidar 1) who lived to be approximately 30 to 45 years old,

---

*The Kebara hyoid is identical to that of modern humans, suggesting that Neandertals did not differ from modern *H. sapiens* in this key element.

◀ **Figure 13-19**
Excavation of the Tabun Cave, Mt. Carmel, Israel.

Harry Nelson

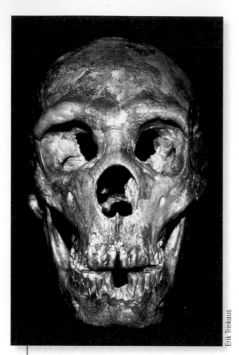
Erik Trinkaus

▲ **Figure 13-20**
Shanidar 1. Does he represent Neandertal compassion for the disabled?

a considerable age for a prehistoric human (**Fig. 13-20**). He is estimated to have stood 5 feet 7 inches tall, with a cranial capacity of 1,600 cm³. The skeletal remains of Shanidar 1 also exhibit several other fascinating features:

> There had been a crushing blow to the left side of the head, fracturing the eye socket, displacing the left eye, and probably causing blindness on that side. He also sustained a massive blow to the right side of the body that so badly damaged the right arm that it became withered and useless; the bones of the shoulder blade, collar bone, and upper arm are much smaller and thinner than those on the left. The right lower arm and hand are missing, probably not because of poor preservation . . . but because they either atrophied and dropped off or because they were amputated. (Trinkaus and Shipman, 1992, p. 340)

Besides these injuries, the man had further trauma to both legs, and he probably limped. It's hard to imagine how he could have performed day-to-day activities without assistance. This is why Erik Trinkaus, who has studied the Shanidar remains, suggests that to survive, Shanidar 1 must have been helped by others: "A one-armed, partially blind, crippled man could have made no pretense of hunting or gathering his own food. That he survived for years after his trauma was a testament to Neandertal compassion and humanity" (Trinkaus and Shipman, 1992, p. 341).

Central Asia

Neandertals extended their range even farther to the east, far into central Asia. A discovery made in the 1930s at the site of Teshik-Tash, in Uzbekistan, of a Neandertal child associated with tools of the Mousterian industry suggested that this species had dispersed a long way into Asia. However, owing to poor archaeological control during excavation and the young age of the individual, the find was not considered

by all paleoanthropologists as clearly that of a Neandertal. New finds and molecular evaluation have provided crucial evidence that Neandertals did in fact extend their geographical range far into central Asia and perhaps even farther east.

DNA analysis of the Teshik-Tash remains shows that they are clearly Neandertal. What's more, other fragments from southern Siberia also show a distinctively Neandertal genetic pattern (Krause et al., 2007a). As we'll see shortly, researchers have recently been able to identify and analyze DNA from several Neandertal specimens. It's been shown that Neandertals and modern humans differ in both their mitochondrial DNA (mtDNA) and nuclear DNA, and these results are extremely significant in determining the evolutionary status of the Neandertal lineage. Moreover, in the case of the fragmentary remains from southern Siberia (dating to 44,000–37,000 ya), it was the DNA findings that provided the key evidence in determining whether the hominin is even a Neandertal. In a sense, this is analogous to doing forensic analysis on our ancient hominin predecessors.

Another Contemporary Hominin?

In 2008 researchers found more fragmentary hominin remains in another cave in the Altai Mountains of southern Siberia. Only a finger bone was found, and it was dated to 48,000–30,000 ya. From such incomplete skeletal remains, accurate anatomical species identification is impossible. In prior years, this seemingly meager find would have been stashed away in a cabinet in a museum or a university laboratory and mostly forgotten. But in the twenty-first century, we have new ways to study bits and pieces of ancient hominins. So the bone was sent to the Max-Planck Institute for Evolutionary Biology in Germany to see if DNA analysis could determine to which species it belongs. No nuclear DNA was recovered, but the entire mitochondrial DNA genome

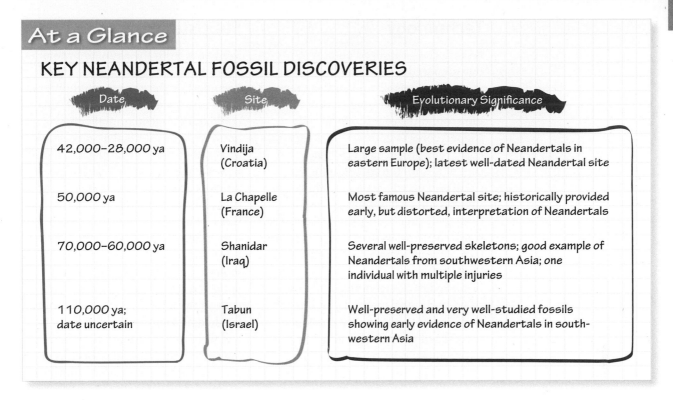

At a Glance

KEY NEANDERTAL FOSSIL DISCOVERIES

Date	Site	Evolutionary Significance
42,000–28,000 ya	Vindija (Croatia)	Large sample (best evidence of Neandertals in eastern Europe); latest well-dated Neandertal site
50,000 ya	La Chapelle (France)	Most famous Neandertal site; historically provided early, but distorted, interpretation of Neandertals
70,000–60,000 ya	Shanidar (Iraq)	Several well-preserved skeletons; good example of Neandertals from southwestern Asia; one individual with multiple injuries
110,000 ya; date uncertain	Tabun (Israel)	Well-preserved and very well-studied fossils showing early evidence of Neandertals in southwestern Asia

was described. The researchers were working on the assumption that it was either a modern *H. sapiens* or a Neandertal (Neandertals having been found only 60 miles away in the other Siberian cave mentioned earlier). The results of the mtDNA analysis produced a big surprise: The finger bone's mtDNA did not match that of either a modern *H. sapiens* or a Neandertal! What's more, the degree of genetic distance suggested to the researchers that the hominin line of this "new" hominin diverged from the modern *H. sapiens*/Neandertal line almost 1 million years ago (Krause et al., 2010). This would strongly suggest that the finger bone came from a completely new species, different from modern humans or Neandertals. The primary researchers chose not to immediately make the "leap" and argue for a new species based solely on molecular evidence. Such an evolutionary designation of a new "molecular" species has never been done, at least not for any primate; but for those hominins that retain enough molecular material, this may well be the future! Another surprising aspect of this find is also difficult to explain.

If there really was another hominin species living in southern Siberia around 40,000 ya, there would have been three different lineages all living in close proximity to each other. How they would have managed to coexist raises many intriguing questions.

Culture of Neandertals

Anthropologists almost always associate Neandertals, who lived in the cultural period known as the Middle Paleolithic, with the **Mousterian** industry—although they don't always associate the Mousterian industry with just Neandertals (since it sometimes is also found with modern humans). Early in the last glacial period, Mousterian culture extended across Europe and North Africa into the former Soviet Union, Israel, Iran, and as far east as central Asia and possibly even China. Also, in sub-Saharan Africa, the contemporaneous Middle Stone Age industry is broadly similar to the Mousterian.

Mousterian Pertaining to the stone tool industry associated with Neandertals and some modern *H. sapiens* groups; also called Middle Paleolithic. This industry is characterized by a larger proportion of flake tools than is found in Acheulian tool kits.

Technology

Neandertals improved on previous prepared-core techniques—that is, the Levallois—by inventing a new variation. They trimmed a flint nodule around the edges to form a disk-shaped core. Each time they struck the edge, they produced a flake, and they kept at it until the core became too small and was discarded. In this way, they produced more flakes per core than their predecessors did. They then reworked the flakes into various forms, including scrapers, points, and knives (**Fig. 13-21**).

Neandertals elaborated and diversified traditional methods, and there's some indication that they developed specialized tools for skinning and preparing meat, hunting, woodworking, and hafting. Even so, in strong contrast to the following cultural period, the Upper Paleolithic, there's almost no evidence that they used bone tools. Still, Neandertals advanced their technology well beyond that of earlier hominins. It's possible that their technological advances helped provide part of the basis for the remarkable changes of the Upper Paleolithic, which we'll discuss in the next chapter. What's more, Neandertals also were quite advanced in exploiting new food resources, as well as fashioning personal adornments.

Subsistence

We know, from the abundant remains of animal bones at their sites, that Neandertals were successful hunters. But while it's clear that Neandertals could hunt large mammals, they may not have been as efficient at this task as Upper Paleolithic modern humans. For example, it wasn't until the beginning of the Upper Paleolithic that the spear-thrower, or atlatl, came into use (see Chapter 14). Soon after that, in Upper Paleolithic groups, the bow and arrow greatly increased efficiency (and safety) in hunting large mammals by putting distance between the hunters and the hunted. Because Neandertals had no long-distance weaponry and were mostly limited to thrusting spears, they may have been more prone to serious injury—a hypothesis supported by paleoanthropologists Thomas Berger and Erik Trinkaus. Berger and Trinkaus (1995) analyzed the pattern of trauma, particularly fractures, in Neandertals and compared it with that seen in contemporary human samples. Interestingly, the pattern in Neandertals, especially the relatively high proportion of head and neck injuries, was most similar to that seen in contemporary rodeo performers. Berger and Trinkaus concluded that "the similarity to the rodeo distribution suggests frequent

▶ **Figure 13-21**
Examples of the Mousterian tool kit, including (from left to right) a Levallois point, a perforator, and a side scraper.

© Randall White

close encounters with large ungulates unkindly disposed to the humans involved" (Berger and Trinkaus, 1995, p. 841).

Recent archaeological discoveries have shown that Neandertals also expanded their range of available foods to include marine resources—a subsistence strategy that had been thought to have developed later on by modern humans during the Upper Paleolithic. From the island of Gibralter, new evidence has shown that some Neandertals gathered shellfish and hunted seals and dolphins, displaying no difference in their hunting behavior from modern humans of the same region (Stringer et al., 2008).

We know much more about European Middle Paleolithic culture than any earlier culture because it's been studied longer and by more scholars. Recently, however, Africa has been a target not only of physical anthropologists but also of archaeologists, who have added considerably to our knowledge of African Pleistocene hominin prehistory. In many cases, the technology and assumed cultural adaptations in Africa were similar to those in Europe and southwest Asia. We'll see in the next chapter that the African technological achievements also kept pace with, or even preceded, those in western Europe.

Speech and Symbolic Behavior

There are a variety of hypotheses concerning the speech capacities of Neandertals, and many of these views are contradictory. While some researchers argue that Neandertals were incapable of human speech, the prevailing consensus has been that they *were* capable of articulate speech and possibly capable of producing the same range of sounds as modern humans.

Recent genetic evidence likely will help us determine when fully human language first emerged (Enard et al., 2002; Fisher and Scharff, 2009). In humans today, mutations in a particular gene (locus) are known to produce serious language impairments. From an evolutionary perspective, what is perhaps most significant is the greater variability seen in the alleles at this locus in modern humans as compared to other primates. One explanation for this increased variation is intensified selection acting on human populations, and as we'll see shortly, DNA evidence from Neandertal fossils shows that these hominins had already made this transformation.

Many researchers are convinced that Upper Paleolithic *H. sapiens* had some significant behavioral advantages over Neandertals and other premodern humans. Was it some kind of new and expanded ability to symbolize, communicate, organize social activities, elaborate technology, obtain a wider range of food resources, or care for the sick or injured? Or was it some other factor? Compared with modern *H. sapiens*, were the Neandertals limited by neurological differences that may have contributed to their demise?

The direct anatomical evidence derived from Neandertal fossils isn't much help in answering these questions. Ralph Holloway (1985) has maintained that Neandertal brains—at least as far as the fossil evidence suggests (from endocasts—both natural and artificial)—aren't significantly different from those of modern *H. sapiens*. What's more, the positioning of the Neandertal vocal tract (determined by the shape of the hyoid bone), as well as other morphological features, doesn't appear to have seriously limited them.

Most of the reservations about advanced cognitive abilities in Neandertals have been based on archaeological data. However, as more archaeological data have been collected and better dating controls applied to a large number of sites bridging the Mousterian–Upper Paleolithic transition, many of the proposed behavioral differences between Neandertals and early modern humans have blurred. For example, it is now known that, like early

A Closer Look

The Evolution of Language

One of the most distinctive behavioral attributes of all modern humans is our advanced ability to use highly sophisticated symbolic language. Indeed, it would be impossible to imagine human social relationships or human culture without language.

When did language evolve? First, we should define what we mean by full human language. As we discussed in Chapter 8, nonhuman primates have shown some elements of language. For example, some chimpanzees, gorillas, and bonobos display the ability to manipulate symbols and a rudimentary understanding of grammar. Still, the full complement of skills displayed by humans includes the extensive use of arbitrary symbols; sophisticated grammar; and a complex, open system of communication.

Most scholars are comfortable attributing such equivalent skills to early members of *H. sapiens*, as early as 200,000–100,000

ya. In fact, some researchers have hypothesized that the elaborate technology and artistic achievements, as well as the rapid dispersal, of modern humans were a direct result of behavioral advantages—particularly full language capabilities. More recently, we have come to appreciate that Neandertal cultural abilities were also quite advanced, and the transition to the more elaborate Upper Paleolithic associated with modern humans was not instantaneous.

Clearly, earlier hominins had some form of complex communication; almost everyone agrees that even the earliest hominins did communicate (and the form was at least as complex as that seen in living apes). What's not generally agreed upon is just when the full complement of human language capacity first emerged. Indeed, the controversy relating to this process will continue to ferment, since there's no clear answer to the question. There's not enough evidence available to fully establish the language capabilities of any fossil hominin. We said in Chapter 8 that there are neurological foundations for language and that these features relate more to brain reorganization than to simple increase in brain size. Also, as far as spoken language is

concerned, alterations within several anatomical structures, including the brain and vocal tract, must have occurred sometime during hominin evolution.

Yet, we have no complete record of fossil hominin brains or their vocal tracts. We do have endocasts, which preserve a few external features of the brain. For example, there are several preserved endocasts of australopiths from South Africa. However, the information is incomplete and thus subject to varying interpretations. (For example, did these hominins possess language? If not, what form of communication did they display?) Evidence from the vocal tract has been even more elusive, although recent finds are helping fill in at least some of the gaps.

In such an atmosphere of fragmentary data, a variety of conflicting hypotheses have been proposed. Some paleoanthropologists argue that early australopiths (3 mya) had language. Others think that such capabilities were first displayed by early *Homo* (perhaps 2 mya). Still others suggest that language didn't emerge fully until the time of *Homo erectus* (2–1 mya), or perhaps it was premodern humans (such as the Neandertals) who first displayed such

H. sapiens, Neandertals sometimes used pigment (probably as body ornamentation) and wore jewelry. The most significant recent finds come from two sites in Spain dating to 50,000–37,000 ya, and both have a Mousterian stone tool industry. Since these sites were occupied *before* modern *H. sapiens* reached this part of Europe, the most likely conclusion is that the objects found were made by Neandertals (Zilhão et al., 2010). The finds include perforated shells, ostensibly drilled to be used as jewelry, as well as natural pigments that were deliberately brought to the site and applied to the shells and some animal bones (see **Fig. 13-22**).

Neandertals and modern humans coexisted in some parts of Europe for up to 15,000 years, so Neandertals didn't disappear suddenly. Nevertheless, shortly after 30,000 ya, they disappear from the fossil and archaeological record. At some point, as a recognizable human group, Neandertals became an evolutionary dead end. Right now, we can't say exactly what caused their disappearance and ultimate replacement by anatomically modern Upper Paleolithic peoples. Indeed, Neandertals didn't really disappear altogether, since a few of their genes still can be found today in many humans groups.

skills. And finally, some researchers assert that language first developed only with the appearance of fully modern *H. sapiens*.

Because the question of language evolution is so fundamental to understanding human evolution (indeed, what it means *to be* human), a variety of creative techniques have been applied to assess the (limited) evidence that's available. We've already mentioned the analysis of endocasts.

To reconstruct speech capabilities in fossil hominins, the physiology of the vocal tract also can provide some crucial hints, especially the position of the voice box (larynx) within the throat. In adult modern humans, the larynx is placed low in the throat, where it can better act as a resonating chamber. Unfortunately, since all the crucial structures within the vocal tract are soft tissue, they decompose after death, leaving paleoanthropologists to their own imagination to speculate about the relative positions of the larynx in life. One way to determine the position of the larynx in long-dead hominins is to look at the degree of flexion at the base of the cranium. This flexion can be directly linked to the placement of the larynx in life, since "it shapes the roof of the voice box" (Klein, 1999). In comparisons of fossil hominin crania, it's been determined that full cranial base flexion similar to that found in modern *sapiens* is not found before *Homo heidelbergensis*.

The tongue is, of course, another crucial structure influencing speech. Because it's a site of attachment for one of the muscles of the tongue, the shape and position of the hyoid bone (**Fig. 1**) can tell us a lot about speech capabilities in earlier hominins. A hyoid located higher up and farther back in the throat allows modern humans to control their tongue much more efficiently and precisely. In the *Australopithecus afarensis* child's skeleton (from Dikika, Ethiopia; see Chapter 11), the hyoid is shaped more like that in a chimpanzee than in a modern human. So, it seems most likely that these early hominins weren't able to fully articulate human speech. The only other hyoid found in a fossil hominin comes from the Neandertal skeleton found at Kebara (Israel), and quite unlike the australopith condition, it resembles modern hyoids in all respects. We thus have some basis for concluding that the tongue musculature of Neandertals may have been much like our own.

Also potentially informative are possible genetic differences between humans and apes in regard to language. As the human genome is fully mapped (especially identifying functional regions and their specific actions) and compared with ape DNA (the chimpanzee genome is now also completely sequenced at a structural level), we might at long last begin to find a key to solving this great mystery.

◄ **Figure 1**
The position of the hyoid bone in the throat, shown in a modern human skeleton.

Burials

Anthropologists have known for some time that Neandertals deliberately buried their dead. Undeniably, the spectacular discoveries at La Chapelle, Shanidar, and elsewhere were the direct results of ancient burial, which permits preservation that's much more complete. Such deliberate burial treatment goes back at least 90,000 years at Tabun. From a much older site, some form of consistent "disposal" of the dead—not necessarily belowground burial—is evidenced. As previously discussed, at the site of Sima de los Huesos in Spain, archaeologists found thousands of fossilized bone fragments in a cave at the end of a deep vertical shaft. From the nature of the site and the accumulation of hominin remains, Spanish researchers are convinced that the site demonstrates some form of human activity involving deliberate disposal of the dead (Arsuaga et al., 1997).

The recent dating of Sima de los Huesos to more than 400,000 ya suggests that Neandertal precursors were already handling their dead in special ways during the Middle Pleistocene. Such behavior was previously thought to have emerged only much later, in the Late Pleistocene. As far as current data

▲ **Figure 13-22**
Upper portion of a bivalve shell that has been perforated and stained with pigment, from the Antón rock-shelter site in Spain (dated around 44,000–37,000 ya). The reddish inner surface (left) is natural, but the yellow colorant on the outer whitish surface (right) was the result of an added pigment.

© João Zilhão

indicate, this practice is seen in western European contexts well before it appears in Africa or eastern Asia. For example, in the premodern sites at Kabwe and Florisbad (discussed earlier), deliberate disposal of the dead is not documented. Nor is it seen in African early modern sites—for example, the Klasies River Mouth, dated at 120,000–100,000 ya (see Chapter 14).

Yet, in later contexts (after 35,000 ya), where modern *H. sapiens* remains are found in clear burial contexts, their treatment is considerably more complex than in Neandertal burials. In these later (Upper Paleolithic) sites, grave goods, including bone and stone tools as well as animal bones, are found more consistently and in greater concentrations. Because many Neandertal sites were excavated in the nineteenth or early twentieth century, before more rigorous archaeological methods were developed, many of these supposed burials are now in question. Still, the evidence seems quite clear that deliberate burial was practiced not only at La Chapelle, La Ferrassie (eight graves), Tabun, Amud, Kebara, Shanidar, and Teshik-Tash, but also at several other localities, especially in France. In many cases, the body's position was deliberately modified and placed in the grave in a flexed posture. This flexed position has been found in 16 of the 20 best-documented Neandertal burial contexts (Klein, 1999).

Finally, as further evidence of Neandertal symbolic behavior, researchers point to the placement of supposed grave goods in burials, including stone tools, animal bones (such as cave bear), and even arrangements of flowers, together with stone slabs on top of the burials. Unfortunately, in many instances,

again due to poorly documented excavation, these finds are questionable. Placement of stone tools, for example, is occasionally seen, but wasn't done consistently. In those 33 Neandertal burials for which we have adequate data, only 14 show potential association of stone tools and/or animal bones with the deceased (Klein, 1999). It's not until the next cultural period, the Upper Paleolithic, that we see a significant behavioral shift, as demonstrated by more elaborate burials and development of art.

Genetic Evidence

With the revolutionary advances in molecular biology (discussed in Chapter 3), fascinating new avenues of research have become possible in the study of earlier hominins. It's becoming fairly commonplace to extract, amplify, and sequence ancient DNA from contexts spanning the last 10,000 years or so. For example, researchers have analyzed DNA from the 5,000-year-old "Iceman" found in the Italian Alps as well the entire nuclear genome from a 4000-year-old Inuit (Eskimo) from Greenland (Rasmussen et al., 2010).

It's much harder to find usable DNA in even more ancient remains, since the organic components, often including the DNA, have been destroyed during the mineralization process. Still, in the past few years, exciting results have been announced about DNA found in more than a dozen different Neandertal fossils dated between 50,000 and 32,000 ya. These fossils come from sites in France (including La Chapelle), Germany (from the original Neander Valley locality), Belgium, Italy, Spain, Croatia, and Russia (Krings et al., 1997, 2000; Ovchinnikov et al., 2000; Schmitz et al., 2002; Serre et al., 2004; Green et al., 2006). As we previously mentioned, recently ascertained ancient DNA evidence strongly suggests that other fossils from central Asia (Uzbekistan and two caves in southern Siberia) dated at 48,000–30,000 ya are also Neandertals (Krause et al., 2007b) or even an entirely different species (Krause et al., 2010).

The technique most often used in studying most Neandertal fossils involves extracting mitochondrial DNA (mtDNA), amplifying it through polymerase chain reaction (PCR; see Chapter 3), and sequencing nucleotides in parts of the molecule. Initial results from the Neandertal specimens show that these individuals are genetically more different from contemporary *Homo sapiens* populations than modern human populations are from each other—in fact, about three times as much.

Major advances in molecular biology have allowed much more of the Neandertal genetic pattern to be determined with the ability to now sequence the entire mtDNA sequence in several individuals (Briggs et al., 2009) as well as big chunks of the *nuclear* DNA (which, as you may recall, contains more than 99 percent of the human genome). In fact, the most exciting breakthrough yet in ancient DNA studies was achieved in 2010 with the completion of the *entire* nuclear genome of European Neandertals (Green et al., 2010). Just a couple of years ago, this sort of achievement would have seemed like science fiction.

This new information has already allowed for crucial (as well as quite surprising) revisions in our understanding of Neandertal and early modern human evolution. Most importantly, we now are able to conclude with confidence that Neandertals interbred with modern *Homo sapiens* (See "New Frontiers in Research" at the end of this chapter).

Moreover, the molecular data provide more precise estimates of when modern humans and Neandertals diverged from one another. The newest evidence from detailed analyses of the entire Neandertal genome suggests that this divergence took place between 440,000 and 270,000 ya. Conclusions from less complete analysis (largely of mtDNA) had hypothesized an earlier divergence, potentially as ancient as 800,000 ya (Green et al., 2006; Noonan et al., 2006). Combined with further refinements in dating early Neandertal-like fossils (from Sima de los Huesos), a more recent divergence date makes good sense. However, further evaluations of ancient DNA and certainly new and well-dated fossil finds may change this conclusion.

What's more, we've already had tantalizing clues of how we differ from Neandertals in terms of specific genes. As the data are further analyzed and expanded, we will surely learn more about the evolutionary development of human anatomy *and* human behavior. In so doing, we'll be able to answer far more precisely that age-old question, What does it mean to be human? (For further discussion, see "New Frontiers in Research" at the end of this chapter).

Trends in Human Evolution: Understanding Premodern Humans

As you can see, the Middle Pleistocene hominins are a very diverse group, broadly dispersed through time and space. There is considerable variation among them, and it's not easy to get a clear evolutionary picture. We know that regional populations were small and frequently isolated, and many of them probably died out and left no descendants. So it's a mistake to see an "ancestor" in every fossil find.

Still, as a group, these Middle Pleistocene premoderns do reveal some general trends. In many ways, for example, it seems that they were *transitional* between the hominins that came before them (*H. erectus*) and the ones that followed them (modern *H. sapiens*). It's not a stretch to say that all the Middle Pleistocene premoderns derived from *H. erectus* forebears and that some of them, in turn, were probably ancestors of the earliest fully modern humans.

Paleoanthropologists are certainly concerned with such broad generalities as these, but they also want to focus on meaningful anatomical, environmental, and behavioral details as well as the underlying processes. So they consider the regional variability displayed by particular fossil samples as significant—but just *how* significant is debatable. In addition, increasingly sophisticated theoretical and technological approaches are being used to better understand the processes that shaped the evolution of later *Homo* at both macroevolutionary and microevolutionary levels.

Scientists, like all humans, assign names or labels to phenomena, a point we addressed in discussing classification in Chapter 5. Paleoanthropologists are certainly no exception. Yet, working from a common evolutionary foundation, paleoanthropologists still come to different conclusions about the most appropriate way to interpret the Middle/Late Pleistocene hominins. Consequently, a variety of species names have been proposed in recent years.

Paleoanthropologists who advocate an extreme lumping approach recognize only one species for all the premodern humans discussed in this chapter. These premoderns are classified as *Homo sapiens* and are thus lumped together with modern humans, although they're partly distinguished by such terminology as "archaic *H. sapiens.*" As we've noted, this degree of lumping is no longer supported by most researchers. Alternatively, a second, less extreme view postulates modest species diversity and labels the earlier premoderns as *H. heidelbergensis* (**Fig. 13-23a**).

At the other end of the spectrum, more enthusiastic paleontological splitters have identified at least two (or more) species distinct from *H. sapi-* *ens*. The most important of these, *H. heidelbergensis* and *H. neanderthalensis*, have been discussed earlier. This more complex evolutionary interpretation is shown in **Figure 13-23b**.

We addressed similar differences of interpretation in Chapters 11 and 12, and we know that disparities like these can be frustrating to students who are new to paleoanthropology. The proliferation of new names is confusing, and it might seem that experts in the field are endlessly arguing about what to call the fossils.

Fortunately, it's not quite that bad. There's actually more agreement than you might think. No one doubts that all these hominins are closely related to each other as well as to modern humans. And everyone agrees that only some of the fossil samples represent populations that left descendants. Where paleoanthropologists disagree is when they start discussing which hominins are the most likely to be closely related to later hominins. The grouping of hominins into evolutionary clusters (clades) and assigning of different names to them is a reflection of differing interpretations—and, more fundamentally, of somewhat differing philosophies.

But we shouldn't emphasize these naming and classification debates too much. Most paleoanthropologists recognize that a great deal of these disagreements result from simple, practical considerations. Even the most enthusiastic splitters acknowledge that the fossil "species" are not true species as defined by the biological species concept (see Chapter 5). As prominent paleoanthropologist Robert Foley puts it, "It is unlikely they are all biological species. . . . These are probably a mixture of real biological species and evolving lineages of subspecies. In other words, they could potentially have interbred, but owing to allopatry [that is, geographical separation] were unlikely to have had the opportunity" (Foley, 2002, p. 33).

Even so, Foley, along with an increasing number of other profession-

▼ **Figure 13-23**

(a) Phylogeny of genus *Homo*. Only very modest species diversity is implied. (b) Phylogeny of genus *Homo* showing considerable species diversity (after Foley, 2002)

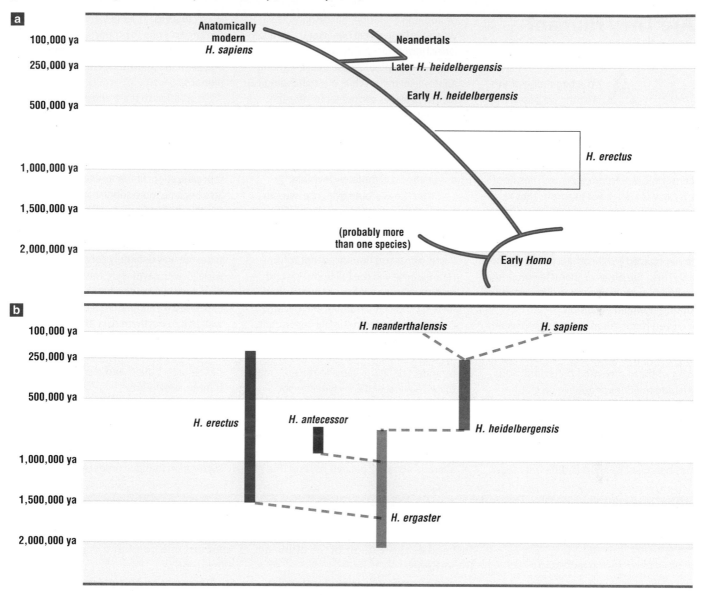

als, distinguishes these different fossil samples with species names to highlight their distinct position in hominin evolution. That is, these hominin groups are more loosely defined as a type of paleospecies (see Chapter 5) rather than as fully biological species. Giving distinct hominin samples a separate (species) name makes them more easily identifiable to other researchers and makes various cladistic hypotheses more explicit—and equally important, more directly testable. The eminent paleoanthropologist F. Clark

Howell, of the University of California, Berkeley, also recognized these advantages but was less emphatic about species designations. Howell recommended the term *paleo-deme* for referring to either a species or subspecies classification (Howell, 1999).

The hominins that best illustrate these issues are the Neandertals. Fortunately, they're also the best known, represented by dozens of well-preserved individuals and also a complete genome. With all this evidence, researchers can systematically

A Closer Look

Are They Human?

At the beginning of this chapter, we posed the question, What does it mean to be human? Applying the term *human* to our extinct hominin predecessors is somewhat tricky. Various prior hominin species share with contemporary *Homo sapiens* a mosaic of physical features. For example, they're all bipedal, most (but not all) have fairly small canine teeth, some are completely terrestrial, and some are moderately encephalized (while others are much more so). Thus, the *physical* characteristics that define humanity appear at different times during hominin evolution.

Even more tenuous are the *behavioral* characteristics frequently identified as signifying human status. The most significant of these proposed behavioral traits include major dependence on culture, innovation, cooperation in acquiring food, full language, and elaboration of symbolic representations in art and body adornment. Once again, the characteristics become apparent at different stages of hominin evolution. But distinguishing when and how these behavioral characteristics became established in our ancestors is even more problematic than analyzing anatomical traits. While the archaeological record provides considerable information regarding stone tool technology, it's mostly silent on other aspects of material culture. The social organization and language capabilities of earlier hominins are as yet almost completely invisible.

From the available evidence, we can conclude that *H. erectus* took significant steps in the human direction—well beyond that of earlier hominins. *H. erectus* vastly expanded hominin geographical ranges, achieved the full body size and limb proportions of later hominins, had increased encephalization, and became considerably more culturally dependent.

H. heidelbergensis (in the Middle Pleistocene) and, to an even greater degree, Neandertals (in the Late Pleistocene) maintained several of these characteristics—such as body size and proportions—while also showing further evolution in the human direction. Most particularly, relative brain size increased further, expanding on average about 22 percent beyond that of *H. erectus* (**Fig. 1**). Notice, however, that the largest jump in proportional brain size occurs very late in hominin evolution—only with the appearance of fully modern humans.

In addition to brain enlargement, cranial shape also was remodeled in *H. heidelbergensis* and Neandertals, producing a more globular shape of the vault as well as suggesting further neurological reorganization. Stone tool technology also became more sophisticated during the Middle Pleistocene, with the manufacture of tools requiring a more complicated series of steps. Also, for the first time, fire was definitely controlled and widely used; caves were routinely occupied; hominin ranges were successfully expanded throughout much of Europe as well as into northern Asia (that is, colder habitats were more fully exploited); structures were built; the dead were deliberately buried; and more systematic hunting took place.

Some premoderns also were like modern humans in another significant way. Analysis of teeth from a Neandertal shows that these hominins had the same *delayed maturation* found in modern *H. sapiens*

test and evaluate many of the differing hypotheses.

Are Neandertals very closely related to modern *H. sapiens*? Certainly. Are they physically and behaviorally somewhat distinct from both ancient and fully modern humans? Yes. Does this mean that Neandertals are a fully separate biological species from modern humans and therefore theoretically incapable of fertilely interbreeding with modern people? Almost certainly not. Finally, then, should Neandertals really be placed in a separate species from *H. sapiens*? For most purposes, it doesn't matter, since the distinction at some point is arbitrary. Speciation is, after all, a *dynamic* process. Fossil groups like the Neandertals represent just one point in this process (see Chapter 5).

We can view Neandertals as a distinctive side branch of later hominin evolution. It is not unreasonable to say that Neandertals were likely an incipient species. Given enough time and enough isolation, they likely would have separated completely from their modern human contemporaries. The new DNA evidence suggests that they were partly on their way, but not yet reaching full speciation from *Homo sapiens*. Their fate, in a sense, was decided for them as more successful competitors expanded into Neandertal habitats. These highly successful hominins were fully modern humans, and in the next chapter we'll focus on their story.

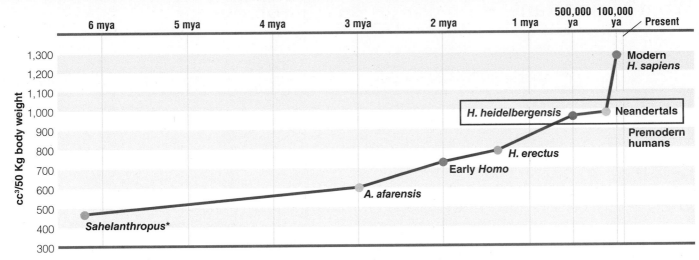

*There are no direct current data for body size in *Sahelanthropus*. Body size is estimated from tooth size in comparison with *A. afarensis*. Data abstracted from McHenry (1992), Wood and Collard (1999), Brunet (2002), and Carroll (2003).

▲ **Figure 1**

Relative brain size in hominins. The scale shows brain size as cm³ per 50 kg of body weight. Premodern humans have a more than 20 percent increase in relative brain size compared to *H. erectus*, but modern humans show another 30 percent expansion beyond that seen in premodern humans.

(Dean et al., 2001). We don't yet have similar data for earlier *H. heidelbergensis* individuals, but it's possible that they, too, showed this distinctively human pattern of development.

Did these Middle and Late Pleistocene hominins have the full language capabilities and other symbolic and social skills of living peoples? It's impossible to answer this question completely, given the types of fossil and archaeological evidence available. Yet, it does seem quite possible that neither *H. heidelbergensis* nor the Neandertals had this entire array of *fully* human attributes. That's why we call them premodern humans.

So, to rephrase our initial question, Were these hominins human? We can answer conditionally: They were human— at least, mostly so.

Summary of Main Topics

- Premodern humans from the Middle Pleistocene show similarities both with their predecessors (*H. erectus*) and with their successors (*H. sapiens*). They've also been found in many areas of the Old World—in Africa, Asia, and Europe.
- Most paleoanthropologists call the majority of Middle Pleistocene fossils *H. heidelbergensis*. Similarities between the African and European Middle Pleistocene hominin samples suggest that they all can

be reasonably seen as part of this same species, but contemporaneous Asian fossils don't fit as neatly into this model.
- Some of the later *H. heidelbergensis* populations in Europe likely evolved into Neandertals, and abundant Neandertal fossil and archaeological evidence has been collected from the Late Pleistocene time span of Neandertal existence, about 130,000–30,000 ya.
- Neandertals are more geographically restricted than earlier pre-

moderns and are found in Europe, southwest Asia, and central Asia.
- Neandertals have been considered quite distinct from modern *H. sapiens*, but recent genetic evidence confirms that some interbreeding took place between these hominins (likely 80,000–50,000 years ago).

In "What's Important," you'll find a useful summary of the most significant premodern human fossils discussed in this chapter.

What's Important

Key Fossil Discoveries of Premodern Humans

DATES	REGION	SITE	HOMININ	THE BIG PICTURE
50,000 ya	Western Europe	**La Chapelle** (France)	Neandertal	Most famous Neandertal discovery; led to false interpretation of primitive, bent-over creature
110,000 ya	Southwestern Asia	**Tabun** (Israel)	Neandertal	Best evidence of early Neandertal morphology in S. W. Asia
130,000 ya	South Africa	**Kabwe** (Broken Hill, Zambia)	*H. heidelbergensis*	Transitional-looking fossil; perhaps a close ancestor of early *H. sapiens* in Africa
?600,000–400,000 ya	Western Europe	**Sima de los Huesos** (Atapuerca, northern Spain)	*H. heidelbergensis* (early Neandertal)	Very early evidence of Neandertal ancestry.
600,000 ya	East Africa	**Bodo** (Ethiopia)	*H. heidelbergensis*	Earliest evidence of *H. heidelbergensis* in Africa—and possibly ancestral to later *H. sapiens*

Critical Thinking Questions

1. Why are the Middle Pleistocene hominins called premodern humans? In what ways are they human?
2. What is the general popular conception of Neandertals? Do you agree with this view? (Cite both anatomical and archaeological evidence to support your conclusion.)
3. Compare the skeleton of a Neandertal with that of a modern human. In which ways are they most alike? In which ways are they most different?
4. What evidence suggests that Neandertals deliberately buried their dead? Do you think the fact that they buried their dead is important? Why? How would you interpret this behavior (remembering that Neandertals were not identical to us)?
5. How are species defined, both for living animals and for extinct ones? Use the Neandertals to illustrate the problems encountered in distinguishing species among extinct hominins. Contrast specifically the interpretation of Neandertals as a distinct species with the interpretation of Neandertals as a subspecies of *H. sapiens*.

New Frontiers in RESEARCH

An exciting and potentially highly informative new direction of research has focused on extracting and analyzing DNA samples from ancient remains. Some of these finds can be extremely ancient, most notably insect tissue embedded in amber (that is, fossilized tree resin). Some of the insect DNA derived from these sources is upward of 120 million years old, and these discoveries, first reported in 1992, were the inspiration for Michael Crichton's *Jurassic Park*.

> ... researchers made a startling breakthrough when they successfully extracted, amplified, and sequenced DNA from a Neandertal skeleton.

Amber provides an unusual and favorable environment for long-term preservation of small organisms—a situation, unfortunately, not applicable to larger organisms such as vertebrates (see Chapter 5). Even so, following the introduction of PCR technology, scientists were able to look for *very* small amounts of DNA that just might still linger in ancient human remains.

In 1986, researchers reported results of sequenced brain DNA obtained from mummified remains found in a Florida bog and dated at 8,000–7,000 ya (Doran et al., 1986). The famous "Iceman" mummy discovered in the Alps in 1991 also yielded widely publicized DNA information about his population origins, shown to be not far from where he died (**Fig. 1**).

No nuclear DNA was identified in the samples just discussed, so researchers used the more plentiful mitochondrial DNA. Their successes gave hope that they could analyze even more ancient remains containing preserved human DNA. And indeed, in 1997, a group of European researchers made a startling breakthrough when they successfully extracted, amplified, and sequenced DNA from a Neandertal skeleton (Krings et al., 1997). As discussed earlier in this chapter, more than a dozen Neandertals ranging in date from 50,000 to 32,000 ya have since yielded enough mtDNA for analysis.

As we've noted, the place of Neandertals in human evolution has been and continues to be a topic of fascination and contention. This is why the Neandertal DNA evidence is so important. Besides, comparing Neandertal DNA patterns with those of early modern humans would be extremely illuminating.

Certainly, numerous early *H. sapiens* skeletons from Europe and elsewhere are still likely to contain some DNA. And indeed, as we'll see in Chapter 14, in just the last few years, several early modern *H. sapiens* individuals have had their DNA sequenced (Caramelli et al., 2003; Kulikov et al., 2004; Serre et al., 2004). These new finds, all coming from Europe or easternmost Asia, extending from France in the west to Russia in the east, support the view that Neandertal (mitochondrial) DNA is somewhat distinct from that of living

Ancient DNA

people *as well as* the first modern *H. sapiens* finds in Europe.

The biggest breakthrough in understanding Neandertal genetics came in 2006, when two teams of researchers announced they had been able to sequence significant portions of nuclear DNA from 38,0000-year-old Neandertal bones (Noonan et al., 2006). Indeed, one

▼ **Figure 1** Iceman.

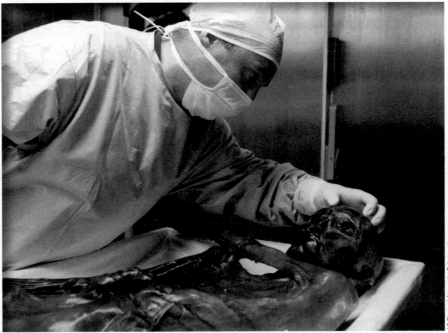

AP Photo / Augustin Ochsenreiter

Ancient DNA (continued)

group (from The Max Planck Institute for Evolutionary Anthropology), using new, high-speed sequencing technology, was able to obtain data for 1 million base pairs (Green et al., 2006). Amazing as this seemed, it was just the beginning.

The new information we can gain from these advances promises to be extraordinary because they'll provide a data base from which to learn a vast amount about Neandertal biology and behavior. For example, are there particular gene differences between Neandertals and modern humans that can help explain alterations in brain organization? And even more intriguing, will genetic changes be discovered that help account for the development of particular fully human behaviors, such as language?

With these new tools and data available, researchers have already begun to answer some of

▼ **Figure 2**

Artist's reconstruction of a Neandertal child, based on a skull found at the Roc-de-Marsal site in France. Note the light skin and reddish hair.

these fascinating but difficult questions. For example, one of the first two nuclear loci identified in Neandertals influences skin and hair pigmentation, and the other is thought to be a crucial locus influencing speech and language.

The pigmentation locus indicates that at least some Neandertals were redheaded and also were likely light-skinned (Lalueza-Fox et al., 2007). These new data help confirm earlier hypotheses suggesting that Neandertals quite likely had light skin (**Fig. 2**).

The second finding relates to the *FOXP2* locus, a genetic region thought to influence speech and language function in modern humans. Interestingly, two distinctive changes in this gene (point mutations) distinguish humans from all other living primates, and these exact same genetic modifications have also been identified in Neandertals (Krause et

al., 2007b). So it appears that this evolutionary change is quite ancient, going back perhaps as far as 400,000 ya. Moreover, it shows that Neandertals did not differ genetically from us in this crucial respect. Did they, then, have full human language? Given that this highly complex behavior is controlled by dozens of genes, we can't really answer this question just yet.

> ... Neandertal DNA is remarkably similar to modern human DNA ...

After more than three years of further work, the Max Planck Institute team, along with a number of new collaborators, announced in 2010 they had been able to sequence the *entire* nuclear genome of Neandertals (Green et al., 2010). Led by Svante Pääbo, the researchers analyzed Neandertal bones of three individuals from the Vindija site in Croatia (dating 44,000–38,000 ya). For all three individuals, the entire nuclear genome was sequenced, providing information on more than 4 billion base pairs. In addition, for further accuracy, and to ensure that their DNA data were generally representative of Neandertals, smaller segments of DNA from Neandertal bones excavated at three other sites in Spain, Germany, and Russia were also sequenced.

When they were satisfied that their Neandertal genome was quite complete and, even more important, accurate (that is, not contaminated by modern people's DNA during laboratory processing), the researchers moved to the next step—comparing the Neandertal genome with that of contemporary humans from different geographical regions. This part of the research provided the biggest surprise.

First of all, Neandertal DNA is remarkably similar to modern human DNA, with 99.84 percent of it being identical. However, to detect those few (but possibly informative)

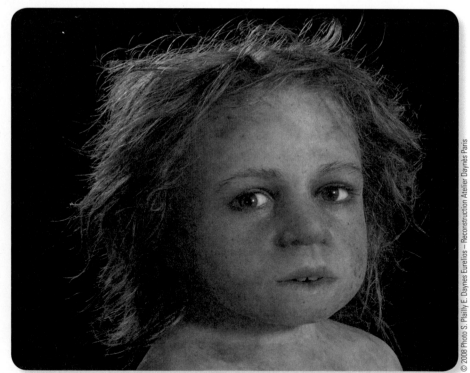

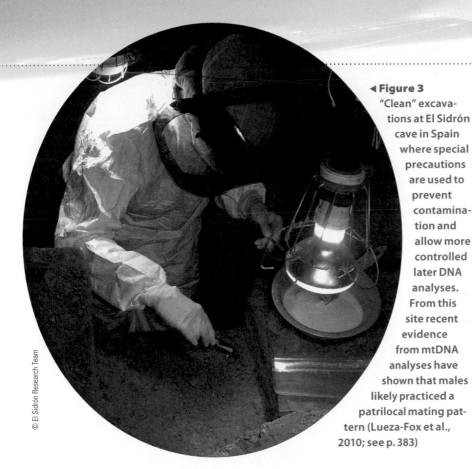

◄ Figure 3

"Clean" excavations at El Sidrón cave in Spain where special precautions are used to prevent contamination and allow more controlled later DNA analyses. From this site recent evidence from mtDNA analyses have shown that males likely practiced a patrilocal mating pattern (Lueza-Fox et al., 2010; see p. 383)

© El Sidrón Research Team

SOURCES

Caramelli, David, Carlos Lalueza-Fox, Cristano Vernesi, et al.

2003 Evidence for a genetic discontinuity between Neandertals and 24,000-year-old anatomically modern Europeans. *Proceedings of the National Academy of Sciences* 100:6593–6597.

Doran, G. H., D. N. Dickel, W.E. Ballinger, Jr., et al.

1986 Anatomical, cellular, and molecular analysis of 8,000-yr-old human brain tissue from the Windover archaeological site. *Nature* 323:803–806.

Green, Richard E., Johannes Krause, Adrian W. Briggs, et al.

2010 A draft sequenc e of the Neandertal genome. *Science* 328:710–722.

Green, Richard E., Johannes Krause, Susan E. Ptak, et al.

2006 Analysis of one million base pairs of Neanderthal DNA. *Nature* 444:330–336.

Krause, Johannes, Carlos Lalueza-Fox, Ludavic Orlando, et al.

2007 The derived *FOXP2* variant of modern humans was shared with Neandertals. *Current Biology* 17:1908–1912.

Krings, M., A. Stone, R. W. Schmitz, et al.

1997 Neandertal DNA sequences and the origin of modern humans. *Cell* 90:19–30.

Kulikov, Eugene E., Audrey B. Poltaraus, and Irina A. Lebedeva

2004 DNA analysis of Sunghir remains. Poster presentation, European Paleopathology Association Meetings, Durham, U.K., August 2004.

Lalueza-Fox, Carles, Hogler Römpler, David Caramelli, et al.

2007 A melanocortin receptor allele suggests varying pigmentation among Neanderthals. *Science Express*, Oct 25, 2007.

Lalueza-Fox, Carles, Antonio Rosas, Almudena Estalrrich, et al.

2011 Genetic evidence for patrilocal mating behavior among Neandertal groups. *Proceedings of the National Academy of Sciences*, 108:250–253.

Noonan, James P. M., Graham Coop, Sridhar Kudaravalli, et al.

2006 Sequencing and analysis of Neanderthal genomic DNA. *Science* 314:1113–1118.

Serre, D., A. Langaney, et al.

2004 No evidence of Neandertal mtDNA contribution to early modern humans. *Plos Biology* 2(3): 313–317.

genes that do differ, the team sequenced the entire genome of five modern individuals (two from Africa and one each from China, France, and New Guinea). To the surprise of almost everyone, the researchers found that many people today still have Neandertal genes! What's more, these Neandertal genes are found only in non-Africans, strongly suggesting that interbreeding occurred between Neandertals and modern *H. sapiens* after the latter had emigrated out of Africa. In fact, all three modern non-African individuals had the same amount of Neandertal DNA—and recall, they come from widely scattered regions (western Europe, China, and the far South Pacific).

The best (and simplest) hypothesis for this genetic pattern is that shortly after modern *H. sapiens* migrants left Africa, a few of them interbred with Neandertals *before* these people and their descendants dispersed to other areas of the world. The best guess is that this intermixing between the two groups occurred in the Middle East, likely sometime between 80,000 and 50,000 ya. DNA data from more individuals, both within and outside of Africa, will help substantiate this hypothesis. For the moment, the degree of interbreeding appears to be small but still significant—about 1 to 4 percent of the total genome for living non-Africans.

A final and ultimately basic question the researchers continued to investigate focused on the specific ways modern people differ genetically from our very close Neandertal cousins (you'll recall that the genomes differ by only .16 percent). Following months of detailed work, the investigators were able to identify 78 specific genetic changes in modern humans that affect protein coding, and only 5 of these loci have more than one alteration. Admittedly, this isn't much of a difference, but these genes are potentially very informative regarding the direction of human evolution over the last several thousand years. Analysis indicates that these genes influence sperm movement, skin physiology (pigmentation and sweating), wound healing, RNA transcription, and cognitive development. Perhaps these are the most important genetic changes that separate us from our closest hominin cousins. Are they the underlying evolutionary foundation of our distinctive "humanity?" The answers are soon to come!

Liang Bua Cave on the Island of Flores (Indonesia) where *Homo floresiensis* was discovered.

14

The Origin and Dispersal of Modern Humans

Key Question

▶ Is it possible to determine when and where modern humans first appeared?

Today, our species numbers more than 6 billion individuals, spread all over the globe, but there are no other living hominins but us. Our last hominin cousin disappeared several thousand years ago. But about 80,000 ya, modern peoples in the Middle East may have encountered beings that walked on two legs, hunted large animals, made fire, lived in caves, and fashioned complex tools. These beings were the Neandertals, and imagine what it would have been like to be among a band of modern people following game into what is now Israel and coming across these other *humans*, so like yourself in some ways, yet so different in others. It's almost certain that such encounters took place, perhaps many times. How strange would it have been to look into the face of a being sharing so much with you, yet being a total stranger both culturally and, to some degree, biologically as well? What would you think seeing a Neandertal for the first time? What do you imagine a Neandertal would think seeing you?

Sometime, probably close to 200,000 ya, the first modern *Homo sapiens* populations appeared in Africa. Within 150,000 years or so, their descendants had spread across most of the Old World, even expanding as far as Australia (and somewhat later to the Americas).

Who were they, and why were these early modern people so successful? What was the fate of the other hominins, such as the Neandertals, who were already long established in areas outside Africa? Did they evolve as well, leaving descendants among some living human populations? Or were they completely swept aside and replaced by African emigrants?

In this chapter, we'll discuss the origin and dispersal of modern *H. sapiens*. All contemporary populations are placed within this species (and the same subspecies as well). Most paleoanthropologists agree that several fossil forms, dating back as far as 100,000 ya, should also be included in the same *fully* modern group as us. In addition, some recently discovered fossils from Africa also are clearly *H. sapiens*, but they show some (minor) differences from living people and could thus be described as *near-modern*. Still, we can think of these early African humans as well as their somewhat later relatives as "us."

These first modern humans, who evolved by 195,000 ya, are probably descendants of some of the premodern humans we discussed in Chapter 13. In particular, African populations of *H. heidelbergensis* are the most likely ancestors of the earliest modern *H. sapiens*. The evolutionary events that took place as modern humans made the transition from more ancient premodern forms and then dispersed throughout most of the Old World were relatively rapid, and they raise several basic questions:

1. When (approximately) did modern humans first appear?
2. Where did the transition take place? Did it occur in just one region or in several?
3. What was the pace of evolutionary change? How quickly did the transition occur?
4. How did the dispersal of modern humans to other areas of the Old World (outside their area of origin) take place?

These questions concerning the origins and early dispersal of modern *Homo sapiens* continue to fuel much controversy among paleoanthropologists. And it's no wonder, for at least some early *H. sapiens* populations are the direct ancestors of all contemporary humans. They were much like us skeletally, genetically, and (most likely) behaviorally. In fact, it's the various hypotheses regarding the behaviors and abilities of our most immediate predecessors that have most fired the imaginations of scientists and laypeople alike. In every major respect, these are the first hominins that we can confidently refer to as *fully* human.

In this chapter, we'll also discuss archaeological evidence coming from the Upper Paleolithic cultures. This

evidence will give us a better understanding of the technological and social developments during the period when modern humans arose and quickly came to dominate the planet.

The evolutionary story of *Homo sapiens* is really the biological autobiography of all of us. It's a story that still has many unanswered questions; but some general theories can help us organize the diverse information that's now available.

Approaches to Understanding Modern Human Origins

In attempting to organize and explain modern human origins, paleoanthropologists have proposed a few major theories that can be summarized into two contrasting views: the *regional continuity model* and various versions of *replacement* models. These two views are quite distinct, and in some ways they're completely opposed to each other. Since so much of our contemporary view of modern human origins is influenced by the debates linked to these differing theories, let's start by briefly reviewing them. Then we'll turn to the fossil evidence itself to see what it can contribute to answering the four questions we've posed.

The Regional Continuity Model: Multiregional Evolution

The regional continuity model is most closely associated with paleoanthropologist Milford Wolpoff, of the University of Michigan, and his associates (Wolpoff et al., 1994, 2001). They suggest that local populations—not all, of course—in Europe, Asia, and Africa continued their indigenous evolutionary development from premodern Middle Pleistocene forms to anatomically modern humans. But if that's true, then we have to ask how so many different local populations around the globe happened to evolve with such similar morphology. In other words, how could anatomically modern humans arise separately in different continents and end up so much alike, both physically and genetically? The multiregional model answers this question by (1) denying that the earliest modern *H. sapiens* populations originated *exclusively* in Africa and (2) asserting that significant levels of gene flow (migration) between various geographically dispersed premodern populations were extremely likely throughout the Pleistocene.

Through gene flow and natural selection, according to the multiregional hypothesis, local populations would *not* have evolved totally independently from one another, and such mixing would have "prevented speciation between the regional lineages and thus maintained human beings as a *single*, although obviously *polytypic* [see Chapter 15], species throughout the Pleistocene" (Smith et al., 1989). Thus, under a multiregional model, there are no taxonomic distinctions between modern and premodern hominins. That is, all hominins following *H. erectus* are classified as a single species: *H. sapiens*.

In light of emerging evidence over the last few years, almost all advocates of the multiregional model aren't dogmatic about the degree of regional continuity. They recognize that a strong influence of modern humans evolving *first* in Africa has left an imprint on populations throughout the world that is still detectable today. Nevertheless, the most recent data suggest that multiregional models no longer tell us anything useful about the origins of modern humans; nor do they seem to offer much regarding the dispersal of modern *H. sapiens*.

Replacement Models

Replacement models all emphasize that modern humans first evolved in Africa and only later dispersed to other parts of the world, where they replaced those hominins already living in these other regions. In recent years, two versions of such replacement models have been proposed, the first emphasizing *complete* replacement. The complete replacement model proposes that anatomically modern populations arose in Africa within the last 200,000 years and then migrated from Africa, completely replacing populations in Europe and Asia (Stringer and Andrews, 1988). It's important to note that this model doesn't account for a transition from premodern forms to modern *H. sapiens* anywhere in the world except Africa. A critical deduction of the original Stringer and Andrews theory argued that anatomically modern humans appeared as the result of a biological speciation event. So in this view, migrating African modern *H. sapiens* could not have interbred with local non-African populations, because the African modern humans were a *biologically* different species. Taxonomically, all of the premodern populations outside Africa would, in this view, be classified as belonging to different species of *Homo*. For example, the Neandertals would be classified as *H. neanderthalensis*. This speciation explanation fits nicely with, and in fact helps explain, *complete* replacement; but Stringer has more recently stated that he isn't insistent on this issue. He does suggest that even though there may have been potential for interbreeding, apparently very little actually took place.

Interpretations of the latter phases of human evolution have recently been greatly extended by newly available genetic techniques, and they've recently been applied to the question of modern human origins. Using numerous contemporary human populations as a data source, geneticists have precisely determined and compared a wide variety of

DNA sequences. The theoretical basis of this approach assumes that at least some of the genetic patterning seen today can act as a kind of window into the past. In particular, the genetic patterns observed today between geographically widely dispersed humans are thought to partly reflect migrations occurring in the Late Pleistocene. This hypothesis can be further tested as contemporary population genetic patterning is better documented.

As these new data have accumulated, consistent relationships are emerging, especially in showing that indigenous African populations have far greater diversity than do populations from elsewhere in the world. The consistency of the results is highly significant, because it strongly supports an African origin for modern humans and some mode of replacement elsewhere. What's more, as we'll discuss in Chapter 15, new, even more complete data on contemporary population patterning for large portions of nuclear DNA further confirm these conclusions.

Certainly, most molecular data come from contemporary species, since DNA is not *usually* preserved in long-dead individuals. Even so, exceptions do occur, and these cases open another genetic window—one that can directly illuminate the past. As discussed in Chapter 13, mtDNA has been recovered from more than a dozen Neandertal fossils.

In addition, researchers have recently sequenced the mtDNA of nine ancient fully modern *H. sapiens* skeletons from sites in Italy, France, the Czech Republic, and Russia (Caramelli et al., 2003, 2006; Kulikov et al., 2004; Serre et al., 2004). MtDNA data, however, are somewhat limited because mtDNA is a fairly small segment of DNA, and it is transmitted between generations as a single unit; genetically it acts like a single gene. Indeed, in just the last few years, comparisons of Neandertal and early modern mtDNA led to some significant misinterpre-

tations. Clearly, data from the vastly larger nuclear genome are far more informative.

As we discussed in Chapter 13, a giant leap forward occurred in 2010 when sequencing of the entire Neandertal nuclear genome was completed. Researchers immediately compared the Neandertal genome with that of people living today and discovered that some populations still retain some Neandertal genes (Green et al., 2010). Without doubt, we can now conclude that some interbreeding took place between Neandertals and modern humans, arguing against *complete* replacement and supporting some form of *partial* replacement.

Partial Replacement Models For a number of years, several paleoanthropologists, such as Günter Bräuer, of the University of Hamburg, suggested that very little interbreeding occurred—a view supported more recently by John Relethford (2001) in what he described as "mostly out of Africa." The new findings from DNA analysis further show that the degree of interbreeding was modest, ranging from 1 to 4 percent in modern populations outside Africa; on the other hand, contemporary Africans have no trace of Neandertal genes, suggesting the interbreeding occurred *after* modern humans migrated out of Africa. This would seem obvious when you consider that (as far as we know) Neandertals never lived anywhere in Africa. For our African ancestors to even have the opportunity to mate with a Neandertal, they would first have to leave their African homeland. Another fascinating discovery is that among the modern people so far sampled (five individuals), the three non-Africans all have some Neandertal DNA. The tentative conclusion from these preliminary findings suggests that the interbreeding occurred soon after modern humans emigrated out of Africa. The most likely scenario suggests that the intermixing occurred around 80,000–50,000 ya, quite possibly in the Middle

East (for further discussion, see "New Frontiers in Research" at the end of Chapter 13).

These results are very new and are partly based on very limited samples of living people. Technological innovations in DNA sequencing are occurring at an amazing pace, making it faster and cheaper. But it is still a challenge to sequence all the 3 billion+ nucleotides each of us has in our nuclear genome. When we have full genomes from more individuals living in many more geographical areas, the patterns of modern human dispersal should become clearer. Did the modern human-Neandertal interbreeding occur primarily in one area, or did it happen in several regions? Moreover, did some modern human populations several thousand years ago interbreed with their Neandertal cousins more than others did? Even more interesting, were there still other premodern human groups still around when modern humans emigrated from Africa—and did they interbreed, too?

From his study of fossil remains, Fred Smith, of Illinois State University, has proposed an "assimilation" model that hypothesizes that more interbreeding did take place, at least in some regions (Smith, 2002). To test these hypotheses and answer all the fascinating questions, we will also need more whole-genome DNA from ancient remains, particularly from early modern human skeletons. This, too, won't be an easy task; remember, it took four years of intensive effort to decode and reassemble the Neandertal genome. Then, too, we need to be aware that DNA thousands of years old can be obtained from hominin remains that are found in environments that have been persistently cold (or at least cool). In tropical areas, DNA degrades rapidly; so it seems a long shot that any usable DNA can be obtained from hominins that lived in many extremely large and significant regions (for example, Africa and Southeast Asia).

The Earliest Discoveries of Modern Humans

Africa

In Africa, several early (around 200,000–100,000 ya) fossils have been interpreted as fully anatomically modern forms (**Fig. 14-2** on p. 408). The earliest of these specimens comes from Omo Kibish, in southernmost Ethiopia. Using radiometric techniques, redating of a fragmentary skull (Omo 1) demonstrates that, coming from 195,000 ya, this is the earliest modern human yet found in Africa—or, for that matter, anywhere (McDougall et al., 2005). An interesting aspect of fossils from this site concerns the variation shown between the two individuals. Omo 1 (**Fig. 14-1**) is essentially modern in most respects (note the presence of a chin; see **Fig. 14-3**, where a variety of modern human cranial characteristics is shown), but another ostensibly contemporary cranium (Omo 2) is much more robust and less modern in morphology.

▼ **Figure 14-1**
Reconstructed skull of Omo 1, an early modern human from Ethiopia, dated to 195,000 ya. Note the clear presence of a chin.

© Milford Wolpoff

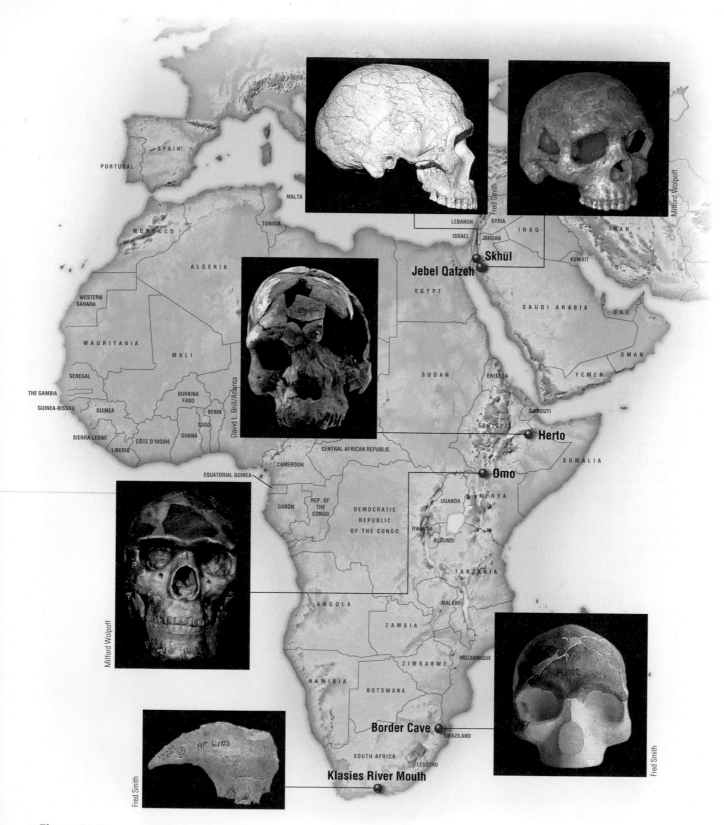

▲ **Figure 14-2**
Modern humans from Africa and the Near East.

Somewhat later modern human fossils come from the Klasies River Mouth on the south coast of Africa and Border Cave, just slightly to the north. Using relatively new techniques, paleoanthropologists have dated both sites to about 120,000–80,000 ya. The original geological context at Border Cave is uncertain, and the fossils may be younger than those at Klasies River Mouth. Although recent reevaluation of the Omo site has provided much more dependable dating, there are still questions remaining about some of the other early African modern fossils. Nevertheless, it now seems very likely that early modern humans appeared in East Africa by shortly after 200,000 ya and had migrated to southern Africa by approximately 100,000 ya. More recently discovered fossils are helping confirm this view.

Herto The announcement in 2003 of well-preserved *and* well-dated *H. sapiens* fossils from Ethiopia has gone a long way toward filling gaps in the African fossil record. As a result, these fossils are helping to resolve key issues regarding modern human origins. Tim White, of the University of California, Berkeley, and his colleagues have been working for three decades in the Middle Awash area of Ethiopia. They've discovered a remarkable array of early fossil hominins (*Ardipithecus* and *Australopithecus*) as well as somewhat later forms (*H. erectus*). From this same area in the Middle Awash, highly significant new discoveries came to light in 1997. For simplicity, these new hominins are referred to as the Herto remains.

These Herto fossils include a mostly complete adult cranium, a fairly complete (but heavily reconstructed) child's cranium, another adult incomplete cranium, and a few other cranial fragments. Following lengthy reconstruction and detailed comparative studies, White and colleagues were prepared to announce their findings in 2003.

What they said caused quite a sensation among paleoanthropologists, and it was reported in the popular press as well. First, well-controlled radiometric dating (^{40}Ar/^{39}Ar) securely places the remains at between 160,000 and 154,000 ya, making these the best-dated hominin fossils from this time period from anywhere in the world. Note that this date is clearly *older* than for any other equally modern *H. sapiens* from anywhere else in the world. Moreover, the preservation and morphology of the remains leave little doubt about their relationship to modern humans. The mostly complete adult cranium (**Fig. 14-4**) is very large, with an extremely long cranial vault. The cranial capacity is 1,450 cm^3, well within the range of contemporary *H. sapiens* populations. The skull is also in some respects heavily built, with a large, arching browridge in front and a large, projecting occipital protuberance in back. The face does not project, in stark contrast to Eurasian Neandertals.

The overall impression is that this individual is clearly *Homo sapiens*—as is the child, aged 6 to 7 years, and the other incomplete adult cranium. White and his team performed comprehensive statistical studies, comparing these fossils with other early *H. sapiens* remains as well as with a large series (over 3,000 crania) from modern populations. They concluded that while not identical to modern people, the Herto fossils are near-modern. That is, these fossils "sample a population that is on the verge of anatomical modernity but not yet fully modern." (White et al., 2003, p. 745). To distinguish these individuals from fully modern humans (*H. sapiens sapiens*), the researchers have placed them in a newly defined subspecies: *Homo sapiens idaltu*. The word *idaltu*, from the Afar language, means "elder."

Further analysis has shown that the morphology of the crania doesn't specifically match that of *any* contemporary group of modern humans. What can we then conclude? First, we can say that these new finds strongly support an African origin of modern humans. The Herto fossils are the

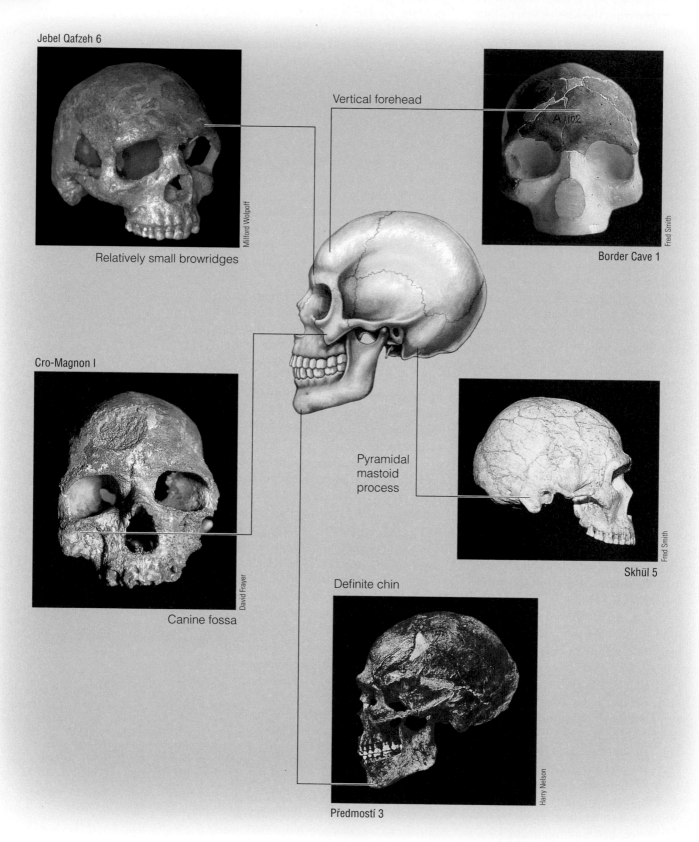

Jebel Qafzeh 6

Relatively small browridges

Vertical forehead

Border Cave 1

Cro-Magnon I

Canine fossa

Pyramidal mastoid process

Skhūl 5

Definite chin

Předmostí 3

▲ **Figure 14-3**
**Morphology and variation in early
specimens of modern *Homo sapiens*.**

right age, and they come from the right place. Besides that, they look much like what we might have predicted. Considering all these facts, they're the most conclusive fossil evidence yet indicating an African origin of modern humans. What's more, this fossil evidence is compatible with a great deal of strong genetic data indicating some form of replacement model for human origins.

The Near East

In Israel, researchers found early modern *H. sapiens* fossils, including the remains of at least 10 individuals, in the Skhūl Cave at Mt. Carmel (**Figs. 14-5** and **14-6a**). Also from Israel, the Qafzeh Cave has yielded the remains of at least 20 individuals (**Fig. 14-6b**). Although their overall configuration is definitely modern, some specimens show certain premodern features. Skhūl has been dated to between 130,000 and 100,000 ya (Grün et al., 2005), while Qafzeh has been

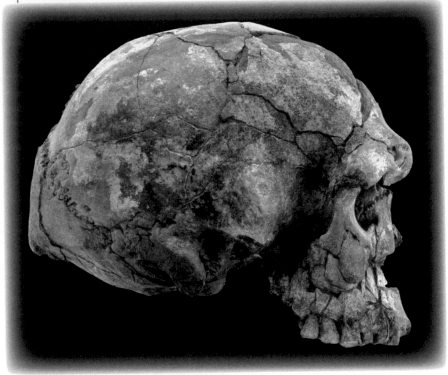

▼ **Figure 14-4**
Herto cranium from Ethiopia, dated 160,000–154,000 ya. This is the best-preserved early modern *H. sapiens* cranium yet found.

© David L. Brill/Atlanta

At a Glance

KEY EARLY MODERN *Homo sapiens* DISCOVERIES FROM AFRICA AND THE NEAR EAST

Date	Site	Hominin	Evolutionary Significance
110,000 ya	Qafzeh (Israel)	H. sapiens sapiens	Large sample (at least 20 individuals); definitely modern, but some individuals fairly robust; early date (>100,000 ya)
115,000 ya	Skhūl (Israel)	H. sapiens sapiens	Minimum of 10 individuals; like Qafzeh modern morphology, but slightly earlier date (and earliest modern humans known outside of Africa)
160,000-154,000 ya	Herto (Ethiopia)	H. sapiens idaltu	Very well-preserved cranium; dated > 150,000 ya, the best-preserved early modern human found anywhere
195,000 ya	Omo (Ethiopia)	H. sapiens	Dated almost 200,000 ya and the oldest modern human found anywhere; two crania found, one more modern looking than the other

▶ **Figure 14-5**
Mt. Carmel, studded with caves, was home to *H. sapiens sapiens* at Skhūl (and to Neandertals at Tabun and Kebara).

▶ **Figure 14-6**
(a) Skhūl 5. (b) Qafzeh 6. These specimens from Israel are thought to be representatives of early modern *Homo sapiens*. The vault height, forehead, and lack of prognathism are modern traits.

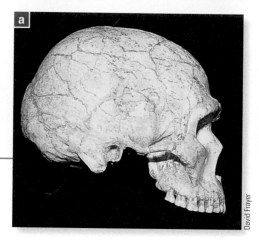

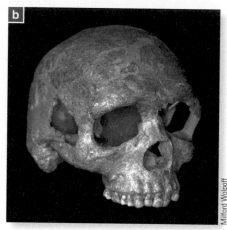

dated to around 120,000–92,000 ya (Grün and Stringer, 1991). The time line for these fossil discoveries is shown in **Figure 14-7**.

Such early dates for modern specimens pose some problems for those advocating the influence of local evolution, as proposed by the multiregional model. How early do the premodern populations—that is, Neandertals—appear in the Near East? A recent chronometric calibration for the Tabun Cave suggests a date as early as 120,000 ya. This dating for these sites, all located *very* close to each other, suggests that there's considerable chronological overlap in the occupation of the Near East by Neandertals and modern humans. This chronological overlap in such a small area is the reason anthropologists have suggested this region as a likely place where Neandertals and modern humans might well have interbred.

Asia

There are seven early anatomically modern human localities in China, the most significant of which are Upper Cave at Zhoukoudian, Tianyuan Cave (very near Zhoukoudian), and Ordos, in Mongolia (**Fig. 14-8**). The fossils from these Chinese sites are all fully modern, and all are considered to be from the Late Pleistocene, with dates probably less than 40,000 ya. Upper Cave at Zhoukoudian has been dated to 27,000 ya, and the fossils consist of three skulls found with cultural remains in a cave site that humans clearly regularly inhabited. Considerable antiquity has also been proposed for the Mongolian Ordos skull, but this dating is not very secure and has therefore been questioned (Trinkaus, 2005).

In addition, some researchers (Tiemel et al., 1994) have suggested that the Jinniushan skeleton discussed in Chapter 12 hints at modern features in China as early as 200,000 ya. If this date—as early as that proposed for direct antecedents of modern *H. sapiens* in Africa—should prove accurate, it would cast doubt on replacement models. This position, however, is a minority view and is not supported by more recent and more detailed analyses.

Just about 4 miles down the road from the famous Zhoukoudian Cave is another cave called Tianyuan, the source of an important find in 2003. Consisting of a fragmentary skull, a few teeth, and several postcranial bones, this fossil is accurately dated by radiocarbon at close to 40,000 ya (Shang et al., 2007). The skeleton shows mostly modern features, but has a few archaic characteristics as well. The Chinese and American team that has analyzed the remains from Tianyuan proposes that they indicate an African origin of modern humans, but there is also evidence of at least some interbreeding in China with resident archaic (that is, premodern) populations. More complete analysis and (with some luck) further finds at this new site will help pro-

vide a better picture of early modern *H. sapiens* in China. For the moment, this is the best-dated early modern *H. sapiens* from China and one of the two earliest from anywhere in Asia.

The other early fossil is a partial skull from Niah Cave, on the north coast of the Indonesian island of Borneo (see Fig. 14-8). This is actually not a new find and was, in fact, first excavated 50 years ago. However, until recent more extensive analysis, it had been relegated to the paleoanthropological back shelf due to uncertainties regarding its archaeological context and dating. Now all this has changed with a better understanding of the geology of the site and new dates strongly supporting an age of more than 35,000 ya and most likely as old as 45,000–40,000 ya, making it perhaps older than Tianyuan (Barker et al., 2007). Like its Chinese counterparts, the Niah skull is modern in morphology. It's hypothesized that some population contemporaneous with Niah or somewhat earlier inhabitants of Indonesia were perhaps the first group to colonize Australia.

▼ **Figure 14-7**
Time line of modern *Homo sapiens* discoveries. Note that most dates are approximations. Question marks indicate those estimates that are most tentative.

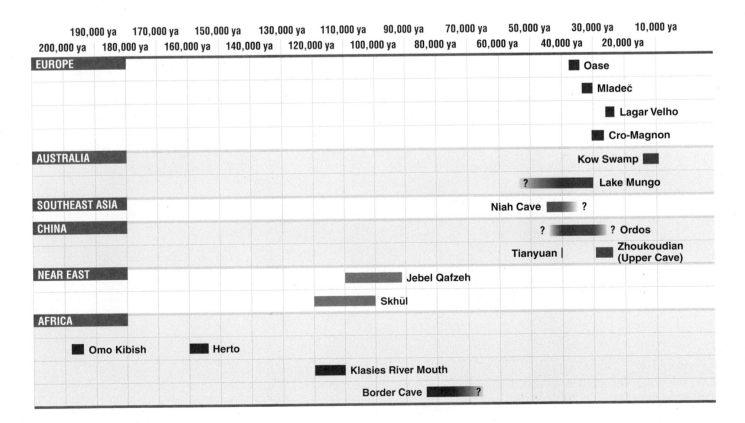

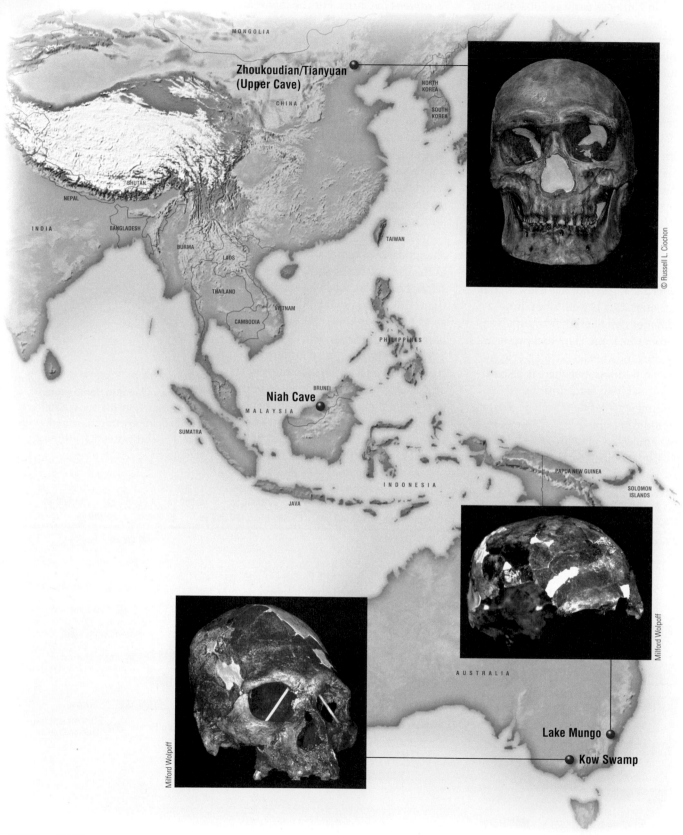

▲ Figure 14-8
Anatomically modern *Homo sapiens*
in Asia and Australia.

Australia

During glacial times, the Indonesian islands were joined to the Asian mainland, but Australia wasn't. It's likely that by 50,000 ya, modern humans inhabited Sahul—the area including New Guinea and Australia. Bamboo rafts may have been used to cross the ocean between islands, and this would certainly have been dangerous and difficult. It's not known just where the ancestral Australians came from, but as noted, Indonesia has been suggested.

Human occupation of Australia appears to have occurred quite early, with some archaeological sites dating to 55,000 ya. There's some controversy about the dating of the earliest Australian human remains, which are all modern *H. sapiens*. The earliest finds so far discovered have come from Lake Mungo, in southeastern Australia (see Fig. 14-8). In agreement with archaeological context and radiocarbon dates, the hominins from this site have been dated at approximately 30,000–25,000 ya. However, newly determined age estimates using electron spin resonance (ESR) and uranium series dating (see Chapter 10) have dramatically extended the suggested time depth to about 60,000 ya (Thorne et al., 1999). The lack of correlation of these more ancient age estimates with other data, however, has some researchers seriously concerned (Gillespie and Roberts, 2000).

Fossils from a site called Kow Swamp suggest that the people who lived there between about 14,000 and 9,000 ya were different from the more gracile early Australian forms from Lake Mungo (see Fig. 14-8). The Kow Swamp fossils display certain archaic cranial traits—such as receding foreheads, heavy supraorbital tori, and thick bones—that are difficult to explain, since these features contrast with the postcranial anatomy, which matches that of living indigenous Australians. Regardless of the different morphology of these later Australians, new genetic evidence indicates that all native Australians are descendants of a *single* migration dating back to about 50,000 ya (Hudjashou et al., 2007).

Central Europe

Central Europe has been a source of many fossil finds, including the earliest anatomically modern *H. sapiens* yet discovered anywhere in Europe. Dated to 35,000 ya, these early *H. sapiens* fossils come from recent discoveries at the Oase Cave in Romania (**Fig. 14-9**). Here, cranial remains of three individuals were recovered, including a complete mandible and a partial skull (**Fig. 14-10**). While quite robust, these individuals are similar to later modern specimens, as seen in the clear presence of both a chin and a canine fossa (see Fig. 14-3; Trinkaus et al., 2003).

Another early modern human site in central Europe is Mladeč, in the Czech Republic. Several individuals have been excavated here and are dated to approximately 31,000 ya. While there's some variation among the crania, including some with big browridges, Fred Smith (1984) is confident that they're all best classified as modern

▼ **Figure 14-9**

Excavators at work within the spectacular cave at Oase, in Romania. The floor is littered with the remains of fossil animals, including the earliest dated cranial remains of *Homo sapiens* in Europe.

© Mircea Gherase

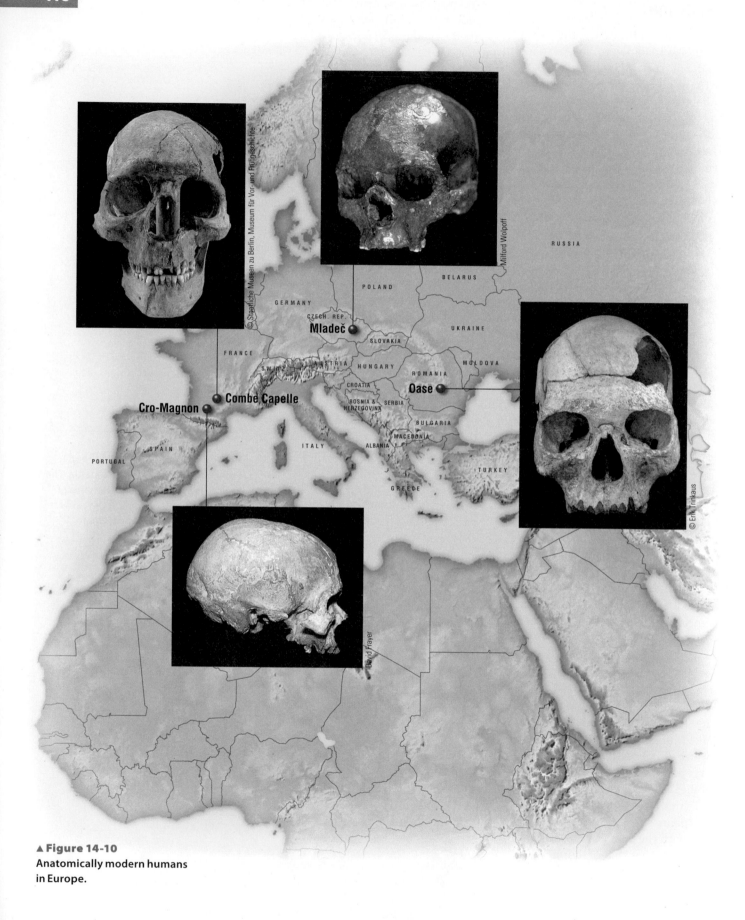

▲ **Figure 14-10**
Anatomically modern humans
in Europe.

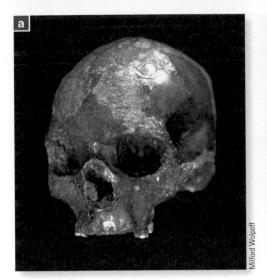

Milford Wolpoff

© Robert Franciscus

◄ Figure 14-11
The Mladeč (**a**) and Dolní Věstonice (**b**) crania, both from the Czech Republic, represent good examples of early modern *Homo sapiens* in central Europe. Along with Oase, in Romania, the evidence for early modern *Homo sapiens* appears first in central Europe before the later finds in western Europe.

H. sapiens (**Fig. 14-11a**). It's clear that by 28,000 ya, modern humans were widely dispersed in central and western Europe (Trinkaus, 2005). Also from the Czech Republic and dated at about 26,000 ya, Dolní Věstonice provides another example of a central European early modern human (see **Fig. 14-11b**).

Western Europe

For several reasons, one of them probably serendipity, western Europe and its fossils have received the most attention. Over the last 150 years, many of the scholars doing this research happened to live in western Europe, and the southern region of France happened to be a fossil treasure trove. Also, early on, discovering and learning about human ancestors caught the curiosity and pride of the local population.

As a result of this scholarly interest, a great deal of data accumulated beginning back in the nineteenth century, with little reliable comparative information available from elsewhere in the world. Consequently, theories of human evolution were based almost exclusively on the western European material. It's only been in more recent years, with growing evidence from other areas of the world and with the application of new dating techniques, that recent human evolutionary

dynamics are being seriously considered from a worldwide perspective.

Western Europe has yielded many anatomically modern human fossils, but by far the best-known sample of western European *H. sapiens* is from the **Cro-Magnon** site, a rock-shelter in southern France. At this site, the remains of eight individuals were discovered in 1868.

The Cro-Magnon materials are associated with an **Aurignacian** tool assemblage, an Upper Paleolithic industry. Dated at about 28,000 ya, these individuals represent the earliest of France's anatomically modern humans. The so-called Old Man (Cro-Magnon 1) became the original model for what was once termed the Cro-Magnon, or Upper Paleolithic, "race" of Europe (**Fig. 14-12**). Actually, of course, there's no such valid biological category, and Cro-Magnon 1 is not typical of Upper Paleolithic western Europeans—and not even all that similar to the other two male skulls found at the site (**Fig. 14-13**).

Most of the genetic evidence, as well as the newest fossil evidence from Africa, argue against continuous local evolution producing modern groups directly from any Eurasian premodern population (in Europe, these would be Neandertals). Still, for some researchers, the issue isn't completely settled. With all the latest evidence, there's no

Cro-Magnon (crow-man´-yon)

Aurignacian Pertaining to an Upper Paleolithic stone tool industry in Europe beginning at about 40,000 ya.

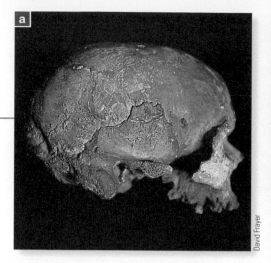

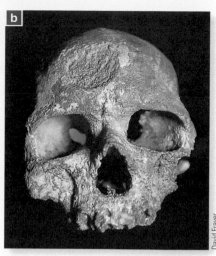

▶ **Figure 14-12**
Cro-Magnon 1 (France). In this specimen, modern traits are quite clear.
(**a**) Lateral view. (**b**) Frontal view.

▶ **Figure 14-13**
Artist's reconstruction of an Upper
Paleolithic modern human, based on
a skull from Chancelade France,
dated around 14,000 ya.

Hybridization in the Fossil Record: What Exactly Were Those Hominins Doing at Lagar Velho?

In 1999, researchers from Portugal announced an exciting discovery from the Lapedo Valley, in central Portugal (Duarte et al., 1999). At the site of Lagar Velho, researchers excavated a burial containing the largely complete skeleton of a 4-year-old child dated to around 24,500 ya (**Fig. 1**). What made this discovery particularly interesting was that the researchers claimed that the Lagar Velho child, as it's been called, represents a hybrid between Neandertals and modern humans—a Paleolithic love child of sorts. That is, the Lagar Velho child's anatomy is suggestive of generations of genetic admixture between indigenous Neandertal populations and modern humans who had migrated into Europe. Researchers looked to several morphological features as evidence of hybridization. For example, the mandible clearly exhibits a chin, which is a telltale sign of modernity. At the same time, though, this region recedes, as in Neandertals. In addition, aspects of the postcrania—such as limb proportions and robusticity of the skeleton—indicate the possible influence of Neandertal genes.

This interpretation of the Lagar Velho skeleton as a combination of both Neandertal and modern human morphology (which resulted from genetic admixture) is highly controversial. Adding to the controversy is the fact that the remains are those of a small child. Most anatomical characteristics used to define fossil species are normally based on adult skeletons, and there's no way to tell what this individual would have looked like once fully grown; we can only make predictions.

This isn't the first time that researchers have interpreted the morphology of hominin fossils as the result of hybridization. Later Neandertals, such as those found at

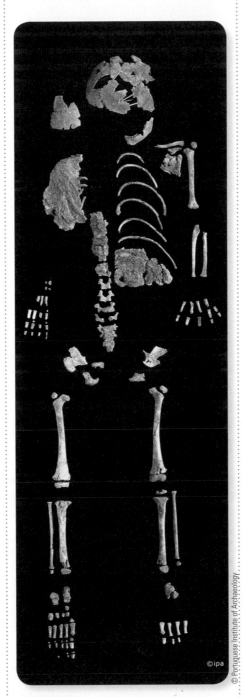

▲ **Figure 1**

The skeleton of the Lagar Velho child thought by some to be a Neandertal–modern human hybrid.

© Portuguese Institute of Archaeology

the sites of St. Césaire, in France, and from the upper levels at the site of Vindija, in Croatia, have also been regarded as the result of genetic admixture. While there's no consensus on whether or not these fossils are actually the product of hybridization, what makes the interpretation of the Lagar Velho remains so important is that they have stimulated significant discussion and research into the concept of genetic admixture in the fossil record. This discussion has led paleoanthropologists to ask some important questions regarding the nature of population hybridization.

Looking for signs of hybridization in the fossil record is a challenging endeavor for the obvious reason that we can't directly observe the breeding habits of fossil hominins. Researchers must therefore turn to other areas of inquiry to begin to understand the nature of genetic barriers that define a species. One type of study that's shedding new light on this issue is exemplified by the research of Trent Holliday, of Tulane University. He and his colleagues have comprehensively investigated hybridization among extant species of primates as well as among other mammals. In particular, Holliday's study of genetic admixture in living animals has allowed researchers to understand not only the genetic markers associated with hybridization but also the morphological differences that result from the pairing of different species. By applying this type of research to the study of modern human origins, we can begin to address and test hypotheses regarding hybridization between Neandertals and modern humans.

As you know, the latest genetic evidence strongly suggests a modest amount of interbreeding dating back perhaps as far as 80,000 ya. Further evidence from the skeletal remains of both Neandertals and early modern individuals can potentially help us determine in what areas hybridization occurred and for how long a period it went on. This information will also help test different versions of replacement models explaining modern human origins.

longer much debate that a *large* genetic contribution from migrating early modern Africans influenced other groups throughout the Old World. What's being debated is just how much admixture might have occurred between these migrating Africans and the resident premodern groups. For those paleoanthropologists (for example, Trinkaus, 2005) who hypothesize that significant admixture (assimilation) occurred in western Europe as well as elsewhere, a recently discovered child's skeleton from Portugal provides some of the best evidence of ostensible interbreeding between Neandertals and anatomically modern *H. sapiens*. This important discovery from the Abrigo do Lagar Velho site was excavated in late 1998 and is dated to 24,500 ya—that's at least 5,000 years more recent than the last clearly identifiable Neandertal fossil. Associated with an Upper Paleolithic industry and buried with red ocher and pierced shell is a fairly complete skeleton of a 4-year-old child (Duarte et al.,

1999). In studying the remains, Cidália Duarte, Erik Trinkaus, and colleagues found a highly mixed set of anatomical features. Many characteristics, especially of the teeth, lower jaw, and pelvis, were like those seen in anatomically modern humans. Yet, several other features—including lack of chin, limb proportions, and muscle insertions—were more similar to Neandertal traits. The authors thus conclude that "the presence of such admixture suggests the hypothesis of variable admixture between early modern humans dispersing into Europe and local Neandertal populations" (Duarte et al., 1999, p. 7608). They suggest that this new evidence strongly supports the partial replacement model while seriously weakening the complete replacement model. The evidence from one child's skeleton, while interesting, certainly isn't going to convince everyone; nevertheless, this finding is intriguing, given the new genetic evidence indicating interbreeding between modern humans and Neandertals.

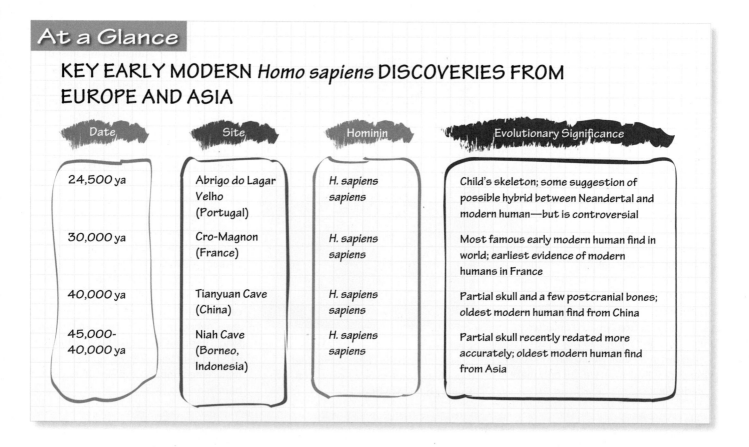

At a Glance

KEY EARLY MODERN *Homo sapiens* DISCOVERIES FROM EUROPE AND ASIA

Date	Site	Hominin	Evolutionary Significance
24,500 ya	Abrigo do Lagar Velho (Portugal)	H. sapiens sapiens	Child's skeleton; some suggestion of possible hybrid between Neandertal and modern human—but is controversial
30,000 ya	Cro-Magnon (France)	H. sapiens sapiens	Most famous early modern human find in world; earliest evidence of modern humans in France
40,000 ya	Tianyuan Cave (China)	H. sapiens sapiens	Partial skull and a few postcranial bones; oldest modern human find from China
45,000–40,000 ya	Niah Cave (Borneo, Indonesia)	H. sapiens sapiens	Partial skull recently redated more accurately; oldest modern human find from Asia

Something New and Different: The "Little People"

As we've seen, by 25,000 years ago, modern humans had dispersed to all major areas of the Old World, and they would soon journey to the New World as well. But at about the same time, remnant populations of earlier hominins still survived in a few remote and isolated corners. We mentioned in Chapter 12 that populations of *Homo erectus* in Java managed to survive on this island long after their cousins had disappeared from other areas (for example, China and East Africa). What's more, even though they persisted well into the Late Pleistocene, physically these Javanese hominins were still very similar to other *H. erectus* individuals.

Even more surprising, it seems that other populations branched off from some of these early inhabitants of Indonesia and either intentionally or accidentally found their way to other, smaller islands to the east. There, under even more extreme isolation pressures, they evolved in an astonishing direction. In late 2004, the world awoke to the startling announcement that an extremely small-bodied, small-brained hominin had been discovered in Liang Bua Cave, on the island of Flores, east of Java (see **Fig. 14-14**). Dubbed the "Little Lady of Flores" or simply "Flo," the remains consist of an incomplete skeleton of an adult female (LB1) as well as additional pieces from approximately 13 other individuals, which the press have collectively nicknamed "hobbits." The female skeleton is remarkable in several ways (**Fig. 14-15**), though surprisingly similar to the Dmanisi hominins. First, she was barely 3 feet tall—as short as the smallest australopith—and her brain, estimated at a mere 417 cm^3 (Falk et al., 2005), was no larger than that of a chimpanzee (Brown et al., 2004). Possibly most startling of all, these extraordinary hominins were still living on Flores just 13,000 ya (Morwood et al., 2004, 2005; Wong, 2009)!

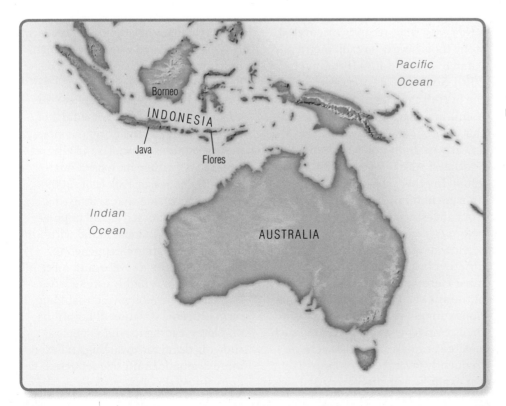

◄ **Figure 14-14**
Location of the Flores site in Indonesia.

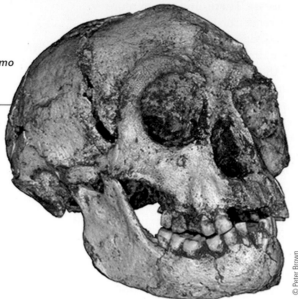

▶ **Figure 14-15**
Cranium of adult female *Homo floresiensis* from Flores, Indonesia, dated 18,000 ya.

© Peter Brown

Where did they come from? As we said, their predecessors were probably *H. erectus* populations like those found on Java. How they got to Flores—some 400 miles away, partly over open ocean—is a mystery. There are several connecting islands, and to get from one to another these hominins may have drifted across on rafts; but there's no way to be sure of this. What's more, these little hominins were apparently living on Flores for a very long time; recently discovered stone tools have been radiometrically dated to at least 1 mya (Brumm et al., 2010). Such an ancient date, as well as the overall similarities to the Dmanisi hominins, suggest to some researchers that *Homo floresiensis* may derive from an early migration of early *Homo* to Southeast Asia (Jungers, 2009; Wong, 2009). In other words, this highly unusual hominin might have evolved from ancestors that left Africa even before *H. erectus* did.

How did they get to be so physically different from all other known hominins? Here we're a little more certain of the answer. Isolated island populations can quite rapidly diverge from their relatives elsewhere. Among such isolated animals, natural selection frequently favors reduced body size. For example, remains of dwarfed ele-

phants have been found on islands in the Mediterranean as well as on some channel islands off the coast of southern California. And perhaps most interesting of all, dwarf elephants *also* evolved on Flores; they were found in the same geological beds with the little hominins. The evolutionary mechanism (called "insular dwarfing") thought to explain such extreme body size reduction in both the elephants and the hominins is an adaptation to reduced resources, with natural selection favoring smaller body size (see Chapter 5; Schauber and Falk, 2008).

Other than short stature, what did the Flores hominins look like? In their cranial shape, thickness of cranial bone, and dentition, they most resemble *H. erectus*, and specifically those from Dmanisi. Still, they have some derived features that also set them apart from all other hominins. For that reason, many researchers have placed them in a separate species, *Homo floresiensis*.

Immediately following the first publication of the Flores remains, intense controversy arose regarding their interpretation (Jacob et al., 2006; Martin et al., 2006). Some researchers have argued that the small-brained hominin (LB1) is actually a pathological modern *H. sapiens* afflicted with a severe disorder (microcephaly and others have been proposed). The researchers who did most of the initial work reject this conclusion and provide some further details to support their original interpretation (for example, Dean Falk and colleagues' further analysis of microcephalic endocasts; Falk et al., 2009).

The conclusion that among this already small-bodied island population the one individual found with a preserved cranium happened to be afflicted with a severe (and rare) growth defect is highly unlikely. Yet, it must also be recognized that long-term, extreme isolation of hominins on Flores leading to a new species showing dramatic dwarfing and even more dramatic brain size reduction is quite unusual.

So where does this leave us? Because a particular interpretation is unlikely, it's not necessarily incorrect. We do know, for example, that such "insular dwarfing" has occurred in other mammals. For the moment, the most comprehensive analyses indicate that a recently discovered hominin species (*H. floresiensis*) did, in fact, evolve on Flores (Nevell et al., 2007; Tocheri et al., 2007; Falk et al., 2008; Schauber and Falk, 2008; Jungers et al., 2009). The more detailed studies of hand and foot anatomy suggest that in several respects the morphology is like that of *H. erectus* (Nevell et al., 2007; Tocheri et al., 2007) or even early *Homo* (Jungers et al., 2009). In any case, the morphology of the Flores hominins is different in several key respects from that of *H. sapiens*, even those who show pathological conditions. There is some possibility that DNA can be retrieved from the Flores bones and sequenced. Although considered a long shot due to poor bone preservation, analysis of this DNA would certainly help solve the mystery.

Technology and Art in the Upper Paleolithic

Europe

The cultural period known as the Upper Paleolithic began in western Europe approximately 40,000 ya (**Fig. 14-16**). Upper Paleolithic cultures are usually divided into five different industries, based on stone tool technologies: Chatelperronian, Aurignacian, Gravettian, Solutrean, and Magdalenian. Major environmental shifts were also apparent during this period. During the last glacial period, about 30,000 ya, a warming trend lasting several thousand years partially melted the glacial ice. The result was that much of Eurasia was covered by tundra and steppe, a vast area of treeless country dotted with lakes and marshes. In many areas in the north, permafrost prevented the growth of trees but permitted the growth, in the short summers, of flowering plants, mosses, and other kinds of vegetation. This vegetation served as an enormous pasture for herbivorous animals, large and small, and carnivorous animals fed off the herbivores. It was a hunter's paradise, with millions of animals dispersed across expanses of tundra and grassland, from Spain through Europe and into the Russian steppes.

Large herds of reindeer roamed the tundra and steppes, along with mammoths, bison, horses, and a host of smaller animals that served as a bountiful source of food. In addition, humans exploited fish and fowl systematically for the first time, especially in southern Europe. It was a time of relative abundance, and ultimately Upper Paleolithic people spread out over Europe, living in caves and open-air camps and building large shelters. We should recall that many of the cultural innovations

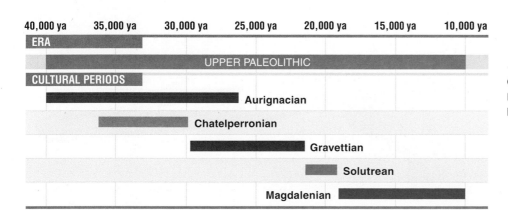

◀ **Figure 14-16**
Cultural periods of the European Upper Paleolithic and their approximate beginning dates.

seen in the Upper Paleolithic had begun with Neandertals (see Chapter 13). Nevertheless, when looking at the entire Upper Paleolithic, there are notable differences. For example, far more elaborate burials are found, most spectacularly at the 24,000-year-old Sungir site near Moscow (**Fig. 14-17**), where grave goods included a bed of red ocher, thousands of ivory beads, long spears made of straightened mammoth tusks, ivory engravings, and jewelry (Formicola and Buzhilova, 2004). During this period, either western Europe or perhaps portions of Africa achieved the highest population density in human history up to that time.

Humans and other animals in most of Eurasia had to cope with shifts in climate conditions, some of them quite rapid. For example, at 20,000 ya, another climatic "pulse" caused the weather to become noticeably colder in Europe and Asia as the continental glaciations reached their maximum extent for this entire glacial period, which is called the Würm in Eurasia.

As a variety of organisms attempted to adapt to these changing conditions, *Homo sapiens* had a major advantage: the elaboration of increasingly sophisticated technology and probably other components of culture as well. In fact, one of the greatest challenges facing numerous Late Pleistocene mammals was the ever more dangerously equipped humans—a trend that continues today.

The Upper Paleolithic was an age of innovation that can be compared

▲ **Figure 14-17**
Skeletons of two teenagers, a male and a female, from Sungir, Russia. Dated 24,000 ya, this is the richest find of any Upper Paleolithic grave.

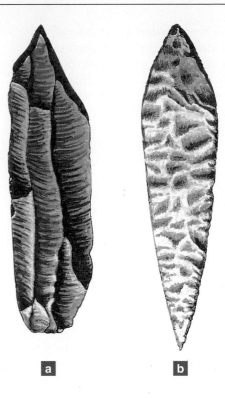

▲ **Figure 14-18**
(a) A burin, a very common Upper Paleolithic tool. **(b)** A Solutrean blade. This is the best-known work of the Solutrean tradition. Solutrean stonework is considered the most highly developed of any Upper Paleolithic industry.

to the past few hundred years in our recent history of amazing technological change. Anatomically modern humans of the Upper Paleolithic not only invented new and specialized tools (**Fig. 14-18**), but, as we've seen, also experimented with and greatly increased the use of new materials, such as bone, ivory, and antler.

▶ **Figure 14-19**
Spear-thrower (atlatl). Note the carving.

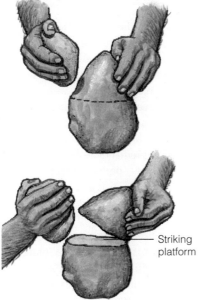

a A large core is selected and the top portion removed by use of a hammerstone.

Striking platform

b The objective is to create a flat surface called a striking platform.

c Next, the core is struck by use of a hammer and punch (made of bone or antler) to remove the long narrow flakes (called blades).

d Or the blades can be removed by pressure flaking.

e The result is the production of highly consistent sharp blades, which can be used, as is, as knives; or they can be further modified (retouched) to make a variety of other tools (such as burins, scrapers, and awls).

Solutrean tools are good examples of Upper Paleolithic skill and likely aesthetic appreciation as well (see Fig. 14-18b). In this lithic (stone) tradition, stoneknapping developed to the finest degree ever known. Using specialized flaking techniques, the artist/technicians made beautiful parallel-flaked lance heads, expertly flaked on both surfaces. The lance points are so delicate that they can be considered works of art that quite possibly never served, nor were they intended to serve, a utilitarian purpose.

The last stage of the Upper Paleolithic, known as the **Magdalenian**, saw even more advances in technology. The spear-thrower, or atlatl, was a wooden or bone hooked rod that extended the hunter's arm, enhancing the force and distance of a spear throw (**Fig. 14-19**). For catching salmon and other fish, the barbed harpoon is a good example of skillful craftsmanship. There's also evidence that bows and arrows may have been used for the first time during this period. The introduction of much more efficient manufacturing methods, such as the punch blade technique (**Fig. 14-20**), provided an abundance of standardized stone blades. These could be fashioned into **burins** (see Fig. 14-18b) for working wood, bone, and antler; borers for drilling holes in skins, bones, and shells; and knives with serrated or notched edges for scraping wooden shafts into a variety of tools.

By producing many more specialized tools, Upper Paleolithic peoples probably had more resources available to them; moreover, these more effective tools may also have had an impact on the biology of these populations. Emphasizing a biocultural interpretation, C. Loring Brace, of the University of Michigan, has suggested that with more effective tools as well as the use of fire allowing for more efficient food processing, anatomically modern

▲ **Figure 14-20**
The punch blade technique.

Magdalenian Pertaining to the final phase of the Upper Paleolithic stone tool industry in Europe.

burins Small, chisel-like tools with a pointed end; thought to have been used to engrave bone, antler, ivory, or wood.

Maybe You *Can* Take It with You

The practice of deliberately burying the dead is an important and distinctive aspect of later human biocultural evolution. We saw in Chapter 13 that Neandertals buried their dead at a number of sites; but we also noted that the assortment of grave goods found in Neandertal burials was pretty sparse.

Something remarkable happened with the appearance and dispersal of modern humans. Suddenly—at least in archaeological terms—graves became much more elaborate. And it wasn't just that many more items were placed with the deceased; it was also the kinds of objects. Neandertal graves sometimes contain a few stone tools and some unmodified animal bones, such as cave bear. But fully modern humans seem to have had more specialized and far more intensive cultural capacities. For example, from 40,000 ya at Twilight Cave, in Kenya, researchers have found 600 fragments of carefully drilled ostrich eggshell beads (Klein and Edgar, 2002). These beads aren't directly associated with a human burial, but they do show an intensification of craft specialization and possibly a greater interest in personal adornment (although Neandertals in Spain at about the same time were doing similar things, but to a somewhat lesser extent; see Chapter 13)

A locale where such elaborate grave goods (including beads) have been found in association with Upper Paleolithic modern human burials is the famous Cro-Magnon site in southwestern France. Likewise, numerous elaborate grave goods were found with human burials at Grimaldi, in Italy.

No doubt, the richest Upper Paleolithic burial sites are those at Sungir, in Russia. Parts of several individuals have been recovered there, dating to about 24,000 ya. Most dramatically, three individuals were found in direct association with thousands of ivory beads and other elaborate grave goods. Two of the individuals, a girl about 9 or 10 years of age and a boy about 12 or 13 years of age, were buried together head to head in a spectacular grave (see Fig. 14-17). The more than 10,000 beads excavated here were probably woven into clothing, a task that would have been extraordinarily time-consuming. The two individuals were placed directly on a bed of red ocher, and with them were two magnificent spears made of straightened mammoth tusks—one of them more than 6 feet (240 cm) long! What's more, there were hundreds of drilled fox canine teeth, pierced antlers, and ivory carvings of animals, as well as ivory pins and pendants (Formicola and Buzhilova, 2004).

Producing all of these items that were so carefully placed with these two young individuals took thousands of hours of labor. Indeed, one estimate suggests that it took 10,000 hours just to make the beads (Klein and Edgar, 2002). What were the Magdalenian people who went to all this trouble thinking? The double burial is certainly the most extravagant of any from the Upper Paleolithic, but another at Sungir is almost as remarkable. Here, the body of an adult male—perhaps about 40 years old when he died—was also found with thousands of beads, and he, too, was carefully laid out on a bed of red ocher.

Sungir is likely a somewhat extraordinary exception; still, far more elaborate graves are often found associated with early modern humans than was ever the case in earlier cultures. At Sungir, and to a lesser extent at other sites, it took hundreds or even thousands of hours to produce the varied and intricate objects.

The individuals who were buried with these valuable goods must have been seen as special. Did they have unique talents? Were they leaders or the children of leaders? Or did they have some special religious or ritual standing? To be sure, this evidence is the earliest we have from human history revealing highly defined social status. Thousands of years later, the graves of the Egyptian pharaohs express the same thing—as do the elaborate monuments seen in most contemporary cemeteries. The Magdalenians and other Upper Paleolithic cultures were indeed much like us. They, too, may have tried to defy death and take it with them!

H. sapiens wouldn't have required the large teeth and facial skeletons seen in earlier populations.

In addition to their reputation as hunters, western Europeans of the Upper Paleolithic are even better known for their symbolic representation (what we today recognize as art). There's an extremely wide geographical distribution of symbolic images, best known from many parts of Europe but now also well documented from Siberia, North Africa, South Africa, and Australia. Given a 25,000-year time depth of what we call Paleolithic art, along with its nearly worldwide distribution, we can indeed observe marked variability in expression.

Besides cave art, there are many examples of small sculptures excavated from sites in western, central, and eastern Europe. Perhaps the most famous of these are the female figurines, popularly known as "Venuses," found at such sites as Brassempouy, in France, and Grimaldi, in Italy. Some of these figures were realistically carved, and the faces appear to be modeled after actual women. Other figurines may seem grotesque, with sexual characteristics exaggerated, perhaps to promote fertility or serve some other ritual purpose.

Beyond these quite well-known figurines, there are numerous other examples of what's frequently called portable art, including elaborate engravings on tools and tool handles (see Fig. 14-19). Such symbolism can be found in many parts of Europe and was already well established early in the Aurignacian, by 33,000 ya. Innovations in symbolic representations also benefited from, and probably further stimulated, technological advances. New methods of mixing pigments and applying them were important in rendering painted or drawn images. Bone and ivory carving and engraving were made easier with the use of special stone tools (see Fig. 14-18). At two sites in the Czech Republic, Dolní Věstonice and Předmostí (both dated at approximately 27,000–26,000 ya), small animal figures were fashioned from fired clay. This is the first documented use of ceramic technology anywhere; in fact, it precedes later pottery invention by more than 15,000 years.

But it wasn't until the final phases of the Upper Paleolithic, particularly during the Magdalenian, that European prehistoric art reached its climax. Cave art is now known from more than 150 separate sites, the vast majority from southwestern France and northern Spain. Apparently, in other areas the rendering of such images did not take place in deep caves. People in central Europe, China, Africa, and elsewhere certainly may have painted or carved representations on rock faces in the open, but these images long since would have disappeared. So we're fortunate that the people of at least one of the many sophisticated cultures of the Upper Paleolithic chose to journey belowground to create their artwork, preserving it not just for their immediate descendants, but for us as well. The most spectacular and most famous of the cave art sites are Lascaux and Grotte Chauvet (in France) and Altamira (in Spain).

In Lascaux Cave, for example, immense wild bulls dominate what's called the Great Hall of Bulls; and horses, deer, and other animals drawn with remarkable skill adorn the walls in black, red, and yellow. Equally impressive, at Altamira the walls and ceiling of an immense cave are filled with superb portrayals of bison in red and black. The artist even took advantage of bulges in the walls to create a sense of relief in the paintings. The cave is a treasure of beautiful art whose meaning has never been satisfactorily explained. It could have been religious or magical, a form of visual communication, or simply art for the sake of beauty.

Inside the cave called Grotte Chauvet, preserved unseen for perhaps 30,000 years, are a multitude of images, including dots, stenciled human handprints, and, most dramatically, hundreds of animal representations. Radiocarbon dating has placed the paintings during the Aurignacian, likely more than 35,000 ya, making Grotte Chauvet considerably earlier than the Magdalenian sites of Lascaux and Altamira (Balter, 2006).

Africa

Early accomplishments in rock art, possibly as early as in Europe, are seen in southern Africa (Namibia) at the Apollo 11 rock-shelter site, where painted slabs have been identified dating to between 28,000 and 26,000 ya (Freundlich et al., 1980; Vogelsang, 1998). At Blombos Cave, farther to the south, remarkable bone tools, beads, and decorated ocher fragments are all dated to 73,000 ya (Henshilwood et al., 2004; Jacobs et al., 2006). The most recent and highly notable discovery from South Africa comes from another cave located at Pinnacle Point, not far from Blombos. At Pinnacle Point, ocher has been found (perhaps used for personal adornment) as well as clear evidence of systematic exploitation of shellfish and use of very small stone blades (microliths). What is both important and surprising is that the site is dated to approximately 165,000 ya, providing the earliest evidence from anywhere of these behaviors thought by many as characteristic of modern humans (Marean et al., 2007). The microliths also show evidence that the stone had been carefully heated, making it easier to modify into such small tools (Brown, 2009; Marean, 2010).

In central Africa, there was also considerable use of bone and antler, some of it possibly quite early. Excavations in the Katanda area of the eastern portion of the Democratic Republic of the Congo (**Fig. 14-21**) have shown remarkable development of bone craftwork. Dating of the site is quite early. Initial results using ESR and TL dating indicate an age as early as 80,000 ya (Feathers and Migliorini, 2001). Preliminary reports have demonstrated that these technological achievements rival those of the more renowned European Upper Paleolithic (Yellen et al., 1995).

Summary of Upper Paleolithic Culture

In looking back at the Upper Paleolithic, we can see it as the culmination of 2 million years of cultural development. Change proceeded incredibly slowly for most of the Pleistocene; but as cultural traditions and materials accumulated, and the brain—and, we assume, intelligence—expanded and reorganized, the rate of change quickened.

Cultural evolution continued with the appearance of early premodern humans and moved a bit faster with later premodern humans. Neandertals in Eurasia and their contemporaries elsewhere added deliberate burials, body ornamentation, technological innovations, and much more.

Building on existing cultures, Late Pleistocene populations attained sophisticated cultural and material heights in a seemingly short (by previous standards) burst of exciting activity. In Europe and southern and central Africa, particularly, there seem to have been dramatic cultural innovations, among them big game hunting with new weapons, such as harpoons, spear-throwers, and eventually bows and arrows. Other innovations included needles, "tailored" clothing, and burials with elaborate grave goods—a practice that may indicate some sort of status hierarchy.

This dynamic age was doomed, or so it seems, by the climate changes of about 10,000 ya. As the temperature slowly rose and the glaciers retreated, animal and plant species were seriously affected, and these changes, in turn, affected humans. As traditional prey animals were depleted or disappeared altogether, humans had to seek other means of obtaining food.

Grinding hard seeds or roots became important, and as humans grew more familiar with propagating plants, they began to domesticate both plants and animals. Human dependence on domestication became critical, and with it came permanent settlements, new technology, and more complex social organization. This continuing story of human biocultural evolution will be the topic of the remainder of this text.

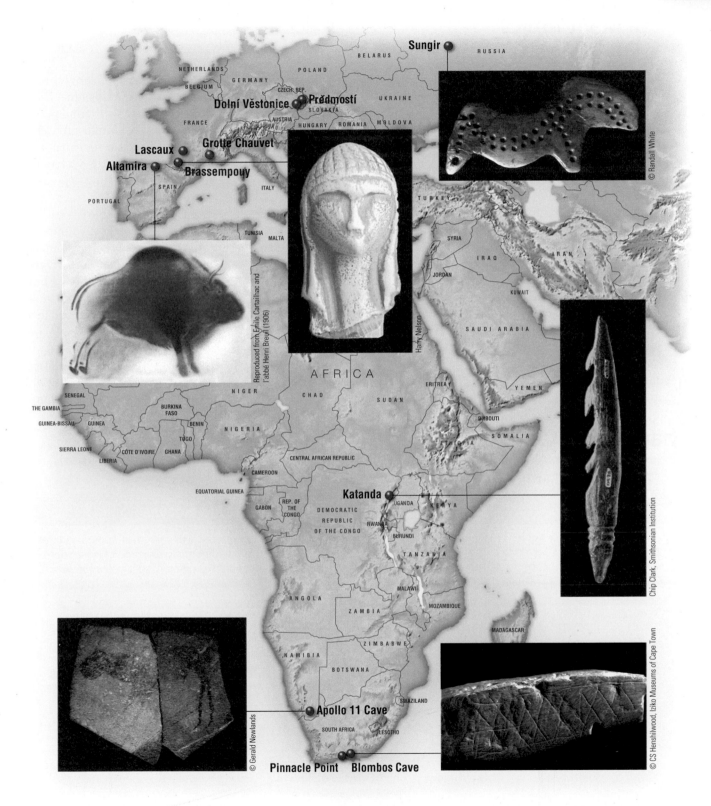

▲ **Figure 14-21**
Symbolic artifacts from the Middle Stone Age of Africa and the Upper Paleolithic in Europe. It is notable that evidence of symbolism is found in Blombos Cave (77,000 ya) and Katanda (80,000 ya), both in Africa, about 45,000 years before any comparable evidence is known from Europe.

Summary
of Main Topics

- Two main hypotheses have been used to explain the origin and dispersal of modern humans:
  —The regional continuity model suggests that different groups of modern people evolved from local populations of premodern humans.
  —Various replacement models, especially those emphasizing partial replacement, suggest that modern humans originated in Africa and migrated to other parts of the world. However, when they came into contact with premodern human groups, they did not completely replace them, but interbred with them to some extent.

- New DNA evidence from ancient Neandertals as well as from modern people demonstrate that some modest interbreeding did take place, probably between 80,000 and 50,000 ya. These findings clearly support a partial replacement model.

- Archaeological finds and some fossil evidence (although the latter is not as well established) also support the view that intermixing occurred between modern *H. sapiens* and Neandertals.

- The earliest finds of modern *H. sapiens* come from East Africa (Ethiopia), with the oldest dating to about 200,000 ya. The second find from Herto is very well dated (160,000 ya) and is the best evidence of an early modern human from anywhere at this time.

- Modern humans are found in South Africa beginning around 100,000 ya, and the first anatomical modern *H. sapiens* are found in the Middle East dating to perhaps more than 100,000 ya.

- The Upper Paleolithic is a cultural period showing many innovations in technology, development of more sophisticated (cave) art, and, in many cases, very elaborate burials rich in grave goods. Similar cultural developments occurred in both Eurasia and Africa.

In "What's Important," you'll find a useful summary of the most significant fossil discoveries discussed in this chapter.

What's Important

Key Fossil Discoveries of Early Modern Humans and *Homo floresiensis*

DATES	REGION	SITE	HOMININ	THE BIG PICTURE
95,000–13,000 ya	Southeast Asia	Flores (Indonesia)	*H. floresiensis*	Late survival of very small-bodied and small-brained hominin on island of Flores; designated as different species (*H. floresiensis*) from modern humans
30,000 ya	Europe	Cro-Magnon (France)	*H. sapiens sapiens*	Famous site historically; good example of early modern humans from France
35,000 ya	Europe	Oase Cave (Romania)	*H. sapiens sapiens*	Earliest well-dated modern human from Europe
110,000 ya	Southwest Asia	Qafzeh (Israel)	*H. sapiens sapiens*	Early site; shows considerable variation
115,000 ya	Southwest Asia	Skhūl (Israel)	*H. sapiens sapiens*	Earliest well-dated modern human outside of Africa; perhaps contemporaneous with neighboring Tabun Neandertal site
160,000–154,000 ya	Africa	Herto (Ethiopia)	*H. sapiens idaltu*	Best-preserved and best-dated early modern human from anywhere; placed in separate subspecies from living *H. sapiens*

Critical Thinking Questions

1. What anatomical characteristics define *modern* as compared with *premodern*, humans? Assume that you're analyzing an incomplete skeleton that may be early modern *H. sapiens*. Which portions of the skeleton would be most informative, and why?

2. What recent evidence supports a partial replacement model for an African origin and later dispersal of modern humans? Do you find this evidence convincing? Why or why not? Can you propose an alternative that has better data to support it?

3. Why are the fossils recently discovered from Herto so important? How does this evidence influence your conclusions in question 2?

4. What archaeological evidence shows that modern human behavior during the Upper Paleolithic was significantly different from that of earlier hominins? Do you think that early modern *H. sapiens* populations were behaviorally superior to the Neandertals? Be careful to define what you mean by "superior."

5. Why do you think some Upper Paleolithic people painted in caves? Why don't we find such evidence of cave painting from a wider geographical area?

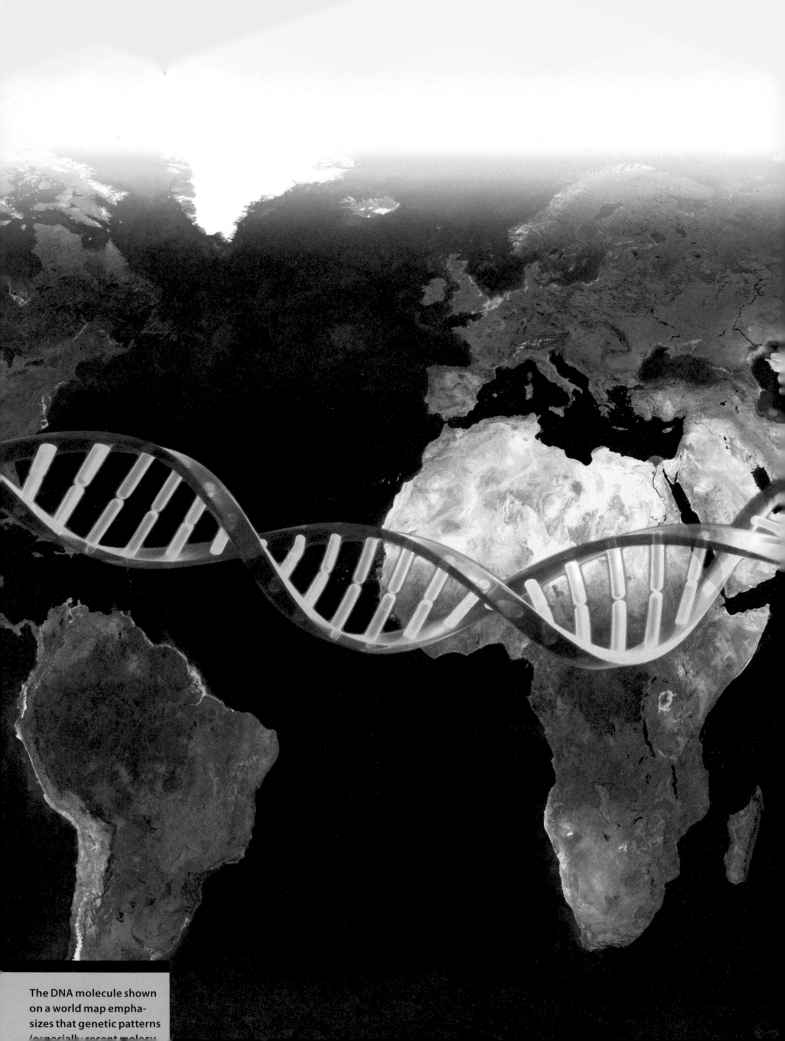

The DNA molecule shown
on a world map empha-
sizes that genetic patterns
(especially recent molecu-

NASA / © iStockphoto.com / James Steidl (DNA)

15

Modern Human Biology: Patterns of Variation

Key Questions

▶ Is evolution still occurring in modern humans?

▶ What is meant by race, and how useful is this concept in understanding the biology and evolution of our species?

At some time or other, you've probably been asked to specify your "race" or "ethnicity" on an application or census form. Did that bother you, and if so, why? Usually, you can choose from a few racial/ethnic categories. Was it easy to pick one? Where would your parents and grandparents fit in?

Notions about human diversity have played an extremely important role in human relations for at least a few thousand years, and they still influence political and social perceptions. While we'd like to believe that informed views have become almost universal, the gruesome tally of genocidal/ethnic cleansing atrocities in recent years tells us tragically that worldwide, we have a long way to go before tolerance becomes the norm.

Unfortunately, there are probably hundreds (if not thousands) of popular misconceptions regarding human diversity, and to make matters worse, many people seem unwilling to accept what science has to say on the subject. Many misconceptions, especially those regarding how race is defined and categorized, are rooted in cultural history over the last few centuries.

In Chapters 3 and 4, we saw how physical characteristics are influenced by the DNA in our cells. We discussed how people inherit genes from their parents and how variations in those genes (alleles) can produce different expressions of traits. We also focused on how the basic principles of inheritance are related to evolutionary change.

In this chapter, we'll continue to deal with topics that directly relate to genetics, namely, biological diversity in humans and how biocultural evolution influences how humans adapt to environmental challenges. After discussing historical attempts to explain human phenotypic variation and racial classification, we'll examine contemporary methods of interpreting diversity. In recent years, several new techniques have emerged that permit direct examination of the DNA molecule, revealing differences among people even at the level of single nucleotides. But as discoveries of different levels of diversity emerge, geneticists have also shown that our species is remarkably uniform genetically, particularly when compared with other species.

Historical Views of Human Variation

The first step toward understanding diversity in nature is to organize it into categories that can then be named, discussed, and perhaps studied. Historically, when different groups of people came into contact with each other, they tried to account for the physical differences they saw. Because skin color was so noticeable, it was one of the more frequently explained characteristics, and most systems of racial classification were based on it.

As early as 1350 B.C., the ancient Egyptians had classified humans based on their skin color: red for Egyptian, yellow for people to the east, white for those to the north, and black for sub-Saharan Africans (Gossett, 1963). In the sixteenth century, after the discovery of the New World, several European countries embarked on a period of intense exploration and colonization in both the New and Old Worlds. One result of this contact was an increased awareness of human diversity.

Throughout the eighteenth and nineteenth centuries, European and American scientists concentrated on describing and classifying biological variation in humans and also in non-human species. The first scientific attempt to describe the newly discovered variation among human populations was Linnaeus' taxonomic classification (see Chapter 2), which placed humans into four separate categories (Linnaeus, 1758). Linnaeus assigned behavioral and intellectual qualities to each group, with the least complimentary descriptions going to sub-Saharan Africans. This ranking system was typical of the period and reflected the almost universal European view

that Europeans were superior to everyone else.

Johann Friedrich Blumenbach (1752–1840), a German anatomist, classified humans into five races. Although Blumenbach's categories came to be described simply as white, yellow, red, black, and brown, he also used criteria other than skin color. What's more, he emphasized that racial categories based on skin color were arbitrary and that many traits, including skin color, weren't discrete phenomena. Blumenbach pointed out that classifying all humans using such a system would completely omit everyone who didn't fall into a specific category. Blumenbach and others also recognized that traits such as skin color showed overlapping expression between groups.

By the mid-nineteenth century, populations were ranked on a scale based primarily on skin color (along with size and shape of the head), again with sub-Saharan Africans at the bottom. The Europeans themselves were also ranked, with northern, light-skinned populations considered superior to their southern, somewhat darker-skinned neighbors in Italy and Greece.

To many Europeans, the fact that non-Europeans weren't Christian suggested that they were "uncivilized" and implied an even more basic inferiority of character and intellect. This view was rooted in a concept called **biological determinism**, which in part holds that there is an association between physical characteristics and such attributes as intelligence, morals, values, abilities, and even social and economic condition. In other words, cultural variations were thought to be *inherited* in the same way that biological variations are. It followed, then, that there are inherent behavioral and cognitive differences between groups and that some groups are by nature superior to others. Unfortunately, many people still hold these views, and following this logic, it's a simple matter to justify the persecution and even

biological determinism The concept that phenomena, including various aspects of behavior (e.g., intelligence, values, morals) are governed by biological (genetic) factors; the inaccurate association of various behavioral attributes with certain biological traits, such as skin color.

enslavement of other peoples simply because their outward appearance differs from what is familiar.

After 1850, biological determinism was a constant theme underlying common thinking as well as scientific research in Europe and the United States. Most people, including such notables as Thomas Jefferson, Georges Cuvier, Benjamin Franklin, Charles Lyell, Abraham Lincoln, Charles Darwin, and Supreme Court justice Oliver Wendell Holmes, held deterministic (and what today we'd call racist) views. Commenting on this usually de-emphasized characteristic of more respected historical figures, the late evolutionary biologist Stephen J. Gould (1981, p. 32) remarked that "all American culture heroes embraced racial attitudes that would embarrass public-school mythmakers."

Francis Galton (1822–1911), Charles Darwin's cousin, shared a growing fear among nineteenth-century Europeans that "civilized society" was being weakened by the failure of natural selection to completely eliminate unfit and inferior members (Greene, 1981, p. 107). Galton wrote and lectured on the necessity of "race improvement" and suggested government regulation of marriage and family size, an approach he called **eugenics**. Although eugenics had its share of critics, its popularity flourished throughout the 1930s. Nowhere was it more attractive than in Germany, where the viewpoint took a horrifying turn. The false idea of pure races was increasingly extolled as a means of reestablishing a strong and prosperous state. Eugenics was seen as scientific justification for purging Germany of its "unfit," and many of Germany's scientists continued to support the policies of racial purity and eugenics during the Nazi period (Proctor, 1988, p. 143), when these policies served as justification for condemning millions of people to death.

But at the same time, many scientists were turning away from racial typologies and classification in favor of a more evolutionary approach. No doubt for some, this shift in direction was motivated by their growing concerns over the goals of the eugenics movement. Probably more important, however, was the synthesis of genetics and Darwin's theories of natural selection during the 1930s. As discussed in Chapter 4, this breakthrough influenced all the biological sciences, and some physical anthropologists soon began applying evolutionary principles to the study of human variation.

The Concept of Race

All contemporary humans are members of the same **polytypic** species, *Homo sapiens*. A polytypic species is composed of local populations that differ in the expression of one or more traits. It's crucial to emphasize that even *within* local populations, there's a great deal of genotypic and phenotypic variation between individuals.

Nevertheless, in discussions of human variation, most people typically have emphasized and grouped together various characteristics, such as skin color, face shape, nose shape, hair color, hair form (curly or straight), and eye color. Those individuals who have particular combinations of these and other traits have been placed together in categories associated with specific geographical localities. Traditionally, such categories have been called *races*.

We all think we know what we mean by the word *race*, but in reality, the term has had various meanings since the 1500s, when it first appeared in the English language. Race has been used synonymously with *species*, as in "the human race." Since the 1600s, race has also referred to various culturally defined groups, and this meaning is still common. For example, you'll hear people say, "the English race" or "the Japanese race," when they actually mean nationality. Another phrase you've probably heard is "the Jewish race," when the speaker is really talking

eugenics The philosophy of "race improvement" through the forced sterilization of members of some groups and increased reproduction among others; an overly simplified, often racist view that's now discredited.

polytypic Referring to species composed of populations that differ in the expression of one or more traits.

A Closer Look

Racial Purity: A False and Dangerous Ideology

During the late nineteenth and early twentieth centuries, a growing sense of nationalism swept Europe and the United States. At the same time, an increased emphasis on racial purity was coupled with the more dangerous aspects of what's known as biological determinism. The concept of pure races is based, in part, on the notion that in the past, races were composed of people who conformed to idealized types and who were similar in appearance and intellect. According to this concept, over time some variation was introduced into these pure races through interbreeding with other groups. Increasingly, this type of "contamination" was seen as a threat to be avoided.

In today's terminology, pure races would be said to be genetically homogenous, or to possess little genetic variation. Therefore, everyone would have the same alleles at most of their loci. Actually, we do see this situation in "pure breeds" of domesticated animals and plants, developed deliberately by humans through selective breeding. We also see many of the detrimental consequences of such genetic uniformity in various congenital abnormalities, such as hip dysplasia in some breeds of dogs.

With our current understanding of genetic principles, we're able to appreciate the potentially negative outcomes of matings between genetically similar individuals. For example, we know that inbreeding increases the likelihood of offspring who are homozygous for certain deleterious recessive alleles. We also know that decreased genetic variation in a species diminishes the potential for natural selection to act, thus compromising that species' ability to adapt to certain environmental fluctuations. What's more, in genetically uniform populations, individual fertility can be seriously reduced, potentially with disastrous consequences for the entire species. So, even if pure human races did exist at one time (and they didn't), it would not have been a genetically desirable condition, and these groups most certainly would have been at an evolutionary disadvantage.

In northern Europe, particularly Germany, and in the United States, racial superiority was increasingly embodied in the so-called Aryan race. *Aryan* is a term that's still widely used, albeit erroneously, with biological connotations. Actually, Aryan doesn't refer to a biological population, as most people who use the term intend it. Rather, it's a linguistic term that refers to an ancient language group that was ancestral to the Indo-European family of languages, and it's the word from which the name Iran is derived.

By the early twentieth century, the "Aryans" had been transformed into a mythical super race of people whose noble traits were embodied in an extremely idealized "Nordic type." The true Aryan was held to be tall, blond, blue-eyed, strong, industrious, and "pure in spirit." Nordics were extolled as the developers of all ancient "high" civilizations and as the founders of modern industrialized nations. (It would appear that the ancient cultures of the Indus Valley, China, Arabia, Mexico, Zimbabwe, Greece, and Rome were unknown.) In

◄ **Figure 1**
Victims of genocide in Rwanda resulting from tribal warfare in 1994.

MSGT Rose Reynolds

about a particular ethnic and religious identity.

So, even though *race* is usually a term with biological connotations, it also has enormous social significance. And there's still a widespread perception that certain physical traits (skin color, in particular) are associated with numerous cultural attributes (such as occupational preferences or even morality). As a result, in many cultural contexts, a person's social identity is strongly influenced by the way he or she expresses those physical traits traditionally used to define "racial groups." Characteristics such as skin color are highly visible, and they make it easy to immediately and

Europe, there was growing emphasis on the superiority of northwestern Europeans as the modern representatives of "true Nordic stock," while southern and eastern Europeans were viewed as inferior.

In the United States, there prevailed the strongly held opinion that America was "originally" settled by Christian Nordics. One wonders how Native Americans could be so conveniently forgotten. Before about 1890, most recent newcomers to the United States had come from Germany, Scandinavia, Great Britain, and Ireland. But by the 1890s, the pattern of immigration had changed. The arrival of increasing numbers of Italians, Turks, Greeks, and eastern European Jews among the thousands of newcomers raised fears that society was being contaminated by immigration from southern and eastern Europe.

Also, in the United States, there were concerns about the large population of former slaves and their descendants. As African Americans left the South to work in the factories of the North, many unskilled white workers felt economically threatened by competition. It was no coincidence that the Ku Klux Klan, which had been inactive for some years, was revived in 1915 and by the 1920s was preaching vehement opposition to African Americans, Jews, and Catholics in support of the supremacy of the white, Protestant "Nordic race." These sentiments were widespread in the general population, although they didn't always take the extreme form advocated by the Klan. One result of these views was the Immigration Restriction Act, passed by Congress in 1924, which was aimed at curtailing the immigration of non-Nordics, including Italians,

Jews, and eastern Europeans, in order to preserve "America's Nordic heritage."

To avoid the further "decline of the superior race," many states practiced policies of racial segregation until the mid-1950s. Particularly in the South, segregation laws resulted in an almost total separation of whites and blacks, except where blacks were employed as servants or laborers. There were also laws against marriage between whites and blacks in over half the states, and unions between whites and Asians were frequently illegal. In several states, marriage between whites and blacks was punishable as either a misdemeanor or a felony, and astonishingly, some of these laws weren't repealed until the late 1950s or early 1960s. Likewise, in Germany by 1935, the newly instituted Nuremberg Laws forbade marriage or sexual intercourse between so-called Aryan Germans and Jews.

The fact that belief in racial purity and superiority led ultimately to the Nazi death camps in World War II is undisputed (except for continuing efforts by certain white supremacist and neo-Nazi organizations). It's one of the great tragedies of the twentieth century that some of history's most glaring examples of discrimination and brutality were perpetrated by people

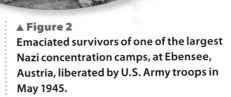

▲ **Figure 2**
Emaciated survivors of one of the largest Nazi concentration camps, at Ebensee, Austria, liberated by U.S. Army troops in May 1945.

who believed their actions to be based in scientific principles. In reality, there's absolutely no evidence to suggest that "pure" human races ever existed. Indeed, such an idea flies in the face of everything we know about natural selection, recombination, and gene flow. The degree of genetic uniformity throughout our species (compared to some other species), as evidenced by mounting data from mitochondrial and nuclear DNA analysis, argues strongly that there has always been gene flow between human populations and that genetically homogenous races are nothing more than fabrication.

superficially place people into socially defined categories. However, so-called racial traits aren't the only phenotypic expressions that contribute to social identity. Sex and age are also critically important. But aside from these two variables, an individual's biological and/or ethnic background is still inevitably a factor that influences how he

or she is initially perceived and judged by others.

References to national origin (for example, African, Asian) as substitutes for racial labels have become more common in recent years, both within and outside anthropology. Within anthropology, the term *ethnicity* was proposed in the early 1950s to avoid the more emotionally charged term *race*. Strictly speaking, ethnicity refers to cultural factors, but the fact that the words *ethnicity* and *race* are used interchangeably reflects the social importance of phenotypic expression and demonstrates once again how phenotype is mistakenly associated with culturally defined variables.

In its most common biological usage, the term *race* refers to geographically patterned phenotypic variation within a species. By the seventeenth century, naturalists were beginning to describe races in plants and nonhuman animals. They had recognized that when populations of a species occupied different regions, they sometimes differed from one another in the expression of one or more traits. But even today, there are no established criteria for assessing races of plants and animals, including humans. As a result, biologists now almost never refer to "races" of other species, but more typically talk about *populations* or, for major subdivisions, *subspecies*.

Before World War II, most studies of human variation focused on visible phenotypic variation between large, geographically defined populations, and these studies were largely descriptive. But in the last 60 years or so, the emphasis has shifted to examining the differences in allele frequencies (and, more basically, DNA differences) within and between populations, as well as considering the adaptive significance of phenotypic and genotypic variation. This shift in focus occurred partly because of the Modern Synthesis in biology and partly because of further advances in genetics.

In the twenty-first century, the application of evolutionary principles to the study of modern human variation has replaced the superficial nineteenth-century view of *race based solely on observed phenotype*. Additionally, the genetic emphasis has dispelled previously held misconceptions that races are fixed biological entities that don't change over

time and that are composed of individuals who all conform to a particular *type*.

Clearly, there are visible phenotypic differences between humans, and some of these differences roughly correspond to particular geographical locations. But we need to ask if there's any adaptive significance attached to these differences. Is genetic drift a factor? What is the degree of underlying genetic variation that influences phenotypic variation? What influence has culture played in the past? These questions place considerations of human variation within a contemporary evolutionary, biocultural framework.

Although, as a discipline, physical anthropology is rooted in attempts to explain human diversity, no contemporary scholar subscribes to pre–Modern Synthesis concepts of races (human or nonhuman) as fixed biological entities. Also, anthropologists recognize that such outdated concepts of race are no longer valid, because the amount of genetic variation accounted for by differences *between* groups is vastly exceeded by the variation that exists *within* groups. Many physical anthropologists also argue that race is an outdated creation of the human mind that attempts to simplify biological complexity by organizing it into categories. So, human races are a product of the human tendency to impose order on complex natural phenomena. In this view, simplistic classification may have been an acceptable approach 100 years ago, but given the current state of genetic and evolutionary science, it's meaningless.

However, even though racial categories based on outwardly expressed variations are invalid, many biological anthropologists continue to study differences in such traits as skin or eye color because these characteristics, and the genes that influence them, can yield information about population adaptation, genetic drift, mutation, and gene flow. Forensic anthropologists, in particular, find the phenotypic criteria associated with race (especially in the skeleton) to have practical applications. Law enforcement agencies frequently call on these scientists to help identify human skeletal remains. Because unidentified human remains are often those of crime victims, identification must be as accurate as possible. The most important variables in such identification are the individual's sex, age, stature, and ancestry ("racial" and ethnic background). Using metric and nonmetric criteria, forensic anthropologists employ various techniques for establishing broad population affinity (that is, a likely relationship) for that individual, and for most

applications their findings are accurate about 80 percent of the time (Ousley et al., 2009).

Another major limitation of traditional classification schemes derives from their inherently *typological* nature, meaning that categories are distinct and based on stereotypes or ideals that comprise a specific set of traits. So in general, typologies are inherently misleading because any grouping always includes many individuals who don't conform to all aspects of a particular type (**Fig. 15-1**). In any so-called racial group, there are individuals who fall into the normal

▲ **Figure 15-1**
Some examples of phenotypic variation among Africans.
(**a**) San (South African).
(**b**) West African (Bantu).
(**c**) Ethiopian.
(**d**) Ituri (central African).
(**e**) North African (Tunisia).

range of variation for another group based on one or several characteristics. For example, two people of different ancestry might differ in skin color, but they could share any number of other traits, including height, shape of head, hair color, eye color, and ABO blood type. In fact, they could easily share more similarities with each other than they do with many members of their own populations.

To blur this picture further, the characteristics that have traditionally been used to define races are *polygenic*; that is, they're influenced by more than one gene and therefore exhibit a continuous range of expression. So it's difficult, if not impossible, to draw distinct boundaries between populations with regard to many traits. This limitation becomes clear if you ask yourself, At what point is hair color no longer dark brown but medium brown, or no longer light brown but dark blond? (Look back at Figure 4-16 for an illustration showing variability in eye color.)

The scientific controversy over race will fade as we enhance our understanding of the genetic diversity (and uniformity) of our species. Given the rapid changes in genome studies, and because very few genes actually contribute to outward expressions of phenotype, dividing the human species into racial categories isn't a biologically meaningful way to look at human variation. But among the general public, variations on the theme of race will undoubtedly continue to be the most common view of human biological and cultural variation. Keeping all this in mind, it's up to anthropologists to continue exploring the issue so that, to the best of our abilities, accurate information about human

variation is available to anyone who seeks informed explanations of complex phenomena (**Fig. 15-2**).

Contemporary Interpretations of Human Variation

Because the physical characteristics (such as skin color and hair form) that are used to define race are *polygenic*, precisely measuring the genetic influence on them hasn't been possible (although geneticists are getting closer; Gibbons, 2010). Physical anthropologists and other biologists who study modern human variation have largely abandoned the traditional perspective of describing superficial phenotypic characteristics in favor of examining differences in the frequencies of genes.

Beginning in the 1950s, studies of modern human variation focused on the various components of blood as well as other aspects of body chemistry. Such traits as the ABO blood types are phenotypes, but they're also direct products of the genotype. (Recall that protein-coding genes direct cells to make proteins, and the antigens on blood cells and many constituents of blood serum are partly composed of proteins; **Fig.15-3**.) During the twentieth century, this perspective met with a great deal of success, as eventually dozens of loci were identified and the frequencies of many specific alleles were obtained from numerous human populations. Even so, in all these cases, it was the phenotype that was observed, and information about the underlying genotype remained largely unobtainable. But beginning in the 1990s, with the advent of genomic studies, new techniques were developed. Now that we can directly sequence DNA, we can actually identify entire genes and even larger DNA segments and make comparisons between individuals and populations. A decade ago, only a small portion of the human genome

▲ **Figure 15-2**
Barack Obama and his family after he was elected president of the United States November 4, 2008. The significance of electing the first African American president cannot be overstated. It was a watershed event that powerfully signaled a major shift in attitudes toward race in the United States.

© Tannen Maury/epa/Corbis

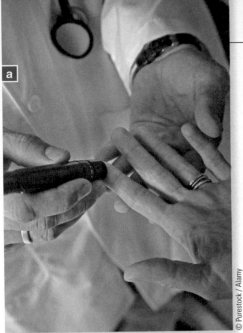

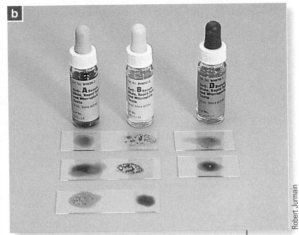

© Purestock / Alamy

Robert Jurmain

▲ **Figure 15-3**

Blood typing. (a) A blood sample is drawn. **(b)** To determine an individual's blood type, a few drops of blood are treated with specific chemicals. Presence of A and B blood type, as well as Rh, can be detected by using commercially available chemicals. The glass slides below the blue- and yellow-labeled bottles show reactions for the ABO system: The blood on the top slide is type AB; the middle is type B; and the bottom is type A. The two samples to the right depict Rh-negative blood (top) and Rh-positive blood (bottom).

was accessible to physical anthropologists, but now we have the capacity to obtain DNA profiles for virtually every human population on earth. And we can expect that in the next decade, our understanding and knowledge of human biological variation and adaptation will dramatically increase.

Human Polymorphisms

Traits (or the DNA sequences that code for them) that differ in expression between populations and individuals are called **polymorphisms**, and they're the main focus of human variation studies. A genetic trait is *polymorphic* if the locus that governs it has two or more alleles. (See Chapter 4 for a discussion of the ABO blood group system governed by three alleles at one locus.). A locus can consist of hundreds of nucleotides or just one nucleotide.

Understanding polymorphisms requires evolutionary explanations, and geneticists use polymorphisms as a principal tool to understand evolutionary processes in modern populations. By using these polymorphisms to compare gene frequencies between different populations, we can begin to reconstruct the evolutionary events that link human populations with one another.

The ABO system is interesting from an anthropological perspective

because the frequencies of the *A*, *B*, and *O* alleles vary tremendously among humans. In most groups, *A* and *B* are rarely found in frequencies greater than 50 percent, and usually their frequencies are much lower. Still, most human groups are polymorphic for all three alleles, but there are exceptions. For example, in native South American Indians, frequencies of the *O* allele reach 100 percent. Exceptionally high frequencies of *O* are also found in northern Australia, and some islands off the Australian coast show frequencies exceeding 90 percent. In these populations, the high frequencies of the *O* allele are probably due to genetic drift (founder effect), although the influence of natural selection can't be entirely ruled out.

Besides ABO, there are many other red blood cell phenotypes, each under the control of a different genetic locus. These include the well-known Rh blood group as well as the less familiar Duffy and MN blood groups. Some antigens on white blood cells are also polymorphic. Called human leukocyte antigens (HLA) in humans, these are crucial to the immune response because they allow the body to recognize and resist potentially dangerous infections. But unlike simple polymorphisms, such as ABO (one locus with three alleles) or MN (one locus with only two alleles), the HLA system

polymorphisms Loci with more than one allele. Polymorphisms can be expressed in the phenotype as the result of gene action (as in ABO), or they can exist solely at the DNA level within noncoding regions.

is governed by perhaps hundreds of alleles at six different loci. Therefore, the HLA system is by far the most polymorphic genetic system known in humans.

Because there are so many HLA alleles, they're useful in showing patterns of human population diversity. For example, Lapps, Sardinians, and Basques differ in HLA allele frequencies from other European populations, and these data coincide with allele fre-

▲ **Figure 15-4**
People in Sardinia, a large island off the west coast of Italy, differ from other European populations in allele frequencies at some loci.

quency distributions for ABO, MN, and Rh (**Fig. 15-4**). Founder effect is the most likely explanation for the distinctive genetic patterning in these smaller, traditionally more isolated groups. Likewise, some of the atypical frequencies of HLA alleles characteristic of certain populations in Australia and New Guinea probably result from founder effect. Natural selection also has influenced the evolution of HLA alleles in humans, especially as related to infectious disease. For example, certain HLA antigens appear to be associated with resistance to malaria and hepatitis B and perhaps to HIV as well. And finally, one physiological and evolutionary influence of HLA concerns male fertility. Data suggest that some HLA antigens are found in higher fre-

quencies in infertile males, suggesting that there may be some influence of two or more HLA loci on sperm production and function (van der Ven et al., 2000).

Another well-studied polymorphism is the ability to taste an artificial substance called phenylthiocarbamide (PTC). While many people perceive PTC as extremely bitter, others don't taste it at all. The mode of inheritance follows a Mendelian pattern, with two alleles (*T* and *t*). The ability to taste PTC is a dominant trait, while the inability to taste it is recessive. So, "nontasters" are homozygous (*tt*) for the recessive allele. The frequency of PTC tasting varies considerably in human populations, and the evolutionary explanation for the patterns of variation isn't clear. But it's possible that perceiving substances as bitter could be advantageous, especially in children, because poisonous plants are often bitter. Thus, heightened sensitivity to bitter substances increases the likelihood that toxic substances will be avoided.

Polymorphisms at the DNA Level

The Human Genome Project has provided considerable insight regarding human variation at the DNA level, and molecular biologists have discovered many previously unknown variations in the human genome. For example, there are thousands of DNA segments called copy number variants (CNVs) where DNA segments are repeated, in some cases just a few times and in other cases hundreds of times. A type of CNV that is repeated only a few times is called a *microsatellite*, and these segments vary tremendously from person to person. In fact, every person has their own unique arrangement that defines their distinctive "DNA fingerprint."

Researchers are expanding their approach to map patterns of variation for individual nucleotides. As you know, point mutations have been rec-

At a Glance

GENETIC POLYMORPHISMS USED TO STUDY HUMAN VARIATION

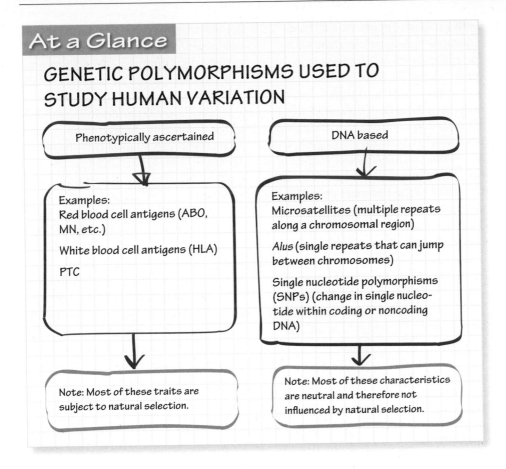

Phenotypically ascertained

Examples:
Red blood cell antigens (ABO, MN, etc.)

White blood cell antigens (HLA)

PTC

Note: Most of these traits are subject to natural selection.

DNA based

Examples:
Microsatellites (multiple repeats along a chromosomal region)

Alus (single repeats that can jump between chromosomes)

Single nucleotide polymorphisms (SNPs) (change in single nucleotide within coding or noncoding DNA)

Note: Most of these characteristics are neutral and therefore not influenced by natural selection.

ognized for some time. But what's only been recently appreciated is that such single-nucleotide changes also frequently occur in *noncoding* portions of DNA. These point mutations, together with those in coding regions of DNA, are all referred to as *single-nucleotide polymorphisms (SNPs)*. From years of detailed analyses, about 15 million SNPs have been recognized. SNPs are dispersed throughout the human genome (the majority found in noncoding DNA), and they're extraordinarily variable (Durbin et al., 2010). So, at the beginning of the twenty-first century, geneticists have gained access to a vast biological "library" that documents the genetic history of our species.

The field of **population genetics** is taking advantage of these new discoveries. While traditional polymorphic traits, such as ABO, are still being studied, researchers are directing more and more attention to the remarkably variable DNA polymorphisms. These molecular applications are now being widely used to evaluate human variation at a microevolutionary level, and this information provides far more accurate measures of within-group and between-group variation than was previously possible. Besides that, we can now use the vast amount of new data to more fully understand very recent events in human population history, including the many roles of natural selection, genetic drift, gene flow, and mutation. As an example of how far the study of human variation has moved toward a molecularly based approach, more than 95 percent of papers dealing with population variation presented at a recent anthropology conference made use of DNA polymorphisms obtained from populations from all over the world.

The most recent and most comprehensive population data regarding worldwide patterns of variation come from analysis of extremely large portions of DNA, called "whole-genome"

population genetics The study of the frequency of alleles, genotypes, and phenotypes in populations from a microevolutionary perspective.

analysis. Three recent studies have evaluated molecular information for the entire genome in more than 1000 total individuals. The first two studies each identified and traced the patterning of more than 500,000 SNPs as expressed in a few dozen populations worldwide (Jakobsson et al., 2008; Li et al., 2008). The most recent study, called the "1000 Genomes Project," is a massive collaboration of more than 400 scientists worldwide, and its preliminary findings reported on close to 15 million SNPs (as well as other DNA variants such and insertions and deletions); indeed, with more detailed sequencing methods and more sophisticated analyses, the researchers conclude they already have discovered the molecular basis for 95% of all fairly common patterns of human variation (Durbin et al., 2010). They have also identified between 50 and 100 gene variants associated with disease. Using the latest techniques, rather than completing scans of human genomes, this study was also able to quite accurately reconstruct the *entire* genome for 179 individuals (with an ultimate goal of completing whole genome sequences for 2,500 people from all around the world). These more complete data, particularly as they are enhanced further, will provide the basis for the next generation of human population genetics studies.

So far, the results of these new studies are highly significant because they confirm earlier findings from more restricted molecular data and they provide new insights. The higher degree of genetic variation seen in African populations as compared to any other geographical group was once again clearly seen. All human populations outside Africa have much less genetic variation than is seen in Africa. These findings further verify the earlier genetic studies (as well as fossil discoveries) that suggest a fairly recent African origin of all modern humans (as discussed in Chapter 14). Moreover, these new data shed light on the genetic relationships between populations worldwide and the nature of

human migrations out of Africa. They also provide evidence of the role of genetic drift (founder effect) in recent human evolution as successively smaller populations split off from larger ones (see "New Frontiers in Research," at the end of this chapter). Finally, preliminary results suggest that the patterning of human variation at the global level may help scientists identify genetic risk factors that influence how susceptible different populations are to various diseases. Specifically, the relative genetic uniformity in non-African populations (for example, European Americans) as compared to those of more recent African descent (for example, African Americans) exposes them to a greater risk of developing disease (Lohmueller et al., 2008). How such information might be put to use, however, is controversial.

All these genetic data, including the more traditional polymorphisms (such as blood groups) and the vast new DNA-based evidence, point in the same direction: Genetically, humans differ individually within populations far more than large geographical groups ("races") differ from each other. Does this mean, as eminent geneticist Richard Lewontin concluded almost 40 years ago, that there's no biological value in the further study of geographical populations (Lewontin, 1972)? Even with all our new information, the answer isn't entirely clear. Some of the recent genetic evidence from patterns of two different types of CNVs (Rosenberg et al., 2002; Bamshad et al., 2003) has found broad genetic correlations that consistently indicate an individual's geographical ancestry. We must consider some important points here, however. These geographically patterned genetic clusters aren't "races" as traditionally defined, and so they aren't closely linked to simple patterns of phenotypic variation (such as skin color). What's more, the correlations are broad, so not all individuals can be easily classified. In fact, many people would probably be misclassified, even when using the best information for dozens of genetic loci.

This debate isn't entirely academic, and it really never has been. Just consider the destructive social impact that the misuse of the race concept has caused over the last few centuries. A contemporary continuation of the debate concerns the relationship of ancestry and disease. It's long been recognized that some disease-causing genes are more common in certain populations than in others (such as the allele that causes sickle-cell anemia). The much more complete data on human DNA patterns have further expanded our knowledge, showing, for example, that some people are more resistant than others to HIV infection (see Chapter 16 for further discussion). Does this mean that a person's ancestry provides valuable medical information in screening or even treating certain diseases?

Some experts argue that such information is medically helpful (e.g., Rosenberg et al., 2002; Bamshad and Olson, 2003; Burchard et al., 2003). What's more, official federal guidelines recently issued by the U.S. Food and Drug Administration recommend collection of ancestry data ("race/ethnic identity") in all clinical trials testing new drugs. Other researchers disagree and argue that such information is at best tenuous (King and Motulsky, 2002) or that it has no obvious medical use (e.g., Cooper et al., 2003). A major difficulty fueling this controversy has been poor communication between biomedical researchers and anthropologists and other evolutionary biologists. To allow for a more balanced and useful approach, anthropologist Clarence Gravlee has argued for adoption of a "more complex biocultural view of human biology" (2009, p. 54).

Even the general public has weighed in on this issue, defeating a 2003 California ballot measure that would have restricted the collection of "racial" (ethnic) information on medical records. There are no easy answers to the questions we've raised, and this is an even stronger argument for an informed public. The subject of race has been contentious, and anthropology and other disciplines have struggled to come to grips with it. Our new genetic tools have allowed us to expand our knowledge at a rate far beyond anything seen previously. But increased information alone doesn't permit us to fully address all human concerns. How we address diversity, both individually and collectively, must balance the potential scientific benefits against a history of social costs.

Population Genetics

As we defined it in Chapter 4, a *population* is a group of interbreeding individuals. More precisely, a population is the group within which an individual is most likely to find a mate. As such, a population is marked by a degree of genetic relatedness and shares a common **gene pool**.

In theory, this is a straightforward concept. In every generation, the genes (alleles) are mixed by recombination and rejoined through mating. What emerges in the next generation is a direct product of the genes going into the pool, which in turn is a product of who is mating with whom.

In practice, however, describing human populations is difficult. The largest human population that can be described is our entire species. All members of a species are *potentially* capable of interbreeding, but are incapable of producing fertile offspring with members of other species. Our species, like any other, is thus a *genetically closed system*. The problem arises not in describing who can potentially mate with whom, but in determining the exact pattern of those individuals who are doing so.

Factors that determine mate choice are geographical, ecological, and social. If individuals are isolated on a remote island in the middle of the Pacific Ocean, there isn't much chance that they'll find a mate outside the immediate vicinity. Such **breeding isolates** are fairly easily defined and are a favorite focus of microevolutionary studies. Geography plays a dominant

gene pool All of the genes shared by the reproductive members of a population.

breeding isolates Populations that are clearly isolated geographically and/or socially from other breeding groups.

role in producing these isolates by severely limiting the range of available mates. But even within these limits, cultural rules can easily play a deciding role by stipulating who is most appropriate among those who are potentially available.

Human population segments are defined as groups with relative degrees of **endogamy** (marrying/mating within the group). But these aren't totally closed systems. Gene flow often occurs between groups, and individuals may choose mates from distant locations. With the advent of modern transportation, the rate of **exogamy** (marrying/mating outside the group) has dramatically increased.

Today, most humans aren't clearly defined as members of particular populations because they don't belong to a breeding isolate. Inhabitants of large cities may appear to be members of a single population; but within the city, there's a complex system of social, ethnic, and religious boundaries that are crosscut to form smaller population segments. Besides being members of these highly open local population groupings, we're simultaneously members of overlapping gradations of larger populations—the immediate geographical region (a metropolitan area or perhaps an entire state), a section of the country, the entire nation, and ultimately the whole species (see **Fig. 15-5**).

After identifying specific human populations, the next step is to find out what evolutionary forces, if any, are operating on them. To determine whether evolution is taking place at a given genetic locus, we measure allele frequencies for specific traits. We then compare these observed frequencies with those predicted by a mathematical model called the **Hardy-Weinberg theory of genetic equilibrium**. This model gives us a baseline set of evolutionary expectations under known conditions.

The Hardy-Weinberg theory establishes a set of conditions in a hypothetical population where no evo-

lution occurs. In other words, no evolutionary forces are acting, and all genes have an equal chance of recombining in each generation (that is, there's random mating of individuals). More precisely, the conditions that such a population would be *assumed* to meet are as follows:

1. The population is infinitely large; this eliminates the possibility of random genetic drift or changes in allele frequencies due to chance.
2. There's no mutation; thus, no new alleles are being added by changes in genes.
3. There's no gene flow; thus, there's no exchange of genes with other populations that could alter allele frequencies.
4. Natural selection isn't operating; thus, specific alleles offer no advantage over others that might influence reproductive success.
5. Mating is random; therefore, there's nothing to influence who mates with whom, and all females are assumed to have an equal chance of mating with any male, and vice versa.

If all these conditions are met, allele frequencies won't change from one generation to the next (that is, no evolution will take place), and as long as these conditions prevail, the population maintains a permanent equilibrium. This equilibrium model provides population geneticists a standard against which they can compare actual circumstances. Notice that the conditions defining the Hardy-Weinberg equilibrium are an idealized, hypothetical state. In the real world, no actual population would fully meet any of these conditions. But don't be confused by this distinction. By explicitly defining the allele frequencies that would be expected if no evolutionary change were occurring (that is, in equilibrium), we establish a baseline with which to compare the allele fre-

endogamy Mating with individuals from the same group.

exogamy Mating pattern whereby individuals obtain mates from groups other than their own.

Hardy-Weinberg theory of genetic equilibrium The mathematical relationship expressing—under conditions in which no evolution is occurring—the predicted distribution of alleles in populations; the central theorem of population genetics.

quencies we actually observe in real human populations.

If the observed frequencies differ from those of the expected model, we can then say that evolution is taking place at the locus in question. The alternative, of course, is that the observed and expected frequencies don't differ enough that we can confidently say that evolution is occurring at a particular locus in a population. In fact, this is often what happens; in such cases, population geneticists aren't able to clearly define evolutionary change at the particular locus under study.

The simplest way to do a microevolutionary study is to observe a genetic trait that follows a simple Mendelian pattern and has only two alleles (A and a). Remember that there are only three possible genotypes: AA, Aa, and aa. Proportions of these genotypes (AA:Aa:aa) are a function of the allele frequencies themselves (percentage of A and percentage of a). To provide uniformity for all genetic loci, a standard notation is employed to refer to these frequencies:

Frequency of dominant allele (A) = p

Frequency of recessive allele (a) = q

Since in this case there are only two alleles, their combined total frequency must represent all possibilities. In other words, the sum of their separate frequencies must be 1:

$$\underset{\substack{\text{(Frequency of}\\ A \text{ alleles)}}}{p} + \underset{\substack{\text{(Frequency of}\\ a \text{ alleles)}}}{q} =$$

1 (100% of alleles at
the locus in question)

To determine the expected proportions of genotypes, we compute the chances of the alleles combining with one another in all possible combinations. Remember, they all have an equal chance of combining, and no new alleles are being added. These probabilities are a direct function of the frequency of the two alleles. The chances of all possible combinations

occurring randomly can be simply shown as:

$$
\begin{array}{r}
p + q \\
\times\ p + q \\
\hline
pq + q^2 \\
p^2 + pq \phantom{{} + q^2} \\
\hline
p^2 + 2pq + q^2
\end{array}
$$

Mathematically, this is known as a binomial expansion and can also be shown as:

$$(p + q)(p + q) = p^2 + 2pq + q^2$$

What we have just calculated is simply:

Allele Combination	Genotype Produced	Expected Proportion in Population
Chances of A combining with A	AA	$p \times p = p^2$
Chances of A combining with a;	Aa	$p \times q = $
a combining with A	aA	$2pq$
		$p \times q = $
Chances of a combining with a	aa	$q \times q = q^2$

Thus, p^2 is the frequency of the AA genotype, $2pq$ is the frequency of the Aa genotype, and q^2 is the frequency of the aa genotype, where p is the frequency of the dominant allele and q is the frequency of the recessive allele in a population.

Calculating Allele Frequencies

We can best demonstrate how geneticists use the Hardy-Weinberg formula by giving an example. Let's assume that a population contains 200 individuals, and we'll use the MN blood group locus as the gene to be measured. The two alleles of the MN locus produce two antigens (M and N) that are similar to the ABO antigens and are also located on red blood cells. Because the M and N alleles are codominant, we can ascertain everyone's phenotype by taking blood samples and testing

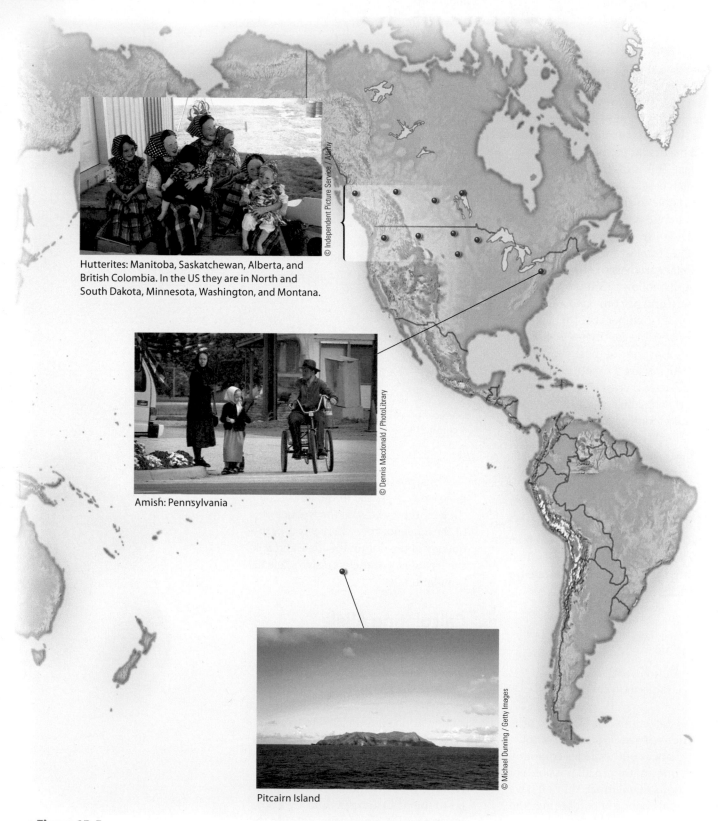

Hutterites: Manitoba, Saskatchewan, Alberta, and British Colombia. In the US they are in North and South Dakota, Minnesota, Washington, and Montana.

Amish: Pennsylvania

Pitcairn Island

▲ Figure 15-5

Examples of population isolates that have been studied by population geneticists. Some of these populations (e.g., Pitcairn Island) became isolated due to geography. Others, such as the Amish, became isolated due to social separation.

Saamis: northern Scandinavia, Finland, and the Kola Peninsula of northern Russia

© Norman Price / Alamy

People of Sardinia

© Peter Turnley / Corbis

Ainu: aborigines of Northern Japan

© Kenneth Garrett / National Geographic Stock

Australian aborigines

© William D. Bachman / Photo Researchers, Inc.

them in a process very similar to that for ABO (see Fig. 15-3). From the phenotypes, we can then directly calculate the observed allele frequencies. So let's see what we can determine.

All 200 individuals are tested, and the observed data for the three phenotypes are as follows:

Genotype	Number of individuals*	Percent	Number of Alleles	
			M	*N*
MM	80	40	160	0
MN	80	40	80	80
NN	40	20	0	80
Totals	200	100	240 + 160	= 400
Proportion			.6 + .4	= 1

_____

*Each individual has two alleles, so a person who's *MM* contributes two *M* alleles to the total gene pool; a person who's *MN* contributes one *M* and one *N*; and a person who's *NN* contributes two *N* alleles. For the *MN* locus, then, 200 individuals contribute 400 alleles.

From these observed results, we can count the number of *M* and *N* alleles and thus calculate the observed allele frequencies:

p = frequency of *M* = .6
q = frequency of *N* = .4

The total frequency of the two alleles combined should always equal 1. As you can see, they do.

Next, we need to calculate the expected genotypic proportions. This calculation comes directly from the Hardy-Weinberg equilibrium formula: $p^2 + 2pq + q^2 = 1$.

p^2	=	(.6)(.6)	=	.36
$2pq$	=	2(.6)(.4) = 2(.24)	=	.48
q^2	=	(.4)(.4)	=	.16
Total				1.00

There are only three possible genotypes: *MM*, *MN*, and *NN*. The total of the relative proportions should equal 1. Again, as you can see, they do.

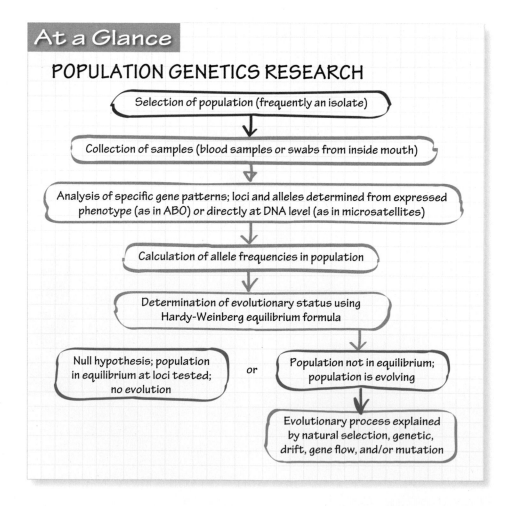

At a Glance

POPULATION GENETICS RESEARCH

Selection of population (frequently an isolate)

↓

Collection of samples (blood samples or swabs from inside mouth)

↓

Analysis of specific gene patterns; loci and alleles determined from expressed phenotype (as in ABO) or directly at DNA level (as in microsatellites)

↓

Calculation of allele frequencies in population

↓

Determination of evolutionary status using Hardy-Weinberg equilibrium formula

Null hypothesis; population in equilibrium at loci tested; no evolution

or

Population not in equilibrium; population is evolving

↓

Evolutionary process explained by natural selection, genetic, drift, gene flow, and/or mutation

Calculating Allele Frequencies: PTC Tasting in a Hypothetical Population

For the PTC tasting trait, it's assumed there are two alleles, T and t. Also, while dominance is displayed, it's incomplete. So it's theoretically possible to ascertain the phenotypes of heterozygotes. To simplify calculations for this example, we assume that all heterozygotes can be ascertained.

In our population of 500 individuals, we find the following observed phenotypic frequencies:

Genotype	Number of Individuals	Percent	Number of Alleles T	t
TT	125	25	250	0
Tt	325	65	325	325
tt	50	10	0	100
Totals	500	100	575	425

Thus, the observed allele frequencies are

$T(p) = .575$
$t(q) = .425$

The expected genotypic proportions are

p^2	=	(.575)(.575)	=	.33
$2pq$	=	2(.575)(.425)	=	.49
q^2	=	(.425)(.425)	=	.18

Now we compare the observed and expected genotypic frequencies:

	Expected Frequency	Expected Number of Individuals	Observed Frequency	Actual Number of Individuals with Each Genotype
TT	.33	165	.25	125
Tt	.49	245	.65	325
tt	.18	90	.10	50

These results show considerable departures of the observed genotypic proportions from those predicted under equilibrium conditions. Both types of homozygotes (*TT* and *tt*) are less commonly observed than expected, while the heterozygote (*Tt*) is more common than expected. A statistical test (called a chi-square) can be performed to test the statistical significance of this difference. The results of this test are shown in Appendix D.

Finally, we need to compare the two sets of data—that is, the observed frequencies (what we actually found in the population) with the expected frequencies (those predicted by Hardy-Weinberg under conditions of genetic equilibrium). How do these two sets of data compare?

	Expected Frequency	Expected Number of Individuals	Observed Frequency	Actual Number of Individuals with Each Genotype
MM	.36	72	.40	80
MN	.48	96	.40	80
NN	.16	32	.20	40

We can see that although the match between observed and expected frequencies isn't perfect, it's close enough statistically to satisfy equilibrium conditions. Since our population isn't a large one, sampling may easily account for the small observed differences. Our population is therefore probably in equilibrium (that is, it's not evolving at this locus).

Of course, the observed allele frequencies do sometimes vary enough from equilibrium predictions to suggest that the population isn't in equilibrium—that is, it's evolving. For example, consider the locus influencing PTC tasting. What makes PTC tasting such a useful characteristic is how easy it is to identify. Unlike blood antigens such as ABO or MN, PTC tasting can be tested by simply having subjects place a thin paper strip on their tongues. This paper contains concentrated PTC, and people either taste it or they don't. So testing is quick, inexpensive, and doesn't involve a blood test. With such an efficient means of screening subjects, we now consider a sample population of 500 individuals. The results from observing the phenotypes and calculations of expected genotypic proportions are shown in "A Closer Look: Calculating Allele Frequencies: PTC Tasting in a Hypothetical Population." You'll find additional examples of population genetics calculations in Appendix D.

Evolution in Action: Modern Human Populations

Once a population has been defined, it's possible to determine whether allele frequencies are stable (that is, in genetic equilibrium) or changing. As we've seen, the Hardy-Weinberg formula provides the tool to establish whether allele frequencies are indeed changing. But what factors cause changes in allele frequencies? There are a number of factors, including:

1. Production of new variation (that is, mutation)
2. Redistribution of variation through gene flow or genetic drift
3. Selection of "advantageous" allele combinations that promote reproductive success (that is, natural selection)

Notice that factors 1 and 2 constitute the first stage of the evolutionary process, as first emphasized by the Modern Synthesis, while factor 3 is the second stage (see Chapter 4). There's also another factor, as implied by the condition of genetic equilibrium that under idealized conditions all matings are random. Thus, an evolutionary alteration (that is, deviation from equilibrium) is called **nonrandom mating**.

Nonrandom Mating

Although sexual recombination doesn't itself alter allele frequencies, any consistent bias in mating patterns can change the genotypic proportions. By affecting genotype frequencies, nonrandom mating causes deviations from Hardy-Weinberg expectations of the proportions p^2, $2pq$, and q^2. It therefore sets the stage for the action of other evolutionary factors, particularly natural selection.

A form of nonrandom mating, called assortative mating, occurs when individuals of either similar phenotypes (positive assortative mating) or dissimilar phenotypes (negative assortative mating) mate more often than expected by Hardy-Weinberg predictions. However, in the vast majority of human populations, neither factor appears to have much influence.

Inbreeding is a second type of nonrandom mating, and it can have important medical and evolutionary consequences. Inbreeding occurs when relatives mate more often than expected. Such matings will increase homozygosity, since relatives who share close ancestors will probably also share more alleles than two unrelated people would. When relatives mate, their offspring have an increased probability of inheriting two copies of potentially harmful recessive alleles from a relative (perhaps a grandparent) they share in common. Many potentially deleterious genes that are normally "masked" in heterozygous carriers may be expressed in homozygous offspring of inbred matings and therefore "exposed" to the action of natural selection. Among offspring of first-cousin matings in the United States, the risk of congenital disorders is 2.3 times greater than it is for the overall population. Matings between especially close relatives (incest) often lead to multiple genetic defects.

All societies have incest taboos that ban matings between close relatives, such as between parent and child or brother and sister. Thus, these mat-

nonrandom mating Pattern of mating in which individuals choose mates preferentially, with mate choice based on criteria such as social status, ethnicity, or biological relationship. In nonrandom mating, an individual doesn't have an equal chance of mating with all other individuals in the group.

inbreeding A type of nonrandom mating in which relatives mate more often than predicted under random mating conditions.

ings usually occur less frequently than predicted under random mating conditions. Whether biological factors also interact to inhibit such behavior has long been a topic of debate among anthropologists. For many social, economic, and ecological reasons, exogamy is an advantageous strategy for hunting and gathering bands. Selective pressures may also play a part, since highly inbred offspring have a greater chance of expressing a recessive genetic disorder and thereby lowering their reproductive fitness. What's more, inbreeding reduces genetic variability among offspring, potentially reducing reproductive success (Murray, 1980). In this regard, it's interesting to note that **incest avoidance** is widespread among vertebrates. Detailed studies of free-ranging chimpanzees indicate that they usually avoid incestuous matings within their family group, although exceptions do occur (Constable et al., 2001). In fact, in most primate species, adults of one sex consistently find mates from groups other than the one in which they were reared (see Chapter 7). As we've seen, recognition of close kin apparently is an ability displayed by several (perhaps all) primates. Primatologists are currently investigating this aspect of our primate cousins. Apparently, both biological factors (in common with other primates) and uniquely human cultural factors have interacted during hominin evolution to produce this universal behavior pattern among contemporary societies.

Human Biocultural Evolution

We've defined *culture* as the human strategy of adaptation. Human beings live in cultural environments that are continually modified by human activity; thus, evolutionary processes are understandable only within this cultural context. We've discussed at length how natural selection operates within specific environmental settings.

For humans and many of our hominin ancestors, this means an environment dominated by culture. For example, the sickle-cell allele hasn't always been an important genetic factor in human populations. Before the development of agriculture, humans rarely, if ever, lived close to mosquito-breeding areas. With the spread in Africa of **slash-and-burn agriculture**, perhaps in just the last 2,000 years, penetration and clearing of tropical rain forests occurred. This deforestation created open, stagnant pools that provided prime mosquito-breeding areas in close proximity to human settlements. DNA analyses have further confirmed such a recent origin and spread of the sickle-cell allele in West Africa. A recent study of a population from Senegal has estimated the origin of the Hb^S mutation in this group at between 2,100 and 1,250 ya (Currat et al., 2002).

So quite recently, and for the first time, malaria struck human populations with its full impact; and it became a powerful selective force. No doubt, humans attempted to adjust culturally to these circumstances, and many biological adaptations also probably came into play. The sickle-cell trait is one of these biological adaptations. But there's a definite cost involved with such an adaptation. Carriers have increased resistance to malaria and presumably higher reproductive success, though some of their offspring may be lost through the genetic disease sickle-cell anemia. So there's a counterbalancing of selective forces with an advantage for carriers only in malarial environments. (The genetic patterns of recessive traits such as sickle-cell anemia are discussed in Chapter 4.)

Following World War II, extensive DDT spraying by the World Health Organization began systematic control of mosquito-breeding areas in the tropics. Forty years of DDT spraying killed millions of mosquitoes; but at the same time, natural selection acted to produce several strains of DDT-resistant mosquitoes (**Fig. 15-6**). Accordingly, especially in the tropics, malaria is

incest avoidance In animals, the tendency not to mate with close relatives. This tendency may be due to various social and ecological factors that keep the individuals apart. There may also be innate factors that lead to incest avoidance, but these aren't well understood.

slash-and-burn agriculture A traditional land-clearing practice involving the cutting and burning of trees and vegetation. In many areas, fields are abandoned after a few years and clearing occurs elsewhere.

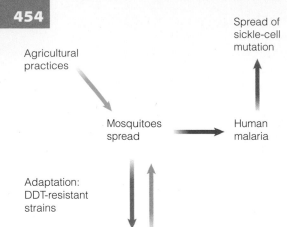

▲ **Figure 15-6**
Evolutionary interactions affecting the frequency of the sickle-cell allele.

again on the rise, with up to 500 million new cases reported annually and more than 1 million people dying each year.

A genetic characteristic (such as sickle-cell trait) that provides a reproductive advantage to heterozygotes in certain environments is a clear example of natural selection in action among human populations. The precise evolutionary mechanism in the sickle-cell example is called a **balanced polymorphism**. A polymorphism, as we've defined it, is a trait with more than one allele at a locus in a population. But when a harmful allele (such as the sickle-cell allele) has a higher frequency than can be accounted for by mutation alone, a more detailed evolutionary explanation is required. In this case, the additional mechanism is natural selection.

This brings us to the second part of the term. By "balanced" we mean the interaction of selective pressures operating on specific alleles in a particular environment (in this case, the sickle-cell alleles in malarial areas). Some individuals (mainly homozygous normals) will die of the infectious disease malaria. Others (homozygous recessives) will die of the inherited disease sickle-cell anemia. Thus, the individuals with the highest reproductive success are the heterozygotes who have sickle-cell trait. These heterozygotes pass both the normal allele (Hb^A) and the sickle-cell allele (Hb^S) to offspring, thus maintaining both alleles at fairly high frequencies. Since one allele in this population won't significantly increase in frequency over the other allele, this situation will become "balanced" and will persist as long as malaria continues to be a selective factor.

Lactose intolerance, which involves an individual's ability to digest milk, is another example of human biocultural evolution. In all human populations, infants and young children are able to digest milk, an obvious necessity for any young mammal. One ingredient of milk is *lactose*, a sugar that's broken down by the enzyme lactase. In most mammals, including many humans, the gene that codes for lactase production "switches off" in adolescence. Once this happens, if a person drinks fresh milk, the lactose ferments in the large intestine, leading to diarrhea and severe gastrointestinal upset. So, as you might expect, adults stop drinking fresh milk. Among many African and Asian populations (a majority of humankind today), most adults are lactose-intolerant (**Table 15-1**). But in other populations, including some Africans and Europeans, adults continue to produce lactase and are able to digest fresh milk. This continued production of lactase is called **lactase persistence**.

Evidence has suggested a simple dominant mode of inheritance for lactase persistence in adults. The environment also plays a role in expression of the trait—that is, whether a person will be lactose-intolerant—since intestinal bacteria can somewhat buffer the adverse effects of drinking fresh milk. Because these bacteria increase with previous exposure, some tolerance can be acquired, even in individuals who genetically are not lactase-persistent.

Throughout most of hominin evolution, milk was unavailable after weaning, so there *may* be a selective advantage to switching off the gene that codes for lactase production. So why can some adults (the majority in some populations) tolerate milk? The distribution of lactose-tolerant populations may provide an answer to this question, and it suggests a powerful cultural influence on this trait.

Europeans, who are generally lactose-tolerant, are partly descended from Middle Eastern populations. Often economically dependent on pastoralism, these groups raised cows and/or goats and probably drank considerable quantities of milk. In such a cul-

balanced polymorphism The maintenance of two or more alleles in a population due to the selective advantage of the heterozygote.

lactase persistence In adults, the continued production of lactase, the enzyme that breaks down lactose (milk sugar). This allows adults in some human populations to digest fresh milk products. The discontinued production of lactase in adults leads to lactose intolerance and the inability to digest fresh milk.

tural environment, strong selection pressures apparently favored lactose tolerance, a trait that has been retained in modern Europeans. Genetic evidence from north-central Europe supports this interpretation. DNA analysis of both cattle and humans suggests that these species have, to some extent, influenced each other genetically. The interaction between humans and cattle resulted in cattle that produce high-quality milk and humans with the ability to digest it (Beja-Pereira et al., 2003). In other words, more than 5,000 ya, populations of north-central Europe were selectively breeding cattle for higher milk yields. And as these populations were increasing their dependence on fresh milk, they were inadvertently selecting for the gene that produces lactase persistence in themselves.

But perhaps even more informative is the distribution of lactose tolerance in Africa, where the majority of people are lactose-intolerant. Groups such as the Fulani and Tutsi have been pastoralists for perhaps thousands of years and have much higher rates of lactase persistence than nonpastoralists (**Fig. 15-7**). Presumably, like their

European counterparts, they've retained the ability to produce lactase because of their continued consumption of fresh milk (Powell and Tishkoff, 2003).

Recent molecular evidence has supported this hypothesis, showing a similar coevolution of humans and cattle in East Africa (Tishkoff et al., 2007). The pattern of DNA mutations (SNPs) in Africa is different from that seen in Europe, strongly suggesting that lactase persistence has evolved independently in the two regions. In fact, the data show that lactase persistence has evolved several times just in East Africa. The importance of cattle domestication in providing milk for human groups was clearly a cultural and dietary shift of major importance. As humans selectively bred cattle to produce more and higher-quality milk, they promoted fairly rapid evolution in these animals. At the same time,

TABLE 15.1	Frequencies of Lactase Persistence

Population Group	Percent
U.S. whites	81–98
Swedes and Danes	>90
Swiss	12
U.S. blacks	70–77
Ibos	99
Bantu	10
Fulani	50
Chinese	1
Thais	1
Asian Americans	<5
Native Australians	85

Source: Lerner and Libby, 1976, Tishkoff et al., 2007.

◀ **Figure 15-7**
Fulani cattle herder with his cattle.

► **Figure 15-8**
Natives of Mongolia rely heavily on milk products from goats and sheep, but they mostly consume these foods in the form of cheese and yogurt.

humans in different areas coevolved through natural selection as allele frequencies shifted to produce higher frequencies of lactase persistence.

As we've seen, the geographical distribution of lactase persistence is related to a history of cultural dependence on fresh milk products. There are, however, some populations that rely on dairying but don't have high rates of lactase persistence (**Fig. 15-8**). It's been suggested that such groups have traditionally consumed their milk in the form of cheese and yogurt, in which the lactose has been broken down by bacterial action.

The interaction of human cultural environments and changes in lactose tolerance in human populations is another example of biocultural evolution. In the last few thousand years, cultural factors have initiated specific evolutionary changes in human groups. Such cultural factors have probably influenced the course of human evolution for at least 3 million years, and today they are of paramount importance.

Summary of Main Topics

- Physically visible traits, traditionally used in attempts to classify humans into clearly defined groups ("races"), have emphasized such features as skin color, hair color, hair form, head shape, and nose shape.
- However, all of these physical characteristics are not only influenced by several genetic loci but are also modified by the environ-ment. As a result, these traditional markers of race aren't reliable indicators of genetic relationships, and they're not biologically useful in depicting patterns of human diversity.
- Since the middle of the twentieth century, more precise techniques have allowed a far better understanding of actual patterns of human variation, beginning with information obtained from the phenotypic expression of Mendelian traits such as blood groups. Population genetics analyses of several of these genetic polymorphisms proved useful in showing broad patterns, such as the high degree of within-population variation and the relatively minor amount of between-population variation.

- Since the 1990s, the development and rapid application of comparative genomics have drastically expanded genetic data. These powerful new tools allow evaluation of human population variation using thousands (or hundreds of thousands) of precisely defined DNA sequences. Such population studies are aimed at reconstructing the microevolutionary population history of our species and understanding the varied roles of natural selection, genetic drift, gene flow, and mutation.

- For humans, of course, culture also plays a crucial evolutionary role. Interacting with biological influences, these factors define the distinctive biocultural nature of human evolution. Two excellent examples of recent human biocultural evolution relate to resistance to malaria (involving the sickle-cell allele) and lactase persistence.

Critical Thinking Questions

1. Imagine you're with a group of friends discussing human diversity and the number of races. One friend says there are three clearly defined races, a second says five, while the third isn't sure. Would you agree with any of them? Why or why not?

2. For the same group of friends mentioned in question 1 (none of whom have had a course in biological anthropology), how would you explain how scientific knowledge fits (or doesn't fit) with their preconceived notions about human races?

3. Explain how the concept of race has developed in the Western world. What are the limitations of this approach? How have current genetic studies changed this view?

4. Explain how modern genetic studies can contribute to our understanding of biological variation in humans. Be as specific as possible.

New Frontiers in RESEARCH

Molecular Applications in Modern Human Biology

As we have shown in Chapters 14 and 15, anthropologists and geneticists are actively investigating human genetic variation in the ancient past as well as attempting to learn more about the patterns of variation seen in contemporary human populations. New techniques are allowing much faster and more economical analyses. The information is expanding exponentially, and researchers are now able to learn vastly more about human variation than just five years ago. These are indeed exciting times to be a student of human biology!

One of the most fascinating areas of study concerns reconstructing the history of human migrations and resultant intermixing of previously more isolated populations. As we've seen, all modern populations ultimately came initially from African ancestors, sometime after 100,000 ya.

Excepting for rare instances of preservation of ancient DNA (see New Frontiers in Research following Chapter 13), all of our information comes from analysis of DNA patterns in living populations. Obviously, a lot of mixing (that is, gene flow) has occurred over the centuries, so the DNA

in many groups reflects a mixed heritage and a complex history of varied migrations. Nevertheless, numerous populations still exist which have remained at least partially isolated, and their DNA tells fascinating stories of migrations dating to the earliest dispersal of modern humans from Africa—or even earlier than that.

So, let's look at what the newest genetic studies can tell us about more ancient patterns of human variation. Geneticist Sarah Tishkoff and colleagues recently examined over 1300 DNA sequences in a genome-wide scan from more than one hundred indigenous African populations (for comparisons, 4 African-American groups as well as 60 other, non-African, populations were also evaluated) (Tishkoff et al., 2009).

Many of the study results confirmed earlier work, but this research included by far the largest and most varied set of African populations yet analyzed. As a result, conclusions are much better substantiated and more detailed regarding genetic variation in light of linguistic, geographic, and subsistence patterning throughout the Africa continent.

> "... their DNA tells fascinating stories of migrations dating to the earliest dispersal of modern humans from Africa..."

Key findings confirm greater genetic diversity within African groups as compared to anywhere else in the world. Moreover, the greatest diversity and highest number of unique genes (called "private alleles") occur among the San population of south-

ern Africa. The San traditionally have been hunter-gatherers, and two other African hunter-gatherer populations show close genetic relationships with the San—suggesting these surviving populations are the most closely related to the earliest modern human African ancestors. Indeed, as we'll see in a moment, the San, in particular, are the closest living descendants in the world to the original modern *H. sapiens*.

Another interesting finding shows that shared language among contemporary groups usually closely parallels degree of genetic relatedness. This reminds us that linguistic studies, as part of a broader biocultural perspective, are crucial to understanding human population history (Campbell and Tishkoff, 2010).

The accuracy of genetic information has continued to improve dramatically in recent years. Standard genetic polymorphisms (such as blood groups) provided some useful information. Data from mtDNA and the Y-chromosome were much better, but subject to misinterpretation. Wider data sets from nuclear DNA are far more accurate, especially when hundreds (or thousands) of DNA segments are used in a "genome-wide" approach (as discussed in the Chapter).

Lastly, the ability to evaluate the *entire* genome of individuals (that is, full sequencing of 3 billion + nucleotides) is the most informative—but also the most expensive. So, only a few studies have yet been able to examine this type of information (one was discussed in the New Frontiers in Research feature following Chapter 13 relating to the Neandertal genetic contribution to modern populations).

Another recent investigation using full genomes also focused on ancestry in African populations. Two South African individuals had their full genomes sequenced and analyzed, one a San, and the other a descendant of Bantu-speaking ancestors. Interestingly, the South African of Bantu descent is quite a well-known individ-

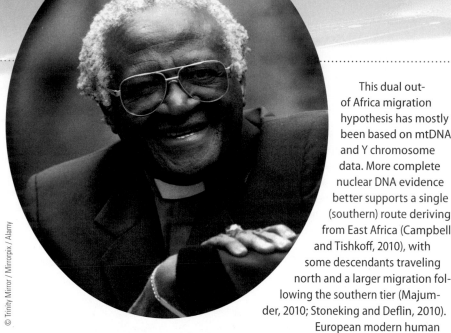

▲ Figure 1

Archbishop Desmond Tutu, who recently had his entire nuclear genome sequenced. This information was compared to other South African individuals from a different ancestry.

© Trinity Mirror / Mirrorpix / Alamy

ual, Archbishop Desmond Tutu (**Fig. 1**). In addition, another 3 San individuals were evaluated for partial genomes (focusing on protein-coding regions) (Schuster et al., 2010).

The results emphasize how genetically diverse are people of San ancestry. In fact, two individuals from this group are as genetically distinct from each other as, for example, is a European from an Asian individual. The degree of unique ('private alleles") found among the San in the study discussed above is much further supported by information from the whole genome investigation in this research. In fact, the researchers found in their small sample of 5 South African men 1.3 million novel DNA differences, not reported previously in other populations. This is quite astounding, as it expands the range of known genetic variants for *Homo sapiens* by more than 10% from what has been reported previously for the whole world.

Based on the best current evidence, major migration(s) of modern humans out of Africa took place 50,000-60,000 ya. One hypothesis proposed two major migration routes. One of these was a "northern" route, up through the Nile Valley in North Africa, directly into the Middle East. A second route suggests a migration from East Africa across the mouth of the Red Sea, into Arabia, then along south Asia (notably southern India), and eventually all the way to Australia, reaching there as early as 50,000 ya (Kayser, 2010).

This dual out-of Africa migration hypothesis has mostly been based on mtDNA and Y chromosome data. More complete nuclear DNA evidence better supports a single (southern) route deriving from East Africa (Campbell and Tishkoff, 2010), with some descendants traveling north and a larger migration following the southern tier (Majumder, 2010; Stoneking and Deflin, 2010). European modern human population history can be traced back to about 45,000 ya, and further genetic data suggest at least 4 subsequent significant migration episodes, culminating in historical times, about 5,000 years ago (Soares et al., 2010). Understanding the origins of New World populations remains perhaps the biggest enigma regarding the worldwide history of major population expansions. Unquestionably, all the genetic data confirm that Native Americans have Asian origins. However, when and by which routes the first Americans arrived and how quickly they spread over North and South America remain unclear and issues of ongoing debate. Nevertheless, more complete molecular data (from contemporary populations as well as ancient DNA) might soon provide much better answers to these nagging questions (O'Rourke and Raff, 2010).

These detailed genetic studies provide huge amounts of new information and stimulate entirely new avenues for future research—with new hypotheses requiring more precise testing. Understanding human population history over the last several thousand years is certainly interesting, but it can be fun too. It's now possible, quite easy, in fact, for you to investigate your own ancestry. A very large international team (sponsored by the National Geographic Society) has assembled genetic data on a wide range of human populations. Thus far, most of the available information comes from genes in mitochondria (mtDNA) and from the Y-chromosome. As mentioned, such genetic data are not as specific or as accurate as more detailed (and more expensive) analyses. Still, the information is quite intriguing and useful, and it's now directly available to the general public. As part of the "Genographic Project," you can send in a bit of your own DNA (from a swab sample inside your cheek) to see what your genes might be able to tell you about your ancestors and where they came from.*

SOURCES

Campbell, Michael C. and Sarah A. Tishkoff
2010   The evolution of human genetic and phenotypic variation in Africa. *Current Biology* 20:R166–R173.

Kayser, Manfred
2010   The human genetic history of Oceania: Near and remote views of dispersal. *Current Biology* 20:R194–R201.

Majumder, Partha P.
2010   The Human Genetic History of South Asia. *Current Biology* 20:R184–R187.

O'Rourke, Dennis H. and Jennifer A. Raff
2010   The human genetic history of the Americas: The final frontier. *Current Biology* 20:R202–R207.

Schuster, Stephan C., Webb Miller, Aakrosh Ratan, et al.
2010   Complete Khoisan and Bantu genomes from southern Africa. *Nature* 463:943-947.

Soares, Pedro, Alessandro Achilli, Ornella Semino, et al.
2010   The archaeogenetics of Europe. *Current Biology* 20:R174–R183.

Stoneking, Mark and Frederick Delfin
2010   The human genetic history of east Asia: Weaving a complex tapestry. *Current Biology* 20:R188-R193

Tishkoff, Sarah A., Floyd A. Reed, Françoise R. Friedlaender, et al.
2010   The genetic structure and history of Africans and African Americans. *Science* 324:1035-1043.

* The National Geographic Society has a Genographic website: (https://www3.nationalgeographic.com/genographic/journey.html). Go to this website to find information about basic genetics and the latest data on patterns of human migrations. You can also send a sample of your own DNA to see what your genetic markers (from mtDNA or the Y-chromosome) might say about your ancestors and where they journeyed.

Modern humans have had to adapt, both culturally and biologically, to extreme environments.

16

Modern Human Biology: Patterns of Adaptation

Key Questions

▶ Can patterns of adaptation in contemporary human populations be linked to the role of natural selection?

▶ What is the main advantage of having less pigmented skin outside the tropics?

▶ Why is the study of SNPs important to understanding human biological adaptation?

▶ How has infectious disease become a selective force in human evolution?

I n previous chapters, we explored the genetic bases for biological variation within and between human populations. We discussed how, as a species, humans are remarkably genetically uniform compared with our closest primate relatives. We've also placed these discussions within an evolutionary framework, emphasizing the roles of natural selection and genetic drift in human evolution. With this foundation, we can turn our attention to some of the many challenges we have faced through our evolutionary journey and consider some of the ways we've met these challenges as a species, as populations, and as individuals.

Early humans migrated out of Africa some 200,000–100,000 ya, and we now permanently inhabit the entire planet except for the oceans, the highest mountain peaks, and Antarctica. But as human populations spread over the earth, they had to cope with variations in ultraviolet (UV) radiation, altitude, temperature, humidity, diet, and infectious disease. All of these factors, plus the fact that populations were separated from one another by enormous distances, have combined to produce many forms of adaptation and variation in our species.

The Adaptive Significance of Human Variation

As you know, when biological anthropologists study human variation, they consider all evolutionary factors. But natural selection favoring adaptive traits was the most important mechanism that produced the variation we see today. We must also bear in mind that to accommodate differences in climate, terrain, and available resources, humans had to adopt lifestyles that differed with regard to technology and diet. As time passed, and especially after the domestication of plants and animals beginning around 14,000 ya, cultural changes, including dietary practices, exerted an even greater degree of selective pressure. Thus, as populational differences in lactose tolerance demonstrate, the interaction between culture and biology became ever more important to human adaptive responses, and this interaction was responsible for changes in the frequencies of many alleles. Since the sequencing of the human genome in 2003, geneticists, armed with an array of new technologies, have been looking at the genes that govern adaptive traits in many populations. Specifically, they've been focusing on single nucleotide polymorphisms, or SNPs, studying how differences in single DNA bases alter gene action and how their frequencies vary between populations. Within the next few years, our understanding of many aspects of human adaptation will increase dramatically, owing to advances in genetic research that will allow the testing not only of long-held hypotheses, but also of new ones.

To survive, all organisms need to maintain the normal functions of internal organs, tissues, and cells. What's more, they must accomplish this task in the context of an ever-changing environment. Even during the course of a single, seemingly uneventful day, there are numerous fluctuations in temperature, wind, solar radiation, humidity, and so on. Physical activity also places **stress** on physiological mechanisms. The body must accommodate all these changes by compensating in some way to maintain internal constancy, or **homeostasis**, and all life-forms have evolved physiological mechanisms that, within limits, achieve this goal.

Physiological response to environmental change is influenced by genetic factors. We've already defined adaptation as a response to environmental conditions in populations and individuals. In a narrower sense, adaptation refers to long-term evolutionary (that is, genetic) changes that characterize all individuals within a population or species.

Examples of long-term adaptations in humans include physiological responses to heat (sweating) or excessive levels of UV light (deeply pigmented skin near the equator). These characteristics are the results of evolutionary change in our species or in populations, and they don't vary

because of short-term environmental change. For example, the ability to sweat isn't lost in people who spend their lives in predominantly cool areas. Likewise, individuals born with dark skin wouldn't become pale, even if they were never exposed to sunlight.

Acclimatization is another kind of physiological response to environmental conditions, and it can be short-term, long-term, or even permanent. The physiological responses to environmental stressors are at least partially influenced by genetic factors, but some can also be affected by the duration and severity of the exposure, technological buffers (such as shelter or clothing), individual behavior, weight, and overall body size.

The simplest form of acclimatization is a temporary and rapid adjustment to an environmental change (for example, tanning). Another example is one you may not know about, although you've probably experienced it: the rapid increase in hemoglobin production that occurs in people who live at lower elevations but travel to higher ones. (It's happened in your own body if you've spent a few days at a ski resort.) In both these examples, the physiological changes are temporary. Tans fade when exposure to sunlight is reduced, and hemoglobin production drops to original levels after returning to lower elevations.

Another type of acclimatization, called developmental acclimatization, results from exposure to an environmental challenge during growth and development. Because this kind of acclimatization is incorporated into an individual's physiology, it isn't reversible. An example of developmental acclimatization is the physiological responses we see in lifelong residents of high altitude.

In this section, we present some of the many examples of how humans respond to environmental challenges. Some of these examples describe adaptations that characterize our entire species; others are shared by most or all members of certain populations.

stress In a physiological context, any factor that acts to disrupt homeostasis; more precisely, the body's response to any factor that threatens its ability to maintain homeostasis.

homeostasis A condition of balance, or stability, within a biological system, maintained by the interaction of physiological mechanisms that compensate for changes (both external and internal).

acclimatization Physiological responses to changes in the environment that occur during an individual's lifetime. Such responses may be temporary or permanent, depending on the duration of the environmental change and when in the individual's life it occurs. The capacity for acclimatization may typify an entire population or species, and because it's under genetic influence, it's subject to evolutionary factors such as natural selection and genetic drift.

Solar Radiation and Skin Color

For many years, skin color has been cited as an example of adaptation through natural selection in humans. In general, pigmentation in indigenous populations prior to European contact (beginning around 1500) followed a particular geographical distribution, especially in the Old World. This pattern pretty much holds true today. As **Figure 16-1** shows, populations with the most pigmentation are found in the tropics, while lighter skin color is associated with more northern latitudes, especially the long-term inhabitants of northwestern Europe.

Three substances influence skin color: hemoglobin, the protein carotene, and, most important, the pigment melanin. Melanin is a granular substance produced by cells called melanocytes, located in the outer layer of the skin (**Fig. 16-2**). Melanin is extremely important because it acts as a built-in sunscreen by absorbing potentially dangerous ultraviolet (UV) rays that are present, but not visible, in

sunlight. So melanin protects us from overexposure to UV radiation, which frequently causes genetic mutations in skin cells. These mutations can lead to skin cancer, which, if left untreated, can eventually spread to other organs and even result in death (see "A Closer Look: Skin Cancer and UV Radiation").

As mentioned earlier, exposure to sunlight triggers a protective mechanism in the form of tanning, the result of temporarily increased melanin production (acclimatization). This response occurs in all humans except albinos, who carry a genetic mutation that prevents their melanocytes from producing melanin. But even people who do produce melanin differ in their ability to tan. For instance, in all populations, women tend not to tan as deeply as men. More importantly, however, people of northern European descent tend to have very fair skin, blue eyes, and light hair. Their cells produce only small amounts of melanin, and when exposed to sunlight, they have almost no ability to increase production. But in areas closest to the equator (the tropics), where the sun's rays

▼ **Figure 16-1**
Geographical distribution of skin color in indigenous human populations. (After Biasutti, 1959.)

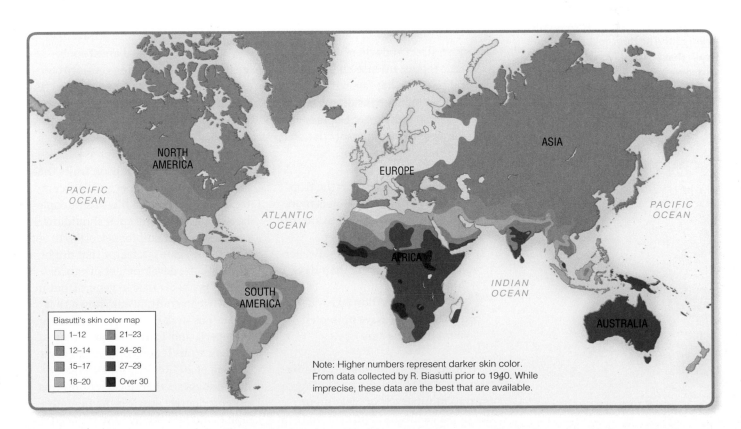

Biasutti's skin color map

1–12	21–23
12–14	24–26
15–17	27–29
18–20	Over 30

Note: Higher numbers represent darker skin color. From data collected by R. Biasutti prior to 1940. While imprecise, these data are the best that are available.

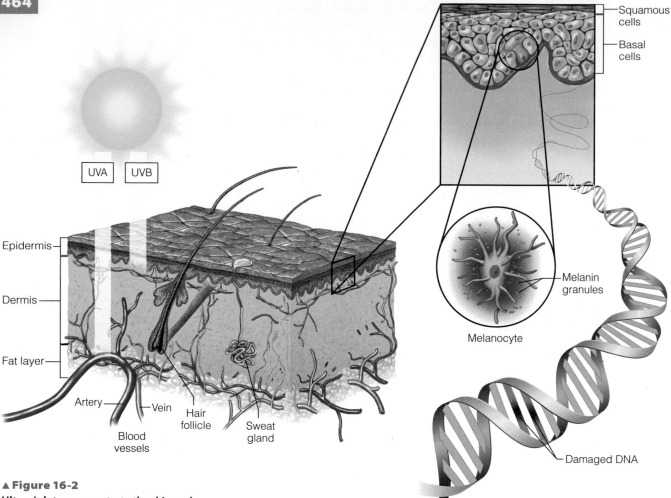

Squamous cells

Basal cells

UVA   UVB

Epidermis

Dermis

Fat layer

Artery

Vein

Hair follicle

Blood vessels

Sweat gland

Melanin granules

Melanocyte

Damaged DNA

▲ **Figure 16-2**
Ultraviolet rays penetrate the skin and can eventually damage DNA within skin cells. The three major types of cells that can be affected are squamous cells, basal cells, and melanocytes.

are most direct and where exposure to UV light is most intense and constant, natural selection has favored deeply pigmented skin. In considering the cancer-causing effects of UV radiation from an evolutionary perspective, keep in mind these three points:

1. Early hominins lived in the tropics, where solar radiation is more intense than in temperate areas to the north and south.
2. Unlike most modern city dwellers, early hominins spent their days outdoors.
3. Early hominins didn't wear clothing that would have protected them from the sun.

Under these conditions, UV radiation was a powerful agent selecting for maximum levels of melanin production as a means of protection from

UV radiation. Physical anthropologists have long considered this protection to be very important because UV radiation is the most common cause of skin cancer. There's an important objection to this hypothesis, however. As we mentioned in Chapter 4, natural selection can act only on traits that affect reproduction. Because cancers tend to occur later in life, after people have had their children, it should theoretically be difficult for selection to act effectively against a factor that might facilitate the development of cancer. This is probably true in general, but in one African study, it was shown that all albinos in dark-skinned populations of Nigeria and Tanzania had either precancerous lesions or skin cancer by the age of 20 (Robins, 1991). This evidence suggests that in early hominins of reproductive age, less pigmented skin could potentially have reduced individual reproductive fitness in regions of intense sunlight.

However, Jablonski (1992) and Jablonski and Chaplin (2000, 2010) disagree that skin cancer was the most important factor and have provided convincing evidence for another, probably more important explanation for heavily pigmented skin in the tropics. This explanation concerns the degradation of folate by UV radiation. Folate is a B vitamin that isn't stored in the body and must be replenished through dietary sources such as leafy green vegetables and certain fruits. Adequate levels of folate are required for cell division, and this is especially important during embryonic and fetal development, when cell division is rapid and ongoing. In pregnant women, insufficient levels of folate are associated with numerous fetal developmental disorders, including **neural tube** defects such as **spina bifida** (Fig. 16-3). The consequences of severe neural tube defects can include pain, infection, paralysis, and even failure of the brain to develop. Given the importance of folate to many processes related to reproduction, it's clear that maintaining adequate levels of this vitamin contributes to individual reproductive fitness.

Studies have shown that UV radiation rapidly depletes folate serum levels both in laboratory experiments and in light-skinned individuals. These findings have implications for pregnant women, children, and the evolution of dark skin in early hominins. Jablonski (1992) has proposed that the earliest hominins may have had light skin covered with dark hair, as is seen in chimpanzees and gorillas (who have darker skin on exposed body parts, such as faces and hands). But as loss of body hair occurred in hominins, dark skin evolved rather rapidly as a protective response to the damaging effects of UV radiation on folate.

The maintenance of sufficient levels of folate and, to a lesser degree, the occurrence of skin cancer have no doubt been selective agents that have favored dark skin in humans living where UV radiation is most intense.

Therefore, we have good explanations for darker skin in the tropics. But what about less pigmented skin? Why do indigenous populations in higher latitudes, farther from the equator, have lighter skin? There are several closely related hypotheses, and recent studies have added strength to these arguments.

As hominins migrated out of Africa into Asia and Europe, they faced new selective pressures. In particular, those populations that eventually occupied northern Europe encountered cold temperatures and cloudy skies, frequently during summer as well as winter. Winter also meant many fewer hours of daylight, and with the sun well to the south, solar radiation was very indirect. What's more, people in these areas wore animal skins and other types of clothing, which blocked the sun's rays. For some time, researchers proposed that because of reduced exposure to sunlight, the advantages of deeply pigmented skin in the tropics no longer applied, and selection for melanin production may have been relaxed.

However, relaxed selection for dark skin doesn't adequately explain the very depigmented skin seen in some northern Europeans. In fact, natural selection appears to have acted very rapidly against darker skin as humans moved to northern latitudes. This is because the need for a physiological UV filter was outweighed by another extremely important biological necessity, the production of vitamin D. The theory concerning the role of vitamin D is called the *vitamin D hypothesis*.

Since the early twentieth century, scientists have known that vitamin D is essential for the mineralization and normal growth of bones during infancy and childhood because it enables the body to absorb calcium (the major source of bone mineral) from dietary sources. Vitamin D is also required for the continued mineralization of bones in adults. Many foods, including

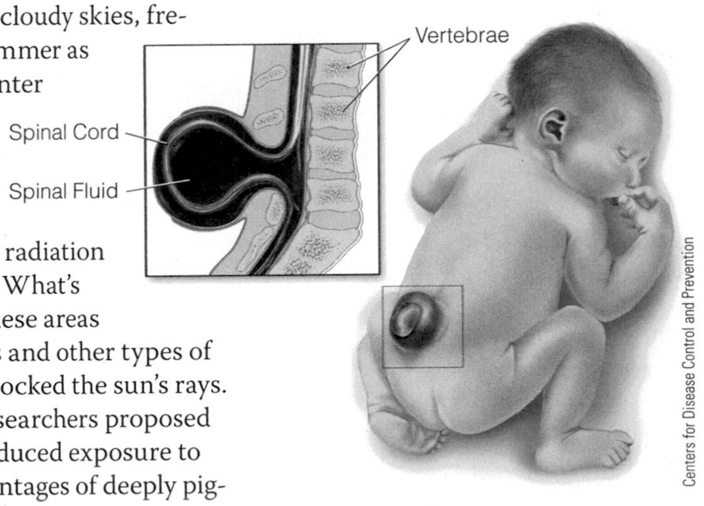

Vertebrae

Spinal Cord

Spinal Fluid

Centers for Disease Control and Prevention

▲ **Figure 16-3**
Spina bifida occurs when the back of the vetebral column (spine) fails to close during embryonic development. It ranges from very mild to lethal. In this illustration the last two lumbar vertebrae have failed to fuse and the spinal cord has protruded through the opening and into the skin.

neural tube In early embryonic development, the anatomical structure that develops to form the brain and spinal cord.

spina bifida A condition in which the arch of one or more vertebrae fails to fuse and form a protective barrier around the spinal cord.

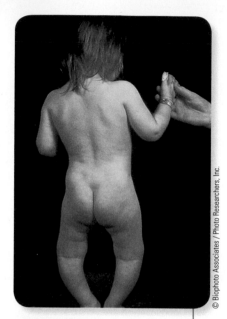

▲ **Figure 16-4**
A child with rickets. Her leg bones have not been properly mineralized due to lack of vitamin D. Thus, they are bowed because they aren't strong enough to support the weight of her upper body.

© Biophoto Associates / Photo Researchers, Inc.

fish oils, egg yolk, butter, cream, and liver, are good sources of vitamin D. But the body's primary source of vitamin D is its own ability to synthesize it through the interaction of UV radiation and a form of cholesterol found in skin cells. Therefore, adequate exposure to sunlight is essential to normal bone growth.

Insufficient amounts of vitamin D during childhood result in rickets, a condition that leads to skeletal deformities, especially in the weight-bearing bones of the legs and pelvis. Thus, people with rickets frequently have bowed legs and pelvic deformities (**Fig. 16-4**). Pelvic deformities are of particular concern for pregnant women, since they can lead to a narrowing of the birth canal. Without surgical intervention, both the mother and her infant can die during childbirth, thus allowing natural selection to act powerfully in favor of any mechanism that provides proper bone mineralization.

In addition to its role in bone mineralization, vitamin D has many other critical functions. In the body, vitamin D is converted to a different molecule called 1,25D, and this molecule can attach directly to DNA, after which it acts as a regulator of more than 1,000 different genes (Tavera-Mendoza and White, 2007). Some of these genes are involved in cell replication, and because 1,25D regulates this activity, it appears to provide some protection against certain cancers, especially prostate and colon cancer (Lin and White, 2004). (Cancer is caused by uncontrolled cell replication.) Moreover, 1,25D reduces inflammation and may eventually be used as a basis for treating certain diseases, including multiple sclerosis (Tavera-Mendoza and White, 2007).

Other genes influenced by 1,25D produce proteins that act as natural antibiotics to kill certain bacteria and viruses, including *Mycobaterium tuberculosis* (*M. tuberculosis*), the bacterium that causes tuberculosis (TB). Liu and colleagues (2006) demonstrated how 1,25D is involved in the destruction of *M. tuberculosis* in infected cells. The fact that exposure

to UV radiation is necessary for vitamin D synthesis probably explains why, in the early twentieth century, TB patients often improved after being sent to sanitariums in sunny locations.

The influence of latitude and skin pigmentation on levels of 1,25D in the body has been shown by epidemiological studies of modern populations. For example, one study revealed that 92 percent of more than 400 girls in several northern European countries were severely deficient in 1,25D during the winter months. Also, the fact that African Americans appear to have about half the amount of 1,25D seen in European Americans illustrates the role of increased pigmentation in reducing vitamin D levels in more northern latitudes (Tavera-Mendoza and White, 2007). This fact is significant because African Americans have a higher incidence of TB than European Americans (Liu et al., 2006).

As you can see, vitamin D is an immensely important factor in the body's response to a number of conditions, many of which influence reproductive success. This evidence substantially supports the vitamin D hypothesis and argues for strong and rapid positive selection for lighter skin in northern latitudes. Furthermore, the vitamin D evidence is strongly supported by recent genetic studies.

At least 100 genetic loci are thought to be involved in pigmentation in vertebrates, and one of the more important ones is *MC1R*, which affects coloration in all mammals (**Fig. 16-5**). In fact, work with DNA from an approximately 43,000-year-old mammoth bone revealed that coat color in mammoths varied from dark to lighter brown (Römpler et al., 2006). The human version of this gene has at least 30 alleles, some of which are associated with red hair combined with fair skin and a tendency to freckle (Lin and Fisher, 2007). As we mentioned in Chapter 13, research on Neandertal DNA has revealed that some Neandertals probably had red hair and fair skin. This research demonstrates the presence of an *MC1R* allele that reduces the amount of pigment in skin and hair, but it's not an allele that's present in modern humans. The fact that less pigmented skin developed in two hominin species, but through different mutations in the same gene, strongly reinforces the hypothesis that there is a significant selective advantage to lighter skin in higher latitudes.

Lastly, evidence for the importance of vitamin D is provided by the recent discovery of yet another gene, called *SCL24A5*, which we'll refer to simply as *SCL* (Lamason et al., 2005). This gene and its effects on pigmentation were first discovered in zebrafish, and just to emphasize (yet again) the concept of biological continuity between species, we'll point out that approximately 68 percent of the sequences of DNA bases in the human and zebrafish SCL genes are the same (Balter, 2007).

Like *MC1R*, the *SCL* gene is involved in melanin production. This gene has two primary alleles that differ by one single base substitution; that is, one allele arose as a point mutation. The original form (allele) of the gene is present in 93 to 100 percent of Africans, Native Americans, and East Asians. However, and most importantly, virtually 100 percent of Europeans and European Americans have the more recent (mutated) allele that inhibits melanin production. These frequencies provide yet more compelling evidence of very strong selection for lighter skin in northern latitudes. In fact, it appears that natural selection favored the mutated allele to the point that it became the only *SCL* allele in northern European populations.

But there's a question that has yet to be answered. (Actually, there are several questions, but we'll mention only one.) In East Asians, the frequency of the original, melanin-producing allele is the same as in sub-Saharan Africans, yet on average, skin color in East Asians is fairly light. Lamason and colleagues (2005) argue that this means that in East Asian populations, there are other, as yet unidentified genes that interact with the *SCL* locus to reduce skin pigmentation. Certainly,

▲ **Figure 16-5**
Artist's conception of wooly mammoths.

several other genes that contribute to skin pigmentation have been identified, but none has yet been shown to have the same degree of variation between populations.

Jablonski and Chaplin (2000) have looked at the potential for vitamin D synthesis in people of different skin color based on the yearly average UV radiation at various latitudes (**Fig. 16-6**). Their conclusions support the vitamin D hypothesis to the point of stating that the requirement of vitamin D synthesis in northern latitudes was as important to natural selection as the need for protection from UV radiation in tropical regions.

Except for a person's sex, more social importance has been attached to skin color than to any other single human biological trait. But there's absolutely no valid reason for this. Aside from its adaptive significance relative to UV radiation, skin color is no more important physiologically than many other biological characteristics. But from an evolutionary perspective, skin color provides an outstanding example of how the forces of natural selection have produced geographically patterned variation as the result of two conflicting selective forces: the need for protection from overexposure to UV radiation, on the one hand, and the need for adequate UV exposure for vitamin D synthesis on the other.

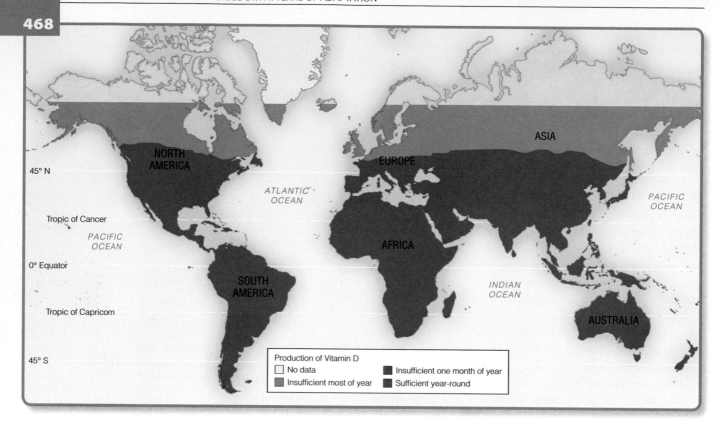

▲ Figure 16-6
Populations indigenous to the tropics (brown band) receive enough UV radiation for vitamin D synthesis year-round. The dark orange band shows areas where people with moderately pigmented skin don't receive enough UV light for vitamin D synthesis for one month of the year. The light orange band shows areas where even light skin doesn't receive enough UV light for vitamin D synthesis during most of the year. (Adapted from Jablonski and Chaplin, 2000, 2002.)

evaporative cooling A physiological mechanism that helps prevent the body from overheating. It occurs when perspiration is produced from sweat glands and then evaporates from the surface of the skin.

The Thermal Environment

Mammals and birds have evolved complex mechanisms to maintain a constant internal body temperature. While reptiles must rely on exposure to external heat sources to raise body temperature and energy levels, mammals and birds have physiological mechanisms that, within certain limits, increase or reduce the loss of body heat. The optimum body temperature for normal cellular functions is species-specific, and for humans it's approximately 98.6°F.

People are found in a wide variety of habitats, with thermal environments ranging from exceedingly hot (in excess of 120°F) to bitter cold (less than −60°F). In such extremes, particularly cold, human life wouldn't be possible without cultural innovations. But even accounting for the artificial environments we live in, such external conditions expose the human body to enormous stress.

Response to Heat All available evidence suggests that early hominins evolved in the warm-to-hot woodlands and savannas of East Africa. The fact that humans cope better with heat (especially dry heat) than they do with cold is testimony to the long-term adaptations to heat that evolved in our ancestors.

In humans, as well as some other species, such as horses, sweat glands are distributed throughout the skin. This wide distribution of sweat glands makes it possible to lose heat at the body's surface through **evaporative cooling**, a mechanism that has evolved to the greatest degree in humans. In fact, perspiration is the most important factor in heat dissipation in humans.

The capacity to dissipate heat by sweating is seen in all human populations to an almost equal degree, with the average number of sweat glands per individual (approximately 1.6 million) being fairly constant. However, there is some variation, since people who aren't generally exposed to hot conditions do experience a period of acclimatization that initially involves significantly increased perspiration rates (Frisancho, 1993). An additional factor that enhances the cooling effects of sweating is increased exposure of the skin through reduced amounts of body hair. We don't know when in our evolutionary history the loss of body hair occurred, but it represents a species-wide adaptation.

Heat reduction through evaporation can be expensive, and indeed dangerous, in terms of water and sodium loss. For example, a person engaged in heavy work in high heat can lose up to 3 liters of water per hour. To appreciate the importance of this fact, consider that losing 1 liter of water is approximately equivalent to losing 1.5 percent of total body weight, and losing 10 percent of body weight can be life threatening. So water must be continuously replaced during exercise in heat.

Basically, there are two types of heat, arid and humid. Arid environments, such as those of the southwestern United States, the Middle East, and parts of Africa, are characterized by high temperatures, wind, and low water vapor. Humid heat, associated with increased water vapor, occurs in regions with a great deal of vegetation and precipitation, conditions found in the eastern and southern United States, parts of Europe, and much of the tropics. Because the increased water vapor in humid climates inhibits the evaporation of sweat on the skin's surface, humans adjust much more readily to dry heat. In fact, people exercising in dry heat may be unaware that they're sweating because the perspiration evaporates as soon as it reaches the skin's surface. While rapid evaporation increases comfort, it can lead to dehydration. Therefore, in dry heat it's important to keep drinking water, even if you aren't particularly thirsty.

Another mechanism for radiating body heat is vasodilation, which occurs when capillaries near the skin's surface widen to increase blood flow to the skin. The visible effect of **vasodilation** is flushing, or increased redness and warming of the skin, particularly of the face. But the physiological effect is to permit heat, carried by the blood from the interior of the body, to be emitted from the skin's surface to the surrounding air. (Some drugs, including alcohol, also produce vasodilation; this accounts for the increased redness and warmth of the face in some people after a couple of drinks.)

Body size and proportions are also important in regulating body temperature. In fact, there seems to be a general relationship between climate and body size and shape in birds and mammals. In general, within a species, body size (weight) increases as distance from the equator increases. In humans, this relationship holds up fairly well, but there are many exceptions.

Two rules that pertain to the relationship between body size, body proportions, and climate are *Bergmann's rule* and *Allen's rule*.

1. *Bergmann's rule concerns the relationship of body mass or volume to surface area.* Among mammals, body size tends to be greater in populations that live in colder climates. This is because as mass increases, the relative amount of surface area decreases proportionately. Because heat is lost at the surface, it follows that increased mass allows for greater heat retention and reduced heat loss. (Remember our discussion of basal metabolic rate and body size in Chapter 7.)

2. *Allen's rule concerns the shape of the body, especially appendages.* In colder climates, shorter appendages, with increased mass-to-surface ratios, are adaptive because they're more effective at preventing heat loss. Conversely, longer appendages, with increased surface area relative to mass, are more adaptive in warmer climates because they promote heat loss.

According to these rules, the most suitable body shape in hot climates is linear with long arms and legs. In

vasodilation Expansion of blood vessels, permitting increased blood flow to the skin. Vasodilation permits warming of the skin and facilitates radiation of warmth as a means of cooling. Vasodilation is an involuntary response to warm temperatures, various drugs, and even emotional states (blushing).

A Closer Look

Skin Cancer and UV Radiation

Even though we know we can't live without it, most people tend to take their skin for granted. The many functions of this complex organ (and skin *is* an organ) are vital to life. Yet most of us thoughtlessly expose our skin to any number of environmental assaults and especially abuse it with overexposure to the sun, practically to the point of charbroiling. For these reasons, we think it's appropriate here to examine a little more closely this watertight, evolutionary achievement that permits us to live on land, just as it allowed some vertebrates to leave the oceans several hundred million years ago.

Skin is composed of two layers, the epidermis and, just beneath it, the dermis (see Fig. 16-2). The upper portion of the epidermis is made up of flattened, somewhat overlapping squamous (scale-like) cells. Beneath these cells, near the base of the epidermis, are several layers of round basal cells. Interspersed within the basal cells are still two other cell types: melanocytes, which produce melanin, and keratinocytes, which are involved in vitamin D synthesis.

Skin cells are continuously produced at the base of the epidermis through mitosis. As they mature, they migrate to the surface, becoming flattened and avascular; that is, they have no direct blood supply. Approxi-

mately one month after forming, skin cells die in a process of genetically directed cellular suicide. The results of this suicidal act are the little white flakes people with dry skin are uncomfortably aware of. (Incidentally, dead skin cells are a major component of common household dust.)

The dermis is composed of connective tissue and many structures, including blood vessels, lymphatic vessels, sweat glands, oil glands, and hair follicles. Together, the epidermis and dermis allow the body to retain fluid, help regulate body temperature, synthesize a number of essential substances, and provide protection from ultraviolet (UV) radiation.

There are three main types of UV radiation, but here we're concerned with only two: UVA and UVB. UVA has the longest wavelength and can penetrate through to the bottom of the dermis, while the medium-length UVB waves usually penetrate only to the basal layer of the epidermis (see Fig. 16-2).

The stimulation of vitamin D production by UVB waves is the only benefit we get from exposure to UV radiation. Following a sunburn, both UVB and UVA rays cause short-term suppression of the immune system. But because UVB is directly absorbed by the DNA within cells, it can potentially cause genetic damage, and this damage can lead to skin cancer.

You know that cancers are tumorous growths that invade organs, a process that often results in death, even after treatment.

But you may not know that a cell becomes cancerous when a carcinogenic agent, such as UV radiation, damages its DNA, and some DNA segments are more susceptible than others. The damage allows the affected cell to divide uncontrollably. Each subsequent generation of cells receives the mutant DNA, and with it, the potential to divide indefinitely. Eventually, cancer cells form a mass that invades other tissues. They can also break away from the original tumor and travel through the circulatory or lymphatic system to other parts of the body, where they establish themselves and continue to divide. For example, cells from lung tumors (frequently caused by carcinogenic agents in tobacco) can travel to the brain or parts of the skeleton and develop tumors in these new sites before the lung tumor is even detectable. (Former Beatle George Harrison died of brain cancer that had spread from his lungs. It's probably no coincidence that he was a heavy smoker when he was young.)

All three types of cells in the epidermis are susceptible to cancerous changes. The most common form of skin cancer is basal cell carcinoma (BCC), which affects about 800,000 people per year in the United States. Fortunately, BCCs are slow growing and, if detected early, can be successfully removed before they spread. They can appear as a raised lump and be uncolored, red-brown, or black (**Fig.1a**).

Squamous cell carcinoma (SCC) is the second most common skin cancer

a cold climate, a more suitable body type is stocky with shorter limbs. Considerable data gathered from several human populations generally conform to these principles. In colder climates, body mass tends, on average, to be greater and characterized by a larger trunk relative to arms and legs. People living in the Arctic tend to be short and stocky, while many sub-Saharan Africans, especially the East African pastoralists, are tall and

linear (**Fig. 16-7**). But there's a lot of human variability regarding body proportions, and not all populations conform so obviously to Bergmann's and Allen's rules.

Response to Cold There are two basic types of physiological responses to cold, those that increase heat production and those that, within limits, retain heat. Of the two, heat retention is more efficient because less ener-

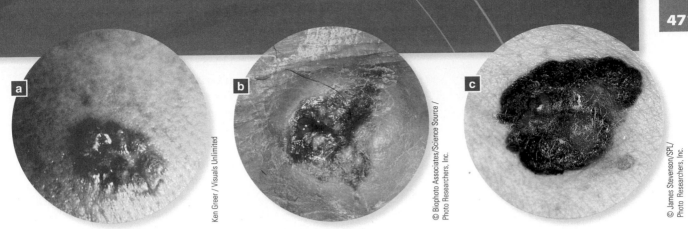

Ken Greer / Visuals Unlimited

© Biophoto Associates/Science Source / Photo Researchers, Inc.

© James Stevenson/SPL/ Photo Researchers, Inc.

▲ **Figure 1**
(**a**) Basal cell carcinoma. (**b**) Squamous cell carcinoma. (**c**) Malignant melanoma.

(**Fig. 1b**). These cancers grow faster than BCCs, but they're also amenable to treatment if detected reasonably early. They usually appear as firm pinkish lesions and may spread rapidly on skin exposed to sunlight.

The third form is malignant melanoma, a cancer of the melanocytes. Melanoma is thought to be caused by UVA radiation, and it accounts for only about 4 percent of all skin cancers. But while it's the least common of the three, melanoma is the fastest growing and the deadliest, killing 30 to 40 percent of affected people. Melanoma looks like an irregularly shaped, very dark or black mole (**Fig. 1c**). In fact, it may be a mole that has changed because some of its cells have been damaged. It's extremely important to notice any changes in a mole or the appearance of a new dark, perhaps roughened spot on the skin and to have it examined as soon as possible. If

a melanoma is less than a millimeter deep, it can be removed before it spreads. But if it has progressed into the dermis, it's likely that it's already spread to other tissues.

Brash and colleagues (1991) and Ziegler and colleagues (1994) determined that the underlying genetic factor in most non-melanoma skin cancers is a mutation of a gene called *p53* located on chromosome 17. This gene produces the protein p53, which prevents any cell (not just skin cells) with damaged DNA from dividing until the damage is repaired. In addition, if the damage to a cell's DNA is too severe to repair, the p53 protein can cause the cell to die. Thus, *p53* is what's known as a tumor suppressor gene (Vogelstein et al., 2000).

Unfortunately, the *p53* gene is itself susceptible to mutation, and when certain mutations occur, it can no longer prevent cancer cells from dividing. Luckily, there are other tumor suppressor genes. In fact, dam-

aged *p53* genes don't appear to be involved in melanoma. Instead, a UV-induced mutation in another tumor suppressor gene on chromosome 9 appears to be the culprit (NCBI, 2003).

BCCs and SCCs tend to appear in middle age, long after the underlying genetic damage occurred during childhood and adolescence. If you've had even one serious sunburn in your life, your odds of developing one of the nonmelanoma skin cancers have increased dramatically. Malignant melanomas can occur at any age, although the DNA damage can precede the development of cancer by several years. The best advice is don't take the threat of skin cancer lightly, and don't overexpose your skin to the sun. Wear a hat and a broad-based sun block that will filter out both UVA and UVB rays. In other words, do your best to protect your tumor suppressor genes—and yourself.

gy is required. This is an important point because energy is obtained from dietary sources. Unless food is abundant, and in winter it frequently isn't, any factor that conserves energy can be beneficial.

An increase in metabolic rate and shivering are short-term responses that generate body heat. Increases in metabolic rate (the rate at which cells break up nutrients into their components) release energy in the form of heat.

Shivering also generates muscle heat, as does voluntary exercise. But both these methods are costly because they require an increased intake of nutrients to provide needed energy. (Perhaps this explains why we tend to have a heartier appetite during the winter and why we also tend to eat more fats and carbohydrates, the very sources of energy we require.)

In general, people exposed to chronic cold (meaning much or most of the

© JTB Photo Communications, Inc. / Alamy

© tbkmedia.de / Alamy

▲ **Figure 16-7**

(a) These Samburu women (and men in the background) have the linear proportions characteristic of many inhabitants of East Africa. The Samburu are cattle herding people who live in northern Kenya. Here they are shown dancing. **(b)** By comparison, these Canadian Inuit women are shorter and stockier. Although the people in these two pictures don't typify everyone in their populations they do serve as good examples of Bergmann's and Allen's rules.

vasoconstriction Narrowing of blood vessels to reduce blood flow to the skin. Vasoconstriction is an involuntary response to cold and reduces heat loss at the skin's surface.

year) maintain higher metabolic rates than people who live in warmer climates. The Inuit (Eskimo) people living in the Arctic maintain metabolic rates between 13 and 45 percent higher than observed in non-Inuit control subjects (Frisancho, 1993). What's more, the highest metabolic rates are seen in inland Inuit, who are exposed to even greater cold stress than coastal populations. Traditionally, the Inuit had the highest animal protein and fat diet of any population in the world. Their diet was dictated by the available resource base, and it served to maintain the high metabolic rates required by exposure to chronic cold.

Vasoconstriction is another short-term response, but instead of producing heat, it minimizes heat loss and therefore is more energy efficient. Vasoconstriction restricts capillary blood flow to the surface of the skin, thus reducing heat loss at the body surface. Because retaining body heat is more economical than creating it, vasoconstriction is very efficient, provided temperatures don't drop below freezing. However, if temperatures do fall below freezing, continued vasoconstriction can lower skin temperature to the point of frostbite or worse.

Long-term responses to cold vary among human groups. For example, in the past, desert-dwelling native Australian populations were subjected to wide temperature fluctuations from day to night. Since they wore no clothing and didn't build shelters, they built sleeping fires to protect themselves from nighttime temperatures that hovered only a few degrees above freezing. Also, they experienced continuous vasoconstriction throughout the night that permitted a degree of skin cooling most people would find extremely uncomfortable. But since there was no threat of frostbite, continued vasoconstriction helped prevent excessive internal heat loss.

By contrast, the Inuit experience intermittent periods of vasoconstriction and vasodilation. This compromise provides periodic warmth to the skin that helps prevent frostbite in below-freezing temperatures. At the same time, because vasodilation is intermittent, energy loss is restricted to retain more heat at the body's core.

Humans, and some other animals, also have a subcutaneous (beneath the skin) fat layer that provides insulation throughout the body. In many overfed populations today, this fat layer is an annoyance to many and a major health issue for others. But in the not-too-distant past, our hunting and gathering ancestors relied on it not only for some protection against the cold but also as a source of nutrients when food was scarce.

These examples illustrate two of the ways adaptations to cold vary among human populations. Obviously, winter conditions exceed our ability to adapt physiologically in many parts of the world. So if they hadn't developed cultural innovations, our ancestors would have remained in the tropics.

High Altitude

Studies of high-altitude residents have greatly contributed to our understanding of physiological adaptation. As you'd expect, altitude studies have focused on inhabited mountainous regions, particularly in the Himalayas, Andes, and Rocky Mountains. Of these three areas, permanent human habitation probably has the longest history in the Himalayas (Moore et al., 1998). Today, perhaps as many as 25 million people live at altitudes above 10,000 feet. In Tibet, permanent settlements exist above 15,000 feet; in the Andes, they can be found as high as 17,000 feet (**Fig. 16-8**).

Because the mechanisms that maintain homeostasis in humans evolved at lower altitudes, we're compromised by the conditions at higher elevations. At high altitudes, many factors result in stress on the human body. These include **hypoxia**, more intense solar radiation, cold, low humidity, wind (which amplifies cold stress), a reduced nutritional base, and rough terrain. Of these, hypoxia causes the most problems for human physiological systems, especially the heart, lungs, and brain.

Hypoxia is caused by reduced barometric pressure. It's not that there's less oxygen in the atmosphere at high altitudes; rather, it's less concentrated. Therefore, to obtain the same amount of oxygen at 9,000 feet as at sea level, people must make certain physiological alterations that increase the body's ability to transport and efficiently use the oxygen that's available.

Reproduction, in particular, is affected through increased infant mortality rates, miscarriage, low birth weights, and premature birth. One cause of fetal and maternal death is preeclampsia, a severe elevation of blood pressure in pregnant women after the twentieth gestational week. In another study of Colorado residents, Palmer and colleagues (1999) reported that among pregnant women living at elevations over 10,000 feet, the prevalence of preeclampsia was 16 percent, compared with 3 percent at around 4,000 feet. In general, the problems related to childbearing are attributed to issues that compromise the vascular supply (and thus oxygen transport) to the fetus.

People born at lower altitudes and high-altitude natives differ somewhat in how they adapt to insufficient amounts of available oxygen. When people born at low elevations travel to higher ones, the process of acclimatization begins within a day or two. These changes include an increase in metabolic rate, respiration, heart rate, and the production of red blood cells. (Red blood cells contain hemoglobin, the protein responsible for transporting oxygen to organs and tissues.)

In high-altitude natives, acclimatization occurs during growth and development. This type of developmental acclimatization is present only in people who grow up in high-altitude areas, not in those who moved there as adults. Compared with populations at lower elevations, lifelong residents of high altitude grow somewhat more slowly and mature later. Other differences include greater lung and heart capacity. People born at high altitudes are also more efficient than migrants at diffusing oxygen from blood to body tissues, and the genes that regulate this ability are beginning to be identified. Developmental acclimatization to high altitude serves as a good example of physiological flexibility by illustrating how, within the limits set by genetic factors, development can be influenced by environmental factors.

But the best evidence for permanent high-altitude adaptation is provided by the indigenous peoples of Tibet, who have been the subject of many studies. These people have inhabited regions higher than 12,000 feet for at least 7,000 (Simonson et al, 2010) and perhaps as long as 25,000 years. Altitude doesn't affect reproduction in Tibetans to the degree it does in other populations. Infants have birth weights

hypoxia Insufficient levels of oxygen in body tissues; oxygen deficiency.

as high as those of lowland Tibetan groups and higher than those of recent (20 to 30 years) Chinese immigrants. This disparity in birth weights may be the result of alterations in maternal blood flow to the uterus during pregnancy (Moore et al., 2006).

Another line of evidence concerns how the body processes glucose (blood sugar). Glucose is critical because it's the only source of energy used by the brain, and it's also used, although not exclusively, by the heart. Both highland Tibetans and the Quechua (inhabitants of high-altitude regions of the Peruvian Andes) burn glucose in a way that permits more efficient oxygen use. This implies the presence of genetic mutations in the mitochondrial DNA because mtDNA directs how cells process glucose. It also indicates that natural selection has acted to increase the

frequency of these advantageous mutations in these groups.

We now have solid evidence that natural selection has acted strongly and rapidly to increase the frequency of certain alleles that have produced adaptive responses to altitude in Tibetans. Ninety percent of Tibetan highlanders possess a mutation (SNP) in a gene called *EPAS1*, which is involved in red blood cell production. In effect, the *EPAS1* mutation inhibits the increased red blood cell production we would expect at high altitude, so Tibetans have red cell counts similar to those of populations living at sea level. Interestingly, the Quechua and other high-altitude residents of the Andes do not have this mutation and have elevated red cell counts compared with lowland inhabitants. But if increased red blood cell production is advantageous

◄ **Figure 16-8**

(a) Namche Bazaar, Tibet, situated at an elevation of over 12,000 feet above sea level. **(b)** La Paz, Bolivia, at just over 12,000 feet, is home to more than 1 million people.

at high altitude, why would selection favor a mutation that acts against it in Tibetans? The answer is that beyond certain levels, elevated numbers of red cells can actually "thicken" the blood and lead to increased risk of stroke, blood clots, and heart attack. In pregnant women, they can also lead to impaired fetal growth and even fetal death. Thus, although the mechanisms aren't yet understood, Tibetans have acquired a number of genetically influenced adaptations to hypoxic conditions while still producing the same amount of hemoglobin we would expect at sea level. Because the mutation is believed to have appeared only around 4,000 ya, its presence throughout most highland Tibetan populations is the strongest and most rapid example of natural selection documented for humans (Yi et al., 2010).

Infectious Disease

Infection, as opposed to other disease categories, such as degenerative or genetic disease, includes pathological conditions caused by microorganisms (viruses, bacteria, fungi, and other one-celled organisms). Throughout the course of human evolution, infectious disease has exerted enormous selective pressures on populations, influencing the frequency of alleles that affect the immune response. Indeed, the importance of infectious disease as an agent of natural selection in human populations cannot be overemphasized. But as important as infectious disease has been, its role in this regard isn't very well documented.

The effects of infectious disease on humans are mediated culturally as well as biologically. Innumerable cultural factors, such as architectural styles, subsistence techniques, exposure to domesticated animals, transportation, and even religious practices, affect how infectious disease develops and persists within and between populations.

Until about 15,000 years ago, all humans lived in small nomadic hunting and gathering groups. These groups rarely stayed in one location more than a few days or weeks at a time, so they had little contact with refuse heaps that house disease **vectors**. But with the domestication of plants and animals, people became more sedentary and began living in small villages. Gradually, villages became towns; and towns, in turn, developed into densely crowded, unsanitary cities.

As long as humans lived in small bands, there was little opportunity for infectious disease to affect large numbers of people. Certainly, people were sometimes infected with various pathogens through contact with animals they killed and butchered; and they were also exposed to infection simply through association with each other. But even if an entire local group or band were wiped out, the effect on the overall population in a given area would have been negligible. Moreover, for a disease to become **endemic** in a population, there must be enough people to sustain it. Therefore, small bands of hunter-gatherers weren't faced with continuous exposure to endemic disease.

But with the advent of settled living and close proximity to domesticated animals, opportunities for exposure to disease increased. As sedentary life permitted larger group size, it became possible for several diseases to become permanently established in some populations. Moreover, exposure to domestic animals, such as cattle and fowl, provided an opportune environment for the spread of several **zoonotic** diseases. The crowded, unsanitary conditions that characterized parts of all cities until the late nineteenth century and that still persist in much of the world today further added to the disease burden borne by human populations.

Tuberculosis, discussed earlier, has been one of the most cited examples of zoonotic disease, believed to have been transmitted from cattle to humans after cattle were domesticated some 10,000 ya. In fact, TB is widely considered to be one of the many prices humans have paid for living in close association with domesticated animals. *Mycobacterium tuberculosis* usually

vectors Agents that transmit disease from one carrier to another. Mosquitoes are vectors for malaria, just as fleas are vectors for bubonic plague.

endemic Continuously present in a population.

zoonotic (zoh-oh-no´-tic) Pertaining to a zoonosis (*pl.*, zoonoses), a disease that's transmitted to humans through contact with nonhuman animals.

Charlotte Roberts

▲ **Figure 16-9**
Portion of a vertebral column from a 17- to 25-year-old male infected with tuberculosis. Most of the bodies of three lower thoracic vertebrae (attached to the ribs) have been destroyed, and the spine has collapsed. This skeleton is from a medieval burial site in England.

infects the lungs. It's spread through sneezing and coughing, and symptoms include coughing, fatigue and fever. Prior to the development of antibiotic therapies, the disease often proved fatal. In addition to the lungs, the bacterium can attack other tissues, including bone. The area of the skeleton most commonly involved is the spine (**Fig. 16-9**), and when this occurs, two or three vertebrae may be destroyed and eventually collapse.

Interestingly, the hypothesis that TB was originally transmitted from cattle to humans has been challenged by genetic evidence that, in fact, cattle may have been exposed to TB through contact with humans, not the other way around (Brosch et al., 2002; Pfister et al, 2008). The cattle-to-human transmission hypothesis is based on the assumption that *Micobacterium bovis*, the bacterial strain that normally infects cattle, gave rise to *M. tuberculosis*, which usually infects humans. Using different techniques, two studies have concluded that *M. bovis* actually evolved from *M. tuberculosis*, indicating that humans were infected first. But it's important to point out that the different strains of TB aren't completely species-specific, so even though the human form may have evolved first, people can also be infected with *M. bovis*. Thus, it's possible that transmission has at times gone in both directions.

Malaria provides perhaps the best-documented example of how disease can act to change allele frequencies in human populations. In Chapter 4, you saw how, in some African and Mediterranean populations, malaria has altered allele frequencies at the locus that governs hemoglobin formation, leading to increased prevalence of sickle-cell anemia. Despite extensive long-term eradication programs, malaria still poses a serious threat to human health. Indeed, the World Health Organization estimates the number of people currently infected with malaria to be between 300 and 500 million worldwide. And this number is increasing as drug-resistant strains of the disease-causing microorganism become more common (Olliaro et al., 1995).

Another example of the selective role of infectious disease is indirectly provided by AIDS (acquired immunodeficiency syndrome). In the United States, the first cases of AIDS were reported in 1981. Since then, perhaps as many as 1.5 million Americans have been infected by HIV (human immunodeficiency virus), the agent that causes AIDS. However, most of the burden of AIDS is borne by developing countries, where 95 percent of all HIV-infected people live (**Fig. 16-10**). According to World Health Organization estimates, between 33 and 35 million people worldwide were living with HIV infection as of November 2009, and more than 25 million had died (UNAIDS/WHO, 2010).

By the early 1990s, scientists were aware of some patients who had been HIV positive for 10 to 15 years but continued to show few if any symptoms. This led researchers to suspect that some individuals are naturally resistant to HIV. This was shown to be true in late 1996 with the publication of two independent studies that demonstrated a mechanism for HIV resistance (Dean et al., 1996; Samson et al., 1996).

These two reports describe a genetic mutation that involves a major receptor site on the surface of certain immune cells, including T4 cells. (Receptor sites are protein molecules that enable HIV and other viruses to invade cells.) As a result of the mutation, the receptor site doesn't function properly and the virus can't enter the cell. Current evidence strongly suggests that people who are homozygous for this allele may be completely resistant to many types of HIV infection. In heterozygotes, infection may still occur; but the course of HIV disease is significantly slowed.

For unknown reasons, the mutant allele occurs mainly in people of European descent, among whom its frequency is about 10 percent. However, the mutation was absent in certain Japanese and West African groups that were studied (Samson

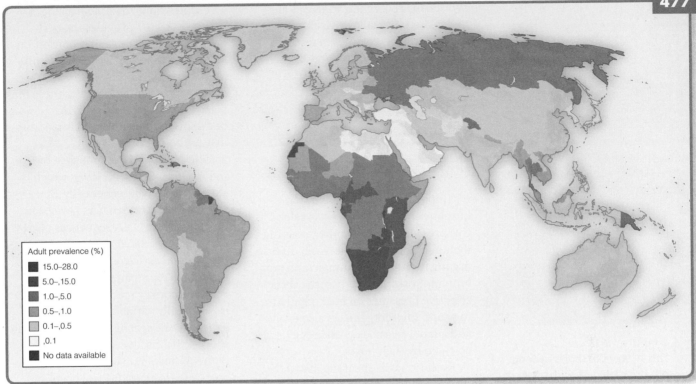

Adult prevalence (%)
- 15.0–28.0
- 5.0–,15.0
- 1.0–,5.0
- 0.5–,1.0
- 0.1–,0.5
- ,0.1
- No data available

▲ **Figure 16-10**

Geographical distribution of HIV infection as of the end of 2004.

et al., 1996). Another research team reported an allele frequency of about 2 percent among African Americans, and they speculated that the presence of the allele in African Americans is due to genetic admixture (gene flow) with European Americans (Dean et al., 1996). They also suggested that this polymorphism exists in Europeans because of selective pressures favoring an allele that originally occurred as a rare mutation. But it's important to understand that the original selective agent was *not* HIV. Instead, it was some other as yet unidentified pathogen that requires the same receptor site as HIV, and some researchers have implicated the virus that causes smallpox. Lalani and colleagues (1999) reported that a poxvirus, related to the virus that causes smallpox, can use the same receptor site as HIV. While this conclusion hasn't yet been proved, it offers a very interesting avenue of research. It may reveal how a mutation that has been favored by selection because it provides protection against one type of infection (perhaps smallpox) can also increase resistance to another (AIDS).

Smallpox, once a deadly viral disease, is estimated to have accounted for 10 to 15 percent of all deaths in parts of Europe during the eighteenth century (**Fig. 16-11**). It's possible that during its long history, smallpox may have altered the frequency of the ABO blood types by selecting against the *A* allele. Smallpox had a higher incidence in people with blood type A or AB than in type O individuals, a fact that may be explained by the presence of an antigen on the smallpox virus that's similar to the A antigen. Thus, when some type A individuals were exposed to smallpox, their immune systems failed to recognize the virus as foreign and didn't mount an adequate immune response. This meant that people with the *A* allele died in greater numbers than those without it. So in regions where smallpox was common in the past, it could have altered allele frequencies at the ABO locus by selecting against the *A* allele.

Smallpox, once a devastating killer of millions, is the only condition to have been successfully eliminated by modern medical technology. By 1977, through massive vaccination programs, the

CDC/Jean Roy

▲ **Figure 16-11**
This 1974 photo shows a young boy in Bangladesh with smallpox. His body is covered with the painful pustules that are typical of the disease. These lesions frequently leave severe scarring on the skin of survivors.

World Health Organization was able to declare the smallpox virus extinct, except for a few colonies in research labs in the United States and Russia.*

The Continuing Impact of Infectious Disease

It's important to understand that humans and pathogens exert selective pressures on each other, creating a dynamic relationship between disease organisms and their human (and non-human) hosts. Just as disease exerts selective pressures on host populations to adapt, microorganisms also evolve and adapt to various pressures exerted on them by their hosts.

Evolutionarily speaking, it's to the advantage of any pathogen not to be so deadly that it kills its host too quickly. If the host dies shortly after becoming infected, the virus or bacterium may not have time to reproduce and infect other hosts. Thus, selection sometimes acts to produce resistance in host populations and/or to reduce the virulence of disease organisms, to the benefit of both. However, members of populations exposed for the first time to a new disease frequently die in huge numbers. This type of exposure was a major factor in the decimation of indigenous New World populations after Europeans introduced smallpox into Native American groups. And it has also been the case with the current worldwide spread of HIV.

---

* Concern over the potential use of the smallpox virus by bioterrorists relates to these laboratory colonies. Although the virus is extinct outside these labs, some officials fear the possibility that samples of the virus could be stolen. Also, there are apparently some concerns that unknown colonies of the virus may exist in labs in countries other than Russia and the United States. Using disease organisms against enemies isn't new. In the Middle Ages, armies catapulted the corpses of smallpox and plague victims into towns under siege, and during the U.S. colonial period, British soldiers knowingly gave Native Americans blankets used by smallpox victims.

Of the known disease-causing organisms, HIV provides the best-documented example of evolution and adaptation in a pathogen. It's also one of several examples of interspecies transfer of infection. For these reasons, we focus much of this discussion of evolutionary factors and infectious disease on HIV.

The type of HIV responsible for the AIDS epidemic is HIV-1, which is extremely variable genetically. Since the late 1980s, researchers have been comparing the DNA sequences of HIV and a closely related virus called *simian immunodeficiency virus (SIV)*. SIV is found in chimpanzees and several African monkey species. Like HIV, SIV is genetically variable, and each strain appears to be specific to a given primate species. SIV produces no symptoms in the African monkeys and chimpanzees that are its traditional hosts, but when injected into Asian monkeys, it eventually causes immune suppression, AIDS-like symptoms, and death. These findings indicate that the various forms of SIV have shared a long evolutionary history (perhaps several hundred thousand years) with a number of African primate species and that these primates have developed ways of accommodating this virus, which is deadly to their Asian relatives. These results also substantiate long-held hypotheses that SIV and HIV evolved in Africa. Furthermore, DNA comparisons have shown that HIV-1 almost certainly evolved from the form of SIV that infects chimpanzees indigenous to western central Africa (Gao et al., 1999).

Unfortunately for both species, chimpanzees are routinely hunted by humans for food in parts of West Africa. So the most probable explanation for the transmission of SIV from chimpanzees to humans is the hunting and butchering of chimpanzees (Gao et al., 1999; Weiss and Wrangham, 1999; **Fig. 16-12**). Thus, HIV/AIDS is a zoonotic disease. The DNA evidence further suggests that there were at least three separate human exposures to chimpanzee SIV, and at some point the virus was altered to the form we call

At a Glance

ZOONOSES AND HUMAN INFECTIOUS DISEASE

Examples

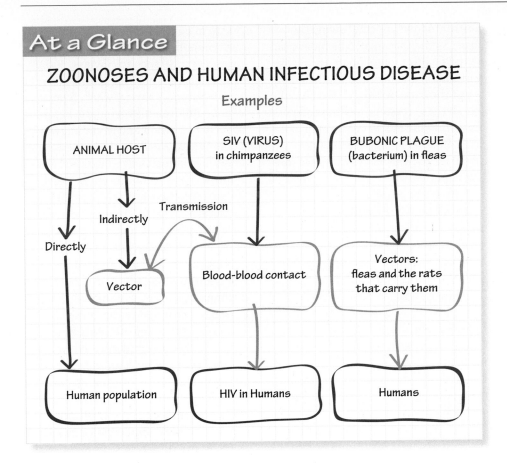

ANIMAL HOST

SIV (VIRUS) in chimpanzees

BUBONIC PLAGUE (bacterium) in fleas

Transmission

Indirectly

Directly

Vector

Blood-blood contact

Vectors: fleas and the rats that carry them

Human population

HIV in Humans

Humans

HIV. Exactly when chimpanzee SIV was transmitted to humans is unknown. The oldest evidence of human infection is a frozen HIV-positive blood sample taken from a West African patient in 1959. Therefore, although human exposure to SIV/HIV probably occurred many times in the past, the virus didn't become firmly established in humans until the latter half of the twentieth century.

Influenza is a contagious respiratory disease caused by various strains of virus. It, too, is a zoonotic disease, and it has probably killed more humans than any other infectious disease. There were two flu pandemics in the twentieth century; the first of these killed an estimated 20 million people in 1918. Moreover, "seasonal flu," which comes around every year, killed 36,000 people annually in the United States during the 1990s (Centers for Disease Control, 2009). Worldwide, it accounts for several hundred thousand deaths every year.

The influenza viruses that infect humans are initially acquired through contact with domestic pigs and fowl (**Fig. 16-13**). For this reason, influenza is frequently referred to as swine or avian (bird) flu, depending on which species transmitted it to humans. In 2009, a new swine flu virus called H1N1 caused great fear of another pandemic, partly because it caused more severe illness in younger people than most flu viruses.

Because swine flu epidemics are less frequent than the seasonal avian flu, people have less resistance when

▼ **Figure 16-12**
These people, selling butchered chimpanzees in West Africa, probably don't realize that by handling this meat they could be exposing themselves to HIV.

confronted with a "new" swine flu virus. Swine flu can also be more deadly, and health professionals are always mindful of, and haunted by, the memory of the catastrophic 1918 pandemic. For all these reasons, health professionals worldwide mobilized an enormous effort in 2009 to prepare for a new swine flu pandemic. Hundreds of millions of doses of vaccine were prepared and distributed, and in the United States alone, more than 100 million doses were made available.

The H1N1 flu epidemic proved not to be as severe as originally feared. By mid-November 2009, about 50 million Americans had been infected (Reinberg, 2009), but most cases were mild. Still, health officials are always on the alert for the possibility of an influenza pandemic, partly because of the ever-present danger presented by close contact between humans, pigs, and domestic fowl.

Until the twentieth century, infectious disease was the number one cause of death in all human populations. Even today, in many developing countries, as much as half of all mortality is due to infectious disease, compared with only about 10 percent in the United States. For example, there are an estimated 1 million deaths due to malaria every year. That figure computes to one malaria-related death every 30 seconds (Weiss, 2002)! Ninety percent of these deaths occur in sub-Saharan Africa, where 5 percent of children die of malaria before age 5 (Greenwood and Mutabingwa, 2002; Weiss, 2002). In the United States and other industrialized nations, with improved living conditions, better sanitation, and the widespread use of antibiotics since the 1940s, infectious disease has given way to heart disease and cancer as the leading causes of death.

Optimistic predictions held that infectious disease would one day be a thing of the past. You may be surprised to learn that in the United States mortality due to infectious disease has actually increased in recent years (Pinner et al., 1996). This increase may partly be due to the overuse of antibiotics. It's estimated that half of all antibiotics prescribed in the United States are used to treat viral conditions such as colds and flu. Because antibiotics are completely ineffective against viruses, antibiotic therapy not only is useless, but may actually have dangerous long-term consequences. There's considerable concern in the biomedical community over the indiscriminate use of antibiotics since the 1950s. Antibiotics have exerted selective pressures on bacterial species that have, over time, evolved antibiotic-resistant strains (an excellent example of natural selection). So in the past few years, we've seen the reemergence of many bacterial diseases, including, pneumonia, cholera, and TB in forms that are less responsive to treatment.

Tuberculosis is now listed as the world's leading killer of adults by the World Health Organization (Colwell, 1996). In fact, the number of TB cases has risen 28 percent worldwide since the mid-1980s, with an estimated 10 million people infected in the United States alone. Although not all infected people develop active disease, in the 1990s an estimated 30 million persons worldwide are believed to have died from TB. One very troubling aspect of the increase in tuberculosis infection

▼ **Figure 16-13**
This woman, selling chickens in a Chinese market, is wearing a scarf over her nose and mouth in an attempt to protect herself from exposure to avian flu.

Hoang Dinh Nam/AFP/Getty Images

is that new strains of *Mycobacterium tuberculosis* are resistant to many antibiotics and other treatments.

Various treatments for nonbacterial conditions have also become ineffective. One such example is the appearance of chloroquin-resistant malaria, which has rendered chloroquin (the traditional preventive medication) virtually useless in some parts of Africa. And many insect species have also developed resistance to commonly used pesticides.

Fundamental to all these factors is human population growth. As it continues to soar, it causes more environmental disturbance and, through additional human activity, increased global warming. Moreover, in developing countries, where as much as 50 percent of mortality is due to infectious disease, overcrowding and unsanitary conditions increasingly contribute to increased rates of communicable illness. It's hard to conceive of a better set of circumstances for the appearance and spread of communicable disease, and it remains to be seen if scientific innovation and medical technology will be able to meet the challenge.

Summary of Main Topics

- Humans have adapted to countless environmental challenges as they evolved and migrated out of Africa to eventually inhabit most of the planet.
- Variation in skin color has enormous adaptive value in response to conflicting selective pressures, all having to do with ultraviolet (UV) radiation. Heavily pigmented skin is adaptive in the tropics because it provides protection from UV radiation, which can cause skin cancer and degrade folate.
- As people moved away from the tropics, dark skin became disadvantageous because a decrease in sunlight meant insufficient exposure to UV radiation for the adequate production of vitamin D.

- In particular, two genes (*MC1R* and *SCL24A5*) have been responsible for the geographical patterning of human skin color.
- Various forms of acclimatization have evolved in humans to accommodate environmental factors like heat, cold, and high altitude. Natural selection favoring several genetic mutations has allowed Tibetan highlanders to adapt to extremely high altitudes. There has been especially rapid and strong selection favoring a particular SNP that permits them to retain red cell counts that are normal for sea-level residents.
- Infectious disease has also played a critical role in human evolution, and the frequencies of certain alleles have changed in various populations in response to diseases such as malaria.
- Cultural innovations and contact with nonhuman animals have altered disease patterns and have increased the spread of infectious diseases. Examples of this type of spread are HIV/AIDS and malaria.
- We humans are still coping with infectious disease as we alter the environment. Certainly, without cultural adaptations, our species never would have left the tropics. But as in the case of sickle-cell anemia, HIV, and many bacterial diseases, some of our cultural innovations themselves have become selective agents.

Critical Thinking Questions

1. If a friend of yours said that skin color is a valuable tool to use in classifying humans, how would you explain that variations in human pigmentation are the result of natural selection in different environments?

2. Why is less pigmented skin a result of conflicting selective factors? What are these factors?

3. How has infectious disease played an important role in human evolution? Do you think it plays a current role in human adaptation? How have human cultural practices influenced the patterns of infectious disease seen today? List as many examples as you can, including some not discussed in this chapter.

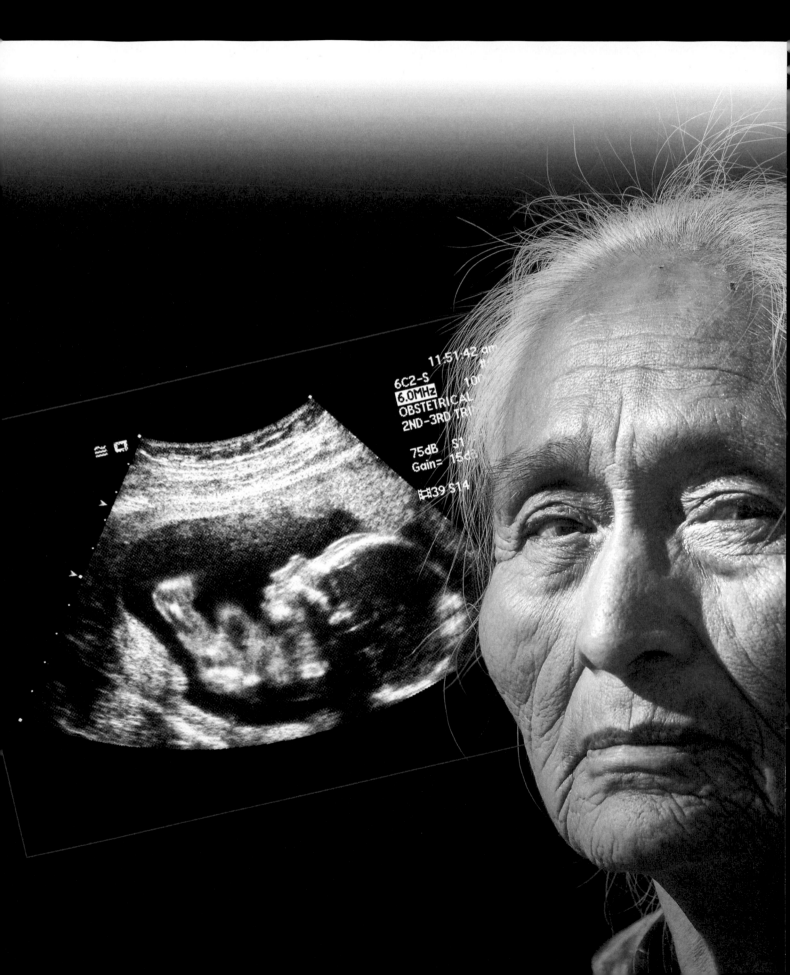

17

The Human Life Course

Key Questions

▶ How does the human growth process illustrate biocultural factors?

▶ How has natural selection acted on aspects of the human life cycle, such as gestation, infancy, adolescence, and longevity?

▶ Will new advances in medicine and technology enable humans to live hundreds of years?

▶ Are humans still evolving?

I n previous chapters, we have seen that modern humans are a highly generalized species. This means that we can live in a great variety of climates, eat a wide variety of foods, and respond to most environmental challenges in myriad ways. For example, as human populations moved into cold northern climates, they were able to respond both physiologically and behaviorally to the environmental challenges they faced. As noted previously, adaptations to cold include physiological responses to conserve or increase heat, such as vasoconstriction of the capillaries, increased metabolic rate, and shivering. Considering these responses from an evolutionary perspective, we can assume that among the earliest human populations inhabiting cold regions of the world, those individuals who had genotypes and phenotypes enabling them to respond physiologically had more surviving offspring to pass along these characteristics. Behavioral and cultural adaptations to cold climates probably included fire, house structures, warm clothing, and hunting for foods that provided energy to withstand the cold. In these examples, we see evidence of human adaptations to cold that are both biological and cultural and that are rooted in evolution.

Biocultural Evolution and the Life Course

A good place to explore the interaction of biology and culture is the human life course. If we consider how a human develops from an embryo into an adult and examine the forces that operate on that process, we will have a better perspective of how both biology and culture influence our own lives and how our evolutionary history creates opportunities and sets limitations.

Of course, cultural factors interact with genetically based biological characteristics to widely varying degrees; these variable interactions influence how characteristics are expressed in individuals. Some genetically based characteristics will be exhibited no matter what the cultural context of a person's life happens to be. If a woman inherits two alleles for albinism, for example, she will be deficient in the

Darren Brode / Shutterstock (left),
David P. Smith / Shutterstock (right)

production of the pigment melanin, resulting in lightly colored skin, hair, and eyes. This phenotype will emerge regardless of the woman's cultural environment. Likewise, the sex-linked trait for hemophilia will be exhibited by all males who inherit it, no matter where they live.

Other characteristics, such as intelligence, body shape, and growth reflect the interaction of environment and genes. We know, for example, that each of us is born with a genetic makeup that influences the maximum stature we can achieve in adulthood. But to reach that maximum stature, we must be properly nourished during growth (including during fetal development), and we must avoid many childhood diseases and other stresses that inhibit growth. What factors determine whether we are well fed and receive good medical care? In the United States, socioeconomic status is probably the primary factor that determines nutrition and health. Socioeconomic status is thus an example of a cultural factor that affects growth. But in another culture, diet and health status might be influenced by whether the individual is male or female. In some cultures, males receive the best care in infancy and childhood and are thus often larger and healthier as adults than are females (**Fig. 17-1**). If there's a cultural value on slimness in women, young girls may try to restrict their food intake in ways that affect their growth; but if the culture values plumpness, the effect on diet in adolescence will likely be different. These are all examples of how cultural values affect growth and development.

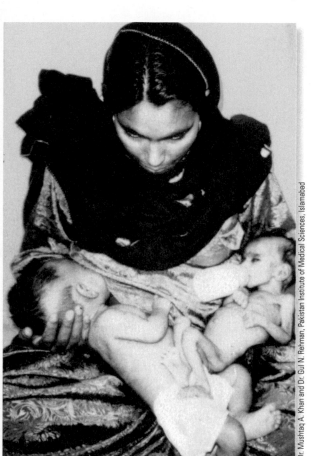

▲ **Figure 17-1**
This is a mother with her twin children. The one on the left is a boy and is breast-fed. The girl, on the right, is bottle-fed. This illustrates both differential treatment of boys and girls in many societies and the potential negative effects of bottle-feeding.

Dr. Mushtaq A. Khan and Dr. Gul N. Rehman, Pakistan Institute of Medical Sciences, Islamabad

growth Increase in mass or number of cells.

development Differentiation of cells into different types of tissues and their maturation.

ossification The process by which cartilage cells are replaced by bone cells in normal growth.

Fundamentals of Human Growth and Development

The terms *growth* and *development* are often used interchangeably, but they actually refer to different processes. **Growth** refers to an increase in mass or number of cells, whereas **development** refers to differentiation of cells into different types of tissues and their maturation. Some cells are manufactured only once and can never be replaced if damaged (for example, nerve cells); some cells are continuously dying and being replaced (skin and red blood cells); and some can be regenerated if damaged (cells in the liver, kidneys, and most glands). One of the most obvious aspects of growth and development occurs in the skeleton. In fact, skeletal growth rates, usually measured as length in infants and height in children and adults, are among the most common gauges of age, health, and maturity in humans.

Bone Growth

Initially, the "skeleton" of the human fetus is made entirely of cartilage. During growth, the cartilage cells are gradually broken down and replaced by bone cells in a process known as **ossification**. A newborn has more than 600 bone segments connected by cartilage, but as she grows, the cartilage will be ossified, resulting in an adult skeleton of approximately 206 bones. **Figure 17-2** shows the process of ossification of the humerus, or upper arm bone. The shaft is referred to as the *diaphysis*, and the ends are called the *epiphyses* (*sing.*, epiphysis). Growth is completed when the epiphyses are completely united with the diaphysis and the cartilage has been fully ossified. At this point, the humerus is a single bone, whereas at age 10, it was made up of 4 bony segments connected by cartilage.

The epiphyses at the ends of long bones unite with their shafts in fairly predictable patterns, enabling an anthropologist to estimate the age at death of young individuals from skeletal remains. For example, growth is completed in the elbow region in most people by approximately age 19 (a bit earlier in girls than in boys). What this means is that the epiphysis on the **distal** end of the humerus has united with the humeral shaft, and the epiphyses at the **proximal** ends of the radius and ulna (lower arm bones) have united with their shafts (**Fig. 17-3**). By age 20 (again with some sex differences), the epiphyses have united in the hip and ankle regions. The epiphyses in the shoulder region do not unite until age 23, and the very last epiphyses to unite are where the collarbone (clavicle) articulates with the breastbone (sternum) at the base of the throat.

Stature

Increased stature is a common indicator of health status in children because it is easy to assess under most circumstances. There are two ways in which increases in height are typically reported in growth studies. One way is to plot a *distance curve*, following a person's height from year to year. (**Fig. 17-4a** is a typical distance curve for height in a healthy American girl.) Obvious growth spurts can be seen in infancy and at puberty. Typically, well-nourished humans grow fairly rapidly during the first two trimesters (6 months) of fetal development, but growth slows during the third trimester. After birth, the rate of development increases and remains fairly rapid for about four years, at which time it decreases again to a relatively slow, steady level that is maintained until puberty. At puberty, there is once again a very pronounced increase in growth. During this so-called **adolescent**

▼ **FIGURE 17-2**
This series depicts the humerus (upper arm bone) at various ages from birth to completion of growth. It shows the ends of the bone (the epiphyses) and the shaft (diaphysis) and different stages of union. The space between the diaphysis and epiphyses is cartilage while growth is continuing.

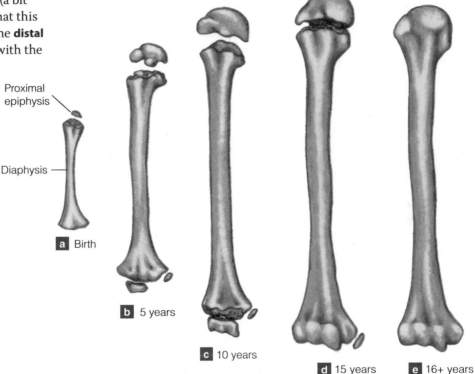

Proximal epiphysis

Diaphysis

a Birth

b 5 years

c 10 years

d 15 years

e 16+ years

growth spurt, Western teenagers typically grow 9 to 10 cm per year. Subsequent to the adolescent growth spurt, the rate of development declines again and remains slower until adult stature is achieved by the late teens.

Another way to describe growth is to plot the amount of increase in height gained each year. This produces a *velocity curve*, which depicts the growth spurts even more clearly (see Fig. **17-4b**). If we were to plot the height velocity curves for a chimpanzee and a baboon, we would see that the curves are different for each species. Some have argued that the human growth curve, with its characteristic spurt at adolescence, is unique to our species. Others argue that chimpanzees show

distal Referring to the part of a bone that is farthest from the point of attachment to the central skeleton.

proximal Referring to the part of a bone that is closest to the point of attachment to the central skeleton.

adolescent growth spurt The period during adolescence when well-nourished teens typically increase in stature at greater rates than at other times in the life cycle.

small but significant spurts at puberty, making their curves similar to those of humans and suggesting that the adolescent growth spurt may be a characteristic that predates the separation of the chimpanzee and human evolutionary paths approximately 7–5 mya. Nevertheless, no other mammal shows this characteristic to the same degree as modern humans. In addition to total height, other parts of the body (for example., limbs, organs) show similar growth curves, with rapid increases in the first trimester of gestation, during the first four years of life, and again at puberty.

Growth curves for boys and girls are significantly different, with the adolescent growth spurt occurring approximately two years earlier in girls than in boys (reflected in the fact that

the ends of the long bones unite earlier in girls than in boys). At birth, there is slight sexual dimorphism in many body measures (for example, height, weight, head circumference, and body fat), but the major divergence in these characteristics does not occur until puberty. **Table 17-1** shows the differences between these measures for boys and girls at birth and at age 18. Boys are slightly larger than girls at birth and are even more so at age 18 except in the last two measures, triceps skinfold and subscapular skinfold. These two measurements give information about body fat and are determined by a special skinfold measuring instrument. The measures in Table 17-1 reflect differences not only in the more obvious characteristics of height and weight, but also in body composi-

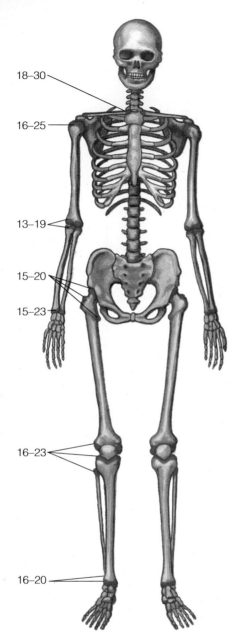

▲ FIGURE 17-3
Ages of epiphyseal union. For example, the epiphyses unite in the elbow between ages 13 and 19.

▶ FIGURE 17-4
Distance and velocity curves of growth in height for a healthy American girl. **(a)** The distance curve shows the girl's height from year to year. **(b)** The velocity curve plots the amount of height gained in a given year.

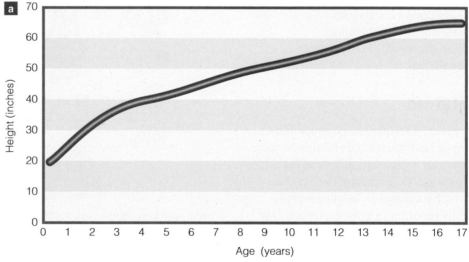

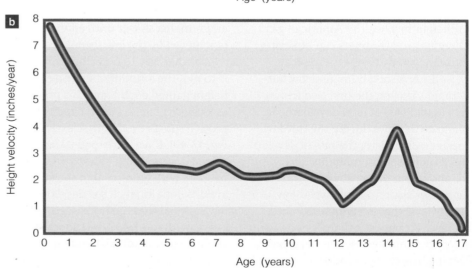

TABLE 17.1	Size at Birth and Age 18 for Boys and Girls Born in the United States			
	Birth		**18 Years**	
	Boys	**Girls**	**Boys**	**Girls**
Length/stature (cm)	49.9	49.3	176.6	163.1
Weight (kg)	3.4	3.3	71.4	58.3
Head circumference (cm)	34.8	34.1	55.9	54.9
Triceps skinfold (mm)	3.8	4.1	8.5	17.5
Subscapular skinfold (mm)	3.5	3.8	10.0	12.0

Source: From Bogin, 1999, p. 65.

tion, with girls generally having more body fat than boys at all ages. As we will see, this body fat is important for reproduction.

An individual's adult stature is influenced by genetics, health, and nutrition. A child who is well-nourished and experiences few childhood illnesses is more likely to reach his or her genetic potential for height than a child who suffers from malnutrition and frequent infectious diseases. In general, members of higher socioeconomic groups in a given population have taller average stature than members of lower socioeconomic groups, reflecting the impact of culture and economic status on the processes of growth and development (Bogin, 1999). Where girls receive less food and medical care than boys during the growing years, the sex differences in stature may be greater than expected. These are examples of how growth is the result of biocultural processes.

Brain Growth

The head is a relatively large part of the body at birth. The continued growth of the brain after birth occurs at a rate far greater than any other part of the body with the exception of the eyeball. At birth, the human brain is about 25 percent of its adult size. By 6 months of age, the brain has doubled in size, reaching 50 percent of adult size, and it reaches near-adult size by age 10 years. At adolescence, the brain displays only a very small growth spurt, making the brain an exception to the growth curves for most other parts of the body. This pattern of brain growth, including the relatively small amount of growth before birth, is unusual among primates and other mammals. By contrast, most mammalian species have typically achieved at least 50 percent of adult brain size before birth. For humans, however, the narrow pelvis that evolved for walking bipedally provides limits on the size of the fetal head that can be delivered through it. That limitation, along with the value of having most brain growth occur in the more stimulating environment outside the womb, has resulted in human infants being born with far less of their total adult brain size than most other mammals.

Delayed brain growth may be particularly important for a species dependent on language. The human brain's language centers develop in the first three years of life, when the brain is rapidly expanding; these three years are considered a critical period for the development of language in the human child. In fact, children who aren't exposed to speech during this period never develop fully normal language skills.

Nutritional Effects on Growth, Development, and Later-Life Health

Nutrition has an impact on human growth at every stage of the life cycle. During pregnancy, for example, a woman's diet can have a profound effect on the development of her fetus and the eventual health of the child. Moreover, the effects are transgenerational, because a woman's own supply of eggs is developed during her own fetal development. So if a woman is malnourished during pregnancy, the eggs that develop in her female fetus may be damaged in a way that affects her future grandchildren's health. And even if a baby girl whose mother was malnourished during pregnancy is well nourished from birth on (as often happens in adoptions), her growth, health, and future pregnancies appear to be com-

promised—a legacy that may extend for several generations (Kuzawa, 2005). Furthermore, nutritional stress during pregancy commonly results in low-birth-weight babies that are at great risk for developing hypertension, cardio-vascular disease, and diabetes later in life (Barker, 1994; Gluckman and Hanson, 2005). Low-birth-weight babies are particularly at risk if they are born into a world of abundant food resources (especially cheap fast food) and gain weight rapidly in childhood (Kuzawa, 2005, 2008). These findings have clear implications for public health efforts that attempt to provide adequate nutritional support to pregnant women and infants throughout the world.

Nutrients needed for growth, development, and body maintenance include proteins, carbohydrates, lipids (fats), vitamins, and minerals. The specific amount that we need of each of these nutrients coevolved with the types of foods that were available to human ancestors throughout our evolutionary history. For example, the specific pattern of amino acids required in human nutrition (the **essential amino acids**) reflects an ancestral diet high in animal protein. We share with many other primates a dependence on dietary sources of organic nutrients such as vitamin C, reflecting a long history of consumption of fruits and other plant parts. In other words, our need for vitamin C coevolved with a diet high in that nutrient. Unfortunately for modern humans, these coevolved nutritional requirements are often incompatible with the foods that are available and typically consumed today. The ancestral diet, while perhaps high in animal protein, was probably lower in fats, particularly saturated fats. The diet was also most likely high in complex carbohydrates (including fiber), low in salt, and high in calcium. We don't need to be reminded that the contemporary diet typically seen in many industrialized societies is just the opposite of the ancestral one. It's high in saturated fats and salt and low in complex carbohydrates, fiber, and calcium (**Table 17-2**). There's

TABLE 17.2 Preagricultural and Contemporary American Dietary Composition		
	Preagricultural Diet	**Contemporary Diet**
Total dietary energy (%)		
Protein	33	12
Carbohydrate	46	46
Fat	21	42
Alcohol	~0	(7–10)
P:S ratio*	1.41	0.44
Cholesterol (mg)	520	300–500
Fiber (g)	100–150	19.7
Sodium (mg)	690	2,300–6,900
Calcium (mg)	1,500–2,000	740
Ascorbic acid (mg)	440	90

*Polyunsaturated: saturated fat ratio.

Source: From *The Paleolithic Prescription*, by S. Boyd Eaton, Marjorie Shostak, and Melvin Konner (New York: Harper & Row, 1988).

Diabetes

What is diabetes? There are actually two different diseases referred to as diabetes. One, the less common, is type 1 diabetes, also called insulin-dependent diabetes mellitus (IDDM), or juvenile-onset diabetes, which occurs when the immune system interferes with the body's ability to produce the insulin that converts sugars (glucose) to energy. This type of diabetes is usually first recognized in childhood and requires lifelong insulin injections to avoid cell damage and death. It's unlikely that children with type 1 diabetes lived very long in the past. Type 2 diabetes, also called non-insulin-dependent diabetes mellitus (NIDDM), is far more common today and has to do with the way insulin is used in the body. Sometimes this is described as "insulin resistance" in that there may be sufficient insulin produced, but the cells are not able to utilize it. This inability results in a buildup of glucose in the bloodstream that can cause a number of complications of the cardiovascular system, kidneys, and nervous system. If untreated, usually with dietary changes, weight control, and exercise, type 2 diabetes can also result in early death.

A few years ago, type 2 diabetes was something that happened to older people living primarily in the developed world. Sadly, this is no longer true. The World Diabetes Foundation estimates that 80 percent of the new cases of type 2 diabetes that appear between now and 2025 will be in developing nations, and the World Health Organization (WHO) predicts that more than 70 percent of *all* diabetes cases in the world will be in developing nations in 2025. Furthermore, type 2 diabetes is now seen in children as young as 4 (Pavkov et al., 2006), and the mean age of diagnosis in the United States dropped from 52 to 46 between 1988 and 2000 (Koopman et al., 2005). In fact, we predict that almost everyone reading this book has a friend or family member who has diabetes. What's happened to make this former "disease of old age" and "disease of civilization" reach what some have described as epidemic proportions?

Several decades ago, geneticist James Neel (1962) proposed that people who develop diabetes have "thrifty genotypes" that served their ancestors well when they lived under alternating feast and famine conditions and engaged in high levels of physical activity. In other words, when food was abundant, people stored extra energy in the form of fat, and when food became scarce, they had energy reserves to rely on. But today, these so called "thrifty genotypes" are nothing but trouble for relatively inactive people who have a constant, overabundant supply of food. Thus, what was formerly an asset (the ability to be thrifty and "save" calories for future use) is now a liability. Recent reviews, however, find the thrifty genotype hypothesis to be an oversimplification, and a "thrifty phenotype hypothesis" has emerged to take its place. According to this view, poor fetal and early postnatal nutrition imposes mechanisms of nutritional thrift on the growing individual, resulting in impaired glucose resistance throughout life (Hales and Barker, 2001). Thus, the long-term consequences of early malnutrition are impaired development of glucose metabolism and a far greater susceptibility to type 2 diabetes. Recognition of the role of early nutrition in predisposing to diabetes suggests that by improving maternal and prenatal health worldwide, we may be able to reduce the incidence of type 2 diabetes in a far more effective way than we can by urging people to change their diets and other aspects of their lifestyles.

---

very good evidence that many of today's diseases in industrialized countries are related to the lack of fit between our diet today and the one with which we evolved (Eaton et.al, 1988, 1999; Cordain, 2002).

Many of our biological and behavioral characteristics evolved because in the past they contributed to survival and reproductive success, but today these same characteristics may be maladaptive. An example is our ability to store fat. This capability was an advantage in the past, when food availability often alternated between abundance and scarcity. Those who could store fat during times of abundance could draw on those stores during times of scarcity and remain healthy, resist disease, and, for women, maintain the ability to reproduce. Today, people with adequate economic resources spend much of their lives with a relative abundance of food. Considering the number of disorders associated with obesity, the formerly positive ability to store extra fat has now turned into a liability. Our "feast or famine" biology is now incompatible with the constant feast many of us indulge in today.

Perhaps no disorder is as clearly linked with dietary and lifestyle behaviors as the form of diabetes mellitus that typically begins in later life. This form is referred to either as type 2 diabetes or NIDDM (non-insulin-

essential amino acids The 9 (of 22) amino acids that must be obtained from the food we eat because they are not synthesized in the body in sufficient amounts.

dependent diabetes mellitus). In 1900, diabetes ranked twenty-seventh among the leading causes of death in the United States; today it ranks seventh. And the threat to world health from this disease is growing, with projections of an increase in incidence between 2010 and 2030 of 20 percent in industrialized countries and 69 percent in developing countries (Shaw et al., 2010). Part of this projected increase will be due to decreases in other causes of death (for example, infectious diseases), but much of it has to do with lifestyle and dietary changes associated with modernization and globalization, especially the decrease in levels of daily activity and increase in dietary intake of fats and refined carbohydrates (Lieberman, 2003).

Noting that our current diets and activity levels are very different from those of our ancestors, proponents of **evolutionary medicine** suggest that diabetes is the price we pay for consuming excessive sugars and other refined carbohydrates while spending our days in front of the TV set or computer monitor. The reason the incidence of diabetes is increasing in developing nations is that these bad habits are spreading to those nations. In fact, we may soon see what can be called an "epidemiological collision" (Trevathan, 2010) in countries such as Zimbabwe, Ecuador, and Haiti, where malnutrition and infectious diseases are rampant but obesity is on the rise, so that people are dying not only from diseases of poverty but also from those more characteristic of wealthier populations.

It's clear that both deficiencies and excesses of nutrients can cause health problems and interfere with childhood growth. Certainly, many people in all parts of the world, both industrialized and developing, suffer from inadequate supplies of food of any quality. We read daily of thousands dying from starvation due to drought, warfare, or political instability. The blame must be placed not only on the narrowed food base that resulted from the emergence of agriculture, but also on the increase

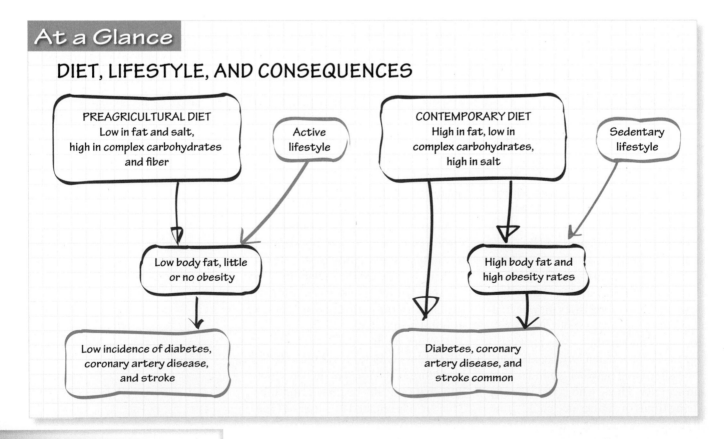

At a Glance

DIET, LIFESTYLE, AND CONSEQUENCES

PREAGRICULTURAL DIET
Low in fat and salt,
high in complex carbohydrates and fiber

Active lifestyle

CONTEMPORARY DIET
High in fat, low in complex carbohydrates, high in salt

Sedentary lifestyle

Low body fat, little or no obesity

High body fat and high obesity rates

Low incidence of diabetes, coronary artery disease, and stroke

Diabetes, coronary artery disease, and stroke common

evolutionary medicine The application of principles of evolution to aspects of medical research and practice.

▲ **FIGURE 17-5**
Some people suffer from an over-abundance of food (left), while others suffer from tragically insufficient amounts of food.

in human population that occurred when people began settling in permanent villages and having more children. Today, the crush of billions of humans almost completely dependent on cereal grains (Cordain, 1999) means that millions face **undernutrition**, **malnutrition**, and even starvation. Even with these huge populations, however, food scarcity may not be as big a problem as food inequality. In other words, there may be enough food produced for all people on earth, but economic and political forces keep it from reaching those who need it most. Of increasing concern are the effects of globalization (including liberalization of trade and agricultural policies) on food security, especially in developing nations, and what has become known as the "Global South." In particular, the adoption of Western diets and lifestyles has contributed to declining health in much of the world (Young, 2004).

In summary, our nutritional adaptations were shaped in environments that included times of scarcity alternating with times of abundance. The variety of foods consumed was so great that nutritional deficiency diseases were rare. Small amounts of animal foods were probably an important part of the diet in many parts of the world. In northern latitudes, after about 1 mya, meat was an important part of the diet. But because meat from wild animals is low in saturated fats, the negative effects of high meat intake that we see

today were rare. Our diet today is often incompatible with the adaptations that evolved in the millions of years preceding the development of agriculture. The consequences of that incompatibility include both starvation and obesity (**Fig. 17-5**).

Other Factors Affecting Growth and Development: Genes, Environment, and Hormones

Although genetic factors set the underlying limitations and potentialities for growth and development, life experience and environmental factors determine how growth and development proceed within those parameters. One way that has historically been used to tease apart genetic and environmental effects on growth is to study monozygotic and dizygotic twins. Monozygotic ("identical") twins come from the union of a single sperm and ovum and share 100 percent of their genes. Dizygotic ("fraternal") twins come from separate ova and sperm and share only 50 percent of their genes, just as any other siblings from the same parents. If monozygotic twins with identical genes but different growth environments are found to have the same

undernutrition A diet insufficient in quantity (calories) to support normal health.

malnutrition A diet insufficient in quality (i.e., lacking some essential component) to support normal health.

stature at various ages (that is, they are highly correlated for stature), then we can conclude that genes are the primary, if not the only, determinants of stature. Most studies of twins reveal that under normal circumstances, stature is "highly correlated" for monozygotic twins, leading to the conclusion that stature is under fairly strong genetic control. Weight, on the other hand, seems to be more strongly influenced by diet, environment, and individual experiences than by genes.

Recent research has called into question some of the earlier twin studies, however. This is because we now know that the way in which gene expression unfolds in the growing individual is influenced by a number of environmental factors that could lead to individuals with identical genotypes having different phenotypes. In other words, identical twins aren't really identical, and they become even more different as they age (Frago et al., 2005; Gluckman et al., 2009). Phenotypic differences emerge in identical twins because of the "software" that provides instructions to the unfolding genotype. These instructions are known as the **epigenome**, and they are responsible for telling liver cells how to be liver cells and heart cells how to be heart cells. All of the cells in our body have the same genes (except the sex cells), but they do different things because of the epigenome. In different individuals, the epigenome may turn off some genes or turn on others, resulting in different phenotypes. This is one of the main ways in which the environment interacts with genes and helps explain why one member of a pair of identical twins may suffer from a genetically based cancer while the other is disease-free. Lifestyle factors are particularly important influences on the epigenome, especially diet and smoking.

The ongoing "nature-nurture debate" has pitted genetic factors against environmental factors in determining how an individual grows, develops, and behaves. The field of **epigenetics** helps to resolve this con-

flict by revealing that structural changes to DNA and associated proteins (without causing changes in the nucleotide sequence) can underlie gene expression. The changes are transmitted through mitosis, so that when they are established during development, they persist with further cell division. In this way, environmental factors (such as smoke or air pollution) can bring about changes during development that affect a person in adulthood, partially explaining differences in disease risk. Although these changes in gene expression are not usually passed on to offspring, there is increasing evidence of epigenetic inheritance that transcends generations (Whitelaw and Whitelaw, 2006). Certainly, research in epigenetics calls into question the whole idea of genetic determinism for many traits.

One of the primary ways in which genes have an effect on growth and development is through their effects on hormones. Hormones are substances produced in one cell that have an effect on another cell. Most hormones are produced by *endocrine* glands and are transported to other cells in the bloodstream; virtually all have an effect on growth. Just above the roof of your mouth are two of the most important organs related to hormone action: the *hypothalamus* and the *pituitary gland*. They are connected to each other and are in almost constant communication. The hypothalamus has been described as the central command center or relay station for all kinds of actions that are going on in the body. The pituitary, on the other hand, is the primary regulator of hormonal interactions related to reproduction, growth, and development. The hypothalamus "tells" the pituitary what to do based on input it receives from throughout the body and brain. There are two parts of the pituitary, the anterior and the posterior. The anterior pituitary produces hormones that regulate reproduction (FSH and LH), milk production (prolactin), metabolism (ACTH), and growth (GH). The posterior pituitary secretes sev-

epigenome The instructions that determine what and how genes are expressed in cells.

epigenetics Changes in phenotype that are not related to changes in underlying DNA.

eral hormones that in turn act on the gonads (ovaries and testes) and the thyroid, adrenal, and mammary glands.

We can use the hormone thyroxine, produced by the thyroid gland in the neck, to illustrate the action of hormones and the communication system among the endocrine glands (**Fig. 17-6**; Crapo, 1985). Thyroxine regulates metabolism and aids in body heat production. When thyroxine levels fall too low for normal metabolism, the brain senses this and sends a message to the hypothalamus. The hypothalamus reacts by releasing a hormone (TRH) that goes to the anterior pituitary, where it stimulates the release of TSH, or thyroid-stimulating hormone. TSH then goes to the thyroid gland, stimulating it to release thyroxine. When the brain senses that the levels of thyroxine are adequate, it sends signals that inhibit the further release of TRH and TSH. In many ways, this process is similar to what your household thermostat does: When it senses that the temperature has dropped too low for comfort, it sends a message to the heating system to begin producing more heat; when the temperature reaches or exceeds the preset level, the thermostat sends another message to turn the heat off.

Two other hormones that are important in growth include insulin and growth hormone (GH). Insulin, produced by the pancreas, regulates the use of glucose in the body, as noted in our discussion of diabetes. Growth hormone, secreted by the anterior pituitary, promotes growth and has an effect on just about every cell in the body. Tumors and other disorders can result in excessive or insufficient amounts of growth hormone secretion, which in turn can result in gigantism or dwarfism. Short stature is not always due to pathology, however. One group of people who have notably short stature are African Efe pygmies (**Fig. 17-7**). There is evidence that altered levels of growth hormone and its controlling factors interact with nutritional factors and infectious diseases to produce the relatively short adult stature of these people (Shea and Bailey, 1996), providing another example of epigenetics and the interaction of biological and cultural forces. More recent research suggests that their short stature may be due to decreased expression of the receptors for growth hormone and that epigenetic factors such as diet could play a role in modifying how genes are expressed in both African and Philippine pygmies (Dávila et al., 2002; Bozzola et al., 2009).

Another hormone that influences growth and development is cortisol, which is elevated during stress. Up to a point, cortisol elevation is adaptive, but if the response is prolonged or severe, there appear to be negative effects on health and behavior (Flinn, 1999; Flinn and England, 2003). Under conditions of chronic emotional and psychosocial

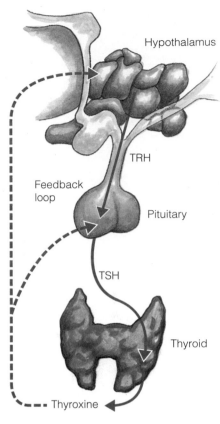

▲ **FIGURE 17-6**

Example of a feedback loop. When thyroxine levels in the blood fall too low, the hypothalamus releases TRH (thyrotropin-releasing hormone), which goes to the anterior pituitary, triggering the release of TSH (thyroid-stimulating hormone). TSH causes thyroxine to be released from the thyroid gland. Release of TRH and TSH is then inhibited.

◄ **FIGURE 17-7**

Charles Knowles of the Wildlife Conservation Network stands beside three Mbuti (Efe) staff members of the Okapi Conservation Project.

stress, cortisol levels may remain high and suppress normal immune function. This means that a child living in a stressful situation is more vulnerable to infectious diseases and may experience periods of slowed growth if the stress is prolonged.

Life History Theory

As noted in earlier chapters, primatologists and other physical anthropologists view primate and human growth and development from an evolutionary perspective, with an interest in how natural selection has operated on the life cycle from conception to death, a perspective known as *life history theory*. Why, for example, do humans have longer periods of infancy and childhood compared with other primates (**Fig. 17-8**)? What accounts for differences seen in the life cycles of such closely related species as humans and chimpanzees? Life history research seeks to answer such questions (e.g., Mace, 2000; Hawkes and Paine, 2006).

Life history theory begins with the premise that an organism has only a certain amount of energy available for growing, maintaining life, and reproducing. Energy invested in one

of these processes is not available for another. So the entire life course is a series of trade-offs among life history traits, such as length of gestation, age at weaning, time spent in growth to adulthood, adult body size, and length of life span. Life history theory provides the basis for understanding how fast an organism will grow and to what size, how many offspring can be produced, how long gestation will last, and how long an individual will live. Crucial to understanding life history theory is its link to the evolutionary process: It is the action of natural selection that shapes life history traits, determining which traits will succeed or fail in a given environment. It's not clear whether life history theory works in contemporary human populations (Strassman and Gillespie, 2002), but it's a useful guide for examining the various life cycle phases from evolutionary and ecological perspectives.

Not all animals have clearly demarcated phases in their lives; moreover, among mammals, humans have more such phases than do other species. Protozoa, among the simplest of animals, have only one phase; many invertebrates have two:larval and adult. Most primates have four phases: gestation, infancy, juvenile (usually called child-

▼ **FIGURE 17-8**
Primate life cycle stages.

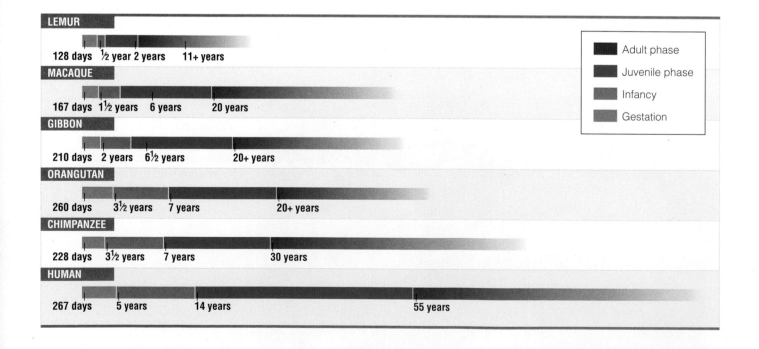

hood in humans), and adult. Apes, humans, and perhaps monkeys have a phase between the juvenile, or childhood, phase and adulthood that is referred to as adolescence (the teenage years, in humans). Finally, for humans there is the addition of a sixth phase in women, the postreproductive years following **menopause**. One could argue that during the course of primate evolution, more recently evolved forms have longer life spans and more divisions of the life span into phases, or stages.

Most of these life cycle stages are well marked by biological transitions. The prenatal phase begins with conception and ends with birth; infancy is the period of nursing; childhood, or the juvenile phase, is the period from weaning to sexual maturity (puberty in humans); adolescence is the period from puberty to the end of growth; adulthood is marked by the birth of the first child and/or the completion of growth; and menopause is recognized as having occurred one full year after the last menstrual cycle. These biological markers are similar among higher primates, but for humans, there is an added complexity: They occur in cultural contexts that define and characterize them. Puberty, for example, has very different meanings in different cultures. A girl's first menstruation (**menarche**) is often marked with ritual and celebration, and a change in social status typically occurs with this biological transition. Likewise, menopause is often associated with a rise in status for women in non-Western societies, but it's commonly seen as a negative transition for women in many Western societies. As we'll see, collective and individual attitudes toward these life cycle transitions affect an individual's growth and development.

Pregnancy, Birth, and Infancy

The biological aspects of conception and gestation can be discussed in a fairly straightforward way, drawing from what is known about reproductive biology at the present time: A sperm fertilizes an egg; the resulting zygote travels through a uterine (fallopian) tube to become implanted in the uterine lining; and the embryo develops until it's mature enough to survive outside the womb, at which time birth occurs. But this is clearly not all there is to human pregnancy and birth. Female biology may be similar the world over, but cultural rules and practices are the primary determinants of who will get pregnant, as well as when, where, how, and by whom.

Once a pregnancy has begun, there's much variation in how a woman should behave, what she should eat, where she should and should not go, and how she should interact with other people. Almost every culture known, including our own, imposes dietary restrictions on pregnant women. Many of these appear to serve an important biological function, particularly that of keeping the woman from ingesting toxins that would be dangerous for the fetus. (Alcohol is a good example of a potential toxin whose consumption in pregnancy is discouraged in the United States.) The food aversions to coffee, alcohol, and other bitter substances that many women experience during pregnancy may be evolved adaptations to protect the embryo from toxins. The nausea of early pregnancy may also function to limit the intake of foods potentially harmful to the embryo at a critical stage of development (Profet, 1988; Williams and Nesse 1991; but see Pike, 2000).

Birth is an event that's celebrated with ritual in almost every culture studied. In fact, the relatively little fanfare associated with childbirth in the United States is unusual by world standards. Because risk of death for both mother and child is so great at birth, it's not surprising that it's surrounded with ritual significance. Perhaps, because of the high risk of death, we tend to think that birth is far more difficult for humans than it is for other mammals. But since almost all primate infants

menopause The end of menstruation in women, usually occuring at around age 50.

menarche The first menstruation in girls, usually occuring in the early to mid-teens.

have large heads relative to body size, birth is challenging to many primates (**Fig. 17-9**). For humans, the pelvis is narrow as an adaptation to bipedalism, so the birth canal presents an even tighter squeeze for the infant during delivery.

The combination of a narrow pelvis, adapted for bipedalism, and a large brain may explain an unusual behavior that humans exhibit: a tendency to seek assistance at birth. Although it is certainly possible to deliver an infant alone, a survey of world cultures reveals that it is far more common for women to deliver their infants in the presence of others (Rosenberg and Trevathan, 2001). So for humans, birth is a life cycle event that typically takes place in the context of culture; it's a social rather than a solitary event, unlike that for most other mammals.

Infancy is defined for mammals as the period when breast-feeding takes place, typically lasting about three to four years in humans. When we consider how unusual it is for a mother to breast-feed her child for even a year in the United States or Canada, this figure may surprise us. But considering that three or four years of breast-feeding is the norm for chimpanzees, gorillas, orangutans, and women in foraging societies, most anthropologists conclude that three years was the norm for most humans in the evolutionary past (Stuart-Macadam and Dettwyler, 1995). Other lines of evidence confirm this pattern, including the lack of other foods that infants could consume until the origin of agriculture and the domestication of milk-producing animals. In fact, if the mother died during childbirth in preagricultural populations, it's very likely that the child died also, unless there was another woman available who could nurse the child. Jane Goodall has noted that this

▶ **FIGURE 17-9**
The relationship between the average diameter of the birth canal of adult females and average head length and breadth of newborns of the same species. (After Jolly, 1985.)

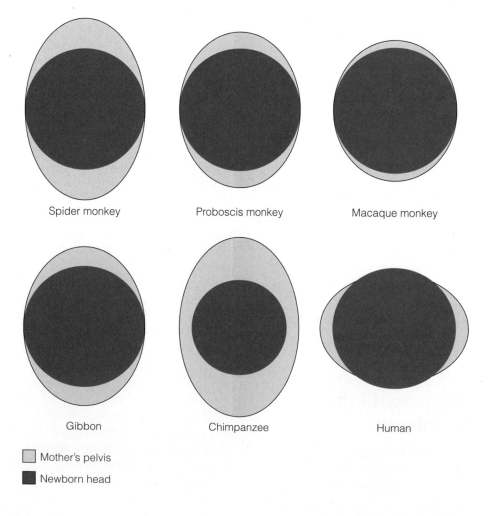

Spider monkey   Proboscis monkey   Macaque monkey

Gibbon   Chimpanzee   Human

☐ Mother's pelvis
■ Newborn head

is also true for chimpanzees: Infants who are orphaned before they are weaned do not usually survive. Even those orphaned after weaning are still emotionally dependent on their mothers and exhibit clinical signs of depression for a few months or years after the mother's death, assuming they survive the trauma (Goodall, 1986).

Human milk, like that of other primates, is extremely low in fats and protein. Such a low nutrient content is typical for species in which mothers are seldom or never separated from their infants and nurse in short, frequent bouts. Not coincidentally, prolonged, frequent nursing suppresses ovulation in marginally nourished women (Konner and Worthman, 1980), especially when coupled with high activity levels and few calorie reserves (Ellison, 2001). Under these circumstances, breast-feeding can help maintain a four-year birth interval, during which infants have no nutritional competition from siblings. Thus, nursing served as a natural birth control mechanism in the evolutionary past, as it does in some populations today. The importance of adequate nutrients during the period of rapid brain growth cannot be overestimated, so it's not surprising that there are many cultural practices designed to ensure successful nursing.

Breast milk also provides important antibodies that contribute to infant survival. Throughout the world, breast-fed infants have far greater survival rates than those who are not breast-fed or who are weaned too early. The only exception is in societies where scientifically developed milk substitutes are readily available and appropriately used, and even then, important antibodies and other immune factors are not passed to the infants. Furthermore, there is increasing evidence that breast-feeding may be protective against later-life obesity, types 1 and 2 diabetes, and hypertension (Pollard, 2008).

Humans have unusually long childhoods and a slowed growth process, reflecting the importance of learning for our species (Bogin, 2006). Childhood is the time between weaning and puberty; it is a time when growth in stature is occurring, the brain is completing its growth, and technical and social skills are being acquired. For most other mammals, once weaning has occurred, getting food is left to individual effort. Humans may be unique in the practice of providing food for juveniles (Lancaster and Lancaster, 1983). In the course of human evolution, it's possible that provisioning children between weaning and puberty may have doubled or even tripled the number of offspring that survived to adulthood (Table 17-3). This long period of extended child care probably enhanced the time for learning technological and social skills, also contributing to greater survival and reproductive success. It is during childhood that the roles of fathers, older siblings, grandmothers, and other kin become very significant. While mothers are highly involved with caring for new infants,

TABLE 17.3	Providing for Juveniles	
	Percent of Those Who Survive	
	Weaning	**Adolescence**
Lion	28	15
Baboon	45	33
Macaque	42	13
Chimpanzee	48	38
Provisioned macaques	82	58
Human populations		
!Kung*	80	58
Yanomamo†	73	50
Paleoindian‡	86	50

*Hunting and gathering population of southern Africa.
†Horticultural population of South America.
‡Preagricultural people of the Americas.
Source: Adapted from Lancaster and Lancaster, 1983.

the socialization and child care of other children often fall to other family or community members. Clearly, family environment, stress, and other biosocial factors have a major impact on children's health (Flinn, 1999, 2008; **Fig. 17-10**).

Onset of Reproductive Functioning in Humans

For most animals, the juvenile, or childhood, stage ends when adulthood begins. For humans and apes, and possibly some monkeys, there's an additional life cycle stage called adolescence. This is a period of extremely rapid growth in humans (the "adolescent growth spurt") that is not seen in other primates (Bogin, 1999). A number of biological events mark the transition to adolescence for both males and females. These include increase in body size, change in body shape, and the development of testes and penes in boys and breasts in girls. Hormonal changes are the driving forces behind all these physical alterations, especially increased testosterone production in boys and increased estrogen production in girls. During this time after

reproductive functioning begins, individuals may be mature in some ways but immature in others. For example, an adolescent girl of 14 may be capable of bearing children, but she is not yet fully grown herself and is often too immature socially and economically to successfully raise a child.

The onset of menarche in girls is affected by several factors, including genetic patterns (girls tend to become mature at about the same age as their mothers), nutrition, stress, and disease. You'll remember from our discussion of life history theory that energy must be allocated among growth, body maintenance, and reproduction. During childhood, most resources are directed toward growth; but at some point, the body switches to allocating more energy to reproduction, and for girls, this shift is somewhat abrupt. What "tells" the body that it's time to direct more energy to reproduction and less (or none) to growth? An early hypothesis was that the switch occurred when a girl had accumulated a certain amount of body fat (Frisch, 1988). This proposal made sense because of a trend toward lower age of menarche that has been noted in affluent human populations in the last

▶ **FIGURE 17-10**
Human children require several years of extensive parental care following weaning.

© Alan Abraham / Corbis

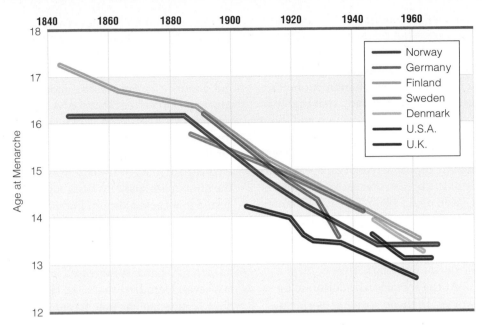

◄ FIGURE 17-11

The secular trend in age of menarche in Europe.

Source: Wood, James W., 1994 *Dynamics of Human Reproduction*, New York: Aldine de Gruyter, original redrawn from Eveleth, P. B. and J. M. Tanner, 1976. *Worldwide Variation in Human Growth*, Cambridge: Cambridge University Press.)

hundred years (**Fig. 17-11**) and the tendency for girls who are very active and thin to mature later than those who are heavier and less active. An alternative view that seems to fit the data better is Ellison's (2001) proposal that the critical growth parameter is not body fat but skeletal growth, specifically growth of the pelvis. We've already seen what a tight squeeze it is for the human infant to pass through the birth canal; just imagine what it would be like for an 8-year-old girl to try to give birth! Thus, it's not only fat that's important for reproduction, but completion of skeletal growth as well.

Life history theory predicts the timing of reproduction under favorable circumstances. For example, if early maturity results in higher numbers of surviving offspring, then it is predicted that natural selection would favor those members of a population who mature earlier. Until the advent of settled living, it's likely that females became pregnant as soon as they were biologically able to do so, that is, as soon as they had finished growing. This would have been advantageous because individual life expectancy would have been low. Paleodemographic studies indicate a mortality rate of at least 50 percent in subadults in preindustrial populations; and of the half that survived to adulthood, most did not survive to age 50. Considering the reality of short life spans combined with the long period of infant dependency, producing offspring as early as possible may have contributed to the reproductive success of females, particularly early hominin females. By giving birth as soon as she reached sexual maturity, an early hominin female enhanced her chances of rearing at least one offspring to the point it could survive without her.

Grandmothers

Pregnancy and child care occupy much of a woman's adult life in most cultures, as they likely did throughout hominin evolution. For most women in developed countries, the years from menarche to menopause are marked by monthly menstruation except when they are pregnant or nursing. A woman who never becomes pregnant may have as many as 400 cycles between menarche and menopause. Because reliable contraceptives were unavailable in the past, this high number of menstrual cycles is probably a relatively recent phenomenon. It's been suggested, in fact, that highly frequent menstrual cycling and the associated cell turnover rates may be implicated in several cancers of the female reproductive organs, especially of the breast, uterus, and ovaries (Eaton et al., 1994). During the course of human evolution, females may have had as few as 60 menstrual cycles in their entire lives unless they were sterile or not sexually active.

At the social level, adulthood for women in the majority of world cultures means, in addition to caring for children, participation in economic activities. Adulthood for men typically includes activities related to subsistence, religion, politics, and family. Women may be equally or less involved in these activities, depending on the culture.

For women, menopause, or the end of menstruation, is a sign that they're entering a new life cycle phase. Estrogen and progesterone production begin to decline toward the end of the reproductive years until ovulation (and thus menstruation) ceases altogether. This occurs at about age 50 in all parts of the world. Throughout human evolution, few women lived much past menopause, but today, this event occurs when women have as much as one-third of their active and healthy lives ahead of them. No other female primates have such a long postreproductive period. Female chimpanzees and monkeys experience decreased fertility in their later years, but most continue to have reproductive cycles until their deaths. Occasional reports of menopause in apes and monkeys have been noted, but it's far from a routine and expected event. In fact, in 2010, a 56-year-old chimpanzee at a Kansas zoo surprised everyone by giving birth to a healthy female infant 22 years after her last birth.

Why do human females cease reproducing and then live such a long time when they can no longer reproduce? There are two questions here, one about cessation and one about living for so long after cessation. A theory regarding cessation of ovulation (menopause) suggests that it wasn't itself favored by natural selection; rather, it is an artifact of the extension of the human life span. It's been suggested that the maximum life span of the mammalian egg is 50 years (you'll recall that all the ova are already present before birth). Thus, although the human life span has increased in the last several hundred years, the reproductive life span has not. To put it another way, the long postreproductive years and associated menopause in women have been "uncovered" by our extended life expectancy resulting from the reduction in many causes of death (Sievert, 2006). Another proposal to explain menopause is that so much energy is needed "up front" for reproduction in the early years that there's nothing left over by the time a woman reaches 50.

One theory for a long postreproductive life relates to parenting. Because it takes about 12 to 15 years before a child becomes independent, it's argued that females are biologically "programmed" to live 12 to 15 years beyond the birth of their last child (Mayer, 1982). This suggests that the maximum human life span for preagricultural humans was about 65 years, a figure that corresponds to what's known for contemporary hunter-gatherers and for prehistoric populations. One final explanation for the long postreproductive period in human females has been proposed by behavioral ecologists and is known as the "grandmother hypothesis." This proposal argues that natural selection may have favored this long period in women's lives because by ceasing to bear and raise their own children, postmenopausal women are freed to provide high-quality care for their grandchildren. (**Fig. 17-12**). In other words, an older woman would do more to increase her lifetime fitness by enhancing the survival of her older grandchildren (who share one-quarter of her genes) through provisioning and direct child care than by having her own, possibly low-quality, infants (Hawkes et al., 1997; but see Peccei, 2001). This is an example of the trade-offs considered by life history theory.

Aging and Longevity

Postreproductive years are physiologically defined for women, but "old age" is a very ambiguous concept. In the United States, we tend to associate old age with physical ailments and decreased activity. Thus, a person who's vigorous and active at age 70 might not be regarded as "old," whereas another who's frail and debilitated at age 55 may be considered old.

One reason we're concerned with this definition is that old age is generally regarded negatively and is typically unwelcome in the United States, a culture noted for its emphasis on youth. This attitude is quite different from that of many other societies, where old age brings with it wealth, higher status, and new freedoms, particularly for women. This is because high status is often correlated with knowledge, experience, and wisdom, which are themselves associated with greater age in most societies. Such has been the case throughout most of history, but today, in technologically developed countries, information is changing so rapidly that older people may no longer control the most relevant knowledge.

By and large, people are living longer today than they did in the past because they aren't dying from infectious disease. Currently, the top five killers in the United States, for example, are heart disease, cancer, stroke, accidents, and chronic obstructive lung disease. Together these account for more than 65 percent of deaths (Heron, 2010). All these conditions are considered "diseases of civilization" in that

◄ **FIGURE 17-12**
Senior Hadza woman and grandchild.

James F. O'Connell

most can be accounted for by conditions in the modern environment that weren't present in the past. Examples include cigarette smoke, air and water pollution, alcohol, automobiles, high-fat diets, and environmental carcinogens. It should be noted, however, that the high incidence of these diseases is also a result of people living to older ages because of factors such as improved hygiene, regular medical care, and new medical technologies. Compared with most other animals, humans have a long life span (**Table 17-4**). The maximum life span potential, estimated to be about 120 years, probably hasn't changed in the last several thousand years. But life expectancy at birth (the average length of life) has increased significantly in the last 100 years, owing to advances in standard of living, hygiene, and medical care. The most important advance is probably the treatment and prevention of infectious diseases, which typically take their toll on the young (Crews and Harper, 1998).

To some extent, aging is something we do throughout our lives (Finch, 2007). But we usually think of aging as **senescence**, the process of physiological decline in all systems of the body that occurs toward the end of the life course. Actually, throughout adulthood, there's a gradual decline in our cells' ability to synthesize proteins, in immune system function, in muscle mass (with a corresponding increase in fat mass) and strength, and in bone mineral density (Lamberts et al., 1997). This decline is associated with an increased risk for the chronic degenerative diseases usually listed as the causes of death in industrialized nations.

As you know, most causes of death that have their effects after the reproductive years won't be subjected to the forces of natural selection. What's more, in evolutionary terms, reproductive success isn't measured by how long we live. Instead, as we have emphasized throughout this textbook, it's measured by how many offspring we produce. So organisms need to survive only long enough to produce offspring and rear them to maturity. Most wild animals die young of infection, starvation, predation, injury, and cold. Obviously, there are exceptions to this statement, especially in larger-bodied animals. Elephants, for example, may live over 50 years, and we know of several chimpanzees at Gombe that have survived into their 40s or even 50s.

Here's one explanation for why humans age and are affected by chronic degenerative diseases like atherosclerosis, cancers, and hypertension: Genes that enhance reproductive success in earlier years (and thus were favored by natural selection) may have detrimental effects in later years. These are referred to as **pleiotropic genes**, meaning that they have multiple effects at different times in the life span or under different conditions (Williams, 1957). For example, genes that enhance the function of the immune system in the early years may also damage tissue so that cancer susceptibility increases in later life (Nesse and Williams, 1994). An example of this may be a gene responsible for lipid transport known as apolipoprotein E (apoE). One variant of this gene enhances immune function early in life but appears to be associated with increased risk of Alzheimer's and cardiovascular disease. In populations in which infectious agents are common, this variant is advantageous, but in populations where infectious diseases are rare and people live longer, the variant that protects against Alzheimer's and cardiovascular disease would be more beneficial (Finch and Sapolsky, 1999).

In another view of aging and pleiotropy, anticancer mechanisms operating in early life may have opposite effects in later life (Hornsby, 2010). What's more, epigenetic mechanisms affect not only aging itself but the diseases associated with aging. Current research on these mechanisms points to possible epigenetic-based therapies and prevention strategies for dealing with the negative consequences of the aging process (Gravina and Vijg, 2010).

TABLE 17.4	Maximum Life Spans for Selected Species	
Organism	**Approximate Maximum Life Span (in years)**
Bristlecone pine	5,000
Tortoise	170
Rockfish	140
Human	120
Blue whale	80
Indian elephant	70
Gorilla	39
Domestic dog	34
Rabbit	13
Rat	5

Source: From "The Biology of Human Aging," by William A. Stini; in C. G. N. Mascie-Taylor and G. W. Lasker (eds.), *Applications of Biological Anthropology to Human Affairs* (Cambridge, UK: Cambridge University Press, 1991, p. 215).

senescence Decline in physiological function usually associated with aging.

Pleiotropy may help us understand evolutionary reasons for aging, but what are the causes of senescence in the individual? Much attention has been focused recently on free radicals, highly reactive molecules that can damage cells. These by-products of normal metabolism can be protected against by antioxidants such as vitamins A, C, and E and by a number of enzymes (Kirkwood, 1997). Ultimately, damage to DNA can occur, which in turn contributes to the aging of cells, the immune system, and other functional systems of the body. Additionally, there is evidence that programmed cell death is also a part of the normal processes of development that can obviously contribute to senescence.

The mitochondrial theory of aging proposes that the free radicals produced by the normal action of the cell's mitochondria as by-products of daily living (for example, eating, breathing, walking) contribute to declining efficiency of energy production and accumulating mutations in mitochondrial DNA (mtDNA). When the mitochondria of an organ fail, there's a greater chance that the organ itself will fail. In this view, as mitochondria lose their ability to function, the body ages as well (Loeb et al., 2005; Kujoth et al., 2007). Two of the most promising strategies for enhancing health in later life are calorie reduction and aerobic exercise, both of which appear to improve mitochondrial function in later life (Lanza and Nair, 2010).

Another hypothesis for senescence is known as the "telomere hypothesis." In this view, the DNA sequence at the end of a chromosome, known as the telomere, is shortened each time a cell divides (**Fig. 17-13**). Cells that have divided many times throughout the life course have short telomeres, eventually reaching the point at which they can no longer divide and are unable to maintain healthy tissues and organs. Changes in telomere length have also been implicated in cancers and other diseases associated with aging (Oeseburg et al., 2010). In the laboratory, the enzyme telomerase can lengthen telomeres, allowing the cell to continue to divide. For this reason, the gene for telomerase has been called the "immortalizing gene." But this may not be a good thing, since the only cells that can divide indefinitely are cancer cells. Although this research isn't likely to lead to a lengthening of the life span, it may contribute to a better understanding of cellular functions and cancer.

Far more important than genes in the aging process, however, are lifestyle factors, such as smoking, physical activity, diet, and medical care. Life expectancy at birth varies considerably from country to country and among socioeconomic classes within a country. Throughout the world, women have higher life expectancies than men. A Japanese girl born in 2008, for example, can expect to live to age 86, a boy to age 79. Girls and boys born in that same year in the United States have life expectancies of 81 and 76, respectively. In contrast to these children in industrialized nations, girls and boys in Mali have life expectancies of only 50 and 48, respectively (data from World Health Organization). Many African nations have seen life expectancy drop below 40 due to deaths from AIDS. For example, before the AIDS epidemic, Zimbabweans had a life expectancy of 65 years; today, life expectancy in Zimbabwe is less than 37 (**Fig 17-14**). Unfortunately, some scholars are now predicting a leveling off or even a decline in life expectancy in nations like the United States because of rising rates of obesity and related health problems (Olshansky et al., 2005).

One consequence of improved health and longer life expectancy in conjunction with declining birth rates is an aging population, leading in some parts of the world to a shift toward older median ages and greater numbers of people older than 65 than younger than 20. In demographic terms, these two groups represent dependent categories, and there's increasing concern about the decline in the number

▲ FIGURE 17-13
Telomeres are repeated sequences of DNA at the ends of chromosomes, and the sequences appear to be the same in all animals. They stabilize and protect the ends of chromosomes, and as they shorten with each cell division, the chromosomes eventually become unstable.

pleiotropic genes Genes that have more than one effect; genes that have different effects at different times in the life cycle.

of working-aged adults available to support the younger and older segments of a population. In other words, the dependency ratio is increasing, with significant consequences for local and global economies.

Are We Still Evolving?

In many ways, it seems that culture has enabled us to transcend most of the limitations our biology imposes on us. But that biology was shaped during millions of years of evolution in environments very different from those in which most of us live today. There is, to a great extent, a lack of fit between our biology and our twenty-first-century cultural environments. Our expectations that scientists can easily and quickly discover a "magic bullet" to enable us to resist any disease that arises have been painfully dashed as death tolls from AIDS reach catastrophic levels in many parts of the world.

Socioeconomic and political concerns also have powerful effects on our species today. Whether you die of starvation or succumb to disorders associated with overconsumption depends

a great deal on where you live, what your socioeconomic status is, and how much power and control you have over your life—factors not related to biology. These factors also affect whether you'll be killed in a war or spend most of your life in a safe, comfortable community. Your chances of being exposed to one of the "new" pathogens such as HIV, SARS, or tuberculosis have a lot to do with your lifestyle and other cultural factors. But your chances of dying from the disease or failing to reproduce because of it still have a lot to do with your biology. The 4.3 million children dying annually from respiratory infections are primarily those in the developing world, with limited access to adequate medical care—clearly a cultural factor. But in those same areas, lacking that same medical care, are millions of other children who aren't getting the infections or aren't dying from them. Presumably, among the factors affecting this difference is resistance afforded by genes. It is clear that human gene frequencies are still changing from one generation to the next in response to selective agents such as disease; thus, our species is still evolving.

We can't predict whether we will become a different species or become

▼ **FIGURE 17-14**
Changes in life expectancy due to AIDS in seven African nations. (From United Nations Population Division, 1998.)

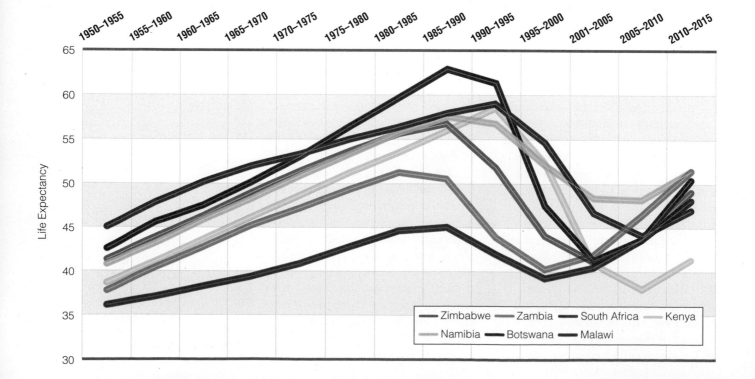

extinct as a species (remember, that is the fate of almost every species that has ever existed). Will our brains get larger, or will our hands evolve solely to push buttons? Or will we change genetically so that we no longer have to eat food? This is the stuff of science fiction, not anthropology. But as long as new pathogens appear or new environments are introduced by technology, there's little doubt that just like every other species on earth, the human species will either continue to evolve or become extinct.

Culture has enabled us to transcend many limits imposed by our biology. Today, people who never would have been able to do so in the past are surviving and having children. This in itself means that we are evolving. How many of you would be reading this text if you had been born under the health and economic conditions prevalent 500 years ago?

Summary of Main Topics

- The human life course is an excellent place to examine the interaction of culture and biology, given that patterns of human growth and nutritional requirements result from millions of years of biological evolution and thousands of years of cultural evolution.
- Our contemporary diets are often out of sync with our evolved nutritional needs, resulting in a number of diseases and disorders that affect an increasing number of people in both the developed and developing worlds.
- Life history theory provides a way of examining how natural selection has operated on the human life course from conception to old age.
- For a number of reasons resulting from our evolutionary history, human infants are relatively undeveloped at birth, especially in brain size, and require intense parental investment to reach adulthood and independence.
- Factors that affect the onset of reproductive functioning in women include skeletal growth processes, genes, environment, hormones, diet, and patterns of energy expenditure.
- Although rare among mammals, human females live relatively long and healthy lives after they have ceased reproducing; their role as grandmothers helps explain the selective value of postreproductive females.
- There appears to be an upper limit to human longevity, and there are a number of theories for why we age and ultimately die.
- As long as factors like disease differentially affect individuals and populations, evolutionary processes will continue for all species, including humans.

Critical Thinking Questions

1. Do you think it's possible to study humans without studying culture? Can we study humans only as cultural animals, or do we need to know something about human biology to understand behavior?
2. Compare and contrast the human preagricultural diet with that seen today in places like the United States. Discuss at least one major health consequence of what has been termed the "lack of fit" between the diet to which humans have evolved and the one many people now consume.
3. Briefly discuss some of the theories for why humans age. Do you think it will be possible to extend the human life span to longer than 125 years? Why or why not?
4. The authors of this text claim that humans are still subjected to the forces of evolution. Do you agree? What is the evidence for or against that claim?

Computerized model of the Arctic ice sheet. Its extent has been shrinking dramatically in recent years, losing as much as one million square miles of ice in just the last three decades.

Conclusion: Why It Matters

Key Questions

▶ What impacts have humans had on the planet and what can we do about those that are potentially negative?

▶ Given the enormous challenges we face as a species, is there any good news about our future?

By reading this book, you have accompanied us through geological time to the present state of *Homo sapiens*: 225 million years of mammalian evolution, 65 million years of primate evolution, 6 million years of hominin evolution, and 2 million years of evolution of the genus *Homo*. So, what do you think now? Are we just another mammal—or just another primate? In most ways, of course, we *are* like other mammals and primates. But as we have emphasized throughout the text, modern human beings are the result of *biocultural evolution*. In other words, modern human biology and behavior have been shaped by the biological and cultural forces that operated on our ancestors. In fact, it would be fruitless to attempt an understanding of modern human biology and diversity without considering that humans have evolved in the context of culture. It would be like trying to understand the biology of fish without considering that they live in water.

In the last few chapters, we saw how the choices we make as cultural animals have profound effects on our health and on the health of other people. Although culture and technology have allowed us to adapt beyond our biology, they have also impacted other species and, indeed, the planet. The human species now has the ability to preserve or destroy a significant portion of the earth's life-forms—the results of billions of years of evolution. Here we will briefly discuss some of the challenges that have emerged as a result of our own actions. While many people refuse to believe that humans are responsible for global climate change, the overwhelming consensus among climate scientists is that we are, and this fact really is an "inconvenient truth."

Although physical anthropology textbooks don't usually dwell on the topics included here, we feel that it's important to consider them, however brief and simplified our treatment must be. We are living during a critical period in the earth's history. Indeed, the future of much of life as we know it will be decided in the next few decades, and these decisions will be irrevocable. Therefore, it's crucial that we, as individuals, cities, and nations, make wise decisions, and to do this we must be well informed. We also think that it's important to consider these problems from

NASA

an anthropological perspective. This is something not usually done in the media and certainly not by politicians and heads of state. But if we are truly to comprehend the impact that human activities have had on the planet, then surely we must consider our biological and cultural evolution.

Human Impact on the Planet and Other Life-Forms

By most standards, *Homo sapiens* is a successful species. There are currently almost 7 billion human beings living on this planet. Even so, we and all other multicellular organisms contribute only a small fraction of all the cells on the planet—most of which are bacteria. So if we see life ultimately as a competition among reproducing organisms, bacteria are the winners, hands down.

Nevertheless, no matter what criterion for success is used, there's no question that *Homo sapiens* has had an inordinate impact on the earth and all other forms of life. In the past, humans had to respond primarily to challenges in the natural world; today the greatest challenges for our species (and all others) are the vastly altered environments of our own making.

Increasing population size is perhaps the single most important reason that our impact has been so great. As human population pressure increases, more and more land is converted to crops, pasture, and construction, providing more opportunities for still more humans and fewer (or no) habitats for most other species.

Scientists estimate that around 10,000 years ago, only about 5 million people inhabited the earth (not even half as many as live in Los Angeles County or New York City today). By the year 1650, there were perhaps 500 million, and by 1800, around 1 billion (**Fig. C-1**). Today we add 1 billion people to the world's population approximately every 11 years. That comes out to 90 to 95 million every year and roughly a quarter of a million every day— or more than 10,000 an hour.

The rate of growth is not equally distributed among all nations. The

▼ **FIGURE C-1**
Growth curve (orange) depicting the exponential growth of the human population. The vertical axis shows the world population in billions. It wasn't until 1804 that the population reached 1 billion, but the numbers went from 5 to 6 billion in 12 short years. Population increase occurs as a function of some percentage (in developing countries, the annual rate is over 3 percent). With advances in food production and medical technologies, humans are undergoing a population explosion, as this figure illustrates.

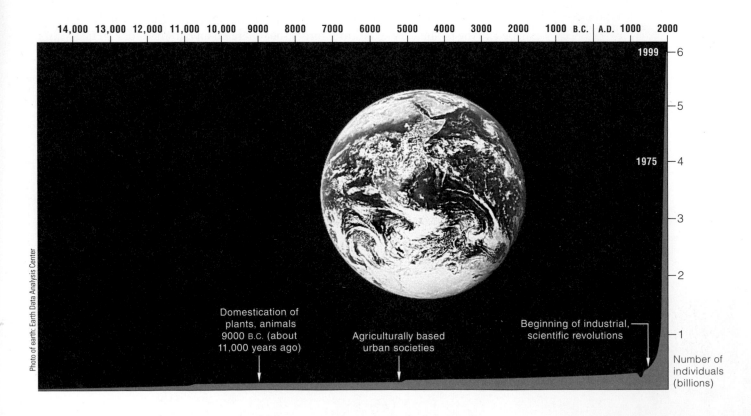

Photo of earth: Earth Data Analysis Center

Domestication of plants, animals 9000 B.C. (about 11,000 years ago)

Agriculturally based urban societies

Beginning of industrial, scientific revolutions

Number of individuals (billions)

◄ **FIGURE C-2**
Stumps of recently felled forest trees are still visible in this newly cleared field in the Amazon.

most recent United Nations report on world population notes that 95 percent of population growth is occurring in the developing world. Likewise, resources are not distributed equally among all nations. Only a small percentage of the world's population, located in a few industrialized nations, control and consume most of the world's resources. A 2009 study estimated that 48 percent of the world's population exists on less than $2 per day (Population Reference Bureau, 2009).

Humans and the Impact of Culture

For most of human history, technology remained simple, and the rate of culture change was slow. From the archaeological record, it appears that around 15,000 ya, influenced in part by climate change (not induced by human activity) and the extinction of many large-bodied prey species, some human groups began to settle down, abandoning their nomadic lifestyles. Moreover,

by about 10,000 ya (and probably earlier), some peoples had learned that by keeping domestic animals and growing crops, they had more abundant and reliable food supplies. The domestication of plants and animals is seen as one of the most significant events in human history, one that was eventually to have far-reaching consequences for the entire planet. Human impact on local environments increased dramatically as soon as people began to live in permanent settlements.

Unfortunately, humans began to exploit, and increasingly depend on, nonrenewable resources. Forests can be viewed as renewable resources, provided they're given the opportunity for regrowth. But in many areas, forest clearing was virtually complete and was inevitably followed by soil erosion, frequent overgrazing, and overcultivation, which in turn led to further soil erosion (**Fig. C-2**). Therefore, in those areas, trees became a nonrenewable resource, perhaps the first resource to have this distinction.

Destruction of natural resources in the past has also had severe consequences for people living today.

▶ **FIGURE C-3**
Pakistani villagers move to higher ground as the Indus River flooded in 2010. The floods were partially due to years of deforestation and dam building.

In 1990, a typhoon and subsequent flooding killed over 100,000 people in Bangladesh, and the flooding was at least partly due to previous deforestation in parts of the Himalayas of northern India. There is also evidence that continued erosion and flooding in China are partly the result of deforestation that occurred in the past. And millions of people in Pakistan were affected by flooding in 2010 that resulted in part from deforestation and dam building along tributaries of the Indus River. The flooding affected one-fifth of the country and set back years of infrastructure development (**Fig. C-3**).

Global Climate Change

Consider for a moment the fact that much of the energy used for human activities is derived from the burning of fossil fuels, such as oil and coal. The burning of fossil fuels releases carbon dioxide into the atmosphere, and this, in turn, traps heat. Increased production of carbon dioxide and other *greenhouse gases*, such as methane and chlorofluorocarbons (CFCs), is of great concern to many in the scientific community, who anticipate dramatic climate change in the form of global warming. Deforestation, particularly in the tropics, also contributes to global warming, since we're reducing

the number of trees available to absorb carbon dioxide.

Certainly, there have been dramatic climatic fluctuations throughout earth's history that had nothing to do with human activity. Furthermore, many of these fluctuations were sudden and had devastating consequences. But even if the current warming were part of a natural cycle, scientists are concerned that human-produced greenhouse gases could tip the balance toward a catastrophic global climate change. In fact, ice core data show that there is significantly more carbon dioxide in the earth's current atmosphere than at any other time in the last 600,000 years.

Global warming is the result of the interactions of thousands of factors, and the consequences of these interactions aren't possible to predict with complete accuracy. Nevertheless, the strong consensus among most scientists is that we can expect dramatic fluctuations in weather patterns along with alterations in precipitation levels. The results of changing temperatures and rainfall include loss of agricultural lands due to desertification in some regions and flooding in others; rising sea levels inundating vast coastal areas throughout the world; increased human hunger; extinction of numerous plant and animal species;

and altered patterns of infectious disease. Regarding the latter, health officials are particularly concerned about the spread of mosquito-borne diseases, such as malaria, dengue fever, and yellow fever, as warmer temperatures increase the geographical range of mosquitoes.

There has been international recognition of the enormity of the problem, and unprecedented international cooperation has begun. All this is happening because virtually every world government understands the gravity of the impending crisis. This is true despite what many radio or TV commentators and even some members of Congress would want you to believe.

In December 2009, a U.N.-sponsored International Convention on Climate Change took place in Copenhagen, Denmark, and was attended by close to 200 countries (**Fig. C-4**). Leading up to this meeting, worldwide expectations ran high that earlier agreements (reached in 1997 at a prior international convention in Kyoto, Japan) would be expanded and strengthened with more rigorous binding agreements to cut carbon emissions.

The world looked especially to the United States for leadership and, even more, signs of real commitment. Yet, despite President Obama's increased attention to this issue, nothing substantive occurred in Copenhagen. Most world leaders indicated that they were fully prepared to commit to major cuts in carbon emissions. But widespread lack of trust in American willingness to make real political commitments (that is, serious legislation passed by Congress) as well as weak support from China led to no formal and certainly no binding agreements. Instead, only a broad statement of goals was made, with no mechanisms to ensure that even these would be met.

Deep disappointment from every corner of the planet greeted the lack of progress in Copenhagen. Where we go from here is not clear, but one thing is certain: The climate will continue to change. It will likely be at least five years before another truly global effort can be made. What will come of that? And will it be in time?

Impact On Biodiversity

According to biologist Stephen Palumbi (2001), humans are the "world's greatest evolutionary force." What Palumbi means is that we humans, like no other species before

▼ **FIGURE C-4**
Closing remarks at the International Convention on Climate Change held in Copenhagen in December 2009.

▶ **FIGURE C-5**
Feral goats, introduced into the Galápagos Islands, threaten the habitat of the Giant Galápagos Tortoise.

Tui De Roy/Minden Pictures/National Geographic Stock

us, have a profound effect on the evolutionary histories of almost all forms of life, including the potential to alter global ecology and destroy ourselves and perhaps all life on earth. Even massive evolutionary catastrophes and mass extinctions did not wreak the havoc that may result from modern human technology.

The geological record indicates that in the last 570 million years, there have been at least 15 mass extinction events, two of which altered all of the earth's ecosystems (Ward, 1994). The first of these occurred some 250 mya and resulted from climate change that followed the joining of all the earth's landmasses into one supercontinent. The second event happened around 65 mya and radically altered the prior 150 million years of evolutionary processes that, among other things, had produced the dinosaurs. This mass extinction is believed by many researchers to have resulted from climate changes following the impact of an asteroid.

A third major extinction event, perhaps of the same magnitude, is occurring now, and according to some scientists, it may have begun in the late Pleistocene or early **Holocene** (Ward, 1994). Unlike all other mass extinc-

tions, this one hasn't been caused by continental drift, climate change (so far), or collisions with asteroids. Today it's due to the activities of a single species, *Homo sapiens*.

For at least the past 15,000 years, human activities such as hunting and clearing land for cultivation have taken their toll on nonhuman species, but today species are disappearing at an unprecedented rate. Hunting, which occurs for reasons other than acquiring food, continues to be a major factor. Competition with introduced non-native species, such as pigs, goats, and rats, has also contributed to the problem (**Fig. C-5**). But in many cases, the most important single cause of extinction is habitat reduction. (In some regions, though, the importance of habitat loss has now become secondary to the hunting that supplies the bushmeat trade; see Chapter 6 for a discussion of more specific impacts on nonhuman primates.)

Habitat loss is a direct result of the burgeoning human population and the resulting need for building materials, grazing and agricultural land, and ever-expanding living areas for people (**Fig. C-6**). We're all aware of the risk to such visible species as elephants, pandas, rhinoceroses, tigers, and moun-

Holocene The most recent epoch of the Cenozoic. Following the Pleistocene, it's estimated to have begun 10,000 years ago.

tain gorillas, to name a few. These risks are real, and within your lifetime, some of these species will certainly become extinct, at least in the wild. But the greatest threat to biodiversity is to the countless unknown species that live in the world's rain forests. By the year 2022, half the world's remaining rain forests will be gone if destruction continues at its current rate. This will result in a loss of between 10 and 22 percent of all rain forest species, or 5 to 10 percent of all plant and animal species on earth (Wilson, 1992).

Should we care about the loss of biodiversity? If so, why? In truth, many people don't seem very concerned. What's more, in explaining why we should care, we usually point out the benefits (known and unknown) that humans may derive from wild species of plants and animals. An example of such a benefit is the chemical taxol (derived from the Pacific yew tree), which may be an effective treatment for ovarian and breast cancer.

The United Nations also recently organized a large international conference to address pressing issues concerning biodiversity. The conference (an extension of the Convention on Biological Diversity) took place October 2010 in Nagoya, Japan, and was attended by representatives from 193 countries. Unlike the lack of agreement that characterized the conference on global climate change, the results from the biodiversity meeting are quite encouraging. Conference members agreed to increase cooperation and to share financial benfits that come from the development of new drugs from wild plants and animals. What's more, they produced an impressive list of significant international goals to be reached by 2020, including: to reduce to half or bring close to zero the rate of loss of all natural habitats; to reduce pollution to levels that are not detrimental to ecosystems and biodiversity; to conserve at least 17 percent of terrestrial areas and 10 percent of coastal and marine areas in protected zones; to prevent the extinction of known threatened species; and to restore at least 15 percent of degraded ecosystems.

▼ **FIGURE C-6**
(a) Agricultural fields in China's Yunnan Province and **(b)** aerial view of Sao Paulo. The fields and city occupy land that was formerly home to hundreds of plants and animals that no longer live there.

© iStockphoto.com / josemoraes

© iStockphoto.com / Jiaxi Shen

Acceleration of Evolutionary Processes

Another major impact of human activities is the acceleration of the evolutionary process for hundreds of life-forms. Many of these changes have occurred over a single human generation (that is, during the lifetime of many people living today)—not the millions of years usually associated with evolution. As noted earlier, our use of antibiotics has dramatically altered the course of evolution of several infectious diseases to the point that many have become resistant to our antibiotics. Human-invented antibiotics have now become the most significant selective factors causing many bacteria to evolve into more virulent forms. It's even likely that human technology and lifestyles are responsible for the deadly nature of some of the so-called new diseases that have arisen in recent decades, such as HIV-AIDS, dengue hemorrhagic fever, Legionnaires' disease, Lyme disease, and resistant strains of tuberculosis, *Staphylococcus*, and *E. coli*. We could reach a point where we have no antibiotics strong enough to fight dangerous bacteria that live and constantly mutate in our midst. For example, each one of us has billions of beneficial bacteria in our digestive tracts. We couldn't live without these bacteria, but some can and occasionally do mutate into varieties that cause serious illness. Without antibiotics, these and many other bacteria in our environment would have the ability to drastically increase mortality due to infectious disease.

A similar phenomenon has occurred with the overuse and misuse of insecticides and pesticides on agricultural crops (Palumbi, 2001). As mentioned previously, perhaps the best-known insecticide to have altered the course of a species' evolution is DDT. When this insecticide was first developed, it was hailed as the best way to reduce malaria, eliminating the mosquitoes that transmit the disease. DDT was highly effective when it was first applied to mosquito-ridden areas; but soon, mosquitoes had evolved resistance to the powerful agent, rendering it almost useless in the fight against malaria. Moreover, the use of DDT proved disastrous to many bird species, including the bald eagle (**Fig C-7**). In the 1970s, its use was curtailed, even banned in some countries, but the failure of other efforts to treat malaria has led to a recent call to begin using DDT again.

From these examples, it's clear that the human-caused accelerated process of evolution is something that can result in great harm to our species and planet. Certainly, none of the scientists developing antibiotics, insecticides, pesticides, and other biological tools intend to cause harm. But unless they understand the evolutionary process, they may not be able to foresee the long-term consequences of their work. As the great geneticist Theodosius Dobzhansky (1973) said, "Nothing in biology makes sense except in the light of evolution." Indeed, we can't afford even a single generation of scientists who lack the knowledge about the process of evolution. If human actions can cause an organism to evolve from a relatively benign state to a dangerously virulent state, then there is no reason why we can't turn that process around. In other words, it is theoretically possible to direct the course of evolution of a dangerous organism like HIV to a more benign, less harmful state (Ewald, 1999). But using evolution to solve health problems requires that medical researchers have a very sophisticated understanding of the evolutionary process; unfortunately, evolutionary theory isn't usually offered as part of medical training.

U.S. Government

▲ FIGURE C-7
DDT almost caused the extinction of the American Bald Eagle, the bird featured on the Great Seal of the United States.

Looking for Solutions

The problems facing our planet reflect an adaptive strategy gone awry. Indeed, it would seem that we no longer enjoy a harmonious relationship with culture. Instead, culture has become the environment in which we live, and every day that environment becomes increasingly hostile. All we need to do is examine the very air we breathe to realize that we have overstepped our limits (**Fig. C-8**).

Can the problems we've created be solved? Perhaps, but any objective assessment of the future offers little optimism. Climate change, air pollution, depletion of the ozone layer, and loss of biodiversity are catastrophic problems in a world of about 7 billion people. How well does the world *now* cope with feeding, housing, and educating its inhabitants? What quality of life do the majority of the world's people enjoy right now? What kind of world have we wrought for the other organisms that share our planet as many are steadily isolated into fragments of what were once large habitats? If these concerns aren't currently overwhelming enough, what kind of world will we see in the year 2050, when the world's population could

▼ **FIGURE C-8**
Today, air pollution is a worldwide problem. **(a)** Two Vietnamese girls using scarves as protective masks. **(b)** Sunrise over Delhi, India. **(c)** Toronto, Canada, in the gloom. **(d)** Sunset over Beijing, China. **(e)** A smoggy day in Los Angeles.

reach 10 billion? Among other consequences of this population growth, the world's food production may need to double in order to adequately feed everyone (something we don't do now). Since our window of opportunity shrinks every year, industrialized nations must immediately help developing countries adopt fuel-efficient technologies that allow them to raise their standard of living without increasing their output of greenhouse gases. Furthermore, family planning must be adopted to slow population growth. In most societies, however, behavioral change is very difficult, and sacrifice on the part of the developing world alone wouldn't adequately stem the tide. It's entirely too easy for someone from North America to ask that the people of Bangladesh control their rate of reproduction (it runs two to three times that of the United States). But consider this: The average American uses an estimated 400 times the resources consumed by a resident of Bangladesh (Ehrlich and Ehrlich, 1990)! Like it or not, much of the responsibility for the world's problems rests squarely on the shoulders of the industralized West.

Is There Any Good News?

Now that you are thoroughly depressed about the potentially gloomy future of the earth and our species, is there any good news? In 2000, heads of state from almost 150 countries agreed to support a set of Millennium Development Goals (MDGs) that would help reduce human misery throughout the world. Here are the eight goals:

1. Eradicate extreme poverty and hunger.
2. Achieve universal primary education.
3. Promote gender equity and empower women.
4. Reduce child mortality.
5. Improve maternal health.
6. Combat HIV/AIDS, malaria, and other diseases.
7. Ensure environmental sustainability.
8. Build a global partnership for development.

These goals set measurable targets that can be examined year by year to see how close we come to meeting them. There will be immense and expensive challenges, but this international agreement seems a good start toward concerted cooperative effort to solve the major problems of the world today, and it goes a long way toward encouraging partnerships between rich and poor nations. Unfortunately (and this is *not* good news), the world economic slowdown and increasing food insecurity have slowed progress toward meeting the goals and in some cases reversed progress (United Nations Dept. of Economic and Social Affairs, 2008). Partly because of this, the target date for meeting the MDGs has been revised to 2015, and there is renewed hope that this worldwide commitment to the most vulnerable people and places on the planet can be met. One interesting development that may have far-reaching impact is a milestone that was reached in 2009: The number of cell phone subscriptions per 100 people worldwide reached 50 percent (United Nations Dept. of Economic and Social Affairs, 2010).

Although world population growth continues, it appears that the rate of growth has slowed somewhat. It's common knowledge among economists that as income and education increase, family size decreases, and as infant and child mortality rates decrease, families are having fewer children. In fact, one of the best strategies for reducing family size and thus world population is to educate girls and women. Educated woman are more likely to be in the labor force and are better able to provide food for their families, seek health care for themselves and their children, delay marriage, and use family planning

With decreases in family size and improvements in education and employment opportunities for both men and women throughout the world, we are also likely to see improvements in environmental conservation and habitat preservation. A generally recognized phenomenon is that habitat destruction and poverty often go hand in hand. Although successes in Costa Rica can't be replicated everywhere, this small nation has been a model for making environmental concerns integral to social and economic development. Ecotourism, built on preserving the nation's abundant and beautiful natural resources, has now become its primary industry. Today, Costa Rica's poverty levels are the lowest in Central America.

Annually since 2005, leaders from both developing and developed countries have come together to discuss new ways of reducing global poverty, especially in sub-Saharan Africa. Additionally, some of the wealthiest individuals in the world (including Bill and Melinda Gates, George Soros, Warren Buffet, Richard Branson, and Ted Turner) have begun to invest their personal fortunes (or in the case of former U.S. presidents Carter and Clinton, their diplomatic talents and charisma) in reducing poverty and poor health and in trying to achieve global peace and prosperity. Lastly, the degree of international cooperation shown at the 2010 conference on biodiversity is a hopeful development that could be a foundation for slowing species extinctions and maintaining natural habitats.

What should be obvious is that only by working together can nations and individuals of the world hope to bring about solutions to the world's problems. As we argued earlier in the book, despite occasional evidence to the contrary, cooperation may have been more important in human evolution than conflict. These international efforts illustrate how strongly we believe that to be the case. The question now is whether or not we have the collective will to see that our admirable goals are met. Many people believe that it's our only hope.

Studies of human evolution have much to contribute to our understanding of how we, as a single species, came to exert such control over the destiny of our planet. It's a truly phenomenal story of how a small apelike creature walking on two feet across the African savanna challenged nature by learning to make stone tools. From these humble beginnings came large-brained humans who, instead of stone tools, have telecommunications satellites, computers, and nuclear arsenals at their fingertips. The human story is indeed unique and wonderful. Our two feet have carried us not only across the plains of Africa, but onto the polar caps, the ocean floor, and even across the surface of the moon! Surely, if we can accomplish so much in so short a time, we can act responsibly to preserve our home and the wondrous creatures who share it with us.

Appendix A

Atlas of Primate Skeletal Anatomy

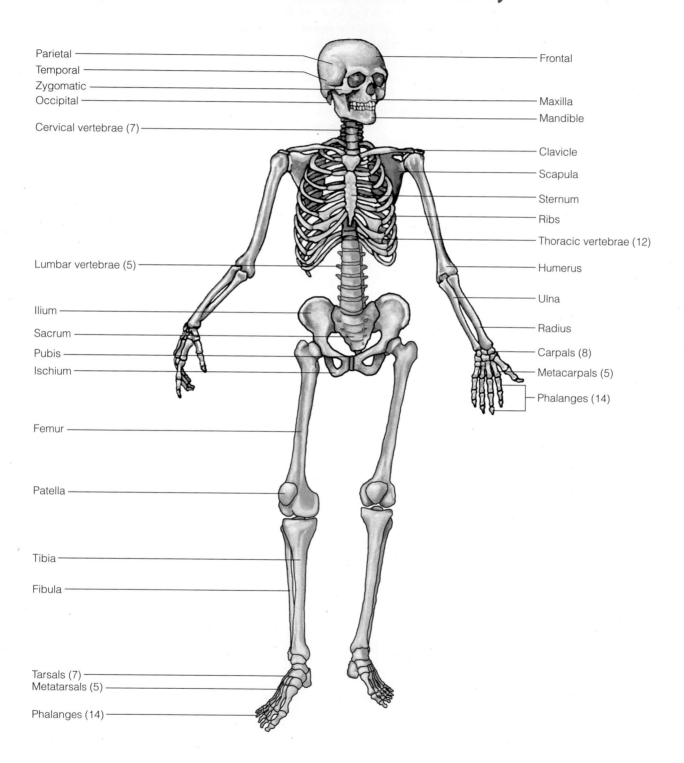

Parietal

Temporal

Zygomatic

Occipital

Cervical vertebrae (7)

Lumbar vertebrae (5)

Ilium

Sacrum

Pubis

Ischium

Femur

Patella

Tibia

Fibula

Tarsals (7)

Metatarsals (5)

Phalanges (14)

Frontal

Maxilla

Mandible

Clavicle

Scapula

Sternum

Ribs

Thoracic vertebrae (12)

Humerus

Ulna

Radius

Carpals (8)

Metacarpals (5)

Phalanges (14)

▲ **Figure A–1**

Human skeleton (*Homo sapiens*)— bipedal hominin.

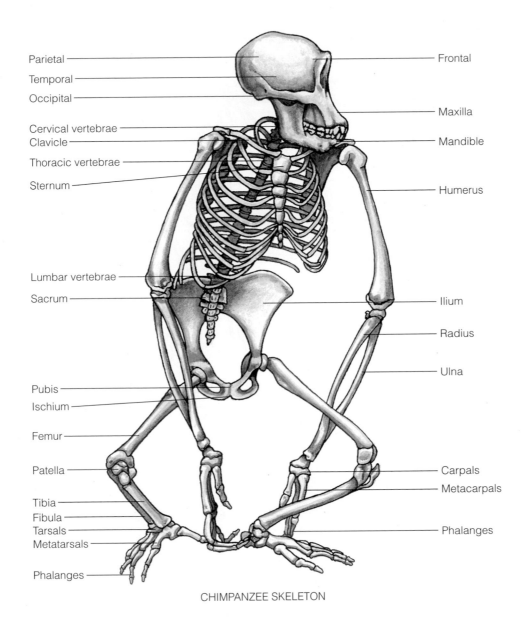

Parietal

Temporal

Occipital

Cervical vertebrae

Clavicle

Thoracic vertebrae

Sternum

Lumbar vertebrae

Sacrum

Pubis

Ischium

Femur

Patella

Tibia

Fibula

Tarsals

Metatarsals

Phalanges

Frontal

Maxilla

Mandible

Humerus

Ilium

Radius

Ulna

Carpals

Metacarpals

Phalanges

CHIMPANZEE SKELETON

▲ **Figure A-2**
**Chimpanzee skeleton (*Pan troglodytes*)—
knuckle-walking ape.**

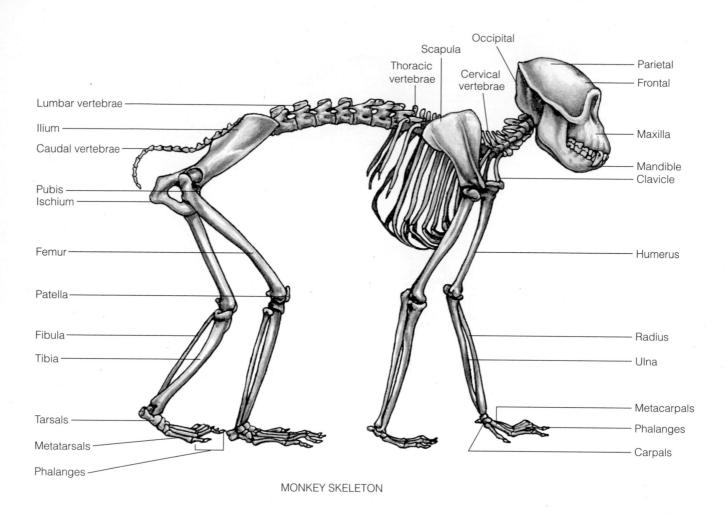

MONKEY SKELETON

▲ **Figure A-3**
Monkey skeleton (rhesus macaque;
Macaca mulatta)—a typical
quadrupedal primate.

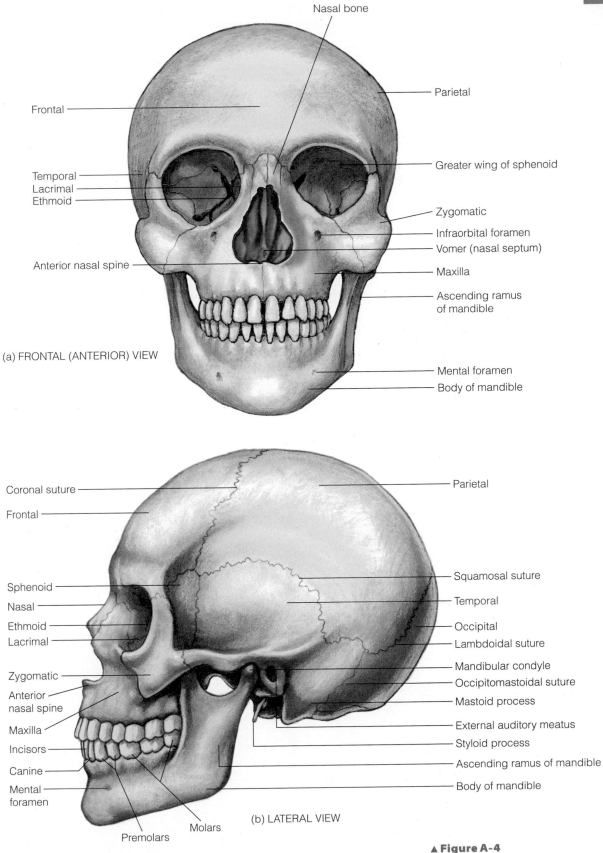

Nasal bone

Frontal

Parietal

Temporal
Lacrimal
Ethmoid

Greater wing of sphenoid

Zygomatic

Infraorbital foramen

Vomer (nasal septum)

Anterior nasal spine

Maxilla

Ascending ramus of mandible

(a) FRONTAL (ANTERIOR) VIEW

Mental foramen

Body of mandible

Coronal suture

Parietal

Frontal

Squamosal suture

Sphenoid

Temporal

Nasal

Ethmoid

Occipital

Lacrimal

Lambdoidal suture

Zygomatic

Mandibular condyle

Anterior nasal spine

Occipitomastoidal suture

Maxilla

Mastoid process

Incisors

External auditory meatus

Canine

Styloid process

Ascending ramus of mandible

Mental foramen

Body of mandible

Premolars

Molars

(b) LATERAL VIEW

▲ **Figure A-4**
Human cranium.

(continued on next page)

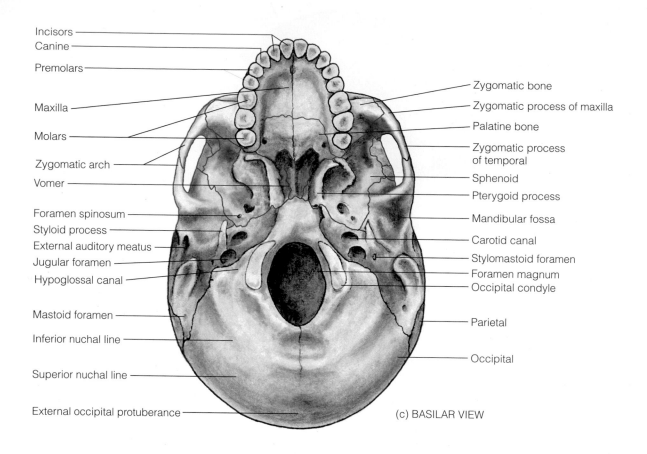

Incisors

Canine

Premolars

Maxilla

Molars

Zygomatic arch

Vomer

Foramen spinosum

Styloid process

External auditory meatus

Jugular foramen

Hypoglossal canal

Mastoid foramen

Inferior nuchal line

Superior nuchal line

External occipital protuberance

Zygomatic bone

Zygomatic process of maxilla

Palatine bone

Zygomatic process of temporal

Sphenoid

Pterygoid process

Mandibular fossa

Carotid canal

Stylomastoid foramen

Foramen magnum

Occipital condyle

Parietal

Occipital

(c) BASILAR VIEW

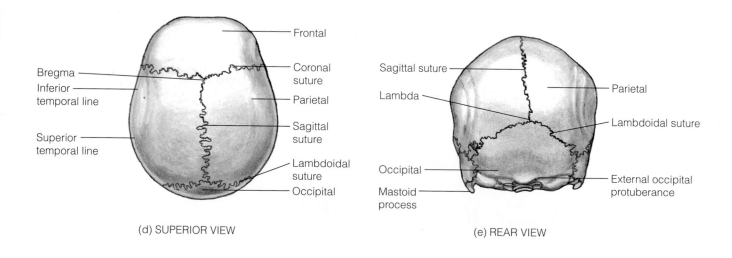

Frontal

Coronal suture

Parietal

Sagittal suture

Lambdoidal suture

Occipital

Bregma

Inferior temporal line

Superior temporal line

(d) SUPERIOR VIEW

Sagittal suture

Lambda

Occipital

Mastoid process

Parietal

Lambdoidal suture

External occipital protuberance

(e) REAR VIEW

▲ **Figure A-4**
Human cranium.

(continued)

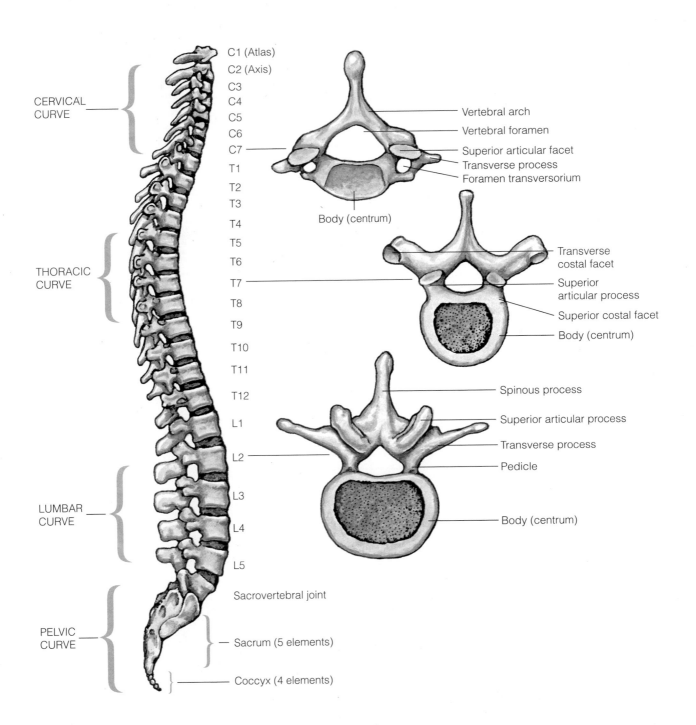

CERVICAL
CURVE

THORACIC
CURVE

LUMBAR
CURVE

PELVIC
CURVE

C1 (Atlas)
C2 (Axis)
C3
C4
C5
C6
C7
T1
T2
T3
T4
T5
T6
T7
T8
T9
T10
T11
T12
L1
L2
L3
L4
L5

Sacrovertebral joint

Sacrum (5 elements)

Coccyx (4 elements)

Vertebral arch
Vertebral foramen
Superior articular facet
Transverse process
Foramen transversorium

Body (centrum)

Transverse
costal facet
Superior
articular process
Superior costal facet
Body (centrum)

Spinous process
Superior articular process
Transverse process
Pedicle
Body (centrum)

▲ **Figure A-5**
**Human vertebral column (lateral view)
and representative cervical, thoracic,
and lumbar vertebrae (superior views).**

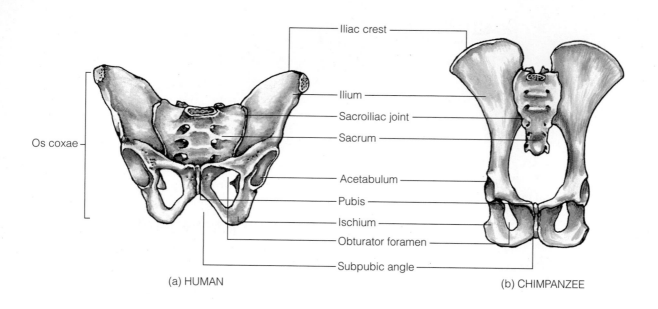

(a) HUMAN

Iliac crest
Ilium
Sacroiliac joint
Sacrum
Acetabulum
Pubis
Ischium
Obturator foramen
Subpubic angle

Os coxae

(b) CHIMPANZEE

▲ **Figure A-6**
Pelvic girdles.

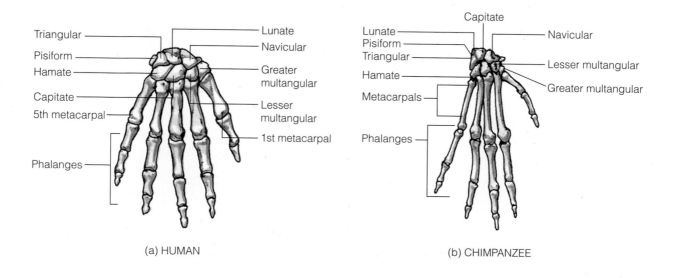

(a) HUMAN

Triangular
Pisiform
Hamate
Capitate
5th metacarpal
Phalanges

Lunate
Navicular
Greater multangular
Lesser multangular
1st metacarpal

(b) CHIMPANZEE

Lunate
Pisiform
Triangular
Hamate
Metacarpals
Phalanges

Capitate
Navicular
Lesser multangular
Greater multangular

▲ **Figure A-7**
Hand anatomy.

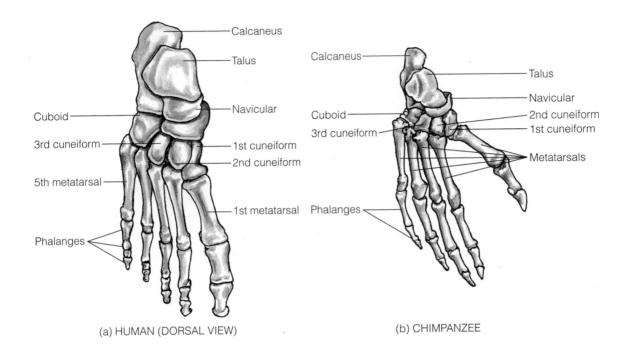

(a) HUMAN (DORSAL VIEW)

(b) CHIMPANZEE

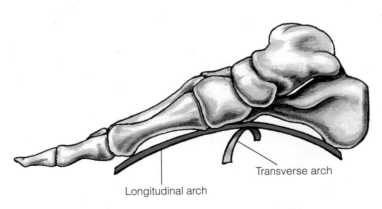

Transverse arch

Longitudinal arch

(c) HUMAN (MEDIAL VIEW)

▲ **Figure A-8**
Foot (pedal) anatomy.

LEMURIFORMS

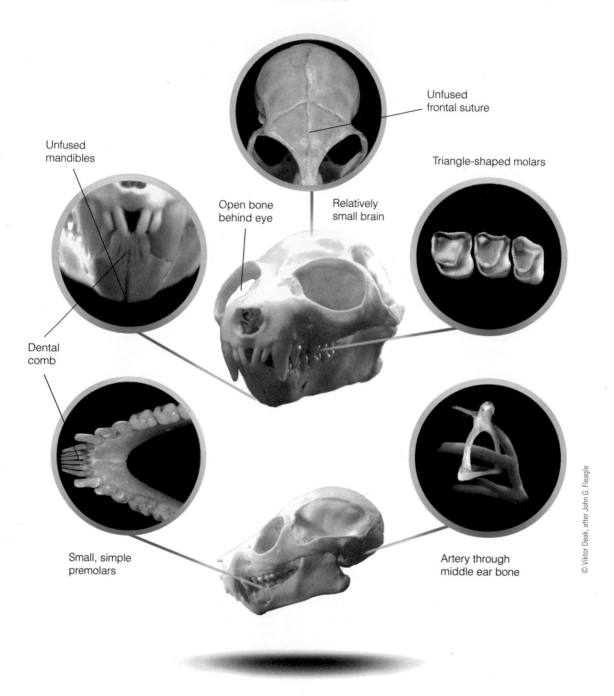

Unfused
frontal suture

Unfused
mandibles

Triangle-shaped molars

Open bone
behind eye

Relatively
small brain

Dental
comb

Small, simple
premolars

Artery through
middle ear bone

© Viktor Deak, after John G. Fleagle

▲ **Figure A-9A**
**Lemuriform anatomy. Refer to At a
Glance: Lemuriforms vs. Anthropoids,
Chapter 9, p. 257.**

ANTHROPOIDS

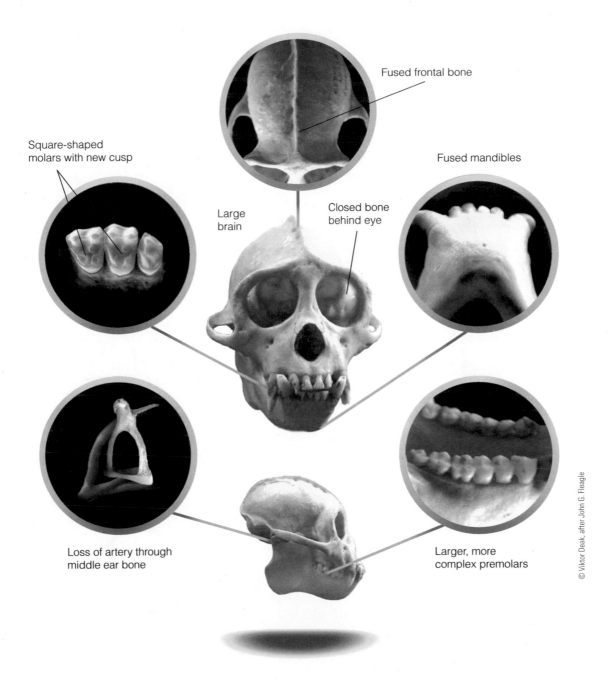

Fused frontal bone

Square-shaped
molars with new cusp

Fused mandibles

Large
brain

Closed bone
behind eye

Loss of artery through
middle ear bone

Larger, more
complex premolars

▲ **Figure A-9B**
**Anthropoid anatomy. Refer to At a
Glance: Lemuriforms vs. Anthropoids,
Chapter 9, p. 257.**

New World Monkeys

Old World Monkeys

Sideways-facing nostrils

Downward-facing nostrils

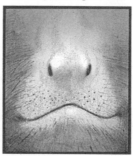

Three
premolars

No ear tube

Two
premolars

Ear tube

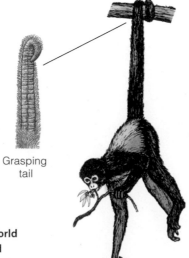

Grasping
tail

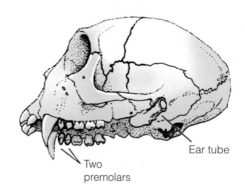

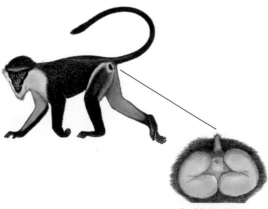

Ischial callosities

▲ **Figure A-10**
**Comparison of New World
Monkey and Old World
Monkey anatomy. Refer to
At a Glance: New World
Monkeys vs. Old World
Monkeys, Chapter 9, p. 259.**

Adapted from John G. Fleagle and Stephen Nash, Stony Brook University, New York

Old World Monkeys

Apes

Narrow nose

Narrow palate

Broad nose

Broad palate

Smaller brain

Larger brain

Bilophodont molars

Simple molars with Y-5 pattern

Tail

Longer torso

Shorter torso

No tail

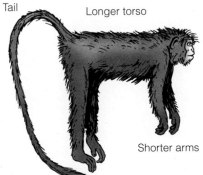

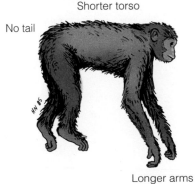

Shorter arms

Longer arms

▲ **Figure A-11**

Comparison of Old World Monkey and ape anatomy. Refer to At a Glance: Old World Monkeys vs. Apes, Chapter 9, p. 259.

Adapted from John G. Fleagle and Stephen Nash, Stony Brook University, New York

Appendix B
Taxonomy of Living and Selected Extinct Primates

ORDER: **Primates**
    SEMIORDER: **Plesiadapiformes**
        SUPERFAMILY: **Plesiadapoidea**
          FAMILY: Plesiadapidae
            GENUS: *Plesiadapis*
          FAMILY: Carpolestidae
            GENUS: *Carpolestes*
          FAMILY: Purgatoriidae
            GENUS: *Purgatorius*

    SEMIORDER: **Euprimates**
      SUBORDER: **Strepsirhini**
        INFRAORDER: **Adapiformes**
          SUPERFAMILY: **Adapoidea**
            FAMILY: Notharctidae
              GENUS: *Cantius*
            FAMILY: Adapidae
              GENUS: *Afradapis*
              GENUS: *Adapis*
              GENUS: *Darwinius*
            FAMILY: Amphipithecidae
        INFRAORDER: **Lemuriformes**
          SUPERFAMILY: **Lemuroidea**
            FAMILY: Cheirogaleidae
            FAMILY: Lemuridae
            FAMILY: Lepilemuridae
              GENUS: *Megaladapis*
            FAMILY: Indriidae
              GENUS: *Archaeoindris*
            FAMILY: Daubentoniidae
              GENUS: *Daubentonia*
            FAMILY: Archaeolemuridae
              GENUS: *Archaeolemur*
          SUPERFAMILY: **Lorisoidea**
            FAMILY: Galagidae
            FAMILY: Lorisidae

SUBORDER: **Haplorhini**

  INFRAORDER: **Omomyiformes**

    SUPERFAMILY: **Omomyoidea**

      FAMILY: Omomyidae

        SUBFAMILY: Anaptomorphinae

          GENUS: *Teilhardina*

        SUBFAMILY: Microchoerinae

          GENUS: *Necrolemur*

        SUBFAMILY: Omomyinae

          GENUS: *Shoshonius*

  INFRAORDER: **Tarsiiformes**

    SUPERFAMILY: **Tarsioidea**

      FAMILY: Tarsiidae

  INFRAORDER: **Anthropoidea**

    SUPERFAMILY: *Incertae sedis**

      FAMILY: *Incertae sedis*

        GENUS: *Altiatlasius*

    SUPERFAMILY: **Parapithecoidea**

      FAMILY: Parapithecidae

        GENUS: *Apidium*

        GENUS: *Parapithecus*

        GENUS: *Biretia*

    PARVORDER: **Platyrrhini**

    SUPERFAMILY: **Ateloidea**

      FAMILY: Pitheciidae

      FAMILY: Atelidae

      FAMILY: Cebidae

        GENUS: *Cebus*

      FAMILY: *Incertae sedis*

        GENUS: *Branisella*

        GENUS: *Homunculus*

    PARVORDER: **Catarrhini**

    SUPERFAMILY: **Saadanioidea**

      FAMILY: Saadanniidae

        GENUS: *Saadanius*

    SUPERFAMILY: **Propliopithecoidea**

      FAMILY: Oligopithecidae

        GENUS: *Catopithecus*

      FAMILY: Propliopithecidae

        GENUS: *Aegyptopithecus*

*Latin phrase meaning "of uncertain placement"; this designation is used for a taxonomic group where its broader relationships are unknown or undefined, meaning it cannot be reliably assigned to a recognized group at this time.

SUPERFAMILY: **Cercopithecoidea**

    FAMILY: Victoriapithecidae

        GENUS: *Victoriapithecus*

    FAMILY: Cercopithecidae

      SUBFAMILY: Cercopithecinae

        GENUS: *Macaca*

        GENUS: *Papio*

        GENUS: *Theropithecus*

      SUBFAMILY: Colobinae

        GENUS: *Colobus*

        GENUS: *Presbytis*

        GENUS: *Nasalis*

SUPERFAMILY: **Pliopithecoidea**

    FAMILY: *Incertae sedis*

        GENUS: *Lomorupithecus*

    FAMILY: Pliopithecidae

        GENUS: *Pliopithecus*

SUPERFAMILY: **Proconsuloidea**

    FAMILY: Proconsulidae

        GENUS: *Proconsul*

        GENUS: *Micropithecus*

SUPERFAMILY: **Hominoidea**

    FAMILY: Hylobatidae

        GENUS: *Yuanmoupithecus*

        GENUS: *Hylobates*

    FAMILY: Hominidae

      SUBFAMILY: Kenyapithecinae

        GENUS: *Kenyapithecus*

      SUBFAMILY: Ponginae

        GENUS: *Sivapithecus*

        GENUS: *Gigantopithecus*

        GENUS: *Lufengpithecus*

        GENUS: *Pongo*

      SUBFAMILY: Homininae

        GENUS: *Dryopithecus*

        GENUS: *Anoiapithecus*

        GENUS: *Ouranopithecus*

        GENUS: *Nakalipithecus*

        GENUS: *Chororapithecus*

        GENUS: *Gorilla*

        GENUS: *Pan*

Appendix C

Summary of Early Hominin Fossil Finds from Africa

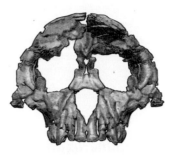

Ardipithecus

Taxonomic designation: *Ardipithecus ramidus*; earlier species designated as *Ardipithecus kadabba*

Year of first discovery: 1992

Dating: Earlier sites, 5.8–5.6 mya; Aramis, 4.4 mya

Fossil material: Earlier materials: Jaw fragment, isolated teeth, 5 postcranial remains. Later sample (Aramis): partial skeleton, 110 other specimens representing at least 36 individuals

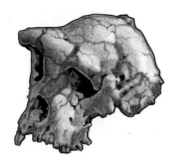

Sahelanthropus

Taxonomic designation: *Sahelanthropus tchadensis*

Year of first discovery: 2001

Dating: ~7–6 mya

Fossil material: Nearly complete cranium, 2 jaw fragments, 3 isolated teeth

Orrorin

Taxonomic designation: *Orrorin tugenensis*

Year of first discovery: 2000

Dating: ~6 mya

Fossil material: 2 jaw fragments, 6 isolated teeth, postcranial remains (femoral pieces, partial humerus, hand phalanx). No reasonably complete cranial remains yet discovered.

Location of finds: Toros-Menalla, Chad, central Africa

Location of finds: Lukeino Formation, Tugen Hills, Baringo District, Kenya, East Africa

Location of finds: Middle Awash region, including Aramis (as well as earlier localities), Ethiopia, East Africa

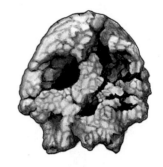

Australopithecus anamensis

Taxonomic designation:
Australopithecus anamensis

Year of first discovery: 1965 (but not recognized as separate species at that time); more remains found in 1994 and 1995

Dating: 4.2–3.9 mya

Fossil material: Total of 22 specimens, including cranial fragments, jaw fragments, and postcranial pieces (humerus, tibia, radius). No reasonably complete cranial remains yet discovered.

Australopithecus afarensis

Taxonomic designation:
Australopithecus afarensis

Year of first discovery: 1973

Dating: 3.6–3.0 mya

Fossil material: Large sample, with up to 65 individuals represented: 1 partial cranium, numerous cranial pieces and jaws, many teeth, numerous postcranial remains, including partial skeleton. Fossil finds from Laetoli also include dozens of fossilized footprints.

Kenyanthropus

Taxonomic designation:
Kenyanthropus platyops

Year of first discovery: 1999

Dating: 3.5 mya

Fossil material: Partial cranium, temporal fragment, partial maxilla, 2 partial mandibles

Location of finds: Kanapoi, Allia Bay, Kenya, East Africa

Location of finds: Laetoli (Tanzania), Hadar/Dikika (Ethiopia), also likely found at East Turkana (Kenya) and Omo (Ethiopia), East Africa

Location of finds: Lomekwi, West Lake Turkana, Kenya, East Africa

Australopithecus garhi

Taxonomic designation:
Australopithecus garhi
Year of first discovery: 1997
Dating: 2.5 mya
Fossil material: Partial cranium, numerous limb bones

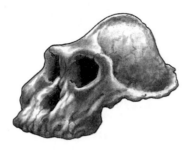

Paranthropus aethiopicus

Taxonomic designation:
Paranthropus aethiopicus (also called *Australopithecus aethiopicus*)
Year of first discovery: 1985
Dating: 2.4 mya
Fossil material: Nearly complete cranium

Paranthropus boisei

Taxonomic designation:
Paranthropus boisei (also called *Australopithecus boisei*)
Year of first discovery: 1959
Dating: 2.2–1.0 mya
Fossil material: 2 nearly complete crania, several partial crania, many jaw fragments, dozens of teeth. Postcrania less represented, but parts of several long bones recovered.

Location of finds: Bouri, Middle Awash, Ethiopia, East Africa

Location of finds: West Lake Turkana, Kenya

Location of finds: Olduvai Gorge and Peninj (Tanzania), East Lake Turkana (Koobi Fora), Chesowanja (Kenya), Omo (Ethiopia)

Paranthropus robustus

Taxonomic designation:
Paranthropus robustus
(also called *Australopithecus robustus*)

Year of first discovery: 1938

Dating: ~2–1 mya

Fossil material: 1 complete cranium, several partial crania, many jaw fragments, hundreds of teeth, numerous postcranial elements

Australopithecus africanus

Taxonomic designation:
Australopithecus africanus

Year of first discovery: 1924

Dating: ~3.0?–2.0 mya

Fossil material: 1 mostly complete cranium, several partial crania, dozens of jaws/partial jaws, hundreds of teeth, 4 partial skeletons representing significant parts of the postcranium

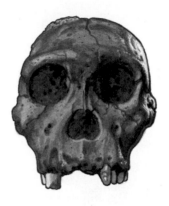

Australopithecus sediba

Taxonomic designation:
Australopithecus sediba
(also called *Homo sediba*)

Year of first discovery: 2008

Dating: 1.95-1.78 mya

Fossil material: 2 partial skeletons
(Note: further fossils remains still in cave but not yet published)

Location of finds: Kromdraai, Swartkrans, Drimolen, Cooper's Cave, possibly Gondolin (all from South Africa)

Location of finds: Taung, Sterkfontein, Makapansgat, Gladysvale (all from South Africa)

Location of finds: Malapa Cave (South Africa)

Early *Homo*

Taxonomic designation:
Homo habilis

Year of first discovery: 1959/1960

Dating: ?2.4–1.8 mya

Fossil material: 2 partial crania, other cranial pieces, jaw fragments, several limb bones, partial hand, partial foot, partial skeleton

Location of finds: Olduvai Gorge (Tanzania), Lake Baringo (Kenya), Omo (Ethiopia), Sterkfontein (?) (South Africa)

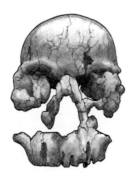

Early *Homo*

Taxonomic designation:
Homo rudolfensis

Year of first discovery: 1972

Dating: 1.8–1.4 mya

Fossil material: 4 partial crania, 1 mostly complete mandible, other jaw pieces, numerous teeth, a few postcranial elements (none directly associated with crania)

Location of finds: East Lake Turkana (Koobi Fora), Kenya, East Africa

Abbreviations Used for Fossil Hominin Specimens

For those hominin sites where a number of specimens have been recovered, standard abbreviations are used to designate the site as well as the specimen number (and occasionally museum accession information as well).

Abbreviation	Explanation	Example
AL	Afar locality	AL-288-1
LH	Laetoli hominin	LH 4
OH	Olduvai hominin	OH 5
KNM-ER (or simply ER)	Kenya National Museums, East Rudolf*	ER 1470
KNM-WT (or simply WT)	Kenya National Museums, West Turkana	WT 17000
Sts	Sterkfontein, main site	Sts 5
Stw	Sterkfontein, west extension	Stw 53
SK	Swartkrans	SK 48

* East Rudolf is the former name for Lake Turkana; the abbreviation was first used before the lake's name was changed. All these fossils (as well as others from sites throughout Kenya) are housed in Nairobi at the National Museums of Kenya.

Appendix D

Population Genetics: The Math of Microevolution

Part A. Further Examples Using the Hardy-Weinberg Equilibrium Formula

Example 1. Hemoglobin Beta Locus In West Africa

As discussed in Chapter 15, there is a high frequency of the Hb^S allele in parts of West Africa. One study (see p. 451) in a Senegalese group found a frequency of the Hb^S allele at 12 percent.

What follows is a hypothetical example for a Senegalese population of 4,000 individuals. Ascertainment is done on all individuals at 6 months of age. Because of incomplete dominance, all three phenotypes (and therefore all three genotypes) can be determined.

Observed frequencies:

	Number of Individuals	Hb^A Alleles	Hb^S Alleles
$Hb^A Hb^A$	3,070	6,140	——
$Hb^A Hb^S$	905	905	905
$Hb^S Hb^S$	25	——	50
Totals	4,000	7,045	955

Allele frequencies:

$Hb^A = p = 7,045/8,000 = .881$

$Hb^S = q = 955/8,000 = .119$

Expected genotypic frequencies:

$Hb^A Hb^A = p^2 = (.881)(.881) = .776$

$Hb^A Hb^S = 2pq = 2(.881)(.119) = .210$

$Hb^S Hb^S = q^2 = (.119)(.119) = .014$

Comparison of expected and observed frequencies:

	Expected Frequency	Expected No. Individuals	Observed Frequency	Observed No. Individuals
$Hb^A Hb^A$	.776	3,105	.767	3,070
$Hb^A Hb^S$	.210	839	.227	905
$Hb^S Hb^S$	.014	57	.006	25

As you can see, there is a noticeable difference between the expected and observed frequencies. There are fewer actual (observed) individuals of both homozygotes than expected and more heterozygotes than expected. Indeed, when performing a statistical test (see Part 2 of this appendix), the difference is statistically significant.

We can extend the example further. Let us assume that we again ascertain allele frequencies in this same population 30 years later, at which point there are 3,000 survivors.

Observed phenotypic frequencies:

	Number of Individuals	Hb^A Alleles	Hb^S Alleles
Hb^AHb^A	2,123	4,246	——
Hb^AHb^S	875	875	875
Hb^SHb^S	2	——	4
Totals	3,000	5,121	879

Allele frequencies:

$Hb^A = p = 5,121/6,000 = .854$

$Hb^S = q = 879/6,000 = .146$

Expected genotypic frequencies:

$Hb^AHb^A = p^2 = (.854)(.854) = .729$

$Hb^AHb^S = 2pq = 2(.854)(.146) = .249$

$Hb^SHb^S = q^2 = (.146)(.146) = .021$

Comparison of expected and observed frequencies:

	Expected Frequency	Expected No. Individuals	Observed Frequency	Observed No. Individuals
Hb^AHb^A	.729	2,188	.708	2,123
Hb^AHb^S	.249	748	.292	875
Hb^SHb^S	.021	64	.001	2

In this adult sample, the differences between the expected and observed frequencies are even greater than they were for the infant sample (and are even more highly statistically significant; see Part 2). Moreover, these differences are in the same direction as before: There are fewer homozygotes and more heterozygotes than expected under equilibrium conditions. A likely explanation for this pattern of allele frequencies would focus on natural selection. At age 6 months, there are slightly fewer Hb^AHb^A homozygotes than expected and considerably fewer Hb^SHb^S homozygotes than expected. Correspondingly, there are many more heterozygotes (Hb^AHb^S) than expected. These differences could arise from differential mortality of Hb^AHb^A individuals due to malaria (likely in early infancy) and Hb^SHb^S individuals due to sickle-cell anemia occurring both *in utero* and during early infancy.

These same factors would continue throughout childhood and early adulthood, so that by age 30, the effects of differential mortality due to both malaria and sickle-cell anemia are even more dramatic. While hypothetical, these figures represent a good example of how natural selection could operate on this population.

Example 2. Adenosine Deaminase (ADA) in a Sri Lankan Population

ADA is an enzyme present in many types of cells. The locus producing this enzyme has two common codominant alleles, A^1 and A^2. There are also very rare mutant alleles that can cause a fatal form of inherited immune deficiency.

From actual data derived from a polymorphic population in Sri Lanka,* the following observed frequencies were found. (*Note:* Because the alleles are codominant, the three phenotypes correspond directly to the three genotypes.)

Observed frequencies:

	Number of Individuals	A^1 Alleles	A^2 Alleles
A^1A^1	113	226	——
A^1A^2	38	38	38
A^2A^2	3	——	6
Totals	154	264	44

Allele frequencies:

$A^1 = p = 264/308 = .857$

$A^2 = q = 44/308 = .143$

Expected genotypic frequencies:

$A^1A^1 = p^2 = (.857)(.857) = .734$

$A^1A^2 = 2pq = 2(.857)(.143) = .249$

$A^2A^2 = q^2 = (.143)(.143) = .020$

Comparison of expected and observed frequencies:

	Expected Frequency	Expected No. Individuals	Observed Frequency	Observed No. Individuals
A^1A^1	.734	113	.734	113
A^1A^2	.245	38	.247	38
A^2A^2	.020	3	.019	3

As you can clearly see, the expected and observed frequencies are nearly identical (in fact, the raw frequencies are identical). There is thus a probability of 1.0 that the null hypothesis is correct and a 0 percent confidence limit in rejecting the null hypothesis. This population at this locus thus appears to be in equilibrium. Such is often the case in actual population genetics studies, especially when the sample size is small.

Example 3. Determining the Number of Heterozygous Carriers for PKU in a Hypothetical Population

Another way to apply the Hardy-Weinberg formula is to first *assume* equilibrium and then work the formula in reverse. For example, for many recessive traits where there is complete dominance (or nearly complete dominance), traditionally it has been impossible to ascertain the heterozygotes directly. However, if we make certain assumptions, we can use the formula to estimate the number of heterozygotes (that is, carriers) in a population.

Let us assume that we are studying PKU in a group of 20,000 students at a university. PKU is an autosomal recessive disorder with an overall frequency in the United States of approximately 1/10,000 (see p. 87). In some subgroups (for example, individuals of European descent), the frequency of PKU is higher.

In our hypothetical student population, we find two individuals with PKU (which was treated when the individuals were children). Because PKU is an autosomal recessive, the number of PKU homozygotes (2/20,000, or .0001) is equal to q^2.

If $q^2 = .0001$, then

$q = .01$ and $p = .99$

The frequency of the heterozygote is $2pq$:

$2(.99)(.01) = .0198$

The estimated number of carriers for PKU in the university student sample is

(.0198)(20,000) = 198

An interesting pattern is evident here. In the entire population, there is a total of 200 individuals who possess at least one PKU allele. Of these, the vast majority (99 percent) are carriers.

Example 4. Applying the Hardy-Weinberg Formula to ABO, a More Complex Genetic System

In Chapter 15 and in the three examples given so far in this appendix, we have used examples of loci with only two alleles (and therefore just three possible genotypes). However, many loci are more complex, having three or more alleles. For example, ABO has three alleles and six genotypes (see p. 88).

How do we utilize the Hardy-Weinberg equilibrium formula for a locus like ABO? First, there are three alleles, so the allele frequencies are designated as:

Frequency of $A = p$
Frequency of $B = q$
Frequency of $O = r$

Under equilibrium conditions, the genotypic frequencies would be calculated as follows:

$$(p + q + r)^2 = 1$$

This is an expansion of a trinomial (rather than the binomial used in a two-allele system). With a three-allele system like ABO, the genotypic frequency formula is

$$p^2 + 2pq + 2pr + 2qr + q^2 = r^2 = 1$$

There are six terms in this formula, each one representing a different genotype:

Term	Genotype Represented
p^2	AA
$2pq$	AB
$2pr$	AO
$2qr$	BO
q^2	BB
r^2	OO

We will not include actual numbers here. We simply wish to illustrate that population genetics calculations can be considerably more complex than implied by our earlier examples.

Part B. Statistical Evaluation: Testing Hardy-Weinberg Results

Following are the results using statistical tests comparing the expected and observed frequencies for the relevant examples shown in Chapter 15 as well as those discussed in this appendix. The test used is the chi-square (χ^2), which assumes that two variables are independent. In our examples, this independence is tested against a null hypothesis stating that there is equilibrium (in other words, the expected and observed frequencies do not differ any more than would be the case strictly as a result of chance). Further details concerning statistical approaches can be found in any introductory statistics text.

In the data tables that follow, all figures are shown as *raw* frequencies.

MN Data (from Chapter 15, p. 448) Contingency Table:

Observed frequencies	80	80	40
Expected frequencies	72	96	32

$\chi^2 = 2.76, p = .251$

The generally accepted confidence limit for rejection of the null hypothesis is less than or equal to .05. Thus, in this case, we cannot confidently reject the null hypothesis.

PTC Tasting Data (from Chapter 15, p. 449) Contingency Table:

Observed frequencies	125	325	50
Expected frequencies	165	245	90

$\chi^2 = 28.17, p < .0000$

This result is highly significant and allows us to reject the null hypothesis with a great deal of confidence. We are able to say there is less than 1 chance in 10,000 that the null hypothesis applies to these data.

Hemoglobin Beta Locus (Example 1, this appendix) Contingency Tables:

At 6 months:

Observed frequencies	3,070	905	25
Expected frequencies	3,105	839	57

$\chi^2 = 15.18, p = .0005$

This is a highly significant result that allows us to reject the null hypothesis with high confidence.

At Age 30:

Observed frequencies	2,123	875	2
Expected frequencies	2,188	748	64

$\chi^2 = 69.16, p < .0000$

This result is even more highly significant than at age 6 months, as there has been further disruption of equilibrium expectations (that is, greater evidence of evolutionary shifts in allele frequencies).

Glossary

acclimatization Physiological responses to changes in the environment that occur during an individual's lifetime. Such responses may be temporary or permanent, depending on the duration of the environmental change and when in the individual's life it occurs. The capacity for acclimatization may typify an entire population or species, and because it's under genetic influence, it's subject to evolutionary factors such as natural selection and genetic drift.

Acheulian (ash´-oo-lay-en) Pertaining to a stone tool industry from the Early and Middle Pleistocene; characterized by a large proportion of bifacial tools (flaked on both sides). Acheulian tool kits are common in Africa, Southwest Asia, and western Europe, but they're thought to be less common elsewhere. Also spelled Acheulean.

adaptation An anatomical, physiological, or behavioral response of organisms or populations to the environment. Adaptations result from evolutionary change (specifically, as a result of natural selection).

adaptive niche An organism's entire way of life: where it lives, what it eats, how it gets food, how it avoids predators, and so on.

adaptive radiation The relatively rapid expansion and diversification of life-forms into new ecological niches.

adolescent growth spurt The period during adolescence when well-nourished teens typically increase in stature at greater rates than at other times in the life cycle.

affiliative Pertaining to amicable associations between individuals. Affiliative behaviors, such as grooming, reinforce social bonds and promote group cohesion.

allele frequency In a population, the percentage of all the alleles at a locus accounted for by one specific allele.

alleles Alternate forms of a gene. Alleles occur at the same locus on paired chromosomes and thus govern the same trait. But because they're different, their action may result in different expressions of that trait.

allometry Also called scaling; the differential proportion among various anatomical structures (e.g., the size of the brain in proportion to overall body size during the development of an individual). Scaling effects must also be considered when comparing species.

alloparenting A common behavior in many primate species whereby individuals other than the parent(s) hold, carry, and in general interact with infants.

allopatric Living in different areas. The allopatric pattern is important in the divergence of closely related species from each other and from their shared ancestral species because it leads to reproductive isolation.

altruism Behavior that benefits another individual at some potential risk or cost to oneself.

amino acids Small molecules that are the components of proteins.

analogies Similarities between organisms based strictly on common function, with no assumed common evolutionary descent.

ancestral Referring to characters inherited by a group of organisms from a remote ancestor and thus not diagnostic of groups (lineages) that diverged after the character first appeared; also called primitive.

anthropocentric Viewing nonhuman organisms in terms of human experience and capabilities; emphasizing the importance of humans over everything else.

anthropoids Members of the primate infraorder Anthropoidea (pronounced "an-throw-poid´-ee-uh"), which includes monkeys, apes, and humans.

anthropology The field of inquiry that studies human culture and evolutionary aspects of human biology; includes cultural anthropology, archaeology, linguistics, and physical, or biological, anthropology.

anthropometry Measurement of human body parts. When osteologists measure skeletal elements, the term *osteometry* is often used.

antigens Large molecules found on the surface of cells. Several different loci govern various antigens on red and white blood cells. (Foreign antigens provoke an immune response.)

anvils Surfaces on which an object such as a palm nut, root, or seed is placed before being struck with another object such as a stone.

applied anthropology The practical application of anthropological and archaeological theories and techniques. For example, many biological anthropologists work in the public health sector.

arboreal Tree living; adapted to life in the trees.

artifacts Objects or materials made or modified for use by hominins. The earliest artifacts are usually tools made of stone or, occasionally, bone.

Aurignacian Pertaining to an Upper Paleolithic stone tool industry in Europe beginning at about 40,000 ya.

australopiths A colloquial name referring to a diverse group of Plio-Pleistocene African hominins. Australopiths are the most abundant and widely distributed of all early hominins and are also the most completely studied.

autonomic Pertaining to physiological responses that aren't under voluntary control. An example in chimpanzees would be the erection of body hair during excitement. Blushing is a human example. Both convey information regarding emotional states; but neither behavior is deliberate, and communication is not intended.

autosomes All chromosomes except the sex chromosomes.

balanced polymorphism The maintenance of two or more alleles in a population due to the selective advantage of the heterozygote.

behavior Anything organisms do that involves action in response to internal or external stimuli; the response of an individual, group, or species to its environment. Such responses may or may not be deliberate, and they aren't necessarily the result of conscious decision making (which is absent in single-celled organisms, insects, and many other species).

behavioral ecology The study of the evolution of behavior, emphasizing the role of ecological factors as agents of natural selection. Behaviors and behavioral patterns are favored by natural selection when they increase the reproductive fitness of individuals (i.e., they're adaptive) in specific environmental contexts.

bilophodont Referring to molars that have four cusps oriented in two parallel rows, resembling ridges, or "lophs." This trait is characteristic of Old World monkeys.

binocular vision Vision characterized by overlapping visual fields provided by forward-facing eyes. Binocular vision is essential to depth perception.

binomial nomenclature (*binomial*, meaning "two names") In taxonomy, the convention established by Carolus Linnaeus whereby genus and species names are used to refer to species. For example, *Homo sapiens* refers to human beings.

bioarchaeology The study of skeletal remains from archaeological sites.

biocultural evolution The mutual, interactive evolution of human biology and culture; the concept that biology makes culture possible and that developing culture further influences the direction of biological evolution; a basic concept in understanding the unique components of human evolution.

biological continuity A biological continuum. When expressions of a phenomenon continuously grade into one another so that there are no discrete categories, they exist on a continuum. Color is one such phenomenon, and life-forms are another.

biological determinism The concept that phenomena, including various aspects of behavior (e.g., intelligence, values, morals) are governed by biological (genetic) factors; the inaccurate association of various behavioral attributes with certain biological traits, such as skin color.

biological species concept A depiction of species as groups of individuals capable of fertile interbreeding but reproductively isolated from other such groups.

biostratigraphy A relative dating technique based on the regular changes seen in evolving groups of animals as well as the presence or absence of particular species.

bipedally On two feet; walking habitually on two legs.

blanks In archaeology, stones suitably sized and shaped to be further worked into tools.

brachiation Arm swinging, a form of locomotion used by some primates. Brachiation involves hanging from a branch and moving by alternately swinging from one arm to the other.

breeding isolates Populations that are clearly isolated geographically and/or socially from other breeding groups.

burins Small, chisel-like tools with a pointed end; thought to have been used to engrave bone, antler, ivory, or wood.

catarrhine Member of Catarrhini, a parvorder of Primates, one of the three major divisions of the suborder Haplorhini. It contains the Old World monkeys, apes, and humans.

catastrophism The view that the earth's geological landscape is the result of violent cataclysmic events. Cuvier promoted this view, especially in opposition to Lamarck.

Chatelperronian Pertaining to an Upper Paleolithic industry found in France and Spain, containing blade tools and associated with Neandertals.

Chordata The phylum of the animal kingdom that includes vertebrates.

Christian fundamentalists Adherents to a movement in American Protestantism that began in the early twentieth century. This group holds that the teachings of the Bible are infallible and that the scriptures are to be taken literally.

chromatin The form of DNA that is present when a cell is not dividing. Microscopically, chromatin appears as a granular substance; when it condenses prior to cell division, it forms chromosomes.

chromosomes Discrete structures composed of DNA and proteins found only in the nuclei of cells. Chromosomes are visible under magnification only during certain phases of cell division.

chronometric dating (*chrono*, meaning "time," and *metric*, meaning "measure") A dating technique that gives an estimate in actual numbers of years; also known as absolute dating.

clade A group of organisms sharing a common ancestor. The group includes the common ancestor and all descendants.

cladistics An approach to classification that attempts to make rigorous evolutionary interpretations based solely on analysis of certain types of homologous characters (those considered to be derived characters).

cladogram A chart showing evolutionary relationships as determined by cladistic analysis. It's based solely on interpretation of shared derived characters. It contains no time component and does not imply ancestor-descendant relationships.

classification In biology, the ordering of organisms into categories, such as orders, families, and genera, to show evolutionary relationships.

clones Organisms that are genetically identical to another organism. The term may also be used to refer to genetically identical DNA segments, molecules, or cells.

codominance The expression of two alleles in heterozygotes. In this situation, neither allele is dominant or recessive, so they both influence the phenotype.

codons Triplets of messenger RNA bases that code for specific amino acids during protein synthesis.

communication Any act that conveys information, in the form of a message, to another individual. Frequently, the result of communication is a change in the recipient's behavior. Communication may not be deliberate, but may instead be the result of involuntary processes or a secondary consequence of an intentional action.

complementary In genetics, referring to the fact that DNA bases form pairs (called base pairs) in a precise manner. For example, adenine can bond only to thymine. These two bases are said to be complementary because one requires the other to form a complete DNA base pair.

conspecifics Members of the same species.

context The environmental setting where an archaeological trace is found. Primary context is the setting in which the archaeological trace was originally deposited. A secondary context is one to which it has been moved (such as by the action of a stream).

continental drift The movement of continents on sliding plates of the earth's surface. As a result, the positions of large landmasses have shifted drastically during the earth's history.

core Stone reduced by flake removal. A core may or may not itself be used as a tool.

core area The portion of a home range containing the highest concentration and most reliable supplies of food and water. The core area is frequently the area that will be most aggressively defended.

cortex Layer. In the brain, the cortex is the layer that covers the cerebral hemispheres, which in turn cover more primitive, or older, structures related to bodily functions and the sense of smell. The cortex is composed of nerve cells called neurons, which communicate with each other and send and receive messages to and from all parts of the body.

crown group All of the taxa that come after a major speciation event. Crown groups are easier to identify than stem groups because the members possess the clade's shared derived traits.

culture Behavioral aspects of human adaptation, including technology, traditions, language, religion, marriage patterns, and social roles. Culture is a set of learned behaviors transmitted from one generation to the next by nonbiological (i.e., nongenetic) means.

cusps The bumps on the chewing surface of premolars and molars.

cytoplasm The semifluid, gel-like substance contained within the cell membrane. The nucleus and numerous structures involved with cell function are found within the cytoplasm.

data (*sing.*, *datum*) Facts from which conclusions can be drawn; scientific information.

dental formula Numerical device that indicates the number of each type of tooth in each side of the upper and lower jaws.

derived (modified) Referring to characters that are modified from the ancestral condition and thus diagnostic of particular evolutionary lineages.

development Differentiation of cells into different types of tissues and their maturation.

direct percussion Striking a core or flake with a hammerstone.

displays Sequences of repetitious behaviors that serve to communicate emotional states. Nonhuman primate displays are most frequently associated with reproductive or agonistic behavior.

distal Referring to the part of a bone that is farthest from the point of attachment to the central skeleton.

diurnal Active during the day.

DNA (deoxyribonucleic acid) The double-stranded molecule that contains the genetic code. DNA is a main component of chromosomes.

dominance hierarchies Systems of social organization wherein individuals within a group are ranked relative to one another. Higher-ranking individuals have greater access to preferred food items and mating partners than do lower-ranking individuals. Dominance hierarchies are sometimes referred to as pecking orders.

dominant In genetics, describing a trait governed by an allele that's expressed in the presence of another allele (i.e., in heterozygotes). Dominant alleles prevent the expression of recessive alleles in heterozygotes. (This is the definition of *complete* dominance.)

ecological niche The position of a species within its physical and biological environments. A species' ecological niche is defined by such components as diet, terrain, vegetation, type of predators, relationships with other species, and activity patterns, and each niche is unique to a given species. Together, ecological niches make up an ecosystem.

ecological species concept The concept that a species is a group of organisms exploiting a single niche. This view emphasizes the role of natural selection in separating species from one another.

empathy The ability to identify with the feelings and emotions of others.

empirical Relying on experiment or observation; from the Latin *empiricus*, meaning "experienced."

encephalization The proportional size of the brain relative to some other measure, usually an estimate of overall body size, such as weight. More precisely, the term refers to increases in brain size beyond what would be expected given the body size of a particular species.

endemic Continuously present in a population.

endogamy Mating with individuals from the same group.

endothermic (*endo*, meaning "within" or "internal") Able to maintain internal body temperature by producing energy through metabolic processes within cells; characteristic of mammals, birds, and perhaps some dinosaurs.

environmental determinism An interpretation that links simple environmental changes directly to a major evolutionary shift in an organism. Such explanations tend to oversimplify the evolutionary process.

enzymes Specialized proteins that initiate and direct chemical reactions in the body.

epigenetics Changes in phenotype that are not related to changes in underlying DNA.

epigenome The instructions that determine what and how genes are expressed in cells.

epochs Categories of the geological time scale; subdivisions of periods. In the Cenozoic

era, epochs include the Paleocene, Eocene, Oligocene, Miocene, and Pliocene (from the Tertiary Period) and the Pleistocene and Holocene (from the Quaternary Period).

essential amino acids The 9 (of 22) amino acids that must be obtained from the food we eat because they are not synthesized in the body in sufficient amounts.

ethnocentric Viewing other cultures from the inherently biased perspective of one's own culture. Ethnocentrism often results in other cultures being seen as inferior to one's own.

ethnographies Detailed descriptive studies of human societies. In cultural anthropology, an ethnography is traditionally the study of a non-Western society.

Euarchonta The superorder designated for the sister (closely related) orders of tree shrews, flying lemurs, and primates.

eugenics The philosophy of "race improvement" through the forced sterilization of members of some groups and increased reproduction among others; an overly simplified, often racist view that's now discredited.

euprimates "True primates." This term was coined by Elwyn Simons in 1972.

evaporative cooling A physiological mechanism that helps prevent the body from overheating. It occurs when perspiration is produced from sweat glands and then evaporates from the surface of the skin.

evolution A change in the genetic structure of a population. The term is also frequently used to refer to the appearance of a new species.

evolutionary medicine The application of principles of evolution to aspects of medical research and practice.

evolutionary systematics A traditional approach to classification (and evolutionary interpretation) in which presumed ancestors and descendants are traced in time by analysis of homologous characters.

exogamy Mating pattern whereby individuals obtain mates from groups other than their own.

exons Segments of genes that are transcribed and are involved in protein synthesis. (The prefix *ex* denotes that these segments are expressed.)

fertility The ability to conceive and produce healthy offspring.

fitness Pertaining to natural selection, a measure of the relative reproductive success of individuals. Fitness can be measured by an individual's genetic contribution to the next generation compared with that of other individuals. The terms genetic fitness, reproductive fitness, and *differential reproductive success* are also used.

fixity of species The notion that species, once created, can never change; an idea diametrically opposed to theories of biological evolution.

flake Thin-edged fragment removed from a core.

flexed The position of the body in a bent orientation, with arms and legs drawn up to the chest.

forensic anthropology An applied anthropological approach dealing with legal matters. Forensic anthropologists work with coroners and others in identifying and analyzing human remains.

fossils Traces or remnants of organisms found in geological beds on the earth's surface.

founder effect A type of genetic drift in which allele frequencies are altered in small populations that are taken from, or are remnants of, larger populations.

frugivorous (fru-give´-or-us) Having a diet composed primarily of fruits.

gametes Reproductive cells (eggs and sperm in animals) developed from precursor cells in ovaries and testes.

gene A sequence of DNA bases that specifies the order of amino acids in an entire protein, a portion of a protein, or any functional product (e.g., RNA). A gene may be made up of hundreds or thousands of DNA bases organized into coding and noncoding segments.

gene flow Exchange of genes between populations.

gene pool All of the genes shared by the reproductive members of a population.

genetic Having to do with the study of gene structure and action and the patterns of inheritance of traits from parent to offspring. Genetic mechanisms are the foundation for evolutionary change.

genetic drift Evolutionary changes, or changes in allele frequencies, that are produced by random factors in small populations. Genetic drift is a result of small population size.

genome The entire genetic makeup of an individual or species. In humans, it's estimated that each individual possesses approximately 3 billion DNA bases.

genotype The genetic makeup of an individual. Genotype can refer to an organism's entire genetic makeup or to the alleles at a particular locus.

genus (*pl.*, genera) A group of closely related species.

geological time scale The organization of earth history into eras, periods, and epochs; commonly used by geologists and paleoanthropologists.

glaciations Climatic intervals when continental ice sheets cover much of the northern continents. Glaciations are associated with colder temperatures in northern latitudes and more arid conditions in southern latitudes, most notably in Africa.

grade A grouping of organisms sharing a similar adaptive pattern. Grade isn't necessarily based on closeness of evolutionary relationship, but it does contrast organisms in a useful way (e.g., *Homo erectus* with *Homo sapiens*).

grooming Picking through fur to remove dirt, parasites, and other materials that may be present. Social grooming is common among primates and reinforces social relationships.

growth Increase in mass or number of cells.

habitual bipedalism Bipedal locomotion as the form of locomotion shown by hominins most of the time.

half-life The time period in which one-half the amount of a radioactive isotope is converted chemically to a daughter product. For example, after 1.25 billion years, half the 40K remains; after 2.5 billion years, one-fourth remains.

haplorhines (hap-lore´-ines) Members of the primate suborder Haplorhini, which includes tarsiers, monkeys, apes, and humans.

Haplorhini (hap´-lo-rin-ee) The primate suborder that includes tarsiers, monkeys, apes, and humans. (Colloquial form: haplorhine.)

Hardy-Weinberg theory of genetic equilibrium The mathematical relationship expressing—under conditions in which no evolution is occurring—the predicted distribution of alleles in populations; the central theorem of population genetics.

hemispheres The two halves of the cerebrum that are connected by a dense mass of fibers. (The cerebrum is the large rounded outer portion of the brain.)

hemoglobin A protein molecule that occurs in red blood cells and binds to oxygen molecules.

heterodont Having different kinds of teeth; characteristic of mammals, whose teeth consist of incisors, canines, premolars, and molars.

heterozygous Having different alleles at the same locus on members of a pair of chromosomes.

Holocene The most recent epoch of the Cenozoic. Following the Pleistocene, it's estimated to have begun 10,000 years ago.

home range The total area exploited by an animal or social group; usually given for one year or for the entire lifetime of an animal.

homeobox genes An evolutionarily ancient family of regulatory genes that directs the development of the overall body plan and the segmentation of body tissues.

homeostasis A condition of balance, or stability, within a biological system, maintained by the interaction of physiological mechanisms that compensate for changes (both external and internal).

hominins Colloquial term for members of the evolutionary group that includes modern humans and now extinct bipedal relatives.

hominoids Members of the primate superfamily (Hominoidea) that includes apes and humans.

homologies Similarities between organisms based on descent from a common ancestor.

homoplasy (*homo*, meaning "same," and *plasy*, meaning "growth") The separate evolutionary development of similar characteristics in different groups of organisms.

homozygous Having the same allele at the same locus on both members of a pair of chromosomes.

hormones Substances (usually proteins) that are produced by specialized cells and that travel to other parts of the body, where they influence chemical reactions and regulate various cellular functions.

Human Genome Project An international effort aimed at sequencing and mapping the entire human genome, completed in 2003.

hybrids Offspring of parents who differ from each other with regard to certain traits or certain aspects of genetic makeup; heterozygotes.

hypotheses (*sing.*, hypothesis) A provisional explanation of a phenomenon. Hypotheses require verification or falsification through testing.

hypoxia Insufficient levels of oxygen in body tissues; oxygen deficiency.

inbreeding A type of nonrandom mating in which relatives mate more often than predicted under random mating conditions.

incest avoidance In animals, the tendency not to mate with close relatives. This tendency may be due to various social and ecological factors that keep the individuals apart. There may also be innate factors that lead to incest avoidance, but these aren't well understood.

intelligence Mental capacity; ability to learn, reason, or comprehend and interpret information, facts, relationships, and meanings; the capacity to solve problems, whether through the application of previously acquired knowledge or through insight.

interglacials Climatic intervals when continental ice sheets are retreating, eventually becoming much reduced in size. Interglacials in northern latitudes are associated with warmer temperatures, while in southern latitudes the climate becomes wetter.

interspecific Between species; refers to variation beyond that seen within the same species to include additional aspects seen between two different species.

intragroup (*intra*, meaning "within") Within the group, as opposed to between groups (intergroup).

intraspecific Within species; refers to variation seen within the same species.

introns Segments of genes that are initially transcribed and then deleted. Because they aren't expressed, they aren't involved in protein synthesis.

ischial callosities Patches of tough, hard skin on the buttocks of Old World monkeys and chimpanzees.

island-hopping Traveling from one island to the next.

K-selected Pertaining to K-selection, an adaptive strategy whereby individuals produce relatively few offspring, in whom they invest increased parental care. Although only a few infants are born, chances of survival are increased for each individual because of parental investments in time and energy. Examples of nonprimate K-selected species are birds and canids (e.g., wolves, coyotes, and dogs).

karyotype The chromosomes of an individual, or what is typical of a species, viewed microscopically and displayed in a photograph. The chromosomes are arranged in pairs and according to size and position of the centromere.

knappers People (frequently archaeologists) who make stone tools.

lactase persistence In adults, the continued production of lactase, the enzyme that breaks down lactose (milk sugar). This allows adults in some human populations to digest fresh milk products. The discontinued production of lactase in adults leads to lactose intolerance and the inability to digest fresh milk.

last common ancestor (LCA) The final evolutionary link between two related groups.

Late Pleistocene The portion of the Pleistocene epoch beginning 125,000 ya and ending approximately 10,000 ya.

lateralized Localized to one side of the brain. Lateralization is the functional specialization of the hemispheres of the brain for specific activities.

life history traits Characteristics and developmental stages that influence rates of reproduction. Examples include longevity, age at sexual maturity, and length of time between births.

lithic (*lith*, meaning "stone") Referring to stone tools.

locus (*pl.*, loci) (lo'-kus, lo-sigh') The position or location on a chromosome where a given gene occurs. The term is sometimes used interchangeably with *gene*.

lumbar Pertaining to the lower back. The lumbar area is longer in monkeys than it is in humans and apes.

macroevolution Changes produced only after many generations, such as the appearance of a new species.

Magdalenian Pertaining to the final phase of the Upper Paleolithic stone tool industry in Europe.

malnutrition A diet insufficient in quality (i.e., lacking some essential component) to support normal health.

matrilines Groupings of females who are all descendants of one female; a female, her daughters, granddaughters, and their offspring. Matrilines also include dependent male offspring. Among macaques, some matrilines are dominant to others, so that members of dominant matrilines have greater access to resources than do members of subordinate matrilines.

meiosis Cell division in specialized cells in ovaries and testes. Meiosis involves two divisions and results in four daughter cells, each containing only half the original number of chromosomes. These cells can develop into gametes.

menarche The first menstruation in girls, usually occuring in the early to mid-teens.

Mendelian traits Characteristics that are influenced by alleles at only one genetic locus. Examples include many blood types, such as ABO. Many genetic disorders, including sickle-cell anemia and Tay-Sachs disease, are also Mendelian traits.

menopause The end of menstruation in women, usually occuring at around age 50.

messenger RNA (mRNA) A form of RNA that's assembled on a sequence of DNA bases. It carries the DNA code to the ribosome during protein synthesis.

metabolism The chemical processes within cells that break down nutrients and release energy for the body to use. (When nutrients are broken down into their component parts, such as amino acids, energy is released and made available for the cell to use.)

microevolution Small changes occurring within species, such as changes in allele frequencies.

microliths (*micro*, meaning "small," and *lith*, meaning "stone") Small stone tools usually produced from narrow blades punched from a core; found especially in Africa during the latter part of the Pleistocene.

microwear Polishes, striations, and other diagnostic microscopic changes on the edges of stone tools.

Middle Pleistocene The portion of the Pleistocene epoch beginning 780,000 ya and ending 125,000 ya.

mineralization The process in which parts of animals (or some plants) become transformed into stone-like structures. Mineralization usually occurs very slowly as water carrying minerals, such as silica or iron, seeps into the tiny spaces within a bone. In some cases, the original minerals within the bone or tooth can be completely replaced, molecule by molecule, with other minerals.

mitochondria (*sing.*, mitochondrion) Structures contained within the cytoplasm of eukaryotic cells that convert energy, derived from nutrients, to a form that can be used by the cell.

mitochondrial DNA (mtDNA) DNA found in the mitochondria. Mitochondrial DNA is inherited only from the mother.

mitosis Simple cell division; the process by which somatic cells divide to produce two identical daughter cells.

molecules Structures made up of two or more atoms. Molecules can combine with other molecules to form more complex structures.

monophyletic Referring to an evolutionary group (clade) composed of descendants all sharing a common ancestor.

morphological Pertaining to the form and structure of organisms.

morphology The form (shape, size) of anatomical structures; can also refer to the entire organism.

mosaic evolution A pattern of evolution in which the rate of evolution in one functional system varies from that in other systems. For example, in hominin evolution, the dental system, locomotor system, and neurological system (especially the brain) all evolved at markedly different rates.

motor cortex The areas of the brain's cortex involved with movement. The motor cortex is located at the back of the frontal lobe and is composed of cells that send information to muscle cells throughout the body.

Mousterian Pertaining to the stone tool industry associated with Neandertals and some modern *H. sapiens* groups; also called Middle Paleolithic. This industry is characterized by a larger proportion of flake tools than is found in Acheulian tool kits.

multidisciplinary Pertaining to research involving mutual contributions and cooperation of experts from various scientific fields (i.e., disciplines).

mutation A change in DNA. The term can refer to changes in DNA bases (specifically called point mutations) as well as to changes in chromosome number and/or structure.

natal group The group in which animals are born and raised. (*Natal* pertains to birth.)

natural selection The most critical mechanism of evolutionary change, first described by Charles Darwin; refers to genetic change or changes in the frequencies of certain traits in populations due to differential reproductive success between individuals.

neocortex The more recently evolved portions of the cortex of the brain that are involved with higher mental functions and composed of areas that integrate incoming information from different sensory organs.

neural tube In early embryonic development, the anatomical structure that develops to form the brain and spinal cord.

nocturnal Active during the night.

noncoding DNA DNA that does not direct the production of proteins. However, such DNA segments may produce other important molecules, so the term *noncoding DNA* is not really accurate.

nonrandom mating Pattern of mating in which individuals choose mates preferentially, with mate choice based on criteria such as social status, ethnicity, or biological relationship. In nonrandom mating, an individual doesn't have an equal chance of mating with all other individuals in the group.

nuchal torus (nuke'-ul) (*nucha*, meaning "neck") A projection of bone in the back of the cranium where neck muscles attach. These muscles hold up the head.

nucleotides Basic units of the DNA molecule, composed of a sugar, a phosphate, and one of four DNA bases.

nucleus A structure (organelle) found in all eukaryotic cells. The nucleus contains chromosomes (nuclear DNA).

obligate bipedalism Bipedalism as the *only* form of hominin terrestrial locomotion. Since major anatomical changes in the spine, pelvis, and lower limb are required for bipedal locomotion, once hominins adapted this mode of locomotion, other forms of locomotion on the ground became impossible.

olfaction The sense of smell.

omnivorous Having a diet consisting of many food types, such as plant materials, meat, and insects.

orthograde Referring to an upright body position. This term relates to the position of the head and torso during sitting, climbing, etc., and doesn't necessarily mean that an animal is bipedal.

ossification The process by which cartilage cells are replaced by bone cells in normal growth.

osteology The study of skeletal material. Human osteology focuses on the interpretation of the skeletal remains from archaeological sites, skeletal anatomy, bone physiology, and growth and development. Some of the same techniques are used in paleoanthropology to study early hominins.

paleoanthropology The interdisciplinary approach to the study of earlier hominins—their chronology, physical structure, archaeological remains, habitats, and so on.

paleomagnetism Dating method based on the earth's shifting magnetic pole.

paleopathology The branch of osteology that studies the evidence of disease and injury in human skeletal (or, occasionally, mummified) remains from archaeological sites.

paleoprimatologists Anthropologists specializing in the study of the nonhuman primate fossil record.

paleospecies Species defined from fossil evidence, often covering a long time span.

pedigree chart A diagram showing family relationships. It's used to trace the hereditary pattern of particular genetic (usually Mendelian) traits.

phenotypes The observable or detectable physical characteristics of an organism; the detectable expressions of genotypes, frequently influenced by environmental factors.

philopatric Remaining in one's natal group or home range as an adult. In most species, members of one sex disperse from their natal group as young adults, and members of the philopatric sex remain. In most nonhuman primate species, the philopatric sex is female.

phylogenetic species concept Splitting many populations into separate species based on an identifiable parental pattern of ancestry.

phylogenetic tree A chart showing evolutionary relationships as determined by evolutionary systematics. It contains a time component and implies ancestor-descendant relationships.

phytoliths (*phyto*, meaning "hidden," and *lith*, meaning "stone") Microscopic silica structures formed in the cells of many plants, particularly grasses.

pigment In reference to polygenic inheritance, molecules that influence the color of skin, hair, and eyes.

placental A type (subclass) of mammal. During the Cenozoic, placentals became the most widespread and numerous mammals and today are represented by upward of 20 orders, including the primates.

platyrrhines Members of Platyrrhini, a parvorder of Primates, one of the three major divisions of the suborder Haplorhini. It contains only the New World monkeys.

pleiotropic genes Genes that have more than one effect; genes that have different effects at different times in the life cycle.

pleiotropy The capacity of a single gene to influence several phenotypic expressions.

Pleistocene The epoch of the Cenozoic from 1.8 mya until 10,000 ya. Frequently referred to as the Ice Age, this epoch is associated with continental glaciations in northern latitudes.

Plio-Pleistocene Pertaining to the Pliocene and first half of the Pleistocene, a time range of 5–1 mya. For this time period, numerous fossil hominins have been found in Africa.

point mutation A change in one of the four DNA bases.

polyandry A mating system characterized by an association between a female and more than one male (usually two or three), with whom she mates. Among nonhuman primates, this pattern is seen only in marmosets and tamarins.

polygenic Referring to traits that are influenced by genes at two or more loci. Examples include stature, skin color, eye color, and hair color. Many (but not all) polygenic traits are influenced by environmental factors such as nutrition and exposure to sunlight.

polymerase chain reaction (PCR) A method of producing thousands of copies of a DNA sample.

polymorphisms Loci with more than one allele. Polymorphisms can be expressed in the phenotype as the result of gene action (as in ABO), or they can exist solely at the DNA level within noncoding regions.

polyphyletic Referring to an evolutionary group composed of descendants with more than one common ancestor (and thus not a true clade).

polytypic Referring to species composed of populations that differ in the expression of one or more traits.

population Within a species, a community of individuals where mates are usually found.

population genetics The study of the frequency of alleles, genotypes, and phenotypes in populations from a microevolutionary perspective.

postcranial Referring to all or part of the skeleton not including the skull. The term originates from the fact that in quadrupeds, the body is posterior to the head; the term literally means "behind the head."

pressure flaking A method of removing flakes from a core by pressing a pointed implement (e.g., bone or antler) against the stone.

primate paleontology The study of fossil primates, especially those that lived before the appearance of hominins.

primates Members of the mammalian order Primates (pronounced "pry-may´-tees"), which includes lemurs, lorises, tarsiers, monkeys, apes, and humans.

primatology The study of the biology and behavior of nonhuman primates (lemurs, lorises, tarsiers, monkeys, and apes).

principle of independent assortment The distribution of one pair of alleles into gametes does not influence the distribution of another pair. The genes controlling different traits are inherited independently of one another.

principle of segregation Genes (alleles) occur in pairs because chromosomes occur in pairs. During gamete formation, the members of each pair of alleles separate, so that each gamete contains one member of each pair.

principle of superposition In a stratigraphic sequence, the lower layers were deposited before the upper layers. Or, simply put, the stuff on top of a heap was put there last.

prosocial behaviors Actions that benefit another individual even when there is no reward to the performer. Prosocial behaviors include sharing, assisting, and comforting and in humans are motivated in part by empathy and compassion.

protein synthesis The manufacture of proteins; the assembly of chains of amino acids into functional protein molecules. Protein synthesis is directed by DNA.

proteins Three-dimensional molecules that serve a wide variety of functions through their ability to bind to other molecules.

proximal Referring to the part of a bone that is closest to the point of attachment to the central skeleton.

punctuated equilibrium The concept that evolutionary change proceeds through long periods of stasis punctuated by rapid periods of change.

quadrupedal Using all four limbs to support the body during locomotion; the basic mammalian (and primate) form of locomotion.

quantitatively Pertaining to measurements of quantity and including such properties as size, number, and capacity. When data are quantified, they're expressed numerically and can be tested statistically.

r-selected Pertaining to r-selection, an adaptive strategy that emphasizes relatively large numbers of offspring and reduced parental care (compared with K-selected species). K-selection and r-selection are relative terms (e.g., mice are r-selected compared with primates but K-selected compared with most fish).

random assortment The chance distribution of chromosomes to daughter cells during meiosis. Along with recombination, random assortment is an important source of genetic variation (but not new alleles).

recessive Describing a trait that isn't expressed in heterozygotes; also refers to the allele that governs the trait. For a recessive allele to be expressed, an individual must have two copies of it (i.e., the individual must be homozygous).

recognition species concept A depiction of species in which the key aspect is the ability of individuals to identify members of their own species for purposes of mating (and to avoid mating with members of other species). In theory, this type of selective mating is a component of a species concept emphasizing mating and is therefore compatible with the biological species concept.

recombination   The exchange of genetic material between paired chromosomes during meiosis; also called *crossing over*.

regulatory genes   Genes that influence the activity of other genes. Regulatory genes direct embryonic development and are involved in physiological processes throughout life. They are extremely important to the evolutionary process.

replicate   To duplicate. The DNA molecule is able to make copies of itself.

reproductive strategies   The complex of behavioral patterns that contributes to individual reproductive success. The behaviors need not be deliberate, and they often vary considerably between males and females.

reproductive success   The number of offspring an individual produces and rears to reproductive age; an individual's genetic contribution to the next generation.

reproductively isolated   Pertaining to groups of organisms that, mainly because of genetic differences, are prevented from mating and producing offspring with members of other such groups. For example, dogs cannot mate and produce offspring with cats.

rhinarium   (rine-air´-ee-um) The moist, hairless pad at the end of the nose seen in most mammalian species. The rhinarium enhances an animal's ability to smell.

ribosomes   Structures composed of a form of RNA called ribosomal RNA (rRNA) and protein. Ribosomes are found in a cell's cytoplasm and are essential to the manufacture of proteins.

ritualized behaviors   Behaviors removed from their original context and sometimes exaggerated to convey information.

RNA (ribonucleic acid)   A single-stranded molecule similar in structure to DNA. Three forms of RNA are essential to protein synthesis: messenger RNA (mRNA), transfer RNA (tRNA), and ribosomal RNA (rRNA).

sagittal crest   A ridge of bone that runs down the middle of the cranium like a short Mohawk. This serves as the attachment for the large temporal muscles, indicating strong chewing.

savanna   (also spelled savannah) A large flat grassland with scattered trees and shrubs. Savannas are found in many regions of the world with dry and warm-to-hot climates.

science   A body of knowledge gained through observation and experimentation; from the Latin *scientia*, meaning "knowledge."

scientific method   An approach to research whereby a problem is identified, a hypothesis (provisional explanation) is stated, and that hypothesis is tested by collecting and analyzing data.

scientific testing   The precise repetition of an experiment or expansion of observed data to provide verification; the procedure by which hypotheses and theories are verified, modified, or discarded.

sectorial   Adapted for cutting or shearing; among primates, refers to the compressed (side-to-side) first lower premolar, which functions as a shearing surface with the upper canine.

selective breeding   A practice whereby animal or plant breeders choose which individual animals or plants will be allowed to mate based on the traits (such as coat color or body size) they hope to produce in the offspring. Animals or plants that don't have the desirable traits aren't allowed to breed.

selective pressures   Forces in the environment that influence reproductive success in individuals.

semiorder   The taxonomic category above suborder and below order.

senescence   Decline in physiological function usually associated with aging.

sensory modalities   Different forms of sensation (e.g., touch, pain, pressure, heat, cold, vision, taste, hearing, and smell).

sex chromosomes   In mammals, the X and Y chromosomes.

sexual dimorphism   Differences in physical characteristics between males and females of the same species. For example, humans are slightly sexually dimorphic for body size, with males being taller, on average, than females of the same population. Sexual dimorphism is very pronounced in many species, such as gorillas.

sexual selection   A type of natural selection that operates on only one sex within a species. Sexual selection results from competition for

mates, and it can lead to sexual dimorphism regarding one or more traits.

shared derived   Relating to specific character traits shared in common between two life-forms and considered the most useful for making evolutionary interpretations.

sickle-cell trait   Heterozygous condition where a person has one Hb^A allele and one Hb^S allele. Thus they have some normal hemoglobin.

sickle-cell anemia   A severe inherited hemoglobin disorder in which red blood cells collapse when deprived of oxygen. It results from inheriting two copies of a mutant allele. The type of mutation that produces the sickle-cell allele is a point mutation.

sister groups   Two new clades that result from the splitting of a single common lineage.

slash-and-burn agriculture   A traditional land-clearing practice involving the cutting and burning of trees and vegetation. In many areas, fields are abandoned after a few years and clearing occurs elsewhere.

social structure   The composition, size, and sex ratio of a group of animals. Social structure is the result of natural selection in a specific habitat, and it influences individual interactions and social relationships. In many species, social structure varies, depending on different environmental factors. Thus, in primates, social structure should be viewed as flexible, not fixed.

somatic cells   Basically, all the cells in the body except those involved with reproduction.

speciation   The process by which a new species evolves from an earlier species. Speciation is the most basic process in macroevolution.

species   A group of organisms that can interbreed to produce fertile offspring. Members of one species are reproductively isolated from members of all other species (i.e., they cannot mate with them to produce fertile offspring).

spina bifida   A condition in which the arch of one or more vertebrae fails to fuse and form a protective barrier around the spinal cord.

stable carbon isotopes   Isotopes of carbon that are produced in plants in differing proportions, depending on environmental conditions. By analyzing the proportions of the isotopes contained in fossil remains of animals (who ate the plants), it's possible to reconstruct aspects of ancient environments (particularly temperature and aridity).

stem group All of the taxa in a clade before a major speciation event. Stem groups are often difficult to recognize in the fossil record, since they don't often have the shared derived traits found in the crown group.

stereoscopic vision The condition whereby visual images are, to varying degrees, super-imposed. This provides for depth perception, or viewing the external environment in three dimensions. Stereoscopic vision is partly a function of structures in the brain.

strategies Behaviors or behavioral complexes that have been favored by natural selection because they're advantageous to the animals that perform them. Examples include actions that enhance an animal's ability to obtain food, rear infants, or increase its social status. Ultimately, strategies influence reproductive success.

stratigraphy Study of the sequential layering of deposits.

strepsirhines (strep-sir´-rines) Members of the primate suborder Strepsirhini, which includes lemurs and lorises.

Strepsirhini (strep´-sir-in-ee) The primate suborder that includes lemurs and lorises. (Colloquial form: strepsirhine.)

stress In a physiological context, any factor that acts to disrupt homeostasis; more precisely, the body's response to any factor that threatens its ability to maintain homeostasis.

subfossil Bone not old enough to have become completely mineralized as a fossil.

superorder A taxonomic group ranking above an order and below a class or subclass.

sympatric Living in the same area; pertaining to two or more species whose habitats partly or largely overlap.

tandem repeats Short, adjacent segments of DNA within a gene that are repeated several times.

taphonomy (*taphos*, meaning "tomb") The study of how bones and other materials came to be buried in the earth and preserved as fossils. Taphonomists study the processes of sedimentation, the action of streams, preservation properties of bone, and carnivore disturbance factors.

taxonomy The branch of science concerned with the rules of classifying organisms on the basis of evolutionary relationships.

terrestrial Living and locomoting primarily on the ground.

territorial Pertaining to the protection of all or a part of the area occupied by an animal or group of animals. Territorial behaviors range from scent marking to outright attacks on intruders.

territory The portion of a home range actively defended against intrusion, particularly by members of the same species.

theory A broad statement of scientific relationships or underlying principles that has been substantially verified through the testing of hypotheses.

thermoluminiscence (TL) (ther-mo-loo-min-ess´-ence) Technique for dating certain archaeological materials (such as stone tools) that were heated in the past and that release stored energy of radioactive decay as light upon reheating.

theropods Small- to medium-sized ground-living dinosaurs, dated to approximately 150 mya and thought to be related to birds.

transfer RNA (tRNA) A type of RNA that binds to specific amino acids and transports them to the ribosome during protein synthesis.

undernutrition A diet insufficient in quantity (calories) to support normal health.

uniformitarianism The theory that the earth's features are the result of long-term processes that continue to operate in the present just as they did in the past. Elaborated on by Lyell, this theory opposed catastrophism and contributed strongly to the concept of immense geological time.

Upper Paleolithic A cultural period usually associated with modern humans, but also found with some Neandertals, and distinguished by technological innovation in various stone tool industries. Best known from western Europe, similar industries are also known from central and eastern Europe and Africa.

variation In genetics, inherited differences among individuals; the basis of all evolutionary change.

vasoconstriction Narrowing of blood vessels to reduce blood flow to the skin. Vasoconstriction is an involuntary response to cold and reduces heat loss at the skin's surface.

vasodilation Expansion of blood vessels, permitting increased blood flow to the skin. Vasodilation permits warming of the skin and facilitates radiation of warmth as a means of cooling. Vasodilation is an involuntary response to warm temperatures, various drugs, and even emotional states (blushing).

vectors Agents that transmit disease from one carrier to another. Mosquitoes are vectors for malaria, just as fleas are vectors for bubonic plague.

vertebrates Animals with segmented, bony spinal columns; includes fishes, amphibians, reptiles (including birds), and mammals.

worldview General cultural orientation or perspective shared by members of a society.

zoonotic (zoh-oh-no´-tic) Pertaining to a zoonosis (*pl.*, zoonoses), a disease that's transmitted to humans through contact with nonhuman animals.

zygomatics Cheekbones.

zygote A cell formed by the union of an egg cell and a sperm cell. It contains the full complement of chromosomes (in humans, 46) and has the potential of developing into an entire organism.

Bibliography

Abzhanov, A., W. Kuo, C. Hartmann, et al.
2006   The calmodulin pathway and the evolution of elongated beak morphology in Darwin's finches. *Nature* 442:563–567.

Abzhanov, A., M. Protas, B. R. Grant, et al.
2004   *Bmp4* and morphological variation of beaks in Darwin's finches. *Science* 305:1462–1465.

Aiello, L. C.
1992   Body size and energy requirements. In: *The Cambridge Encyclopedia of Human Evolution*, J. Jones, R. Martin, and D. Pilbeam (eds.), pp. 41–45. Cambridge, England: Cambridge University Press.

Aiello, L. C., and J. C. K. Wells
2002   Energetics and the evolution of the genus *Homo*. *Annual Review of Anthropology* 31:323–338.

Alba, D. M., S. Moyà-Solà, et al.
2010   A New Species of *Pliopithecus gervais*, 1849 (Primates: Pliopithecidae) from the Middle Miocene (MN8) of Abocador de Can Mata (els Hostalets de Pierola, Catalonia, Spain). *American Journal of Physical Anthropology* 141:52–75.

Alemseged, Z., F. Spoor, W. H. Kimbel, et al.
2006   A juvenile early hominin skeleton from Dikika, Ethiopia. *Nature* 443:296–301.

Ali, J. R., and M. Huber
2010   Mammalian biodiversity on Madagascar controlled by ocean currents. *Nature* 463:653–656.

Altmann, J., G. Hausfater, and S. A. Altmann
1988   Determinants of reproductive success in savannah baboons, *Papio cynocephalus*. In: *Reproductive Success*, T. H. Clutton-Brock (ed.), pp. 403–418. Chicago: University of Chicago Press.

Anderson, R. P., and C. O. Handley
2002   Dwarfism in insular sloths: Biogeography, selection, and evolutionary rate. *Evolution* 56:1045–1058.

Andrews, P.
1984   An alternative interpretation of the characters used to define *Homo erectus*. *Cour Forschungist Senckenb* 69:167–175.

Ankel, F.
1965   Der canalis sacralis als indikator für die lange der caudelregion der primaten. *Folia Primatologica* 3:263–276.

Arnason, U., A. Gullberg, et al.
2000   Molecular estimates of primate divergences and new hypotheses for primate dispersal and the origin of modern humans. *Hereditas* 133:217–228.

Arsuaga, J.-L., C. Lorenzo, A. Gracia, et al.
1999   The human cranial remains from Gran Dolina Lower Pleistocene site (Sierra de Atapuerca, Spain). *Journal of Human Evolution* 37:431–457.

Arsuaga, J.-L., I. Martinez, A. Gracia, et al.
1997   Sima de los Huesos (Sierra de Atapuerca, Spain): the site. *Journal of Human Evolution* 33:109–127.

Ascenzi, A., I. Biddittu, et al.
1996   A calvarium of late *Homo erectus* from Ceprano, Italy. *Journal of Human Evolution* 31:409–423.

Asfaw, B., W. H. Gilbert, Y. Beyene, et al.
2002   Remains of *Homo erectus* from Bouri, Middle Awash, Ethiopia. *Nature* 416:317–320.

Asfaw, B., T. D. White, and G. Suwa
1994   *Australopithecus ramidus*, a new species of hominid from Aramis, Ethiopia. *Nature* 371:306.

Ashley-Koch, A., Q. Yang, et al.
2000   Sickle hemoglobin (HbS) alleles and sickle cell disease. *American Journal of Genetics* 151:839–845.

Aureli, F., C. M. Schaffner, et al.
2006   Raiding parties of male spider monkeys: Insights into human warfare? *American Journal of Physical Anthropology* 131:486–497.

Badrian, A., and N. Badrian
1984   Social organization of *Pan paniscus* in the Lomako Forest, Zaire. In: *The Pygmy Chimpanzee*, R. L. Susman (ed.), pp. 325–346. New York: Plenum Press.

Badrian, N., and R. K. Malenky
1984   Feeding ecology of *Pan paniscus* in the Lomako Forest, Zaire. In: *The Pygmy Chimpanzee*, R. L. Susman (ed.), pp. 275–299. New York: Plenum Press.

Bajpai, S., R. F. Kay, et al.
2008   The oldest Asian record of Anthropoidea. *Proceedings of the National Academy of Sciences* 105:11093–11098.

Balter, M.
2006   Radiocarbon dating's final frontier. *Science* 313:1560–1563.

Balter, M.
2007   Zebrafish researchers hook gene for human skin color. *Science* 310:1754–1755.

Balter, M.
2010   Candidate human ancestor from South Africa sparks praise and debate. *Science* 328:154–155.

Bamshad, M. J., and S. E. Olson
2003   Does race exist? *Scientific American* 289:78–85.

Bamshad, M. J., S. Wooding, et al.
2003   Human population genetic structure and inference of group membership. *American Journal of Human Genetics* 72:578–589.

Barker, D. J. P.
1994   *Mothers, Babies, and Disease in Later Life*. London: BMJ Publishing Group.

Barker, G., H. Barton, M. Bird, et al.
2007   The human revolution in lowland tropical Southeast Asia: The antiquity and behavior of anatomically modern humans at Niah Cave (Sarawak, Borneo). *Journal of Human Evolution* 52:243–261.

Bartlett, T. Q., R. W. Sussman, and J. M. Cheverud
1993   Infant killing in primates: A review of observed cases with specific references to the sexual selection hypothesis. *American Anthropologist* 95:958–990.

Barton, R. A. and R. L. M. Dunbar
1997   Evolution of the social brain. In: *Machiavellian Intelligence*, A. Whiten and R. Byrne (eds.). Cambridge, England: Cambridge University Press.

Beall, C. M.
2007   Two routes to functional adaptation: Tibetan and Andean high-altitude natives. *Proceedings of the National Academy of Sciences, U.S.A.* 104 Supp 1:8655–8660.

Beard, C.
2004   *The Hunt for the Dawn Monkey: Unearthing the Origins of Monkeys, Apes, and Humans.* Berkeley: University of California Press.

Beard, K. C.
2008   The oldest North American primate and mammalian biogeography during the Paleocene-Eocene Thermal Maximum. *Proceedings of the National Academy of Sciences, USA* 105:3815–3818.

Bearder, S. K.
1987   Lorises, bush babies & tarsiers: Diverse societies in solitary foragers. In: *Primate Societies*, B. B. Smuts, D. L. Cheney, and R. M. Seyfath (eds.), pp. 11–24. Chicago: University of Chicago Press.

Begun, D,. and A. Walker
1993   The Endocast. In: *The Nariokotome* Homo erectus *Skeleton*, A. Walker and R. E. Leakey (eds.), pp. 326–358. Cambridge, MA: Harvard University Press.

Begun, D. R.
1994   Relations among the great apes and humans: New interpretations based on the fossil great ape *Dryopithecus*. *Yearbook of Physical Anthropology* 37:11–63.

Begun, D. R.
2002   The Pliopithecoidea. In: *The Primate Fossil Record*, W. C. Hartwig (ed.), pp. 221–240. Cambridge, UK: Cambridge University Press.

Begun, D. R.
2003   Planet of the Apes. *Scientific American* 289:74–83.

Behrensmeyer, A. K., N. E. Todd, et al.
1997   Late Pliocene faunal turnover in the Turkana Basin, Kenya and Ethiopia. *Science* 278:1589–1594.

Behrensmeyer, A. K., D. Western, et al.
1979   New perspectives in vertebrate paleoecology from a recent bone assemblage. *Paleobiology* 5(1): 12–21.

Beja-Pereira, A., G. Luikart, P. R. England, et al.
2003   Gene-culture coevolution between cattle milk protein genes and human lactase genes. *Nature Genetics* 35:311–313.

Benefit, B. R., and M. L. McCrossin
1997   Earliest known Old World monkey skull. *Nature* 388:368–371.

Berger, L. R., D. J. de Ruiter, S. E. Churchill, et al.
2010   *Australopithecus sediba*: A new species of *Homo*-like australopith from South Africa. *Science* 328:195–204.

Berger, T. D., and E. Trinkaus
1995   Patterns of trauma among the Neandertals. *Journal of Archaeological Science* 22(6): 841–852.

Bergman, T. J., J. C. Beehner, et al.
2003   Hierarchical classification by rank and kinship in baboons. *Science* 302:1234–1236.

Bermijo, M., J. Rodriguez, et al.
2006   Ebola outbreak killed 5000 gorillas. *Science* 314:1564.

Bermudez de Castro, J. M., J. Arsuaga, E. Carbonell, et al.
1997   A hominid from the Lower Pleistocene of Atapuerca, Spain. Possible ancestor to Neandertals and modern humans. *Science* 276:1392–1395.

Bermudez de Castro, J. M., M. Martinon-Torres, E. Carbonell, et al.
2004   The Atapuerca sites and their contribution to the knowledge of human evolution in Europe. *Evolutionary Anthropology* 13:25–41.

Bernor, R. L.
2007   New apes fill the gap. *Proceedings of the National Academy of Sciences* 104:19661–19662.

Biasutti, R.
1959   Razze e Popoli della Terra. *Turin: Unione-Tipografico-Editrice.*

Binford, L. R.
1981   *Bones. Ancient Men and Modern Myths.* New York: Academic Press.

Binford, L. R.
1983   *In Pursuit of the Past.* New York: Thames and Hudson.

Binford, L. R., and C. K. Ho
1985   Taphonomy at a distance: Zhoukoudian, "the cave home of Beijing Man." *Current Anthropology* 26:413–442.

Binford, L. R., and N. M. Stone
1986a   The Chinese Paleolithic: An outsider's view. *AnthroQuest* 1:14–20.

Binford, L. R., and N. M. Stone
1986b   Zhoukoudian: A closer look. *Current Anthropology* 27:453–475.

Bininda-Emonds, R. P. Olaf, M. Cordillo, et al.
2007   The delayed rise of present-day mammals. *Nature* 446:507–512.

Bischoff, J. L., R. W. Williams, R. J. Rosebauer, et al.
2007   High-resolution U-series dates from the Sima de los Huesos hominids yields 600+/−66 kyrs: Implications for the evolution of the early Neanderthal lineage. *Journal of Archaeological Science* 34:763–770.

Bloch, J. I., and D. M. Boyer
2002   Grasping primate origins. *Science* 298:1606–1610.

Bloch, J. I., and M. T. Silcox
2001   New basicrania of Paleocene-Eocene Ignacius: Re-evaluation of the plesiadapiform-dermopteran link. *American Journal of Physical Anthropology* 116:184–198.

Bloch, J. I., M. T. Silcox, et al.
2007   New Paleocene skeletons and the relationship of plesiadapiforms to crown-clade primates. *Proceedings of the National Academy of Sciences USA* 104(4): 1159–1164.

Blumenschine, R. J.
1986   *Early Hominid Scavenging Opportunities.* Oxford, Bar International Series 283.

Blumenschine, R. J.
1995   Percussion marks, tooth marks, and experimental determinants of the timing of hominid and carnivore access to long bones at FLK *Zinjanthropus*, Olduvai Gorge, Tanzania. *Journal of Human Evolution* 29:21–51.

Blumenschine, R. J., and J. A. Cavallo
1992   Scavenging and human evolution. *Scientific American* 267:90–96.

Blumenschine, R. J., and C. R. Peters
1998   Archaeological predictions for hominid land use in the paleo-Olduvai Basin, Tanzania, during lowermost Bed II times. *Journal of Human Evolution* 34:565–607.

Boaz, N. T., and A. K. Behrensmeyer
1976   Hominid taphonomy: Transport of human skeletal parts in an artificial fluviatile environment. *American Journal of Physical Anthropology* 45:56–60.

Boaz, N. T., and R. L. Ciochon
2001   The scavenging of *Homo erectus pekinensis*. *Natural History* 110(2): 46–51.

Boesch, C.
1996   Social grouping Tai chimpanzees. In: *Great Ape Societies*, W. C. McGrew, L. Marchant, and T. Nishida (eds.), pp. 101–113. Cambridge, UK: Cambridge University Press.

Boesch, C., and H. Boesch
1989   Hunting behavior of wild chimpanzees in the Tai National Park. *American Journal of Physical Anthropology* 78:547–573.

Boesch, C., and H. Boesch-Achermann
2000   *The Chimpanzees of the Tai Forest*. New York: Oxford University Press.

Boesch, C., P. Marchesi, et al.
1994   Is nut cracking in wild chimpanzees a cultural behaviour? *Journal of Human Evolution* 26:325–338.

Bogin, B.
1999   *Patterns of Human Growth*, 2nd ed. Cambridge, UK: Cambridge University Press.

Bogin, B.
2006   Modern human life history: The evolution of human childhood and fertility. In: *The Evolution of Human Life History*, K. Hawkes and R. R. Paine (eds.). Santa Fe, NM: SAR Press.

Borries, C., K. Launhardt, C. Epplen, et al.
1999   DNA analyses support the hypothesis that infanticide is adaptive in langur monkeys. *Proceedings of the Royal Society of London Series B-Biological Sciences* 266:901–904.

Bower, B.
2003   The ultimate colonists. *Science News* 164:10–12.

Bozzola M., P. Travaglino, N. Marziliano, et al.
2009   The shortness of Pygmies is associated with severe under-expression of the growth hormone receptor. *Molecular Genetics and Metabolism* 98:310–313.

Brace, C. L., H. Nelson, and N. Korn
1979   *Atlas of Human Evolution*, 2nd ed. New York: Holt, Rinehart & Winston.

Brain, C. K.
1981   *The Hunters or the Hunted? An Introduction to African Cave Taphonomy*. Chicago: University of Chicago Press.

Brash, D. E., J. A. Rudolph, et al.
1991   A role for sunlight in skin cancer: UV-induced P53 mutations in squamous cell carcinoma. *Proceedings of the National Academy of Sciences USA* 88:10124–10128.

Breuer, T., M. Ndoundou-Hockemba, V. Fishlock, et al.
2005   First observations of tool use in wild gorillas. *PloS Biology* 3(11): e380. doi: 10.1371/journal.pbio.0030380

Briggs, A., J. M. Good, R. E. Green, et al.
2009   Targeted retrieval and analysis of five Neandertal mtDNA genomes. *Science* 325:318–320.

Bromage, T. G., and C. Dean
1985   Re-evaluation of the age at death of immature fossil hominids. *Nature* 317:525–527.

Brosch, R., S. V. Gordo, M. Marmiesse, et al.
2002   A new evolutionary scenario for the *Mycobacterium tuberculosis* complex. *Proceedings of the National Academy of Sciences* 99:3684–3689.

Brown, K. S., C. W. Marean, A. I. R. Herries, et al.
2009   Fire as an engineering tool of early modern humans. *Science* 325:859–862.

Brown, P., T. Sutikna, M. K. Morwood, et al.
2004   A new small-bodied hominin from the Late Pleistocene of Flores, Indonesia. *Nature* 431:1055–1061.

Brumm, A., G. M. Jensen, G. D. van den Bergh, et al.
2009   Hominins on Flores, Indonesia, by one million years ago. *Nature* 464:748–752.

Brunet, M., F. Guy, et al.
2002   A new hominid from the Upper Miocene of Chad, Central Africa. *Nature* 418:145–151.

Bshary, R., and R. Noe
1997   Red colobus and diana monkeys provide mutual protection against predators. *Animal Behavior* 54:1461–1474.

Buchan, J. C., S. C. Alberts, et al.
2003   True paternal care in a multi-male primate society. *Nature* 425:179–180.

Bunn, H. T.
1981   Archaeological evidence for meat-eating by Plio-Pleistocene hominids from Koobi Fora and Olduvai Gorge. *Nature* 291:574–577.

Burchard, E. G., E. Ziv, et al.
2003   The importance of race and ethnic background in biomedical research and clinical practice. *New England Journal of Medicine* 348:1170–1175.

Campbell, C. J.
2006   Lethal intragroup aggression by adult male spider monkeys (*Ateles geoffroyi*). *American Journal of Physical Anthropology* 68:1197–1201.

Campbell, M. C., and S. A. Tishkoff
2010   The evolution of human genetic and phenotypic variation in Africa. *Current Biology* 20:R166–R173.

Cantalupo, C., and W. D. Hopkins
2001   Asymmetric Broca's area in great apes: A region of the ape brain is uncannily similar to one linked with speech in humans. *Nature* 414:505–505.

Caramelli, D., C. Lalueza-Fox, C. Vernesi, et al.
2003   Evidence for genetic discontinuity between Neandertals and 24,000-year-old anatomically modern humans. *Proceedings of the National Academy of Sciences* 100:6593–6597.

Caramelli, D., C. Lalueza-Fox, S. Condemi, et al.
2006   A highly divergent mtDNA sequence in a Neandertal individual from Italy. *Current Biology* 16(16): R630–R632.

Carbonell, E., J. M. Bermuda de Castro, J. M. Pares, et al.
2008   The first hominin of Europe. *Nature* 452:465–469.

Cartmill, M.
1972   Arboreal adaptations and the origin of the order Primates. In: *The Functional and Evolutionary Biology of Primates*, R. H. Tuttle (ed.), pp. 97–122. Chicago: Aldine-Atherton.

Cartmill, M.
1990   Human uniqueness and theoretical content in paleoanthropology. *International Journal of Primatology* 11:173–192.

Cartmill, M.
1992   New views on primate origins. *Evolutionary Anthropology* 1:105–111.

Catlett, K. K., G. T. Schwartz, et al.
2010   "Life History Space": A multivariate analysis of life history variation in extant and extinct malagasy lemurs. *American Journal of Physical Anthropology* 142:391–404.

Centers for Disease Control
2009   www.cdc.gov/flu/about/disease

Chatterjee, H. J.
2006   Phylogeny and biogeography of gibbons: A dispersal-vicariance analysis. *International Journal of Primatology* 27:699–712.

Chen, F. C. and W.-H. Li
2001   Genomic divergences between humans and other hominoids and the effective population size of the common ancestor of humans and chimpanzees. *American Journal of Human Genetics* 68:444–456.

Cheney, D. L., R. M. Seyfarth, et al.
1988   Reproductive success in vervet monkeys. In: *Reproductive Success*, T. H. Clutton-Brock (ed.), pp. 384–402. Chicago: University of Chicago Press.

Cheng, Z., M. Ventura, X. She, P. Khaitovich, T. Graves, et al.
2005   A Genome-wide comparison of recent chimpanzee and human segmental duplications. *Nature* 437:88–93.

Chimpanzee Sequencing and Analysis Consortium.
2005   Initial sequence of the chimpanzee genome and comparison with the human genome. *Nature* 437:69–87.

Chin, S. Y.
2008   Personal Communication, Ascension Health.

Ciochon, R. L.
2009   The mystery ape of Pleistocene Asia. *Nature* 459:910–911.

Ciochon, R. L., and E. A. Bettis
2009   Asian *Homo erectus* converges in time. *Nature* 458:153–154.

Ciochon, R. L., and A. B. Chiarelli
1980a   *Evolutionary Biology of the New World Monkeys and Continental Drift.* New York: Plenum Press.

Ciochon, R. L., and A. B. Chiarelli
1980b   Paleobiogeographic perspectives on the origin of Platyrrhini. In: *Evolutionary Biology of the New World Monkeys and Continental Drift*, R. L. Ciochon and A. B. Chiarelli (eds.), pp 459–493. New York: Plenum Press.

Ciochon, R. L., and R. S. Corruccini (eds.)
1983   *New Interpretations of Ape and Human Ancestry.* New York: Plenum Press.

Ciochon, R. L., and G. F. Gunnell
2002   Eocene primates from Myanmar: Historical perspectives on the origin of Anthropoidea. *Evolutionary Anthropology* 11:156–168.

Ciochon, R. L., F. Huffman, et al.
2009   Rediscovery of the *Homo erectus* bed at Ngandong: Site formation of a Late Pleistocene hominin site in Asia. *American Journal of Physical Anthropology* (Supplement 48):110.

Ciochon, R. L., J. J. Olsen, and J. James
1990   *Other Origins: The Search for the Giant Ape in Human Prehistory.* New York: Bantam.

Clark, A. G., S. Glanowski, et al.
2003   Inferring nonneutral evolution from human-chimp-mouse orthologous gene trios. *Science* 302:1960–1963.

Clarke, R. J., and P. V. Tobias
1995   Sterkfontein Member 2 foot bones of the oldest South African hominid. *Science* 269:521–524.

Clemens, W. A.
2004   *Purgatorius* (Plesiadapiformes, Primates?, Mammalia), A Paleocene immigrant into Northeastern Montana: Stratigraphic occurrences and incisor proportions. *Bulletin of Carnegie Museum of Natural History* 36.

Colwell, R. R.
1996   Global climate and infectious disease: The cholera paradigm. *Science* 274:2025–2031.

Conroy, G. C.
1997   *Reconstructing Human Origins. A Modern Synthesis.* New York: W. W. Norton.

Constable, J. L., M. V. Ashley, et al.
2001   Noninvasive paternity assignment in Gombe chimpanzees. *Molecular Ecology* 10:1279–1300.

Cooper, R. S., J. S. Kaufman, et al.
2003   Race and genomics. *New England Journal of Medicine* 348:1166–1170.

Cordain, L.
1999   Cereal grains: Humanity's double-edged sword. *World Review of Nutrition and Diet* 84:19–73.

Cordain, L.
2002   *The Paleo Diet: Lose Weight and Get Healthy by Eating the Food You Were Designed to Eat.* New York: Wiley.

Crapo, L.
1985   *Hormones: The Messengers of Life.* New York: W. H. Freeman.

Crews, D. E., and G. J. Harper
1998   Ageing as part of the developmental process. In: *The Cambridge Encyclopedia of Human Growth and Development*, S. J. Ulijaszek (ed.), pp. 425–427. Cambridge, UK: Cambridge University Press.

Crook, J. H., and J. S. Gartlan
1966   Evolution of primate societies. *Nature* 210:1200–1203.

Cummings, M.
2000   *Human Heredity. Principles and Issues*, 5th ed. St. Paul, MN: Wadsworth/West.

Currat, M., G. Trabuchet, D. Rees, et al.
2002   Molecular analysis of the beta-globin gene cluster in the Niokholo Mandenka population reveals a recent origin of the beta(S) Senegal mutation. *American Journal of Human Genetics* 70:207–223.

Curtin, R., and P. Dolhinow
1978   Primate social behavior in a changing world. *American Scientist* 66:468–475.

Daeschler, E. B., N. H. Shubin, and F. A. Jenkins Jr.
2006   A Darwinian tetrapod-like fish and the evolution of the tetrapod body plan. *Nature* 440:757–763.

Dalton, R.
2007   Oldest gorilla ages our joint ancestor. *Nature News* 448:844–845.

Darwin, C.
1859   *On the Origin of Species. A Facsimile of the First Edition.* Cambridge, MA: Harvard University Press (1964).

Darwin, F.
1950   *The Life and Letters of Charles Darwin.* New York: Henry Schuman.

Dávila N., B. T. Shea, K. Omoto, et al.
2002   Growth hormone binding protein, insulin-like growth factor-I and short stature in two pygmy populations from the Philippines. *Journal of Pediatric Endocrinology and Metabolism* 15:269–276.

Day, M. H., and E. H. Wickens
1980   Laetoli Pliocene hominid footprints and bipedalism. *Nature* 286:385–387.

de Bonis, L., and G. D. Koufos
1994   Our ancestors' ancestor: *Ouranopithecus* is a Greek link in human ancestry. *Evolutionary Anthropology* 3:75–83.

de Heinzelin, J., J. D. Clark, et al.
1999   Environment and behavior of 2.5-million-year-old Bouri hominids. *Science* 284:625–629.

de Ruiter, D. J., R. Pickering, C. M. Steininger, et al.
2009   New *Australopithecus robustus* fossils and associated U-Pb dates from Cooper's Cave (Gauteng, South Africa). *Journal of Human Evolution* 56:497–513.

de Waal, F.
1982   *Chimpanzee Politics.* London: Jonathan Cape.

de Waal, F. B. M.
1987   Tension regulation and nonreproductive functions of sex in captive bonobos (*Pan paniscus*). *National Geographic Research* 3:318–335.

de Waal, F.
1989   *Peacemaking Among Primates.* Cambridge, MA: Harvard University Press.

de Waal, F.
1999   Cultural primatology comes of age. *Nature* 399:635–636.

de Waal, F. B. M.
2007   With a little help from a friend. *PLoS Biology* 5:1406–1408.

de Waal, F., and F. Lanting
1996   *Good Natured. The Origins of Right and Wrong in Humans and Other Animals.* Cambridge, MA: Harvard University Press.

de Waal, F., and F. Lanting
1997   *Bonobo: The Forgotten Ape.* Berkeley: University of California Press.

de Waal, F., and F. Lanting
2005   *Our Inner Ape.* New York: Penguin Group.

Deacon, T. W.
1992   The human brain. In: *The Cambridge Encyclopedia of Human Evolution*, S. Jones, R. Martin and D. Pilbeam (eds.), pp. 115–123. Cambridge, UK: Cambridge University Press

Dean, C., M. G. Leakey, D. Reid, et al.
2001   Growth processes in teeth distinguishing modern humans from *Homo erectus* and earlier hominins. *Nature* 414:628–631.

Dean, M., M. Carrington, C. Winkler, et al.
1996   Genetic restriction of HIV-1 infection and progression to AIDS by a deletion allele of the CKR5 structural gene. *Science* 273:1856–1862.

Dean, M. C., and B. H. Smith
2009   Growth and development of the Nariokotome youth, KNM-ER-15000. In: *The First Humans. Origin and Evolution of the Genus* Homo, F. E. Grine, J. J. Fleagle, and R. E. Leakey (eds.), pp. 101–120. New York: Springer.

Delson, E., I. Tattersall, I., J. Van Couvering, and A. Brooks (eds.)
2000   *Encyclopedia of Human Evolution and Prehistory*, 2nd ed. New York: Garland Publishing.

Demuth, J. P., T. D. Bie, J. E. Stajich, N. Christianini, and M. W. Hahn
2006   The evolution of mammalian gene families. *PLoS ONE* 1(1): e85. doi: 10.1371/journal.pone.0000085

Deragon, J. M., and P. Capy
2000   Impact of transposable elements on the human genome. *Annals of Medicine* 32:264–273.

Desmond, A., and J. Moore
1991   *Darwin.* New York: Warner Books.

DeVore, I., and S. L. Washburn
1963   Baboon ecology and human evolution. In: *African Ecology and Human Evolution*, F. C. Howell and F. Bourlière (eds.), pp. 335–367. New York: Viking Fund Publication.

Dirks, P. H. G. M., J. M. Kibii, B. F. Kuhn, et al.
2010   Geological setting and age of *Australopithecus sediba* from southern Africa. *Science* 328:205–208.

Dobzhansky, T.
1973   Nothing in biology makes sense except in the light of evolution. *American Biology Teacher* 35:125–129.

Dominy, N. J., and P. W. Lucas
2001   Ecological importance of trichromatic vision to primates. *Nature* 410:363–366.

Doran, G. H., D. N. Dickel, W. E. Ballinger, Jr., et al.
1986   Anatomical, cellular, and molecular analysis of 8,000-yr-old human brain tissue from the Windover archaeological site. *Nature* 323:803–806.

Doran, D. M., and A. McNeilage
1998 Gorilla ecology and behavior. *Evolutionary Anthropology* 6:120–131.

Duarte, C., J. Mauricio, P. B. Pettitt, et al.
1999 The early Upper Paleolithic human skeleton from the Abrigo do Lagar Velho (Portugal) and modern human emergence in Iberia. *Proceedings of the National Academy of Sciences USA* 96:7604–7609.

Dunbar, R.
2001 Brains on two legs: Group size and the evolution of intelligence. In: *Tree of Origin: What Primate Behavior Can Tell Us about Human Social Evolution*, pp. 173–191. Cambridge, MA: Harvard University Press.

Dunbar, R. I. M.
1998 The social brain hypothesis. *Evolutionary Anthropology* 6:178–190.

Durbin, R. M.
2010 A map of human genome variation from population scale sequencing. *Nature* 467:1061–1073.

Eaton, S. B., S. B. Eaton III, and M. J. Konner
1999 Paleolithic nutrition revisited. In: *Evolutionary Medicine*, W. Trevathan, J. J. McKenna and E. O. Smith (eds.), pp. 313–332. New York: Oxford University Press.

Eaton, S. B., M. C. Pike, R. V. Short, et al.
1994 Women's reproductive cancers in evolutionary context. *Quarterly Review of Biology* 69:353–367.

Eaton, S. B., M. Shostak, and M. Konner
1988 *The Paleolithic Prescription*. New York: Harper and Row.

Eberhart, G. M.
2002 *Mysterious Creatures: A Guide to Cryptozoology*. Santa Barbara, CA.: ABC-CLIO.

Ehret, G.
1987 Left-hemisphere advantage in the mouse-brain for recognizing ultrasonic communication calls. *Nature* 325:249–251.

Ehrlich, P. R., and A. H. Ehrlich
1990 *The Population Explosion*. New York: Simon & Schuster.

Ellison, P. T.
2001 *On Fertile Ground: A Natural History of Human Reproduction*. Cambridge, MA: Harvard University Press.

Enard, W., M. Przeworski, S. E. Fisher, et al.
2002 Molecular evolution of FOXP2, a gene involved in speech and language. *Nature* 418:869–872.

Ewald, P. W.
1999 Evolutionary control of HIV and other sexually transmitted viruses. In: *Evolutionary Medicine*, W. R. Trevathan, E. O. Smith, and J. J. McKenna (eds.). New York: Oxford University Press.

Falguères, C., J. J. Bahain, Y. Yokoyama, et al.
1999 Earliest humans in Europe: The age of TD6 Gran Dolina, Atapuerca, Spain. *Journal of Human Evolution* 37:343–352.

Falk, D.
1990 Brain evolution in *Homo*: The 'Radiator' Theory. *Behavioral and Brain Sciences* 13:333–344.

Falk, D., C. Hildebolt, K. Smith, et al.
2005 The brain of LB1, *Homo floresiensis*. *Science* 308:242–245.

Falk, D., C. Hildebolt, K. Smith, et al.
2008 LB1 did not have Laron Syndrome. *American Journal of Physical Anthropology, Supplement* 43:95 (abstract).

Falk, D., C. Hildebolt, K. Smith, et al.
2009 LM1's virtual endocast, microcephaly, and hominin brain evolution. *Journal of Human Evolution* 57:597–607.

Feathers, J. K. and E. Migliorini
2001 Luminescence dating at Katanda: A reassessment. *Quaternary Science Reviews* 20:961–966.

Fedigan, L. M.
1983 Dominance and reproductive success in primates. *Yearbook of Physical Anthropology* 26:91–129.

Finch, C. E.
2007 *The Biology of Human Longevity Inflammation, Nutrition, and Aging in the Evolution of Life Spans*. London: Academic Press.

Finch, C. E., and R. M. Sapolsky
1999 The evolution of Alzheimer disease, the reproductive schedule, and apoE isoforms. *Neurobiology of Aging* 20:407–428.

Fisher, S. E., and C. Scharff
2009 FOXP2 as a molecular window into speech and language. *Trends in Genetics* 25:166–177.

Fleagle, J.
1999 *Primate Adaptation and Evolution*, 2nd ed. New York: Academic Press.

Flinn, M.
2008 Why words can hurt us: social relationships, stress and health. In: *Evolutionary Medicine and Health*, W. R. Trevathan, E. O. Smith, and J. J. McKenna (eds.), pp. 242–258. New York: Oxford University Press.

Flinn, M. V.
1999 Family environment, stress, and health during childhood. In: *Hormones, Health, and Behavior*, C. Panter-Brick and C. M. Worthman (eds.), pp. 105–138. Cambridge, UK: Cambridge University Press.

Flinn, M. V., and B. G. England
2003 Childhood stress: Endocrine and immune responses to psychosocial events. In: *Social and Cultural Lives of Immune Systems*, James MacLynn Wilce (ed.), pp. 107–147. London: Routledge Press.

Foley, R. A.
1991 How many hominid species should there be? *Journal of Human Evolution* 20:413–427.

Foley, R. A.
2002 Adaptive radiations and dispersals in hominin evolutionary ecology. *Evolutionary Anthropology* 11(Supplement 1): 32–37.

Fondon, J. W., and H. R. Garner
2004 Molecular origins of rapid and continuous morphological evolution. *Proceedings of the National Academy of Sciences* 101:18058–18063

Formicola, V., and A. P. Buzhilova
2004   Double child burial from Sunghir (Russia): Pathology and inferences for Upper Paleolithic funerary practices. *American Journal of Physical Anthropology* 124:189–198.

Foster, J. B.
1964   Evolution of mammals on islands. *Nature* 202: 234–235.

Fouts, R. S., D. H. Fouts, and T. T. van Cantfort
1989   The infant Loulis learns signs from cross-fostered chimpanzees. In: *Teaching Sign Language to Chimpanzees*, R. A. Gardner (ed.) pp. 280–292. Albany: State University of New York Press.

Fraga, M. F., E. Ballestar, M. F. Paz, et al.
2005   Epigenetic differences arise during the lifetime of monozygotic twins. *Proceedings of the National Academy of Sciences* 102:10604–10609.

Fragaszy, D., P. Izar, et al.
2004   Wild capuchin monkeys (*Cebus libidinosus*) use anvils and stone pounding tools. *American Journal of Primatology* 64:359–366.

Franzen, J. L., P. D. Gingerich, et al.
2009   Complete primate skeleton from the Early Eocene of Messel in Germany: Morphology and paleobiology. *PLoS ONE* 4:e5723.

Freundlich, J. C., H. Schwabedissen, and E. Wendt
1980   Köln radiocarbon measurements II. *Radiocarbon* 22:68–81.

Frisancho, A. R.
1993   *Human Adaptation and Accommodation*. Ann Arbor: University of Michigan Press.

Frisch, R. E.
1988   Fatness and fertility. *Scientific American* 258:88–95.

Galik, K., B. Senut, M. Pickford, et al.
2004   External and internal morphology of the bar, 1002'00 *Orrorin tugenensis* femur. *Science* 305:1450–1453.

Gao, F., E. Bailes, D. L. Robertson, et al.
1999   Origin of HIV-1 in the chimpanzee *Pan troglodytes troglodytes*. *Nature* 397:436–441.

Garcia, T., G. Féraud, C. Falguères, et al.
2010   Earliest human remains in Eurasia: New ^{40}Ar/^{39}Ar dating of the Dmanisi hominid-bearing levels, Georgia. *Quaternary Geochronology* 5:443–451.

Gardner, R. A., B. T. Gardner, and T. T. van Cantfort (eds.)
1989   *Teaching Sign Language to Chimpanzees*. Albany: State University of New York Press.

Garner, K. J., and O. A. Ryder
1996   Mitochondrial DNA diversity in gorillas. *Molecular Phylogenetics and Evolution* 6(1): 39–48.

Gebo, D. L., L. MacLatchy, et al.
1997   A hominoid genus from the early Miocene of Uganda. *Science* 276:401–404.

George, I., H. Cousillas, H. Richard, et al.
2002   Song perception in the European starling: Hemispheric specialization and individual variations. *C.R. Biol.* 325:197–204.

Ghiglieri, M. P.
1984   *The Chimpanzees of Kibale Forest*. New York: Columbia University Press.

Gibbons, A.
2010   Tracing evolution's recent fingerprints. News Focus, *Science* 329:740–742.

Gibson, D., J. Glass, C. Lartique, et al.
2010   Creation of a bacterial cell controlled by a chemically synthesized genome. Science Express: www.sciencemag.org/cgi/content/abstract/science.1190719

Gilbert, W. H., and B. Asfaw (eds.)
2008   Homo erectus: *Pleistocene Evidence from the Middle Awash, Ethiopia*. Berkeley: University of California Press.

Giles, J., and J. Knight
2003   Dolly's death leaves researchers woolly on clone ageing issue. *Nature* 421:776.

Gillespie, B., and R. G. Roberts
2000   On the reliability of age estimate for human remains at Lake Mungo. *Journal of Human Evolution* 38:727–732.

Gingerich, P. D., K. D. Rose, et al.
2008   Oldest North American primate. *Proceedings of the National Academy of Sciences USA* 105(23): E30–E31.

Gluckman, P., A. Beedle, and M. Hanson
2009   *Principles of Evolutionary Medicine*. Oxford, UK: Oxford University Press.

Gluckman, P. D., and M. Hanson
2005   *The Fetal Matrix: Evolution, Development, and Disease*. New York: Cambridge University Press.

Godfrey, L. R., W. L. Jungers, et al.
2006   Ecology and extinction of Madagascar's subfossil lemurs. In: *Lemurs Ecology and Adaptation*, L. Gould and M. L. Sauther (eds.), pp. 41–64. New York: Springer.

Godfrey, L. R., M. R. Sutherland, et al.
1990   Size, space, and adaptation in some subfossil lemurs from Madagascar. *American Journal of Physical Anthropology* 81:45–66.

Goodall, J.
1986   *The Chimpanzees of Gombe*. Cambridge, MA: Harvard University Press.

Goodman, S., and H. Schütz
2000   The lemurs of the northeastern slopes of the Réserve Spéciale de Manongarivo. *Lemur News* 5:30–33.

Goodman, S. M.
2008   Conservation priorities on Madagascar: Synergy between surveys and geological history in understanding patterns. *South African Journal of Botany* 74:358.

Goodman, S. M., J. P. Benstead, H. Schutz (eds.)
2003   *The Natural History of Madagascar*. Chicago: University of Chicago Press.

Gossett, T. F.
1963   *Race, the History of an Idea in America*. Dallas: Southern Methodist University Press.

Gould, S. J.
1981   *The Mismeasure of Man*. New York: W.W. Norton.

Gould, S. J.
1985   Darwin at sea—and the virtues of port. In: *The Flamingo's Smile. Reflections in Natural History*, S. J. Gould (ed.), pp. 347–359. New York: W.W. Norton.

Gould, S. J.
1987   *Time's Arrow, Time's Cycle*. Cambridge, MA: Harvard University Press.

Gould, S. J.
1994   *Hen's Teeth and Horse's Toes*. New York: W.W. Norton.

Gould, S. J., and N. Eldredge
1977   Punctuated equilibria: The tempo and mode of evolution reconsidered. *Paleobiology* 3:115–151.

Grant, P. R.
1982   Variation in the size and shape of Darwin's finch eggs. *Auk* 99:5–23.

Graves, R. R., R. C. McCarthy, A. C. Lupo, et al.
2010   New estimates of stature and body mass for KNM-WT 15000. *American Journal of Physical Anthropology, Supplement* 50:115 (abstract).

Gravina, S., and J. Vijg
2010   Epigenetic factors in aging and longevity. *European Journal of Physiology* 459:247–258.

Gravlee, C. C.
2009   How race becomes biology: Embodiment of social inequality. *American Journal of Physical Anthropology* 139:47–57.

Green, R. E., J. Krause, et al.
2006   Analysis of one million base pairs of Neanderthal DNA. *Nature* 444:330–336.

Green, R. E., J. Krause, A. W. Briggs, et al.
2010   A draft sequence of the Neandertal genome. *Science* 328:710–722.

Greene, J. C.
1981   *Science, Ideology, and World View*. Berkeley: University of California Press.

Greenwood, B., and T. Mutabingwa
2002   Malaria in 2000. *Nature* 415:670–672.

Gregory, J. M., P. Huybrecths, et al.
2004   Threatened loss of the Greenland Ice-sheet. *Nature* 428:616.

Gros-Louis, J., H. Perry, et al.
2003   Violent coalitionary attacks and intraspecific killing in wild White-faced Capuchin Monkeys (*Cebus capucinus*). *Primates* 44:341–346.

Gross, L.
2006   Scientific illiteracy and the partisan takeover of biology. *PLoS Biology* 4(5): 206.

Groves, C. P.
2001   Why taxonomic stability is a bad idea, or why are there so few species of primates (or are there?). *Evolutionary Anthropology* 10:191–197.

Grün, R., and C. B. Stringer
1991   ESR dating and the evolution of modern humans. *Archaeometry* 33:153–199.

Grün, R., C. B. Stringer, F. McDermott, et al.
2005   U-series and ESR analysis of bones and teeth relating to the human burials from Skhūl. *Journal of Human Evolution* 49:316–334.

Haile-Selassie, Y., G. Suwa, and T. D. White
2004   Late Miocene teeth from Middle Awash, Ethiopia, and early hominid dental evolution. *Science* 303:1503–1505.

Hales, C. N., and D. J. P. Barker
2001   The thrifty phenotype hypothesis. *British Medical Bulletin* 60:5–20.

Hare, B., and S. Kwetuenda
2010   Bonobos voluntarily share their own food with others. *Current Biology* 20(5):R230–R231

Harlow, H. F.
1959   Love in infant monkeys. *Scientific American* 200:68–74.

Harlow, H. F., and M. K. Harlow
1961   A study of animal affection. *Natural History* 70:48–55.

Harrison, T.
2002   Late Oligocene to middle Miocene catarrhines from Afro-Arabia.In: *Primate Fossil Record*. W. Hartwig (ed.), pp. 311–338. Cambridge, UK: Cambridge University Press.

Harrison, T.
2010   Apes among the tangled branches of human origins. *Science* 327:532–534.

Harrison, T., X. Ji, et al.
2008   Renewed investigations at the late Miocene hominoid locality of Leilao, Yunnan, China. *American Journal of Physical Anthropology* 135(S46): 113.

Harrison, T., X. Ji, and D. Su
2002   On the systematic status of the late Neogene hominoids from Yunnan Province, China. *Journal of Human Evolution* 43:207–227.

Hawkes, K., J. F. O'Connell, and N. G. Blurton Jones
1997   Hadza women's time allocation, offspring provisioning, and the evolution of long postmenopausal life spans. *Current Anthropology* 38:551–577.

Hawkes, K., and R. R. Paine
2006   *The Evolution of Human Life History*. Santa Fe, NM: SAR Press.

Heaney, L. R.
1978   Island area and body size of insular mammals: Evidence from the tri-colored squirrel (*Callosciurus prevosti*) of Southeast Asia. *Evolution* 32:29–44.

Heizmann, E., and D. R. Begun
2001   The oldest European hominoid. *Journal of Human Evolution* 41:465–481.

Henshilwood, C. S., F. d'Errico, M. Vanhaeren, et al.
2004   Middle stone age shell beads from South Africa. *Science* 304:404.

Henzi, P., and L. Barrett
2003   Evolutionary ecology, sexual conflict, and behavioral differentiation among baboon populations. *Evolutionary Anthropology* 12:217–230.

Hernandez-Aguilar, R. A., J. Moore, et al.
2007   Savanna chimpanzees use tools to harvest the underground storage organs of plants. *Proceedings of the National Academy of Sciences* 104:19210–19213.

Heron, M.
2010   Deaths: Leading causes for 2006. *National Vital Statistics Reports* 58(14):1–100.

Hershkovitz, P.
1977   *Living New World Monkeys (Platyrrhini): With an Introduction to Primates*. Chicago and London: University of Chicago Press.

Higham, T., C. B. Ramsey, I. Karavanic, et al.
2006   Revised direct radiocarbon dating of the Vindija G$_1$ Upper Paleolithic Neandertals. *Proceedings of the National Academy of Sciences* 103:553–557.

Hill, A.
2007   Introduction. In: *Hominin Environments in the East African Pliocene: An Assessment of the Faunal Evidence*, R. Bobe, Z. Alemseged, and A. K. Behrensmeyer (eds.), pp. xvii–xx. Dordrecht, The Netherlands: Springer.

Hodgson, J. A., K. N. Sterner, et al.
2009a   Successive radiations, not stasis, in the South American primate fauna. *Proceedings of the National Academy of Sciences USA* 106:5534–5539.

Hodgson, J. A., L. Pozzi, et al.
2009b   Molecular divergence dates suggest an origin of crown primates near the K/T boundary. *American Journal of Physical Anthropology* 138(S48): 227

Hodgson, J. A., K. N. Sterner, et al.
2008   Phylogenetic relationship of the Platyrrhini inferred from complete mitochondrial genome sequences. *American Journal of Physical Anthropology* S46:118–119.

Hoffstetter, R.
1972   Relationships, origins, and history of the ceboid monkeys and the caviomorph rodents: A modern reinterpretation. In: *Evolutionary Biology*, T. Dobzhansky, T. M. K. Hecht, and W. C. Steere (eds.), pp. 323–347. New York: Appleton-Century-Crofts.

Holloway, R. L.
1983   Cerebral brain endocast pattern of *Australopithecus afarensis* hominid. *Nature* 303:420–422.

Holloway, R. L.
1985   The poor brain of *Homo sapiens neanderthalensis*. In: *Ancestors, The Hard Evidence*, E. Delson (ed.), pp. 319–324. New York: Alan R. Liss.

Hornsby, P. J.
2010   Senescence and life span. *European Journal of Physiology* 459:291–299.

Horvath, J. E., D. W. Weisrock, et al.
2008   Development and application of a phylogenetic toolkit: Resolving the evolutionary history of Madagascar's lemurs. *Genome Research* 18:489–499.

Horvath, J. E., and H. F. Willard
2007   Primate comparative genomics: Lemur biology and evolution. *Trends in Genetics* 23:173–182.

Hou, Y., R. Potts, Y. Baoyin, et al.
2000   Mid-Pleistocene Acheulean-like stone technology of the Bose Basin, South China. *Science* 287:1622–1626.

Houle, A.
1998   Floating islands: A mode of long-distance dispersal for small and medium-sized terrestrial vertebrates. *Diversity and Distribution* 4:201–219.

Houle, A.
1999   The origin of platyrrhines: An evaluation of the Antarctic scenario and the floating island model. *American Journal of Physical Anthropology* 109:541–559.

Howell, F. C.
1999   Paleo-demes, species clades, and extinctions in the Pleistocene hominin record. *Journal of Anthropological Research* 55:191–243.

Hrdy, S. B.
1977   *The Langurs of Abu*. Cambridge, MA: Harvard University Press.

Hrdy, S. B., C. Janson, and C. van Schaik
1995   Infanticide: Let's not throw out the baby with the bath water. *Evolutionary Anthropology* 3:151–154.

Hudjashou Georgi, T. K., Peter A. Underhill, et al.
2007   Revealing the prehistoric settlement of Australia by Y Chromosome and mtDNA Analysis. *Proceedings of the National Academy of Sciences USA* 104:8726–8730.

Hunt, G. R.
1996   Manufacture and use of hook-tools by New Caledonian crows. *Nature* 379:249–251.

International Human Genome Sequencing Consortium
2001   Initial sequencing and analysis of the human genome. *Nature* 409:860-921.

International SNP Map Working Group
2001   A map of human genome sequence variation containing 1.42 million single nucleotide polymorphisms. *Nature* 409:928–933.

IUCN
2008   http://www.iucnredlist.org/apps/redlist/details/15932/0

Izawa, K., and A. Mizuno
1977   Palm-fruit cracking behaviour of wild black-capped capuchin (*Cebus apella*). *Primates* 18:773–793.

Jablonski, N. G.
1992   Sun, skin colour, and spina bifida: An exploration of the relationship between ultraviolet light and neural tube defects. *Proceedings of the Australian Society of Human Biology* 5:455–462.

Jablonski, N. G., and G. Chaplin
2000   The evolution of human skin coloration. *Journal of Human Evolution* 39:57–106.

Jablonski, N. G., and G. Chaplin
2002   Skin deep. *Scientific American* 287:74–81.

Jablonski, N. G., and G. Chaplin
2010   Human skin pigmentation as an adaptation to UV radiation. *Proceedings of the National Academy of Sciences* 107:8962–8968.

Jacob, T., E. Indriati, et al.
2006   Pygmoid Australomelonesian *Homo sapiens* skeletal remains from Liang Bua, Flores: Population affinities and pathological anomalies. *Proceedings of the National Academy of Sciences USA* 103:13421–13426.

Jacobs, Z., G.A.T. Duller, A.G. Wintle, and C.S. Henshilwood
2006   Extending the chronology of deposits at Blombos Cave, South Africa, back to 140 ka using optical dating of single and multiple grains of quartz. *Journal of Human Evolution* 51:255–273.

Jakobsson, M., S. W. Scholz, P. Scheet, et al.
2008   Genotype, haplotype and copy-number variation in worldwide human populations. *Nature* 451:998–1003.

Janečka, J. E., W. Miller, et al.
2007   Molecular and genomic data identify the closest living relative of primates. *Science* 318:792–794.

Janson, C. H.
1990   Ecological consequences of individual spatial choice in foraging groups of brown capuchin monkeys, *Cebus apella*. *Animal Behaviour* 40:922–934.

Janson, C. H.
2000   Primate socio-ecology: The end of a golden age. *Evolutionary Anthropology* 9:73–86.

Jerison, H. J.
1973   *Evolution of the Brain and Behavior*. New York: Academic Press.

Jia, L., and W. Huang
1990   *The Story of Peking Man*. New York: Oxford University Press.

Jolly, A.
1985   *The Evolution of Primate Behavior*, 2nd ed. New York: Macmillan.

Jolly, C. J.
1970   The seed-eaters: A new model of hominid differentiation based on a baboon analogy. *Man, New Series* 5:5–26.

Jolly, C. J.
1993   Species, subspecies, and baboon systematics. In: *Species, Species Concepts, and Primate Evolution*, W. H. Kimbel and L. B. Martin (eds.), pp. 67–107. New York: Plenum Press.

Jungers, W. L., L. R. Godfrey, E. L. Simons, and P. S. Chatrath
1997   Phalangeal curvature and positional behavior in extinct sloth lemurs (Primates, Palaeopropithecidae). *Proceedings of the National Academy of Sciences USA* 94:11998–12001.

Jungers, W. L., W. E. H. Harcourt-Smith, R. E. Wunderlich, et al.
2009   The Foot of *Homo floresiensis*. *Nature* 459:81–84.

Kano, T.
1992   *The Last Ape. Pygmy Chimpanzee Behavior and Ecology*. Stanford, CA: Stanford University Press.

Kappeler, P. M.
2000   Lemur origins: Rafting by groups of hibernators? *Folia Primatologica* 71:422–425.

Kappelman, J., M. Alcicek, N. Kazanci et al.
2008   First *Homo erectus* from Turkey and implications for migration into temperate Eurasia.

Kay, R. F., C. Schmitt, et al.
2004   The paleobiology of Amphipithecidae, South Asian late Eocene primates. *Journal of Human Evolution* 46:3–25.

Kayser, M.
2010   The human genetic history of Oceania: Near and remote views of dispersal. *Current Biology* 20:R194–R201.

Keeley, L. H., and N. Toth
1981   Microwear polishes on early stone tools from Koobi-Fora, Kenya. *Nature* 293:464–465.

Kelley, R. I., D. Robinson, et al.
2002   Amish lethal microcephaly: A new metabolic disorder with severe congenital microcephaly and 2-ketoglutaric aciduria. *American Journal of Medical Genetics* 112:318–326.

Keynes, R.
2002   *Darwin, His Daughter and Human Evolution*. New York: Riverhead Books.

Kimbel, W. H., T. D. White, and D. C. Johanson
1988   Implications of KNM-WT-17000 for the evolution of 'robust' *Australopithecus*. In: *Evolutionary History of the Robust Australopithecines* (Foundations of Human Behavior), F. E. Grine (ed.), pp. 259–268. Somerset, NJ: Aldine Transaction.

King, B. J.
1994   *The Information Continuum*. Santa Fe, NM: School of American Research.

King, B. J.
2004   *Dynamic Dance: Nonvocal Communication in the African Great Apes*. Cambridge, MA: Harvard University Press.

King, M. C., and A. G. Motulsky
2002   Mapping human history. *Science* 298: 2342–2343.

Kirk, E. C., and E. L. Simons
2001   Diets of fossil primates from the Fayum Depression of Egypt: A quantitative analysis of molar shearing. *Journal of Human Evolution* 40:203–229.

Kirkwood, T. B. L.
1997   The origins of human ageing. *Philosophical Transactions of the Royal Society of London B* 352:1765–1772.

Klein, R. G.
1999   *The Human Career. Human Biological and Cultural Origins*, 2nd ed. Chicago: University of Chicago Press.

Klein, R. G. and B. Edgar
2002   *The Dawn of Human Culture*. New York: Wiley.

Konner, M. J., and C. M. Worthman
1980   Nursing frequency, gonadal functioning, and birth spacing among !Kung hunter-gartherers. *Science* 207:788–791.

Koopman, R. J., A. G. Mainous, V. A. Diaz, et al.
2005   Changes in age at diagnosis of type 2 diabetes mellitus in the United States, 1988 to 2000. *Annals of Family Medicine* 3(1): 60–69.

Kramer, A.
1993   Human taxonomic diversity in the Pleistocene: Does *Homo erectus* represent multiple hominid species? *American Journal of Physical Anthropology* 91:161–171.

Krane, S., Y. Itagaki, et al.
2003   "Venom" of the slow loris: Sequence similarity of prosimian skin gland protein and Fel d 1 cat allergen. *Naturwissenschaften* 90(2):60–62.

Krause, J., C. Lalueza-Fox, et al.
2007b   The derived FOXP2 variant of modern humans was shared with Neandertals. *Current Biology* 17:1908–1912.

Krause, J., L. Orlando, D. Serre, et al.
2007a   Neanderthals in central Asia and Siberia. *Nature* 449:902–904.

Krause, J., Q. Fu, J. M. Good, et al.
2010   The complete mitochondrial DNA genome of an unknown hominin from southern Siberia. *Nature* 464:894–896.

Krings, M., C. Capelli, et al.
2000   A view of Neandertal genetic diversity. *Nature Genetics* 26:144–146.

Krings, M., A. Stone, R. W. Schmitz, et al.
1997   Neandertal DNA sequences and the origin of modern humans. *Cell* 90(1): 19–30.

Kroeber, A. L.
1928   Sub-human cultural beginning. *Quarterly Review of Biology* 3:325–342.

Krützen, M., J. Mann, M. R. Heithaus, et al.
2005   Cultural transmission of tool use in bottlenose dolphins. *Proceedings of the National Academy of Sciences, USA* 102(25): 8939–8943.

Kujoth, G. C., P. C. Bradshaw, S. Haroon, and T. A. Prolla.
2007   The role of mitochondrial DNA mutations in mammalian aging. *PLoS Genetics* 3:e24.

Kulikov, E. E., Audrey B. Poltaraus, and Irina A. Lebedeva
2004   DNA analysis of Sunghir remains: Problems and perspectives. Poster presentation. European Paleopathology Association Meetings, Durham, UK, August 2004.

Kummer, H.
1968   *Social Organization of Hamadryas Baboons*. Chicago: University of Chicago Press.

Kunimatsu, Y., M. Nakatsukasa, et al.
2007   A new Late Miocene great ape from Kenya and its implications for the origins of African great apes and humans. *Proceedings of the National Academy of Sciences* 104:19220–19225.

Kuzawa, C. W.
2005   The fetal origins of developmental plasticity: Are fetal cues reliable predictors of future nutritional environments? *American Journal of Human Biology* 17:5–21.

Kuzawa, C. W.
2008   The developmental origins of adult health: Intergenerational inertia in adaptation and disease. *Evolutionary Medicine and Health: New Perspectives*, W. R. Trevathan, E. O. Smith, and J. J. McKenna (eds.), pp. 325–349. New York: Oxford University Press.

Lack, D.
1966   *Population Studies of Birds*. Oxford, UK: Clarendon.

Lahr, M. M., and R. A. Foley
1998   Towards a theory of modern human origins: Geography, demography, and diversity in recent human evolution. *Yearbook of Physical Anthropology*. 41:137–176.

Lai, C. S. L., S. E. Fisher, et al.
2001   A forkhead-domain gene is mutated in a severe speech and language disorder. *Nature* 413:519–523.

Lakshminarayan, V. R., and L. R. Santos
2008   Capuchin monkeys are sensitive to others' welfare. *Current Biology* 20(5):R230–231.

Lalani, A. S., J. Masters, et al.
1999   Use of chemokine receptors by poxviruses. *Science* 286:1968–1971.

Lalueza-Fox, C., H. Römpler, D. Caramelli, et al.
2007   A melanocortin receptor allele suggests varying pigmentation among Neanderthals. *Science Express* Oct. 25, 2007.

Lalueza-Foxa, C., A. Rosas, A. Estalrrich, et al.
2011   Genetic evidence for patrilocal mating behavior among Neandertal groups. *Proceedings of the National Academy of Sciences*, 108:250–253.

Lamason, R. L., M-A. P. K. Mohideen, J. R. Mest, et al.
2005   SLC24A5, a putative cation exchanger, affects pigmentation in zebrafish and humans. *Science* 310:1782–1786.

Lamberts, S. W. J., A. W. van den Beld, and A. J. van der Lely
1997   The endocrinology of aging. *Science* 278:419–424.

Lancaster, J. B., and C. S. Lancaster
1983   Parental investment: The hominid adaptation. In: *How Humans Adapt: A Biocultural Odyssey*, D. J. Ortner (ed.), pp. 33–66. Washington, DC: Smithsonian Institution Press.

Lanza, I. R., and K. S. Nair
2010   Mitochondrial function as a determinant of life span. *European Journal of Physiology* 459:277–289.

Leakey, M. D.
1971   Remains of *Homo erectus* and associated artifacts in Bed IV at Olduvai Gorge, Tanzania. *Nature* 232:380–383.

Leakey, M. D., and R. L. Hay
1979   Pliocene footprints in Laetolil beds at Laetoli, Northern Tanzania. *Nature* 278:317–323.

Lepre, C. J., and D. V. Kent
2010   New magnetostratigraphy for the Olduvai Subchron in the Koobi Fora Formation, northwest Kenya, with implications for early *Homo*. *Earth and Planetary Science Letters* 290:362–374.

Lerner, I. M., and W. J. Libby
1976   *Heredity, Evolution, and Society*. San Francisco: W. H. Freeman.

Leroy, E. M., B. Kumulungui, et al.
2005   Fruit bats as reservoirs of Ebola virus. *Nature* 438:575–576.

Leroy, E. M., P. Rouquet, et al.
2004   Multiple Ebola virus transmission events and rapid decline of central African wildlife. *Science* 303:387–390.

Lewontin, R. C.
1972   The apportionment of human diversity. In: *Evolutionary Biology*, T. Dobzhansky (ed.), pp. 381–398. New York: Plenum.

Li, J. Z., Devin M. Absher, H. Tang, et al.
2008   Worldwide human relationships inferred from genome-wide patterns of variation. *Science* 319:1100–1104.

Li, T. Y., and D. A. Etler
1992   New middle Pleistocene hominid crania from Yunxian in China. *Nature* 357:404–407.

Lieberman, L. S.
2003　Dietary, evolutionary, and modernizing influences on the prevalence of type 2 diabetes. *Annual Review of Nutrition* 23:345–377.

Lin, D. R., and J. H. White
2004　Pleiotropic actions of vitamin D. *BioEssays* 26(1): 21–28.

Lin, J. Y., and D. E. Fisher
2007　Melanocyte biology and skin pigmentation. *Nature* 445:843–850.

Linnaeus, C.
1758　*Systema Naturae*. Holmiae: Laurentii Salvii.

Linnen, C. R., E. P. Kingsley, J. D. Jensen, and H. E. Hoekstra
2009　On the origin and spread of an adaptive allele in deer mice. *Science* 325:1095–1098.

Liu, P.T., S. Stenger, H. Li, et al.
2006　Toll-like receptor triggering of a vitamin D-mediated human antimicrobial response. *Science* 311:1770–1773.

Lofgren, D. L.
1995　The bug creek problem and the Cretaceous-Tertiary transition at McGuire Creek, Montana. *University of California Publications in Geological Sciences* 140:1–185.

Lohmueller, K. E., Amit R. Indap, S. Schmidt, et al.
2008　Proportionally more deleterious genetic variation in European than in African populations. *Nature* 451:994–997.

Lomolino, M. V.
2005　Body size evolution in insular vertebrates: Generality of the island rule. *Journal of Biogeography* 32:1683–1699.

Lordkipandize, D., Tea Jashashuil, A. Vekua, et al.
2007　Postcranial evidence from early *Homo* from Dmanisi, Georgia. *Nature* 449:305–310.

Lordkipandize, D., A. Vekua, R. Ferring, and P. Rightmire
2006　A fourth hominid skull from Dmanisi, Georgia. *The Anatomical Record: Part A* 288:1146–1157.

Lovejoy, C. O.
1981　The origin of man. *Science* 211:341–350.

Lovejoy, C. O.
2009　Reexamining human origins in light of *Ardipithecus ramidus. Science* 326:74e1–74e8.

Lovejoy, C. O., B. Latimer, G. Suwa, et al.
2009a　Combining prehension and propulsion: The foot of *Ardipithecus ramidus. Science* 72e1–72e8.

Lovejoy, C. O., G. Suwa, S. W. Simpson, et al.
2009b　The great divides: *Ardipithecus ramidus* reveals the postcrania of our last common ancestors with African great apes. *Science* 326:100–106.

Lycett, S. J., M. Collard, and H. E. Hoekstra
2009　On the origin and spread of an adaptive allele in deer mice. *Science* 425:1095–1098.

Lycett, S., M. Collard, and W. McGrew
2010　Are behavioral differences among wild chimpanzee communities genetic or cultural? An assessment using tool-use data and phylogenetic methods. *American Journal of Physical Anthropology* 142:461–467.

Mace, R.
2000　Evolutionary ecology of human life history. *Animal Behaviour* 59:1–10.

MacKinnon, J., and K. MacKinnon
1980　The behavior of wild spectral tarsiers. *International Journal of Primatology* 1:361–379.

Majumder, P. P.
2010　The human genetic history of South Asia. *Current Biology* 20:R184–R187.

Manson, J. H., and R. W. Wrangham
1991　Intergroup aggression in chimpanzees and humans. *Current Anthropology* 32:369–390.

Marean, C. M.
2010　When the sea saved humanity. *Scientific American* 303 (August):54–61.

Marean, C. W., Miryam Bar-Matthews, J. Bernatchez, et al.
2007　Early human use of marine resources and pigment in South Africa during the Middle Pleistocene. *Nature* 449:905–908.

Marivaux, L., P.-O. Antoine, et al.
2005　Anthropoid primates from the Oligocene of Pakistan (Bugti Hills): Data on early anthropoid evolution and biogeography. *Proceedings of the National Academy of Sciences USA* 102:8436–8441.

Marris, E.
2006　Bushmeat surveyed in Western cities. Illegally hunted animals turn up in markets from New York to London. *News@Nature.com*. doi: 10.1038/news060626-10

Martin, R. D.
1990　*Primate Origins and Evolution: A Phylogenetic Reconstruction*. Princeton, NJ: Princeton University Press.

Martin, R. D., A. M. MacLarnon, J. C. Phillips, and W. B. Dobyns
2006　Flores hominid: New species or microcephalic dwarf? *The Anatomical Record: Part A* 288A:1123–1145.

Martin, R. D., C. Soligo, et al.
2007　Primate origins: Implications of a Cretaceous ancestry. *Folia Primatologica* 78:277–296.

Mayer, P.
1982　Evolutionary advantages of menopause. *Human Ecology* 10:477–494.

Mayr, E.
1970　*Population, Species, and Evolution*. Cambridge, MA: Harvard University Press.

Mayr, E.
1981　*The Growth of Biological Thought*. Cambridge, MA: Harvard University Press.

McBrearty, S., and N. G. Jablonski
2005　First fossil chimpanzee. *Nature* 437:105–108.

McCall, R. A.
1997　Implications of recent geological investigations of the Mozambique channel for the mammalian colonization of Madagascar. *Proceedings of the Royal Society of London Series B-Biological Sciences* 264:663–665.

McCollum, M. A., B. A. Rosenman, et al.
2010　The vertebral formula of the last common ancestor of African apes and humans. *Journal of Experimental*

Zoology Part B: Molecular and Developmental Evolution 314B:123–134.

McCrossin, M. L., and B. R. Benefit.
1994   Maboko Island and the evolutionary history of Old World monkeys and apes. In: *Integrative Paths to the Past: Paleoanthropological Advances in Honor of F. C. Howell*, R. S. Corruccini and R. L. Ciochon (eds.), pp. 95–122. Englewood Cliffs, NJ: Prentice-Hall.

McCrossin, M. L., B. R. Benefit, et al.
1998   Fossil evidence for the origins of terrestriality among Old World monkeys and apes. In: *Primate Locomotion: Recent Advances*, E. Strasser, J. G. Fleagle, H. M. McHenry, and A. L. Rosenberger (eds.), pp. 353–396. New York: Plenum.

McDougall, I., F. H. Brown, and J. G. Fleagle
2005   Stratigraphic placement and age of modern humans from Kibish, Ethiopia. *Nature* 433:733–736.

McGraw, W. S., and R. Bshary
2002   Association of terrestrial mangabeys (*Cercocebus atys*) with arboreal monkeys: Experimental evidence for the effects of reduced ground predator pressure on habitat use. *International Journal of Primatology* 23:311–325.

McGrew, W. C.
1992   *Chimpanzee Material Culture. Implications for Human Evolution.* New York: Cambridge University Press.

McGrew, W. C.
1998   Culture in nonhuman primates? *Annual Review of Anthropology* 27:301–328.

McGrew, W. C., and E. G. Tutin
1978   Evidence for a social custom in wild chimpanzees? *Man, New Series* 13:234–251.

McHenry, H.
1988   New estimates of body weight in early hominids and their significance to encephalization and megadontia in "robust" australopithecines. In: *Evolutionary History of the Robust Australopithecines* (Foundations of Human Behavior), F. E. Grine (ed.), pp. 133–148. Somerset, NJ: Aldine Transaction.

McHenry, H.
1992   Body size and proportions in early hominids. *American Journal of Physical Anthropology* 87:407–431.

McKusick, V. A. (with S. E. Antonarakis et al.)
1998   *Mendelian Inheritance in Man*, 12th ed. Baltimore, MD: Johns Hopkins University Press.

McNulty, K. P.
2010   Apes and tricksters: The evolution and diversification of humans' closest relatives. *Evolution: Education and Outreach* 3:40–46.

McPherron, S. P., Z. Alemseged, C. W. Marean, et al.
2010   Evidence of stone-tool-assisted consumption of animal tissue before 3.39 million years ago at Dikika, Ethiopia. *Nature* 466:857–860.

Miles, H. L. W.
1990   The cognitive foundations for reference in a signing orangutan. In: *Language and Intelligence in Monkeys and Apes: Comparative Developmental Perspectives*,

S. T. Parker and K. R. Gibson (eds.), pp. 511–539. New York: Cambridge University Press.

Miller, E. R., B. R. Benefit, et al.
2009   Systematics of early and middle Miocene Old World monkeys. *Journal of Human Evolution* 57:195–211.

Miller, E. R., G. F. Gunnell, et al.
2005   Deep time and the search for anthropoid origins. *Yearbook of Physical Anthropology*. 48:60–95.

Mitani, J. C., D. P. Watts, and S. J. Amsler
2010   Lethal intergroup aggression leads to territorial expansion in wild chimpanzees. *Current Biology* 20(12):R507–R508.

Moore, L. G., S. Niermeyer, and S. Zamudio
1998   Human adaptation to high altitude: Regional and life-cycle perspectives. *Yearbook of Physical Anthropology* Suppl. 27:25–64.

Moore, L. G., M. Shriver, L. Bemis, and E. Vargas
2006   An evolutionary model for identifying genetic adaptation to high altitude. *Advances in Experimental Medicine and Biology* 588:101–118.

Morwood, M. J., P. Brown, T. Jatmiko, et al.
2005   Further evidence for small-bodied hominins from the Late Pleistocene of Flores, Indonesia. *Nature* 437:1012–1017.

Morwood, M. J., R. P. Soejono, R. G. Roberts, et al.
2004   Archaeology and age of a new hominin from Flores in eastern Indonesia. *Nature* 431:1087–1091.

Moura, A. C. A., and P. C. Lee
2004   Capuchin tool use in Caatinga dry forest. *Science* 306:1909.

Moyà-Solà, S., D. M. Alba, et al.
2009   A unique Middle Miocene European hominoid and the origins of the great ape and human clade. *Proceedings of the National Academy of Sciences* 106:9601–9606.

Murray, R. D.
1980   The evolution and functional significance of incest avoidance. *Journal of Human Evolution* 9:173–178.

Muttoni, G., G. Scardia, D. Kent, et al.
2009   Pleistocene magnetochronology of early hominin sites at Ceprano and Fontana Ranuccio, Italy. *Earth and Planetary Science Letters* 286:255–268.

Nakatsukasa, M., and Y. Kunimatsu
2009   *Nacholapithecus* and its importance for understanding hominoid evolution. *Evolutionary Anthropology* 18:103–119.

Nakatsukasa, M., C. V. Ward, et al.
2004   Tail loss in *Proconsul heselonsi*. *Journal of Human Evolution* 46:777–784.

Napier, J.
1967   The antiquity of human walking. *Scientific American* 216:56–66.

Neel, J. V.
1962   Diabetes mellitus: A thrifty genotype rendered detrimental by "progress"? *American Journal of Human Genetics* 14:353–362.

Nesse, R. M., and G. C. Williams
1994   *Why We Get Sick. The New Science of Darwinian Medicine.* New York: Vintage Books.

Nevell, L., A. Gordon, and B. Wood
2007   *Homo floresiensis* and *Homo sapiens* size-adjusted cranial shape variations. *American Journal of Physical Anthropology, Supplement* 14:177–178 (abstract).

News in Brief
2007   Congolese government creates bonobo reserve. *Nature* 450:470. doi: 10.1038450470f

Nishida, T.
1991   Comments: Intergroup aggression in chimpanzees and humans by J. H. Manson and R. Wrangham. *Current Anthropology* 32:369–390, 381–382.

Nishida, T., N. Corp, M. Hamai, et al.
2003   Demography, female life history, and reproductive profiles among the chimpanzees of Mahale. *American Journal of Primatology* 59:99–121.

Nishida, T., M. Hiraiwa-Hasegawa, T. Hasegawa, and Y. Takahata
1985   Group extinction and female transfer in wild chimpanzees in the Mahale National Park, Tanzania. *Zeitschrift Tierpsychologie—Journal of Comparative Ethology* 67:284–301.

Nishida, T., H. Takasaki, and Y. Takahata
1990   Demography and reproductive profiles. In: *The Chimpanzees of the Mahale Mountains*, T. Nishida (ed.), pp. 63–97. Tokyo: University of Tokyo Press.

Nishida, T., R. W. Wrangham, J. Goodall, and S. Uehara
1983   Local differences in plant-feeding habits of chimpanzees between the Mahale Mountains and Gombe National Park, Tanzania. *Journal of Human Evolution* 12:467–480.

Noe, R., and R. Bshary
1997   The formation of red colobus-diana monkey associations under predation pressure from chimpanzees. *Proceedings of the Royal Society of London Series B-Biological Sciences* 264:253–259.

Noonan, J. P., G. Coop, S. Kudaravalli, D. Smith, et al.
2006   Sequencing and analysis of Neanderthal genomic DNA. *Science* 314:1113–1118.

Nowak, R. M.
1999   *Walker's Primates of the World*. Baltimore, MD: Johns Hopkins University Press.

Oakley, K.
1963   Analytical methods of dating bones. In: *Science in Archaeology*. D. Brothwell and E. Higgs (eds.). New York: Basic Books.

Oates, J. F., M. Abedi-Lartey, W. S. McGraw, et al.
2000   Extinction of a West African red colobus monkey. *Conservation Biology* 14:1526–1532.

Oates, J. F., R. A. Bergl, J. Sunderland-Groves, and A. Dunn
2007   *Gorilla gorilla* ssp. Diehli. *2007 IUCN Red List of Threatened Species*.

Oeseburg, H., R. A. de Boer, W. H. van Gilst, and P. van der Harst
2010   Telomere biology in health aging and disease. *European Journal of Physiology* 459:259–268.

Olliaro, P., J. Cattani, et al.
1995   Malaria, the submerged disease. *Journal of the American Medical Association* 275:230–233.

Olshansky, S. J., D. J. Passaro, et al.
2005   A potential decline in life expectancy in the United States in the 21st Century. *New England Journal of Medicine* 352:1138–1145.

Ottoni, E. B., and P. Izar
2008   Capuchin monkey tool use: Overview and implications. *Evolutionary Anthropology* 17:171–178.

O'Rourke, D. H., and J. A. Raff
2010   The human genetic history of the Americas: The final frontier. *Current Biology* 20:R202–R207.

Ousley, S., R. Jantz, and D. Freid
2009   Understanding race and human variation: Why forensic anthropologists are good at identifying race. *American Journal of Physical Anthropology* 139:68–76.

Ovchinnikov, I. V., A. Gotherstrom, G. P. Romanova, et al.
2000   Molecular analysis of Neanderthal DNA from the northern Caucasus. *Nature* 404:490–493.

Padian, K. and L. M. Chiappe
1998   The origin of birds and their flight. *Scientific American* 278:38–47.

Pagel, M., C. Venditti, and A. Meade
2006   Large punctuational contribution of speciation to evolutionary divergence at the molecular level. *Science* 314:119–121.

Paine, M.
2001   Source of the Australasian tektites? *Meteorite*, from http//www.meteor.co.nz/.

Palmer, S. K., L. G. Moore, D. Young, et al.
1999   Altered blood pressure course during normal pregnancy and increased preeclampsia at high altitude (3100 meters) in Colorado. *American Journal of Obstetrics and Gynecology* 180:1161–1168.

Palumbi, S. R.
2001   *The Evolution Explosion: How Humans Cause Rapid Evolutionary Change*. New York: W.W. Norton.

Pares, J. M., and A. Perez-Gonzalez
1995   Paleomagnetic age for hominid fossils at Atapuerca archaeological site, Spain. *Science* 269:830–832.

Park, E.
1978   The Ginsberg Caper: Hacking it as in Stone Age. *Smithsonian* 9:85–96.

Pavkov, M. E., P. H. Bennett, et al.
2006   Effect of young-onset type 2 diabetes mellitus on incidence of end-stage renal disease and mortality in young and middle-aged Pima Indians. *Journal of the American Medical Association* 296:421–426.

Peccei, J. S.
2001   Menopause: Adaptation or epiphenomenon? *Evolutionary Anthropology* 10:43–57.

Pennisi, E.
2005   Why do humans have so few genes? *Science* 309:80.

Penny, D.
2004   Our relative genetics. *Nature* 427:208–209.

Peres, C. A.
1990   Effects of hunting on western Amazonian primate communities. *Biological Conservation* 54(1): 47–59.

Perez, V. R., L. R. Godfrey, et al.
2005   Evidence of early butchery of giant lemurs in Madagascar. *Journal of Human Evolution* 49:722–742.

Perkins, S.
2003   Learning from the present. *Science News* 164:42–44.

Pfister, L.-A., M. S. Rosenberg, and A. C. Stone
2008   Full genome comparisons of *Mycobacterium*: Insight into the origin of TB and leprosy. Paper presented at the 77th annual meeting of the American Association of Physical Anthropologists.

Phillips, K. A.
1998   Tool use in wild capuchin monkeys (*Cebus albifrons trinitatis*). *American Journal of Primatology* 46:259–261.

Phillips-Conroy, J. E., C. J. Jolly, P. Nystrom, and H. A. Hemmalin
1992   Migration of male hamadryas baboons into anubis groups in the Awash National Park, Ethiopia. *International Journal of Primatology* 13:455–476.

Pickford, M., and B. Senut
2001   The geological and faunal context of late Miocene hominid remains from Lukeino, Kenya. *Comptes Rendus de l'Académie des Sciences, Ser. 11A, Earth and Planetary Science* 332:145–152.

Pike, I. L.
2000   The nutritional consequences of pregnancy sickness: A critique of a hypothesis. *Human Nature* 11:207–232.

Pilbeam, D.
1982   New hominoid skull material from the Miocene of Pakistan. *Nature* 295:232–234.

Pilbeam, D.
1996   Genetic and morphological records of the Hominoidea and hominid origins: A synthesis. *Molecular Phylogenetics and Evolution* 5(1): 155–168.

Pilbeam, D., M. D. Rose, et al.
1990   New *Sivapithecus* humeri from Pakistan and the relationship of *Sivapithecus* and *Pongo*. *Nature* 348:237–239.

Pinner, R. W., S. M. Teutsch, L. Simonson, et al.
1996   Trends in infectious diseases mortality in the United States. *Journal of the American Medical Association* 275:189–193.

Pollard, T. M.
2008   *Western Diseases: An Evolutionary Perspective.* Cambridge, UK: Cambridge University Press.

Pollard, T., and N. Unwin
2008   Impaired reproductive function in women in Western and "Westernizing" populations: An evolutionary approach. In: *Evolutionary Medicine and Health: New Perspectives*, W. R. Trevathan, E. O. Smith, and J. J. McKenna (eds.), pp. 169–181. New York: Oxford University Press.

Population Reference Bureau
2009   2009 World Population Data Sheet. http://www.prb.org/Publications/Datasheets/2009/2009wpds.aspx

Poremba, A., M. Malloy, et al.
2004   Species-specific calls evoke asymmetric activity in the monkey's temporal poles. *Nature* 427:448–451.

Potts, R.
1984   Home bases and early hominids. *American Scientist* 72:338–347.

Potts, R.
1991   Why the Oldowan? Plio-Pleistocene toolmaking and the transport of resources. *Journal of Anthropological Research* 47:153–176.

Potts, R.
1993   Archeological interpretations of early hominid behavior and ecology. In: *The Origin and Evolution of Humans and Humanness*, D. T. Rasmussen (ed.), pp. 49–74. Boston: Jones and Bartlett.

Potts, R., and P. Shipman
1981   Cutmarks made by stone tools on bones from Olduvai Gorge, Tanzania. *Nature* 291:577–580.

Potts, R., and R. Teague
2003   Heterogeneity in large-mammal paleocommunities and hominin activities in the southern Kenya rift valley during the mid-Pleistocene (1.2–0.4 Ma). *Abstracts, Paleoanthropology Society Annual Meetings.* Tempe, AZ.

Poux, C., P. Chevret, et al.
2006   Arrival and diversification of caviomorph rodents and platyrrhine primates in South America. *Systematic Biology* 55:228–244.

Poux, C., and E. J. Douzery
2004   Primate phylogeny, evolutionary rate variations, and divergence times: a contribution from the nuclear gene IRBP. *American Journal of Physical Anthropology* 124:1–16.

Powell, K. B., and S. A. Tishkoff
2003   The evolution or lactase persistence in African populations. *American Journal of Physical Anthropology* Supplement 36:170.

Proctor, R.
1988   From anthropologie to rassenkunde. In: *Bones, Bodies, Behavior. History of Anthropology* (Vol. 5), W. J. Stocking, Jr. (ed.), pp. 138–179. Madison: University of Wisconsin Press.

Profet, M.
1988   The evolution of pregnancy sickness as a protection to the embryo against Pleistocene teratogens. *Evolutionary Theory* 8:177–190.

Pruetz, J. D., and P. Bertolani
2007   Savanna chimpanzees, *Pan troglodytes verus*, hunt with tools. *Current Biology* 17:412–417.

Pusey, A., J. Williams, and J. Goodall
1997   The influence of dominance rank on the reproductive success of female chimpanzees. *Science* 277:828–831.

Raaum, R. L., K. N. Sterner, et al.
2005   Catarrhine primate divergence dates estimated from complete mitochondrial genomes: Concordance with fossil and nuclear DNA evidence. *Journal of Human Evolution* 48:237–257.

Rafferty, K. L., A. Walker, et al.
1995   Postcranial estimates of body weight in *Proconsul*, with a note on a distal tibia of *P. major* from Napak, Uganda. *American Journal of Physical Anthropology* 97:391–402.

Rak, Y., A. Ginzburg, and E. Geffen
2007   Gorilla-like anatomy on *Australopithecus afarensis* mandibles suggests *Au. afarensis* link to robust australopiths. *Proceedings of the National Academy of Sciences* 104:6568–6572.

Rasmussen, D. T.
2007   Fossil record of the primates from the Paleocene to the Oligocene. In: *Handbook of Paleoanthropology*,

W. Henke and I. Tattersall (eds.), pp. 889–920. Part 2: Primate Evolution and Human Origins. New York: Springer.

Rasmussen, M., Y. Li, S. Lindgreen, et al.
2010   Ancient human genome sequence of an extinct Palaeo-Eskimo. *Nature* 463:757–762.

Reinberg, S.
2009   Swine flu has infected 1 in 6 Americans:CDC. *U.S. News and World Reports.* www.usnews.com/health [posted December 10, 2009].

Relethford, J. H.
2001   *Genetics and the Search for Modern Human Origins.* New York: Wiley-Liss.

Renne, P. R., W. D. Sharp, et al.
1997 ^{40}Ar/^{39}Ar dating into the historic realm: Calibration against Pliny the younger. *Science* 277:1279–1280.

Reno, P. L., R. S. Meindl, et al.
2003   Sexual dimorphism in *Australopithecus afarensis* was similar to that of modern humans. *Proceedings of the National Academy of Sciences USA* 100:9404–9409.

Reno, P. L., R. S. Meindl, et al.
2005   The case is unchanged and remains robust: *Australopithecus afarensis* exhibits only moderate skeletal dimorphism: A reply to Plavcan et al., 2005. *Journal of Human Evolution* 49:279–288.

Rhesus Macaque Genome Sequencing and Analysis Consortium.
2007   Evolutionary and biomedical insights from the rhesus macaque genome. *Science* 316:222–234.

Richmond, B. G., and W. L. Jungers
2008   *Orrorin tugenensis* femoral morphology and the evolution of hominin bipedalism. *Science* 319:1662–1665.

Riddle, R. D., and C. J. Tabin
1999   How limbs develop. *Scientific American* 280:74–79.

Ridley, M.
1993   *Evolution.* Boston: Blackwell Scientific Publications.

Rightmire, G. P.
1998   Human evolution in the Middle Pleistocene: The role of *Homo heidelbergensis. Evolutionary Anthropology* 6:218–227.

Rightmire, G. P.
2004   Affinities of the Middle Pleistocene cranium from Dali and Jinniushan. *American Journal of Physical Anthropology, Supplement* 38:167 (abstract).

Robins, A. H.
1991   *Biological Perspectives on Human Pigmentation.* Cambridge, UK: Cambridge University Press.

Römpler, H., N. Rohland, et al.
2006   Nuclear gene indicates coat-color polymorphism in mammoths. *Science* 313:62–64.

Rosenberg, K., and W. Trevathan
2001   The evolution of human birth. *Scientific American* 285:72–77.

Rosenberg, N. A., J. K. Pritchard, et al.
2002   Genetic structure of human populations. *Science* 298:2381–2385.

Ross, C. F.
2000   Into the light: The origin of Anthropoidea. *Annual Review of Anthropology* 29:147–194.

Ross, C. F., M. Henneberg, et al.
2004   Curvilinear, geometric and phylogenetic modeling of basicranial flexion: Is it adaptive, is it constrained? *Journal of Human Evolution* 46:185–213.

Rossie, J. B., and L. MacLatchy
2006   A new pliopithecoid genus from the early Miocene of Uganda. *Journal of Human Evolution* 50:568–586.

Rossie, J. B., X. Ni, and K. C. Beard
2006   Cranial remains of an Eocene tarsier. *Proceedings of the National Academy of Sciences USA* 103:4381–4385.

Rouquet, P., J. Froment, et al.
2005   Wild animal mortality monitoring and human Ebola outbreaks, Gabon and Republic of Congo. *Emerging Infectious Diseases* 11:283–290.

Rovner, I.
1983   Plant opal phytolith analysis: Major advances in archaeobotanical research. In: *Advances in Archaeological Method and Theory*, M. B. Schiffer (ed.), pp. 225–266. New York: Academic Press.

Rudran, R.
1973   Adult male replacement in one-male troops of purple-faced langurs (*Presbytis senex senex*) and its effect on population structure. *Folia Primatologica* 19:166–192.

Ruff, C. B., and A. Walker
1993   The body size and shape of KNM-WT 15000. In: *The Nariokotome* Homo erectus *Skeleton*, A. Walker and R. E. Leakey (eds.), pp. 234–265. Cambridge, MA: Harvard University Press.

Ruff, C. B., A. Walker, et al.
1989   Body mass, sexual dimorphism and femoral proportions of *Proconsul* from Rusinga and Mfangano Islands, Kenya. *Journal of Human Evolution* 18:515–536.

Ruff, C.
2010   Body size and body shape in early hominins—implications of the Gona pelvis. *American Journal of Physical Anthropology, Supplement* 50:203 (abstract).

Ruvolo, M., D. Pan, et al.
1994   Gene trees and hominoid phylogeny. *Proceedings of the National Academy of Sciences USA* 91:8900–8904.

Sagan, C.
1977   *The Dragons of Eden: Speculations on the Evolution of Human Intelligence.* New York: Random House.

Samson, M., F. Libert, B. J. Doranz, et al.
1996   Resistance to HIV-1 infection in Caucasian individuals bearing mutant alleles of the CCR-5 chemokine receptor gene. *Nature* 382:722–725.

Sargis, E. J., D. M. Boyer, et al.
2007   Evolution of pedal grasping in Primates. *Journal of Human Evolution* 53(1):103–107

Sarmiento, E. E.
2010   Comment on the paleobiology and classification of *Ardipithecus ramidus. Science* 328:1105-b.

Sarmiento, E. E., and J. F. Oates
2000   The Cross River gorilla: A distinct subspecies *Gorilla gorilla diehli* Matschie 1904. *American Museum Novitates* 3304:1–55.

Savage-Rumbaugh, S.
  1986   *Ape Language: From Conditioned Responses to Symbols.* New York: Columbia University Press.

Savage-Rumbaugh, S., and R. Lewin
  1994   *Kanzi: The Ape at the Brink of the Human Mind.* New York: Wiley.

Savage-Rumbaugh, S., K. McDonald, et al.
  1986   Spontaneous symbol acquisition and communicative use by pygmy chimpanzees (*Pan paniscus*). *Journal of Experimental Psychology: General* 115:211–235.

Schauber, A. D., and D. Falk
  2008   Proportional dwarfism in foxes, mice, and humans: Implications for relative brain size in *Homo floresiensis*. *American Journal of Physical Anthropology, Supplement* 43:185 (abstract).

Schmitz, R. W., D. Serre, G. Bonani, et al.
  2002   The Neandertal type site revisited: Interdisciplinary investigations of skeletal remains from the Neander Valley, Germany. *Proceedings of the National Academy of Sciences USA* 99:13342–13347.

Schuster, S. C., W. Miller, A. Ratan, et al.
  2010   Complete Khoisan and Bantu genomes from southern Africa. *Nature* 463:943–947.

Schwartz, J. H.
  1984   What is a tarsier? In: *Living Fossils.* Niles and Steven M. Stanley Eldridge (eds.), pp. 38–49. New York: Springer Verlag.

Scriver, C. R.
  2001   *The Metabolic and Molecular Bases of Inherited Disease.* New York: McGraw Hill.

Seehausen, O.
  2002   Patterns of fish radiation are compatible with Pleistocene dessication of Lake Victoria and 14,600 year history for its cichlid species flock. *Proceedings of the Royal Society of London (Biological Science)* 269:491–497.

Seiffert, E. R., J. M. G. Perry, et al.
  2009   Convergent evolution of anthropoid–like adaptations in Eocene adapiform primates. *Nature* 461:1118–1121.

Seiffert, E. R., E. L. Simons, et al.
  2003   Fossil evidence for an ancient divergence of lorises and galagos. *Nature* 422:421–424.

Seiffert, E. R., E. L. Simons, et al.
  2005a   Additional remains of *Wadilemur elegans*, a primitive stem galagid from the late Eocene of Egypt. *Proceedings of the National Academy of Science USA* 102:11396–11401.

Seiffert , E., E. Simons, et al.
  2005b   Basil anthropoids from Egypt and the antiquity of Africa's higher primate radiation. *Science* 310:300–304.

Seiffert, E. R., E. L. Simons, et al.
  2010   A fossil primate of uncertain affinities from the earliest late Eocene of Egypt. *Proceedings of the National Academy of Sciences* 107:9712–9717.

Semaw, S., M. J. Rogers, J. Quade, et al.
  2003   2.6-million-year-old stone tools and associated bones from OGS-6 and OGS-7, Gona, Afar, Ethiopia. *Journal of Human Evolution* 45:169–177.

Senut, B., M. Pickford, D. Grommercy, et al.
  2001   First hominid from the Miocene (Lukeino Formation, Kenya). *Comptes Rendus de l'Académie des Sciences, Ser. 11A, Earth and Planetary Science* 332:137–144.

Serre, D., A. Langaney, M. Chech, et al.
  2004   No evidence of Neandertal mtDNA contribution to early modern humans. *Plos Biology* 2:313–317.

Seyfarth, R. M., D. L. Cheney, and P. Marler
  1980a   Monkey responses to three different alarm calls. *Science* 210:801–803.

Seyfarth, R. M., D. L. Cheney, and P. Marler
  1980b   Vervet monkey alarm calls: Semantic communication in a free-ranging primate. *Animal Behaviour* 28:1070–1094.

Shang, H., H. Tong, S. Zhang, et al.
  2007   An early modern human from Tianyuan Cave, Zhoukoudian, China. *Proceedings of the National Academy of Sciences USA* 104:6573–6578.

Shaw, J. E., R. A. Sicree, and P. Z. Zimmet
  2010   Global estimates of the prevalence of diabetes for 2010 and 2030. *Diabetes Research and Clinical Practice* 87(1):4–14.

Shea, B. T., and R. C. Baily
  1996   Allometry and adaptation of body proportions and stature in African pygmies. *American Journal of Physical Anthropology* 100:311–340.

Shen, G., X. Gao, B. Gao, and D. E. Granger
  2009   Age of Zhoukoudian *Homo erectus* with $^{26}Ar/^{10}Be$ burial dating. *Nature* 458:198–200.

Shindler, K.
  2006   *Discovering Dorothea: The Life of the Pioneering Fossil-Hunter Dorothea Bate.* London: Harper Collins Ltd.

Shipman, P.
  1983   Early hominid lifestyle. hunting and gathering or foraging and scavenging? In: *Animals and Archaeology*, J. Clutton-Brock and C. Grigson (eds.), pp. 31–51. Vol. I: Hunters and Their Prey. London: Brit. Arch. Rpts.

Shreeve, J.
  2009   Oldest skeleton of human ancestor found. *National Geographic News* October 1, 2009. http://news.nationalgeographic.com/news/2009/10/091001-oldest-human-skeleton-ardi-missing-link-chimps-ardipithecus-ramidus.html.

Shubin, N. H., E. B. Daeschler, and F. A. Jankins, Jr.
  2006   The pectoral fin of *Tiktaalik roseae* and the origin of the tetrapod limb. *Nature* 440:764–771.

Shubin, N., C. Tabin, and S. Carroll
  1997   Fossils, genes, and the evolution of animal limbs. *Nature* 388:639–648.

Sievert, L. L.
  2006   *Menopause: A Biocultural Perspective.* New Brunswick, NJ: Rutgers University Press.

Sigé, B., J.-J. Jaeger, et al.
  1990.   *Altiatlasius koulchii* n. gen. et sp., primate omomyide du Paleocene superieur du Maroc, et les origines des euprimates. *Palaeontographica A* 214:31–56.

Silcox, M. T.
  2001   *A Phylogenetic Analysis of Plesiadapiformes and Their Relationship to Euprimates and Other Archontans.*

Unpublished PhD dissertation, Johns Hopkins University School of Medicine, Baltimore, MD.

Silcox, M. T.
2007   Primate taxonomy, plesiadapiforms, and approaches to primate origins. In: *Primate Origins: Adaptations and Evolution*, M. J. Ravosa and M. Dagosto (eds.), pp. 143–178. New York: Plenum Press.

Silcox, M. T.
2008   The biogeographic origins of primates and euprimates: East, west, north, or south of Eden? In: *Mammalian Evolutionary Morphology: A Tribute to Frederick S. Szalay (Vertebrate Paleobiology and Paleoanthropology)*, E. J. Sargis and M. Dagosto (eds.), pp. 199–231. New York: Springer Science.

Silk, J. B., S. C. Alberts, and J. Altman
2003   Social bonds of female baboons enhance infant survival. *Science* 302:1231–1234.

Silk, J. B., S. F. Brosman, J. Vonk, et al.
2005   Chimpanzees are indifferent to the welfare of unrelated group members. *Nature* 437:1357–1359.

Simons, E. L.
1972   *Primate Evolution: An Introduction to Man's Place in Nature*. New York: MacMillan.

Simons, E. L.
1976   The fossil record of primate phylogeny. In: *Molecular Anthropology: Genes and Proteins in the Evolutionary Ascent of the Primates*, M. Goodman (ed.), pp. 35–62. New York: Plenum Press.

Simons, E. L., F. Ankel-Simons, et al.
2009   Outrage at high price paid for a fossil. *Nature* 460:456.

Simonson, T., Y. Yang, C. Huff, et al.
2010   Genetic evidence for high-altitude adaptation in Tibet. *Science* 329:72–75.

Simpson, S. W., J. Quade, N. E. Levin, et al.
2008   A female *Homo erectus* pelvis from Gona, Ethiopia. *Science* 322:1089–1092.

Skaletsky, H., T. Kuroda-Kawaguchi, et al.
2003   The male-specific region of the human Y chromosome is a mosaic of discrete sequence classes. *Nature* 423:825-U2.

Smith, F. H.
2002   Migrations, radiations and continuity: Patterns in the evolution of Late Pleistocene humans. In: *The Primate Fossil Record*, W. Hartwig (ed.), pp. 437–456. New York: Cambridge University Press.

Smith, F. H., A. B. Falsetti, and S. M. Donnelly
1989   Modern human origins. *Yearbook of Physical Anthropology* 32:35–68.

Smith, F. H., E. Trinkaus, P. B. Pettitt, et al.
1999   Direct radiocarbon dates for Vindija G1 and Velika Pécina Late Pleistocene hominid remains. *Proceedings of the National Academy of Sciences* 96:12281–12286.

Smith, T., K. D. Rose, and P. Gingerich
2006   Rapid Asia-Europe-North America geographic dispersal of earliest Eocene primate *Teilhardina* during the Paleocene-Eocene thermal maximum. *Proceedings of the National Academy of Sciences USA* 103:11223–11227.

Smuts, B.
1985   *Sex and Friendship in Baboons*. Hawthorne, NY: Aldine de Gruyter.

Snyder, M., and M. Gerstein
2003   Genomics. Defining genes in the genomics era. *Science* 300:258–260.

Soares, P., A. Achilli, O. Semino, et al.
2010   The archaeogenetics of Europe. *Current Biology* 20:R174–R183.

Soligo, C., and R. D. Martin
2007   The first primates: A reply to Silcox et al. (2007). *Journal of Human Evolution* 53:325–328

Soligo, C., O. Will, S. Tavaré, et al.
2007   New light on the dates of primate origins and divergence. In: *Primate Origins: Adaptations and Evolution*, M. J. Ravosa and M. Dagosto (eds.), pp. 29–49. New York: Springer.

Sponheimer, M., and J. A. Lee-Thorp
1999   Isotopic evidence for the diet of an early hominid. *Australopithecus africanus*. *Science* 283:368–370.

Sponheimer, M., B. H. Passey, D. J. de Ruiter, et al.
2006   Isotopic evidence for dietary variability in the early hominin *Paranthropus robustus*. *Science* 314:980–982.

Spoor, F., M. G. Leakey, P. N. Gathago, et al.
2007   Implications of new early *Homo* fossils from Ileret, East of Lake Turkana, Kenya. *Nature* 448:688–691.

Srivastava, M., O. Simakov, J. Chapman, et al.
2010   The *Amphimedon queenslandica* genome and the evolution of complexity. *Nature* 466:720–726.

Stanford, C.
1999   *The Hunting Apes: Meat Eating and the Origins of Human Behavior*. Princeton, NJ: Princeton University Press.

Stanford, C.
2001   The ape's gift: Meat-eating, meat-sharing, and human evolution. In: *Tree of Origin*, F. deWaal (ed.), pp. 95-117. Cambridge, MA: Harvard University Press.

Starin, E. D.
1994   Philopatry and affiliation among red colobus. *Behaviour* 130:253–270.

Steiper, M. E., and N. M. Young
2006   Primate molecular divergence dates. *Molecular Phylogenetics and Evolution* 41:384–394.

Steiper, M. E., and N. M. Young
2008   Timing primate evolution: lessons from the discordance between molecular and paleontological estimates. *Evolutionary Anthropology* 17:179–188

Steklis, H. D.
1985   Primate communication, comparative neurology, and the origin of language reexamined. *Journal of Human Evolution* 14:157–173.

Stelzner, J., and K. Strier
1981   Hyena predation on an adult male baboon. *Mammalia* 45:259–260.

Sterner, K. N., R. L. Raaum, et al.
2006   Mitochondrial data support an odd-nosed colobine clade. *Molecular Phylogenetics and Evolution* 40:1–7.

Stevens, N. J., and C. P. Heesy
2006   Malagasy primate origins: Phylogenies, fossils, and biogeographic reconstructions. *Folia Primatologica* 77:419–433

Stini, W. A.
1991   Body composition and longevity: Is there a longevous morphotype? *Medical Anthropology* 13:215–229.

Stoneking, M., and F. Delfin
2010   The human genetic history of East Asia: Weaving a complex tapestry. *Current Biology* 20:R188–R193.

Strassmann, B. I., and B. Gillespie
2002   Life-history theory, fertility and reproductive success in humans. *Proceedings of the Royal Society of London Series B-Biological Sciences* 269(1491): 553–562.

Straus, L. G.
1995   The Upper Paleolithic of Europe: An overview. *Evolutionary Anthropology* 4:4–16.

Strier, K. B.
2003   *Primate Behavioral Ecology*. Boston: Allyn and Bacon.

Stringer, C. B., and P. Andrews
1988   Genetic and fossil evidence for the origin of modern humans. *Science* 239:1263–1268.

Stringer, C. B., J. C. Finlayson, R. N. E. Barton, et al.
2008   Neanderthal exploitation of marine mammals in Gibralter. *Proceedings of the National Academy of Sciences* 105:14319–14324.

Struhsaker, T. T.
1967   Auditory communication among vervet monkeys (*Cercopithecus aethiops*). In: *Social Communication Among Primates*, S. A. Altmann (ed.). Chicago: University of Chicago Press.

Struhsaker, T. T., and L. Leland
1979   Socioecology of five sympatric monkey species in the Kibale forest, Uganda. In: *Advances in the Study of Behavior*, J. S. Rosenblatt, R. A. Hinde, C. Beer, and M.C. Busnel (eds.), pp. 159–229. New York: Academic Press.

Struhsaker, T. T., and L. Leland
1987   Colobines: Infanticide by adult males. In: *Primate Societies*, B. Smuts, D. L. Cheney, R. M. Seyfarth, et al. (eds.), pp. 83–97. Chicago: University of Chicago Press.

Stuart-Macadam, P. and K. A. Dettwyler
1995   *Breastfeeding: Biocultural Perspectives*. Hawthorne, NY: Aldine de Gruyter.

Sturm, R. A., D. L. Duffy, et al.
2008   A single SNP in an evolutionary conserved region within intron 86 of the HERC2 gene determines human blue-brown eye color. *American Journal of Human Genetics* 82:424–431.

Sugiyama, Y.
1965   Short history of the ecological and sociological studies on non-human primates in Japan. *Primates* 6:457–460.

Sumner, D. R., M. E. Morbeck, and J. Lobick
1989   Age-related bone loss in female Gombe chimpanzees. *American Journal of Physical Anthropology* 72:259.

Suomi, S. J., S. Mineka, and R. D. DeLizio
1983   Short-and long-term effects of repetitive mother-infant separation on social development in rhesus monkeys. *Developmental Psychology* 19:710–786.

Susman, R. L. (ed.)
1984   *The Pygmy Chimpanzee: Evolutionary Biology and Behavior*. New York: Plenum.

Susman, R. L., J. T. Stern, and W. L. Jungers
1985   Locomotor adaptations in the Hadar hominids. In: *Ancestors: The Hard Evidence*, E. Delson (ed.), pp. 184–192. New York: Alan R. Liss.

Sussman, R. W.
1991   Primate origins and the evolution of angiosperms. *American Journal of Primatology* 23:209–223.

Sussman, R. W., J. M. Cheverud, and T. Q. Bartlett
1995   Infant killing as an evolutionary strategy: reality or myth? *Evolutionary Anthropology* 3:149–151.

Suwa, G., R. T. Kono, S. Katch, B. Asfaw, and Y. Beyene
2007   A new species of great ape from the late Miocene epoch in Ethiopia. *Nature* 448:921–924.

Swisher, C. C., W. J. Rink, S. C. Anton, et al.
1996   Latest *Homo erectus* of Java: Potential contemporaneity with *Homo sapiens* in Southwest Java. *Science* 274:1870–1874.

Switek, B. J.
2009   A discovery that will change everything (!!!) … or not. http://scienceblogs.com/laelaps/2009/05/a_discovery_that_will_change_e.php.

Switek, B. J.
2010   Ancestor or adapiform? *Darwinius* and the search for our early primate ancestors. *Evolution: Education and Outreach*. doi: 10.1007/s12052-010-0261-xOnline First™

Tavaré, S., C. R. Marshall, et al.
2002   Using the fossil record to estimate the age of the last common ancestor of extant primates. *Nature* 416:726–729.

Tavera-Mendoza, L. E. and J. H. White
2007   Cell defenses and the sunshine vitamin. *Scientific American* 297(5): 62–72.

Teresi, D.
2002   *Lost Discoveries. The Ancient Roots of Modern Science—from the Babylonians to the Maya*. New York: Simon and Schuster.

Thieme, H.
1997   Lower Palaeolithic hunting spears from Germany. *Nature* 385:807–810.

Thorne, A., R. Grün, G. Mortimer, et al.
1999   Australia's oldest human remains: Age of the Lake Mungo 3 skeleton. *Journal of Human Evolution* 36:591–612.

Tiemel, C., Y. Quan, and W. En
1994   Antiquity of *Homo sapiens* in China. *Nature* 368:55–56.

Tishkoff, S. A., F. A. Reed, et al.
2007   Convergent adaptation of human lactase persistence in Africa and Europe. *Nature Genetics* 39(1): 31–40.

Tishkoff, S. A., F. A. Reed, F. R. Friedlaender, et al.
2010   The genetic structure and history of Africans and African Americans. *Science* 324:1035–1043.

Tobias, P.
1971   *The Brain in Hominid Evolution*. New York: Columbia University Press.

Tobias, P.
1983   Recent advances in the evolution of the hominids with especial reference to brain and speech. Pontifical Academy of Sciences, *Scrita Varia* 50:85–140.

Tocheri, M. W., Caley M. Orr, S. G. Larson, et al.
2007   The primitive wrist of *Homo floresiensis* and its implications for hominin evolution. *Science* 317:1743–1745.

Tornow, M. A.
2008   Systematic analysis of the Eocene primate family Omomyidae using gnathic and postcranial data. *Bulletin of the Peabody Museum of Natural History*: 43–129

Trevathan, W.
2010   *Ancient Bodies, Modern Lives: How Evolution Has Shaped Women's Health*. New York: Oxford University Press.

Trinkaus, E.
2005   Early modern humans. *Annual Review of Anthropology* 34:207–230.

Trinkaus, E., S. Milota, R. Rodrigo, et al.
2003   Early modern human cranial remains from Pestera cu Oase, Romania. *Journal of Human Evolution* 45:245–253.

Trinkaus, E., and P. Shipman
1992   *The Neandertals*. New York: Alfred A. Knopf.

UNAIDS/WHO
2010   http://www.who.int/hiv/data/fast_facts/en/index .html

Ungar, P. S., and R. F. Kay
1995   The dietary adaptations of European Miocene catarrhines. *Proceedings of the National Academy of Sciences USA* 92:5479–5481.

United Nations Dept. of Economic and Social Affairs
2008   Millennium Development Goals Report 2008. http:// www.un.org/en/development/desa/news/statistics/ mdg-2008.shtml.

United Nations Dept. of Economic and Social Affairs
2010   Millennium Development Goals Report 2010. http:// www.un.org/en/development/desa/news/statistics/ mdg-2010.shtml.

United Nations Population Division
1998   *World Population Prospects: The 1998 Revision*.

Van Bocxlaer, B., D. Van Damme, et al.
2008   Gradual versus punctuated equilibrium evolution in the Turkana Basin molluscs: Evolutionary events or biological invasion? *Evolution* 62:511–520.

van der Ven, K., R. Fimmers, et al.
2000   Evidence for major histocompatability complex-mediated effects on spermatogenesis in humans. *Human Reproduction* 15:189–196.

van Schaik, C. P., M. Ancrenaz, G. Bogen, et al.
2003   Orangutan cultures and the evolution of material culture. *Science* 299:102–105.

Van Valen, L.
1973   Pattern and the balance of nature. *Evolutionary Theory* 1:31–49.

Venter, J. C., M. D. Adams, E. W. Myers, et al.
2001   The sequence of the human genome. *Science* 291:1304–1351.

Vialet, A., L. Tianyuan, D. Grimaud-Herve, et al.
2005   Proposition de reconstitution du deuxième crâne d'*Homo erectus* de Yunxian (Chine). *Comptes rendus. Palévol* 4:265–274.

Vigilant, L., M. Hofreiter, H. Siedel, and C. Boesch
2001   Paternity and relatedness in wild chimpanzee communities. *Proceedings of the National Academy of Sciences USA* 98:12890–12895.

Vignaud, P., P. Duringer, H. MacKaye, et al.
2002   Geology and palaeontology of the Upper Miocene Toros-Menalla hominid locality, Chad. *Nature* 418:152–155.

Villa, P.
1983   *Terra Amata and the Middle Pleistocene Archaeological Record of Southern France*. University of California Publications in Anthropology, Vol, 13. Berkeley: University of California Press.

Visalberghi, E.
1990   Tool use in *Cebus. Folia Primatologica* 54:146–154.

Visalberghi, E. D. F., E. Ottoni, et al.
2007   Characteristics of hammer stones and anvils used by wild bearded capuchin monkeys (*Cebus libidinosus*) to crack open palm nuts. *American Journal of Physical Anthropology* 132:426–444.

Vogelsang, R.
1998   *The Middle Stone Age Fundstellen in Süd-west Namibia*. Köln: Heinrich Barth Institut.

Vogelstein, B., D. Lane, et al.
2000   Surfing the p53 network. *Nature* 408:307–310.

Vrba, E. S.
1992   Mammals as a key to evolutionary theory. *Journal of Mammalogy* 73(1): 1–28.

Wakayama, S., H. Ohta, T. Hikichi, et al.
2008   Production of healthy cloned mice from bodies frozen at −20°C for 16 years. *Proceedings of the National Academy of Sciences* 105:17318-17322

Walker, A.
1991   The origin of the genus *Homo*. In: *Evolution of Life*, S. Osawa and T. Honjo (eds.), pp. 379–389. Tokyo: Springer-Verlag.

Walker, A., and R. E. Leakey
1993   *The Nariokotome* Homo erectus *Skeleton*. Cambridge, MA: Harvard University Press.

Walker, A.
1976   Remains attributable to *Australopithecus* from East Rudolf. In: *Earliest Man and Environments in the Lake Rudolf Basin*, Y. Coppens (ed.), pp. 484–489. Chicago: University of Chicago Press.

Walker, J., R. A. Cliff, and A. G. Latham
2006   U-Pb isoptoic age of the Stw 573 hominid from Sterkfontein, South Africa. *Science* 314:1592–1594.

Waller, D. K., A. Correa, T. M. Vo., et al.
2008   The population-based prevalence of achondroplasia and thanatophoric dysplasia in selected regions of the US. *American Journal of Medical Genetics* 146A(18):2385–2389.

Walsh, P. D., K. A. Abernethy, M. Bermejo, et al.
2003   Catastrophic ape decline in western equatorial Africa. *Nature* 422:611–614.

Ward, C. V.
    2005   Torso morphology and locomotion in *Proconsul nyanzae*. *American Journal of Physical Anthropology* 92:321–328.

Ward, P.
    1994   *The End of Evolution*. New York: Bantam.

Ward, S., B. Brown, et al.
    1999   *Equatorius*: A new hominoid genus from the middle Miocene of Kenya. *Science* 285:1382–1386.

Warren W. C., L. W. Hillier, J. A. Marshall, et al.
    2008   Genome analysis of the platypus reveals unique signatures of evolution. *Nature* 453:175–183.

Washburn, S. L., and Irven DeVore
    1961   The social life of baboons. *Scientific American* 204:62–71.

Waterston, R. H., K. Lindblad-Toh, E. Birney, et al. (Mouse Genome Sequencing Consortium)
    2002   Initial sequencing and comparative analysis of the mouse genome. *Nature* 421:520–562.

Watson, J. D., and F. H. C. Crick
    1953a   Genetical implications of the structure of the deoxyribonucleic acid. *Nature* 171:964–967.

Watson, J. D., and F. H. C. Crick
    1953b   A structure for deoxyribonucleic acid. *Nature* 171:737–738.

Weiner, J. S.
    1955   *The Piltdown Forgery*. London: Oxford University Press.

Weiner, S., Q. Xu, P. Goldberg, et al.
    1998   Evidence for the use of fire at Zhoukoudian, China. *Science* 281:251–253.

Weir, A., J. Chappell, et al.
    2008   Shaping of hooks in New Caledonian crows. *Science* 297: 981.

Weiss, R. A., and R. W. Wrangham
    1999   From *Pan* to pandemic. *Nature* 397:385–386.

Weiss, U.
    2002   Nature insight: Malaria. *Nature* 415:669.

Westergaard, G. C., and D. M. Fragaszy
    1987   The manufacture and use of tools by capuchin monkeys (*Cebus apella*). *Journal of Comparative Psychology* 101:159–168.

White, T. D.
    1986   Cut marks on the Bodo cranium: A case of prehistoric defleshing. *American Journal of Physical Anthropology* 69:503–509.

White, T. D., B. Asfaw, D. DeGusta, et al.
    2003   Pleistocene *Homo sapiens* from Middle Awash, Ethiopia. *Nature* 423:742–747.

White, T. D., B. Asfaw, Y. Beyene, et al.
    2009   *Ardipithecus ramidus* and the paleobiology of early hominids. *Science* 326:75–86.

White, T. D., G. WoldeGabriel, B. Asfaw, et al.
    2006   Asa Issie, Aramis and the origin of *Australopithecus*. *Nature* 440:883–889.

White, T. D., G. Suwa, and C. O. Lovejoy
    2010   Response to comment on the paleobiology and classification of *Ardipithecus ramidus*. *Science* 328:5982.

Whitelaw, N. C., and E. Whitelaw
    2006   How lifetimes shape epigenotype within and across generations. *Human Molecular Genetics* 15:R131–R137.

Whiten, A., J. Goodall, W. C. McGrew, et al.
    1999   Cultures in chimpanzees. *Nature* 399:682–685.

Wildman, D. E., N. M. Jameson, et al.
    2009   A fully resolved genus level phylogeny of neotropical primates. *Molecular Phylogenetics and Evolution* 53:694–702.

Wildman, D. E., M. Uddin, G. Liu, et al.
    2003   Implications of natural selection in shaping 99.4% nonsynonymous DNA identity between humans and chimpanzees: Enlarging genus *Homo*. *Proceedings of the National Academy of Sciences USA* 100:7181–7188.

Williams, B. A., R. F. Kay, and E. C. Kirk
    2010   New perspectives on anthropoid origins. *Proceedings of the National Academy of Sciences* 107:4797–4804.

Williams, G. C.
    1957   Pleiotropy, natural selection, and the evolution of senescence. *Evolution* 11:398–411.

Williams, G. C., and R. M. Nesse
    1991   The dawn of Darwinian medicine. *The Quarterly Review of Biology* 66:1–22.

Williams, J. M.
    1999   *Female Strategies and the Reasons for Territoriality in Chimpanzees. Lessons from Three Decades of Research at Gombe*. Unpublished Ph.D. Thesis, University of Minnesota.

Wilmut, I., A. E. Schnieke, J. McWhir, et al.
    1997   Viable offspring derived from fetal and adult mammalian cells. *Nature* 385:810–813.

Wilson, E. O.
    1992   *The Diversity of Life*. Cambridge, MA: The Belknap Press of Harvard University Press.

Wilson, M. L., W. R. Wallauer, et al.
    2004   New cases of intergroup violence among Chimpanzees in Gombe National Park, Tanzania. *International Journal of Primatology* 25:523–549.

Wolpoff, M. H., J. Hawks, D. Frayer, and K. Hunley
    2001   Modern human ancestry at the peripheries: A test of the replacement theory. *Science* 291:293–297.

Wolpoff, M. H., B. Senut, M. Pickford, and J. Hawks
    2002   Paleoanthropology (communication arising): *Sahelanthropus* or '*Sahelpithecus*'? *Nature* 419:581–582.

Wolpoff, M. H., A. G. Thorne, et al.
    1994   Multiregional evolutions: A world-wide source for modern human populations. In: *Origins of Anatomically Modern Humans*, M. H. Nitecki and D. V. Nitecki (eds.), pp. 175–199. New York: Plenum Press

Wong, K.
    2009   Rethinking the hobbits of Indonesia. *Scientific American* 301 (November):66–73.

Woo, J. K.
    1966   The skull of Lantian Man. *Current Anthropology* 7:83–86.

Wood, B.
1991   *Koobi Fora Research Project IV: Hominid Cranial Remains from Koobi Fora.* Oxford: Clarendon Press.

Wood, B.
1992   Origin and evolution of the genus *Homo. Nature* 355:783–790.

Wood, B.
2010   Reconstructing human evolution: Achievements, challenges, and opportunities. *Proceedings of the National Academy of Sciences* 107(Suppl. 2):8902–8909.

Wood, B., and M. Collard
1999a   The human genus. *Science* 284:65–71.

Wood, B., and M. Collard
1999b   The changing face of genus *Homo. Evolutionary Anthropology* 8:195–207.

World Health Organization
2010   World Health Statistics 2010.

Wrangham, R., A. Clark, and G. Isabiryre-Basita
1992   Female social relationships and social organization of Kibale forest chimps. In: *Topics in Primatology,* W. McGrew T. Nishida, P. Marler, et al. (eds.), pp. 81–98. Tokyo: Tokyo University Press.

Wrangham, R. W.
1980   An ecological model of female-bonded primate groups. *Behaviour,* 75:262–300.

Wrangham, R. W.
1999   The evolution of coalitionary killing. *Yearbook of Physical Anthropology* 42:1–30.

Wrangham, R. W., and B. B. Smuts
1980   Sex differences in the behavioural ecology of chimpanzees in Gombe National Park, Tanzania. *Journal of Reproduction and Fertility* 28:13–31.

Wright, P. C., E. L. Simons, et al.
2003   *Tarsiers: Past, Present, and Future.* New Brunswick, NJ: Rutgers University Press.

Wu, R., and X. Dong
1985   *Homo erectus* in China. In: *Palaeoanthropology and Palaeolithic Archaeology in the People's Republic of China,* R. Wu and J. W. Olsen (eds.), pp. 79–89. New York: Academic Press.

Wu, R., and J. W. Olsen (eds.)
1985   *Palaeoanthropology and Palaeolithic Archaeology in the People's Republic of China.* Orlando, FL: Academic Press.

Wu, X., and F. E. Poirier
1995   *Human Evolution in China.* New York: Oxford University Press.

Wu, X. J., L. A. Schepartz, et al.
2006   Endocranial cast of Hexian *Homo erectus* from South China. *American Journal of Physical Anthropology* 130:445–454.

Wuethrich, B.
1998   Geological analysis damps ancient Chinese fires. *Science* 281:165–166.

Xu, Q., and Q. Lu
2007   *Series monograph III:* Lufengpithecus—*An Early Member of Hominidae.* Beijing: Science Press.

Yellen, J. E., A. S. Brooks, E. Cornelissen, et al.
1995   A Middle Stone-Age worked bone industry from Katanda, Upper Semliki Valley, Zaire. *Science* 268:553–556.

Yi, X, Y. Liang, E. Huerta-Sanchez, et al.
2010   Sequencing of 50 human exomes reveals adaptation to high altitude. *Science* 329:75–78.

Yoder, A. D., M. M. Burns, et al.
2003   Single origin of Malagasy Carnivora from an African ancestor. *Nature* 421:734–737.

Yoder, A. D., M. Cartmill, et al.
1996   Ancient single origin for Malagasy primates. *Proceedings of the National Academy of Sciences* 93:5122–5126.

Yokoyama, Y, C. Falguères, F. Sémah, et al.
2008   Gamma-ray spectrometric dating of late *Homo erectus* skulls from Ngandong and Sambungmacan, Central Java, Indonesia. *Journal of Human Evolution* 55:274–277.

Young, D.
1992   *The Discovery of Evolution.* Cambridge, UK: Natural History Museum Publications, Cambridge University Press.

Young, E. M.
2004   Globalization and food security: novel questions in a novel context? *Progress in Development Studies* 4:1–21.

Zalmout, I. S., W. J. Sanders, et al.
2010   New Oligocene primate from Saudi Arabia and the divergence of apes and Old World monkeys. *Nature* 466:360–365.

Zhang, F., S. L. Kearns, P. J. Orr, et al.
2010   Fossilized melanosomes and the colour of Cretaceous dinosaurs and birds. *Nature* 463:1075–1078.

Zhang, J. Z., Y. P. Zhang, et al.
2002   Adaptive evolution of a duplicated pancreatic ribonuclease gene in a leaf-eating monkey. *Nature Genetics* 30:411–415.

Zhu, R. X., Z. S. An, R. Potts, et al.
2003   Magnetostratigraphic dating of early humans in China. *Earth Science Reviews* 61:341–359.

Ziegler, A., A. S. Jonason, et al.
1994   Sunburn and P53 in the onset of skin-cancer. *Nature* 372:773–776.

Zilhão, J., D. E. Angeluccib, E. Badal-García, et al.
2010   Symbolic use of marine shells and mineral pigments by Iberian Neandertals. *Proceedings of the National Academy of Sciences* 107:1023–1028.

Photo Credits

This page constitutes an extension of the copyright page. We have made every effort to trace the ownership of all copyrighted material and to secure permission from copyright holders. In the event of any question arising as to the use of any material, we will be pleased to make the necessary corrections in future printings. Thanks are due to the following authors, publishers, and agents for permission to use the material indicated.

iv, © The Print Collector / Alamy; **vi**, © iStockphoto.com / Doug Berry; **vii**, © 2010 Photo E. Daynes – Reconstruction Atelier Daynès Paris; **ix**, NASA / © iStockphoto.com / James Steidl (DNA); **xi**, © Robert Greisen; **xii**, © iStockphoto.com / Tomasz Zachariasz; **4**, Courtesy, Peter Jones; **5**, © NASA; **6**, (a) Lynn Kilgore; (b) NASA/Space Telescope Science Institute; (c) Museum of Primitive Art and Culture, Peace Dale, RI; (d) © iStockphoto.com / Ravi Tahilramani; (e) Lynn Kilgore; (f) © iStockphoto.com / Justin Horocks; **8**, (a) © ephotocorp / Alamy; (e) Wally Wecker, University of Wisconsin-Madison; brainmuseum.org; (f) Reproduced from Emile Cartailhac and l'abbé Henri Breuil (1906); (g) ©iStockphoto.com / Mayumi Terao; **9**, (b) Wally Wecker, University of Wisconsin-Madison; brainmuseum.org; (c) Noemi Spagnoletti/EthoCebus Project; (d) © 2009 Photo E. Daynes – Reconstruction Atelier Daynès Paris; (h) © iStockphoto.com / Christopher Badzioch; (i) © Dr. Stanley Flegler / Visuals Unlimited; **12**, (a) © Kenneth Garrett/NGS Image Collection; (b) © Russell L. Ciochon; **13**, Lynn Kilgore; **14**, top, © Tom McCarthy / Photo Edit; bottom, Kathleen Galvin; **15**, (a) Robert Jurmain; (b) Nelson Ting; **16**, (a & b) Lynn Kilgore; **17**, (a) © Reuters / Corbis; (b) U.S. Army Corp of Engineers and the Regime Crime Liaison Office; **18**, Linda Levitch; **19**, (a) © Cyril Ruoso / PhotoLibrary; (b) Julie Lesnik; **20**, (a) Dr. Soo Young Chin; (b) Nanette Barkey; **29**, © The Bridgeman Art Library; **30**, Johannes van Loon, "Scenographia systematis mundani Ptolemaici", nla.map-nk10241, National Library of Australia; **32**, American Museum of Natural History; **33**, Mathieu-Ignace van Brée (1773–1839); **34**, With permission from the Master of Haileybury; **35**, top, © National Portrait Gallery, London; (a & b) Lynn Kilgore; **36**, The Natural History Museum, London; **37**, © Bettmann / Corbis; **38**, © Gordon Chancellor; **39**, (1st finch) Tui De Roy / Minden Pictures; (2nd finch) Mark Moffett / Minden Pictures; (3rd finch) D. Parer & E. Parer-Cook/ Auscape/ Minden Pictures; (4th finch) Tui De Roy / Minden Pictures; bottom, Robert Jurmain; **40**, (Wolf) © Corbis / Superstock; (Dogs surrounding wolf) Lynn Kilgore and Lin Marshall; Great dane, Eric Isselée / Shutterstock; Chihuahua, © iStockphoto.com / Marcin Pikula; Yorkshire terrier, © iStockphoto.com / Eriklam; **41**, top, National Portrait Gallery, London; bottom, © Russell L. Ciochon; **43**, (a) Perennou Nuridsany / Photo Researchers, Inc.; (b) Michael Willmer Forbes Tweedie / Photo Researchers, Inc.; **47**, © Bettmann / Corbis; **50**, Equinox Graphics / Photo Researchers, Inc.; **52**, Courtesy, Dr. Michael S. Donnenberg; **53**, Professors P. Motta and T. Naguro/SPL/Photo Researchers, Inc.; **54**, A. Barrington Brown / Photo Researchers, Inc.; **55**, The Novartis Foundation; **63**, (a–c) Lynn Kilgore; **64**, (a & b) © Dr. Stanley Flegler / Visuals Unlimited; **67**, © Biophoto Associates / Photo Researchers, Inc.; **69**, CNRI/Photo Researchers, Inc.; **76**, Cellmark Diagnostics,

Abingdon, UK; **77**, (a–e) Advanced Cell Technology, Inc., Worcester, Massachusetts; **78**, (a & b) © J. Craig Venter Institute; **81**, © Spencer Grant / Alamy; **82**, (a) © iStockphoto.com / stocksnapper; (b) © Cassandra Tiensivu; bottom, Raychel Ciemma and Precision Graphics; **90**, Dennis McDonald / Photoedit; **91**, (a) Reuters / STR / Landov; (b) © Juniors Bildarchiv / Alamy; **94**, (c) Ray Carson, University of Florida News and Public Affairs; **95**, (a–f), Lynn Kilgore; (g) Robert Jurmain; **99**, Reprinted, with permission, from the Annual Review of Genetics, Volume 10 ©1976 by Annual Reviews www.annualreviews.org; **101**, (a) © iStockphoto.com / Waldemar Dabrowski; (b) © 2004 National Academy of Sciences, U.S.A. Photo by Dr. John Fondon; **104**, Lynn Kilgore; **110**, Peter Menzel / Photo Researchers, Inc.; **127**, (a) © John Cancalosi / Alamy; (b) © Phil Degginger / Alamy; (c) Elwyn Simons; (d) © Marvin Dembinsky Photo Associates / Alamy; (e) © Shoshannah White / Aurora Photos; (f) © Russell L. Ciochon; **128**, Kazuo Unno / Minden Pictures; **130**, © iStockphoto.com / EvansArtsPhotography; **134**, left, © Tom McHugh / Photo Researchers, Inc.; right, © iStockphoto.com / Michael Sacco; **136**, © Nigel J. Dennis; Gallo Images / Corbis; **139**, left & right, © iStockphoto.com / Tomasz Zachariasz; **140**, (a & b) Lynn Kilgore; **142**, © Ingo Arndt / Minden Pictures; **145**, (a–e) Lynn Kilgore; **147**, © iStockphoto.com / Steve Geer; **148**, Lynn Kilgore; **149**, Lynn Kilgore; **150**, Howler species: © Arco Images GmbH / Alamy; Spider monkey: © Michel Lefèvre / PhotoLibrary; Prince Bernhard's titi: Marc van Roosmalen; Marmosets and tamarins: © Arco Images GmbH / Alamy; Muriqui: Andrew Young; White-faced capuchins: © Jay Dickman/Corbis; Squirrel monkey: © Kevin Schafer/Corbis; Uakari: R. A. Mittermeier/Conservation International; **151**, Baboon: Courtesy, Bonnie Pedersen/Arlene Kruse; Macaque: Courtesy, Jean De Rousseau; Gibbon: Lynn Kilgore; Tarsier: © Steve Bloom Images / Alamy; Orangutan: © Rolf Nussbaumer Photography / Alamy; Langur: © Cyril Ruoso / PhotoLibrary; Lemur: Courtesy, Fred Jacobs; Loris: © Ian Butler / Alamy; Cercopithecus: Robert Jurmain; Colobus: Robert Jurmain; Galago: © DLILLC / Corbis; Chimpanzee: Courtesy, Arlene Kruse/ Bonnie Pedersen; Mountain gorilla: Lynn Kilgore; **152**, (a & b) © Russell L. Ciochon; **153**, (a–d) Stephen Nash; **154**, Lynn Kilgore; **157**, Fig. 6-9, Lynn Kilgore; Fig. 6-10, © Diane France; **158**, left, Cyril Ruoso / JH Editorial / Minden Pictures; bottom, Fred Jacobs; **159**, top left, © Ian Butler / Alamy; top right, © DLILLC / Corbis; bottom, © Steve Bloom Images / Alamy; **161**, top left, © Andrew Young; top right, © Kevin Schafer / Corbis; center right, Marc van Roosmalen; bottom right, R. A. Mittermeier / Conservation International; bottom left, © Jay Dickman / Corbis; **162**, top, © Arco Images GmbH / Alamy; bottom, © Arco Images GmbH / Alamy; **163**, © Michel Lefèvre / PhotoLibrary; **164**, top, Robert Jurmain; (a) © Corbis Super RF / Alamy; (b) © Thomas Dobner 2006 / Alamy; **165**, top, Nelson Ting; bottom, © ian cruickshank / Alamy; **167**, top, Gerry Ellis / Minden Pictures; (a) © Rolf Nussbaumer Photography / Alamy; (b) Thomas Marent / Minden Pictures; **169**, (a) © imagebroker / Alamy; (b) © Duncan Usher / Alamy; **170**, (a) Thomas Marent / Minden Pictures; (b) Lynn Kilgore; **171**, © Morales / PhotoLibrary; **172**, Ellen Ingmanson; **173**, Lynn Kilgore; **177**, (a) John Oates; (b) Getty Images / Jenny

Researchers, Inc.; West Turkana: National Museums of Kenya, copyright reserved; Sima del Elefante: Javier Trueba / Madrid Scientific Films / Photo Researchers, Inc.; **343**, Zhoukoudian: © Russell L. Ciochon; Lantian, Hexian, Ngandong: Milford Wolpoff; Trinii: Courtesy, S. Sartano; Sangiran: © Russell L. Ciochon; **346**, Zhoukoudian: © Russell L. Ciochon; Sangiran 17: Milford Wolpoff; Ngandong 5: © Russell L. Ciochon; Zhoukoudian: © Russell L. Ciochon; ER 3733: Milford Wolpoff; O.H. 9: Pascal Goetgheluck / Photo Researchers, Inc.; **347**, Pascal Goetgheluck / Photo Researchers, Inc.; **348**, (a) Kenya Museums of Natural History; (b) © 2008 Photo P. Plailly E. Daynes Eurelios – Reconstruction Atelier Daynès Paris; **350**, (a–c) David Lordkipanidze; **351**, top, David Lordkipanidze; bottom, S. Sartano; **353**, © Russell L. Ciochon; **354**, © Russell L. Ciochon; **356**, Zhoukoudian Museum, China and © Russell L. Ciochon; **357**, © Russell L. Ciochon; **358**, (a & B) Milford Wolpoff; **360**, © Giorgio Manzi; **361**, William Turnbaugh; **363**, © Russell L. Ciochon; **366**, 2010 Photo E. Daynes – Reconstruction Atelier Daynès Paris; **370**, Milford Wolpoff; **371**, © Robert Franciscus; **372**, top, © 2010 Photo E. Daynes – Reconstruction Atelier Daynès Paris; bottom, Milford Wolpoff; **374**, Arago: Courtesy, H. DeLumley; Steinheim: Milford Wolpoff; Petralona: Milford Wolpoff; Bodo: © Robert Franciscus, University of Iowa; Florisbad: Courtesy, Günter Bräuer; Kabwe: Milford Wolpoff; **375**, Jinniushan: © Russell L. Ciochon; Dali: Milford Wolpoff; **376**, (a) Milford Wolpoff; (b) © Russell L. Ciochon; **381**, Shanidar I: Erik Trinkaus; Gibraltar: © Robert Franciscus, University of Iowa; Amud 1: Milford Wolpoff; La Chapelle: Courtesy, Fred Smith; St. Césaire: Harry Nelson; La Ferrassie 1: Courtesy, Fred Smith; **382**, St. Césaire: Harry Nelson; La Ferrassie: Courtesy, Fred Smith; Krapina/Vindija: Milford Wolpoff; Amud: Milford Wolpoff; Shanidar: Erik Trinkaus, Washington University, St. Louis; Tabun/Kebara: Courtesy, Fred Smith; La Chapelle: Courtesy, Fred Smith; Gibraltar: © Robert Franciscus, University of Iowa; **383**, left, © 2010 Photo E. Daynes – Reconstruction Atelier Daynès Paris; center, Fred Smith; right, Harry Nelson; **384**, (a & b) Fred Smith; **385**, Harry Nelson; **386**, Erik Trinkaus; **388**, © Randall White; **392**, © João Zilhão; **399**, AP Photo / Augustin Ochsenreiter; **400**, © 2008 Photo P. Plailly E. Daynes Eurelios – Reconstruction Atelier Daynès Paris; **401**, © El Sidrón Research Team; **402**, © John Stanmeyer/VII/Corbis; **407**, Milford Wolpoff; **408**, Skhūl, Courtesy, Fred Smith; Jebel Qafzeh: Milford Wolpoff; Herto: David L. Brill/Atlanta; Border Cave: Courtesy, Fred Smith; Klasies River Mouth, Courtesy, Fred Smith; Omo: Milford Wolpoff; **410**, Jebel Qafzeh 6: Milford Wolpoff; Border Cave 1: Courtesy, Fred Smith; Skhūl 5: Courtesy, Fred Smith; Předmostí; Harry Nelson; Cro-Magnon I: David Frayer; **411**, David L. Brill/Atlanta; **412**, top, David Frayer; (a) David Frayer; (b) Milford Wolpoff; **414**, Zhoukoudian/Tianyuan: © Russell L. Ciochon; Lake Mungo: Milford Wolpoff; Kow Swamp: Milford Wolpoff; **415**, ©Mircea Gerhase; **416**, Combe Capelle: © Staatliche Museen zu Berlin, Museum fur Vor- und Fruhgeschichte; Mladeč: Milford Wolpoff; Oase: © Erik Trinkaus, Washington University, St. Louis; Cro-Magnon: David Frayer; **417**, (a) Milford Wolpoff; (b) © Robert Franciscus, University of Iowa; **418**, (a & b) David Frayer; bottom, © 2009 Photo S. Plailly – Reconstruction Atelier Daynès Paris; **419**, © Portuguese Institute of Archaeology; **422**, © Peter Brown; **424**, N. O. Bader; **429**, Altamira: Reproduced from Emile Cartailhac and l'abbé Henri Breuil (1906); Brassempouy:

Harry Nelson; Sungir: © Randall White, New York University; Katanda: Courtesy, Chip Clark, Smithsonian Institution; Blombos Cave: © CS Henshilwood, Iziko Museums of Cape Town; Apollo 11 Cave: © Gerald Newlands, University of Calgary; **432**, (map) NASA; (DNA) © iStockphoto.com / James Steidl; **436**, MSGT Rose Reynolds; **437**, © Bettmann / Corbis; **439**, (a) © Peter Johnson / Corbis; (b) © Charles & Josette Lenars / Corbis; (c) © Gallo Images / Corbis; (d) © Otto Lang / Corbis; (e) Lynn Kilgore; **440**, © Tannen Maury/epa/Corbis; **441**, (a) © Purestock / Alamy; (b) Robert Jurmain; **442**, © Peter Turnley / Corbis; **448**, top, © Independent Picture Service / Alamy; center, © Dennis Macdonald / PhotoLibrary; bottom, © Michael Dunning / Getty Images; **449**, top, © Norman Price / Alamy; center left, © Peter Turnley / Corbis; center right, © Kenneth Garrett / National Geographic Stock; bottom, William D. Bachman / Photo Researchers, Inc.; **455**, © Atlantide Phototravel / Corbis; **456**, © Michael S. Yamashita / Corbis; **459**, © Trinity Mirror / Mirrorpix / Alamy; **460**, Frans Lemmen / Getty Images; **465**, Centers for Disease Control and Prevention; **466**, © Biophoto Associates / Photo Researchers, Inc.; **467**, © INTERFOTO / Alamy; **471**, (a) Ken Greer / Visuals Unlimited; (b) © Biophoto Associates/Science Source/Photo Researchers, Inc.; (c) © James Stevenson/SPL/Photo Researchers, Inc.; **472**, (a) © JTB Photo Communications, Inc. / Alamy; (b) © tbkmedia.de / Alamy; **474**, (a) © iStockphoto.com / Rafal Belzowski; (b) © iStockphoto.com / Danny Warren; **476**, Charlotte Roberts; **478**, CDC/Jean Roy; **479**, © Karl Ammann; **480**, Hoang Dinh Nam/AFP/Getty Images; **482**, (ultrasound) Darren Brode / Shutterstock; (Native American) David P. Smith; **484**, Dr. Mushtaq A. Khan and Dr. Gul N. Rehman, Pakistan Institute of Medical Sciences, Islamabad; **491**, left, © Digital Vision / Getty Images; right, © Peter Turnley / Corbis; **493**, Wildlife Conservation Network; **498**, © Alan Abraham / Corbis; **501**, James F. O'Connell; **506**, NASA; **508**, (photo of earth) Earth Data Analysis Center; **509**, © iStockphoto.com / Joseph Luoman; **510**, AP Photo / Mohammad Sajjad; **511**, UN Photo / Mark Garten; **512**, Tui De Roy/Minden Pictures/National Geographic Stock; **513**, (a) © iStockphoto.com / Jiaxi Shen; (b) © iStockphoto.com / josemoraes; **514**, U.S. Government; **515**, (a) © iStockphoto.com / nolimitpictures; (b) © iStockphoto.com / Allen Goodreds; (c) © iStockphoto.com / Glenn Rogers; (d) © iStockphoto.com / Dave Logan; © iStockphoto.com / Tyler Oliver; **526**, © Viktor Deak, after John G. Fleagle; **527**, © Viktor Deak, after John G. Fleagle; **528**, Adapted from John G. Fleagle and Stephen Nash, Stony Brook University, New York; **529**, Adapted from John G. Fleagle and Stephen Nash, Stony Brook University, New York

Index